STRATEGY, POLICY, & CENTRAL MANAGEMENT

NINTH EDITION

William H. Newman

Director, Strategy Research Center
Graduate School of Business
Columbia University

James P. Logan

Professor of Management and Policy
College of Business and Public Administration
The University of Arizona

W. Harvey Hegarty

Associate Professor of Administrative Studies and
Director, Executive MBA Program
Graduate School of Business
Indiana University

Published by

G50   **SOUTH-WESTERN PUBLISHING CO.**

CINCINNATI   WEST CHICAGO, IL   DALLAS   PELHAM MANOR, NY   PALO ALTO, CA

To the memory of
SAMUEL BRONFMAN
and his belief in
the creative capacity
of independent
business enterprise.

PREFACE

Company strategy, when well developed, is the overriding plan of action for an enterprise. For managers, such strategy can be a powerful tool for focusing and controlling diverse operations. For professors of business, company strategy has a further attraction; its study provides a challenging way to integrate many facets of a business school curriculum. This unifying quality is the main reason why a course on strategy (or "business policy") is usually the capstone requirement in the education of future business managers.

All too often, however, the potential benefits of strategy are not realized. In company situations, strategic planning may fail to be converted into well-timed action. And in business schools, the strategy course may stop with industry and company analysis only. This book, by contrast, emphasizes how both managers and professors can capture the full potential of strategy.

Three features of the book provide this broader, integrating scope: (1) linking business-unit strategy downward into policies of functional departments and upward into corporate design; (2) tying strategic plans to essential steps for execution; and (3) applying these two concepts—described in the text material—to an array of real-life cases.

Integrating Strategy with Functional Policy and with Operating Design

The structure of this book helps students integrate functional and other courses into a comprehensive view of an enterprise by:

1. linking business-unit strategy (Part 1) to policy for marketing, research and development, production, human resources, and finance (Part 2);
2. linking business-unit strategy and policy (Parts 1 and 2) to the strategy of a diversified corporation with respect to portfolio, mergers and acquisitions, and corporate inputs (Part 3); and
3. linking strategy and policy (Parts 1, 2, and 3) to management structure—organizing, programming, leading, and controlling—in Parts 4 and 5.

The combined effect of systematic attention to all these elements and their linkages is a fitting together of otherwise disconnected subjects. From the focal point of managing a business-unit, we build bridges up, down, and across. Students must understand the full array of these interconnections if the strategy (or "business policy") course is to fill its role in integrating the normal curriculum.

Following Through from Planning to Execution

The book transforms "strategy" from a planning exercise to a basis for managerial action. In practice, strategy is useful only if it can be executed effectively. We develop this crucial mating of formulation and implementation by:

1. Treating company strategy as a four-part concept. The formulation is incomplete until it moves from (a) selecting a domain, and (b) finding a source of differential advantage, on to (c) picking strategic thrusts, and (d) specifying target results. These last two elements are action-oriented and lead to more specific planning of near-term steps. Moreover, the two tend to force consideration of tough competitive situations.
2. Dealing systematically with execution, because even a four-part, action-oriented strategy requires persistent follow-through: supporting policy, tailored organization, suitable human and other resources, appropriate leadership style, and reinforcing controls and rewards. These topics occupy a significant part of this book because they are crucial elements in strategic management. If they cannot be fitted to the strategy then the strategy should be reconsidered.

Students, as well as managers, need an appreciation of this full cycle—from selecting a strategy to controlling results. With such a grasp of the ties between planning and execution, they can see the relevance and the impact of strategy on many jobs—both high and low in the organization.

Our aim, then, is to provide the student with a conceptual model that promotes both *synthesis* and *relevance*.

Using Cases To Build Insights and Skills in Applying Concepts

The text material—about half of the book—provides a framework for thinking in an integrated way about strategic management. We have worked hard to make this framework and its many supporting concepts clear. Nevertheless, we realize that practice in applying such concepts adds greatly to understanding when and how to use them. So the other half of the book is devoted to carefully selected cases—forty-three in all.

The number and variety of cases give professors many options in the way they can use these teaching aids. There are:

- end-of-chapter cases;
- integrating cases at six places throughout the book;
- comprehensive cases covering the entire range of the book.

While each case is related to adjacent text issues, almost every case raises additional issues. Consequently, the cases provide frequent opportunities to stress integration among the factors involved.

Also, the variety of settings provide professors the flexibility to emphasize different sorts of business. Twenty cases deal with small firms (fewer than 100 employees). Nine are multinationals or foreign-based companies. Fourteen of the firms are in service industries. Since a choice must be made, a professor can opt to give frequent attention to small business, or high-tech firms, or financial services, or international companies.

Over 60 percent of the cases are either new or substantially revised in this edition of the book. All involve lively, contemporary problems. With them, the policy course can be tied to the current dynamic business world.

Acknowledgements

Many people have contributed to this publication. The basic model around which the text is organized is a lineal descendant of the diagnostic approach to company-wide problems used by James O. McKinsey, founder of the preeminent consulting firm. Recent modifications of the model reflect studies made at the Strategy Research Center of the Graduate School of Business, Columbia University. The cases come directly or indirectly from a large number of business executives who are willing to share their knowledge and experience with tomorrow's prospective leaders.

Specifically, we want to acknowledge permission from the Executive Programs of the Graduate School of Business, Columbia University, to reproduce cases first written for their use. Our colleagues at Columbia have been very helpful. Melvin Anshen, an indefatigable case writer, is the author of the original versions of Crosby Home Security Company, "QuiknEasy" Sauce, Reed Shoe Company, and Sci-Tech Associates. Donald C. Hambrick provided background data for Maytag's Niche and White's Future. Kathryn Rudie Harrigan provided background data for McFadden's and Solar Engineering Supply. For this cooperation we are most grateful.

Our thanks also go to Camilla Koch who, in the face of many other duties and distractions, has skillfully transformed rough notes and vague instructions into a clear and well-organized manuscript. Our high regard for strategy execution comes in part from observing this miracle.

William H. Newman
James P. Logan
W. Harvey Hegarty

CONTENTS

LIST OF CASES

End of Chapter
Integrating
Comprehensive

(International and foreign-based cases marked with *)

1 SOCIAL RESPONSIBILITY AND CENTRAL MANAGEMENT

Western nations, and especially the United States, rely on thousands of independent enterprises to convert resources into desired goods and services. Moreover, these enterprises provide most of the initiative for improving and adapting this flow of goods and services to new wants. Consequently, successful management of these enterprises is vital to many people and, in fact, to the survival of our pluralistic society.

Not all companies succeed. Some leaders of past eras, such as International Harvester and the Pennsylvania Railroad, barely survive, while upstarts such as Apple Computers or Merrill Lynch financial services take center stage—at least for a short time. The rise or fall of small firms is even more uncertain and challenging.

Why do some companies succeed where others fail? And, in light of the vital role of independent enterprises in our pluralistic system, how should a company be run to best serve the needs of society? More specifically, what can you or I do to help in the basic resource conversion process?

This book helps you answer such questions. It focuses on (1) the overall management of (2) separate enterprises. Although we shall deal mostly with private, profit-seeking companies, the same approach and many of the same factors apply to not-for-profit ventures. The key tasks of central managers in both types of enterprises are alike. Management problems are affected more by the kind of services provided and by the size of operations—as we shall frequently note throughout the book—than by the form of ownership. The critical task for each firm is to find a unique niche where it can render distinctive service.

Conceptual Framework

To set the stage, this first chapter explains three related viewpoints that we shall use throughout the book:

1. Socially responsible action for a business enterprise, we shall argue, is that course that enables the enterprise to function as a dynamic resource converter on a continuing basis.

1

2. Central management[1] is the group within each enterprise that designs a particular course that enables the firm to perform in such a socially responsible fashion.
3. To assist central management to fulfill this role, an analytical framework is presented. This framework—which also forms the structure of our book—aids in sorting numerous influences and issues into a related sequence of thought and in building a coherent view of total company activities. In other words, the framework assists central management to act in a socially responsible manner.

Each of these viewpoints needs elaboration because their application is much more complex than this simple, abstract statement suggests.

ACTING IN A SOCIALLY RESPONSIBLE MANNER

A business firm, like any other social institution, can endure only if it continues to contribute to the needs of society. And in our current topsy-turvy world, the actions of business firms, like all other facets of "the establishment," are being challenged. "Why should business wield so much power over the use of materials, labor, capital, and other resources?" is a typical probe. It is important, then, that present—and aspiring—business managers understand how the companies they direct help meet social needs.

The concept of social responsibility is far from clear. Some idealists would like to include every reform that is socially desirable. But business executives have neither the competence nor the means to undertake improvements in prisons, churches, classrooms, and other areas remote from their normal activity. So, to give practical meaning to the idea, we need an approach to social responsibility for business managers that relates to actions and outcomes directly affected by executive decisions.

A useful approach is to think of a manager as a *resource converter*. From the viewpoint of society, an enterprise justifies its existence by converting resources into desired outputs. (1) Resource inputs of labor, materials, ideas, government support, capital, and the like are converted by a firm into (2) outputs of goods, services, employment, stimulating experiences, markets, and other things desired by those who provide the inputs. The job of central managers is to design and maintain a converting mechanism that will generate continuing flows of these inputs and outputs.

An auto garage, for instance, converts labor, parts, machinery, and capital into auto repair services, jobs, rent, etc. Likewise, a poultry farmer converts chicks, feed, labor, equipment, and other resources into outputs of eggs, meat,

---

[1]Central managers (or central management) include all the senior executives who concentrate on running the enterprise as an integrated whole. We prefer the term "central management" rather than "top management" because it is more descriptive and also because it carries less connotation of social status and use of power.

jobs, a market for grain, and a profit on capital. Civilized society depends on a continuing flow of such conversions. And when we talk of the social responsibility of business managers, we are mainly concerned about the effectiveness and the side effects of resource conversions.

This concept of central managers dealing primarily with resource conversion puts the emphasis on constructive action. Three basic elements are involved: (1) building continuing exchange flows with resource suppliers, (2) designing an internal conversion technology, and (3) integrating and balancing the external and internal flows.

Building Continuing Exchange Flows with Resource Suppliers

The relationship with each resource supplier always involves an exchange. Figure 1-1 shows these flows for five typical outside groups. For a specific company there will be a wider variety of subgroups, but the underlying concept is the same. Each group of contributors provides a needed resource and receives in exchange part of the outflow of the enterprise.

FIGURE 1-1.
ENTERPRISE = RESOURCE CONVERTER

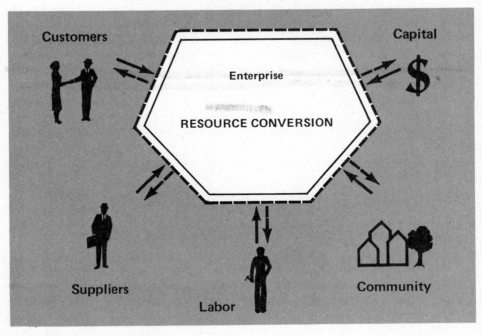

Much more than money is involved. Typically, an array of conditions provides the basis for continuing cooperation. Employees, for instance, are concerned about meaningful work, stability of employment, reasonable supervision, future opportunities, and a whole array of fringe benefits in addition to their paychecks. Suppliers of materials want a continuing market, sure and prompt payment, convenient delivery times, quality standards suited to their facilities, minimum returns, and the like. Investors are concerned about uncertainty of repayment, security, negotiability of their claims, veto of major changes, and perhaps some share in the management. For each resource contributor, mutual agreement about the conditions under which the exchange will continue is subject to evolution and periodic renegotiation.

Because a steady flow of resources is necessary, wise central managers will

1. *predict changes* in conditions under which each resource group will be willing and able to continue its cooperation,
2. conceive and promote *revised exchange* of inputs and outputs that will (a) be attractive to the resource group and (b) be viable for the enterprise,
3. start discussions of changes *early* to allow time for psychological as well as technical adjustments, and
4. assist and work with *other agencies* concerned with the change.

Central managers devote a substantial part of their efforts to negotiating—or guiding their subordinates in negotiating—these agreements covering the bases of cooperation. It is a never-ending process because in our dynamic world the needs of resource suppliers shift, their power to insist on fulfilling their needs changes, and the value of. their contributions to the enterprise varies. In fact, most of the widely discussed "social responsibility" issues deal with some modification of previous conditions of cooperation, such as those shown in Table 1-1.

TABLE 1-1.
SOME "SOCIAL RESPONSIBILITY" ISSUES

Input Group	Reason Prompting a Change
Labor	"Equal opportunity" for women and minorities
Investors	Inflation protection; public disclosure of informantion
Community	Environmental protection; growth in employment opportunities
Suppliers of materials	Predictable, long-run markets
Customers	"Consumerism" pressures for quality guarantees, informative labeling

The real core of social responsibility of a business executive is the maintenance of resource flows on mutually acceptable terms. And this is a very difficult assignment in times of rapidly changing values and expectations—as the succession of labor disputes and energy supply crises illustrates. But note that social responsibility, at least in our view, is not something new, tacked onto an executive's job. Rather, it is reflected in the recognition of shifting social needs and the approach an executive takes in adapting to them. Thus, when we examine adjustments to environmental changes, in Parts 1, 2, and 3, we shall be dealing repeatedly with questions about what is socially responsible action.

Designing an Internal Conversion Technology

Each enterprise, large or small, must maintain a balance between the outputs it generates and the satisfaction it has agreed to provide its suppliers of resources. For instance, promises of stable employment must be compatible with protection promised to suppliers of capital. Such ability to make ends meet depends, partly, on the skill of executives in devising a *conversion technology* suited to their particular company. The way the resources are converted strongly affects the outputs available. So, in addition to negotiating agreements assuring the continuing availability of resources, central managers must design internal systems to effectively utilize the resources.

Every enterprise has its technology for converting resources into outputs. For example, a school has its teaching technology, an insurance company has its technology for policy risks, and a beauty shop has its technology for shaping unruly hair.

This internal conversion technology involves much more than mechanical efficiency. The desired outputs, as we have already noted, include interesting jobs, low capital risks, minimum pollution of the environment, improved job opportunities for women and minorities, and a host of other features. Consequently, devising a good internal conversion technology is a very complex task.[2] This selection of an internal conversion technology is one of the key elements in each company's strategy—as we will see in Chapter 5.

Integrating and Balancing the External and Internal Flows

Important as attracting resources and designing conversion technologies may be, it is the *combination* of (1) responding to new "needs" of resource contributors and (2) restricting total responses to what total output permits that

---

[2]In abstract symbols, the technology should meet the following conditions: With each resource contributor designated by subscripts 1, i, e, s, c, . . . n and

S = satisfactions required by a resource contributor
C = contributions by a resource contributor
CT = conversion technology
O = total output of satisfactions
then:

$$O = (S1 + Si + Se + Ss + Sc . . . Sn)$$
$$O = fCT (C1 + Ci + Ce + Cs + Cc . . . . Cn)$$

And as viewed by each resource contributor:

$$Sx > Cx$$

poses the final challenge to central management. Socially responsible executives must respond quickly enough to the everchanging desires of resource contributors to maintain a continuing flow of needed resources, and at the same time, they must keep their enterprise alive by generating the right quantity and mix of outputs to fulfill commitments. If they do not, some key resource will be withdrawn and the enterprise will collapse.

Community hospitals, to cite a not-for-profit service example, must keep their technology up to date; this includes both putting patient records on computers and installing sophisticated diagnostic and treatment equipment. At the same time, employees want higher wages and shorter hours. The main squeeze, however, arises from a reduction in the average number of days patients are staying in hospitals; patients want excellent service—but less of it—so hospital income is not keeping pace with improved technology and higher wages. Somehow, hospital central managers must reconcile these *combined* pressures.

Throughout this book we shall be exploring ways in which companies can effectively cope with such a dynamic environment—partly by adjusting the exchanges of inputs and outputs with resource groups, and partly by reshaping their conversion technology to generate desired outputs. A recurring theme will be anticipating pressures for change. By adjusting promptly to new conditions, a company usually increases its "output" and thereby makes a greater social contribution.

Considering a company as a resource converter uses a broad social viewpoint. We suggest that this is a better way to conceive of "the purpose of a company" than the more common cliche "to make a profit." Indeed, every successful resource converter must make a profit in order to continue to attract capital. But this is a narrow oversimplification. To survive, a company must also provide attractive employment, be a good customer, earn continuing support of governments and the community, and serve customers well. The task for central management is to find a way to do all these things simultaneously while keeping abreast of changes in each field.

An approach to this complex task is outlined at the close of this chapter and is elaborated throughout the book.

The Business-Unit Versus Diversified Corporations

The best way to understand the strategic problems involved in business is to think first in terms of a company making a single line of products which are sold to a set of similar customers. Such an enterprise faces the full array of transactions—with employees, suppliers, customers, governments. It must wisely allocate resources, assume risks, make trade-offs between alternative courses of action—all with an eye to future service, balance, and survival—as indicated in the preceding pages.

A diversified corporation, of course, has several different lines of business. RCA Corporation, for instance, recently has had business-units in broadcasting (NBC), transportation (Hertz), international communications, color TV sets, and large electronic products. Nevertheless, we can consider the strategy and policy problems related to each product line as though that segment of the corporation were a separate enterprise. Each such division has its own competitors, its own opportunities and threats, and its own strategy. It may draw on corporate resources, but the survival of that part of the total business depends upon how well it adapts to its particular environment.

For convenience in this book we shall call such a product division a "company" (or occasionally "firm," "business-unit," or "enterprise"), regardless of its actual legal status. This usage emphasizes the importance of managing a product division of a large corporation with the same vigor and adaptability as a truly independent single-line company.

The senior executives of a diversified corporation do face an additional set of strategic issues which are distinct from those of their "companies." They must decide which companies to expand and which to contract; perhaps they will launch or acquire new firms; and they must devise ways to help their companies operate successfully. This overriding level we call "corporate management."

Because companies are on the firing-line—where products and services must stand up to competition and where the ability to attract resources is really tested—the primary emphasis in this entire book is on managing these basic businesses. We will consider corporate management in Part 3 and again in Part 4, but only after planning and organizing for the underlying companies have been explored. Contrary to occasional popular criticism of a large corporation, socially responsible actions of business originate largely at the operating level.

CENTRAL MANAGEMENT VIEWPOINT

Integrated, Timely Action

Central management is concerned with the total enterprise—the "whole business." As already noted, an array of interactions with external groups must be negotiated, and internal systems that utilize available resources to best advantage must be designed. When dealing with such matters, central management takes its own unique perspective. Other executives will be confronted with the same problems, but with a more specialized viewpoint.

Central managers give particular attention to interdependence. Commitments to customers must be reconciled with vacation schedules for employees; automated production must not generate air pollution; high-risk research and price competition may cause an unbearable cash squeeze—these examples only suggest the many *interrelationships* between different aspects of a company's operations. Somehow, someone must develop an *integrated* course of action.

Specialized attention to segments of a firm's activities is also necessary, of course. With the knowledge explosion, specialists are essential. But as specialists deal with ever-narrower scopes, the task of integration becomes more difficult and more vital. A major distinctive characteristic of the central management viewpoint is this relating of parts to the whole, integrating them into a *balanced, workable* plan.

A second distinctive concern of central management is setting *priorities* for the enterprise. A robust firm in our volatile environment has many different options, yet only a few can be pursued. People in marketing, finance, research, and other functional fields naturally differ in their recommendation of the best path to follow. Also, some people are more sensitive to social needs than others, and eagerness to take risks will vary. So, to achieve concerted, unified action, one or two objectives must be singled out and plans for achieving these goals must be specified. This process clarifies the *mission* to be sought. Optimum results are obtained only when such guidance is clearly accepted throughout the organization.

Central management, then, focuses on missions and priorities on the one hand, and on interrelationships, functional integration, and a balanced plan of action on the other.

But being aware of central management's point of view still leaves us with a practical question: How can we (and central managers) proceed to "analyze" such intricately involved situations?

NEED FOR ANALYTICAL FRAMEWORK

Even the preceding terse description indicates that the task of central management is complex. And, as with any complex situation, a tested approach that divides the complicated mass into simpler elements can be very helpful. The approach outlined in this book is basically a framework for thinking about central management issues. It expedites analysis, and it assists in forming a synthesis of action to be taken.

Of course, any single approach must be adapted and amplified to fit the peculiarities of a specific company. In a small importing firm, for instance, organization may be relatively unimportant, whereas political outlook is crucial. On the other hand, the senior executives in a young electronics company may be predominantly concerned about technology and additional sources of capital.

Most useful is an approach that draws attention to a limited (comprehensible) number of *basic issues* in a *systematic arrangement* and, at the same time, is reasonably complete in the *potential opportunities* for improvement it flags or suggests. Such a way of thinking about central management problems is more important than an exhaustive listing of all possible difficulties.

Future-Oriented Approach

To maintain a forward-looking view of the central management job, the following approach is very useful:

1. Design company *strategy* on the basis of continuous matching of (a) anticipated opportunities and problems in the industry with (b) distinctive company strengths—and limitations.
2. Amplify and clarify this strategy in *policy*, which serves as a more specific guide to executives in the various functional divisions of the company.
3. When a diversified corporation is involved, plan for a *balanced portfolio strategy* covering the several business-units (companies), and modify the strategies and policies of the business-units to fit into this consolidated plan.
4. Set up an *organization* to carry out the strategy and policy. This involves making clear who does what and developing key personnel who can push forward in the direction singled out in the strategy.
5. Guide the *execution* of the strategy and policy through the organization. This calls for programming, activating, and controlling the operations.

Since this division of tasks of central management will be used throughout the book, the nature of each section should be recognized from the start. So let us take a closer look at what is involved.

Analyzing the Outlook for the Company

Many factors impinge on the future development of any enterprise. Some cities grow; others decay. New ways to control insect pests may obsolete chemical plants; new social mores may obsolete college dormitories. Inflation distorts cost structures; cable TV changes shopping habits; war in the Middle East creates new shortages of petroleum supply—this list of opportunities and problems could go on and on.

A practical way to bring some kind of order out of this array of environmental changes is to concentrate on an industry. This industry may be one the company is already in or one that it is thinking about entering. The aim of these industry analyses is to predict growth, profitability, and especially the key factors for future success.

Turning to the specific company, its strengths and limitations relative to its competitors should be carefully assessed. Then, by matching the company strengths with key factors for success in the industry, the outlook for the company can be predicted. For even sharper analysis, the way key actors in the environment are likely to respond to company moves can be predicted. This sequence of analysis is elaborated in Chapters 2, 3, and 4.

Of course, the company need not stand still. It can take steps to alter its strengths, and by its actions it may modify the services or the prices of the entire industry. Similarly, an industry occasionally makes a dent in the environment. For instance, business representatives participate in debates on national priorities and help shape guidelines for protection of our natural environment. On balance, however, each company must adapt to its environment. And corporate management must find distinctive services to provide in such environments.

Designing Company Strategy

Armed with the forecast of the world in which the company will operate, central management shifts to active, positive thinking: "What are we going to do about it?" "What should be the mission of our unique enterprise, and what steps do we have to take to fulfill that goal?"

Picking the right mission obviously is crucial. It is also difficult. To be most useful, the master strategy should (1) identify the particular services—that is, the product-market *domain*—which the company will promote; (2) select a basic resource conversion technology by which these services will be created—a technology that hopefully will give the company some *differential advantage* as a supplier; (3) with this concept of its economic and social mission, determine the major *thrusts* necessary to move the company from its present course to the desired one; and finally, (4) establish the *criteria* and the standards that will be used to measure achievement. No strategy is complete without all four of these dimensions being clarified.

A critical judgment in designing strategy is what to accept as unchangeable. Every company possesses (or can attract) only limited resources, and it has to be careful that the goals it sets are achievable. In addition to sensing a future opportunity, central management must realistically assess the cost of grasping the opportunity in terms of people, outside help, money, and other resources. It must then decide whether "that is something we can do." This issue, along with other aspects of strategy formulation, is explored in Chapter 5.

Establishing Policy

Strategy concentrates on basic directions, major thrusts, and overriding priorities. The full implication of the strategy, however, is clarified by thinking through the more detailed policy that guides execution of the strategy. Central managers of each company must actively participate in shaping policy (1) partly because working through the policy implications is an excellent way to check the practicality of a basic concept and (2) especially to make sure that the intent of strategy is correctly interpreted into the work of the various departments of the company.

Almost all companies need policy guidance on product lines, customers, and sales promotion. Likewise, the implication of strategy on research and development, production, and procurement should be expressed in policy. In the human resource area, policy on selection, compensation, and industrial relations helps build the desired personnel strength; financial policy regarding allocation and sources of capital shape money resources. Each of these fields is examined in Part 2. A significant role of policy is to indicate the direction and degree of emphasis these and other sensitive fields should receive in order to effectively project company strategy.

Most attention in this book is directed toward change—adapting to new opportunities and pressures. Nevertheless, during the time any given strategy is in effect, consistent integrated action is highly important. Policy is a major tool of central management for securing such consistent behavior. Policy permeates the numerous daily activities of a firm and helps establish a normal, predictable pattern of behavior.

Strategy for Diversified Corporations

A company, as we are using that term, focuses on a particular type of business, say life insurance or video cassette recorders. Each of such businesses has its own markets, technology, competitors, and other distinctive features. Therefore, strategy and policy must be fitted to that business—as just outlined.

A diversified corporation, however, faces a different set of issues. It has a family of business-units. It must decide which of these businesses to expand and which to contract. Capital and other scarce resources must be allocated to the various businesses. Mergers or divestments may be arranged. Perhaps ways can be found for one of its business-units to help another. And, the inputs which the corporation will provide to give its businesses a differential advantage over their competitors should be strengthened. These issues will be explored in Part 3.

Note that the "company" or business-unit continues to be the primary building block for managerial planning. The strength of any diversified corporation rests predominantly on its separate businesses. They are the sources of growth, earnings, stability, etc. And each of these business-units gains strength through its own strategy and policy. For this reason, it is wise first to develop a strategy and policy for each business-unit which will enable that business to adapt best to its opportunities and threats. Then a combined corporate strategy and policy for all the businesses can be devised as a superstructure.

Building an Organization

Strategy and policy, at both the business-unit and corporate levels, are carried out by an organization. Unless this organization is well designed for its tasks, the plans, however sound, may lead to mediocre results. In fact, if the strategy relies on, say, pioneering in a new field, an ineffective organization that failed in such leadership could bring disaster.

The way in which activities are combined into sections and departments will affect the choice of problems to receive first attention, the speed of coordination, and the cost of performing the service. Decentralization is well suited to a strategy stressing local service, but it encounters difficulty with computerized production scheduling. A strategic decision to expand internationally alters the optimum power and location of staff units. Product diversification usually modifies the range of decisions that can be made wisely in the senior corporate office. As these examples indicate, central management must appraise the company organization in terms of where tasks critical to the success of its strategy can be performed most effectively.

In most enterprises these adjustments in organization design are highlighted in deliberate "reorganizations." The enterprise goes through a series of *stages*, moving first from a "one-person show" to a set of specialized departments. Then as volume and diversity increase, a third kind of structure becomes necessary; separate, self-contained product or regional divisions are established. Finally, if diversification continues, a conglomerate structure is needed.

Especially for strategy choices—which often shape the destiny of a business—somebody has to have the last say. And as corporations grow, oversight is needed. So, a critical part of central managerial structure is the board of directors. Also vital are executives with qualities and experience that fit the organization design. These and related organization issues are examined in Part 4.

Guiding Execution

With strategy, policy, and organization decided, the stage is set. Actual achievement, however, awaits the action. Central management necessarily relies heavily on junior executives for immediate supervision of operations. But senior executives can never fully divest themselves of leadership in the execution phase of purposeful endeavor. As explained in Part 5, this phase includes specific programming of nonrepetitive work, communicating and motivating, and exercising control over the rate and the quality of performance.

Substantial amounts of time are necessary for this make-happen effort. Many people, inside the company and out, have to be contacted personally, and unexpected difficulties inevitably call for on-the-spot adjustments. But during the process the executives are accumulating both information and a subjective feel for the actual performance of company services that are immensely valuable in planning the following cycles of activity.

Interaction and Evolution

Figure 1-2 depicts the broad division of central management tasks that we have briefly described—analyzing company outlook, designing strategy, establishing policy, setting up organization, and guiding execution.

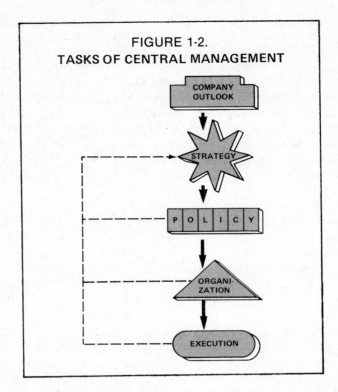

FIGURE 1-2.
TASKS OF CENTRAL MANAGEMENT

Three qualifications to the simple sequence shown in the chart should be made explicit. First, in a going concern each phase influences all the others to some degree. Firmly established policy or organization, for instance, may make a proposed strategy easy (or difficult) to put into action; in that case, policy or organization influences the choice of strategy. Such a "reverse flow" is suggested by the light line on the side of the chart. Nevertheless, while some of this "reverse flow" is always present, the primary sequence for a dynamic service enterprise is the one emphasized on the chart and used as the structure of this book.

Second, for diversified corporations a separate analysis of outlook, strategy, and policy will be necessary for each business-unit. And in the process of combining these business-unit plans into a balanced corporate plan, some constraints and modifications of the strategy or policy of a business-unit may arise.

Third, a neatly integrated package of strategy, policy, organization, and execution does not stay neat. The environment changes. Even the company's own success creates the need for revision. Consequently, the broad process described must be repeated and repeated again. Minor adjustments and refinements will be occurring most of the time. Major reshuffling, however, is expensive in both financial and human terms; so, like tooling-up for a new automobile model, a particular design should be followed long enough to learn how to use it well and to recoup the investment. But it is recognized that sooner or later retooling will be necessary.

These qualifications—the interaction between parts and the need for successive revisions—do not diminish the usefulness of the basic model proposed. Quite the opposite, these added complexities make an analytical framework even more valuable as an aid to orderly thinking.

The versatility of the model is further developed in Chapter 23 where it aids in the examination of managing multinational enterprises. Coming at the end of the book, Chapter 23 also serves as a review of the step-by-step breakdown in Parts 1 through 5.

QUESTIONS FOR CLASS DISCUSSION

1. As a sample illustration of the resource conversion model of an enterprise, consider the daily (weekly) student paper of your university. (a) What resource inputs are converted into what outputs of satisfaction? (b) For each main resource contributor, what is the two-way exchange? That is, what are the characteristics of the input which the paper wants (function, time, quality, etc.) and what are the characteristics of the satisfactions that the paper gives in exchange?

2. The president of the Ford Motor Company has said that a part of his firm's higher wage rates and thus higher labor costs per automobile than those of Japanese firms can be explained by the refusal of the Japanese firms to pass on to their workers as much of their sales revenue as do American firms, thus lessening the relative welfare and living standards of the Japanese assembly workers. Does this seem an action of irresponsible labor relations by the Japanese management and a harm to the employees' welfare?

3. "Where were you *last* year?" the K-Mart buyer said to the Plasto Company president who was offering lamps for the Christmas rush at bargain prices. The buyer already knew the answer, that Plasto had been busy with Sears, Roebuck & Co.'s business, and so he turned the president away empty-handed. During the previous year Sears had abandoned a price-cutting campaign designed to attract customers in an effort to improve profit margins. Sales dropped and Sears cut orders to its suppliers sharply. Plasto went from feast to famine as its sales were cut in half. Efforts by Plasto to find new customers have not been successful. Other lamp manufacturers appear to have cut their own prices by at least 20 percent. Have Sears' actions been socially responsible? K-Mart's? Plasto's? Other lamp manufacturers'?

4. (a) Foreign corporations own all or substantial blocks of the stock of several U.S. businesses. Examples include Lever Brothers, Shell Oil, A&P, Ciba-Geigy Pharmaceuticals, BIC Pens. Do you believe that such U.S. businesses are less responsive to U.S. social problems (unemployment, inflation, consumer protection, and the like) than are locally owned companies? (b) Do you believe that businesses in Europe or developing countries which are owned by U.S. corporations are responsive to the social problems in the countries in which they are located? (c) What is your general conclusion about socially responsible behavior of multinational corporations?

5. The vast majority of a group of about 200 managers of publicly traded stock corporations, when questioned, believed their objective (in return for suitable compensation) was to maximize the profit to the stockholders. When the managers were questioned more closely about this single-minded objective, many qualifications and doubts were added. Under difficult conditions (major recessions, substantial loss of market share, sudden new environmental demands made by the state, a tight squeeze on cash flow when prices dropped) personal and organizational survival became far more important to managers than the interest of shareholders. Explain this change.

6. Eastern Airlines, one of the largest U.S. carriers, has had a series of disputes with its employees' unions. In the early 1980s, a string of deficits totaling over $400 million coupled with heavy commitments for new, more efficient planes brought on a financial crisis. To make ends meet, Eastern demanded a 20 percent cut in labor costs (labor consumes 37 percent of Eastern's revenues) in exchange for a 20 percent share in future profits. The machinists' union especially was bitterly opposed, although Eastern's president insisted that this offer was much better than the alternative of bankruptcy. (A reorganization following bankruptcy would undoubtedly provide fewer jobs, a major overhaul of work rules, and lower take-home pay—though the pay would still be high in terms of the average for all U.S. industry.) (a) In this situation, what is Eastern's social responsibility to its millions of riders? its 37,000 employees? its bankers who are lending money to keep this company afloat? the communities it serves? (b) Is the management of Eastern justified in holding out for the cut in labor costs at the expense of poisoned labor relations in the future and the possible reactions of embittered employees? (c) Should Eastern be prepared to take a long strike over the labor cost question which would lead to a major loss in revenues and almost certain bankruptcy?

7. The chairman of Hoffman-LaRoche (a large pharmaceutical manufacturer), when asked about the disclosure of operating information to the stockholders, was able to say, "This has nothing to do with them." Explain.

8. Explain *your* understanding of the phrase, "social responsibility."

9. Social standards change. We praised pioneers for clearing land and draining swamps, but now similar action may be illegal. Likewise, legislation and company practice protecting women workers was hailed as a social triumph fifty years ago; now such practice is unfair discrimination. (a) Is it the responsibility of company central managements to decide what social standards should be in their own organi-

zations? (b) Since a new standard often affects previous jobs, markets, financial returns, and other prevailing resource conversion patterns, should central management work to accept some standards, such as equal employment opportunity in hiring; keep others from the past, such as seniority in firing; and reject others, such as long, flowing hair for men working in sales?

10. When England "nationalized" its coal mines (in effect, the government became the stockholder of the mines), how was the social responsibility of the managers of the mines changed? In answering, please focus on responsibilities to interests other than the new stockholder.

11. The Nestlé company, a Swiss-owned firm which operates worldwide, was pressured by a group of shareholders who demanded that a Swiss be appointed to the top operating post in the company when a Frenchman retired as managing director. The two chief candidates for the post—who had both managed large subsidiaries of Nestlé very successfully—were non-Swiss. Were the shareholders acting in their own interest? Explain.

CASE 1
Snowbird Snowmobiles

You are sizing up a potential job as assistant to the president of Snowbird Snowmobiles, Inc. and have gathered the following information from key persons.

Marketing V.P. "Snowmobiling has become a major winter sport. It offers healthy, family-oriented winter activity, easily obtained by millions of Americans. Few other outdoor activities are available in the winter that do not require exceptional physical fitness.. . . . There are already about four million snowmobiles in the U.S. and Canada. With three active users per machine, that means around twelve million people are enjoying the thrill of skimming over the snow going places they could never reach before.

"In some ways, snowmobiling is a cross between skiing and motorcycling, except that it is easier and safer than either of these sports. There is nothing like it for speed, and power, and fun. And it fills a niche of a winter sport everyone can enjoy. Snowmobiling has had a phenomenal growth in about fifteen years. Already, according to the National Sporting Goods Association, people are spending over half as much for snowmobiling equipment as skiing equipment. There are lots of local clubs with visiting back and forth.

TABLE 1.
RETAIL SALES OF SPORTING EQUIPMENT

Summer

Camping appliances	$463 million
Fishing tackle	608 million
Golf clubs, balls, bags	704 million
Tennis rackets, balls, strings	799 million
Water skis	114 million

Winter

Bowling balls	116 million
Ice skates & hockey equipment	92 million
Skis, boots, bindings	505 million
Snowmobiles	267 million

"Currently we are still recovering from too rapid, undisciplined growth. Ask the E.P.A. rep; she can give you that story. Five years ago there were forty-eight companies selling snowmobiles. They flooded the market and couldn't maintain service. Then the bubble burst. Within two years over a third of the companies folded. But then competition got really rough. Last year there were only eleven in business, and now we are seven! Unfortunately, the bankrupt companies left a lot of unsold inventory in dealers' hands. So price competition has been fierce. Maybe one or two more companies will withdraw, but most of us believe the shakeout is over. With the underlying growth in snowmobiling, five or six companies could have very satisfactory volume.

TABLE 2.
NEW PRODUCTS SOLD (number)

Year	Industry	Snowbirds	Share
Near-term future	(250,000–		
(Company Estimate)	300,000)	(65,000)	(25)%
This year	200,000	48,000	24
Last year	250,000	45,000	18
Two years ago	300,000	45,000	15
Peak—five years ago	500,000	60,000	12

"Product improvement has been substantial. The noise level is now a mere fraction of what it was in the early days. Machines are more rugged with an average life of seven years, up from three. Safety is improved. We have been leaders in this, but all surviving companies have made vast improvements. Of course, this has contributed to increasing the retail price of a good snowmobile to over $2,000."

Representative of U.S. Environmental Protection Agency. "A few years ago snowmobiles were a major headache—noisier than an airplane and dashing all over the place. Protests came from all directions, and the hot-rod snowmobilers were just as vociferous. But there has been improvement and we are getting fewer complaints.

"The noise now is like a garden tractor, thanks to an industry association standard. We have a regulation calling for an even lower standard, but have temporarily postponed its effective date to see how the public reacts to the present machines.

"Damage to the natural terrain is still being debated. Originally we included snowmobiles along with other off-the-road vehicles (such as dune-buggies, which are tearing up fragile desert ecology) in exclusion from national parks and other public lands. Two considerations lead to postponing that regulation also. As the industry association claims, we do not yet have hard evidence that snowmobiles have any lasting effect on the ground or vegetation. Apparently, when the snow melts, their tracks go with it. More important, a whole network of snowmobile tracks have been established—75,000 miles; and most snowmobilers stick to the tracks. We are continuing to keep an eye on what happens because there are a lot of people who think we should outlaw snowmobiles except in remote areas and for commercial purposes. Safety is outside our jurisdiction, but I understand it also is improving. Fatalities last year were down to 121. Partly that reflects better equipment. Mostly it is safety training by local clubs. When people skim a few inches over a slick surface at fifty miles an hour in a lightweight vehicle (about 300 pounds), the driver better know how to dodge a tree or rock."

Production V.P. "Some things we can act on—like engineering in better quality—but in the plant we have to take what volume comes. We have capacity to produce at least 50 percent more machines than we did last year, which means our overhead is high. That particularly hurts because we also have seasonal valleys. To limit investment in inventory, our policy is to work short shifts or shut down entirely. I personally think this uncertainty about when there will be work is why we have a union. Here in St. Cloud [Minnesota] the workers have few opportunities to find other work during layoffs.

"We also watch our parts inventory which can get out of hand because we buy our engines from Japan and all the machined parts and accessories from some distance. To most of our suppliers we're a small customer. But by concentrating all purchases of a particular item with a single supplier we can get quick deliveries when we need them.

"Actually our competitors are in the same fix. The largest company, Bombardier, is located in a small town in Canada and I guess they have more delivery problems than we do. But their labor rates are lower than ours.

"Our three models—Stag, Stallion, Silver Fox—are similar in construction and in many of their parts so that does not complicate production very much. I came up through production and know the operations. We did bring in several engineers to work on new designs and quality; they are very important in our picture."

Finance V.P. "Here's our income statement and balance sheet in condensed form. A couple of items may not be clear.

"In addition to snowmobiles, we sell a fine line of snowmobile clothing including gloves and helmets. We subcontract the manufacture of this clothing but perform all other functions ourselves. As you see, the income from all the supplementary items adds significantly to snowmobile sales, and we would like to see this grow.

TABLE 3.
BALANCE SHEET (in millions)

Cash	$ 2	Accounts payable	$ 7
Accounts receivable	4	Bank loan	5
Inventory	29	Accrued items	3
Current assets	35	Current liabilities	15
Plant & equipment, net	12	Mortgage loan	4
		Paid-in-capital	20
		Retained earnings	8
	$47		$47

"Due to industry conditions, profit margins are unsatisfactory. When the industry moves beyond the liquidation of weak companies and demand picks up, the profit ratio should change dramatically. The two projections on the income statement show what should happen with even conservative assumptions.

"Our inventory is high. Part of the explanation is that we continue to own all the inventory held by our distributors. In this respect, they are like manufacturers' agents and we sell directly to many small dealers. This arrangement helps us get wide distribution without operating our own regional offices. Even so, the inventory is too high. If we could cut it five million we could pay off the bank loan.

"Nevertheless, we are in a strong financial position. A public stock issue back in the boom days gives us all the equity capital we need—at least so long as we stick to the snowmobile business."

President. "You've talked with our top people, except for the person we brought in to manage our clothing line. It's a lean organization, and that is part of the reason we are talking to you. There is just no slack to devote to unusual problems; we don't have time to think about what we might do differently.

"We have come through a very stormy period, and are now Number 2 in the industry. It is time for the tide to turn, and when it does we want to take full advantage of the position we have worked hard to achieve."

TABLE 4.
INCOME STATEMENT
(financial data in millions)

	Last year actual	1–3 year projection	3–5 year projection
Assumptions:			
Industry volume (1,000 units)	200	250	300
Companies in industry	7	6	6
Snowbird share of market	24%	26%	30%
Inflation rise (total from last year)	—	20%	40%
Gross profit margin	21%	23%	24%
Financial results:			
Snowmobile sales	$64	$103	$168
Sales of parts, accessories, & clothing	18	29	47
Total sales	82	132	215
Cost of goods sold	65	102	163
Gross profit	17	30	52
Marketing expense	7	11	18
General & administrative expense	7	10	15
Interest expense	1	2	4
Total expenses	15	23	37
Operating profit	2	7	15
Income taxes	1	4	8
Net profit	$ 1	$ 3	$ 7

Questions

1. As part of the process of evaluating you, the president of Snowbird asks you to submit any recommendations you have for improving future prospects for the company.
2. If you were offered the job, at a reasonable salary, would you take it? Why?

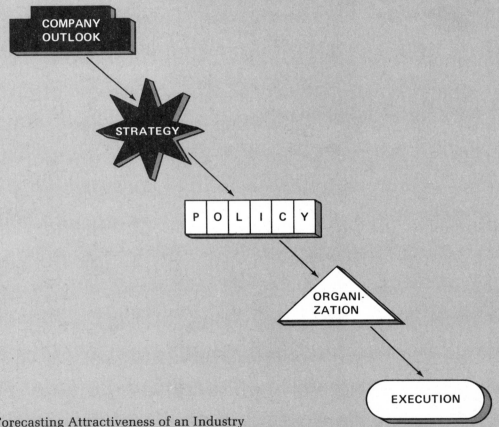

Part 1

DETERMINING BUSINESS-UNIT STRATEGY

COMPANY OUTLOOK

STRATEGY

P O L I C Y

ORGANI-ZATION

EXECUTION

2 FORECASTING ATTRACTIVENESS OF AN INDUSTRY

Wise strategy is based on a hard, objective look at the setting—the environment—in which our enterprise will operate. We should know whether our industry is declining (rural post offices), mature (fast-food restaurants), or in the early stages of major growth (office automation). More than volume of output is involved. Shifts in quality of services, fierceness of competition, government opposition or support, opportunities to be unique may sharply constrain what is possible for us to do.

This chapter gives you a point-of-view and framework for marshaling such data about the attractiveness of an industry. Then, in following chapters, our particular strengths and our options in this environment will be examined.

DYNAMIC FORCES AFFECTING BUSINESS

A sharp cutback in gasoline supplies would upset our economy. People could not get to work, vacation resorts would close, railroads would be rejuvenated, social relations would become more provincial—to mention only a few of the ramifications.

Similarly, the rise of independent nations in Africa is much more than a local political matter. World sources of raw materials are jeopardized; potential new markets for such items as radios and pharmaceuticals are created; fair-employment practices in, say, Detroit, become even more crucial in foreign diplomacy; added strain is placed on satellite communications.

These examples of change illustrate a major problem for modern executives: adapting the direction and the operation of their enterprises to shifts in the environment. To identify shifts that may create opportunities or threats for a specific enterprise, regular scanning of four sources of change is desirable: technological, social, political, and economic. Predicting both the significant change *and* its impact on our operations is necessary. Some current illustrations follow.

Technological Changes

Electronic Computers. The dramatic development of computers has become the classic example of a new generation of technology. Computer capabilities have

been increasing tenfold every three or four years. Meanwhile the minimum size
has dropped from that of a freight car to a wristwatch. Clearly, the physical
capabilities have outrun our knowledge of how to use this electronic wonder.

The new uses that will have the most influence on business strategy still lie
in the future. Banks, for example, may maintain a whole set of books for depositors, pay their bills, and provide subtotals for use on annual income tax returns.
And these changes may contribute to a rearrangement of our financial institutions. Medical diagnosis, traffic control, libraries, and chemical analysis are
among the many other possibilities. Eventually the postal clerk sorting mail may
be as obsolete as a telegraph operator.

Manipulative Biology. Potentially more upsetting than electronic advances are
the technological advances in biology. By tinkering with the DNA structure of a
reproductive cell, new living forms can be created. One hopeful prospect is
transferring genetic information among species of plants, enabling the design of
hardy plants which contain high protein. Such plants could substantially
improve the world food supply, especially for countries where the present diet is
deficient in protein.

A related technique is cloning—producing identical copies. Thus, a prize-
winning bull or cow might be duplicated over and over again. This process coupled with the use of surrogate mothers could quickly change animal husbandry
throughout the world.

One disturbing aspect of manipulative biology is the possibility of applying
such techniques to human beings. Even the idea of being able to predetermine
the sex of a new baby has caused intense debate. So as often happens, technological developments become entwined with social and political pressures.

Energy and Resources. The difficulty of maintaining a balance between the
accelerating use and the supply of natural resources is illustrated by basic
energy. Our insatiable appetite for electrical energy may outstrip the supply that
can be economically produced. For Europe and Japan especially, the uncertain
supply of oil from the Middle East has stepped up construction of nuclear power
plants. In the United States, we can postpone heavy reliance on nuclear plants
by turning back to coal. But the required investment in any shift away from oil
is tremendous. As a result, manufacture of products requiring high-energy
inputs is moving out of our traditional industrial centers.

Perhaps the supply of fresh pure water, rather than energy, will become the
bottleneck on expansion. Most large metropolitan areas in the country face serious water shortages, and the decline in water tables suggests that the problem
may be more than lack of adequate facilities. Clearly, we are going to need new
technologies to help us use water more effectively.

At the same time, control of water pollution is essential. Both communities
and industries will have to use new techniques to hold down contamination.

One of our greatest potential resources is the ocean. It contains vast mineral resources and has a virtually untapped capacity to support both animal and plant life.

Social Changes

Like technology, the social environment of a company presents both opportunities and obstacles. Also like technology, part of the changes can be foreseen—the forces that will generate them are already known. The nature, magnitude, and timing of other social changes are shrouded in uncertainty.

Population. A few years ago, estimates of U.S. population growth to 300 million by the turn of the century were common. These estimates were based on a high birth rate in the 1950s and early 1960s. Recently, attitudes toward family formation, birth control, and responsibility of rearing children have contributed to a sharp drop in the birth rate. Now the century-end population is often predicted at 260 million, with a stable population shortly thereafter. This drop sharply reduces the demand for elementary schools.

More striking in recent years has been a move from downtown areas to the suburbs. This move to the outskirts has not only helped boom housing and the construction industry, it has also revolutionized retail selling. Concurrently, it has created mass need for urban renewal. The older areas in the central cities typically house our lowest income group; this leads to overcrowding and poor maintenance. And such conditions foster social deterioration—frustration, indifference, drug addiction, crime. Slums are not new. Those of the 19th century were far worse physically, but usually they had more social resilience.

Workforce. Women are the most dynamic element in our workforce. Not only are they over 40 percent of all entries into the workplace, but also they are moving into many jobs previously held only by men—from bank tellers to corporate directors. Only a generation ago "progressive" labor laws sought to protect women; now *any* differentiation is illegal. This shift in social and legal values greatly enlarges the supply of able people for key posts.

Managers must also learn to deal with a number of potentially productive employees whose lifestyles and values sharply curtail the importance they attach to their jobs. Employment of such men and women will never be satisfactory to either the individual or the company until some concurrence on worthwhile goals is achieved.

Pluralism. In place of dominant national values, people are becoming more involved with particular groups. Such groups may focus around ethnic background, athletic or cultural interest, religion, occupation, physical handicap, even age (the population 65 years or older will increase 20 percent during the 1980s). Improved communication and ease of travel enable dispersed people to form strong social bonds. Often these groups want special services or products, and are becoming differentiated markets. And their existence may complicate political action.

Political Changes

Government Policy. Government action impinges on business in a variety of ways. Most obvious is direct regulation—dealing with such issues as antitrust, fair trade (advertising, pricing, and the like), sale of securities, labor relations, minimum wages, or air pollution. On the other hand, nearly every kind of business benefits, at least indirectly, from import restrictions, subsidies, research grants, financial aids, or other forms of assistance.

Overriding partisan politics is war. Apart from the question of sheer survival, a major war drastically alters allocation of resources and the activities companies are permitted to perform. Consequently, one of the elements in every company strategy is what provision, if any, should be made for the possibility of war.

International Development. The birth of a new nation or a new government in power occurs almost monthly. We are witnessing the formation of many new states especially in Africa; and throughout the world feelings of nationalism are strong. At the same time, radio, movies, magazines, and travel have greatly expanded the aspirations of "have not" nations. This inherently unstable situation is complicated by the "have" nations in their jockeying for influence and for economic or military advantage.

In this milieu the businessperson faces contradictory factors. Great human need and perhaps the incentive for investment are countered by occasional confiscation of mines and oilwells, import quotas, and similar acts. The result is widely fluctuating risk in dealing with developing countries.

Inflation and Unemployment. Permeating and confusing all these changes is inflation. Annual price and wage increases of 5 to 10 percent have become almost normal. In many countries 10 to 15 percent is considered modest.

Government efforts to restrain inflation clash with very strong pressures to increase, rather than decrease, expenditures. Most stubborn is high unemployment. Few governments, of any political persuasion, are prepared to take firm anti-inflationary action if it means increasing the demoralizing burden of unemployment. In addition, military budgets are sacrosanct and social security payments irreversible. Politically acceptable cutbacks are indeed very hard to find.

One of the main ways to check inflation is to increase productivity—i.e., generate more output with a given input of resources. And it is enterprise managers—the resource converters we described in Chapter 1—who carry the initiative in improving productivity! No single company can sweep back the inflationary tide, but each productivity advance helps.

Economic Changes

Economic forces have received primary attention in business analysis—and also in most business school courses. Since we make repeated use of these concepts later in this chapter and elsewhere in the book, only a reminder of their importance is needed here.

Macro Shifts. The long upward trend which we experienced in gross national product has introduced an assumption of *growth* in most strategic planning. But in the United States and other Western countries that growth rate has slowed down. So, a fundamental question is how "mature" our economy has become and how much underlying growth we can assume in the future.

Of course, cyclical fluctuations confuse the picture. It is hard to perceive trends while riding a roller coaster. Yet the feasibility of a specific strategic thrust is strongly affected by timing it to fit recovery or recession.

Differences Among Economic Segments. Within the total economy, some segments fare better than others. For example, per capita income is growing faster in the Sun Belt than in New England. Services are expanding much more than manufacturing output. Although total farm production continues to lead in productivity, farm employment has dropped to less than 3 percent of the workforce.

The Economic Fate of Industries. A study of national economic accounts (which we recommended for all strategic planners) reveals two contrasting forces. Industries are interdependent; the growth of, say, housing construction is affected by employment in government agencies and in consumer goods industries, and likewise it affects the demand for lumber and doorbells. Despite this interdependence, industries do rise or fall over time: autos replace passenger trains, men's straw hats just disappear.

Prices and Profits. All these shifts in macro movements, in economic segments, and in industries have an impact on prices of specific goods and services and on annual profits of specific companies. The general economic forces are only part of the strategy picture, but they are irrepressible. As in navigating a ship, the pilot must reckon with the tide and the current.

Stress and Strain

Change, the theme of this chapter so far, produces stress in any individual or organization that goes through it. Pouring new wine into old bottles builds pressure that must be planned for beforehand or mopped up after the explosion.

The turret lathe operator who must develop new skills when electronic controls are added to the machine, the company that must change its organization structure when new products are added, the downtown hotel that finds its survival threatened by motels, and the stockbrokerage firm that loses clients to banks and mutual funds—all must plan for some adaptation of their way of operating.

The uncertainties from the international political scene and from changes in government policy often bring a feeling of uneasy tension combined with frustration—a feeling that unmanageable forces might be taking one toward some impending disaster and that there is nothing to be done about it. Psychiatrists occasionally call ours an Age of Anxiety.

Management has the never-ending task of providing enough stability and continuity of action to permit efficient performance and, at the same time, of adjusting company operations to the array of changes suggested in the preceding pages. The socially responsible response to a dynamic, imperfect world is to identify tasks that need doing and then to do them well.

FRAMEWORK FOR INDUSTRY ANALYSIS

Dynamic changes, like those just noted, can be baffling. There are so many shifts we are unsure which ones are important to us. So, we need a method for (1) singling out critical developments and (2) relating these forces to plans for our enterprise. One of the best ways to do this is to concentrate on the outlook for the industry in which we are operating—and also the outlook for any other industry that we might go into. Looking at the industry brings the picture into focus.

The future of every industry depends upon (1) the continuing demand for its output, (2) conditions affecting the supply of these goods and services, and (3) competitive conditions within the industry. Important topics in each of these dimensions are indicated in the following outline. With this framework we can relate most critical environmental changes directly to our industry, *and* we have a device for combining the varied influence of many different changes.

We will examine the nature of each of these topics in the following pages. All subheadings may not be important for a particular industry, and others may be added, but the underlying approach applies to large and small, profit and not-for-profit, and new and old industries.

Outlook for Industry
A.   Demand for Products or Services of the Industry
    1.   Long-run growth or decline
    2.   Stability of demand for products
    3.   Stage in product life cycle
B.   Supply of Products or Services
    1.   Capacity of the industry
    2.   Availability of needed resources
    3.   Volatility of technology

DEMAND FOR PRODUCTS OR SERVICES OF THE INDUSTRY

Long-Run Growth or Decline

The end uses of an industry's products provide a key to future demand. For instance, if the familiar flashlight battery were used only for flashlights, the demand would be stable and mature. Actually, small dry cells are used in portable radios, cassettes, action toys, emergency lights, and a variety of gadgets. Thus, the resulting high growth rate depends on a rising popularity of the portable entertainment devices.

Dry cells illustrate two other aspects of demand that may be significant. First, dry batteries have a *derived demand.* They are used only in association with some other product, and it is the popularity of these other products that leads to the demand for dry batteries. Manufacturers can do little to influence total industry sales; instead, their sales efforts focus on increasing their share of the market.

Second, the *focus of research and development effort* is not on new devices that will increase the demand for batteries. Of course, the manufacturers are glad to provide data to the designers of toys and radios, but these end products involve such different considerations that the battery manufacturers feel they have little to contribute. Instead, research by battery manufacturers is directed toward reduction of cost and improvement of quality.

After the possible uses of a product or a service of an industry have been explored, it is often desirable to classify potential customers by type and area. Thus the customers for automobile insurance may be grouped as private and commercial, and they may be further divided between regions. Then, any major changes affecting these customers can be related easily to our industry.

Stability of Demand for Products

Demand for a product or a service may be steady and predictable or it may be volatile and uncertain. The following factors give insight regarding stability.

Substitutes. The desire for the utility or satisfaction rendered by a product may be reasonably stable, yet the demand for the product itself may be quite unstable because of increased or decreased use of substitutes that render this same satisfaction. Ballpoint and felt-tip pens have reduced the demands for pencils. Atomic energy could replace crude oil. In each case the issue is not so much a decline in the demand for the service as the substitution of one product for another.

Durability of Products. Durable products have wide fluctuations in demand. Once constructed, houses, airports, and washing machines render services over a period of time, and consequently the demand for such products is more active during *periods of original construction* than during periods when existing facilities are merely being replaced. Also, the replacement of durable goods can often be postponed for a substantial period of time. For these reasons the demand for durable products tends to fluctuate over wider ranges than does the demand for such things as food, clothing, travel, and entertainment, which must be replenished to render additional services. Speculation may play a part in fluctuations of demand for almost any product; however, the more durable the product, the more lasting the maladjustment that may result from the unwarranted speculation.

Necessity Versus Luxury. Necessities, such as food and medical care, will enjoy a more stable demand than products such as swimming pools and foreign travel that are generally purchased only when people have funds over and above what is necessary for the first class of goods. However, attitudes toward services do switch. For example, air-conditioning or long-distance telephoning have moved from luxury to necessity for many users. Interactive cable TV may someday become a "necessity."

Stage in Product Life Cycle

Many products and services pass through a life cycle, as shown in Figure 2-1. Although the phases vary widely in length, experience with an array of products—from penicillin to automatic pinsetters in bowling alleys—does show that the concept is a useful analytical tool. Clearly, when electric refrigerators are already in 90 percent of the homes, growth prospects are much lower than for microwave ovens; refrigerators have reached the maturity phase. A shift from maturity to decline typically occurs when a substitute product or service appears on the scene—witness what happened to the small-town newspaper.

In addition to a way of predicting demand, the life-cycle concept bears directly on key factors for success. In the growth phase, a company can take risks with overcapacity and even with quality in an effort to establish a market position; profit margins will permit production inefficiencies. By contrast, in the maturity phase, efficient use of plant and close attention to production costs become much more important.

FIGURE 2-1.
CLASSICAL PRODUCT LIFE CYCLE

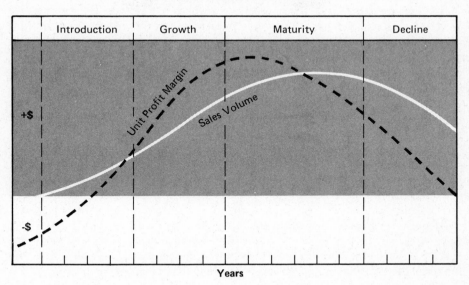

Every future shift in technology, social behavior, politics, and economic forces will increase or decrease the demand picture for at least some industries. Both small and large firms will feel the impact. Anticipating those impacts that will affect us is a crucial part of effective management.

SUPPLY OF PRODUCTS OR SERVICES

The outlook for profitable operations in an industry depends not only on the demand, but also on the available supply and cost of bringing such products or services to the market.

Capacity of the Industry

In a dynamic business system, some industries are likely to have excess capacity while others have inadequate capacity. At one stage, sulfa was the wonder antibiotic drug and pharmaceutical producers expanded greatly to meet the urgent demand. Then penicillin and Aureomycin came along, and the sulfa producers found themselves with a large capacity that could not be used. In the finance field, stockbrokers have been plagued with excess capacity when interest in stock speculation declines. In addition to such drops in demand, excess capacity may result from overexpansion. Sometimes a field of business such as personal computers or resort hotels looks so attractive that too many firms enter it.

Inadequate capacity is common in any expanding industry. If a new service like retirement villages meets with wide public acceptance, the original facilities may not be able to fill the demand. When capacity of an industry is scarcely adequate to meet demand, most companies will enjoy profitable operations. Products will find a ready market, prices will be firm, and a high level of operation will permit spreading overhead costs over many units.

In contrast, excess capacity will have a depressing influence on the outlook for an industry, for it may lead to low prices, low rates of operation, and a high proportion of sales expense.

The seriousness of excess capacity depends, in part, upon how large depreciation, interest, and other expenses connected with the facilities are in relation to total costs. If, as in the chemical fertilizer industry, these overhead charges are a high percentage of total expenses, individual companies may cut prices to low levels in an attempt to secure volume and at least some contribution above out-of-pocket expenses toward the fixed burden. On the other hand, if the bulk of expense goes for materials and labor, the excess capacity will have much less effect on supply and price because the relation between out-of-pocket costs and prices will be the controlling influence—whether the plant is busy or not.

Availability of Needed Resources

The sheer existence of an adequate supply of raw materials may be a factor in the outlook of a few industries, notably those depending upon a natural resource such as timber, crude oil, iron ore, or other minerals. In most cases, however, the problem is the price at which the materials can be obtained.

Future material costs depend on world demand, on new sources of supply—often from developing nations—and/or on production technology, as in the dramatic drop in the cost of computer chips. The number of suppliers is also important; with only a few available, they are more likely to exact high prices and stipulate terms of delivery. And if those few form an alliance, as the OPEC countries did, their bargaining position is further enhanced.

The seriousness of rising costs will depend upon the industry's (or company's) ability to pass such an increase on to its customers in the form of higher prices. Some industries, such as health services, can maintain their margins, whereas industries which face substitutes may be unable to raise their prices. Several pay-TV programs, for example, probably cannot raise their prices to protect their profit margins—although the evidence here is not yet clear.

The supply of labor may pose issues similar to those in materials. In a given region, skilled labor may be so scarce that expansion will be very difficult. Or, the costs of labor and of output restrictions may contribute to non-competitive costs—as has been the case in the U.S. shoe industry.

While materials and labor are most likely to be critical in an industry forecast, the availability of each needed resource should be assessed—as the resource converter model discussed at the beginning of Chapter 1 implies.

Volatility of Technology

Industries vary in the frequency with which new products are introduced and the frequency of changes in processing technology. For example, technology jumps quickly in the pharmaceutical, space, and urban-renewal industries.

When confronted with such volatile technology, managers must give close attention to research and development (R & D). They must be prepared to move promptly when either their own efforts or their competitors' create important innovations. The frequency of change means that market positions are insecure; consequently, caution in making capital investments is required. Success depends, in part, on being agile.

Social Constraints

Companies must act in a socially acceptable manner or face all sorts of delays and harassment. Having the facilities, resources, and technology to supply a desired service or product is not enough. In addition, all the activities of a company are expected to meet various social norms.

The catch is that these norms are not clearly defined. They keep changing, and various segments of society have quite different views on what is acceptable. Moreover, some industries, such as manipulative biology, are under more pressures than others.

Vague though the standards may be, the outlook for an industry should include the constraints within which that industry is—or will be—expected to operate. For example, the norms may relate to:

- pollution of the air, water, ground, etc.
- environmental protection—e.g., strip mining
- equal opportunity in employment, steady jobs
- dealing with people who are unpopular with strong pressure groups— communists, South Africans, Israelis, R.O.T.C., those involved in abortion clinics, etc.
- integrity, honesty, "questionable payments," and the like

The potential seriousness of social constraints is indicated by the prolonged delay they have imposed on the creation of a positive energy program for the country.

Inflation Vulnerability

Inflation may hurt an industry in several ways. Most common is costs rising faster than selling prices—a danger already noted.

Inflation may cause dislocation of sales volume. The demand for some products, especially non-durable luxuries, is "price elastic" and consumers simply do not buy when they feel the price is too high. In contrast, real estate and other durable products may have a speculative boom—and a later collapse.

Still another likely impact of inflation, which is less obvious at first, is inability to generate replacement capital. Sales may be made at what appears to be an attractive profit margin above the actual costs; but when the inventory and equipment have to be replaced, the money taken in is insufficient to cover the new prevailing costs. The longer the production cycle and the more capital-intensive the technology, the more likely such a capital shortage is to arise.

In summary, we see that demand for its services or products is only part of an industry's forecast. The ability to effectively meet the demand depends upon how well the industry will be able to cope with problems of resource availability, volatility of technology, social constraints, and vulnerability to inflation.

COMPETITIVE CONDITIONS IN THE INDUSTRY

The framework thus far has suggested that the outlook for an industry will be determined by the balance of various forces bearing on demand and supply. Competitive conditions within the industry will often affect the manner and the rapidity with which these forces work themselves out.

Government Support and Regulation

Even the most ardent advocates of "American individualism" will admit that the forces of demand and supply should not be given free sway in the contemporary business world. Both restraints and assistance are likely to be inserted by government bodies.

Forecasting the nature of restraints is difficult. In the Reagan era, for instance, control over several ethical drugs was increased and AT&T was broken up; at the same time airlines and truckers were given much more freedom for individual action. So, in this arena, specific national and state predictions are necessary.

Also, governments often provide *special advantages* to particular industries. Our merchant marine is heavily subsidized; many other industries are protected from foreign competition by tariffs; agricultural products have been granted large subsidies. In order to qualify for such special advantages, it is often necessary for the industry to conform to stipulations and regulations of the government. This is particularly true in the agricultural industries where the whole program of subsidies is associated with a plan for controlled production and marketing.

Such government action is frankly and deliberately designed to modify the underlying forces of demand and supply. It is part of the composite picture of the outlook for any industry.

Industry Leadership

The voluntary actions of members of an industry likewise affect the way demand and supply work out.

The *attitude* of the managements of companies in an industry can affect the future profitability of the entire industry. Some managers are likely to engage in any activities that might give them an immediate benefit, regardless of the future repercussions of such actions. In contrast, the typical managers in other industries are more "statesmanlike." They tend to adhere strictly to an accepted code of business ethics and are inclined to take a long-run industry viewpoint in their actions.

Organized cooperative effort also has a significant effect upon the outlook for some industries. There are literally hundreds of *trade associations*, which are the central agencies for such voluntary action. Many of these associations do little more than sponsor an annual convention and perhaps publish a trade paper. Others, like insurance associations, engage in research and compilation of information of interest to its members, lobby in national or state legislatures, conduct public relations campaigns, and promote fair trade practices.

Underlying these traditional patterns of leadership and cooperation are economic forces that shape the nature of competition in an industry. We turn to this form of competitive analysis in the next section.

FORECASTING COMPETITION WITHIN AN INDUSTRY

Two strong forces affecting "statesmanship" versus "dog-eat-dog" competition in an industry are (1) the mobility of competitors in and out of the industry, and (2) the relative bargaining power of key players in the industry.

Barriers to Mobility

Professor Michael E. Porter[1] and others report that the competitive structure in an industry is determined at least in part by the ease of entry and exit. This concept gives us a tool for forecasting how competition is likely to develop in our industry.

---

[1]Michael E. Porter, *Competitive Strategy: Techniques for Analyzing Industries and Competitors* (New York: The Free Press, 1980). See especially Chapters 1, 7, and 12.

Entry Barriers. The basic idea is that, especially in a growing industry, the more difficult it is for new competitors to enter, the more stable and profitable the industry is likely to be. Consider, for example, women's apparel. Almost anyone with a knowledge of dressmaking and enough capital to buy materials and rent sewing machines can enter the industry. The result is very sharp price competition, style piracy, widely fluctuating inventories, and frequent failure.

A less obvious example of ease of entry has prevailed in the passenger airline business. Planes are readily available for rent, maintenance and repair can be subcontracted to shops of the major operators, experienced pilots are looking for work, airport counter space can be rented. So, very little capital is needed to organize charter flights, and—with government deregulation—firms such as People Express and New York Air can grasp significant shares of selected markets with their low-price, low-cost service.

In contrast, other industries are very difficult to enter. Kodak, for instance, has such an established reputation for high-quality film combined with an effective widespread distribution network that new suppliers of film face almost insurmountable barriers. (Note that film developing and printing is much easier to enter and is subject to volatile price competition.)

Potential barriers to entry include:

1. Economies of scale. When large volume significantly cuts per unit costs, entry may be discouraged because years of losses would be necessary before any new firm could expect to achieve such a volume of sales. These economies of scale may exist in marketing or other functions as well as production.
2. Product differentiation. A distinctive product or service—including brand identification—makes entry difficult.
3. Large capital requirements. The high cost of building a new hospital, for example, is one of the factors that restrains newcomers from entering into a locality with existing facilities.
4. Customers' switching costs. If customers of an existing company have a large investment in training employees to use and maintain products or services of that company, switching to a new supplier will be resisted.
5. Access to distribution channels. Loyal dealers and retailers can be a distinct advantage to existing firms; newcomers may have to rely on less experienced distributors or embark on finding and training a whole new set.
6. Superior technology. Firms already in an industry may have patented processes or expertise based on long experience. Unless the newcomer can somehow overcome this cost advantage its profit margin will be squeezed.
7. Favorable access to raw materials or favorable location. In the fast-food industry, for example, new entrants may have difficulty finding good locations not already occupied by older companies. DeBeers Company may have preempted most of the supply of gem-quality diamonds.

When a combination of such factors discourages new firms from entering an industry, the competitive pressures are stabilized; there is less chance that some aggressive newcomer will rock the boat.

Exit Barriers. The situation differs if industry demand is falling rather than growing. Here the mobility issue is how fast competitors will leave. If available supply shrinks as fast as industry volume drops, then normal competition is likely to continue. However, when industry capacity substantially exceeds demand cut-throat competition is apt to emerge. Therefore in declining industries we need to predict barriers to exit.

Among the reasons why companies may be loath to cut capacity or withdraw entirely are these:

1. Durable and specialized assets. Manufacturers of cement, for example, hold heavy investments in mills that have no alternative use. Consequently, the manufacturers are under severe pressure to continue producing cement at whatever price may be had.
2. High costs of exit. Termination pay for employees or warranty obligations on products may be so large that shutting down costs more than fighting for the remaining business.
3. Impact on related operations. A faltering product may be continued as a service to customers who buy other, more profitable products from the same supplier. Or, a vertically integrated firm may stay in a declining market because this volume helps to keep its raw material plant busy.
4. Managers' emotional commitment. Like loyalty to a losing team, managers who have spent years perfecting a product or service may refuse to give up. Professors of Greek keep on offering courses in Greek syntax.
5. Social pressures. The closing of a business throws people out of work, may disrupt a town, and may provoke government sanctions. For instance, often railroads are not permitted to abandon service to declining communities.

Several alternative strategies are available for what Harrigan calls, "playing an end game."[2] Nevertheless, high barriers to exit are likely to create very volatile competition in declining industries.

Relative Bargaining Power

In addition to entry and exit barriers, the future competitive structure of an industry will be partly shaped by the relative power of key players—an issue that we will examine in Chapter 4. Generally, when a single firm dominates an industry, it sets a continuing stable pattern. But when several strong aggressive companies clash, all sorts of actions and responses should be anticipated.

Not only competition among suppliers is involved. If only a few customers buy most of the output—as automobile manufacturers do for purchased parts—they can drive very tough bargains on specifications, delivery, and prices. Similarly, if one or two suppliers of critical services or raw materials have relatively strong bargaining power, they may be able to influence where and how competition takes place. For instance, when du Pont first introduced nylon yarn, it influenced the quality of products made of nylon and the consumer service.

---

[2]See K. R. Harrigan, *Strategies for Declining Businesses* (Lexington, MA: D.C. Heath and Company, 1980).

We can, then, make reasonable predictions about the nature of competition in an industry if we consider—in addition to demand and supply factors—entry and exit barriers along with the relative power of key players.

When applying these concepts, the focus should be specific business segments where interdependence of various participants is strong. Categories such as steel, or food, or health services are too broad to be of much use in strategic management.

SUMMARY

The base from which a company strategy should be developed is an insightful assessment of (1) dynamic conditions in the environment where the company operates, (2) prospects for its industry generally, (3) strengths and weaknesses of the company to compete in that industry, and (4) the likely responses of key actors in the industry to strategic moves that it initiates. We have considered the first two topics in this chapter; we will examine the third and fourth topics in the next two chapters.

Strategy is concerned with future action in a dynamic environment. Obviously, predicting what that environment is likely to be is a vital step in this process. However, such prediction is difficult for business managers partly because they face so many interrelated variables. One useful way to simplify environmental forecasting is to focus on industries—the industry in which we now operate and any other industry we consider entering.

A time-tested framework for analyzing an industry covers (1) demand for its products and services, (2) supply of those products and services, and (3) competitive conditions within the industry. In the last few pages we have stressed competitive analysis because in the past its prediction has received much less attention than the other aspects of industry outlook. But all three warrant continuing attention by top executives.

The next step is a careful look at how our company fits into the predicted scene.

QUESTIONS FOR CLASS DISCUSSION

1. Select an industry in which you are considering taking a job. Develop an "outlook" for that industry using the framework outlined in this chapter. Do you still want to work in that industry?

2. "The growing mood of conservatism in American society is probably related to the maturation of the population and the waning of the youth culture," said Jeffrey Evans of the National Institute of Child Health and Human Development, as quoted in *Business Week.* Do you agree that the American population is maturing? (The median age in 1970 was 28 years; in 1984, 31 years; and, in 2000, is predicted to be 36 years.) What "youth culture" could be waning? Will the mood of conservatism then continue growing? How might this affect dress designs? Shoe designs? The sale of surfboards? Travel by train? Pension funds?

3. (a) Assume that the president of a mobile home manufacturing company asks you, "What are the half dozen key factors in the environment that I should watch in order to anticipate the growth or decline in our industry?" Give your answer. (b) Do the same for eggs.

4. For years the restaurant industry has attracted small entrepreneurs; it is an arena where entry and exit have been relatively rapid. How do you think the growth of fast-food chains has affected restaurant competition in the locality in which you live? Use concepts from this chapter to prepare an outlook for the restaurant industry in your locality.

5. As the birth rate in the United States (babies per thousand population) dropped steadily since 1955 and as the absolute number of births declined after 1960, so also did the prospects and fortunes of manufacturers of baby food. Rivalry increased as sales and profits dropped. Swift and Co. (the meat-packing and food division of Esmark Corporation) first stepped up the pace of rivalry by increasing advertising allowances to retailers and dropping its prices. Both Beech-Nut Corporation and H. J. Heinz followed the price cuts, while Gerber Products ("Our business is babies") retaliated by adding new products, selling at a premium price, and cutting some of its costs through vertical integration. Eventually the price competition became so severe that Swift and Co. left the market and discontinued making and selling baby foods, while Beech-Nut went through two changes of ownership and was finally sold off at a give-away price to become a privately held corporation. With Beech-Nut's costs down, it cut some prices and began to advertise its juice line heavily. Gerber's followed the price cuts (as did Heinz) but kept a premium price position. Eventually market shares were estimated to be: Gerber's—69 percent, Heinz—16 percent, Beech-Nut—12 percent, and private labels—3 percent. H. J. Heinz had already closed several baby food plants and the one remaining was operating at 75 percent of capacity. An executive said, "Even using some fairly generous projections for the late 1980s, the market will be much less than it was in 1960." (a) Explain why Beech-Nut and Heinz stayed in the game as long as they did. (b) What are the exit barriers for the baby-food industry? (c) Explain why Gerber's has increased its market share. (d) Can you find Heinz and Beech-Nut baby food in your local supermarket? A private-label brand?

6. In the past, international agreements to restrict the world supply of a basic product, such as rubber, coffee, or copper, have fallen apart within a few years. Either discord among the supplying countries and/or new sources of supply have led to

renewed competition. (a) Do you think such agreements will be more stable in the future? Use crude oil or bauxite (aluminum ore) as an example. (b) After answering (a), appraise the method you used to make your forecast. What are the strengths and the weaknesses of that forecasting method?

7. (a) "From 1985 to 1990, major problems are likely to arise from the labor surplus that will be caused by the enormous size of the 25- to 44-year-old group as it bulges through the economic arteries." So say many demographers. What will happen to the competition for jobs? Will blacks, other minorities, women, and older people face continuing difficulties in the marketplace? Will those who have jobs try to protect them by tightening seniority and by shortening the hours of work? (b) "In the 1990s, the problems will begin to shift. As the much smaller age group born in the 1960s and 1970s moves up the job ladder, labor shortages will develop." Will you have difficulty finding a job? (c) "Then, after the turn of the century, as the baby-boom generation retires, the ratio of dependents to active workers will increase, straining the ability of the economy to support nonworkers." What will this mean for company pension plans? For jobs for those older than 65? For the design of jobs and tasks in business?

8. (a) Compare what you consider to be the key success factors in the following industries: aerospace, auto repair, cigarettes, coal mining, cosmetics, electric utilities, ski resorts, women's dresses. (b) In which industry would you prefer to build your career?

9. Some years ago bowling became a very popular pastime. New large bowling alleys were constructed in all parts of the country, and companies making bowling alley equipment prospered. Many people still bowl, but the rapid growth has stopped; both equipment manufacturers and alleys are in financial difficulties. (a) What characteristics of demand are illustrated in the experience of the bowling industry? (b) To what extent do you think skiing will have a similar experience? Explain the similarities and dissimilarities present.

10. (a) Most high schools are facing a decline in enrollment, reflecting a drop in birth rate. Does the discussion at the close of this chapter on "barriers to exit" have any application to this school situation? What is happening in your community? (b) The decline in birth rate also affects producers of baby foods, basketballs, and braces for straightening teeth. Compare the outlook for these products with the outlook for public high school education.

CASE 2
Happy Hunting in Retail Financial Services

The financial marketplace is in the process of dramatic change. Banks and bankers are pushing well outside their traditional roles, and nonbank organizations are aggressively moving into bank territory. The theme is complete financial services. Here are a few examples of moves by well-known firms.

- Merrill Lynch, the largest stockbrokerage firm, offers a "cash management account" which includes a checking account, Visa card, brokerage services, loans to finance purchases, and automatic transfer of uninvested balances into a money market account.
- So successful is this package that it has been closely matched by Crocker National Bank in California and Citibank in New York.
- Prudential, the largest life insurance company in the U.S., acquired a leading stockbrokerage firm—Bache Group, Inc.—and formed Prudential-Bache Securities. The aim is to combine the selling of life insurance and securities. Moreover, Prudential continues to branch out by buying a small commercial bank in Georgia.
- Sears, Roebuck, the largest American "mail order" retailer, has long sold automobile insurance. This is being expanded to include life insurance and stockbrokerage. You will be able to buy chicken-wire fence and Class A preferred stock in the same store.
- Savings banks can now offer checking accounts and make commercial loans of up to 20 percent of their assets.
- Dreyfus Corp., a leading seller of money market funds, has purchased a small New Jersey bank as an avenue into the consumer loan business. It also bought a small life insurance company to market "universal life insurance" (a type of policy that combines a tax deferred savings plan with low-cost term insurance). To enter real estate mortgage lending, Dreyfus seeks to buy a savings and loan association in Virginia.
- Bank of America, the largest U.S. commercial bank, has purchased the giant discount stockbroker Charles Schwab & Company with the intent of selling stocks in its many branches throughout California.
- Citibank has started to *insist* that customers with balances under $5,000 must use machines rather than human tellers. "This gives them faster service," explains a Citibank vice president. "We are redefining what a bank is." Citibank now sees its branch network as a mechanism to "sell products."[3]

The list could go on and on. Not all these moves have yet been approved by government regulatory authorities. Indeed the invasion of new turf may be partly motivated by a desire to sidestep traditional constraints, and who will be permitted to do what is still unsettled. No one doubts, however, that the institutional structure that was fashioned over many years is being shaken to its roots.

Nature of This Case

This case poses the question, "What new combinations of retail services will be attractive domains for financial service companies in the next decade?" You

---

[3]One month after this statement was made, *The New York Times* noted: "Citibank, Under Pressure, Ending Limit on Access to Tellers." A Citibank senior vice president stated: "The policy did smack a little of class distinction, which is not consistent with our interest in serving customers. There was some bad publicity, and publicity can crystallize public opinion."

are asked to assume that you are consultants to the senior managers of a large commercial bank; they want your predictions of the winning combinations that will emerge from the reshuffle that is taking place.

The term "retail" narrows our attention to services that you and I might use as individuals for our personal financial needs. So, we will temporarily set aside the large and complex financing activities for businesses and not-for-profit organizations. These commercial operations are also in a state of flux, and there is some overlap between retail and commercial services. Nevertheless, the retail area is sufficiently large and distinct to justify very careful scrutiny.

As background, first, traditional institutions and services will be very briefly described. Then, important environmental changes which challenge the traditional pattern will be summarized.

Traditional Institutions and Services

John Horne, a marketing supervisor for a pharmaceutical company, is a typical user of *retail* financial services. During the last ten years, he has dealt with eleven separate organizations. Our question is whether the activities of these organizations should be recombined in a nontraditional way.

1. Commercial Bank. Horne makes frequent use of his *checking account* with the First National Bank. Both his income and larger disbursements are in the form of checks. This simplifies transactions, reduces the risk and trouble of handling large amounts of currency and coins, creates a record of each transaction, and gives him a monthly summary statement.

On a few occasions, Horne did talk with someone at the bank about a *personal loan*—for a new automobile and a mortgage on his home. However, as noted below, he ended up using specialists. Also, Horne is considering naming the *trust department* of the bank as the administrator of his estate.

2. Savings and Loan Association. For years Horne has set aside small amounts of money in his *savings account* at the Community Savings & Loan Association. These are reserves for "a rainy day," and they earn a conservative rate of interest.

In addition, Horne financed the purchase of his home with a *real estate mortgage loan* from the Community S & L. The Community S & L invests most of the money it receives from depositors in such home mortgages. (Its alternative is purchase of government bonds.)

3. Investment Bank. Horne has had only one direct contact with an investment banking firm—when he bought a $25,000 tax-exempt bond. Typically, investment banks help corporations and government bodies raise capital, often underwriting (guaranteeing) that the issue will be sold. Investment banks may sell part of such new issues directly to individual investors, but most of the contact with the retail market is through stockbrokers. For instance, Horne resold that tax-exempt bond through his stockbroker.

4. Stockbroker. To share in the ownership (and profits) of American business, Horne dealt with the stockbrokerage firm of Bull & Bear, Inc. A specific account executive at Bull & Bear advised Horne on what and when to *buy or sell particular securities*. The broker would also buy or sell future contracts for commodities (or other items) if Horne wished to carry that kind of risk. And, Bull & Bear would arrange a loan which would enable Horne to trade on the margin.

5. Real Estate Broker. Each time Horne has *bought or sold a home* he has relied upon a local real estate broker to find the other party to the deal—and to give advice on price, financing, etc. A different local broker was involved in each of these transactions.

6. Life and Health Insurance Companies. During the early years of his working career, Horne bought from a Metropolitan Life Insurance Company agent several *life insurance policies* that included a large element of savings as well as pure insurance. Later, after his family expanded and inflation increased the dollar amount of protection needed, he bought term insurance and *health and accident insurance* from an agent for Travelers Insurance Co. The health and accident policy supplements the Blue Cross Blue Shield coverage provided by Horne's employer.

7. Casualty Insurance Company. *Automobile insurance* has been an essential financial service for Horne, as *fire and related insurance* has been on his home. Horne obtained both of these coverages from a neighbor who runs a local insurance agency; the company actually issuing the policies is State Farm Mutual Insurance Co.

8. Consumer Credit Companies. For each automobile he has purchased, Horne has used the *installment purchase plan* of the automobile manufacturer. However, for several large appliances he used the *consumer finance* division of CIT.

9. Credit Card Company. Because Horne travels a lot, he finds credit cards a real convenience. For several years he has carried both American Express and Visa cards.

10. Tax Accountant. Early in his career, Horne got into a row with the Internal Revenue Service about his traveling expenses. Since that time he has relied upon a public accountant to prepare his *income tax returns*. This accountant has also called attention to investment possibilities which would lower Horne's taxable income.

11. Lawyer. Lawyers have turned up in most of Horne's major financial moves. In addition to drafting a *will* and preparing papers for a *large gift*, a lawyer has handled each of the *real estate transactions*. Horne also recognized the importance of lawyers when his sister went through *divorce* proceedings and when his father's estate was settled.

A Collection of Services. This list of retail financial services is only suggestive. In each of the fields mentioned, the services were packaged in a wide variety of ways for the purpose of attracting customers. This product diversity increased the choices confronting a customer like John Horne.

Of course, technicalities exist in each field. Specialization and the skills derived from it are necessary to deal with them effectively. Moreover, each field is regulated separately by federal or state bodies. A primary aim of the regulatory commissions is to protect customers against excessive risk, misrepresentation, and malpractice. A side effect of this regulation has been professional barriers between the various segments of financial services.

Each of the agents John Horne dealt with, or at least the agent's company, profited by an increase in the volume of transactions. Horne himself had to decide how much of each service to buy, and what constituted a balance best suited to his situation.

Winds of Change

Several powerful forces are upsetting the established pattern of financial services. The aura of stability—the Rock of Gibralter symbol—is being challenged. These changes will significantly affect the optimum combinations of financial services.

Technology. Computerized bookkeeping has altered the internal technology of banks, brokers, and insurance companies. The minimum efficient size of an office is larger. On the other hand, the capability to handle large masses of transactions rapidly has also jumped. Access to memory files combined with localized display terminals potentially make the improved bookkeeping immediately available to anyone in the organization.

Electronic communication is the essential handmaiden of the computer. Communication satellites make national, even international, networks economically feasible. Indeed, a national credit file on millions of consumers is already being used by a number of consumer credit organizations. Fiber optics "wire" will greatly increase the capability of transmission lines to carry facsimile copies of documents.

Credit cards, or some comparable identification device, combined with national communication networks and computerized bookkeeping might make our present check-clearing system obsolete.

Automated bank teller machines permit individuals to obtain cash at convenient locations twenty-four hours a day. Terminals can be placed in retail stores so that a customer (with a bank balance or good credit standing) can pay for merchandise with a direct charge to his or her bank account. Or monthly charges—or deposits—can be made directly without the customer doing anything.

When interactive TV connections are made to homes, financial services will be one of the possible uses.

Government Action. Two kinds of action by governmental bodies are having a profound effect on financial service companies—market price interest rates and deregulation.

For years, tradition, usury laws, and Federal Reserve action kept interest rates within a fairly narrow range. Changes in rates were more significant as a signal of tightness or availability of credit than as a price for the use of capital. Then the dam broke.

Inflation forced interest rates to unprecedented levels because the rates had to include provision for a drop in the value of money during the loan period. Double-digit inflation alone made traditional (and legal) interest ceilings obsolete. In addition, the Federal Reserve Board decided that the most efficient way to allocate money while trying to restrain the overall price level was to give market forces free rein. Individuals and businesses could get money if they were willing to pay more for it than other users. For instance, mortgage dealers or auto finance companies had to increase their offer (interest rate) if they wanted more funds. This bow to Friedman economics has added volatility to interest rates—and mobility to capital.

At the same time that interest rates started to bounce about madly, the federal government embarked on a deregulation policy. Traditional and legal boundaries for who (what type of institution) should do what are crumbling. For instance, stockbrokerage companies have invaded the checking account business of commercial banks; and through their money market funds, they raided the savings banks. Retail store chains and brokerage firms are selling life insurance. Commercial banks can now be stockbrokers (but not yet underwriters). Insurance companies have countered by going into the brokerage business. And the list could go on.

Substantial regulation remains, especially those measures intended to protect the consumer. However, often the new entrants into a field are not covered by the regulations of the traditional provider.

The holding company device has become a more common legal mechanism to circumvent restrictions imposed on operating companies. A subsidiary may continue to comply with state or federal regulations, while the parent company expands into new businesses or new territories.

To curtail size, many states for years had sharp restrictions on the number of branch locations a commercial bank could operate; these state constraints are now being relaxed. Now great concern centers on nationwide banking—an arrangement prohibited since the establishment of commercial banks in the United States. One side of the argument is that brokerage houses, credit card companies, consumers' finance companies, and other kinds of businesses that are taking on commercial banking functions are already operating nationally. So in self-defense the commercial banks should be permitted to do likewise.

No one knows how far and how fast the deregulation movement will go. There is no doubt, however, that many new combinations of services are already legally feasible. And further realignments are considered likely.

Deregulation does not mean complete *laissez-faire*. Integrity of and public confidence in institutions dealing with money are vital for any complex society. Consequently, there is no movement to get rid of our deposit insurance. Reliable public data on companies issuing securities and insurance policies and on companies accepting deposits continues to be expected. Furthermore, devices to provide relief of special pressing needs—such as the IRAs or All-Savers certificates—will not disappear. Nevertheless, the underlying current is running toward greater freedom for companies to design their own packages of services.

Social Change. Combined with new technology and shifts in government action are a third cluster of forces. The *user* of retail financial services is also changing. The attitude toward personal debt is just one example. Pride in being thrifty and in saving is being replaced by a willingness to go into debt—not only debt for a house but for anything from clothing to vacations.

Personal checks or credit card chits are the common "medium of exchange" instead of currency and coins. In fact, with direct deposits and direct billing even checks may pass out of fashion. "Hard cash" is now a figure of speech, no longer a necessity of life that you and I work for. And when each of us has our own personal computer, with the press of a button we can flip from a daily update of our personal net worth to a score in the latest computer game—without feeling much difference in reality.

A much larger segment of the population now plays the income-tax game. Both state and national contests are available. With more two-income families the calculations and deductions become trickier. IRAs and other tax shelters are designed to appeal to the plumber and school teacher.

Indeed, the individual is confronted with both the opportunity and the need to understand an array of financial services. Somehow he or she has to fit together and balance "goodies" from several different sources. The following alternatives have already been suggested:

- checking accounts—with diverse provisions
- savings accounts—with diverse provisions
- life insurance and annuities—of numerous sorts
- casualty insurance—fire, auto, liability, etc.
- investments—bonds, stocks, commodities, antiques, options, etc.
- real estate and personal property—purchase and maintenance
- credit cards
- personal loans—secured and unsecured
- income tax counsel and assistance
- wills, trusts, estates
- legal services—from alimony to zoning

Question

The numerous changes taking place in the financial arena create threats and opportunities. Ten years from now, many firms will have disappeared while others will have risen to national prominence. A critical factor in such future success will focus on desired services and especially on combinations of services which have synergistic benefits.

The CEO of a large commercial banks asks you, "What new combinations of retail services will be attractive domains for financial service companies in the next decade?" How do you respond?

3 ASSESSING A COMPANY'S COMPETITIVE STRENGTHS

Success comes from matching opportunity with capability. The industry analyses, discussed in the preceding chapter, may flag an array of opportunities (and threats). The next part of the puzzle, then, is to examine the particular strengths and weaknesses of our company to grasp these opportunities.

FRAMEWORK FOR COMPANY ANALYSIS

As in the study of an industry, numerous facts about a company can be obtained. To help give meaning to these facts, and to aid in relating company data to industry data, the following framework is useful.

Position of Company in Its Industry

A. Market Position of the Company
1. Relation of company sales to total industry and to leading competitors
2. Relative appeal of company products
3. Strength of the company in major markets
B. Supply Position of the Company
1. Comparative access to resources
2. Unique productivity advantages
3. R & D strength
C. Special Competitive Considerations
1. Relative financial strength
2. Community and government relations
3. Ability and values of company managers
D. Conclusions
Comparative strengths and weaknesses of the company in terms of key success factors identified in your analysis of the industry outlook

Several refinements are important when using this framework. First, the significance of each heading in a specific situation depends on the technology and basis of competition in the industry and on the strategy pursued by the company. Thus, R & D capability is crucial in the fast evolving personal computer field, but unimportant to a Paris restaurant. Similarly, access to low-cost raw materials (bauxite) is vital for a company producing virgin aluminum, but unimportant to firms producing secondary (recycled) aluminum. Although the weights for each topic may differ greatly, the underlying model does help to diagnose most company strengths and weaknesses.

Second, for strategic planning, we are particularly concerned about a company's strength *relative* to its competitors. Occasionally in a new venture there may be doubt whether the company can operate at all—perhaps the local farmers will refuse to pool their land in a cooperative. Usually, however, the issue is whether our company can perform as well or better than competitors.

Finally, we must define carefully just who a relevant competitor is. We compete to obtain capital, for example, with quite different firms than we do to obtain customers for our goods and services. Likewise a hospital's competitors for patients to fill up its beds are a different set than its competitors for nursing staff; there will be some—but not complete—overlap and a hospital's relative standing in the two markets may differ a lot.

The relevant competition will also depend on a company's strategy—on what it wants to do. The local fuel dealer in Oshkosh cares little about who sells fuel in Madison, but if it becomes a wholesaler then competitors in both cities are likely to be the same. Moreover, potential competition must be weighed. New firms may enter the business, substitute products may reduce customers, separate industries may bid away resources. So, when we weigh relative strengths and weaknesses, we should consider all the principal rivals for the resources and patronage that we would like to have.

With these qualifications in mind, the main headings and subheadings can be a significant aid in putting facts about a company into a meaningful structure.

MARKET POSITION OF THE COMPANY

The survival of each enterprise depends upon providing goods or services that people want. Therefore, an essential part of the basis for company strategy is knowing how well—relative to competitors—those needs are being fulfilled.

Relation of Company Sales to Total Industry and to Leading Competitors

The ups and downs of a total industry often obscure how well a specific company is being managed. A revealing way to screen out such external influences is to watch company sales as a percentage of its total industry and to watch its major competitors.

A dramatic example of loss of industry position is Univac—the computer subsidiary of Sperry Rand Corporation. Although its forebearer was the leading pioneer in digital computers, Univac failed to capture the lion's share of the market. Here was a company very technically oriented. It was good at product development, but slow in exploiting commercially sound products. Its competitors, notably IBM, were more sensitive to customer needs and had stronger marketing organizations. As soon as the key to success embraced the market as well as the laboratory, Univac slipped.

A company's share of its target market typically is closely related to its profitability. The Strategic Planning Institute has found that for a wide range of businesses, higher market share is linked to higher profits. (See Figure 3-1.) This relationship probably reflects economies based on greater experience, economies of scale, and relative bargaining power. Clearly, the "little guy" must find a distinctive niche in order to prosper.

Hospitals, banks, and even churches or professional athletic teams can use the market share concept. Measurement may be more difficult and profit may not be the goal, but the tie to viability is much the same.

Relative Appeal of Company Products

The market position of a company is strongly influenced by the quality and the distinctiveness of its products. The TV set that has unique engineering features, the motel that serves good food, the hospital equipment that has dependability and durability, or the airline with a good on-time record is the product that will improve its position in the market. The important characteristics from the *user's point of view* should be determined and the company's products appraised in terms of these characteristics. In this process it is necessary to distinguish between various price ranges, because the controlling characteristics may not be the same for, say, low-priced shoes and high-priced shoes.

Sometimes the past success of a company is attributable to a single product, whereas future success in the industry must be built upon an *ability to develop new products.* For example, the Mead Johnson Company has enjoyed very large sales of its prepared baby cereal Pablum, but possible substitutes or changes in ideas regarding child feeding made this single product an inadequate base for maintenance of a leading position in the industry. This company, fully recognizing the danger, developed a wide line of baby foods and then hit upon another winner—Metrecal.

The importance of a full line of products depends on both customer buying habits and the appeal the company elects to stress. When buying men's shirts—or skis—the customer expects to find a full range of sizes and would like an array of colors in each size. In contrast, the manager of a mutual fund or theater production may focus on providing the best single product that appeals to a particular segment of the market. In the medical field there is debate about whether doctors, and clinics, should be generalists or specialists.

FIGURE 3-1.

RELATION OF MARKET SHARE TO PROFITABILITY

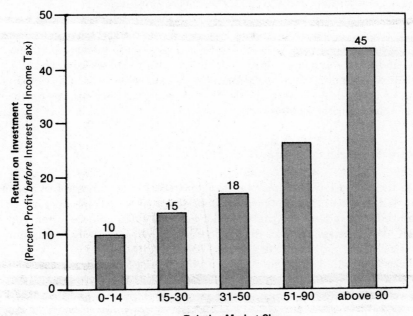

Source: Strategic Planning Institute.
This chart and later ones are based on confidential data covering the experience of over 1,000 highly diversified business-units. In its PIMS Program, the Institute makes very sophisticated statistical analyses of over 50 variables affecting profits and cash flow. Only a few of the simple relationships are shown on these charts, but the inferences are consistent with the more elaborate findings.

Strength of the Company in Major Markets

A company's position in its industry is also affected by its reputation in major markets. For instance, some motels cater to commercial travelers and business conferences, while competitors carefully nurture the tourist trade. Supplementary services and sales promotion help to focus on their target market.

Often the reputation of a firm varies by area as well as by type of customer. This is illustrated by different brands of coffee. Many local brands exist that are known in only one metropolitan area or perhaps one region; even the nationally advertised brands experience substantial differences in consumer acceptance in different sections of the country. In the same way, a particular manufacturer of farm machinery may have a strong *dealer organization* in the corn-belt states but have weak dealers and acceptance in the cotton states.

Reputation is an intangible thing including, in addition to being known, a prominence for giving service, for offering a good buy in terms of product and price, and for fair dealings. Many companies, as already indicated, have a niche in the industry where they are outstanding. For purposes of forecasting, the problem is to identify those areas or types of trade from which a company will obtain its business and then consider the prospects for such groups on the basis of the outlook for the general industry.

Unique Strengths of Small Businesses

In the discussion of market position and other issues, most of our examples are large companies. This is normal practice because such companies are quickly recognized by readers and the behavior of such companies is often generally known. Nevertheless, most of the concepts described also apply to medium- and small-sized firms.

Market position of small firms is a good example. If the little firm plays a "me too" game and tries to do the same things as much bigger companies, the little one is sure to get bruised and may not survive. However, if the little firm can carve out a special niche with a distinct product or a distinct set of customers then we have a big frog in a little puddle. And the evidence indicates that such distinctive performance pays off even in small puddles.

The key is, first, to find a distinctive product or service, not offered by bigger firms, which a relatively small group of customers want strongly enough to buy separately and probably to pay a somewhat higher price. An alternative is to focus on the needs of a particular group of customers who want tailored service not available from large companies. Then, second, the small firm must concentrate on delivering the distinctive product or service within bounds acceptable to the selected market segment.

Examples of successful small businesses are all around us, especially in the service sectors. In products, for instance, the leading manufacturer of horseshoe nails enjoys a much wider profit margin than do big producers of building nails. For years, Crown Cork & Seal Company has focused on aerosol and beverage cans only; for these products its engineering and delivery service is outstanding. And Crown Cork has been consistently more profitable than larger, more diversified container manufacturers.

In services, many localities are favored with a restaurant that continues to be crowded because it serves exceptionally good food. Among magazines, the leading special-interest publications have moved far ahead of the general reader magazines (except for Number 1, *Reader's Digest*). The Mayo Clinic attracts patients to Rochester, Minnesota, from all over the nation because of its outstanding diagnostic service.

So, mere size is not the critical dimension. When analyzing market position, we learn more from observing whether a firm is at or near the top of a separable market segment.

SUPPLY POSITION OF THE COMPANY

The position of a firm in its industry depends upon its ability to deal with supply factors as well as with demand or market factors. Its relative supply position influences the extent and the direction of company expansion and may be the key to survival itself.

Comparative Access to Resources

Ready and inexpensive access to *raw materials* is a major asset for companies using bulky products. The newsprint mills of Canada, for instance, now have a controlling advantage over their former competitors in Wisconsin, Michigan, or the New England states because the virgin timber in the latter areas has been cut off and logs—or pulp—must be transported long distances to the mills. In fact, most of the remaining mills in these areas have turned to specialty paper products to counteract the disadvantage of their location.

Location with respect to *labor* is sometimes a definite advantage or disadvantage to a company. Minimum-wage legislation and union activity have greatly reduced geographic differentials in wage rates within the United States, so "cheap labor" is now obtainable only in foreign countries. Occasionally a company located in a rural area is at a disadvantage if expansion requires that skilled workers must be induced to move from the cities.

In some industries, location close to *markets* is crucial. This is obvious for retail stores for which buyer traffic may mean the difference between success or failure. Printing firms that wish to serve advertising agencies must locate nearby so as to provide the necessary speed in service. For heavy products like cement, shipping expense becomes a significant factor.

Industry analysis, already discussed, should have indicated the significance—or the insignificance—of a favorable location with respect to raw materials, labor, or markets.

Favorable access to resources and customers may arise from ownership or contractual ties as well as from physical location. A primary advantage sought in *vertical integration* of ore mines and steel plants, of oil wells, refineries, and filling stations, is assured supply. In times of inflation, favorable costs also arise from vertical ties. Of course, in dynamic industries vertical ties can become an oppressive burden. So, when analyzing the supply position of a company, its long-term commitments both upstream and downstream should be compared with those of major competitors.

Unique Productivity Advantages

"Experience is a great teacher." The second time we perform a task it is easier than the first, the third time easier than the second, and so on. In fact, experience is so important for complex activities that cost estimates and output schedules in the aircraft and space industries are adjusted for the number of times a particular product has been produced, and The Boston Consulting Group has developed a whole theory of competitive behavior on the concept.

According to the *experience-curve* theory, the company with the most cumulative experience (a result of high-market position) should have the lowest production costs. Personal learning plus opportunities to specialize and automate should lead to higher productivity. In practice, newcomers may catch up, especially when product designs are changed or new processing technology becomes available. A critical question is whether companies have made maximum use of the opportunities to lower cost that the experience curve provides.

In fact, some firms develop poor work habits, instead of good ones, and these become entrenched in *work rules and social structure.* Then, becoming relatively efficient is an almost insurmountable task—as current difficulties in some steel plants, insurance offices, stockbrokerage houses, and hospitals clearly attest. In contrast, a few firms have a strong tradition—like the Japanese—of persistently looking for ways to increase productivity.

A further consideration is that a company's facilities may become outmoded. The prime issue is whether the plant can make products suited to the trends in demand. To take an example from a service industry, high-ceiling hotel rooms without air-conditioning no longer serve the lodging market satisfactorily. Bowling alleys as a form of entertainment are in a similar fix.

Often such *outmoded facilities* are doubly disadvantageous because other companies are also likely to have excess equipment for the declining products; therefore, profit margins tend to be narrow, especially in contrast to margins on the expanding products that may be in short supply.

Flexibility of equipment is often a factor in operating costs. For example, large jet planes such as the Boeing 747 are efficient for transatlantic and cross-continental flights, but they are expensive and hard to handle on short runs where traffic is lighter. Smaller, flexible planes cost more to operate per passenger mile than a 747 when the latter is fully loaded on a long flight, but they have decided advantages in filling varying needs. Again, the crucial point is having equipment suited to the market the company wants to serve.

R & D Strength

If the industry analysis indicates that research and development is a key success factor, then any company staking its future in that domain must have access to current technology. The need is well recognized in pharmaceuticals and electronics, but also is vital in some divisions of agriculture, communications, energy, office equipment, space—to name just a few examples.

Small companies cannot afford broad-ranging, basic research. However, even a tiny technically oriented firm may be a pioneer in a very specific application. Also, licensing is common practice in some industries, in which case an ability to qualify as a licensee is crucial.

As with access to resources and productivity, a company must assess its R & D strengths relative to competitors as a basis for its strategy.

SPECIAL COMPETITIVE CONSIDERATIONS

Three further considerations, in addition to market and supply factors, throw light on the ability of an enterprise to grasp new opportunities: namely, financial strength, community and government relations, and ability and values of company executives.

Relative Financial Strength

Adequate capital provides one of the necessary means to put plans of the business administrator into action. A company may enjoy a distinctive product, an unusually low cost, or some other advantage over its competitors; but virtually every type of expansion requires additional capital for inventory and accounts receivable if not also for fixed assets. Moreover, if a firm is to maintain its position, it must have sufficient financial strength to withstand depressions and aggressive drives by competitors for choice markets. Competition may force a company to expand the variety of products offered for sale, to establish district warehouses and local sales organizations, or to buy new equipment. All of this requires capital.

The simplest way for a company to meet these capital requirements is from its own cash balances, which may be larger than necessary for day-to-day operations. Most concerns, however, do not carry large amounts of idle cash (or nonoperating assets readily convertible into cash, such as government securities), so financial strength is primarily a question of ability to borrow new capital or to secure it from stockholders. Ability to raise new capital will reflect not only past and probable future earnings, but also the existing debt structure and fixed charges of the company. So, the entire financial structure of the company should be examined, particularly if there are likely to be major readjustments in industry operations.

Community and Government Relations

Governments are formally required to treat everyone alike. Nevertheless, over time one company may have antagonized governmental officials while another firm carefully developed good rapport. Also important, representatives of a company may have learned governmental procedures and the particular issues which are sensitive. Friendships help, but even more significant is identification with a cause that is cherished by a block of voters (along the lines considered in the next chapter). The overall effect is that companies do differ in their ability to work with governments.

Community relations are even more intangible. For a variety of reasons a company may (or may not) be regarded as a "good citizen." Then when special police protection, a zoning variance, or perhaps prompt resolution of a complaint is needed, opposition does not automatically arise. Most of the time, for most companies good community and government relations lead simply to a permissive situation, but at times of crises the right to continue operating may be at stake.

Ability and Values of Company Managers

The most important single factor influencing the position of a company in its industry is the ability of its executives. The executives of a business turn potential sales into actual sales, keep costs in line, and face the endless stream of new and unanticipated problems. Consider two well-publicized examples. In the early 1980s the "tough" conservative approach of the CEO of International Harvester brought the company to the brink of bankruptcy. During the same period, an aggressive, confident CEO of the Chrysler Corporation narrowly saved the number three U.S. auto producer from bankruptcy.

The qualities desired for executives are numerous and vary to some extent for different types of companies; for example, the manager of a specialty shop needs a style sense, whereas the head of a hospital must have the ability to supervise a diverse collection of professional employees. Outstanding research capability or a willingness to take risks might be the key to success.

A related issue is whether entrenched executives are so committed to the existing company strategy that they will be unable to change. This sort of commitment clearly restricts the strategic options that realistically can be considered. Executives of competitors may likewise have strong commitments that shape their range of possible actions.

No single executive should be expected to have all the talents required, but within the management group there should be vision, creativeness, supervisory ability, human understanding, diligence, and other qualities essential to the planning, direction, and control of the enterprise. In fact, partly due to age and to the personal motivations of people in central management posts, the capacities of company managements differ sharply.

In predicting the future of a business, it is also necessary to consider the extent to which success is dependent on a few individuals and the provision that has been made for a succession of capable leadership. This is crucial in the outlook for a small "one-man company."

COMPANY CAPABILITY TO ADAPT STRATEGICALLY

Readiness to Change

The framework just described helps to identify a company's strengths and weaknesses relative to its competitors. First, the market position of the company, then its comparative strengths as a supplier, and finally its power as a competitor should be carefully assessed. These are vital answers to the question: Where do we now stand?

Knowing "where we are at" aids in planning for the future. We can build on our strengths, and we can circumvent or buttress our weaknesses. Note, however, that the analysis of strengths and weaknesses is intended to be a snapshot—a picture as of a moment in time. Because of this balance-sheet character, it is inherently static. Our subsequent planning, then, tends to focus on moving from one fixed position to another fixed position. Such neat, clear-cut planning is basic to progress on many fronts.

Frequently, however, strategic change is more messy than making well-timed moves from position A to position B sounds. Uncertainty abounds—about how the external world will change, about our ability to execute plans, about counter moves by competitors for customers and resources. Much of the change is incremental—small steps to test the water, or delaying actions until forecasts become more reliable. And to deal with these less clear-cut situations, our analysis of company strengths and weaknesses needs to be supplemented.

Two supplements to the basic study of existing strengths and weaknesses are especially valuable: (1) strategic positioning, which is described in the next few pages, and (2) key actor analysis, which is the subject of the following chapter. By adding these two perspectives a company can significantly increase its capability to deal with irrepressible changes.

Strategic Positioning

Strategic positioning deals with acquiring at an early date a tangible or intangible asset which will later place the company in an advantageous position. A very simple example is buying extra land around an office or plant so that expansion at some indefinite future time will be relatively easy.

Developing intangible assets may be a significant form of strategic positioning. A small industrial-scale company, for instance, employed an electrical engineer several years before anyone knew just how his skills might be applied. Actually, it was a fortuitous move, because having such an engineer already familiar with company products enabled the company to move into electronic controls and weighing systems ahead of competitors.

Another example is U.S. firms establishing business relations with mainland Chinese enterprises. Sometimes the potential short-run trade is attractive, but more often the aim is to build a relationship that could be the foundation of large future transactions if and when foreign exchange and other factors become more favorable.

Three kinds of strategic positioning warrant attention.

Defensive Positioning. The aim here is to avoid being squeezed by a powerful supplier, customer, or competitor. Petroleum companies, for example, may acquire leases on crude oil properties in their own country, primarily as protection against exorbitant demands such as OPEC imposed in the 1970s. Amax Aluminum retained leases on large Australian bauxite deposits partly as a protection against the large firms that were currently supplying its reduction plants. Similarly, one reason some companies do not utilize all their ability to borrow capital is to save some borrowing capacity for a "rainy day."

Prepared Opportunism. This is a posture of preparedness—being ready to act if and when conditions are right, as in the China trade example cited above. Many banks and other financial institutions made moves of this sort in the early 1980s. Large New York banks established ties with banks in the midwest and far west. If legislation permitting national banking is passed, these ties could be converted into national networks. Insurance companies bought real estate brokerage firms, and so on. While some of these affiliations were converted into combined activities immediately, uncertainty about the future structure of the industry was so great that most affiliations simply remained as a readiness to act.

Preemptive Positioning. I. C. MacMillan has defined this strategy as a move by a company "ahead of its adversaries which allows the company to secure an advantageous position from which it is difficult to be dislodged."[1] The folklore example is the rancher who buys up land that probably will be a necessary access to the primary water supply. Then as more cattle are brought into the outlying regions, the rancher has an asset which must be included in development plans.

A modern parallel is the current scramble for cable TV franchises and for preferred network channels. At present, it is unclear whether an increase in available channels or other changes in technology will undermine the national networks. Also, the use of cable TV connections for interactive programs is uncertain. Nevertheless, several large companies are investing heavily to preempt positions in this form of mass communication.

The current value of any of these forms of positioning—defensive, prepared opportunism, or preemption—is difficult to place on a financial balance sheet. They are a type of "contingency" investment which defies the conventional ROI (return on investment) justification. And yet they might be vital to the future of the company.

---

[1] I. C. MacMillan, "Preemptive Strategies" (Working paper, Strategy Research Center, Graduate School of Business, Columbia University, 1983.)

Our conclusion is that strategic positioning should be included in the assessment of the strengths and weaknesses of a company. Although many positioning moves may turn out to be of little value, for the execution of a particular strategy a few of these early actions may be crucial. Other companies will be jockeying for position. We need to know, in addition to our current demand and supply position, how well poised we are—relative to competitors—to strike off in new directions.

SUMMARY

Wise strategy calls for an adroit mating of opportunity and threats in our industry with the strengths and weaknesses of our particular company. We have focused here on the second part of this coupling—with an emphasis on our strengths compared with other firms which might want the same customers or the same resources.

A useful framework for this company evaluation is: (1) How strong is our market position? Are we big or small in the total picture? Are our products distinctive? Do we have unusual strength with particular customers or in special localities? (2) Do we have advantages in supplying the market? For instance, favorable location and access to materials? Is our productivity high and our cost low? Does our R & D strength enable us to pioneer in new products or new technology? (3) Are we a strong competitor—due to unusual financial strength, favorable government relations, or exceptionally well qualified and dedicated executives?

Answers to these questions will provide basic information about the kind of strategy that is likely to succeed for us. However, to provide a stronger future orientation and to suggest strengths and weaknesses in striking out in new directions, our readiness to make new moves should also be assessed. In this connection, three kinds of strategic positioning are important: defensive possibilities, prepared opportunism, and preemptive moves.

A further impact to strategy formulation is predicting how key actors in our industry will respond to our initiatives. That is the subject of the next chapter.

 ## QUESTIONS FOR CLASS DISCUSSION

1. (a) Using the framework presented in this chapter, describe the position and relative strengths and weaknesses of an independent (non-chain) restaurant which you frequently patronize. (b) How do you explain this restaurant's ability to survive in face

of competition from McDonald's? (c) Will McDonald's and other chains eventually take over the restaurant business?

2. Assume that you have decided to open a new carwash in your city. Your alternatives on production methods range from a hand operation with only hoses, brushes, and rags as equipment to a fully automatic tunnel that can be run by an individual who collects money as the cars enter. (a) Would you invest in the capital-intensive process or the labor-intensive process? (b) Does your answer to (a) imply a general view that new operations in your city in any line of business should be as capital-intensive (or labor-intensive) as technology will permit? (c) What other competitive strengths do you believe will be crucial to your success in your new venture?

3. "Gazing 20 Years Into Future" was a headline on a *Wall Street Journal* article about Control Data Corporation and its founder, William C. Norris. The company grew— in 25 years—into a computer and financial-services giant that earned $155 million on sales of $4.3 billion. It makes one of the fastest super-computers in the world. Its peripheral computer products are so advanced that other computer companies use them. It has, however, entered ventures—because of its founder's ideas—that lose money. These ventures (growing vegetables hydroponically on rooftops, importing Yugoslavian wine, and providing health care on Indian reservations) are "position- ing the company for prosperity for years to come" and are showing corporate Amer- ica how to solve social problems. "I don't think in terms of 10 years. I think in terms of 20 years; 10 years is a very, very short length of time," said Mr. Norris. "Address- ing these basic needs . . . it takes longer to get a return."

Control Data for over 20 years has invested about $900 million in its teaching and training system, Plato, which has yet to show a profit. "Countertrade," carried out by Control Data Commerce International, imports goods from Eastern Bloc nations so that they have hard currency with which to buy its computers. This sub- sidiary is expected to lose money for many years.

High energy costs, believes Mr. Norris, will eventually make transporting vege- tables long distances too expensive. So Control Data invests in research and develop- ment work on hydroponics—growing plants in nutrient-rich water in greenhouses.

Mr. Norris says that he would rather be remembered for his ventures into urban-renewal projects and developing small businesses in central cities than as a computer pioneer and entrepreneur. "That's much more significant, and that was always one of my ambitions—to do something important."

(a) Does your college or university use the Plato system? How effective is it? (b) What do you think of Control Data's positioning for the long run? (c) Should the firm stick to large computers—a business in which it does well?

4. Select an independent, local commercial bank located either in your home commu- nity or in your college community. Assume that officers of the bank believe that the chances are at least 50-50 that the U.S. Congress will pass a new law permitting banks to operate nationally (instead of being confined to a single state). What should the bank that you selected do to position itself strategically to deal with such national banking?

5. Company analysis outlined in this chapter focused on profit enterprises. To test the applicability of the same approach to nonprofit enterprises, use the outline to analyze the outlook for your university or college.

6. Assume that your aunt has been president of Early Learning Associates for several years. (Early Learning Associates is a prestige distributor of equipment and materials to kindergartens, nursery schools, and day-care centers. Through its professional selection of products and its 15 field representatives—each with 200 key school accounts—Early Learning stresses the educational benefits of its products. Competing jobbers typically are mere order-takers and quite willing to supply items that merely entertain children.)

    Your aunt agrees with industry experts that (a) government support for day-care centers and Head Start programs will diminish during the next five years, but (b) the number of families with preschool children and both parents working (or single-parent homes with that parent working) will increase.

    How might Early Learning Associates position itself in anticipation of these trends? What are its chief options? Which do you recommend?

7. Coca-Cola Co., Atlanta, entered the U.S.-wide wine industry in 1977 by spending about $100 million to buy Taylor Wine (a famous, old, New York State company) and two smaller California vineyards. Despite hostility expressed by other winemakers and predictions that Coca-Cola would soon fail as had other outsiders, such as Pillsbury Co., the entry succeeded and Coke did the unheard-of by establishing a volume of three million cases within two years and by taking market share away from premium brands such as Almaden (owned by National Distillers and Chemical Corp.), Seagram's Paul Masson, and United Vintners (a Heublein subsidiary). Coke advertised heavily ($11 million in one year) and standardized the taste of its California wines with considerable success. It also invested $35 million in a large, new winery in California. A Coke executive said, "By 1990, U.S. wine consumption will be at 4.3 gallons per capita, compared with two gallons today. That's twice the growth rate for any other beverage, including soft drinks."

    The industry reacted to Coke by doubling and tripling advertising expenditures. E & J Gallo Co. began a costly campaign to market premium and varietal wines while reducing marketing emphasis on its cheap wines like Thunderbird and Pagan Pink Ripple. Gallo maintained its 27 percent market share, but had to resort to some heavy price discounting to do so.

    Then, in 1982, Seagram formed a special wine unit to combine efforts on its brands—Gold Seal, Paul Masson, Barton and Guestier wines of France, and Browne Vintners. Mary E. Cunningham, former vice-president of Bendix Corp., had directed a project to coordinate Seagram's worldwide wine business and develop a worldwide strategy. The new unit was, in part, a result of her work.

    In 1983, wine consumption changed from growth at a 6 percent annual rate to no growth and imported wines presented an even greater challenge because of the strength of the U.S. dollar. In the meantime, Coke's Taylor California Cellars increased sales by 15 percent per year and took over third place in sales volume in the wine industry.

Then Coke's chairman, Mr. Goizeuta, elected in 1980, decided that its wine operations should be sold to Seagram by taking up a Seagram offer which allowed Coke to "fully recapture" its investment in the wine business—about $210 million. Coke was in and out in six years and joined Beatrice Foods, Pillsbury Co., and Jos. Schlitz Brewing in trying the wine business, souring on it, and bailing out. The president of another wine company said: "The return on assets in the wine business is not the 30 percent to 35 percent (Coke) is used to in the syrup business. Gaining share and trying to compete with E & J Gallo left Coke with, eventually, the number two position in the wine industry (32 million gallons) but profits of $6 million on $220 million in sales." One industry observer said: "Wall Street's desire for immediate returns made Coke unwilling to make the kind of long-term investment spending that was necessary to build the brands. Had they stayed for five more years, they would have been a key leader in a large and profitable industry."

Seagram immediately went from sixth in the industry to a strong second place with an 11 percent market share. The president of Seagram's wine company stated: "We believe you can make money in this business in two ways: Remain a small boutique winery, or become large and achieve economies of scale."

(a) Explain entry barriers and exit barriers in the three segments of the wine industry—boutiques, jug wines, and premium table wines sold in a nationwide market. (b) What can Seagram do over the long haul that Coca-Cola could not? (c) Appraise Coke's initial strategic positioning and its entry behavior.

8. Recent reports are that at least fourteen different Japanese companies are in or are entering the personal computer field. It is anticipated that several of these producers will seek a large share of the U.S. personal computer market, and some observers fear that the Japanese will eventually dominate the market as they do in cameras and radios.

(a) What strategic positioning should a full-line U.S. computer manufacturer undertake to forestall the Japanese invasion? (b) What strategic positioning should U.S. producers specializing in personal computers—like Apple—undertake to forestall the Japanese invasion?

CASE 3
Maytag's Niche

For years the Maytag Company outperformed other firms in the major appliance industry by concentrating on laundry equipment—clothes washers and dryers. Now it is considering joining its major competitors with a "full line" strategy. What prompts Maytag to switch from a highly successful strategy to be like its competitors? Is it wise?

Industry Developments

The major appliance industry (except microwave ovens) is mature. In the United States most potential users of various kinds of big-ticket products already own them. Consequently, sales of new equipment is predominantly for replacement. And because the equipment is durable, much of this replacement can be deferred until consumers are in a mood to buy.

Even this replacement business is very large, however. Table 1 shows that millions of each type of major appliances are made and sold each year. During the mid-1980s this volume will increase faster than real Gross National Product rises because users will be catching up with postponed replacements.

TABLE 1.
MAJOR APPLIANCE STATISTICS

	Units Shipped[a] Millions in 1981	Approximate % Installed in New Buildings[b]	Price Index 1982[c] 1967 = 100
Clothes Washers	4.6	3	206
Dryers	3.2	4	
Refrigerators	5.5	12	
Freezers	1.8	0	196
Ranges (all types)	4.4	40	216
Microwave Ovens	4.4	1	—
Dishwashers	2.5	40	187
Disposers	3.2	44	196
Compactors	.2	31	—
Total	29.8	18%	203
All Commodities			299

[a]Source: *Association of Home Appliance Manufacturers*
[b]Based on 1979 Housing Industry Dynamics Survey of Builder Installation Practices.
[c]Source: *Bureau of Labor Statistics*

Demand for major appliances is also affected by residential construction. New apartments and homes may have some appliances already installed by the builder. As the second column of the foregoing table indicates, this practice is especially significant in the sale of ranges, dishwashers, waste disposers, and trash compactors.

Maturity in product design is another important characteristic of major appliances. Competing brands of, say, refrigerators or dishwashers differ very little in function and appearance. Moreover, they are increasingly more alike in terms of durability and need for repair. Basically, the quality of all brands remaining on the market is good; differentiation on this basis is hard to achieve.

And to survive, each producer must have low costs. The major companies are taking steps to reduce their costs even more than they already have—as we note later in this case. Efficient production is now a requirement. However, it is becoming more and more difficult to achieve a major advantage over competitors via cost reductions. "Everybody who is anybody" is doing it.

One combined effect of these trends—maturity in demand, similar products, sustained efforts to reduce costs—has been very sharp competition. Ninety percent of the firms making major appliances at the end of World War II have disappeared. Fewer than twenty-five now survive, and several of these are in shaky condition.

Part of the same picture is a squeeze on prices. During the fifteen years from 1967 to 1982, producer prices of all commodities about tripled, whereas major appliances only doubled. The price indexes for various types of appliances, shown in Table 1, all reveal approximately the same thing. In terms of real dollars, prices of major appliances have dropped sharply—while quality was improving and most input costs were rising. That's a tough setting in which to earn a profit.

The large survivors now all have a more or less full line of major appliances. General Electric and Whirlpool developed their products internally; White Industries and Magic Chef are consolidations of formerly separate companies. A full line is related to present-day marketing. Competition has weeded out thousands of small appliance dealers. Instead, *retail* sales are now made largely either through regional chains of appliance outlets or independent operators who carry stocks of many brands. To get space on the floors of these retailers and the support of their salespeople, a full line of well-known brands is a significant advantage.

To reach the *builder* market, companies submit bids for kitchen packages designed according to the builder's specifications. While this is a price-competitive game, a line of coordinated products and/or a well-known brand name are distinct advantages. For instance, the builder can point to "a G.E. kitchen."

It is into this industry setting that the Maytag Company must position itself.

Maytag's Heritage

Throughout its history, Maytag has placed primary attention on high-quality laundry equipment. Its dependability and durability have enabled Maytag to stay aloof of competitive pricing—by charging a margin at least twice that of the industry generally. Over 60 percent of Maytag's customers are previous Maytag users.

This quality stance has been enhanced by (1) reliance, for many years, on a network of dealers who sold only Maytag equipment, and (2) the highest advertising budget per unit in the industry. The TV ads have featured the old lonely repairman with nothing to do because the Maytag equipment is so well-made.

Maytag's focus on a high-quality, high-priced niche has made the company the outstanding exception in the industry in terms of profitability. It has earned, on average, an attractive return on investment in the face of the maturity pressures described above. The record of the last five years is shown in Table 2.

TABLE 2.
MAYTAG FINANCIAL DATA
(in millions of dollars, except ratios)

	1982	1981	1980	1979	1978
Net Sales	441	409	349	369	325
Cost of Products Sold	296	282	231	238	209
Profit before Income Tax	69	68	65	83	70
Net Income	37	37	36	45	37
% Profit before Tax to Net Sales	15.6	16.6	18.6	22.4	21.5
Total Assets	274	229	235	203	181

Moreover, Maytag is in a strong financial position. Traditionally, it had no long-term debt. Its present long-term obligations of $22 million (11 percent of equity) were added to finance the acquisition of Jenn-Air and could be repaid out of the cash account.

Maytag's production costs appear to be in the approximate range of its major competitors. However, the company has not embarked on a major program for further reduction, as have G.E. and Whirlpool. Maytag's location in Newton, Iowa, places it in an area where the protestant ethic of responsibility and hard work is still extant.

Winds of change

In view of Maytag's resilience during the maturing of the major appliance industry, why should it be considering a change in strategy now? The data already presented gives several reasons for at least a reassessment.

As competitors improve their quality, Maytag may have increasing difficulty sustaining its reputation for *superior* dependability and durability. The shifting patterns of retailing major appliances may reduce the availability and effectiveness of small, exclusive dealers. Perhaps partly for these reasons, Maytag's margin of profit before tax has declined from 22.4 percent in 1979 to 15.6 percent in 1982. Furthermore, the survivors of the shakeout in the industry are in fighting trim and looking for new ways to increase market share. The major appliance industry is no place to rest on one's laurels.

To assist in predicting competition in the future, Maytag should take a hard look at the strengths and likely plans of its main competitors. Table 3 gives the

market leaders in Maytag's present product lines and in closely related lines
which Maytag might enter.

Table 3.
Share of U.S. Market

Clothes Washers		Dryers (Electric)		Refrigerators		Freezers	
Whirlpool	43%	Whirlpool	44%	G.E./Hotpoint	30%	Whirlpool	32%
G.E./Hotpoint	18	G.E./Hotpoint	17	Whirlpool	29	White	30
Maytag	18	Maytag	16	White	22	Admiral	22
White	15	White	15	Others	19	Amana	12
Others	6	Others	8			Others	4
	100%		100%		100%		100%

Ranges (Electric)		Ranges (Gas)		Microwave Ovens		Dishwashers	
G.E./Hotpoint	32%	Magic Chef	22%	G.E./Hotpoint	14%	Design & Mfg.	45%
Others	36	Raytheon	22	Litton	13	G.E./Hotpoint	22
White	16	Tappan	18	Raytheon	13	Hobart	16
Whirlpool	9	Roper	14	Sharp	11	Whirlpool	9
MagicChef	7	Others	24	Others	49	Others	8
	100%		100%		100%		100%

Disposers		Compactors	
In-Sink-Erator	55%	Whirlpool	47%
G.E./Hotpoint	20	G.E./Hotpoint	30
Hobart	8	Hobart	10
Tappan	8	Others	13
	100%		100%

Source: *Appliance Manufacturer*

Future threats appear to be most likely from Whirlpool, General Electric, White
Consolidated Industries, and Magic Chef (in view of its recent acquisitions of
Admiral and Norge). Recent activities of each of these corporations along with
their 1982 sales and operating income in major appliances throw some light on
their strengths relative to Maytag.

Whirlpool Corporation. With sales of over $2.1 billion and profits before
income tax of $174 million, Whirlpool is clearly number two in major appli-
ances. Years ago, Whirlpool made appliances only for Sears, Roebuck & Co.,
and still about half its output goes to Sears. This volume helps lower costs. Nevertheless, Whirlpool is spending $148 million, the single biggest investment in
its history, to overhaul its washing machine factory and to redesign its washer to
cut weight and parts. Whirlpool is a leader in new uses of electronics for con-

trols. In marketing, Whirlpool has a reputation for helping dealers—with financing, inventories, etc. The company is in strong financial condition.

General Electric. The industry leader with $2.9 billion appliance sales, G.E. is an aggressive competitor in almost all segments. After some soul-searching about the low profitability of the industry, G.E. embarked in 1981 on a $1 billion five-year modernization of its plants. It intends to pioneer in the use of robotics to cut costs. Heavy advertising of the total line, price rebates, surprise tactics, and sharp bidding in the builder market indicate that G.E. aims to increase its market share even further. It has ample capital resources.

White Consolidated Industries. Originally a sewing machine company, White is now a diversified conglomerate. Its major appliance lines, with combined sales totaling $1.3 billion and operating income of $77 million, include a variety of once-famous trade names: Frigidaire, Philco, Bendix, Hamilton, Kelvinator, Gibson, Easy. White's strategy has been to buy unprofitable companies (or divisions of large corporations like GM or Westinghouse) at liquidation prices, and then cut costs drastically. To promote sales, White frequently gives the salespeople of dealers a five- to twenty-dollar "spiff" for each White produce sold. Whether such gutsy treatment of costs, pricing, and selling will bring lasting returns remains to be seen. Availability of capital depends on what other deals White enters.

Magic Chef. In the late 1970s, Magic Chef transformed itself from a range company to a full-line producer of major appliances—primarily by the acquisition of the Admiral refrigerator and the Norge laundry businesses. Sales of $513 million and operating income of $7 million reflect retail distribution of a full line of products under both the Magic Chef and the Admiral names and substantial sales for private label distribution. Magic Chef has invested large amounts to modernize its production facilities. A refrigerator equipped with a stir freezer to make ice cream illustrates Magic Chef's attempts to differentiate its products with special features. Although Magic Chef does have some long-term debt, it is in sound financial condition.

Most other remaining manufacturers in the major appliance industry focus on only one or two kinds of appliances, often selling their products under their own brands and for private labeling by companies that wish to promote a more complete line of products. *The* growth product is the microwave oven—produced by several companies (including Japanese) with still half its potential market untapped.

Maytag's Diversification Moves

Maytag appears to be experimenting with diversification rather than embarked on a clear-cut program. It has recently made two acquisitions. One is Jenn-Air, the leading manufacturer of indoor cooking grills that include a special vented exhaust. These grills appeal to the upper income market (compatible with Maytag's) but are predominantly a custom builders' item (not a normal outlet for Maytag). The other is Hardwick Stove Company, a manufacturer of ranges predominantly for private label sale. Hardwick is making twenty models of ranges to be sold under the Maytag label. This venture will test whether Maytag's prestige and ability to charge premium prices for laundry equipment can be transferred to another line of product where leading brands are already entrenched.

Questions

1. What are Maytag's strengths and weaknesses relative to its competitors in the home laundry equipment business?
2. What are Maytag's strengths and weaknesses relative to its competitors as a potential full-line supplier of major appliances?
3. Do you recommend that Maytag (a) manufacture and sell only laundry equipment, (b) manufacture and sell most types of major appliances, (c) or something in-between? Please specify.

4 PREDICTING RESPONSES OF KEY ACTORS

In the preceding two chapters, we treated the external dynamics as unresponsive forces to which a firm should adjust. A lot of change and uncertainty might prevail, but the presumption was that our actions would not alter the environment. This chapter adds another dimension.

It looks at the way key people are likely to respond to fresh actions which we or other persons initiate. To at least a limited degree, each of us tries to reshape our world. So we need to predict responses and counter-responses to initiatives we or our peers thrust into the system. The wisdom of any strategic move depends in part on the resistance and retaliation, or the cooperation, which that move is likely to evoke.

After distinguishing between passive and hostile environments, this chapter deals with two issues: How are key actors likely to respond to our thrusts? In light of that predicted response, what kind of alignments among actors should we try to establish?

HOSTILE VERSUS PASSIVE ENVIRONMENT

Passive Environment

Our pioneer heritage creates a bias about strategy. In the traditional Western scenario, the physical obstacles were great, but customers liked the new services provided, employees welcomed new and better jobs, and supporting organizations such as railroads cooperated. Despite a few hostile Indians in the background and occasional feuds between the cattle-ranchers and settlers, the environment was basically friendly and benevolent. Our task in that setting would have been to provide the vision, mobilize resources, and share in the hard systematic work of turning opportunity into achievement.

Note that in this view a series of well-planned moves would have overcome the obstacles, and the response of people affected was preset. Occasionally such a relatively simple situation exists, but most strategy today runs into other people's strategy and must deal with their countermoves.

Hostile Environment

In a "hostile" environment several key groups will resist the moves called for in our strategy. In fact, they probably will be aggressively pursuing their own objectives which may include our fitting into *their* plans. How much direct conflict arises will depend, of course, on the strategy we elect. Perhaps some arrangement can be found which will be at least acceptable to two or more groups. But negotiations will be necessary, and in that process our strategy may have to be modified. Everyone is pushing; our aim in this game is to position ourselves so that we are not pushed way off course—or, if we are lucky and smart, occasionally get pulled along toward our goal by others' efforts (like riding the surf).

The scramble for production of wide-body, medium-range jet airplanes—at the end of the 1970s—illustrates this kind of process. Airbus Industries, a joint French-German venture, was several years ahead in the market with its 240-seat model. Boeing countered with a proposed new line of planes (B757, B767) focused on a similar market segment. The physical characteristics of both Airbus and Boeing lines were sharply competitive: lower fuel consumption, less noise, wide-body, medium-range, around 200-passenger size. But much more than plane design was involved in making sales in the important international market. Foreign airlines need the financial backing of their local governments, and that backing could be secured only by recognizing other concerns of the respective governments. To help deal with local employment and nationalism, Boeing negotiated subcontracts for components in Italy and Japan, and for Rolls-Royce engines in England. Airbus, via the French government, courted Spain with support for entry into the Common Market and India with broad trade benefits. Clearly the groups vitally concerned extended beyond the plane producers and airline customers, and an array of interlocking strategies on issues far removed from plane production were involved.

Lease financing of computers is a simpler example of a hostile environment—as we are using the term. For several years financial firms thought lease financing was a splendid investment. The firm with capital to invest located a company that had just made a large purchase of computers. The financial firm bought the computers from the user and leased them back again. In this arrangement the user in effect borrowed capital at favorable terms and usually obtained tax benefits; the lessor found an attractive investment. Soon, however, more people became involved. Smaller manufacturers of computers and peripheral equipment relied on (and often had formal agreements with) leasing firms to help make sales. But these manufacturers also relied on local service companies to maintain their equipment, and this service was vital to keep the equipment running—and the lease viable. Then, users occasionally went bankrupt or their needs changed, so part of the equipment had to be resold; this often brought in a fifth party. The business was complicated by rapid technological change, and by a practice of manufacturers such as Digital Equipment Corporation to lower prices on older models.

Consequently, to be successful in lease financing of computers, a financial firm has to develop formal or informal understandings with equipment manufacturers, service companies, technical consultants, and resale agents, in addition to its direct "customers," the equipment users. Each of these "actors" has a particular environment and a particular strategy, and the terms on which cooperation will be continued have to be negotiated.

In both of these examples, wide-bodied jets and computer leasing, strategy goes beyond selecting an attractive domain. Key parts of the environment are busily pushing their own objectives, and our strategy must be linked to theirs. Directly or indirectly we try to manipulate this environment. In the process our strategy may be modified, especially because the various actions and reactions of other actors are hard to predict.

In a "hostile" environment, strategy must be adroit and adaptive.

Range of Options

Relationships with key actors vary widely. We may elect to fight with a competitor head-on, as Avis does with Hertz. Or the competition may be mixed with cooperation, even to the point where competition is publicly denied, as is the usual relation among universities and among hospitals.

Sometimes a desired result is so expensive or so risky that no one firm wants to seek it alone. So a joint venture focused on a particular outcome is created. The pipeline bringing crude oil from the north slope of Alaska is such a venture. Several pilot plants experimenting with gasification of coal also are jointly sponsored by companies which compete on most other fronts.

In many other relationships mutual dependence is pervasive and continuing. Professional football and the TV networks, for instance, have a durable marriage; clearly the football teams could not operate in their present manner without the broadcast income. Automobile manufacturers and their dealer organizations are likewise dependent on each other.

Coalitions and alliances may be multifaceted. For example, a company in the specialized business of insuring real estate titles is valuable to—and also dependent on the goodwill of—mortgage lenders, surveyors, real estate brokers, and, in some areas, local lawyers who make the title search. In this arena, exchange of favors and mutual trust is vital to success. Similarly, in the growing field of solid-waste disposal, strategy must recognize the interaction between equipment manufacturers (and their maintenance organizations), trash collectors, environmental control agencies, bond underwriters, and users of the output such as steam for utility generators.

Society is increasingly complex and interdependent, in terms of technology, trade, regulation, and geographic scope. External alignments must fit these trends and change with them. And as just illustrated, there are a variety of choices in the way the relationships will be structured.

ANALYSIS OF KEY ACTORS

Success and, indeed, survival of every business depends upon either obtaining the support or neutralizing the attacks of key actors in its environment. We live in a highly interdependent world. And to steer a course through this ever-changing structure, we need a keen insight into the behavior of those actors who affect our fate.

Who Must Be Considered?

Resource suppliers and customers interact directly with the business. As suggested in the discussion of the *resource converter model* in Chapter 1, included here are employees, material suppliers, bankers, stockholders, governmental agencies, other community groups. Because all these contributors are more or less dependent on our company, they are often called "stakeholders." An exchange relationship typically exists—a trading of inducements for inputs; so for actors in these groups we are concerned with both what we give up and what we get in return.

Of course, as indicated in Figure 4-1, each stakeholder will have its own array of suppliers and customers. We are only one part of the network. The stakeholder is trading on many fronts, just as we are doing. Consequently, to anticipate the response to our inducements, we should understand the stakeholder's relationships with its other resource suppliers and customers.

Competitors are also important—competitors for *resources* and competitors for *customers*. But note that, unlike our relations with stakeholders, we rarely deal directly with competitors. Rather, we focus on wooing stakeholders. We try to offer inducements that will be more attractive than those offered by our rival(s) by (1) improving our package and/or (2) undercutting what our rival offers. Since our rival is playing the same game, it is important to predict how the rival will respond to our efforts to attract a continuing, growing flow of orders or resources. The rival might upset our best laid plans.

Government regulators and *interest group representatives* are a third set of potential key actors. However, for present purposes they can be treated as a special class of stakeholder.

As a practical matter, only *key* actors in the above groups warrant close analysis. A key actor is a stakeholder or competitor who in relation to us has a lot of *power*—a customer who buys over 25 percent of our output, the only available supplier of fuel for our plant, a competitor who has the capability of hiring away our engineering staff, a regulatory agency that approves the quality

FIGURE 4-1.
STAKEHOLDER ANALYSIS

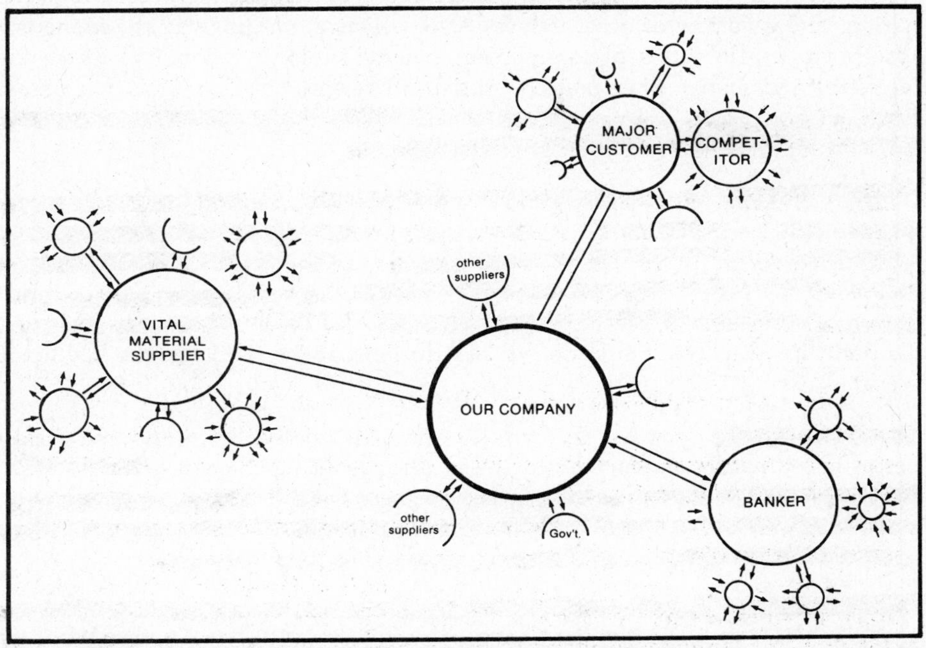

of our new products. Sometimes likely future entrants into the arena will be key actors.

For most purposes we can treat a total company—a supplier, a customer, or a competitor—as a single key actor. As in the legal concept of a corporation, we assume that the company is an independent being with a mind of its own. Occasionally in critical situations we go a step further and look inside the company at the specific persons who are key actors within that organization. But normally it is company actions that are our main concern.

What Will Guide Behavior of Key Actors?

Because we want to predict what key actors are likely to do if left alone, how they will respond to our initiatives, and often how we can modify their behavior, it behooves us to know what makes them tick. How do they normally behave, and what might cause them to change?

Goals, Values, and Beliefs. Each key actor is motivated by a set of goals or aspirations—with respect to size, type of business, place in the industry, status, profitability, and the like. Efforts to achieve these goals will be conditioned by a willingness to take risks, loyalty to friends, importance attached to service to the nation, and a variety of other values. Also, beliefs about the way the monetary system works, the future of communism, new technology, reliability of first-line workers, and many other matters guide and restrain decisions of that actor. Because these goals, values, and beliefs influence strongly what the actor will do, we should learn all we can about this mind set.

Patterns of Behavior. A key actor, like any of us, operates in a specific socio-economic system, and has a going enterprise with its particular resources and established relationships with external groups. (We should know what these are.) Inevitably there will be *patterns of behavior*—normal responses to normal pressures. This established flow gives us a base for predicting future behavior. To understand it, we should do our best to look at the world as the key actor sees it.

Capability Profile. Just as we appraise our own relative strengths and weaknesses in estimating our own outlook—see the preceding chapter—so too should we size up the strengths and weaknesses of each key actor. Such a "capability profile" of our competitors is especially valuable. This assessment will tell us what is *possible* for the key actor to do and where its limitations lie.

Future Pressures. For these actors, what *new pressures and opportunities* are likely to arise (shifts in their markets, cost changes, new technology, etc.), and how are they likely to react? In particular, what will be absorbing most of their attention? what internal or external resource limitations will they confront? what commitments which restrict their options are they likely to make? what are their chief risks? what could upset their plans?

Experience indicates that a surprising amount of information about any organization operating in the public sphere can be assembled by systematic observation. Speeches, press releases, published data, announced plans, positions taken on controversial issues—when regularly pulled together and analyzed—give a broad picture. And many kinds of alignments with key actors provide personal contacts which are an additional source of data. More subtle is assessing the personalities of important executives, and the values they cherish. But even here, insights can be picked up directly and indirectly.

Such a key actor assessment serves several purposes. (1) The predicted behavior indicates what the actor is likely to try to impose on other actors—including us. (2) From the assessment, events or actions which will appeal to the actor can be surmised, and also weaknesses and vulnerabilities. These conclusions can be very useful in negotiating a desired alignment with that actor. (3) More specifically, the likely reaction of the actor to particular strategic moves that we might initiate can be predicted.

What Is the Relative Power of Key Actors?

Power, in the present context, is the ability of key actors to modify the conduct of others and, on the other hand, their ability to prevent someone else from modifying their conduct. Obviously, relative power will affect which actor can pursue a strategy with the least concession to others.

In relationships between business organizations, power is based largely on an *ability to restrict the flow of desired inputs on attractive terms*. Thus, if OPEC can withhold needed crude oil it has a lot of power over petroleum refineries, or if a bank can call in necessary loans it has power over the borrower. To simplify the discussion, we will consider a large customer withholding an order, or a governmental agency withholding approval, as other examples of restriction of a desired input.

When we start analyzing power relationships, we soon see that there are degrees of power, costs of exercising power, and all sorts of countervailing power. For example, the degree of power I have over you depends on the number of good *alternative* sources you can turn to for the input I am providing. The fewer and less attractive the alternatives you have, the greater is my power. So one consideration in designing strategy is its effect on the number of alternatives which will remain open to you and to me. For instance, you may be a large and prestigious customer but I will hesitate to sell you a third of my output if there are few ways to replace this volume in the event you threaten to withdraw.

Of course, the other side of the coin is that I have power over you, *if* you lack alternative sources of supply. Or, if through the help of my friends, the teamsters, I can delay your use of alternative sources, the impact is similar. Coalitions gain strength when, directly or indirectly, their membership can narrow the number of options various actors have.

The kind of power we are discussing is *potential*; only rarely is it actually exercised. In fact, most people are reluctant to use their power—for several reasons. The person being pressured may call up countervailing power and will start to develop new alternatives (coal or solar energy, for instance, as alternatives for crude oil); future friendship and trust will be lost; a reputation for harsh dealings may spoil relationships with other suppliers. On the other hand, total reluctance to use power can undercut the influence of a person who will soon be regarded as a "paper tiger." Consequently, in assessing power we have to consider willingness to use it as well as capability.

In summary, the analytical approach just outlined gives a basis for setting up external alignments. First, key actors are identified—the external organizations or individuals whose continuing cooperation is vital to our strategic moves. Second, for each key actor an assesment is made of his or her motivations, strengths and weaknesses, probable future behavior, and likely response to our actions. Third, the relative power of each key actor to pursue a particular course is estimated. This analysis provides insights about present and probable

future behavior of the human forces in our environment; these are the dynamic
elements from which a realistic interaction strategy must be forged.

CHOICE OF ALIGNMENTS

As when a nation designs its international strategy, a look first at the simpler one-to-one relationships shows the varying colored pieces that must be fitted into the overall mosaic.

One-to-One Relationships with Stakeholders

A business-unit's relations with its diverse resource suppliers and customers
are sure to take different forms. They range from close cooperation to sharp
conflict. The matrix shown in Figure 4-2 suggests a way to deal with this array.

FIGURE 4-2.

AN APPROACH TO ONE-TO-ONE RELATIONSHIPS
(with a key supplier or customer)

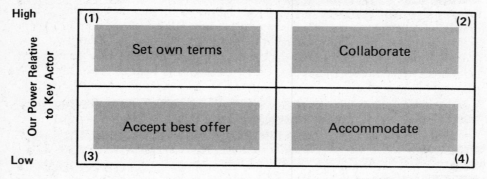

Note: The matrix is not intended to show the array of options
for dealing with competitors. When to fight, stall, ignore, or defend is
a study in itself. However, the kind of key actor analysis already
recommended does provide essential information for competitive
strategy and tactics.

When Cooperation Is Likely To Pay Off. On one axis of the matrix we show the
benefits to us of cooperating with a specific key actor. Our interests may be
highly interdependent, as between Pratt & Whitney and Boeing in designing
engines for the new wide-bodied jets; or, at the other extreme, the interest may
be too small to warrant more than routine treatment.

The other axis reflects relative power—our ability to impose our will on the other actor compared with the actor's capacity to make us conform to his or her will. Availability of alternatives and backup resources are the usual sources of such power. Sears, Roebuck and a small South Carolina manufacturer of dungarees are a classical example of the range on this scale.

The descriptions in the quadrants merely suggest the kind of relationship with a key supplier or customer that we can readily achieve under the different conditions. Of course, each actor will view the situation from a unique perspective, and may prefer a course of action different from ours. So some negotiation and testing of power may be necessary.

When the benefits of working together predominate (the righthand side of the matrix), cooperative alignments are called for. The more dynamic and uncertain the environment, the more attractive will be joint efforts with financiers, equipment suppliers, customers, regulatory agencies, and so on. The electronics and computer industries grew rapidly partly because collaboration has been the prevailing relationship between suppliers and users. In contrast, the energy program in the late 1970s moved at a snail's pace, in part because collaboration between interested parties proved very hard to sustain. (Governmental and public concern dealt more with who-would-get-what than with pooling resources to confront the monumental task.)

Relative power obviously affects the kind of joint action it is wise to seek. Two comparatively strong actors—for instance, Texas Instruments and GM approaching computerization of automobiles—can work as roughly equal partners. However, if one firm is weak relative to the other, it will probably have to accommodate—fit into the changing situation as best it can, accepting the dictates of the stronger actor as constraints while trying to develop some capabilities which will be attractive to the dominant partner.

While these two considerations, relative power and potential benefits of cooperation, provide insight into desirable one-to-one alignments, other factors deserve careful attention. Are the stakes high or low? If low, perhaps a modification of the traditional relationship does not warrant the expense. Legislation may prohibit certain kinds of joint effort. Past experience with either fighting or collaborating sets the stage for future alignments. Because all such factors are likely to vary from actor to actor, the optimum path to pursue in each relationship calls for particular attention.

Use of Supplier Analysis. A specific case will illustrate how the type of analysis just outlined clearly shaped the strategy of one company, Ethicon Sutures, at a critical stage in its development. Ethicon manufactures surgical sutures for stitching-up operations ranging from delicate eye repair to leg amputations. For years, surgeons threaded sutures through the eye of the needle used. (The needles, of course, vary greatly in size and shape.) Then a new kind of needle was invented that could be crimped at the factory onto the end of a piece of suture. This arrangement saved the trouble of threading the needle, but much more important, it reduced the hole that was pierced to draw the suture through the tissue.

Ethicon adopted a strategy of featuring the new needle-suture combination, each encased in a sterile container. But it ran into difficulty obtaining needles. Its primary needle supplier dealt chiefly in textile needles; surgical needles were a sideline. So when Ethicon asked this supplier to devise a technology to make the new type of needle, the supplier expressed reluctance and insisted on large volumes of each size and shape. Moreover, to increase volume the supplier reserved the right to sell needles to other suture companies. A second supplier, also focusing on textile needles, was even less interested; and a third, much smaller manufacturer lacked capital to tool up and also lacked the quality control so important for the surgical market.

In terms of the matrix, the primary supplier had substantial power over Ethicon but did not see much benefit in close collaboration, so its relations with Ethicon fell in the first quadrant. Ethicon was in a weak bargaining position, yet the outcome of negotiations was vital to its new strategy. Further analysis of the R & D activity of the primary supplier indicated that this company intended to move away from the needle business. So Ethicon predicted that long-run prospects were poor for getting the relationship into quadrant 4, let alone quadrant 2.

Consequently, Ethicon decided it could not risk staying so dependent on an uninterested supplier. It first explored a joint venture with the smaller company to make one or two sizes of the new needle, but soon worked out an arrangement to acquire a stockholder position in the company. That enabled Ethicon to establish a collaborative relation with the company—quadrant 2. Several years were needed to develop the capability of this company to make the various kinds of needles with the necessary quality. And, as Ethicon cut back on purchases of traditional needles, its old suppliers became even less interested in maintaining prompt delivery and quality. All this slowed Ethicon's growth and delayed pushing its new product across the total market. But in the end Ethicon escaped from its dependent and therefore weak position.

Degrees of Collaboration

Economic theory and much of the business literature is preoccupied with competition. We are conditioned to think in terms of zero-sum games. A broader view of society, however, highlights the mechanisms by which people cooperate. The miracle of modern civilization is the way specialized outputs are combined, traded, and combined again to generate sophisticated services and goods. So when we talk of collaboration as one form of external alignment, we are dealing with a fundamental phenomenon.

Collaboration between key actors varies in degree.

1. *Informal mutual aid* is the most common. You help me as a neighborly act;

later I probably return the favor. Sociologist Peter Blau observes that this sort of cooperation permeates social relations; it differs from economic exchanges in the unspecified nature of the return help, and it requires a high amount of trust that mutually supportive actions will be continued.[1] This is the foundation of goodwill with employees, suppliers, customers, bankers, and a host of other points in the environment.

2. *Formal agreements* covering the scope and nature of cooperation become necessary when advance commitments are large and when many individuals must have a consistent understanding about the relationship.

3. *Joint ventures* break out a particular area for intense collaborative activity and provide for a pooling of knowledge and resources related to that activity. The joint venture may be a temporary consortium for a large project, such as the construction of a dam, or it may be a corporation with indefinite life.

4. *Mergers* carry collaboration to the extreme where separate identity is sacrificed for the benefits of central direction of the combined activities.[2]

Many other variations are possible. Nevertheless, these four degrees of collaboration clearly indicate the profound impact that external alignments can have on the process of strategy formulation.

Collaboration implies some sharing of decision-making. When American Motors undertakes selling Renault automobiles in the U.S., and probably using some Renault parts in its own production, American Motors' strategy in the U.S. clearly will include Renault inputs and vice versa. And under accommodation, the adjustment of our initial plans is likely to be even greater. In other words, strategic planning involves dynamic give-and-take in which more than our own interests must be considered.

Of course, managers of a business-unit may choose to limit the extent of collaboration. Crown Cork & Seal, for instance, as a point of strategy, rarely installs can-making equipment in customers' plants—as do its leading competitors—because it wishes to retain greater flexibility. This successful company builds strong informal ties to its suppliers and customers but minimizes formal agreements.

The alignment with each key actor is a separate, unique relationship. The approach to shaping these relations outlined thus far stresses a one-to-one analysis because each key actor is important to us and each presents a distinct set of factors and opportunities. Nevertheless, a *collective view* of all of a company's external alignments is also desirable.

A company develops a reputation for aggressiveness, for fair dealings, for consistency, and the like, so the way one actor is treated raises expectations in other dealings. For example, in its early history, Sears, Roebuck & Co. had a reputation for squeezing its suppliers once they became highly dependent on

---

[1]See Peter M. Blau, *Exchange and Power in Social Life* (New York: John Wiley & Sons, 1964).

[2]An economist, Oliver E. Williamson, has argued in *Markets and Hierarchies*, (New York: The Free Press, 1975), that merged operations are more effective than competitive markets for handling exchange when mutual trust is vital. Mutual trust is necessary, he says, when uncertainty is high and key actors are few (two features of a hostile environment we listed at the opening of this chapter).

Sears' purchase orders. Later, Sears adopted a strategy of assuring its efficient suppliers that they could earn reasonable profits; to carry out this strategy, close collaboration in product design and production scheduling is often undertaken. Not every one of Sears' thousands of suppliers agrees with the application, but the policy is clear: it does not use its power for short-run benefits, but rather for building a reputation as an attractive customer.

It is entirely possible to be ruthless in some spheres and cooperative in others—say, purchasing and labor relations—but some public rationalization of such behavior is desirable in order to create an aura of reliability, even integrity.

The combined set of alignments must also be weighed in terms of the total demands on resources. Few business-units have the personnel and capital to support several aggressive fights at the same time. In fact, even simultaneously maintaining close collaboration in several different areas may create severe problems of internal coordination. So, while the very essence of strategy deals with change, it is often advisable to ration or stagger the volatility.

Coalitions

The careful analysis of each key actor recommended early in this chapter provides the underlying data base upon which the various relationships are built. That same bank of data may suggest desirable alliances or coalitions. A coalition is an agreement among at least three actors on joint action; often some of the actors have only indirect relationships with each other.

Circumstances Leading to Coalitions. Often a business-unit discovers that by itself it cannot bring about the changes it desires. It lacks the necessary power. To reach its objectives it rallies allies. In practice this use of allies in coalitions is much more common than generally realized.

Quite diverse organizations may form a coalition around a common cause. For example, the "gun lobby" which opposes restrictions on private ownership and use of guns is supported by strange bedfellows: hunters, people who want guns to protect their homes, criminals, and firms with a commercial interest in the sale of guns and ammunition. Acting separately they would have limited impact on Congress, but their united strength has been remarkably potent.

In the gun lobby example, each participant has a direct concern about the outcome. A variation is found in the support of tariff barriers. Here, trading of support is common—I'll support your protection if you'll support mine. Such mutual helping of friends is found in all sorts of business situations, from the sale of consulting services to "professional courtesy" among doctors. We are not suggesting that participants in such coalitions are cavalier about giving their support, although some may be; considerable effort may be devoted to deserving the support. Rather, the point is that coalitions are necessary to achieve the desired impact.

As already noted, the allies may embrace people who are only indirectly involved. Thus, in the finance company example cited at the beginning of this chapter, equipment manufacturers, service agencies, and resale brokers are all included in the coalition. All are required to make the purchase and lease-back practice a viable business, and each actor has to adopt a strategy regarding the coalitions to be joined.

Basically, when coalitions are formed, one or more business-units recognize that they cannot passively wait until the people with whom they have direct dealings are all set to act. Instead, they actively sponsor a whole chain of events by several different agencies. Consider a grain dealer wishing to sell feed to cat-fish raisers. Taking a cue from the way frying chickens are now raised and mar-keted by the millions, the grain dealer has to interest farmers in mass production of catfish in artificial lakes. This is appealing because catfish are very efficient converters of grain feed into meat. But to market the output, local "factories" are necessary to clean, cut, package, and freeze the meat. Refrigerated trucks must take the frozen fish to wholesale distribution points. And a marketing com-pany has to sell the product either to "fish and chips" and other restaurants or to a slowly emerging retail-store market. These are the main actors, although the cooperation of zoologists, government inspectors, and others is also essential.

The way such a new industry is developed and the successful entrepreneurs establish themselves is through a coalition. Perhaps one enterprise will under-take two or more steps, but complete vertical integration is unlikely. So some-one has to appreciate what conditions are necessary to attract collaborators into each step, and then induce related actors to adjust their activities in a way that will create these conditions. The leading and profitable firms in this new busi-ness will be those who have mastered the art of forming and guiding coalitions.

Coalition in the Health Field. Coalitions may be vital in all sorts of settings. For example, an old hospital located in the downtown section of a typical city faced a dismal outlook. Its leading doctors and full-paying patients were moving to the suburbs; a proud history carried with it outmoded facilities; Medicaid patients could not provide or attract resources for rebuilding. The bold new strategy was to become a teaching hospital focusing on specialities; this would attract a high-quality staff, and full-paying patients would be sent for special treatment on referral from suburban hospitals. However, a wide array of allies were needed. The state medical authorities had to bow to local political pressure for a teaching hospital in that part of the state. The Veterans Administration had to locate one of its new health centers on an adjacent site, providing an addi-tional volume of use of the specialty capabilities. The city had to clear land for new buildings and help finance a closed (safe) parking garage. The trustees had to raise additional funds for upgrading the plant. And this hospital complex had to be a significant part of a broad plan for revitalizing the downtown section of the city.

Throughout several years of planning and development, the critical job of the hospital administrators was to keep all the contributing elements in back of the plan. This proved to be predominantly a political task. Alternative suggestions were made frequently, usually with sponsorship from competing locations. To meet these challenges, some modifications in the original strategy were negotiated. A continuing promotional effort has been necessary to sustain commitment to the venture at national, state, and local levels. Withdrawal of support at any one of these levels would probably kill the plan.

Coalitions may be necessary for survival, as the above examples indicate. We suggest that they be approached as elaborations of the simpler direct alignments every enterprise must cultivate. A coalition network is indeed more complicated since more actors are involved and inducements to cooperate may come from third parties, but the analysis of motivations and options of each key actor is still the starting point.

SUMMARY

Predicting the behavior of key actors is an important supplement to judgment about the industry and company outlook recommended in the previous chapters. The broader forecasts about the setting in which company action will take place are indeed essential; but those forecasts pass over the more specific help or hindrance which can be expected from other people who are also active in that same setting. A forecast of likely moves of at least the key actors should be added to our total assessment.

Especially useful is a prediction of the responses and counter-responses of key actors to our own initiatives. The business environment is not inert and passive. Instead, many firms are each pushing their own programs, and these firms may welcome or oppose what we try to do. The ensuing negotiations may then modify previous drives. A whole array of alignments with stakeholders and competitors will be developed. Obviously, we should try to anticipate how this dynamic give-and-take process will work out.

Such a careful analysis of our competitors, our major suppliers, and our major customers will provide valuable input into the decision-making of central management. It probably will influence the design of strategy and the choice of policy.

An approach for predicting the responses of key actors has been outlined in this chapter. First comes careful analysis—leading to capability profiles—of key actors: *who* must be considered, *what* motivates each one, what is the *relative power* of each. Then with this background, the likely alignments are predicted. Among the possible arrangements which should be considered are (1) simple one-to-one relationships, (2) varying degrees of collaboration where joint action appears feasible, and (3) coalitions.

The next chapter will discuss how these forecasts, along with those from Chapters 2 and 3, are used to design a strategy for a business-unit.

We should note, again, that strategy formulation does not follow a simple sequence. Instead, it is iterative. Forecasts suggest possible strategies; analysis of these strategies calls for further forecasts; these new forecasts point to other alternatives; and so on. This recycling is especially true of key actor analysis because we are specifically concerned with the way competitors and stakeholders are likely to respond to various strategic moves that we are contemplating. The recommended approach continues to be useful throughout. But the first application rarely will provide all the estimates which will eventually be needed.

QUESTIONS FOR CLASS DISCUSSION

1. To practice key actor analysis, select a student organization that you know well (coop laundry, mid-city tutoring, artist concert series, radio station, or the like). Who are the key actors within and outside the organization that primarily determine its continuing success? For three of these key actors, use the outline suggested in the chapter to determine the main factors that will influence their future behavior. What power does each of the three have?

2. Boeing invested $3 billion in developing its new series of wide-bodied planes—the 757 and 767 briefly discussed in the opening of this chapter. This sum was twice the net worth of the company. Make a list of the dozen most important key actors Boeing should have analyzed prior to embarking on such a large program. (If you don't know company names, at least identify them by function.) Explain why you selected these actors.

3. (a) Where would you place each of the following on the matrix appearing in this chapter? Assume that you are the first actor named in each pair: (1) a Chevrolet dealer in relation to the Chevrolet Division of GM; (2) your school cafeteria in relation to you; (3) the Springfield Hospital in relation to the union which is the certified bargaining agent for nurses in the hospital; (4) Exxon and the prime contractor building a supertanker for you. (b) Do the descriptive words in the quadrant selected in each situation suggest what you think the relationship would be?

4. (a) Had you been Ernest Gallo shortly before Coca-Cola left the wine business, what would have been your analysis of Coke's wine company as a key actor (see question 7 of Chapter 3 for some data), and your analysis of the environment of your company? To increase market share slightly, Gallo advertised its premium varietal wines on TV (spending three times the dollars spent just four years earlier), reduced wholesale prices, and offered big promotional discounts to retailers. Coke matched all these actions. All other American firms in the wine industry lost market share as the

two leaders tried harder. (b) As the president of Coke's wine company, what would have been your analysis of E & J Gallo Co. and your analysis of the environment? Would you have tried to persuade your chairman, Mr. Goizeuta of Coca-Cola, that your company was well-positioned (1) to fight further with Gallo, (2) for long-run sales and profits?

5. In the Ethicon example described in the chapter, the company needed especially designed sterile containers as well as special needles. The containers were to be molded plastic tubes, which could be produced by quite a few firms. What degree of collaboration should Ethicon seek in obtaining these containers?

6. MacMillan observes, "Coalition members do not join the coalition without bringing with them their demands, and the support of these members could easily be given to alternative coalitions.. . . Each member will, therefore, make a set of demands on the coalition to commit itself to certain goals.. . . However, it is often impossible for the coalition to satisfy *all* the demands of *all* its members.. . . A potential member will join only if he feels that the policy commitments of the coalition will promote his own goals, and he will stay only as long as he expects the coalition to be successful."[3] Use the hospital example appearing near the end of this chapter to illustrate MacMillan's points.

7. Assume that you wish to establish a "Teen Canteen" in your home community (a place for senior high school students to meet in the late afternoons and evenings to buy snacks and dance). Describe the *alliance* that would have to be established to make the project viable.

8. At one point in its struggle to survive in the steel industry in the United States, the largest firm in the industry, U.S. Steel Corporation, won major concessions from the United Steel Workers Union—reduced wage rates and more flexible work rules in a 41-month contract (a contract of unusual length). The company's position was that the concessions were necessary to preserve jobs. U.S. Steel also lobbied extensively and strenuously with the U.S. Tariff Commission and the White House, seeking administrative action (and higher duties) against foreign steel that was, said the company, heavily subsidized by the foreign governments.

    Subsequently, U.S. Steel announced that it was seeking an agreement with the government-owned British Steel Corp. whereby British Steel would invest $100 million in U.S. Steel's Fairless works near Trenton, New Jersey, and would also supply semi-finished steel ingots and slabs to the U.S. firm for further processing. This would allow U.S. Steel to close its outmoded and costly open-hearth furnaces that turned blast-furnace iron into steel and thus cut its costs by 10 percent. British Steel could then keep open a Scottish plant which employed

---

[3] I. C. MacMillan, *Strategy Formulation: Political Concepts* (St. Paul: West Publishing Company, 1978).

4,000 workers and which had been mentioned as one that the British government might close to halt British Steel's large losses. British Steel had earlier been cited as one of the more heavily subsidized foreign producers.

Predict the reactions to the proposed agreement of the following actors in U.S. Steel's network: U.S. Steel's management, the USW leaders, the White House, the U.S. Tariff Commission, the British Ministries of Labour and Industry, members of the British parliament of the party not then in power, and purchasing agents of large steel users in the United States.

CASE 4
PACCAR Truck Leasing

A Seattle banker comments, "Although we are a long way from Detroit, our local customer—PACCAR—is one of the few companies in the automobile and truck industry to have uninterrupted profits over the last ten years. Now, the top managers are thinking of moving into a related activity, full-service leasing, and that is a very different ballgame. I just hope some of the giants don't knock them for a loop."

The present position of PACCAR and its new frontier are described in the following paragraphs.

PACCAR's Present Niche

PACCAR Inc. has been adept at keeping pace with changes in the transportation industry. As overland freight shifted from railroads to trucks, PACCAR made a corresponding change. Originally a freight car and lumbering equipment manufacturer, PACCAR's primary business now is building heavy-duty trucks. Currently, well over 80 percent of its $1.2 billion sales and its $32 million net income comes from the manufacture and sale of Class 8 diesel trucks (gross weight of 33,000 pounds and over).

Another striking feature of PACCAR in this troubled industry is its strong financial position, as shown in Table 1. The parent company has virtually no long-term debt and its current ratio is 2.6. Net income did fall sharply during the recent depression, but it was the dwindling freight car volume that showed the steepest decline.

PACCAR makes only the Class 8 trucks, using the trade names of Peterbilt and Kenworth. These trucks sell for $50,000 to $80,000 each. They are made to customer specifications including such features as CB radios, air-conditioning, bunks for sleeping, and an array of controls over the enginer and the brakes.

TABLE 1.
SELECTED FINANCIAL DATA FOR PACCAR, INC.
(in millions except per share data)

	1982	1978	1973
Sales	$1,230	$1,552	$ 766
Net income	32	87	42
Total assets	807*	613	
Long-term debt	13	21	18
Stockholders' equity	584	393	203
Net income per share common stock	4.16	9.56	5.20

*Over 40 percent of these assets are invested in or loaned to PACCAR financing affiliates.

Actually PACCAR manufactures (in six regional plants) only the tractor part of a tractor-trailer rig; trailers are sold separately by other companies. Customers include all sorts of manufacturing companies, big and small, which ship their products all over the country.

Most of PACCAR's competitors in the Class 8 field also make smaller trucks. International Harvester—clearly the largest producer—makes many kinds of trucks, construction equipment, and all sorts of agricultural equipment. A former "blue chip" company, International Harvester got into a severe financial crisis following a long strike and is in a selective retrenchment program. Mack Trucks, which competes with PACCAR's combined output of Peterbilt and Kenworth trucks for second place in the Class 8 field (each has about one-sixth of the total), also makes middle-weight trucks. Mack Truck has a checkered financial history and is now controlled by a foreign conglomerate.

The half-dozen remaining producers, below the top three, have their main base in other fields and moved into Class 8 as an extension from these operations. For example, Ford, GM, and Mercedes (a worldwide truck supplier outside the U.S.) only offer more standardized trucks than the three leaders.

PACCAR's survival and success in its selected niche reflects largely three related strengths:

1. Built-in product quality. Engineering specifications and care in production create a truck that on the average is more trouble-free and lasts longer than competing products. And such performance is important where dependable delivery is vital to the user. There is cost to achieve this quality, so PACCAR trucks are priced at a premium over competitors'.
2. Reputation among drivers as "the Cadillac" of the industry. Long-haul truck drivers are a breed apart—self-reliant, independent, proud, clannish, dependable. They are the modern Knights of the Road. Most of the time they work without supervision, and must cope reliably with a variety of situations. As a result, they feel that they deserve the best, and they take pride in driving a Cadillac.
3. A strong distribution and service network. PACCAR has 250 independent

dealers who both sell and offer full maintenance and repair service.[4] This network is crucial in keeping Peterbilt and Kenworth trucks in top operating condition and in making emergency repairs rapidly.

In addition, PACCAR does have a subsidiary company that helps customers finance their purchases. This affiliate benefits from the strong financial standing of its parent, and in turn extends credit in about one-third of the truck sales.

The Impact of Truck Leasing

However, the world does not stand still. The depression of the early 1980s cut sales of the entire truck manufacturing industry to 56 percent of its 1978 total. Deregulation of commercial carriers led to rate-cutting and lower income in their ranks. High interest rates discouraged purchase of all capital goods—including trucks. Consequently, new alignments and new ways to improve efficiency are being sought throughout the transporation sector.

One development is a sharp rise in the full-service leasing, instead of buying, of trucks by companies that want to transport their products. Estimates indicate that by 1983 a third of Class 8 trucks sold were on full-service lease to actual users; this figure was expected to increase to 48 percent by 1987, and one prediction foresaw 80 percent by 1992.

Under a typical full-service lease, a separate company owns the truck and maintains it in good running condition. The user pays rent on a monthly and mileage basis. It's similar to your renting a passenger car at an airport, except that large truck rentals often extend from three to five years. *Full-service* leasing also includes a variety of other services which simplify life for the traffic manager at the user company. Such services may include: logistics studies, full insurance, multistate vehicle licensing, multistate tax reporting, a fuel program, preventive maintenance, emergency repair, substitute vehicles, extra trucks for peak needs, parking-storage-washing, driver recruiting and testing. Recently the Interstate Commerce Commission removed one more restraint; now it is permissible for a leasing company to provide the driver as well. This involves the delicate tasks of supervising and motivating those Knights of the Road.

Note that full-service leasing differs from merely financing a purchase. Under full-service, the leasing company carries the risks and takes over special administrative burdens—tasks that few users are well suited to perform. Instead, the user avoids a diverting chore and can concentrate on its main line of business. Other attractions may include tax benefits, avoiding a capital appropriation hassle, balance sheet effects, and improved productivity through the use of the expertise and scale economies of the leasing firm. The user is buying an array of services, not just borrowing money to pay for the initial cost of the truck.

---

[4]Basically, the relationship of a dealer to PACCAR is like that of an automobile agency to its supplier of cars—for example, a Ford agency to the Ford Motor Company.

PACCAR has to decide how far it wants to get into this leasing business. Major competitors already exist. The largest truck leasing firm, in all size trucks as well as Class 8's, is Ryder—a firm with 600 locations that has an annual revenue of $2 billion. Hertz-Penske also is active in heavy-duty truck leasing (this operation is completely separate from Hertz auto rentals).

A sharp constraint on entry into heavy-duty truck leasing is the need for a far-flung servicing network. Many of the automobile leasing firms can take care of light trucks—a field where Japanese competition is expected to increase; but they lack the capability to handle large trucks. Firms such as Saunders, Gelco, and Rollins do support their heavy-duty truck leasing through contracts with a network of independent repair shops. And a couple of associations of independent leasing companies do have reciprocal servicing agreements. However, such arrangements are difficult to maintain on a nationwide basis, especially when the leasing companies undertake to maintain all kinds of trucks.

How and why should PACCAR get into this leasing business? For over eighty years, PACCAR has been a manufacturer of large transportation vehicles, not an operator of transportation fleets. A senior marketing executive answers:

"We should go into leasing for defensive reasons and to grasp an opportunity. If we don't, as the leasing companies become stronger they will take over our close relationships with users. Our chances to give distinctive services would be replaced by sharp price competition for just truck orders from the leasing companies. Then with our premium prices we would rapidly lose volume. Many of our dealers would lose the truck sales they need to survive, and our service organization would disintegrate.

"Instead, we can treat our existing dealer and service organization as an asset. We can put those dealers who wish into the leasing business. They are competent business people and know their customers well. We will have to create a central staff of experts who can provide all sorts of technical assistance to the dealers—contract forms, insurance leads, logistic studies, personnel training, etc. The setup for truck maintenance and repair is already in place.

"Our experience shows that a large number of users in our niche are willing to pay for quality, and quality will be even more important in full-service leasing. Also good drivers like our trucks.

"Leasing through the dealers is something we must do and can do well."

A financial executive of PACCAR is more skeptical. He points out: "There are a lot of risks in leasing. Both working capital and equipment costs are laid out first. Then you have to do everything right to keep the rental payments flowing back in. Not all our dealers are willing and able to take that sizable risk. A large dealer would have millions outstanding, you realize.

"You would be taking on a major education task—converting dealers and their salespeople to a new kind of business. When they stub their toes we would have an obligation to help bail them out. And if very many stub their toes, there goes our reputation for quality service.

"One other angle bothers me. The more we compete with the leasing companies the less likely they are to buy our trucks. We would be boxing ourselves out of what you predict will be the largest part of the market. Just last week one of our plant managers asked me what we were doing to *improve* our chances of shipping to the large leasing companies."

Questions

1. List the key actors in this situation. For a representative sample of the actors you list, prepare a "key actor analysis" as proposed in this chapter.
2. To what extent, if any, should PACCAR enter into truck leasing?

5

SELECTING BUSINESS-UNIT STRATEGY

For a short period a company may simply drift along just doing what is customary. Or if the competition is tough, it may react to each new crisis as seems best at the moment. Only if it is lucky and has a lot of resources will such passive or "fire-fighting" behavior enable the enterprise to survive very long in today's turbulent environment. The constructive alternative is to be *proactive* instead of *reactive*. This requires company managers to energetically forestall trouble and seize new opportunities. They must provide positive, future-oriented direction to company activities. An essential part of such proactive behavior is the development of a *master strategy* for the business-unit as a whole.

The three preceding chapters on industry outlook, company strengths, and likely behavior of key actors outline the array of forces that should be considered in designing master strategy. They set the stage. The next step is for the central managers of the business-unit to decide how their companies can best adapt to the anticipated opportunities and threats. A business-unit strategy normally should indicate:

1. *Domain sought.* What products or intangible services will the business-unit sell to what group of customers?
2. *Differential advantage in serving that domain.* On what basis—e.g., access to raw materials, better personnel, new technology, or low costs and prices—will the business-unit seek an advantage over competitors in providing its products or services?
3. *Strategic thrusts necessary and their approximate timing.* For the business-unit to move from its present position to where it wants to be—as laid out in 1 and 2—which moves will be made early and which can be deferred?
4. *Target results expected.* What financial and other criteria will the business-unit use to measure its success, and what levels of achievement are expected?[1]

Too often statements of strategy deal with only a single dimension. A new market or a desired financial return on investment, for instance, may be labeled as "our company strategy." Such a goal may indeed be part of the strategy, but its narrowness robs strategy of a needed balanced operational quality. A company strategy should be a well-conceived, practical commitment. To achieve this realistic quality, all four of the elements just listed should be carefully con-

---

[1]By listing targets as the fourth element, rather than the first, we place emphasis on the operational content of strategy. The more abstract goals, such as growth, usually serve better as criteria for acceptability than as guides for action. In practice, possible strategies are debated back and forth so often that no clear priority exists between target results and mission.

sidered. The resulting strategy will then be an *integrated*, forward-looking plan. This integration is depicted in Figure 5-1.

Although strategy has many dimensions to consider—domain sought, differential advantage, strategic thrusts, and target results—it need not be detailed and comprehensive. Rather, strategy should concentrate on *key* factors necessary for success and on *major* moves to be taken by the particular company at the current stage in its development. The selectivity of key points, and by implication the designation of other points as supportive, gives strategy much of its value as a planning device.

Full elaboration of plans is a necessary sequel to selecting company strategy, as we shall see in Parts 2 and 3. The role of strategy, however, is primarily to identify missions and to set forth major ways of achieving distinctiveness—our focus in this chapter.

DOMAIN SOUGHT

Product/Market Scope

The starting point in clarifying the mission of almost any enterprise is to define the services it will provide. It may design and manufacture a broad range of physical products or it may merely sell advice. But to continue to exist, it must provide some package of services for which some segment in society is prepared to pay. For example, after carefully examining the anticipated growth in the use of computers for billing retail customers, two enterprising IBM salespeople set up their own firm that (1) leases time on a central computer and (2) assists medium-sized stores in adapting their records and procedures to make use of this service. Note that this young firm has a sharp definition of the kind of computer work it will undertake and the kind of customers it seeks. This definition is a vital element in its strategy.

Attractive Industries

Most business-units have their resources and strengths so deeply committed to an industry that they have only limited choice in this matter. Nevertheless, a careful analysis of that industry outlook, as suggested in Chapter 2, provides an essential basis for deciding whether to harness a favorable underlying trend or to seek unusual segments in a mature or declining situation. For example, most companies dealing with mobile homes are trying to increase their industry position. In contrast, the senior managers of the former Illinois Central Railroad are seeking ways to get rid of their railroad operations. (In recent years, less than 20 percent of I. C. Industries' operating profits came from railroading.)

A redefinition of one's industry sometimes suggests an attractive domain. A

FIGURE 5-1.

FOUR ESSENTIAL PARTS OF A BUSINESS-UNIT STRATEGY

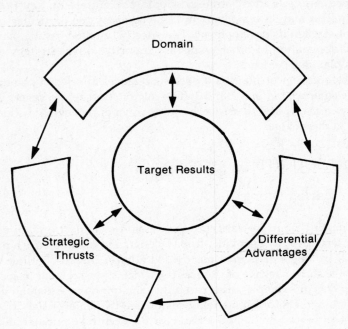

typical example is O. M. Scott & Sons, which found the outlook for its grass seed business not very attractive. By redefining its industry from grass seed to "lawn care" it uncovered many untapped opportunities in fertilizers and herbicides. A glass-bottle firm has significantly shifted the nature of its business by thinking in terms of containers.

Finding Niche Suited to Company Strengths

The chief domain issue for most companies, however, is picking a propitious niche in its industry. The niche may be a segment of the total products (or services) offered by the industry, or it may be a selected group of customers defined by a characteristic such as size, income, or location. Obviously, each business tries to select a niche where the growth and profit prospects are attractive, and also where it has strengths relative to competitors.

The Franklin National Bank switched the domain it sought during its exciting history. Starting as just a small country bank on Long Island, it grew under the guidance of a single CEO to become the thirteenth largest bank in the United

States. Its first domain was commercial banking serving consumers and local business in the limited area of Long Island. Having become the leading bank in this domain, Franklin National expanded its goals (as soon as the state law permitted). It then moved into Manhattan and sought to become a truly national and international bank with an array of services matching Citibank, Chase Manhattan, and the other giants. This enlarged domain drastically altered the character of the bank, with results which we explore in the next sections.

Even a basic product, such as coal, raises strategy questions. The Island Creek Coal Company, to cite a specific case, has large deposits of coal especially suited for the production of steel. Clearly the company should serve these metallurgical customers. But the recent growth in coal demand is in generating electricity. Island Creek is handicapped in serving this large market because its coal must be dug in high-cost underground mines and because electric utilities are unwilling to pay a premium for the high quality of Island Creek coal. So Island Creek must decide whether to (1) concentrate only on metallurgical customers who will pay a premium, (2) sell its high-quality coal to utilities at low prices, (3) try to capture some of the utility business by buying strip mines and learning a new technology, or (4) hold onto its reserves until techniques for converting coal into gas and gasoline become practical.

Clear identification of a desired domain enables a business to concentrate on the particular activities necessary to serve that domain well. Especially important is anticipating changes in demand, supply, and regulation in the domain and preparing in advance to meet these new requirements. A secondary benefit of a well-defined domain is that it provides a guide for what *not* to do. Activities which are irrelevant to serving the domain can be pushed aside.

The desired domain does not remain static. The nature of markets and competition in those markets frequently change. Products mature. A business may achieve a dominant position in one niche and have to look elsewhere for growth. But until a change is decided upon, the selected domain provides positive direction to other business-unit planning.

Multiple Niches

The strategic advances of picking a niche very carefully does not necessarily mean that a company should confine its activities to a single niche. As a firm grows, it frequently spots an additional service it can provide effectively. Thus, an auditing firm may also do consulting on management information systems.

Such expansion is desirable because it secures synergistic benefits. *Synergy* arises when two actions performed jointly produce a greater result than they would if performed independently. A simple example is building a restaurant with a motel; the restaurant makes the motel a more convenient place to stop, and the motel contributes business to the restaurant; the total business is larger than it would be if the two units were located 5 miles apart. Often this is called the "2 + 2 = 5" effect.

Because synergy is often involved in considering multiple niches, a framework for thinking about it is desirable. The *expansion matrix* depicted in Figure 5-2 suggests that growth arising from finding new customers for present products leads in quite different directions from adding different products for existing customers. Thus, the producer of Eveready flashlight batteries took virtually the same product from the United States to many developing countries and expanded its use from flashlights to portable radios and toys. In contrast Head Ski Company went from skis to ski-wear and then to tennis rackets and summer sport clothing—all to the same (or a closely related) group of customers.

As a firm moves further away from its present customers and/or its present products, the prospects for synergistic benefits diminish. At the extreme (lower right corner), if new customers are to require completely different products, synergy almost disappears; the firm is thus involved in unrelated "conglomerate" expansion.

Naturally, a firm will seek combinations of niches that supplement or reinforce each other in a synergistic way. Managers should be aware, however, that negative synergy can occur; perhaps "2 + 2 = 3." A women's dress shop almost went bankrupt because of this problem. The shop had a long and successful record of serving middle-aged and older women. Its inventory and sales personnel matched that niche well. Then the shop decided to cater also to young women. It purchased the latest style clothing and featured it in window displays. Also, several much younger salespersons were added to the staff. The net effect of trying to serve both niches was to annoy the former customers and fail to attract younger women because of the store's reputation for being conservative if not stodgy. Sales dropped and unsold inventory skyrocketed. The synergy was negative.

FIGURE 5-2.

EXPANSION MATRIX

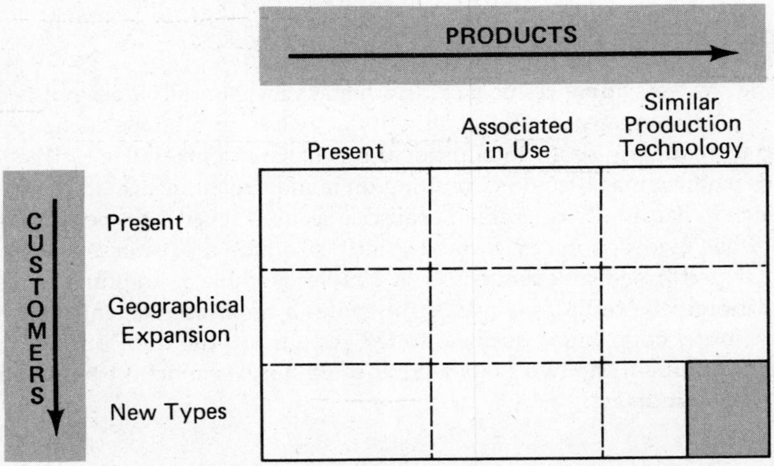

If a business-unit elects to serve two or more niches, it is highly desirable to analyze and plan for each separately. In this way, the benefits that come from concentrated attention will not be lost. When and if the volume of work in a single niche can support its own organization, and if economies of scale permit separate marketing and production activities, the creation of an additional business-unit may be wise. The desirability of having two or more separate but related business-units is discussed in Chapter 14 as a portfolio issue.

Early writers on business strategy gave almost exclusive attention to this task of finding attractive niches suited to company strengths and to building a large market share in each niche. Indeed, selection of domain is crucial to success. Experience with strategic management, however, shows clearly that being well situated in an attractive market is not enough. Business-unit strategy should include three additional elements.

DIFFERENTIAL ADVANTAGE IN SERVING SELECTED DOMAIN

The second essential pillar in a company strategy is identifying one or more bases in which superiority over competitors will be sought. If our particular enterprise is to continue to attract customers and resources, we must perform at least some parts of the total industry task with distinction. New product design, quick deliveries, low production costs, better personnel policies, fewer fights with environmentalists—these examples only suggest the many possibilities.

Franklin National Bank, to return to that example, differentiated itself during its Long Island growth phase by (1) promptly opening branches in expanding residential areas, and (2) offering unusual services first. (Its "firsts" included parking for customers, drive-in windows, evening hours, prompt FHA home mortgage loans, and the like.) However, when the bank moved to Manhattan, it found itself in a "me too" situation, running hard to catch up with the services offered by established competitors. Consequently, the primary differential advantage it found itself forced to adopt was the granting of higher-risk loans. And this latter practice led directly to Franklin National's collapse.

A company may seek a differential advantage in *any* of its external relations or in its internal resource conversion technology. The resource converter model, discussed briefly in Chapter 1, suggests the possibilities. The strategic requirement is to become—somehow, in at least a few respects—a favorable supplier in the selected domain. Several commonly used ways of getting at least some comparative advantage are highlighted in the following paragraphs.

Products and Services Tailored for Selected Niches

Having selected a niche which is growing fast or is being inadequately served by competing suppliers, a company may adjust its products and services to suit the particular needs of customers in that niche. Familiar examples are radio stations which focus on sophisticated listeners by programming classical music or on Hispanic listeners by offering Spanish-language programs. Such stations then have a differential advantage for advertisers who want to reach those particular audiences.

Pioneer Life, a medium-sized insurance company, revamped a large part of its operations for a similar purpose. Pioneer could not compete successfully with large insurance companies for most *group* business (group life, insured pension plans, group health and disability, and the like). However, the large companies were giving little attention to clients with fewer than 200 employees. Such small clients usually lacked an insurance specialist on their own staff, and they were often confused by government tax and reporting requirements and by union requests for insurance as a fringe benefit. So Pioneer decided to cater to this niche.

To build a differential advantage in serving the smaller clients, Pioneer: (1) selected and trained agents (salespersons) to advise small companies on *all* aspects of employee insurance; (2) prepared an array of standard options suited to small companies from which an insurance plan for a specific client could be quickly assembled; (3) wrote computer programs which store employment and vital statistics on company employees, and quickly calculate costs of various kinds of insurance; (4) designed a monthly (or quarterly) report form for the client showing the contributions and status of insurance coverage on each employee; and (5) reorganized internally so that group insurance became a self-contained business-unit within Pioneer. Of course, this kind of service is expensive on a per employee basis, but Pioneer is now able to relieve smaller clients of almost all of their headaches in this technical area of employee insurance.

High Volume-Low Cost

A very different approach to differential advantage is to seek high volume which, it is hoped, will result in low cost per unit. The low cost, in turn, will enable the company to set a lower selling price—or spend more on promotion and service—than its competitors can afford.

The classic concept of high volume leading to low cost has been popularized by the Boston Consulting Group. B.C.G. talks of large market share, which gives a company higher volume than its competitors, and of the "experience curve," which explains why costs can be expected to drop as a result of that higher volume. More specifically, the argument is that a company (like a person) learns from experience; each time the cumulative output doubles, cost per unit should drop, say 30 percent. Indeed, experience in production of aircraft and electronic components, two well-known examples, conforms with the theory.

Fortunately, for small firms and newcomers the B.C.G. theory is subject to a variety of qualifications. For instance, with a new product or a new production technology, a company may start with as much "experience" as its more prominent competitors. Nevertheless, the central point remains. Using some relevant concept of volume, a company can seek a differential advantage by playing the high volume-low cost game.

Distinctive Research and Development

In some industries, such as pharmaceuticals or electronics, strong company research and development is regarded as the touchstone for success. Especially for firms that hope to serve new technical markets, an imaginative engineering department is vital. Two college professors, who set up a firm to design and install equipment to control air pollution of chemical processing plants, considered their research program as a key element in the firm's basic strategy.

But what is good for one firm is not necessarily wise for another. For instance, a leading British cement company relies on very good customer service, not on distinctive products, to win business from competitors. Hence it spends no money on product research; its engineering is focused on reducing operating costs. In contrast, many advertising agencies rely heavily on their ability to create unusual campaigns. For them, as for fashion dress manufacturers, creative design is the main way they try to differentiate themselves from competitors.

Favorable Strength in Resources

A company may gain an advantage in serving a particular niche by having greater strength in key resources, such as scarce raw materials, unusual people, or cash for investment. For strategic planning, an ability to acquire the resource quickly is almost the same as having it in hand. Of course, to provide a differential advantage the resource must be vital in serving the niche, and it must be readily available to competitors. In times of inflation, having timberlands can be a comparative advantage to a paper company. Whether owning a tomato farm places a catsup plant in a superior position depends upon the availability and price of tomatoes for competitors.

Access to capital creates a distinct advantage in some circumstances. For instance, large sums of risk capital must be available for any firm engaged in exploring the ocean floor. Small equipment companies have difficulties expanding into niches where end-products are leased rather than sold. Even urban renewal firms have discovered that one requirement for growth is equity capital. Again, the underlying question is, "Do we have, or can we get, the financing needed? And in this respect, will we be at any advantage or disadvantage relative to others serving the same need?"

In service operations, personnel is *the* critical resource. For this reason one of the leading management consulting firms insists that staff members devote 10 percent of their working time to training and development, even though billable work for clients is available. The aim is to have the best staff in the profession fully informed on the latest developments. A secondary benefit is that this training appeals to the professional pride of the individuals, and that aids morale and recruiting. Of course, any enterprise can benefit or suffer from the relative capability of its management and technical team. Realistic strategic planning should always take this resource into account.

Choice in Emphasis

Many potential sources of differential advantages exist. The preceding examples only suggest the possibilities. As a practical matter, any single company becomes ineffective if it tries to excel on all fronts. Instead, a key feature of strategy is selection of a few ways in which the company seeks to distinguish itself.

A few examples will highlight this feature of strategy. IBM has always stressed customer service, customer orientation in product design, and liberal treatment of its employees. Humble Oil rose to prominence because it gave high priority to acquiring an advantageous crude oil supply. Merck and Boeing stressed building better mousetraps—ethical pharmaceuticals and aircraft, respectively. Conglomerates derive their differential advantage predominantly by the way they raise capital.

Each company singles out perhaps one, but more likely a few areas having synergistic ties. In these areas it tries to develop a relationship with the resources that is more favorable than that of its competitors. Typically, it establishes a new symbiotic relationship between a key group of resources and the internal technology of the company. If the company is wise (or lucky), it selects relationships for emphasis which will become especially important strengths in the future competition within its industry.

In the numerous external relationships not selected as a source of differential advantage, a company "satisfices"; that is, it merely seeks to be acceptable but not to excel. Often a company is too small to attempt any more than following general industry practice; its location, history, personal preferences of key executives, or existing resource base may not provide a good springboard; or management may deliberately decide that effort applied in other directions will be more rewarding. These secondary relationships cannot be neglected; they must be adequately maintained, like Herzberg's hygiene factors. Moreover, the secondary relationships should be designed so that they support or at least are compatible with the primary features of the selected strategy.

Of course, over time a company may shift its choice of areas in which it seeks differential advantage. Critical factors for success change; the company changes; new opportunities for distinctiveness emerge. Adapting to these opportunities by adjusting the emphasis placed on sources of distinction is a crucial aspect of successful strategy. Unless a business-unit can devise a strategy which couples obtainable differential advantage with an attractive domain, the domain is likely to be captured by a competitor.

 # STRATEGIC THRUSTS

Normally a gap exists between the present position of a business-unit and the domain and differential advantages it seeks. Obstacles to closing that gap will vary in magnitude and over time, and the business-unit will have limited personnel, capital, existing external relationships, and other resources to use in dealing with these obstacles. Consequently, a third basic strategic consideration is deciding what major thrusts to make and how fast to press for changes. Besides identifying what these major thrusts should be, this element of strategy also involves steering a course between too-much-too-soon and too-little-too-late.

Major Steps to Be Taken

A few years ago, Crown Cork & Seal Company faced a threat to its strong position in high-pressure cans. The aluminum companies began producing a two-piece aluminum can. This new can had a differential advantage over the conventional three-piece steel can such as Crown Cork, American, Continental, and National can companies were making. It was lighter in weight, it had less possibility of leaky seams, and it avoided the remote chance of producing lead poisoning from lead on the seams, and it enabled printing on the can that looked slightly better. Crown Cork did not want to switch to the aluminum can because it would then find itself buying raw material (roughly half the cost) from companies which would also be its competitors for the end-product. A possible alternative was a two-piece steel can.

So a new thrust, vital to maintaining Crown Cork's position in the can business, was forged: the development of a low-cost technology to manufacture a two-piece steel can. This involved high-speed drawing of a thin steel sheet into the sides and bottom of the can, a task previously believed impractical. A complicating factor was that Crown Cork's low-overhead policy meant that it normally spent very little on manufacturing-process R & D. So a joint engineering venture with steel companies, which also had a substantial stake in the outcome, was launched. Five years later a technology that involved both steel-making and can-making emerged. The two-piece steel can became a viable competitor with the two-piece aluminum can.

A second issue then arose. How fast should Crown Cork convert to manufacturing two-piece steel cans? A large investment in machinery was involved; the technology could change; excess three-piece capacity would create price pressure in the total market; and the environmental agitation against nonreturn-

able containers could swing demand back to glass bottles. In spite of these drawbacks, Crown Cork decided to beat its competitors in building two-piece steel
can lines. As a result of this second thrust, the company already has over half of
the installed capacity for making the new steel cans.

Clearly, these two moves have been crucial points of Crown Cork's strategy. They illustrate what we have called "thrusts" and what some other people
term "initiatives," or "key programs." A strategic thrust is a vital, positive
undertaking which moves a company toward its differential advantage in its
desired domain.

Failure to include thrusts in a strategic plan may leave the selected objectives floating; it is probably the major "missing link" in moving strategy from
ideas to action. This was a contributing weakness in Franklin National Bank's
move into Manhattan. In addition to taking risky loans, Franklin National failed
to tool up to do the broader business it said it wanted. There was no thrust
focused on developing and/or acquiring a pool of talented personnel necessary
for the new tasks. And there was only slow recognition of the need to modify
the informal centralized organization which had suited Long Island. The necessary shift to a complex, sophisticated organization needed by a major bank of
world stature posed so many difficulties that it should have been set up as an
explicit thrust. By contrast, note that when Citibank adopted its strategy to go
after more business from "world corporations," it recognized the organization
and personnel hurdles and established thrusts to overcome them.

Timing of Thrusts

The sequence and timing of thrusts may be tricky. Some actions obviously
must precede others, for example, land acquisition before plant construction.
But often a strategic choice can be made. When British Petroleum moved into
the U.S. market, the company deferred heavy commitment in marketing until a
source of U.S. crude was in sight. To have started marketing alone and relied
completely on local purchases of finished products would have exposed the company to very high risks. In this situation, we can also note that building or
acquiring refining capacity came even later; clearly, refining capacity was not
regarded as a critical factor and it could be manipulated later without paying
high penalties.

A different sequence is being followed by a manufacturer of fiberglass
boats. A low selling price is a key feature of the marketing strategy, and in order
to achieve costs permitting this low price, a large modern plant is necessary.
Starting up such a plant is clearly a strategic thrust. However, the company's
current sales are not large enough to keep an optimum-sized plant busy. Nevertheless, the management decided to build the plant in order to be in a strong
competitive position. While market demand is being built up, the company has
taken on several subcontracts at break-even prices and is even selling some boat

hulls to another boat builder to help cover overhead costs of the plant. Here is an instance of moving first into large-scale production facilities, hoping that demand will catch up.

Even after a sequence has been selected, the manager has to decide how fast to move. It is quite possible to be too early. A leading East Coast department store, for example, correctly predicted a major shift of population to the suburbs, and it became a leader in establishing suburban branches. However, at the time it selected branch locations, few of the large modern shopping centers with their vast parking spaces were in existence. Consequently, the store established branches in locations that are now being passed by. The irony of the situation is that the management of this store had more foresight than several of its competitors, yet because it moved too soon, it is now at a relative disadvantage in suburban operations.

In these examples, and in most other timing decisions, the likely response of other key actors to company moves is a significant consideration. As we noted in Chapter 4, the possibility of gaining cooperation or of provoking countermoves depends upon the involvement of the other actors at the time we initiate our moves.

Although difficult to do wisely, the timing of thrusts does provide a desirable "flexibility" in the execution of strategy. Delaying or even shifting the sequence of major moves permits postponing heavy commitments. This introduces a degree of flexibility without a total change in strategy with each shift in the wind.

In dealing with thrusts, even more than with differential advantages, a business-unit should be highly *selective*. Highlighting the critical moves, in contrast to all sorts of minor maneuvers, is a significant part of the guidance strategy provides.

TARGET RESULTS EXPECTED

The three elements of company strategy just described deal primarily with what to do, when, and, by implication, what not to do. They are guides to more detailed planning and action which are to follow. This emphasis leaves out one important dimension of strategy. If these things are done (and the environment is largely as predicted), what results are expected?

A small manufacturer of testing instruments for metallurgical industries, for instance, adopted a strategy of major commitment to research in the use of lasers. Translated into targets or anticipated results, this research commitment meant aiming for (1) a breakthrough in testing equipment in two to five years, (2) a reputation as a technical leader in this field within three years, and (3) reaching a break-even point in company profit and loss during the next three to five years. Note how much clearer the strategy is when we state *both* the means (laser research) and the ends (the three targets).

There are several reasons why strategy should include some statement of anticipated results. The people who must endorse the strategy, especially those who contribute resources, can reasonably hold back until they get some feel for what the situation is likely to be as a consequence of all this activity. Also, the individuals designing the strategy will have their personal objectives and values, and they, too, will be concerned about how results are expected to match these criteria. By no means least important, target results set the stage for shorter-run goals and controls which are essential ingredients of effective implementation.

How does the senior manager who is responsible for the selection of strategy decide, "O.K., that's it"? Fundamentally, the process involves: (1) selecting the criteria for judging the strategy, (2) translating and stating the expected results of the strategy in terms of these criteria, and (3) deciding whether the expected results (the targets) meet acceptable minimum levels of achievement and are better than expected results of alternative targets.

Criteria to Be Considered

Several criteria are often used to evaluate a strategy, such as:

1. return on investment (usually this is profit related to financial investment, but it might be the return on any critically scarce resources)
2. risk of losing investment of scarce resources
3. company growth (in absolute terms or as a percentage of the market)
4. contribution to social welfare (in one or more dimensions)
5. stability and security of employment and earnings (of all employees and/or of executives)
6. prestige of the company and of company representatives
7. future control (or influence) over company decisions

Different individuals naturally stress one or two of the above criteria—finance people the return on investment, research people the company prestige, marketing people the company growth, and so forth—and occasionally they may wish to add other criteria such as cash flow or international balance of payments. Fortunately, doing well on one criterion does not necessarily detract from all of the others. A specific strategy has not one but a whole set of results, and the only practical way to judge a strategy is to consider several criteria simultaneously. To expedite the evaluation process, three or four of these various criteria should be singled out as dominant in the specific situation.

Expressing Strategy in Terms of Criteria

Meaningful strategies must be conceived in *operational* terms, such as products to sell, markets to reach, materials to acquire, research to perform, and the like. However, such actions take on value only as they contribute to desired results. And the pertinent results are defined by the criteria just discussed.

So to relate a strategy to the selected criteria, a conversion or translation is needed. For instance, the actions contemplated in a strategy have to be expressed in anticipated costs and revenues, which give us an estimated profit. Similarly, the proposed actions have to be restated in terms of human resources to estimate their effect on stability of employment (if that is one of the key criteria). And likewise for other criteria.

These restatments of anticipated results become the targets at which the strategy is aimed. But since the success of any strategy is never certain, these targets will be surrounded by many "ifs" and "maybes." Often they should be expressed as a range, not a single point, with subjective probabilities attached. Nevertheless, tentative though the estimates may be, this is the basis on which a strategy will be evaluated.

Are Targets Acceptable?

Now, with criteria selected and the anticipated results of strategy expressed in terms of these criteria, the manager is in a position to say, "Let's go" or "That's not good enough." Rarely is there a choice among several strategies, each of which is quite attractive. Instead, the pressing question is whether any proposed plan is acceptable at all. The reason for this scarcity of attractive choices is that all of us have *high aspirations,* at least for one or two criteria. Thirty percent profits, no real risk, worldwide prestige, half of industry sales— any and all of these may be part of our dreams. The blunt facts are that few of these dreams will be realized by any strategy we can conceive. So we have to decide what *level of achievement* will be acceptable for each of our criteria.

This picking of acceptable levels is complicated by differences in values held by key executives. For instance, Strategy A may promise a 30 percent return on capital but with a 15 percent chance of complete loss and a sure transfer of ownership; whereas Strategy B promises only a 15 percent return on capital but with small risk of total loss and little danger of change in control of the company. Many quantitative techniques exist for computing optimal combinations. Reality, however, indicates that personal perceptions and values strongly affect the decision. The chair of the board—say, a wealthy person and a large stockholder—may prefer Strategy A; while the president, who came up from the ranks and owns little stock, may prefer Strategy B. Or, if the chairperson likes the prestige of the position and the president thinks the chairperson is too conservative, the preferences may be reversed.

It is difficult to generalize about whose values will predominate. Generally, the most active and aggressive senior executives will establish the pattern, *provided* their objectives meet at least the minimum acceptable requirement of each interest group whose withdrawal of support could paralyze the company. In the language of Chapter 1, the "output" of the strategy must enable the company to fulfill at least minimum needs of resource contributors.

Thus, while there is no simple resolution of how high targets should be, we obviously should not evade the translation of operational plans into key targets (or vice versa). A strategy expressed in terms of targets alone is little more than wishful thinking. On the other hand, an operational strategy that is not translated into targets is primarily an article of faith. A well-developed strategy has *both* an operational plan and targets.

SUMMARY

Company strategy deals with the basic ways a business-unit seeks to take optimum advantage of its environment. As we saw in Chapter 2, changes in technology, politics, social structure, and economics create opportunities and problems. To bring these environmental factors into sharper focus, we urged that they be woven into industry analyses. Such industry studies identify growth and profit prospects, and also the key factors necessary for future participation in the growth. Still more pointed is an analysis of company strengths and weaknesses outlined in Chapter 3, and a matching of these against the key success factors for each industry. The final narrowing, proposed in Chapter 4, calls for an analysis of key actors and their likely responses to our moves.

Armed with this background, central management selects its strategy. The strategy indicates (1) the *domain* to be sought, (2) our *differential advantages* in serving that domain, (3) *strategic thrusts* necessary to move from our present position to the desired one, and (4) *target results* to be achieved. These elements interact and should reinforce each other.

This master plan evolves, of course. As the environment changes, some uncertainties become realities and new uncertainties arise. And the company strategy may be shifted to take advantage of the new situation. Competitors are also responding to the same environment, and their actions may open up—or require—adjusted action. Meanwhile the company itself moves forward and/or runs into snags, so it has new internal information and modified strengths and weaknesses. Inevitably the strategy needs reassessment.

Nevertheless, at any point in time, and hopefully for a long enough span to translate plans into action, the main elements of strategy remain stable. With this overriding guidance, central management moves to elaboration and implementation of the scheme (as we do in the next parts of the book).

Small companies benefit from well-conceived strategies fully as much as large ones. Their strengths and options differ, but their flexibility and growth rate can be greater.

QUESTIONS FOR CLASS DISCUSSION

1. Wilda Winters is a well-known landscape architect in the San Francisco Bay area. She is often employed by building architects to plan the layout and planting around commercial buildings and "Silicon Valley" plants—especially on irregular terrain. These contacts lead to private jobs for homeowners—mostly long-range plans that integrate gradual growth with seasonal beauty. Also, she has two small annual retainers with community governments.

   Winters is discussing the formation of a corporation with B. P. Green Associates—landscape contractors who primarily have annual contracts for full responsibility for maintenance of the grounds surrounding large business establishments. Green Associates also seeks jobs of grading and planting around new construction which frequently includes installing sprinklers and drains.

   The rationale back of the Winters/Green proposal is (a) more steady income for Winters, and (b) entry into "big time" landscaping for Green—hopefully replacing some of the routine lawn mowing.

   Assume that you are a partner in B. P. Green Associates. (You do the financial and accounting work; this job is paying your way through school.) Do you recommend going ahead with the new corporation? Are there any strategy issues that you want resolved first?

2. (a) The number of farmers in the United States continues to decline (31 million in 1940, 16 million in 1960, 7 million in 1980, and 5 million in 1984). Does this mean that there are no attractive niches in the farm industry? (b) Briefly outline what you believe would be a successful master strategy for a farmer in your home state.

3. Uniroyal is the third largest producer of rubber tires in the United States. It manages to sell a plurality of the tires purchased by GM for new cars and trucks, but it has no other special distinction. Its costs are about average for the industry. Its sales are especially weak in truck and off-highway tires and in the replacement market. Uniroyal has a relatively heavy debt and thus high interest charges which help lower its profits. Clearly Uniroyal must do better in the tire business to improve its profits and balance sheet.

   Trends in the total market include tires that last longer than tires formerly did, and thus replacement tire sales have been about level during the past ten years. Truck production accounts for more of the increase in tires for new vehicles than does auto production.

   Possibilities for Uniroyal include trying for a larger share of passenger tire business from GM, penetrating the after-market more by lowering prices or by increasing dealer discounts, focusing on replacement tires for small and medium-sized trucking firms by opening a network of truck-service centers while focusing research and development expenditures on truck tires, or gradually liquidating the tire business by cutting out all advertising and shutting down the higher-cost plants as rapidly as possible to increase profits per unit while sales decline.

(a) Does Uniroyal have any differential advantage that you know about? (b) From the possibilities just mentioned, what do you believe will be the most suitable domain for Uniroyal? (c) Should Uniroyal invest $15 million over the next year to set up 30 truck-service centers and then repeat this for two more years? Each center would produce about $3 million per year in sales and turn an operating profit of about 12 percent. Corporate research and development expenditures could be cut from $25 million to $20 million by spending only for truck-tire research. (d) Is there a mix of strategies for the different market segments that appears suitable to you?

4. Several airlines have purchased resort hotels at locations they serve. For instance, Eastern Airlines bought hotels in Puerto Rico. (a) Use this development to *illustrate* each of the four elements in company strategy discussed in this chapter. (The aim of the question is to show the meaning of strategy, so make assumptions about the local situation if you need to.) (b) Now assume the airline decided to go out of the hotel business (its hotels were losing money) and sold one of them to you. How would this change in ownership affect the strategy you would recommend for the hotel?

5. Use each of the boxes in Figure 5-1 to identify possible alternative ways of expanding for (a) a company in the office furniture manufacturing business, or (b) a medical "clinic" consisting of five doctors concentrating on pediatrics.

6. One company's statement of objectives calls for "a decent return to stockholders, an example to the community of corporate citizenship, payment of better than a living wage and stability of employment for all employees, honorable treatment of suppliers, and the willingness to undertake business risks to provide an example of dynamic management." How can the concept of a "strategy" as outlined in this chapter help sharpen the meaning and the focus of such a statement?

7. Assume that you have just been appointed manager of the leading bookstore on your campus, with a free hand to make any changes you believe desirable. Outline the strategy you intend to follow.

8. "Continuing education" (education of people already employed in business for five to twenty-five years) will become much more important during the next decade. Two reasons are (a) a decline in the college-age pool of potential students, and (b) rapid technological changes which will make obsolescent much of what we are learning today. Assuming that this forecast is correct, what changes, if any, in its present strategy should your school make?

9. "After Slow Start, Gene Machines Approach a Period of Fast Growth and Steady Profits"—so read the headline and Leon Wood, president of Applied Biotechnol-

ogies, thought he agreed. His machines make DNA—the basic raw material of the genetic code and the essential raw material in the growing business of genetic engineering. The Biotechnologies machines sell for about $40,000 each and allow users to turn out ten strands of DNA (deoxyribonucleic acid) each week—ten times the rate of manual production. The gene machine is a chemical robot. Housed inside a suitcase-sized metal cabinet containing a maze of computer-controlled valves and bottles holding the chemical ingredients of DNA, it pumps the chemicals in a programmed sequence onto a glass column, where the strand of DNA "grows." Having a machine is like having an earth-mover to build a dam. The manual method was like using a shovel.

Applied Biotechnologies has worked its cash flow up to a point that successfully covers its heavy debt and interest payments and it expects to soon show a profit. With five other competitors in the gene-machine game, Leon Wood expects to have a significant market share and steady profits in competition with the three independent manufacturers (subsidized by venture capital companies) and the two subsidiaries of large pharmaceutical firms. His problem is to decide whether or not to try to make and sell the chemicals used in the DNA machine. "Shall we imitate Gillette?" he asks. Doing so would put him in a different game—competing with chemical companies like Merck and DuPont and also searching out new resource suppliers. "We would have the same customers, but different suppliers of raw materials and of money. Perhaps our salesforce would need to be different also. We know how to build the machine but we don't know, as yet, how to make the chemicals."

What is your evaluation of a strategy for Applied Biotechnologies that would mean a somewhat varied domain and an uncertain differential advantage?

CASE 5
COLUMBIA JOURNAL OF WORLD BUSINESS

The *Columbia Journal of World Business* (*CJWB*) is a quarterly magazine published by the Graduate School of Business at Columbia University. Its main target readers are managers in multinational companies—although 70 percent of the actual subscriptions come from the companies, libraries, consultants, and other "corporate" subscribers. One distinctive feature of the *CJWB* is student responsibility; both the editing of articles and the business operations are handled by MBA students.

Now entering its third decade of publication, *CJWB* is an established professional journal. It has a subscription base of about 4,000, 70 percent in the U.S. and 30 percent abroad. The objectives served by *CJWB* include: contributing to the professional competence of international managers, helping to maintain Columbia's reputation as a center for the study of international business, and providing a group of MBA students with practical experience in running a small business.

Enter a new Dean of the Business School! Like most university deans, this one has more ways to spend money than he has money coming in, so he is looking for painless ways to cut outlays. CJWB breaks even financially on an incremental cost basis (added income generated by CJWB equals added disbursements created by the CJWB), but it contributes little to university overhead. This disagreeable fact puts CJWB in the marginal category, financially. Moreover, like a normal newly-appointed, self-assured manager, the dean is looking for changes in the School's activities that he can make. Consequently, a reassessment of the strategy and operations of the CJWB is in order.

In the strategy area, a clarification and wider acceptance of the mission of CJWB is desirable. A clearly related issue is the effectiveness of students to execute such a strategy.

Linking Academic Research and Managerial Effectiveness

The market domain currently sought by CJWB—top and middle managers of multinational corporations—is growing. In spite of cyclical and political ups and downs, world trade is rising. As the dominance of free-wheeling raw material firms is giving way to more localized production and to more joint ventures, the need for skillful managers of diverse national origins becomes more pressing. So, CJWB has a significant market to serve.

But what is CJWB's differential advantage in serving this market? The general news media are filled with flash reports on international political and economic developments. Several weekly or monthly magazines are designed to provide commentaries on specific companies or markets, and to give "how to" advice. *World Business Weekly, International Business,* and *International Management* each have circulations four to six times as large as CJWB. Clearly, the *Columbia Journal* should not try to compete directly with these publications.

CJWB's distinction lies in linking scholarly research to managerial effectiveness. The aim here is to draw from research an array of new approaches, concepts, and potential solutions that managers can use in their practice. No other publication concentrates on this niche.

This central theme does not rule out articles by practitioners. They often do penetrating research, and past issues of CJWB contain many well-documented studies from people in the business world. Broad observations and objective analyses are no monopoly of professors.

To serve this niche requires (1) a translation of scholarly reports into an action mode and into clear, ordinary English. On the other hand, (2) company studies often have a narrow purpose; such studies need to be identified, generalized, and often camouflaged. In other words, a significant editorial task is involved in preparing the raw material for the target audience. Incidentally, students are more adept at (1), whereas a professor or a widely acquainted editor is usually needed as an intermediary for (2).

The new dean has discovered that *CJWB*'s mission, as just defined, is better understood and endorsed by the *Journal*'s staff than by professors in the School of Business. For example, one professor said, "I've never read the *Journal* much and don't have specific examples in mind, but I am concerned about its impact on the School's reputation. *CJWB* is not refereed! Only refereed journals can assure good scholarship." Another professor commented, "The purpose of our School is to do research. As soon as we try to seek popularity with managers our standards go down the drain." Note that for this faction of the faculty, the process of "refereeing" is the dominating test of an acceptable journal; to them, serving a selected market niche is a secondary consideration.

"Refereeing" in this context has a specific meaning. All manuscripts submitted for publication have the name of the author removed and are then sent to at least two scholars for blind review. These referees may recommend rejection, major or minor changes, or publication. The names of referees are withheld from the author to assure an unbiased evaluation.

In connection with the implied suggestion that *CJWB* become a refereed journal, a senior faculty member observed, "Refereeing could be very helpful. Difficulty arises, however, when the standards used by referees differ from the objectives of *CJWB*. The typical refereeing practice, unfortunately, guarantees inbreeding, because a clique of referees impose their personal biases on what gets published. Unless an author conforms to the current fashion regarding jargon, format, citations, etc., the manuscript is turned down. Young professors facing the tenure gauntlet must conform because their records must show publications in refereed journals."

The implications of refereeing manuscripts for *CJWB* have not been spelled out, partly because not all the faculty take as purist a position as the first two quoted above. One of the student editors has noted, "Most of our job would be taken over by the referees. After they approved an article, we wouldn't dare do anything except routine editing and marking for the printer."

Role of Students

Another perspective on possible changes in the *CJWB* comes from the students. To what extent should the *Journal* be shaped by the interests and competence of the students who run it?

The concept of a student-run *CJWB* comes partly from law school reviews. All major law schools have such publications operated by their students. Articles in the reviews are often influential in the legal profession, and positions on a law review staff are very prestigious and open career opportunities for students who win these assignments.

The comparison of *CJWB* and law school reviews is not close, however, for two reasons. (1) An MBA program covers only two school years whereas an LL.B. program runs three years. The shorter time leads to faster turnover of the *CJWB* staff, and continuity of effort becomes a serious problem. Jobs are scarcely learned before it is time to leave; projects such as sales promotion are planned by one person and then left for someone else—who may not agree with the plan—to carry out. (2) The business and publications activities are major tasks in the *CJWB* setup, whereas law review tasks are almost solely editorial.

The operation of *CJWB*—like most magazine publication—is divided into two distinct parts. The editors are responsible for the content: obtaining articles, editing material into a form suitable for each issue of the particular publication, instructing the printer, and proofreading. In contrast, the business manager is concerned with building circulation, sustaining accurate subscription lists, billing, corresponding with subscribers, obtaining advertisements, mailing, selling reprints, and the like.

On both the editorial and business sides, a hierarchy of jobs has been set up, with new students doing the more specialized tasks as they pick up information about the total operation. A total of about twenty students are involved at any one time. For all students, work on the *CJWB* is in addition to regular courses, and usually it has second priority to papers and exams (and job interviews).

Two continuing "editors-in-chief" are provided by the School, each on a part-time basis. One is a professor who is largely concerned with relations of the faculty with the *Journal*. He encourages other members of the faculty to submit articles, develop material for a "focus issue," comment on manuscripts, and "bird-dog" possible contributions by business managers. The second editor-in-chief oversees the work of the student staff; she provides a crucial continuity of policy, selects and helps train people for key positions, watches scheduling of work, and otherwise assures that the ball keeps rolling. Because of the high turnover, this is a pivotal job.

In practice, student editors are more effective in dealing with manuscripts after they are submitted than in getting the right authors to write the right kind of articles. Some, though not all, faculty members can perform the latter role; one effective device is to have a professor invite contributions to a "focus issue" on a timely subject. For example, several articles in a particular issue might deal with international banking, transfer of technology, East-West trade, debt payments by less developed countries, or comparative management practices. Obviously, when inviting a person to write an article, care is necessary to maintain consistency with the strategy for *CJWB*.

While invited articles have made a distinctive contribution to *CJWB*, in recent years they account for less than 25 percent of the total content—and a much smaller percentage of manuscripts received. Most manuscripts are simply sent to *CJWB* by professors or practitioners who would like to have their writing published in a prestigious journal.

On the business side, students carry almost all the load. Inevitably, much of this work is routine. Writing letters about the billing procedure, for instance, gets a bit boring after the 173rd time. MBA students are more intrigued with throwing out existing systems and starting new ones than they are with fine-tuning the old ones. But for *CJWB* subscribers reliability is more important than originality. Also, as noted above, well-designed market research and promotion programs have lacked follow-through by subsequent generations of student managers; this has undoubtedly contributed to a recent lack of growth in the number of subscribers.

The hands-on experience that the business managers of *CJWB* get is valuable to them, but much of it is not very thrilling. Nevertheless, students who serve on the staff of the *Journal* are proud of their accomplishments and feel strongly that the venture belongs to them.

A proposal that keeps reappearing is to turn the *business* part of *CJWB* operations over to a commercial publisher. Several firms publish a whole series of professional journals, and by combining the routine activities they benefit from economies of scale. Commercial publishers also contend that they would be more effective in selling subscriptions and selling advertising space. In this way, they would expect to make *CJWB* not only self-supporting but profitable. Of course, any such partnership between Columbia and a commercial publisher would have to be based on a clear definition of strategy, especially with respect to domain and differential advantage.

Another possibility is to give the students an opportunity to share in the profits earned by *CJWB*. This would require a way to balance short-run and long-run results.

Question

What, if anything, should the new dean do about the *Columbia Journal of World Business*?

Part 2

DEFINING
MAJOR
POLICY

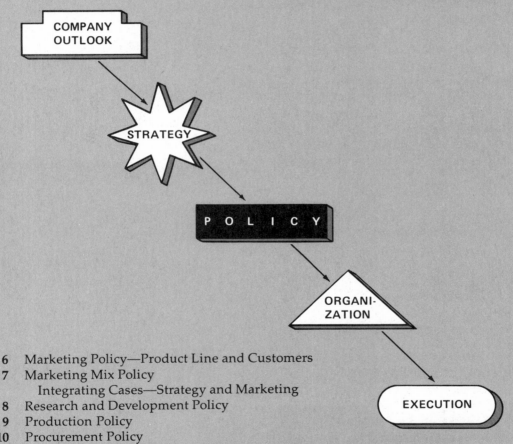

COMPANY OUTLOOK

STRATEGY

POLICY

ORGANI-ZATION

EXECUTION

6 MARKETING POLICY—PRODUCT LINE AND CUSTOMERS

Relation of Policy to Strategy

Strategy, as defined in Chapter 5, takes a broad, total company view and singles out major targets for company action. Its strength arises from highly selective concentration on a few critical issues. To achieve this necessary perspective and emphasis, strategy sets aside a whole array of issues "to be considered later." Policy deals with an important group—though not all—of these issues that were temporarily set aside.

A policy is a standing plan; it is used over and over to guide specific actions. For example, if a company adopts a policy to sell only for cash, all employees give a consistent answer to any customer asking for credit. Every company needs policy covering many aspects of its operations in order to simplify decision-making and to give predictability and consistency to actions taken at different times by different people.

In addition, policy serves a key role in spelling out, clarifying, and testing strategy. Frequently strategy is stated in such general terms that its interpretation can be varied. A carefully selected policy sharpens the meaning of the strategy and guides specific decisions in a direction that supports the strategy. In a sense, no strategy has really been thought through until its implications for policy (and programs) have been explored. Sometimes as our planning follows through from a tentative strategy to more specific policy we encounter a stumbling block that causes us to go back and revise the strategy. In the end, each should support the other. To be sure, some policy is adopted for administrative convenience and is not affected one way or the other by a change in strategy; our focus here, however, is on policy that does directly help implement strategy.

Basic Policy Issues

Since each company has its own unique strategy, its policy will also be individually tailored. However, virtually every firm faces a similar set of issues, and an analysis of policy can be expedited and improved by a systematic exploration of these basic issues. A convenient sequence for analysis is:

1. marketing policy,
2. research and development policy,

3. production and procurement policy,
4. human resources policy, and
5. financial policy.

These groups are interrelated, and it is impossible to make final decisions for one group without considering other groups. Some companies may have still other policies for specialized activities. Nevertheless, the sequence does provide a logical approach to overall company activities, so in this Part the chapters are arranged to illustrate this flow of analysis.

Market Segmentation

Market segmentation is one of the primary options that a manager has in formulating business-unit strategy. It involves focusing effort on a select segment of a broader market. The segment may be a particular type of customer, a narrow range of products, a special end use, or a place and method of purchase. The reasons for focusing on such a segment include finding a niche where competitors are few and weak, and concentrating resources to provide distinctly better and more finely tuned services than do competitors.

The next decade will probably witness more and more market segmentation. Sharper competition in a slow-growth economy will force companies to be more selective in their efforts. Also, the drift in our social structure toward pluralism invites segmentation.

Often such segmentation is treated narrowly as strictly a marketing concern. In this book, however, we include selecting a segment—a niche—as part of business-unit strategy. It is an important element in defining domain as explained in Part 1. The definition of a company's domain has profound effects far beyond marketing and requires continuing attention by top management of the business.

In this chapter we assume that the market segmentation issue is being dealt with as a part of overall strategy. Here we turn attention to policy refinement of a selected strategy in the areas of product line and customers.

PRODUCT LINE

Although the domain part of company strategy defines the type of product or service to be sold—such as mobile home sites, textbooks, or sneakers—rarely does it provide answers to the following questions: How many *different* sizes, grades, and shapes of the product will be carried in the line? Just how can our products be made *distinctive* from those of competitors? Should we *change* product design frequently, say, every spring, or stick with a tested model? We need standard answers—policy—on such issues for two reasons: first, to build a desired and consistent interpretation of strategy, and second, because many marketing, production, and financial activities will be affected by the simplicity or the elaborateness of our product line.

Variety of Products

For each strategic niche, a company must decide what variety of products will be offered to its customers. This is a recurring and often controversial issue as markets change, competition grows, and new technology becomes available.

Cost of Diversity. Customers are continually asking for products that are smaller, stronger, of another voltage, or otherwise different from what is offered, and sales representatives will contend that the sales volume could be increased materially if they had a larger variety of products to sell.

One manufacturer of soaps yielded to this pressure. Whenever the sales manager noted that competitors were offering a new soap or that a number of customers had requested a soap that differed in color, shape, fragrance, or composition, a new product meeting these specifications would be introduced. Examination of sales records showed that sales of most of these new products were satisfactory for several months but would gradually dwindle. Apparently the initial sales were largely due to the enthusiasm of the sales representatives for a new product and a willingness on the part of the retailers to try an original stock to see how the product would sell. After this original distribution, however, most new products were discovered to have no unique appeal. This particular company, therefore, had a large number of products for which the sales volume was inadequate to justify the cost of manufacturing, warehousing, and selling. Only by careful study was the company able to reduce the number of items carried to comparatively few products that really had significant differences. It then concentrated its attention on selling these products rather than dissipating its effort on unnecessary additions to its line.

One way to deal with this recurring controversy is to fix a limit on the number of items. Then any proposal for a new item must be accompanied by a recommendation to drop an existing one. While exceptions may be necessary, this plan has the advantage of forcing attention to pruning along with justifying the new item.

Need for Complete Line. Sometimes the customer wants to buy a variety of products from the same source. For example, each of us expects the druggist to be able to fill within a few hours any prescription our doctor may write. The druggist, in turn, expects the same kind of complete line service from drug wholesalers. Since a single slow delivery is likely to result in a long-time loss in patronage, a complete line is very important.

In contrast, a policy to concentrate on only a few items may be wise for a firm seeking distinction as a specialist. A paper company may sell only newsprint, for example, or a firm may specialize in putting out fires at oil and gas wells. By focusing on a narrow line, costs can be reduced, and if the product is sold in *large enough units* to warrant separate action by customers, the lack of a complete line may be no serious handicap. A narrow line policy relies on specialization to achieve a competitive advantage in pricing, unique service, or concentrated attention. One way to look at product line is suggested by Figure 6-1.

FIGURE 6-1.

PROFITABILITY OF NARROW VS. WIDE PRODUCT LINES IN VARIOUS STAGES OF PRODUCT LIFE CYCLE

(A narrow product line tends to give low profit in early or middle stages of the cycle)

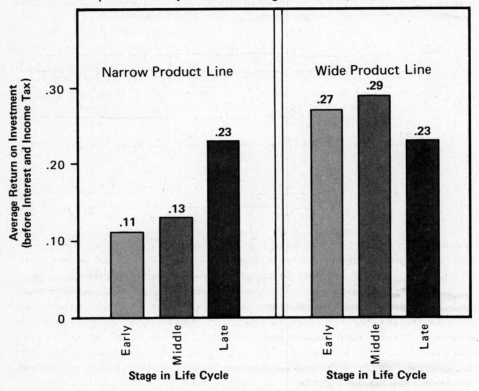

Source: Strategic Planning Institute.

Ways of Customizing Products. A middle position may be feasible. Perhaps some variety can be offered without too much added expense. Common practice with automobiles or refrigerators, for instance, is to have a standard product in two or three sizes, with other options to choose from, such as color and accessories. The number of variations is strictly limited, and the optional items are available only by paying a premium. While inventory and production scheduling are complicated by this practice, it does give the customer some choice.

Product Differentiation

Variety of products is one way to seek differential advantage. A related and perhaps less costly possibility is to offer "better" products—that is, better in the eyes of our desired set of customers. This raises a question: In what respects will a company try to make its products distinctive? Usually the company will have a standard answer, because it wants a continuing and consistent reputation in the market and because its engineers and production people need guidance on what to emphasize.

What Is Quality? Quality cannot be defined exactly. The purchaser of garden tools may define quality in terms of *durability*, while the buyer of a fashionable dress may be more interested in richness of *appearance*. For medical products, quality usually refers to *purity*; customers will pay a premium for a product they feel confident is pure. *Dependability* is crucial in the space industry. So, if a company seeks distinctiveness on the basis of product quality, it must decide the particular characteristics it will stress. Here, desired market segmentation is the key in setting policy.

In television programming there is doubt about how much basic difference the major networks really want. Likewise, universities would like to excel in accepted dimensions but are reluctant to change their services in any way that will be challenged by accrediting bodies. In contrast, Arthur Treacher's Fish and Chips outlets rely on product differences to attract customers away from the more common hamburger chains.

Consumer Recognition of Product Differences. In deciding on the kind of distinctiveness to emphasize, the company must consider not only the desires of its customers but also their ability to appreciate variations in quality. Even purchasers of stereos are limited in their ability to detect differences in tone quality. The company must therefore determine (1) what characteristics of its product its customers feel are important; (2) the extent to which its customers can appreciate the differences in such features and how much they are willing to pay for this extra quality; and (3) whether the cost of producting extra features is more or less than customers are willing to pay for them.

Frequency of Design Change

Related to the question of how product distinction is to be achieved is the troublesome issue of how frequently changes in design should be made.

Costs of Change. Design changes are costly. First come the expenses of technical and marketing research, engineering, testing, and tooling-up for the redesigned product. For simple products, such preparation expenses often amount to thousands of dollars; for complex products, like automobiles or airplanes, they can amount to millions of dollars. GM invested over $2 billion on its line of front-wheel drive cars. Then, manufacturing costs tend to increase if frequent changes are made; new skills have to be learned, production runs are shorter, and overhead builds up.

Next, inventory problems are complicated. Enough, but not too much, of the old product is needed as it is being phased out, and stocks of the new product must be built for an uncertain demand. The same problem arises at each stage in distribution—wholesaler, retailer, and perhaps consumer. In fact, anticipation of new models often leads to wide fluctuations in distributors' inventory and irregular orders for the manufacturer. If the manufacturer wants to keep distribution channels well stocked, it may have to accept return of old merchandise or make price concessions.

The use of computers may reduce the costs of changing production setups and handling a more diversified inventory. To the extent that this kind of automation is developed, adjusting production to the wishes of individual customers will become a practical alternative. Nevertheless, frequent changes in product design will continue to be costly.

Moreover, frequent design changes complicate service problems. The user of the product expects repair parts to be readily available and people servicing the product to understand the idiosyncrasies of each model. As users of foreign products know from bitter experience, adequate service on a product has a significant effect on its usefulness and its resale value.

But these costs of development, manufacture, distribution, and service are only one side of the picture. In setting a policy for frequency of design changes, the manager must also consider the benefits of changing.

Pressures to Change. The most recent style may be so important to consumers that frequent design changes are inevitable. Today even staple products are styled according to the current mode. Kitchenware and bathtubs, which still render the same service they did thirty years ago, are streamlined and styled to the modern taste. Bath towels and sheets come in all colors of the rainbow; even steam hammers are streamlined.

Change may be necessary for more technical reasons. New developments are occurring every year in color television, microfilming, and solid-state controls of machines, to mention only a sample. If customers are to be well served, a company must from time to time adapt its products to such technological developments.

The pressures of style or technology are strong by themselves. Competitors' actions, however, may make the need to change irresistible. When a clearly preferred product is offered by a competitor, a company must respond in some manner, usually be redesigning its own products.

Frequency of Change. Several alternative ways of reconciling the pressures and the costs of redesign of products are available to managers. Annual models are often used for consumer goods. Another tack, more common in industrial goods, is a policy of "product leadership." Here the firm wants to be first on the market with improvements, and new designs are introduced as rapidly as new technology is developed. But as one urban planner observed, "You don't tear down your house every time a new heat pump is invented."

A few firms try the leapfrog approach. Once they have a good design, they stick with it, letting competitors try various modifications. Then when significant improvements are evident, they make a major adjustment—incorporating competitors' advances as well as their own. The presumption here is that production and marketing economies of few changes will more than offset a temporary lag in improvements. This policy works well in those fields where technological change has been slow.

Product Line Policy of a Service Company

The issues regarding product line are easier to grasp when we use physical products as examples. However, most service enterprises face comparable problems. Consider a university. What variety of courses should it offer—aerospace, black studies, Sanskrit? How should it differentiate its services from other universities? What characteristics of quality are significant, and can the consumer recognize the differences? How frequently should programs change? A similar set of questions confront advertising agencies, hospitals, and management consultants. Clearly, these issues are fundamental in developing a viable, continuing relationship between a firm and the people who use its product or service output.

CUSTOMER POLICY

Customer policy, like product policy, is broadly determined by company strategy regarding domain but it needs elaboration and refinement before it gives adequate guidance to daily decision making. Three kinds of issues arise again and again: What body of ultimate consumers does the company wish to serve? What channel of distribution will be most effective in reaching these consumers? And, what limits on size or other characteristics should be placed on customers with whom the company deals directly?

Consumer Sought

Distinction Between Customers and Consumers. Confusion sometimes arises because of failure to distinguish between "customers" and "consumers." The term *consumer* means the one who *uses* a product (or service) for personal satisfaction or benefit; or in the case of industrial materials, the one who so *changes* the form of the product as to alter its identity. A *customer*, on the other hand, is anyone who *buys* goods. A customer may be a consumer, or it may be a dealer who will resell the product to someone else.

The habits and the wishes of the ultimate consumer of a product (or service) are of vital interest to all businesses having anything to do with the product, for a major purpose of economic activity is to create consumer satisfaction. In the original design of a product, during its production, and throughout its distribution, consumer satisfaction is ever a controlling consideration. Consequently, a policy clearly defining the "segments" of consumers sought should be an early decision for every company, even though the company may use middlemen (for example, retailers) to actually sell to those consumers.

Types of Consumers. Various kinds of consumers want services of very different nature. The restaurant catering to business executives offers a different service from the campus kitchen seeking the trade of students. A patent medicine company found as a result of studying its market that a major group of its consumers were people who spoke only foreign languages. These groups were located primarily in large industrial centers and could be reached only by foreign language newspapers and circulars printed in foreign languages.

When a manufacturer of electric-powered hand tools decided to tap the do-it-yourself market in addition to its established market with the professional building trades, it failed to recognize the difference in needs of the two types of customers. The amateurs required more foolproof machines and elementary instruction sheets. After two years of losses, the manufacturer returned to its policy of focusing only on the professional market.

The relation of a company to consumers of its products is normally continuous over a period of years. Reputations are established, and expectations—so vital to careful planning—are built up. Consequently, a company cannot move in and out of a market from week to week. Instead, well-established and relatively stable policies regarding consumers to be served are very useful.

Location of Consumers. The large mail-order houses such as Sears, Roebuck and Montgomery Ward built their businesses with rural consumers—people who had difficulty getting to cities to shop. But conditions have changed. Now there are fewer farmers, and they drive automobiles. One adjustment to this shift has been an impressive expansion of retail stores operated by these companies.

Nevertheless, the mail-order business also continues to prosper. How? Through a shift in definition of potential consumers. The largest mail-order market now is the suburban homemaker, whose children and other duties make shopping a chore, and the "do-it-yourselfer." They find the semiannual catalogs a storehouse of merchandise information and a convenient way to select many items. To be sure, the merchandise offered has been adapted to appeal to the nonfarm consumer, and telephone ordering is replacing the mailed order. But, vital to the planning of what will be offered is a clear concept of where the potential buyers live.

How about exports? In analyzing foreign markets, as any other new markets, the added or *incremental* costs should be balanced against the added income. Once a company has completed its product engineering and is "tooled-up" for production, the cost per unit of turning out an added 5 percent or 10 percent is less than the total average cost of the basic output. If the company has idle capacity in its plant, this incremental cost may be very much lower. So, even though there are difficulties in selling abroad, the net revenue received may still be above the incremental cost. Banks, advertising agencies, and consultants also seek clients abroad, but they are exporting only ideas and services.

Full utilization of an existing strength may be a factor. Most common is adoption of *national distribution* because national advertising of the company—already necessary for part of the market—is reaching consumers in all areas. In these cases, sales promotion considered to be desirable dictates the market scope, rather than consumer policy determining what promotion is feasible. A somewhat similar situation arises when a company invests heavily to acquire technical expertise for a specific problem and then feels impelled to serve all people having this problem regardless of where they are located.

Competitive tactics may also influence policy regarding location of desired consumers. For instance, Company A may immediately follow Company B into a new area because A does not want B to acquire a possible source of strength that might be extended to other markets. On the other hand, if a pattern of normal territories has evolved, Company X may not move into Company Y's home market for fear that Y will reciprocate. Such intangible considerations may result in a firm not pushing its territorial limits just to the point where incremental selling and delivery costs match incremental revenue.

Consumers of a "Small Business." Over the years small businesses have typically catered to local consumers. Dramatic improvements in transportation and communication, however, have undercut the local butcher, baker, and candlestick-maker. National concerns now reach even the remotest consumers, and consumers drive many miles to shop. Local semimonopolies are fast disappearing. Consequently, most small businesses now are seeking more distinction in their products and services, while expanding the geographical location of their potential consumers.

Channels of Distribution

By *channel of distribution* we mean the *steps* by which products are *distributed* from the one who first converts them into usable form to the consumer. Many enterprises, of course, render services rather than manufacture products, for example, airlines, banks, public accountants, and all sorts of retail stores. Because of their nature, such services are almost always sold directly to consumers. But for manufacturers the selection of the proper channels of distribution is a very real problem.

Changes in buying habits, transport, communications, and market locations have modified methods of distribution greatly during recent years. This whole field is in a state of flux, and few companies are justified in assuming that their traditional channels are necessarily the most effective ways of reaching the consumer they prefer. The farsighted choice of the right channel of distribution sometimes becomes a major "differential advantage."

Through Jobbers. Utilizing jobbers (or wholesalers) was long regarded as the orthodox method of distribution. They assemble products from many manufacturers, store them, and sell them to retailers. In so doing, they also assume risks of price change, damage, or obsolescence; they extend credit to retailers; and they sort and ship products according to retailer needs.

All of these functions are essential in the distribution of merchandise; regardless of the channel of distribution used, someone must perform them. When a large part of consumer purchases was secured through small retailers scattered over a wide territory, it was more economical for a manufacturing firm to have the wholesaler perform these services than to undertake them itself.

Today, retailers are larger and many manufacturers have set up distribution systems which deal directly with them. Nevertheless, there are auto supply jobbers who serve repair shops, plumbing supply houses that serve plumbers, and similar specialty jobbers for a particular trade or industry. A baffling issue for every manufacturer is the extent of the use of such distributors; they add at least 20 percent to the selling price of the products.

Direct to Retailers. Distribution by the manufacturing firm direct to retailers has some distinct advantages. By using its own sales representatives to call on retailers, the manufacturer may secure more aggressive selling efforts; a jobber's general-line salespeople sell a wide variety of products and cannot concentrate their efforts upon the sale of one particular product. Dealing with retailers may also enable a manufacturer to ascertain better the consumers' desires, since the retailer has firsthand contact at the final "point-of-sale."

The manufacturing firm exercises more control over the final sale of its goods if it has direct contact with the retailer. Personal relationships and goodwill are tied to the manufacturer, and consequently the firm is not so dependent on the jobber for sales volume. Also, the manufacturer has a better opportunity to influence retail prices, display, and other factors that affect the popularity of the product with the consumer.

The plan of selling direct to retailers, however, may lead to excessive costs if it is used unwisely. If the manufacturing firm eliminates the jobber entirely, it may incur unbearable costs because many retailers buy in such small quantities that the expense of selling and servicing them may exceed the gross profits on the goods they purchase.

Companies that manufacture a variety of products may set up their own *sales branches*. These branches perform in many respects like a jobber, except that they sell only products of the parent company. One firm, for example, has eleven separate manufacturing divisions—each operated like an independent company. The sales division is another fairly independent unit with several branches that perform the functions of a jobber. A sales branch with its own sales staff enables a company to secure improved selling effort and at the same time has a local distributing point.

Direct to Consumers. This plan is usually employed when the product is of such a nature that the salesperson needs a high degree of technical training to sell it, and when technical services must be rendered in connection with the product after it is sold. For example, this plan is used by manufacturers of office equipment such as duplicating machines, postage meters, and computers. Salespeople must be able to operate such equipment to sell it, and the manufacturer must be sure that the equipment is kept in proper repair. For similar reasons most industrial equipment is sold directly to users.

Use of *exclusive dealers,* as is done by automobile manufcturers and many oil companies, combines many advantages of direct sales to consumers while retaining the initiative of local businesspeople. The dealers "run their own business," but to retain a franchise the dealer must join in company sales programs and conform to service standards set by the company. Obviously, the producing company must have a line of products good enough to enable the typical dealer to make a profit or competent people will not apply for dealerships and the whole system will collapse.

Through Brokers or Agents. The broker usually performs only one major function of distribution—selling. As contrasted with the jobber, the broker usually sells only one type of product, or at most only a few closely related products. Although brokers are employed most frequently in the distribution of producer goods, they may also be used in the distribution of consumer goods. For example, brokers are often used by small canneries that do not have sufficient output to justify a full-time sales force. Anyone who has publicly announced an intention to buy a house or a suburban lot knows that brokers are also used in the real estate field. Here, again, it is difficult for buyers and sellers to get together without the aid of someone who is in close contact with the market.

Selecting a Channel of Distribution. Dr. Thomas L. Berg suggests that selecting a channel of distribution be viewed as an organization problem and that the activities analyzed include the total distribution system. More specifically, his approach involves:

1. Listing all actions necessary between producer and consumer—promotion, actual selling, transportation, financing, warehousing, repackaging, risk-taking, installation and repair service, and the like.
2. Grouping these activities into jobs that can be effectively and efficiently performed by separate firms. These firms may be banks or warehouse workers who also do other things, or they may be firms exclusively involved in this particular channel. The crucial matter here is to conceive of jobs (packages of activities) that are the most effective combinations.
3. Defining relationships between the jobs that will assure cooperation and necessary flow of information. Also define how each firm involved is to be compensated for its efforts. And work out necessary, minimum controls to be exercised by various members over other members.

4. On the basis of the organization design (the *policy* adopted by the designer), developing specifications for the firms that are to fill each job.
5. Then moving on to execution of the plan by recruiting people to take the specified jobs (some negotiation may arise here since independent firms will be participants), educating people on how the plan is to work, supervising the day-to-day operations, and exercising necessary controls.[1]

One of the significant aspects of this approach is that the channel of distribution problem is not viewed as a choice between a few predetermined alternatives. Instead, each company should work out a design of the best way to get its products to the consumers it has selected. Also implied is the idea that tasks assigned to participants are apt to need modification as economic and competitive conditions change.

Since a channel of distribution typically creates a complex set of relationships, a policy is needed to provide consistency and stability of action. And top management is vitally concerned because—as experience in the automobile, watch, liquor, and many other industries testifies—a strong, well-designed distribution system may spell the difference between success and failure of the entire enterprise.

Size of Customers

Customers that a company deals with directly may buy in quantities either too small or too large. The company should know how much it costs to serve each type of customer and the amount the customers must buy if their business is to yield a profit to the company. One manufacturing concern, for example, was selling to 8,000 retail accounts. An analysis of these accounts revealed that 55 percent of the total number purchased only 5 percent of its entire sales volume and that none of these 55 percent purchased more than $200 worth of merchandise a year. The company decided to eliminate all such accounts, which it thought, would not develop into better accounts; as a consequence, the number of customers was reduced to 4,000. This enabled the company to reduce its sales staff from 82 to 43 and to make a number of other substantial reductions in selling costs.

In deciding whether to eliminate customers who purchase in small quantities, consideration should be given to the potential as well as present purchases of these customers. If they have the capacity to increase their purchases substantially, it may be desirable not to eliminate them but to concentrate on securing a larger percentage of their trade.

On the other hand, a customer may purchase too much merchandise! If a concern is dependent on one or two customers for most of its business, its posi-

---

[1]See T. L. Berg, "Designing the Distribution System," *The Social Responsibilities of Marketing*, edited by W. D. Stevens (Chicago: American Marketing Association, 1962).

tion is vulnerable because loss of patronage of one such important buyer will disrupt the entire organization. As we noted in Chapter 4, those few customers exercise too much relative power.

Companies in the aerospace industry often depend upon one or two large government contracts for the bulk of their business. Cancellation of or failure to win renewal of such a contract can spell disaster for the firm. Advertising agencies may develop a similar overdependency on one or two large accounts; when an account is "dropped," the agency has to lay off most of its talented employees and may close entirely. Consequently, companies may have a policy that says no more than 20 percent of their business will be done with one customer.

SUMMARY

Company strategy requires elaboration to give it specificity and to put it in more operational terms. Policy is a major instrument for thinking through and sharpening such elaboration. And in this chapter we started a systematic review of key policy that almost always is involved in this "filling in of the broad picture."

Two dimensions that shape the domain part of every master strategy are the products (or services) to be sold and the customers who will buy them. So the discussion in this chapter of policy covering product line and customers is a logical starting point for this phase of company planning.

Sharpening the product area singled out in a master strategy involves policy regarding the variety of products, product differentiation, and frequency of design changes.

Central management should also set up policy regarding the types and the location of final consumers the company hopes to reach, the distribution system to be used in getting products to such consumers, and the upper and lower limits on the size of direct customers. These adjustments to the market are vital to success; they have to be nurtured over time, and they need wise policy guidance for consistency and dependability.

There has been frequent occasion in this chapter to note how customer policy is closely related to many other aspects of a company's activities. For example, the customers sought will affect the kind of sales promotion needed, the size of plant, the type of sales and perhaps production personnel, the need for large accounts receivable, and other phases of operations. These interrelations will become increasingly apparent in subsequent discussion of the other aspects of management and in the analysis of the cases found throughout the book.

QUESTIONS FOR CLASS DISCUSSION

1. For years T. V. Black & Daughter has made parts for automobile brake systems. Recently it has concentrated on a single critical part, made in various sizes and specifications in conformity with designs of the auto manufacturers. About half of the output has gone to the replacement market, and the company has a policy of selling no more than 20 percent of its annual output to a single customer. During the depression of the early 1980s, sales for original equipment dropped sharply and all three of the U.S. auto manufacturers insisted on a price freeze. Nevertheless, T. V. Black & Daughter continued to take some orders at below-cost prices in order to remain on the "approved vendor" lists. Recently Ford has circulated a general statement about its "preferred vendor lists." Ford wants vendors who (a) adopt quality assurance practices that Ford believes will ensure virtually no defects, and who (b) are prepared to cooperate with a "just-in-time" delivery scheduling (which has been so successful for the Japanese). Ford has invited T. V. Black & Daughter to qualify as a preferred vendor—indicating that large orders will be placed with firms on the preferred list. Mr. Black says, "With our present plant management we can easily qualify as a preferred supplier, and Ford might place orders equal to 50 percent of our capacity if we were competitive on price. Running at capacity we surely would make money." Do you recommend that the company go after the Ford business?

2. The 7-eleven convenience stores have moved into the retailing of gasoline in a big way. The move from groceries and related items to self-service gasoline has added about $1.5 billion to the sales of the 7,400-unit chain. How do you explain the success of this unconventional addition to the 7-eleven product line?

3. In addition to gasoline and oil, possibilities for the product line of a filling station include: batteries, tires, antifreeze, oil filters, fan belts, windshield wipers, mufflers, brake linings, tire chains, soft drinks, cigarettes, souvenirs, candy, and an array of repair services ranging from motor tune-ups, front-end repairs, body work, and transmission replacement to greasing and car washing. (a) If you owned and operated a filling station, how would you decide on your product line? (b) If you were the manager of a major oil company's nationwide chain of filling stations, what policy would you establish regarding filling station product lines? What would you insist on? forbid? leave up to the local operator?

4. Name two or more industries (in addition to plumbing and auto supplies mentioned in the chapter) in which specialty jobbers play a major role in distribution. What factors explain this continuing importance of jobbers? If you were a manufacturer in the

industries that you have named, what functions would you want the jobber to perform? What functions that jobbers often perform would you try to reserve for your own organization?

5. Brentano's is the oldest bookstore chain in the country. During the last decade, however, its growth has been modest while two competing chains—B. Dalton and Waldenbooks—have grown dramatically to control about 20 percent of all retail book sales. The new owner-managers of Brentano's intend to "get the company off dead-center." However, they will not follow Dalton's and Waldenbooks' success formula of opening hundreds of branches. Instead, they plan to continue the present emphasis on gift books and related kinds of gifts and on selling such items via a catalog mailed to two million affluent customers. They hope to make better selections, exercise tighter inventory control, and execute more dramatic promotion. Why do you think they want to continue their product and customer policies rather than challenge the upstarts?

6. A product of room air-conditioners for use in homes is having difficulty obtaining adequate distribution. Use the Berg approach outlined on page 125 to build a model of the total distribution system of the industry. Then select places in that system where you believe a company with only 12 percent of the total market could develop some comparative advantage. Assume that the products of all competitors have about the same characteristics and quality.

7. The converter-resource model used in Chapter 1 to discuss social responsibility implied that relationships with each resource group are somewhat similar. Test this notion by applying the product and customer policy issues raised in this chapter to (a) labor and (b) raw material suppliers.

8. The Smith Brothers Memorial Hospital is located in a community that is attracting an increasing number of retirees. In recognition of this population shift, the Hospital trustees have decided that their institution should give emphasis to serving the elderly. What product line and customer policies do you recommend for carrying out this strategy revision?

9. In a speech to a group of financial analysts, the president and chief executive officer of Campbell Soup Company said:
   "We are trying to organize this company to give it some flavor and some vitality for the 1980s. . . . [Our objectives] came from looking at what the good, topnotch food companies have done in the last couple of years and from deciding whether we can play in this game up there with the best. We don't want to be down in the middle stream where we appeared to be. . . . Let's look back at the heritage of this company and see where we take this. . . . I tried to dredge out . . . what the quality of this company was. . . . The first thing . . . is that this is a company that wants to make quality products. We are not in the schlock business. We are also interested in a product line that has value added. We are not in the commodity business. . . .

"[Non-food activities] do not play a role at Campbell Soup. In the immediate five-year plan they do not. But over the long term we've said that we are in a business that is designed to give healthy well-being to people. It is conceivable that we could be involved in bicycles, for instance."

(a) What is wrong with the commodity business—the tomato soup business, for example? Toward what food products should Campbell Soup move?

(b) Should Campbell Soup make and sell bicycles? Explain.

CASE 6
STEIGER'S OPTIONS

Steiger Tractor, Inc., the feisty North Dakota producer of some of the world's largest farm tractors, faces a sharp decline in demand for its product. It needs to determine which options to follow to regain past momentum.

During the last thirty years, U.S. agriculture has far outpaced manufacturing in mechanization and productivity. The number of farms has been cut in half and workers on farms dropped even more. But physical output rose more than 50 percent during the same period. Several factors have contributed to this record—improved seeds and farm animals, more fertilizer and chemical treatment, larger farms, and major increases in mechanization.

TABLE 1.
U.S. FARM TRENDS

Year	Number of Farms (millions)	Acres per Farm (average)	Farm Population (millions)	Output per/hr. (index)	Tractors on Farms (millions)	Horsepower on Farms (millions)
1950	5.6	213	23.0	34	3.4	93
1960	4.0	297	15.6	65	4.7	153
1970	2.9	374	9.7	112	4.6	203
1980	2.7	400	7.2	169	4.9	269

As Table 1 shows, most of the trends are clear, although the rates of change may be slowing down. The number of tractors on farms, for instance, is about stable. Only an increase in the size and power of new tractors has permitted the rise in total horsepower to continue. In 1965, when Steiger was still struggling to produce its big tractors in a converted dairy barn, only 2 percent of all tractors sold had more than 100 horsepower; ten years later almost half the new tractors exceeded this power.

The demand for agricultural equipment, however, fluctuates sharply with the rise and fall of farm prosperity. These cyclical changes, coupled with the natural seasonal change, create a lot of instability in tractor sales, as well see in Table 2.

TABLE 2.
HIGHS AND LOWS IN U.S. TRACTOR SHIPMENTS

Year	Units (thousands)	Value (millions)	Average Unit Value
1955 high	326	$ 519	$ 1,592
1960 low	156	358	2,295
1966 high	270	1,006	3,726
1971 low	165	892	5,406
1974 high	234	1,785	7,628
1978 low	174	2,663	15,305
1979 high	202	3,425	16,998
1982 low	94	2,749	29,307

The decline from 1979 to 1982 has been especially severe. Unit sales fell over 50 percent; high inventories at dealers became static, and costs continued to rise. These pressures helped push two large producers, International Harvester and Massey Ferguson, to the verge of bankruptcy. Even John Deere, the industry leader, lost heavily on its equipment sales. From this perspective, we take a closer look at Steiger Tractor, Inc.

Steiger has carved out a small, distinctive niche in the $3 billion farm tractor industry. The company was founded by two farmers who wanted a versatile, powerful tractor. They were among the first to make a four-wheel drive tractor. Since then, the company has consistently led the industry at the top of the power range, producing over fifteen models varying from 200 to 450 horsepower.

Large four-wheel drive tractors fit with industry trends toward large, mechanized farms. They quickly gained popularity as shown in Table 3, until they constituted 9 to 10 percent of the farm tractors sold in the U.S.

Peak sales of four-wheel drive tractors in the U.S. were close to 11,500 units in 1979, but, because of the depression, the volume is expected to be less than 7,000 in 1982. Steiger has about 20 percent of this market (counting sales under both Steiger's and customers' trade names).

A Steiger tractor is a rugged, sophisticated machine, with a retail price of between $50,000 to $90,000. Like other large tractors, it has power steering, power brakes, hydraulic lifts, etc. The cab is equipped with airconditioning, radio and tape player, noise insulation, wide visibility, adjustable seat—all to ease the very long, strenuous days in the field.

TABLE 3.
RELATIVE IMPORTANCE OF FOUR-WHEEL DRIVE TRACTORS
(Number of Units Sold at Retail in U.S.)

| Year | 2-Wheel Drive | | 4-Wheel Drive | Total Retail Sales |
	40 to 100 horsepower	Over 100 horsepower		
1978	46%	47%	7%	100%
1979	47	45	8	100
1980	49	42	9	100
1981	49	41	10	100
1982	53	38	9	100

Several of Steiger's large competitors also offer four-wheel drives on some of their large tractors. However, Steiger has a unique construction which it claims enables its tractors to get the maximum benefit of a four-wheel drive. A Steiger tractor is "articulated"—its body has a joint in the middle which permits the front and rear axles to move independently of each other in both a horizontal and vertical plane. This articulated body can keep all four wheels on the ground in hilly or uneven terrain and thereby reduce slippage. Moreover, an articulated body significantly reduces a tractor's turning radius.

The advantages of four-wheel drive, and especially of Steiger's articulated body, are (1) reduced soil compaction, (2) improved ability to work in wet fields and otherwise act fast when planting and harvesting should be done, and (3) increased fuel economy. Steiger's 267-gallon fuel tank and lighting system allow twenty hours of uninterrupted running time.

Being a relatively small, unknown company with a single product, Steiger has had to scramble for sales. In addition to selling directly to 350 farm equipment dealers in the U.S., Steiger has sought foreign customers. Australia, with a frontier in its Southwest similar to our West two generations ago, has been the main overseas market. Also, Steiger has sold its articulated tractor to International Harvester, Allis Chalmers, Ford, and others to be marketed under their names through their equipment dealers. The importance of these supplementary channels is indicated in Table 4.

Unfortunately, all three of these markets are in trouble. The farm depression has severely cut sales through Steiger's domestic dealers, as already indicated. A second year of drought has ruptured the farmland boom in Western Australia. And sales to other farm equipment companies are shrinking as they consolidate their lines and stress production in their own under-utilized plants. Clearly, Steiger must do some more scrambling.

In the short-run, Steiger needs volume just to keep its oversized plant in Fargo operating with reasonable efficiency. A layoff of one-third of its 750 employees and unpaid vacations have cut costs but such belt-tightening cannot be pushed much further. Even more important is finding additional business that

TABLE 4.
STEIGER SALES AND NET INCOME
(in millions)

Year	With Steiger Trade Name North America	Overseas	With Customer Trade Name	Total Sales	Net Income
1976	$ 57	$ 11	$ 37	$ 105	$ 4.5
1977	47	11	35	93	- .4
1978	48	9	27	84	-.3
1979	68	13	33	114	6.7
1980	71	20	30	121	5.5
1981	99	27	22	148	6.2
1982	73	28	9	110	.9

will put Steiger in a strong position over a period of years. Moves now should contribute to a wise long-range strategy. Steiger can consider the following options:

1. *Manufacture and sell two-wheel drive tractors.* The aim here would be to break out of Steiger's present narrow specialty. To be successful, a distinctive design would be essential—possibly a tractor already tested in Europe or other overseas area. A design "as good as" those used by Deere, Massey Ferguson, International Harvester, Allis Chalmers, or Ford will not be enough because these large companies are firmly entrenched with ample production capacity and wide distribution networks.

The introduction of such a product also requires finding good farm equipment dealers who would stock and push it. Virtually all strong dealers already have a tractor line around which they have built their reputation. For example, Steiger's present dealers have all added the big four-wheel drive, articulated tractors to the line of the more traditional two-wheel drive tractors. They will not upset this arrangement, or add to it, unless the new product offers distinctive advantages. Moreover, introducing a product like a new tractor takes time and capital. The dealer must stock parts as well as whole tractors. Service people must learn how to repair all features. Farmers themselves must learn how to operate and repair this vital piece of equipment. Confidence all along the distribution channel must be built on satisfactory experience.

2. *Manufacture and sell equipment to be used with Steiger tractors.* Plows, disk harrows, planters, cultivators, even harvesting equipment are possibilities. As with two-wheel drive tractors, such equipment is already in ample supply from well-known companies. Steiger dealers already carry such lines. One option Steiger might consider here is to acquire an existing specialty line company. (In this case there undoubtedly would be a mismatch of dealers presently handling that product with dealers handling Steiger tractors.) Or, Steiger could design new equipment that is uniquely suited to the power and driving capabili-

ties of Steiger tractors. A drawback of this second approach is that the uniqueness would appeal only to owners of high-powered tractors, and this might reduce the size of the potential market to a level at which tooling-up costs could not be justified.

3. *Seek market share of companies withdrawing from articulated tractor market.* The farm equipment market is so depressed that several companies that have been buying articulated tractors from Steiger to sell under their own names will probably drop this product after their existing inventory is sold. Allis Chalmers and Ford, for instance, have not renewed their orders from Steiger (and it is unlikely that they will try to produce this design in their own plants). Steiger can try to capture the sales that such firms might have made. This will not be easy because these large companies will continue to offer regular four-wheel drives, but not the articulated chassis design.

International Harvester is a special case. This company has always been Steiger's largest customer. In the mid-1970s, when Steiger was struggling to become a national supplier, it bought 25 percent of Steiger's output.[2] Recently, however, the fate of International Harvester has changed dramatically. Huge losses are forcing International Harvester to cut outlays and generate cash every way it can. With respect to Steiger, this former blue-chip company wants to get out of a three-year contract to buy a minimum of $10 million of Steiger tractors per year. An International Harvester representative proposes, "If you will relieve us of that obligation, we will arrange for, say, a hundred of our best U.S. and Canadian dealers—in areas where Steiger tractors can be used—to sell your tractors under your name. Maybe you can sell more through them than the $10 million that you expected to get from us. I'm sure the dealers will be glad to sign up with you because they need every sale they can make, and they already know your product even though it had our name on it."

4. *Expand overseas.* The Australian outlook is clouded by severe droughts; this is forcing many large farmers (often with 8,000 to 10,000 acres) into bankruptcy. Also, so much marginal land was plowed up that dust-bowl conditions may have been created. But what of other areas where large-scale, industrialized farming is feasible? Such areas are found in Russia, Argentina, Brazil, and South Africa (Canada is already served from Fargo). Since about 80 percent of the manufacturing cost of a Steiger tractor goes for purchased parts—diesel engine, transmission, air compressors, tires, etc.—it is expensive to assemble Steiger tractors in North Dakota and then export them. Instead, assembly in the country of use makes more sense, as is done in Australia. Of course, local assembly adds to the economic and political risk.

---

[2]In 1974 International Harvester also bought a million shares of Steiger's common stock (about 29 percent of the total) for $5 million. Since that time, IH has placed three of its executives on Steiger's board of directors.

Question

Which of the above options, or others that you suggest, should Steiger pursue to buttress its position in the farm equipment industry? Justify your answer, including an assessment of the long-run risks and advantages.

7
MARKETING MIX POLICY

Strategy and the Consumer

The strategy of a company identifies the domain it seeks—its industry and preferred market niche(s). And perhaps, though not necessarily, the selected differential advantage will further define the way the company will deal with customers. Then product and customer policy do expand and specify the marketing efforts. Essential as all this planning is, however, it is not enough.

The analysis and planning should also take a consumer viewpoint. Management should envisage all the actions necessary to complete the full transformation of company products (or services) into consumer satisfactions.

Rarely does a consumer merely buy a physical product. Instead, the consumer purchases a *package* that fulfills some "need," that provides a psychological pride of ownership and/or consumption, that involves a minimum of anxiety about breakdown or damage, that is considered a "good buy at the price," that can be acquired without great financial upset, that will be delivered when wanted, and so forth. An essential part of a marketing plan, then, is to conceive of a practical package of satisfactions that will appeal to a significant number of consumers.

Normally, providing each of these consumer satisfactions involves a cost. The cost may be a direct expense incurred by the producing company, or it may be a fee or margin charged by a distributor. Keeping these costs within acceptable bounds is, of course, an inherent aspect of designing a viable package of satisfactions.

Marketing Mix

In addition to seeking a winning combination of consumer satisfactions, the central manager must consider how to communicate with the consumer to present an offer. An array of alternative forms of advertising are available for this purpose. And the role of sales representatives and agents in this total distribution process has to be defined.

But advertising and sales staffs involve costs, as do the satisfactions discussed in the previous section. Inevitably, a choice must be made. How much of each—consumer services, higher quality, convenient packages, lower price, advertising, or personal solicitation—should be offered? This allocation among such competing uses for the distribution dollar is called the *marketing mix*.

136

Of course, the particular marketing mix that fits one product in one market will differ from the combination suited to other product-markets. Selling life insurance differs from selling automobile insurance; a marketing mix suited to electric typewriters differs from one for computers. Also, a company may elect to seek a distinct differential advantage. So, basic policies must be determined with respect to:

1. a lean low-cost approach versus a full-service approach
2. sales appeals to be emphasized
3. sales promotion in support of selected appeals

LEAN LOW-COST APPROACH VERSUS FULL-SERVICE APPROACH

An overriding policy affecting the entire design of a marketing mix deals with the total effort and expense to be devoted to embellishing the product or service package offered to consumers. Should we focus on selling an austere, stripped-down product at a low cost or should we strive for more complete consumer satisfaction of some important need?

Digital Equipment Company, for instance, commenced business with the lean low-cost approach. It sold simple, low-cost minicomputers to research laboratories with no accompanying software and no organized repair service. The assumption was that a lot of technically trained customers wanted bare-bones equipment which they could afford and that they already understood how to use and to repair such computers. In contrast, IBM has always provided its customers with user-oriented technical assistance, and it has a service organization that maintains and repairs its computers. The price is high, but if that is an obstacle, IBM will lease the equipment so that the customer pays as the equipment is being used. Digital Equipment Company was not strong enough to challenge IBM on IBM's terms, but it was highly successful in appealing to an untapped market on the basis of low cost-low service.[1]

The forerunners of today's supermarkets had a similar beginning. They sold only case lots of canned goods piled in old warehouses located along railroad tracks. There was no credit, no returns, and the customer carried the boxes out to his or her car. This was during the Great Depression when low prices attracted a lot of customers in spite of the very limited service. Today, farm auctions operate in a similar manner, and the "I can get it wholesale" markets for clothing are not much different.

Of course, the bargain-basement approach need not mean that no service whatsoever will be provided. However, it does imply that in production, as well

---

[1]After its early success, Digital Equipment Company modified its original policy so as to serve other market niches; however, its reputation was founded on a unique marketing approach in the industry at that time.

as in marketing, expenses will be minimized. As in the People Express airline, parsimony is a way of life—at least for a while.

Such a low-expense policy sharply restricts marketing mix options. The catch is that not enough customers may be willing to accept such spartan service for very long. Experience shows that in almost every business that starts out with very low prices, a shift occurs to more service. Running very lean is not a steady state, at least in the U.S. The tough question then becomes how much of which services to add.

SALES APPEALS TO BE EMPHASIZED

Important among the possible sales appeals that a company may choose to emphasize (sooner or later) in its marketing mix are:

1. associated services
2. quality
3. style and packaging
4. company reputation
5. pricing

Except for style and packaging, these appeals can be related to services just as well as to physical goods. Also, they can be used by both small companies and large ones.

Associated Services

Personal Assistance. A recurring question is how much personal assistance to the customer should be a part of the total sales package. For example, a driver who pulls up to a gas pump in Honolulu will find someone checking tire pressure, washing the windows, filling the radiator, and inspecting the battery while the gasoline is being pumped. In contrast, at a New York City "full service" station the driver has to ask to have the windshield washed, and checking tire pressure is clearly a do-it-yourself operation.

A shift is occurring in personal service in the hotel field. Motels grew up with a minimum of personal service, in contrast to the traditional hotels with doormen, bellhops, and room maids. But as motels are becoming more luxurious, they are adding more personal assistance; meanwhile, the large downtown hotels will permit guests to carry their own bags and to find their own rooms. With changing attitudes about personal assistance, matching services to a particular desired clientele calls for sharp perception.

Maintenance and Repair. One of the central pillars of IBM's marketing success is its maintenance service policy. Most of its machines are covered by a contract under which IBM provides regular maintenance service and is available for prompt repair work in the event of a breakdown. Other manufacturers have a less elaborate service organization and often merely maintain a stock of repair parts for all equipment sold during, say, the past twenty years.

Policies on customer service and on channels of distribution are closely related. The further removed manufacturers are from the consumers of their product, the more difficult is control of consumer service. Companies that stress service often find it necessary to maintain their own branches; some television and stereo manufacturers establish exclusive distributorships in order to ensure the quality of repair service available to consumers.

Installment Credit. The day is gone when installment credit is only available on durable goods. Now financing may be arranged on almost any large purchase, and mail-order houses, among others, extend installment credit on an accumulation of small purchases. However, the ease of obtaining credit and the terms on which it is granted vary. Part of the marketing mix, then, is the extent to which a company gets into the financing business. Recently, companies have been turning over more and more of this function to banks, finance companies, and credit card companies; this tends to remove installment credit as a competitive factor.

Equipment leasing is a service provided by some manufacturers. Dental equipment, postal meters, even transponders on a satellite are all available under lease. Many of these lease arrangements are similar to installment credit, calling for periodic payments during the period when the product is being used and giving the customer an option to buy the equipment at the end of the lease. The major difference between leasing and buying is that the leasing customer may return the equipment when it is only partially used. For customers with limited financial resources or fluctuating needs, such leases can be quite attractive.

Prompt Availability. This is a valuable dimension for both products and services. An employer with a potential strike wants consulting advice promptly— not next week. Similarly, a loan from the bank or a delivery of fuel oil have much greater sales value if customers know they can depend on the services being available when needed.

Small local companies can often gain significant advantage by providing this prompt delivery. They can reach the scene of action quickly, they are already familiar with local conditions, and their small size permits considerable flexibility. If larger firms choose to stress availability, they have to set up local representatives or branches and then give the local units both the incentive and the authority to meet unusual customer requirements.

Considerable opportunity for creative variation is available in customer services that a company provides, as these examples show. Some of these services may be so important to customers that they are regarded as part of the product itself. Since they are intimately tied up with the product in the mind of the customer, it is important that their use be integrated with product, customer, and other marketing policies.

Quality as a Sales Appeal

Quality higher than the usual prevailing level can be used as part of the marketing mix.

Extra quality involves extra effort and cost. Strawberry jam made with only pure sugar and no corn syrup has added raw material cost; handrubbed furniture has extra labor cost. A policy to build extra quality into our products, therefore, has to be matched up against other ways to differentiate our total marketing mix. The question is: Does distinctive quality hold strong appeal to the particular customers we are trying to reach?

One limitation to using quality as a sales appeal is that consumers may be unable to detect the difference and may be skeptical about the claims made. So, to clinch the appeal, some companies *guarantee* their products. For instance, one automobile manufacturer extended its guarantee from one year to three years (and on some parts to five years). The move attracted so much attention that competitors were forced to follow. In the meantime, the first company added to its reputation for producing dependable products.

Professional ethics prevent doctors or lawyers from guaranteeing the results of their services. Nevertheless, quality is especially significant in intangible services, so a professional person's reputation for quality work becomes very important.

Emphasis on Style and Packaging

"Pick the right style" is merely a wish, not a policy. However, the degree of emphasis on style in the total selling effort may be a significant policy. A French restaurant, for instance, may go to great lengths to create a Louis XIV decor and atmosphere. A few men's shoe manufacturers stress the latest style, at the sacrifice of durability. Producers of household items—from hand tools to garbage cans—need some guidance on how much to add to design and production expense to have currently popular styles and colors.

Packaging is one means of giving a product stylish appearance, but it may play a more important role in the marketing mix. Packaging can affect the product-service itself, as in the use of aerosol cans for paint. If a product is to be sold through self-service stores, the size, sturdiness, and shelf appeal of the package are critical to success. So, while a package may add significantly to the unit cost, the right kind of package can be an integral part of providing distinctive service for a group of consumers.

Place of a Company's Reputation in Marketing Mix

Banks, insurance companies, and other financial institutions must guard their reputations jealously because this is a major factor in the business they secure. Likewise, a well-regarded brand name is so important in the sale of large kitchen appliances that an unknown company has a hard time breaking into the market. The Whirlpool Corporation, to cite a specific case, for years made appliances for Sears, Roebuck & Company but was unknown to the general public; lacking a reputation with consumers and dealers, it entered into a long-term agreement to use the highly regarded RCA label. Several years later, after the Whirlpool reputation had become established, the association with RCA was dropped.

Even the highly competitive bidding process of the federal government makes allowance for company reputation. A low bid may be rejected if the bidder lacks a demonstrated ability to perform. And for high technology contracts, as in aerospace, reputation is often the deciding factor.

Good reputations are not bought on Madison Avenue. They arise primarily from a sustained willingness to devote extra effort to assure dependability and use of the latest state of the art, to avoid exaggerated claims, and to adjust such errors as do occur in a prompt and liberal fashion. Since conducting activities in this manner is sometimes inconvenient and costly, a policy on the kind of reputation the company desires is necessary. (We might note in passing that a policy on company reputation is very difficult to state in writing; here especially the policy takes on operational meaning through a succession of specific decisions that become a traditional way of operating.) If a company has earned a distinctive reputation, then it is appropriate to reinforce this posture publicly and to incorporate it in the total marketing effort.

Pricing

Providing any or all of the above sales appeals will surely boost company expenses. So an unavoidable issue is how to fit such expenses into prices charged to customers. Moreover, pricing itself is often presented as a sales appeal.

Pricing policy should fit with other company policy and with strategy in three important ways; prices should be related to our costs, to competitors' prices, and to consumers' use of the product.

Guides for Relating Prices to Costs. When we are selling unique products or services—such as a custom-built house, market research data, or leg amputation—charging *cost plus* a customary mark-up is the usual policy. In such situations there is normally a professional relationship between us and the customer. Trust is important, including confidence that our price will be fair.

For standardized products or services, if we are in the favorable position of being a low-cost producer in our industry we may tie prices to total costs in order to discourage new entrants. This is a common practice in the computer industry where the experience curve leads to falling unit costs for firms enjoying high output. Often these firms lower their prices as their costs go down—partly to tap new markets but also to ward off new competitors.

Setting prices to cover total costs (including a normal profit) may provide a comparable internal discipline. If a particular product cannot be sold at a price that "earns its keep" then that product can be dropped—or never launched. Recall that course in Greek syntax! Note, however, that such a policy assumes that resources devoted to producing the product are transferable to more rewarding issues.

When part of our costs are fixed—that is, cannot be cut out or transferred to other uses—we may drop the price below total costs provided the income received makes some contribution to these fixed costs. This kind of pricing has occurred in the aluminum industry during depressions, when demand was too small to utilize existing capacity.

Relating Our Prices to Competitors' Prices. A common policy, especially for smaller firms, is to set a price close to that of a leading company or the industry norm. The aim here is to remove price as a competitive factor in selling.

In retail trade, however, price is often used as a prominent part of the marketing mix. Such slogans as "Our prices can't be beat" and "Buy here and save" proclaim that our prices are low relative to competitors'. Or, a temporary price cut may be a part of a special sales promotion. Such a practice may be defensive—competitors are making price claims and we want to be perceived as offering good values too. Or we may wish to reach a market segment that is price sensitive.

Even when a prestigious firm—the Cadillac of the industry—caters to customers for whom price is not a major consideration, some relation to competitors' prices is common. One accounting firm, for example, had a policy to keep its billing rates within 20 percent of the rates charged by a specific Big Eight firm. A posture of high value for high price—but not exploitation—is usually tied to such a policy.

Prices Recognizing Customers' Use of the Product. Different customers may be charged different prices. For instance, when running shoes are sold to both wholesalers and retailers, the wholesaler normally receives an extra discount in recognition of its work of storing, selling, and financing. Likewise, the plumber who buys a hot water heater to install in your basement pays less than you would buying it directly. Such trade discounts are important in shaping a total distribution system.

A few products have quite distinct end uses. Ordinary humus, for instance, is used on golf courses and also as potting soil for African violet devotees. Even at wholesale the potting soil sells for five times as much as humus for golf courses. Factories pay lower prices for electricity than the householder next door. The service is going into different competitive markets.

Not every customer wants all the services that a company offers. Sometimes, but not always, the company recognizes this difference by *unbundling* the price. Thus, a separate charge is made for annual inspections, long-term credit, and even the Christmas wrapping. Unbundling software from hardware has significantly altered competition in the computer industry.

In all these examples we can see how pricing is an integral part of each marketing mix.

Concluding briefly, no company can stress all the sales appeals we have discussed. Some are incompatible (for example, low price versus high quality and service); others are inappropriate; all involve some expense. In thinking through what combination of appeals makes sense for a particular company, central management should recognize (1) the differences in attractiveness of various appeals to the groups it seeks as customers, and (2) the compatibility, and perhaps synergistic effect, of a particular appeal policy with the product-market emphasis, the differential advantage selected by the company, and other aspects of its master strategy.

SALES PROMOTION IN SUPPORT OF SELECTED APPEALS

A third major ingredient of the marketing mix is sales promotion. Our selected sales appeals, and even a low-price image if that is to be part of our scheme, have to be communicated to our target customers. This can be done with various kinds of advertising and personal solicitation. But again, because there are many possible forms and degrees of such promotional effort, policy guidance is needed.

Advertising

We are bombarded by advertising. No matter whether we walk, drive a car, ride a bus, watch television, read a newspaper or magazine, or open our mail, we are brought face to face with advertising. This creates a difficult situation for management, for it must determine what advertising on its part will justify its cost amid the bewildering array of advertisements by other companies. Major questions of policy with reference to advertising are (1) the purposes for which it is to be used and (2) the media employed to accomplish these purposes.

Analysis shows that advertising is employed for numerous purposes. It also shows that many companies have not given adequate thought to the question of exactly what they are trying to accomplish with their advertising. Let us, then, take a look at the major options.

Purpose of Advertising. Analysis shows that many companies have not thought through exactly what they are trying to accomplish with their advertising beyond emphasizing their selected appeals. Among the major options are the following:

- bringing customers to the place where goods are sold,
- persuading the customers to ask for a specific product,

- assisting a sales representative in making sales when calling on customers,
- producing direct sales via mail or telephone, and
- building institutional goodwill.

In a specific company, the role(s) assigned to advertising will depend on (1) the channel of distribution it has selected, (2) the buying habits of the target customers for its kind of product, and (3) the way it wants those customers to perceive its product. Also, the choice will be influenced by advertising being done by competitors; there will be jockeying to find a way to get the maximum impact within budget limitations.

Choice of Advertising Media. Closely related to a definition of the purpose of advertising is selection of media to be used. Possibilities include:

television	newspapers
radio	trade papers
magazines	direct mail

This list is not intended to be complete. Other types of sales promotion that might be classified as advertising are displays, dealer-helps, and sampling.

The selection among these media involves a delicate choice between economy and effectiveness in reaching objectives. For example, an airline wished to build goodwill among a large number of people and also develop immediate traffic on its planes. For the latter purpose, it confined expenditures to short TV commercials, direct mail to executives known to be frequent travelers along its routes, and circulars to passengers on its planes. However, to develop institutional goodwill, it used magazine ads and general newspaper publicity as the chief media.

For small companies with limited budgets, media choice is strongly influenced by what competitors are doing; there is jockeying to find imaginative ways of attracting attention within the budget limitations.

Personal Solicitation

Although sales representatives have a role in most selling transactions, the extent and purpose of personal solicitation vary greatly.

Differences in the Use of Sales Representatives. Most management consulting firms, for instance, operate on a professional basis and—like doctors—limit their advertising to a few dignified announcements. Such a firm secures its business largely through personal contacts by partners and supervisors, rarely by salespeople employed just for this work.

In contrast, insurance is typically sold by individuals who devote their whole effort to selling.

The selling of ethical pharmaceuticals illustrates another arrangement. Physicians, when they write a prescription, choose what drugs will be purchased.

Consequently, drug manufacturers send "detail reps" to call on physicians and explain the virtues of products made by their particular firm. Since the actual purchase is made by the patient at a drugstore, the detail rep stops in the local drugstores just be to sure products are in stock.

A representative selling industrial equipment, say printing presses, not only knows more about various kinds of equipment than the printing company usually does but also is an expert in the entire technology. Such a person should be qualified as an expert technical advisor. This is in sharp contrast to a ticket-seller at a theater box office.

An Analytical Approach. When deciding what role sales representatives should play—and when thinking about other parts of the marketing mix as well—ask yourself four questions:

1. Who consumes the product or alters it so that its identity is lost?
2. Who makes the final decision as to the products that such a consumer buys?
3. What factors influence those who make final decisions?
4. How is it possible to influence those factors by means of varying the marketing mix?

Need for Synergy

In marketing, no single factor makes a sale. Nor can the several factors—price, other sales appeals, various forms of sales promotion—be considered separately. Instead, each part should complement the other in a synergistic way. Thus, technical bulletins and engineer-trained salespeople or well-styled products and magazine advertising should reinforce each other. Likewise, sales promotion and other policy should be synergistic. IBM's repair service, leasing machines, capital financing, and high-wage policy, for instance, each gives added impact to the other.

The final marketing mix selected need not be complicated if a relatively simple combination fits the basic mission of the company. Here are three examples:

1. Handy & Harman, a leading processor of silver, makes bimetals, brazing compounds, and a variety of other fabricated silver products for industrial uses. To reach the industrial users, it stresses (a) closely controlled quality, (b) engineering advice to customers by sales representatives, backed up by technical bulletins, (c) sales representatives who understand the problems of their respective industries, and (d) company reputation built up over a hundred years. A relatively high amount of money is spent on the first two appeals. In contrast, advertising expenditure is very low (occasional ads in trade journals and Christmas greetings), price is simply kept "in line" with competition, and no thought is given to style.
2. A prominent correspondence school offers courses in computers, programming, mathematics, and a wide variety of semitechnical subjects. It concentrates heavily on advertising in trade and do-it-yourself magazines and by direct mail. A low price is featured—low, that is, in relation to potential earnings resulting from a course. Also, considerable effort goes into "product

design" so that courses are up-to-date and easily grasped by the students. The school has no sales representatives, quality of performance is not stressed, and reputation of the institution is not a major appeal.

3. The Paper Wrapper Company prints and finishes wrappers for bread, candy, and other food products. It obtains business primarily on the basis of low price, willingness to accept short runs, and personal friendships of sales representatives. It does no advertising, provides no technical advice, and gives no special emphasis to style, reputation, or quality.

Each of these companies has a marketing mix carefully designed to fit its master strategy. They differ sharply, but this is a reflection of very different jobs to be done. In each example the marketing approach builds on company strengths and avoids efforts that would create internal strain with other activities of the company.

SUMMARY

In moving a product from the plant to consumers, a variety of activities are undertaken—and each of these involves an expense. The marketing mix policy of a company guides the selection of these activities and the allocation of marketing funds. The aim, of course, is to create a final package of satisfactions that are attractive to the specific groups of customers identified by customer policy.

Services cannot be stored, and so they move directly from their creator to the user. Nevertheless, an array of attributes also surrounds each service. Here, too, there is a marketing mix, and the customer is attracted by the total package of attributes provided.

Components of a marketing mix policy include: (1) an overriding policy on the relative emphasis on low cost versus complete service, (2) sales appeals to be emphasized, and (3) sales promotion support of the selected appeals. Selection of an optimum combination is crucial. It calls for empathy with various target customer groups balanced against realistic understanding of incremental expense.

Policy regarding marketing mix should be compatible—hopefully, also synergistic—with R & D, production, purchasing, personnel, and financial policies. For instance, stress on quality affects production, delivery service is related to purchasing, leasing increases capital requirements, and so forth. So, as we examine these other types of policy in the following chapters, we will often need to think back to the package of customer satisfactions that has been adopted for our marketing mix.

QUESTIONS FOR CLASS DISCUSSION

1. (a) The Bridal Center is a new venture formed by two energetic women to provide advice and other services related to weddings. The product line includes bridal gowns (pre-made or custom-made) and related clothing, dresses for mother of the bride, bridesmaids, rental suits of various styles for the groom and his attendants, invitations and announcements, photographic service, guest books, gift patterns service and acknowledgements, counsel on the entire procedure, counsel on receptions and dinners (references but no catering). The location is in a middle to lower-middle income suburb. What marketing mix do you recommend for the Bridal Center?

   (b) Three blocks away from the Bridal Center is a funeral home. What marketing mix do you recommend for this business? What reasons account for the main differences in your answers to (a) and (b)?

2. The financial vice president of a large oil company which finds, pumps, and transports crude oil to its refineries in the United States and then sells gasoline, lubricating oil, and other products through its owned or leased service stations is fed up with the company's return on its investment, which is lower than that of other oil companies. He proposes that prices of its gasoline be raised 9 percent to restore profitability and to enable increased spending on exploration for new crude oil. The marketing vice president proposes no change in retail prices. She receoommends the company find ways to reduce refinery and transportation costs even further; the company has had success in cutting these costs recently and is just about the most efficient in the industry in transportation and refining—but not in exploration and distribution. "Our competitors won't follow our price increase even though industry demand for gasoline is inelastic."

   The national sales manager proposes that prices be decreased by 10 percent. "This will allow us to recapture the market share that we had in the past and that we have lost by not being the lowest-priced seller in our markets. With a good sales increase we can generate enough revenues to more than cover the increase in variable costs and can make a big contribution to exploration costs."

   Which of these three possible approaches to pricing policy do you think will be most effective?

3. How do you explain the wide range of prices charged by airlines for an almost identical service—transporting someone from X to Y? What policies seem to be in effect? Is there a better way of pricing?

4. What marketing mix would you suggest to South-Western Publishing Co. for selling this textbook, *Strategy, Policy, and Central Management*? Use the outline of this chapter in framing your answer.

5. Two of your friends like outdoor work and have decided to set up a landscape gardening business. They hope to get regular customers for whom they will mow the lawn weekly, trim shrubbery, fertilize, etc. Their location will be in an upper-middle class suburban area north of Cincinnati, focused in a five-mile radius to reduce travel time. They have enough capital for the necessary equipment. "You've studied business," they say, "how should we market our services? Will advertising pay?" What marketing mix do you recommend?

6. Contrast the marketing mix policy that you would recommend for two companies; both make men's shirts but differ in their strategy regarding domain sought. Company C-P sells only high-quality shirts under the brand name of "Arrow." Company E-Z sells much less expensive shirts under any brand name that a wholesale distributor likes.

7. (a) In a period of general inflation, many companies will own buildings and equipment that cost a lot less than their current replacement costs. Also, inventories often will have been purchased at less than replacement costs. In pricing its products, should such a company use actual costs or replacement costs or neither when thinking about its cost-to-price ratio? (b) How would you answer the question if replacement costs of equipment and inventory were below actual costs?

8. Five medical doctors with diverse specialties have established in Cheyenne a private clinic for their joint practice. From society's viewpoint, how should they price their services: (a) On the basis of time devoted to a patient? (b) On the value of the services to the patient? (c) On ability of patients to pay for services? (d) On an annual service charge for all care needed? (e) On an annual service charge, with quantity discounts for families? (f) On fixed charges for each specific kind of service, for instance, tonsillectomy, broken arm, obstetrical care, infected toe, case of pneumonia?

9. The Amsterdam Petroleum Transport Company owned and operated eight T-2 tankers. By today's standards these tankers were small and slow, and they had been operating at a substantial loss (except for brief periods of acute tanker shortage). Estimates showed that a cut in freight rates might increase the volume of business but that, even with the increased volume, depreciation and interest on the capital investment would not be earned. Consequently, the vessels were sold at substantially below their book value to an Algerian concern. The Algerian concern proceeded to cut the freight rates to a point where the tankers were kept reasonably busy. Amsterdam Petroleum Transport protested strongly against the low rates. The Algerian concern replied that, because of the low purchase price and the resulting low depreciation and interest, it was able to operate at these low rates and show a profit. Assuming equal efficiency of operation, should Amsterdam Petroleum Transport have sold the vessels or should it have cut rates to the same level as the Algerian concern?

10. Do you recommend that the sales appeals and sales promotion activities of a motel located close to an airport should differ significantly from those of a motel at a resort such as the Grand Canyon? Explain specifically how.

11. In the pharmaceutical industry, products are divided into proprietary drugs (products with brand names often widely advertised and readily available to consumers) and ethical drugs (products sold by drugstores by prescription from a doctor). Since the purchaser of ethical drugs does not decide which product to buy, special problems of marketing mix arise. Pharmaceutical manufacturers spend large sums sending representatives, called detail persons, to doctors to explain the merits of their products and to encourage the doctors to prescribe such products by the company trade name. (It is unethical for a doctor to accept any financial inducement from a manufacturer or a drugstore.) The cost of detail persons is subject to much debate. Manufacturers of ethical drugs contend that such persons perform a vital educational function; critics recommend use of generic (not company) names and reliance on professional journals to help doctors stay abreast of new discoveries. In addition to detail persons, ethical drug producers can promote their products by publishing research reports and by direct-mail advertising to doctors, stressing quality, pricing, service to drug wholesalers and retailers, etc. (a) Which sales appeals and forms of sales promotion do you believe will be most effective and profitable for a manufacturer? (b) Is the marketing mix you recommend in answer to (a) in the best interest of the consumer? If not, what can be done about it?

12. A method of approach to sales promotion and the marketing mix has been outlined on page 143. Apply this outline to the development of a program for (a) a chocolate pudding mix, (b) folding fishing rods for backpackers and others to carry, (c) sightseeing tours in San Diego, California, and (d) an office building skyscraper to be named for an insurance company that will use one-half of the total space and plans to lease the rest.

13. The steel products division of Pittsburg Equipment, Inc., has just been spun off as a separate company. Lee Reynolds, former plant superintendent, is president. The new company has one major line—heavy steel rollers used in equipment that rolls out metal from an ingot to smooth sheets or other shapes. These vital rollers can be used for copper, brass, aluminum, or other metals but over 90 percent of the company's business is with steel mills which require especially tough, precise, well-tempered rollers. Tremendous pressures and high speeds eventually upset the close tolerances required, leading to a replacement market in addition to the new equipment market. The company is one of three leading producers in the country. Business goes up and down; nevertheless, on the average the company has made some profit.

Pat McCulloch of the Coakley Advertising Agency recently suggested to Reynolds, "Let us take over your entire market research and sales promotion. We have other industrial accounts, and could relieve you of most of your marketing headaches." Do you think Reynolds should turn to an advertising agency for this kind of help? Why or why not?

CASE 7
"QuiknEasy" Sauce[2]

Six weeks ago Eileen Reilly was hired as product manager of "QuiknEasy" sauce, one of the products of the Convenience Food Division of Radford Foods Company. A new Division management has undertaken to bring profitability of the Division up to the company average, and Reilly's appointment is one of the moves made for that purpose.

Reilly's Challenge

Sales and profits of "QuiknEasy" sauce have been slipping for several years, and last year only $155,000 operating profit was earned on $12.3 million sales. This led to the "resignation" of Reilly's predecessor.

The position was an attractive challenge for Reilly. The salary and potential bonus are good for a person only nine years out of college and five years beyond her MBA. And, she can use her experience in an advertising agency (two years) and, more recently, in another food company where she progressed—rather slowly, she felt—to an associate brand manager. Her new boss, John Silver, said:

"This is a turnaround opportunity. Find what's wrong and fix it, and you can move on here to a much bigger product manager job. I don't want to fool you, however, You've got two years. If you strike out, that's when you'll be gone. My head's on the chopping block, too—for the whole Division—and I intend to make good things happen. If I can help you, let me know, but basically this is your job."

The organization of the Convenience Food Division has just been restructured. Under the new setup Reilly has primary profit responsibility for her product line. She has direct control over pricing, advertising, and sales promotion. Actual selling is done by the corporate market department; however, if Reilly wants extra sales or promotion programs she can request them and "pay" the additional cost from her budget. Moreover, Reilly can "buy" services from the Division's market research staff or the product development staff to the extent

---

[2]Adapted from a longer case on Radford Foods Company written by Professor Melvin Anshen, Graduate School of Business, Columbia University.

that she decides is wise. Production of all convenience foods is done by a centralized manufacturing department; products are transferred to product managers at full cost including a planned manufacturing "profit."

In her new job Reilly is assisted by two key people: Peter Selowitz, transferred from the divisional marketing staff in the earlier organization setup, now responsible, under Reilly's direction, for market analysis, pricing, and liaison with the corporate marketing group; and Carl Wilks, transferred from the divisional advertising department, now responsible, under Reilly's direction, for advertising and promotion.

Reilly's Inheritance

"QuiknEasy" sauce, available in beef, chicken, and "Italian-style" flavors, is a dry sauce mix. A user pours the contents of the package of dry ingredients into a cup of boiling water and stirs the mixture for one minute. "QuiknEasy" sauce competes directly with two national brands and several regional brands of similar mixes, as well as grocery chains' private brands. Canned sauces requiring only heating are viewed as indirect competitors.

The downward trend of sales and profits was attributed by divisional management to a variety of causes: increasing popularity of frozen dinners complete with their own sauces, preference of some consumers for prepared sauces requiring no mixing or stirring, intense competition from national and regional dry sauce mixes, and unaggressive and unimaginative marketing administration by the former "QuiknEasy" product manager.

The existing annual budget for "QuiknEasy" sauces was put together by Reilly's immediate boss, Silver, during the interim after the former product manager was discharged. He explains:

"It was our judgment that 'QuiknEasy' has been suffering in sales and profits because it has been overpriced and underadvertised relative to competition. We reduced the selling price the equivalent of two cents a package and increased advertising 15 percent over last year. Reflecting the results of these two actions, we projected a sales increase of 15 percent and a better bottom line than last year. (See first column in Table 1.) The results show some improvement, but not as much as we budgeted. Right now the line is just breaking even.

"You can interpret these results in several different ways. One conclusion might be that the price cut and the increased advertising have only begun to make an impact on consumer perceptions and therefore on sales. Resulting decision: maintain the twin price and advertising strategy and watch what happens through, say, the spring months.

"Another conclusion might be that the price cut is too small—only two cents on a package of mix that usually sells at retail for about twenty-nine cents. Possible decision: cut the price further, another two cents or more. Maybe also put additional advertising pressure behind the line—say, to an annual rate of more than $3 million. Of course, we'd have to get a really big lift in sales to come out with a better bottom line under these conditions of shrinking gross margin percentage and higher advertising dollars. A critical issue here is the extent to which economies of scale in production will bring down the cost-of-goods-sold percentage as sales rise. My guess is that we ought to get a 1 percent savings for each 10 percent increase in sales, exclusive of price changes.

"Third conclusion: the line is mature; it won't respond much to either price-cutting or advertising. Possible decision: cut the advertising way back and enjoy a big fat bottom line for a few years while sales slowly slump. You might speculate that if we stopped all advertising as soon as we could cancel space and time contracts, sales for the balance of this year might not decline more than about 10 percent. That would suddenly make 'QuiknEasy' the most profitable brand in the Division by a huge margin. Then let sales and market share drift on down while we invest part of the profit in new product development or an acquisition.

"Of course, there are other options. Maybe when we concluded that we had an overpriced package of mix we were wrong. What if we put the price up? Could we retain something like the present sales volume with a fatter gross margin? If we could do that and also cut the advertising way down, there'd be a simply beautiful bottom line. At least for a while. Come back and see me when you've got a proposal."

Reilly's Quandary

Since arriving at Radford Food Company Reilly has immersed herself in marketing studies of "QuiknEasy" drawn from the files and updated informally in conversations with knowledgeable staff personnel from the corporate market research group. She also talked with Pete Selowitz and Carl Wilks about their views of the brand's position and prospects. She visited buyers in three major grocery chains to solicit their ideas. She talked to the "QuiknEasy" account executive at the brand's advertising agency. From these and other sources, she has concluded:

1. The total national market for dry sauce mixes last year was valued at about $150 million at producers' prices. The market was growing about 5 percent annually. Sales were heavily concentrated in the ten largest metropolitan market areas. "QuiknEasy" had about a 10 percent share nationally and had been slipping in market share from above 15 percent five years ago.
2. No single cause for the steady decline of market share and dollar sales could be isolated in the research findings. Nor was there any indication of strong consumer attitudes for or against the brand. Most purchasers and users of dry sauce mixes viewed the product class as a convenience item—easy to use when dinner had to be prepared in a hurry, although inferior in flavor to "homemade" sauces. They had much the same attitude toward canned sauces. The big buying motivation was saving time in preparing meals. Among competing brands of dry mixes there were no strongly marked preferences for one brand against another. A common reply to a question probing for perceived distinctions among dry mix brands was, "They're all alike. They taste about the same

TABLE 1.
"QuiknEasy" BUDGETS
EXISTING BUDGET AND REILLY'S PROJECTIONS FOR SELF-FINANCING NEW PRODUCTS
(in Thousand's)

	Existing Present Year Budget[a]	Present Year Revised[b]	Self-Financing New Products					
			1st Year		2nd Year		3rd Year	
			Staple Line	Gourmet Line[c]	Staple Line	Gourmet Line[d]	Staple Line	Gourmet Line
Sales	14,100	12,750	11,250	500	9,000	2,500	7,500	6,000
Costs of Goods Sold	9,500	8,670	7,650	400	6,300	1,750	5,250	3,600
Gross Margin	4,600	4,080	3,600	100	2,700	750	2,250	2,400
Selling Expense	1,100	1,000	900	250	800	400	600	600
Advertising and Promotion Expense	2,700	900	250	250	250	750	200	1,500
Product Development Expense	—	200	—	100	—	—	—	
Administrative Expense	350	350	250	100	250	200	150	300
Operating Profit	450	1,630	2,200	(600)	1,400	(600)	1,300	

[a]Prepared by Silver.
[b]Reflects cash-cow strategy for "QuiknEasy" and investment in development of new gourmet line.
[c]Reflects intensive test marketing.
[d]Assumes favorable consumer acceptance of gourmet line and regional rollout campaign.

and they sell for about the same price." Merchandisers in supermarket chains viewed dry sauce mixes as a product they had to stock because a small but significant share of their customers bought them regularly. But the annual sales volume and dollar gross margin per shelf-foot generated by sauce mixes were too low to get store operators excited about the product or disposed to give it prominent display space. The typical large supermarket carried two brands, of which one was often its own "private" brand. Smaller stores typically stocked only one brand.

Peter Selowitz argues that the two-cent price reduction now in effect is not likely to induce any sales increase beyond the relatively small gain already experienced. A deeper price cut would, he believes, draw more purchasers from competing brands temporarily; this shift would compel competitors to reduce their prices to protect market share. Lower prices for all brands would not, in his judgment, materially enlarge the total market for dry sauce mixes because price is a less important consideration than convenience in their purchase. This conclusion leads him to recommend an increase in price several cents above the level prior to the experimental two-cent cut. "We could raise the gross margin per package without significantly hurting unit sales."

Carl Wilks argues that increased advertising expenditures above the level already budgeted would have two favorable effects: (1) it would induce some customer brand-shifting from competing mixes; (2) it would increase the total market for dry mixes, with much of the increase coming to "QuiknEasy." He favors increasing the advertising budget by at least 20 percent, with all the increment invested in the ten major metropolitan markets.

As Eileen Reilly ponders these findings, opinions, and proposals, she has become increasingly disturbed by the thought that she is in a personal "no-win" situation. The rational decision at the divisional level might well be the present strategy of treating "QuiknEasy" as a cash-cow with the mission of generating profits to invest in other divisional products with attractive sales and profit potential. But if she follows such a course, what would it do to her career? In three years "QuiknEasy" sales might decrease by 25 percent or more. She would be managing a very profitable business headed for extinction.

Reilly's Bright Idea

While turning this problem over in her mind, a new option occurred to Reilly. "QuiknEasy" and competing dry mixes were all offered in varieties of staple sauces and advertised as convenience or time-saving products. What if dry mixes could be formulated for gourmet-type sauces, such as hollandaise, béarnaise, mornay, and béchamel? Here, the issue of fast, convenient preparation would be of small significance compared with the fact that many (possibly most) individuals responsible for daily food preparation are relatively unskilled in preparing such sauces. A supporting consideration might be the widely publicized growing interest in gourmet cooking and its "fit" with emerging life styles.

Many of these nonstaple sauces are difficult to prepare, requiring careful combination of ingredients and close attention in cooking. Would a dry-mix line of gourmet sauces, under "QuiknEasy" or another brand name, be a way to convert a minimum-growth, low-profit situation into a high-growth, high-profit situation?

Intrigued by the notion, she took the idea to the Division's product development staff. After some study and experimentation, the staff's director reported that it is feasible to formulate such a line of sauces. She estimates that developing and testing dry mixes for three gourmet sauce varieties would involve at least six months of work and a cost of about $200,000, which Reilly would have to fund from her budget. The end product, the product development staff believes, would be a convenience version of a "homemade" gourmet concoction, not equal in flavor, taste, and texture to the creation of a skilled amateur chef, but of good quality and as easy to prepare as the present varieties of staple sauces. The costlier ingredients would necessitate a selling price at least double the current "QuiknEasy" price. The product development staff offered no judgment about possible consumer reactions to such a line of sauces.

The potential gains and risks suggested by the gourmet sauce notion added to, rather than simplified, Reilly's problems. One strategic possibility would be to combine a recommendation to treat the existing three sauce types as "cash cows" with a recommendation to assign their enriched bottom line to finance the development and then, if successful, the marketing of a gourmet sauce line. The substantial advertising costs required to launch such a new product would certainly absorb much of the operating profits created by sharply curtailing advertising support for the staple product line, leaving little for the rest of the Division. If she should propose such a venture, get an approval up the line, and then have it fail in the market, she could envision no outcome for herself but discharge and a "loser" reputation to take into the job market.

Reilly is aware that (1) most new food products fail in the market, and (2) new food products that meet with favorable consumer acceptance usually lose money for at least three years while distribution is being rolled out nationally and heavy advertising and promotional support is committed to persuading consumers to make the initial purchase. Assurance from the product development staff that the formulation of a dry-mix line of gourmet sauces would be technically feasible was only the first step in a risky sequence of events. Test marketing would have to be undertaken, with the possibility that consumers would reject the product. If successful in test markets, the line would have to be introduced in major markets with very strong initial advertising and promotional support.

To quantify the possibilities, Reilly projected the present budget for three years as shown in Table 1. This projection assumes (1) a decision to convert the existing staple sauce line to cash-cow status at once, (2) investment in formulating the gourmet line, (3) steady decline of sales for the staple line with drastically curtailed advertising support, (4) test marketing of the gourmet line next year, (5) favorable consumer reception for the gourmet line in test markets, (6) subsequent rollout of the gourmet line with strong advertising and promotional support, and (7) a break-even result for the gourmet line in its third year with the likelihood of substantial profits in future years. She anticipates that the success of the gourmet line would bring one or more competitive offerings into the market.

Considering the list of assumptions that have to be fulfilled to make the venture a success, Reilly wonders if her best personal strategy might be to abandon the gourmet option, recommend converting "QuiknEasy" into a cash-cow serving other divisional investment opportunities, and immediately start looking for a new job.

Questions

1. As an outside consultant, what would you recommend that Radford Food Company do with its "QuiknEasy" line of sauces?
2. If you were in Eileen Reilly's position, what would you propose?

for humans to use in farm animals. This opens up a large market with relatively low R & D expense. In addition to veterinary products for the control and treatment of disease, Hygeia produces a variety of feed supplements. Now about 15 percent of Hygeia's total sales of over a billion dollars come from "agricultural" activities!

Hygeia's agricultural business includes active participation in mass production of poultry. Today, frying chickens are raised in 100,000-chick batches. Thanks to genetic selection, scientific feeding, and strictly controlled environment, friers can be ready for market in ten weeks. Egg production is similarly engineered. Significantly, these mass production methods provide one of the most efficient conversions of cereal grains into protein known on earth.

Of course, two essential features of such operations are drugs for disease control and feed supplements. Hygeia makes both (as do several competitors). Moreover, to keep in contact with the latest developments, Hygeia has a subsidiary focusing on development of new genetic strains in chickens—for faster growth, larger proportion of white meat, more eggs, disease resistance, or other desired characteristics. In the U.S., Hygeia itself does not produce chickens or eggs commercially nor sell chicks for this purpose, but it does have experts familiar with the entire technology.

As part of its international expansion, Hygeia has helped promote modern poultry technology in Europe, Latin America—and now Nigeria.

Potential Market

A British colony until 1960, Nigeria is growing dramatically. It is by far the leading black African country economically. Its large population of over ninety million (growing 2.7 percent per year) coupled with massive foreign exchange from its crude oil exports ($15 billion in 1980) provide a base for all sorts of expansion.

At the time of independence, Nigeria was a relatively poor developing country with only modest agricultural exports. Probably 90 percent of its population relied on the small village economy, almost unchanged for centuries. Political independence provided the drive, and oil the financial means to modernize. Even now the average annual per capita income of about $500 is unevenly distributed, with many village people being very poor.

National plans call for universal education and the improvement of hospitals, roads and airports, electric plants, radio and TV, and industry. Lagos, the capital, already has a population of over a million and so many automobiles that new bridges and a fine elevated highway cannot handle the traffic.

Such a rapid transition naturally creates strains. Politically, the most important task is to unite three major tribal groups: the Hausa-Fulani in the north, Ibo in the east, and Yoruba in the west. They speak many different languages (English is the common language) and traditionally are suspicious of each other. A serious civil war occurred from 1967 to 1969 when Biafra tried unsuccessfully to secede. The constitution provides for democratic government, but a series of military coalitions has been necessary to maintain national unity.

Although significant European influence in Nigeria is only about a century old along the southern coast, the Moslem religion and associated ideas have been present in the northern, more arid, regions since the 12th century. (Kano, for example, was a city state when Europe was still in the Dark Ages.) Nevertheless, society continues to center around the simple village economy with strong emphasis on loyalty to the extended family. Today over three-quarters of the population relies on localized agriculture. The great movement now occurring is from the village to the city, with all the social and economic adjustments tied to such a shift.

The total population growth, and especially the movement to the cities, has created problems of food supplies. Nigeria has much fertile land, but sugar and cereals are being imported. The village society is unsuited to large-scale agricultural technology, and marketing channels are poorly developed. Particularly serious is the shortage of protein foods. The production of peanuts is rising slowly, but the amount of meat going into markets is stable at best.

Therefore, one facet of the national plan is to increase agricultural output. A system of agricultural agents to advise farmers is being established, some research on products and technology is underway, and loans to farmers are available on favorable terms. A major bottleneck in this effort is trained human resources. The number of experts capable of dealing with local farmers is very limited, and farmers with knowledge, skill, and capital needed for modern agriculture are scarce. As usual, pricing presents a dilemma. High prices, which will stimulate farm output, also lead to high food prices for the city dweller who is already caught in inflation. Nigeria, like the U.S., has basically a free price system but resorts to some political control of items that are important in the worker's cost of living.

In this situation, government officials would like to increase substantially the supply of eggs and chickens. And if this can be done without raising the real (adjusted for inflation) prices, that is even more attractive. A relatively small technical staff in the Ministry of Agriculture is working on poultry, and low-interest loans are available to farmers who wish to install modern poultry-raising equipment. A few demonstration farms are in operation, and their results show the advantages of mass production methods. However, the response to date has been limited. The concept of producing eggs or chickens in large quantities is new, and few farmers have a technical background in scientific feeding, disease control, and mechanical equipment.

Product/Customer Issue for Hygeia

Hygeia International is already well established in Nigeria. It has built a "dosage" plant where several hundred different pharmaceutical products (imported) are put into pills, capsules, bottles, and other forms suited to local use. These pharmaceuticals are sold to hospitals, clinics, and drugstores in much the same way as ethical drugs are sold in the U.S.

The sale of Hygeia products is helped by the local company's full cooperation with the "indigenization program" which requires the employment of Nigerians for virtually all positions. Also, to comply with recent laws, 40 percent of the shares of the local company have been sold to Nigerians. A substantial amount of training and technical advice continues to be provided for a fee by Hygeia offices in Europe and in the U.S. Hygeia's policy is to cooperate as fully as it can in the development of medical services in Nigeria.

In the agricultural area Hygeia follows a similar practice. It imports and sells unique medicines and feed supplements, and it is active in technical development. Working closely with government and trade association officials, Hygeia helped set up demonstration sites for poultry colony housing and displays on lighting, ventilation, and feeding routines. It trains farmers on disease control and forecasts epidemics or disease frequency. Also, it has helped establish reliable regional feed mills. As a result of the total cooperative program, the number of egg-laying hens has increased to perhaps three million.

As with human products, Hygeia uses a wide range of services to build a market for its veterinary and feed products. Note, however, that the company does not now operate its own egg-laying colonies nor meat colonies. Nor does Hygeia maintain colonies of "parents"—pedigree chickens which produce the millions of first-line workers. In the U.S., parent colonies are usually operated by separate companies closely linked to genetic development; then fertile eggs or chicks are sold to companies in the meat or egg business. The question now facing Hygeia is whether to integrate forward in Nigeria—that is, actually to produce eggs or meat (sold as live chickens or dressed meat) or to stop with fertile eggs or chicks sold to farmers.

Proposal from Nigeria.
Dear Mr. Livingstone:

This letter outlines a proposed expansion of the agricultural division of our company. Estimates show that this would be a very profitable venture, and it would help meet the food needs of our growing population.

The basic plan is to become a large-scale producer of eggs and of chickens to be sold for meat. The reasons supporting this move are:

1. We already have the necessary technical staff who are fully acquainted with adapting the latest technology to local conditions.
2. There is high potential demand for protein foods, especially eggs, which are less perishable than fresh meat. Considering only our urban population of 15 million people, Nigeria now markets only about 36 eggs per person per year compared with 335 in the United States.
3. Government support is available. Much of the plant cost can be financed with low-interest loans, and other cooperation can be expected.
4. Our success will attract others into the poultry business. Some of the people we

train will leave and start their own operations. This activity, in addition to our
own, will increase the demand for veterinary products and feed supplements.

5. Facilities for egg production can be shifted to birds for meat as marketing channels for live and/or frozen birds develop.

6. During inflation there is some risk that price controls on eggs might squeeze the
   profit margins. However, if eggs become a stable part of urban dwellers' diets,
   we doubt that the government will permit sharp reduction in egg production.
   Therefore, the increased demand for veterinary and feed products will
   continue.

7. To attract and retain good local managers, we plan a series of joint ventures
   with the local manager sharing in the ownership and profits. Each will be a
   separate corporation. Tentatively we are thinking of ten ventures located in the
   environs of the following cities: Lagos (3), Ibadan (2), Benin (2), Kaduna,
   Kano, Makurdi. Three will be parent-stock farms—one each in Lagos, Ibadan,
   and Benin; the others will be commercial egg farms.

8. The financial projection prepared by R. Akobo, our agricultural manager, and
   checked by M. Suleman, our financial manager, is attached. You do not have
   to send us cash; we can simply withhold capital as it becomes needed from
   remittances due on shipments made to us.

I hope you will telex your approval of this proposal in the near future so we
can start negotiations with government officials and possible venture managers.
I feel confident that local stockholders will approve the expansion.

Sincerely yours,

E. P. Murtala, President
Nigerian Hygeia, Ltd.

When Mr. Livingstone received Mr. Murtala's letter, he immediately asked
Hygeia's treasurer and the corporate vice president for agriculture for their comments on the proposal.

The treasurer noted that "the estimated return is well over the 30 percent
hurdle-rate used for domestic investment. Also, with Nigeria's favorable foreign
exchange position, the danger of exchange rate losses is not high. So the main
question relates to political risks—revolution, confiscation, controls on repatria-
tion of profits, arbitrary actions to promote diplomatic ends (e.g., South
Africa), etc. And you are in the best position to assess these risks."

The agriculture vice president replied, in part: "My chief concern is whether
Hygeia should enter into agricultural production. In the U.S., Europe, and most
other locations we confine our activities to *helping others* (local people who
know local problems) improve their output. That posture keeps us out of a lot of
trouble. In particular, we must be sure that what we do in poultry does not
upset sales of livestock veterinary and feed products, or more important, sales of
products for humans. My preference is to enter production only when that is the
only feasible way to start the use of our regular line of products, and to pull out
as soon as local operators are ready to carry on. So I urge you to think of the

TABLE 1.
FINANCIAL SUMMARY
(Based on detailed estimates—amount in thousands of dollars.)

	Parent Stock Farm (day-old chicks)	Comercial Egg Farm (eggs for food)
Land	40	25
Buildings & Equipment	960	440
Development Expenses	100	60
Total fixed investment	1,100	525
Working Capital	500	175
Total investment	1,600	700
Sales[a]	2,300	850
Direct Expenses	870	685
Administration, Sales, etc.	150	45
Operating profit	1,020	120
Income taxes @ 50%[b]	510	60
Net Profit	510	60
Government and Bank Financing	1,000	450
Equity	600	250
Total investment	1,600	700
Return on Equity before Taxes/yr[c]	170%	48%
Return on Equity after Taxes/yr	85%	24%

[a]Sales figures, but not expenses, reduced 20% to allow for contingencies.
[b]Actually most Nigerian taxes will be rebated during first four years.
[c]Figures converted from naira to dollars at rate of 1N = $1.50.
Inflation will increase all estimates, but the proportions should remain the same.

    Estimates are for full-scale operations. It will take two to three years to reach this level. Estimates show both cash and net income break-even by end of first year and, with tax rebate, full recovery of equity by early in third year.

Nigerian proposal only as a sales promotion device. You can decide whether there are better ways to promote sales."

Question

    Assume that you are a personal assistant to Mr. Livingstone, and that he has asked you to study the total Nigerian situation and recommend what he should do regarding Mr. Murtala's proposal. What do you tell Mr. Livingstone?

8 RESEARCH AND DEVELOPMENT POLICY

The creation of services is just as indispensable as their distribution, which we have been examining in preceding chapters. Company strategy embraces both. In fact, it is often the ingenious marriage of producing and marketing that gives a company unique strength. And as with marketing, policy is needed to elaborate and sharpen the broad strategic choices that have been made for the production of services that are to be sold. This amplification of directions for creating services will be discussed in this chapter on research and development policy, and in the following two chapters on production policy and procurement policy.

ROLE OF RESEARCH AND DEVELOPMENT

Some firms quite wisely do virtually no research and development. Others rely on their R & D for survival. Between these two extremes there are many variations in purposes and emphasis. Because of this array of options, policy guidance on the role of research and development is sorely needed.

Scope

This chapter deals with activities from basic research to placing a product on the market or utilizing a new process. We are primarily concerned with *innovation*—the effective application of a new idea. Innovations occur in all kinds of human activity, but here we are focusing on technological changes in products and processes.

Clearly, the business manager is concerned with more than *invention*—the conceiving of a new and useful idea. Invention is an essential part of the total process, but it is only a part. Companies may engage in activities that lead to inventions; but if they do, they must also devote a great deal of effort to converting the invention into a practical application.

Stages

When planning for R & D, a recognition of the stages involved in innovation is helpful. The normal stages of technological innovation follow.

1. Basic research—the scientific investigation of a physical phenomenon without any defined use that might be made of the resulting knowledge.
2. Applied research—studies designed to identify specific potential applications of general knowledge.
3. Development—testing and elaborating a potential application into a model or a set of specifications that demonstrates the physical practicality of a new process or product.
4. Pilot plant or prototype testing—testing the economic as well as the physical feasibility of actually using a model or specifications emerging from the development stage.
5. Manufacturing, tooling, and debugging—designing and assembling new manufacturing equipment, then testing and modifying it until full-scale operations at acceptable efficiencies are possible.
6. Marketing start-up—overcoming any new technical problems of physical distribution and customer use.

Table 8-1 presents an outline of the six stages of technological innovation with respect to output, predictability of results, and types of personnel involved.

TABLE 8-1.
NORMAL STAGES OF TECHNOLOGICAL INNOVATION

Stages	Output	Ability to Predict Results	Kinds of People Involved
1. Basic research	Knowledge	None	Idealists and dreamers—young, professionally oriented
2. Applied research	Directed knowledge, leading to identified applications*	Little	May be prickly personalities
3. Development	Product or process model—operational feasibility	Some	
4. Pilot plant	Cost knowledge—economic feasibility		Engineers—organization oriented
5. Manufacturing, tooling, and debugging	Total operating system, specifications, and process costs	High probability	Persons with efficiency and effectiveness as values
6. Marketing start-up	Product acceptance		

*Many inventions by individual tinkerers arise without benefit of knowledge from basic research; all major inventions sparking the Industrial Revolution were of this sort.

In practice, the separation of these six stages of technological innovation is fuzzy. Problems encountered at any one stage may require backtracking to a previous stage. For instance, a difficulty uncovered in a pilot plant may signal the need for further development or even applied research effort. Similarly, good management practice requires forward bridging. Thus, basic research shades into applied research and applied research shades into development. Especially important in private R & D work is a frequent checking of market potentials and market requirements during all of the stages except basic research.

In setting policy for R & D work, it is important to recognize that research expenses are normally very much smaller than development expenses for a successful project. Statistics on this point are far from precise, but Figure 8-1 does indicate the range in three important industries.

The reasons for high expense in later stages are not hard to find. Many work-hours are required to design and test each of the subparts of a new product or process. Moreover, as the work progresses it must be done on a larger and larger scale, requiring greater inputs of materials and machinery. In some instances, such as the development of penicillin, entirely new processes for acquiring raw material in the quantity and the quality desired have to be invented. The identification and the recording of all the specifications in an experimental model is time-consuming. Clearly, any company that engages in applied research must be prepared to invest substantially larger additional amounts if it is to reap full benefit from its research efforts.

Progress by Increments

A single dramatic invention such as Carlson's Xerography or Land's Polaroid camera catches our attention when we think about innovation. However, it is a mistake to assume that the success of all R & D work depends upon major discoveries. Much more common is a succession of small improvements, one built upon another, that in total add up to a major change. The development of mobile homes and self-service stores are examples of innovations that occurred in this incremental fashion.

This incremental process permits several different companies to participate in an innovation. Frequently one firm builds on the advances of another, and it is possible to enter the game late and still be successful. Of course, a basic invention protected by a patent is of great competitive value, but a great majority of R & D work is not of this character. Most firms advance a step at a time, and R & D success is measured by who is stepping fastest.

Risk Entailed

Both uncertainty and expense permeate the design of all R & D policy. Of course, business expenditures in R & D of about $50 billion per year (one-half of this in government money) produces a stream of new products and processes, but the output of a single company laboratory is by no means sure. For example, laser theory was discovered and published by Charles Towne early in the 1950s. Many different laboratories started applied research with this new concept, but twenty years later only a few significant industrial applications had appeared. R & D managers estimate that less than 20 percent of the ideas that look good enough to move from applied research to development actually end up in a mar-

FIGURE 8-1.

COST DISTRIBUTION OF SUCCESSFUL INNOVATIONS
IN CHEMICAL, ELECTRONIC, AND MACHINERY INDUSTRIES

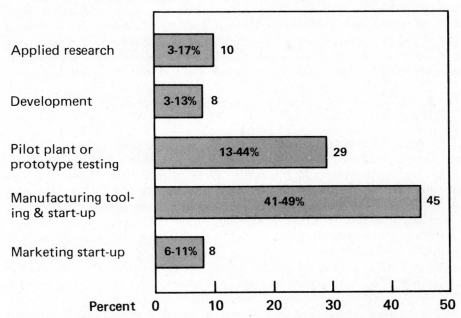

Source: Edwin Mansfield *et al., The Production and Application of New Industrial Technology,* (New York: W. W. Norton & Co., Inc., 1977), p. 71. Lengths of bars show mean percentages of sample cases; numbers within bars show the range.

ketable product (or applied process), and only a part of these are commercially successful. Uncertainty in R & D is real.

Moreover, R & D work is expensive. When technical assistants and other laboratory expenses are added to salary, a scientist or a senior engineer may cost a company from $100,000 to $175,000 a year. Of course the cost of routine engineering is lower, but so is the useful output. Projects that call for a team approach quickly entail a significant investment. Such cost, coupled with uncertainty of outcome, puts pressure on central management to think through carefully how R & D should be used.

Among the key issues for which policy guidance is needed are the following:

1. targets for improvement
2. depth of research effort
3. offensive versus defensive R & D
4. getting R & D done by outsiders
5. limits on total commitment

TARGETS FOR IMPROVEMENT

R & D activities tend to wander. Researchers and engineers must be given considerable freedom to organize their own work, and each person prefers to move in directions that are intellectually exciting to that individual. No company can afford such a diffused effort on a large scale, although occasionally a company does permit its researchers to devote, say, 20 percent of their time to anything that intrigues them. Instead, guideposts—policy—are established to focus the effort. The guides should be directly derived from company strategy.

Product Versus Process Focus

A recurring question is how R & D effort will be divided between developing new and improved products and seeking improvements in production processes. The key to a policy on this matter lies in the *industry analysis*, which we have urged as a prerequisite for drawing up company strategy. In a mature industry where low cost is necessary to meet price competition, for instance, R & D effort on processes may be crucial. On the other hand, newly designed products may be the primary success factor in another industry, so here R & D should focus on products.

A large chemical company used this simple but fundamental approach to sharply alter its R & D targets. For years this company had focused on tonnage production of carbon compounds. It was an efficient producer and maintained a steady position in its segment of a growing industry. Good process R & D was an important contributor to this achievement. Then the oil companies entered the chemical industry on a large scale. In terms of tonnage and low cost, the oil companies had some relative advantages: ready access to low-cost carbon inputs in the form of oil and gas and a large cash flow available for the huge investments needed for new plants. Analysis of these developments led the independent chemical company to conclude that maintaining its position in the tonnage business would probably yield a declining return on its invested capital. Prospects were brighter for complex products that produced special effects and carried greater added value. Consequently, a new strategy was adopted of gradually phasing out the heavy petrol chemicals and replacing this business with new complex products. To implement this strategy the R & D policy was sharply altered. New products became the dominant theme, whereas process research was confined to modifications of existing plants.

Adoption of the policy change just cited was no easy matter. For years the company had prided itself on being an aggressive, successful competitor. The personal careers of several of the key executives were based on this success. To them the policy change was like forfeiting a football game in midseason. Of course, the firm would continue to be a major factor in the segment of the industry these individuals knew so well, probably beyond the date of their retirement, but they were well aware that the change in the R & D policy would probably shape the character of the company in the future.

Many U.S. companies in basic industries—such as automobiles, textiles, and even electronics—are now worried about their future ability to meet foreign price competition. This concern has spurred greater interest in process R & D.

Existing Lines Versus New Lines

A decision to support product research still leaves open the question of what type of product to concentrate on. For example, a jet engine manufacturing company sticks to its existing products. It believes that the future market in this line alone is very large and that technological improvements from company R & D will be the key determinant of who gets the lion's share.

In contrast, Minnesota Mining and Manufacturing Company, makers of Scotch tape, photographic material, and a variety of other products, has achieved considerable success with R & D focused on new lines. The company does have a clear policy about the kinds of products on which money is to be spent. The emphasis is to be on products that are (1) new, (2) patentable, and (3) consumable (heavy repeat business). Here again, the R & D policy is a direct extension of the expansion strategy that this particular company has selected.

One dimension of a product line sometimes covered by R & D policy is the amount of forward integration. For instance, should a transistor manufacturer do research on products using transistors? In its fiber division, the Du Pont company has stayed away from end-products such as hosiery, shirts, and rugs. The R & D people must know enough about the subsequent processing and final consumption of its fibers to build desirable characteristics into its products, but that is as far as its R & D people are expected to go. Incidentally, when there is no clear breaking point, Du Pont does carry its research clear to the consumer level, as in paints. Nevertheless, for years the company's basic policy was to stick to chemical manufacturing. This forward limit has had a significant effect upon the character of Du Pont research and the innovations it has produced.

Process Improvements That Count

In process R & D, as with product R & D, policy guidance on where to focus attention is needed. One approach is to deal only with those aspects of production where significant savings are possible. Thus a farm equipment manufacturer turned down a proposal from its engineering department to develop a new way of heat-treating a special type of steel. Even if the project had been as successful as hoped, it would have cut total manufacturing costs only by a fraction of one percent. The company preferred to concentrate its limited resources where the potential payback was greater.

The number of units affected by a process change is also critical. A large copper company, for instance, devoted substantial effort to finding ways to improve the recovery of copper from its ore-crushing process by just a small percentage. Since millions of tons went through this process, even a small improvement in recovery could be significant. Unfortunately, a special study showed that the R & D department of this company was proceeding with equal zeal on the recovery of other metals that were produced in minor amounts as by-products of the copper operation. The study resulted in a sharper definition of what kind of process improvements to seek.

Policy defining the direction of R & D effort should provide for some degree of freedom, especially in the research stages. Many new discoveries have come through serendipity—finding one thing when looking for another. Penicillin and X ray are examples. However, an interest in bright ideas that may be unrelated to the purposes of the project at hand does not diminish the value of policy about where to put the major effort. With such policy, most of the output will be directly usable by the company. Additional insights are welcome by-products, but they should be treated as by-products.

DEPTH OF RESEARCH EFFORT

Identification of a promising research area still leaves management with a question of depth of effort. For example, does a research interest in vertical take-off planes mean that the company will undertake theoretical research in aerial dynamics or structural properties of lightweight metal? Where on the continuum from a search for new knowledge to practical specifications for a marketable product should a firm focus its efforts?

Basic Research Versus Applied Research

No company authorizes its research department to study anything that intrigues its scientists. Even basic research will be in areas related to the company's strategic mission—biochemistry for pharmaceutical companies, geology for oil companies, and the like. The issue is whether (1) simply to investigate a phenomenon without any specific idea of how the new knowledge acquired will be used (basic research), or (2) to pick a potential application of knowledge—human need—and try to devise ways of meeting this need (applied research). The distinction is like studying the geography of Central Africa just to learn more about it or to identify attractive sites for hydroelectric power plants.

Exceptional Companies in Basic Research.   A few companies have had outstanding success with their policy of doing basic research. A notable example is the work at Bell Telephone Laboratories on semiconductors. Because of a possible connection with solid-state amplifiers, Bell Labs set up a semiconductor basic research group of physicists, chemists, and metallurgists in 1946. In the process of their investigation, they discovered the transistor in 1948, and by 1951 they had developed the theoretical knowledge on which transistors with all their manifold applications are based. In passing, note that the initial effort took over five years of basic research by a whole group of scientists and that ten to fifteen years elapsed before the transistor was in widespread commercial application.

The Du Pont discovery of nylon is another classic example of where basic research paid off. Here, the research was on polymerization and by accident one of the researchers discovered that the fiber formed by pulling a stirring rod out of an experimental batch had unusual flexibility and strength. This led to a change in the direction of the research; but after two years of intensive work, the results were so discouraging that the entire project was almost abandoned. It took seven years after the initial discovery before nylon could be produced on a commercial basis. Just when this undertaking moved from "basic research" to "applied research" is hard to define. But it is clear that the basic research provided the situation in which the intitial discovery was possible.

Occasional commercial success growing out of basic research, however, does not mean that all companies interested in new products and processes should embark on basic research. In fact, most companies have concluded that the costs and the difficulties of basic research make it an unwise investment of company funds. Even large research-minded companies like Union Carbide Corporation and Monsanto Company have recently redirected their R & D efforts to applied market-oriented projects.

Policy Criteria for Basic Research. If a company is going to undertake basic research, it should meet the following criteria: (1) be prepared to take the risk of long periods of research without discovering ideas that have commercial value; (2) have a "payout" period threshold that permits a long time between investment and return (over twenty-five years elapsed between Fleming's discovery of penicillin and its large-scale production); and (3) possess enough capital to exploit discoveries when and if they are made—often millions of dollars are needed after the discovery to bring it into commercial use.

In addition to the three preceding criteria, which are essentially financial, a fourth operating consideration is usually necessary to justify basic research: (4) be sufficiently large in the industry where the discovery is applied to take full advantage of the new concept. This means that the company should have an existing position that will permit it to obtain synergistic benefits when the new product or process is introduced. Of course, a company can license or sell its patents to other companies, or it might enter a new industry in an effort to exloit a discovery it had made; but the return from such use of a new idea is much smaller than enhancing an existing market position or production capability.

Government financing of research can mitigate these rather severe criteria. In the aerospace industry and some other industries, government financing does permit a lot of *applied* research and development. To a much smaller extent, this same approach can be utilized for basic research (typically, however, government funds for this purpose go to universities or other nonprofit research institutes). Of course, government financing means that the company will not have exclusive use of the knowledge obtained, but direct access to scientists familiar with the latest developments might be advantageous for the company.

Applied Research Versus Development

If basic research looks nebulous for a company, maybe it should also back away from applied research. Instead of spending time and money in finding how to accomplish a desired end, perhaps effort could better be concentrated on developing economical methods of utilizing ideas that are already known to work.

The considerations in making this choice are similar to those just listed for basic research, but the risks here are fewer and the payout periods somewhat shorter. The main advantage of sticking to "development" is assurance that results will reinforce existing activity. Thus the outcome can be directed toward strategic objectives (new products or production economy) rather than less predictable outcomes of applied research, which at least occasionally go off on tangents.

One category of applied research has a different twist. A company may develop a store of background knowledge about a phenomenon it often confronts. Then, as specific problems are faced, the research findings expedite solutions. For instance, a relatively small company making automatic materials-handling systems frequently needed to know how different materials (flour, paint, pigment, fertilizer, and cement) flowed; any tendency to lump, dust, or bridge required special design modifications. A research project on all factors affecting the way materials in general flow created a bank of information that enabled the company to give its customers distinctive advice on materials handling. The desirability of such applied research depends, of course, on the kind of service a company seeks to provide. One oil company may study the behavior of lubricants in Arctic temperatures, whereas an oil company selling only to Midwest customers would not bother. Policy guidance, geared into strategy, on how far to push such research is needed.

OFFENSIVE VERSUS DEFENSIVE R & D

Company strategy strongly influences R & D policy in terms of its emphasis on being a leader or a follower.

First with the Best

If company strategy endorses a strong leadership position in any industry where technological change is a significant factor, an aggressive R & D program is essential. Money, time, and executive effort must be devoted toward this end.

Maxwell House Coffee, the largest division of General Foods Corporation, illustrates the price of such leadership. Having won a preeminent position in the U.S. coffee market by pioneering instant coffee, the division might have concentrated on maximizing short-run profits. Instead, the basic strategy was to retain this strong position over the long run, and this required product leadership. Consequently, Maxwell House retained a large research effort on ways to improve its product—notably to capture the aroma of freshly ground coffee. The freeze-dry method of making instant coffee was finally perfected in the laboratory and, despite the company's existing market leadership, additional millions of dollars were spent on tooling-up and introducing this new type of coffee to the consumer. Incidentally, Nestlé developed a freeze-dried coffee about the same time, and if Maxwell had not engaged in "offensive R & D" during the preceding ten years, Nestlé probably would have captured a large piece of the Maxwell House business.

The fact that a company adopts an offensive R & D policy does not, of course, guarantee a dominant position such as Maxwell House gained. RCA, for instance, spent millions of dollars pioneering in color television. It was successful in being an early entry into this vast market but other companies quickly followed, each with its own modifications, so the market has always been shared with half a dozen other leading manufacturers. Also, even a successful R & D effort, to be effective, must be combined with good production and marketing for the investment to pay off. We noted in Chapter 3 that Univac did very well with its offensive program in computer research but then failed to capitalize on its initial technological advantage.

Running a Close Second

The price of being first is high. Many firms, especially those which are not giants in their industries, adopt an R & D policy that they hope will enable them to defend themselves against advances made by competitors. The policy has two phases. First, a systematic scanning—including planned intelligence—of research effort and results by others is maintained in all fields that could seriously upset present competitive strengths. Such surveillance requires a few people of fine technical perception but does not require large outlays of money for laboratory and staff. Second, the company needs unusual competence to perform development work; its engineers must be able to move rapidly and be ingenious in devising methods of accomplishing results someone else has demonstrated as possible. The aim is to match competitors' offerings before the delay seriously upsets market positions.

Such a defensive policy has advantages. The most obvious is avoiding long, unproductive expenses for applied research and perhaps basic research. In addition, typically a new product does not work well in all its early applications; these initial problems create customer dissatisfaction, delays, and perhaps makeshift remedies. For instance, despite all the testing, a really new model of an automobile usually develops a series of weak points that require tedious trips back to the shop. If a second-runner can avoid these difficulties, it may rightfully claim it has the more dependable product. So, for that very large part of innovation that is developed by a series of modifications rather than a dramatic "breakthrough," a defensive R & D policy may not be a serious handicap.

Patents do create difficulties for the company using a defensive R & D policy. Basic patents are the serious ones because they may cut off an entire new area; for example, Hall's patent on electrolytic reduction of aluminum prevented new entry into the basic aluminum business until the patent expired. Patents for modifications or refinements are less troublesome because often the same effect can be achieved in a slightly different way. In some industries, such as pharmaceuticals and automobiles, cross-licensing of the use of patents is fairly common. Nevertheless, the possibility of a patent block is one of the hazards that must be weighed in considering the defensive policy approach.

A Varied Attack

The R & D policy does not have to be the same for all product lines. A medium-sized pharmaceutical company, for example, concluded that it could afford applied research only in two fields—tranquilizers and anesthetics. In seven other areas it adopted a defensive policy of follow-the-leader, and for two older product lines it simply continued production of established items with existing facilities, doing no R & D.

In practice, this mixture of defensive and offensive R & D created some internal misunderstandings. The need to select a limited area for concentrated research was understood, although not everyone agreed on the selections made. Confusion sometimes arose when high priority was given to intensive development effort on one side of the other lines—to catch up with competition. "Why don't they make up their minds whether to stay in that business or not? For six months, all hell breaks loose and then we lapse back into our 'do-nothing' policy." The idea that the company was playing *both* an offensive and a defensive game was hard to accept by people who found themselves shifted suddenly from one project to another. But, to the executives who wanted to get maximum return from a limited R & D budget, the mixed policy made sense.

GETTING R & D DONE BY OUTSIDERS

R & D does not have to be done "in house." As with other inputs desired by a company, the R & D results may be acquired from outsiders. This is the familiar "make-or-buy" issue.

A firm may consider the use of outsiders for several reasons. Much R & D work requires a minimum-sized effort to be effective; the minimum "critical

mass" usually consists of at least two or three scientists, some laborabory technicians, physical facilities, a flow of information and raw materials, travel money,
and overhead services. Also, while an improvement in a product or process may
be desired by an industry, the potential use by a single company may be too
small to justify the cost of the necessary R & D. Or, a company may have a
more attractive use for its funds; a quicker cash flow return will be preferred,
particularly by a company in a tight capital position. For any of these reasons, a
company may hesitate to back a proposal with its own R & D effort, yet
strongly desire the result.

Buying R & D Effort

Like preparing advertising copy, making a computer analysis, or running a
training course, R & D effort can be purchased outside the company.

Tapping Expertise of Others. In many fields, good independent research laboratories have been established to do special research for people who lack their own
facilities. The Battelle Institute, for instance, did development work on Carlson's
Xerox invention (the patent was subsequently sold to what is now Xerox Corporation). The staffs of these institutes often include a wider array of specialists
than many companies can retain on their permanent staff. Especially when a
company only occasionally needs a particular type of R & D work, temporary
access to such experts may be of great help.

Universities are a second major place to buy research effort. Occasionally a
contract is made with the university itself, but more often individual faculty
members are employed to work on projects in their special field of expertise.
Pharmaceutical companies, for instance, frequently support the private research
work of professors in the biochemistry field. The development of one of the oral
contraceptives, to cite a specific instance, was done by university professors on
sponsored research projects. Normally when university facilities are used, the
results of the research must be made public; the sponsor gains by having the task
done and being among the first to know about the results.

Joint Ventures in R & D. If a project will be of value to several companies or
perhaps an entire industry, several companies may join in financing the study.
Currently, several studies on the control of pollution are being handled in this
fashion. In some industries, such as coal and cement, a trade association conducts research for the entire industry. Incidentally, the common practice in the
oil industry of several companies sharing the cost of an exploratory well is a
variation of this general policy of joint ventures in research. In all these
instances, the research cost to a single company is lowered and frequently the
quality of research is improved; the disadvantage—which may not be serious—
is that the results of the research must be shared.

Relying on Others to Do Desired R & D

A firm's outlay for R & D can be even further reduced without sacrificing all of the benefits from such effort. This policy need not be passive; a company can actively encourage and assist work in particular directions.

Pay License or Royalty Fee. In industries where cross-licensing is an established practice, a company can make known in advance its willingness to enter into such agreements. This knowledge, combined with similar assurances from other firms, may encourage a member of the industry or an outsider to conduct research in desired areas. A medium-sized oil company, for instance, concluded that the research it could afford in refining technology was too small to keep it abreast of its competitors. Instead, it publicly announced its willingness to pay substantial royalties for improved technology developed by others. After two decades of experience, the management feels that it has been at no serious technical disadvantage to competitors and that royalty payments, while high, total considerably less than R & D efforts would have to achieve similar results. Obviously, the feasibility of this policy rests upon a prediction that licenses will be available.

Seek Foreign Licenses or Patents. Technical expertise is a significant item in international trade. U.S. companies receive over $1 billion annually in payment for their technical expertise, patent royalties, and the like. The flow into the U.S. is only about a fifth of this size, but it does reflect a potential source of technical ideas.

Often a foreign company lacks the desire or the capital to enter the U.S. market, and it may welcome an opportunity to get some additional return on its technical knowledge and designs. The U.S. company will probably have to take some initiative in working out the agreement, and it must be prepared to do considerable engineering work to adapt the foreign concepts to local conditions (just as is necessary in the reverse flow). Nevertheless, our debt to foreigners for important contributions to products ranging from helicopters to ballpoint pens indicates the potential of this approach.

Encourage Equipment or Materials Suppliers. In a number of industries, the suppliers rather than the fabricators themselves provide most of the innovation. This is clearly true of the textile industry where most R & D activity has been carried on by producers of manufactured fibers and by equipment manufacturers.

A company can encourage such external developments. For equipment, the most common practice is to place an order for an experimental model or to agree to pay a rather high price for the first two or three units of a product that meet certain performance specifications. Vast sums are spent by the U.S. government in this fashion, and most of the high-speed railroad equipment has been developed on this basis. The amount of premium a company must pay for newly designed equipment naturally depends upon the size of the market the manufacturer anticipates if the equipment works well. Incidentally, from the equipment manufacturer's viewpoint, it is getting a customer to help underwrite its R & D expense.

Similar cooperation between customer and supplier can relate to raw materials. If the materials supplier sees a large and continuing market, it will foot most of the development expense. Even in such instances the supplier often wants trial runs in actual production conditions. The user contributes its plant for such testing. In return it hopes to have an edge in the early use of the new material.

Promote Government Research. The U.S. government spends over $25 billion a year to finance R & D work. Most of this goes to defense and space projects, but the remaining amount is still very large. The pressure for use of these funds is tremendous and the allocation is based primarily on potential contribution to public welfare. However, since many companies wish to pioneer in the same directions that the government is promoting, the possibility of having government finance expensive research exists. The production of gasoline from oil shale, improved means to control injurious insects, better urban transportation, use of plankton from the ocean, and less expensive hospital services are merely illustrations of the diversity of government interest in R & D work. A company can actively encourage the government to sponsor research that may make technical contributions of interest to the company.

Of course, if a company's strategy includes seeking the government as a customer, the government may also underwrite company R & D effort. Usually this possibility is open only to companies with strong R & D departments. In this section, however, we have been exploring ways a company could obtain R & D results without having a large research operation of its own.

In conclusion, enough alternatives to in-house research have been mentioned to indicate that a company need not abandon all interest in R & D if it cannot do the work itself. Most of the possibilities for getting others to do desired research involve sharing the results. Nevertheless, when the magnitude or the duration of the necessary effort is beyond the resources of a single company, initiative in getting others to help share the load may bear fruit. Finally, a mixed policy is again possible; a company can do its own R & D in some fields and work with outsiders in others.

LIMITS ON TOTAL COMMITMENT

The wide range of possible R & D effort, which we have already indicated, adds up to a substantial undertaking for most companies. Like most budgets, when one totals all the things it would be desirable to do, the sum can be staggering. Central management has the task of setting some kind of limit that maintains a desired balance of R & D work with other activities of the company. This decision as to "how much" probably involves as much subjective judgment as any faced by central management. The uncertainty of results, what competitors will do, and the contribution of technology to long-range strategy—all are based on intuitive judgment more than on objective facts. Nevertheless, if R & D is to proceed with vigor and on an even keel, guidelines for the magnitude of the effort are needed.

Policy regarding the size of R & D commitment is usually stated in terms of the key considerations that will be used in setting annual appropriations. A useful approach is the following.

Use Percent of Sales or Gross Profit for Maximum Range

To get some kind of a handle on R & D expenditures, central managements often use "percent of sales." Sales volume does indicate the principal cash inflow of the company and thus provides a gross measure of the total annual resources from which outlays for R & D will be drawn. For example, a company with $100 million in sales can undertake more R & D than a company with $10 million in sales.

At best, this is a crude guide. The gross profit on a dollar of sales may be only 15 percent in a distribution firm compared with more than 60 percent in a pharmaceutical firm. Indirect expenses like R & D obviously must come out of the margin remaining after the costs of materials, labor, and other direct expenses are met. Consequently, it makes more sense to relate R & D outlays to gross profit rather than to sales.

Clearly, there is a limit to what proportion of this gross profit a management can allocate to R & D without eroding current profits so much that the company's financial strength is in danger. The permissible maximum depends upon the urgency of other claims upon the company's funds for optional uses. Somewhere in the range of 5 to 20 percent of gross profit—depending upon the industry—is a limit beyond which a company cannot prudently go. While imprecise, this consideration does establish the order of magnitude for the maximum R & D expenditure in a normal year.[1]

Use Competitors' Actions for Minimum Range

In technologically based industries, any company that wishes to maintain (or achieve) a particular position in the market must do enough R & D to keep up with the parade. In other words, the magnitude of the research effort by competitors sets a minimum floor below which it is hazardous to go. Such a mini-

---

[1]For an exceptional project, *new capital* may be brought into the company just to finance the necessary R & D. This is an unusual situation and goes beyond a policy for internal growth.

mum is an approximate figure. No two companies have exactly the same product line. Based on its technological forecasts, a company may decide to pursue an offensive policy with respect to some products, a defensive policy with respect to others, and the phasing out of its remaining products. Allowances must be made for differences in this mix when comparing research efforts of competitors. However, after making such adjustments, a study of competitors' actions does provide some guidance as to the minimum level of R & D that a company with given market targets can safely undertake.

Use "Expected" Profit Between Minimum and Maximum

A third way to set limits on R & D is in terms of "expected" profit. If no uncertainty were present, this would simply involve estimating the total outlays and the total incomes for each project and then, using discounted cash flow or some other appropriate procedure, computing the rate of profit. Unfortunately, both future outlays and incomes are highly uncertain. Theoretically, the decision-maker should think in terms of a frequency distribution for each of these figures, compute "expected" value, adjust for differences in time, and compute the "expected" profit. Rarely does the accuracy of the estimates justify this refined estimating procedure, but the underlying concepts can be used to size up the attractiveness of a series of proposed R & D projects.

Then, if the major R & D projects a company contemplates are ranked according to their attractiveness in terms of expected profits, a cumulative total may be computed running from highly desirable to least desirable proposals. The final step is to see where the cumulative annual expense for these projects falls within the previously established maximum and minimum. If the analysis shows that the company has an ample supply of very attractive projects to utilize the maximum that can be allocated for R & D, a strong case can be made for a policy of spending this maximum amount. On the other hand, if the company would be undertaking projects of marginal attractiveness with an outlay, say, halfway between the maximum and the minimum, then the policy should set an overall limit close to the minimum outlay. The reason for setting the combined total somewhat lower than the expected profit analysis of individual projects suggests is the optimistic bias that almost always exists in such estimates. Experience indicates that the ceiling should be low enough to encourage frequent review of projects in process so that the ones turning out badly can be dropped promptly to make room for exciting proposals that had to be temporarily deferred.

Adjust for Stability and Capacity to Absorb

Two further considerations are important in setting a limit on the total R & D effort. Some stability in the level of activity is highly desired. Effective R & D cannot be expanded and contracted on short notice. Time is required to hire good scientists and engineers, to build facilities, to establish working relationships, and to get a program underway. Consequently, central management should establish a policy that it expects to continue for several years, and the value of momentum should be recognized when changes in policy are considered.

A final factor in setting a limit is the capacity of the company to absorb the output of its R & D department. If the company lacks the capital, the managerial talent, or other resources necessary to exploit, say, two new products a year, then an R & D department that is likely to produce five such ideas is out of balance.

Subjective judgments and imprecision permeate the approach we have just outlined for establishing policy limits on total R & D commitment. Unfortunately, this is inherent in the nature of the problem. Our contention is only that the proposed approach is far better than dealing with this important subject on purely an intuitive basis.

R & D Policy of Small Companies

New venture research firms are exceptions to the constraints on R & D just discussed. For example, in office automation and in software programs for personal computers many of the new products are coming from small companies. Often one or two technically trained individuals start their own firm to *develop* products for a special niche. They simply hope that if they are successful they will be able to attract capital and other resources necessary to exploit their brainchild, or that they can license the concept to larger firms that do have the capability to utilize it.

A majority of small companies, however, lack the risk capital and talent to do much R & D. Instead, they rely on being able to buy or license new ideas that they need. For them a defensive policy is alertness to new developments in their industry coupled with a willingness to adapt rapidly. Indeed, small companies may have the advantage of greater flexibility than large firms in playing this kind of a game.

SUMMARY

R & D needs policy direction in terms of (1) targets for new products and/or processes that are important to company success, (2) the areas in which the company wishes to push back from development work into applied research and possibly basic research, and (3) the areas where an offensive effort is called for and the areas where a defensive posture makes more sense. These guidelines define the mission of R & D activities

Part or possibly all of this R & D mission can be met through the use of outsiders. So, policy is needed on subcontracting, joint ventures, licensing, and encouraging suppliers or governmental research. Here, as in each facet of the mission, a mixed response may be dictated by policy—the approach to be taken depending upon the kind of R & D being considered.

With the scope of R & D effort thus defined, limits on total resource commitments provide a third dimension. Financially, a policy maximum often is a percent of gross profit, the minimum is a sum necessary to keep up with competitors, and within this range "expected" profit of projects sets the level. The capacity of management and other aspects of organization may also set limits.

We have stressed repeatedly the need to relate R & D policy to master strategy. The R & D mission finds its *raison d'etre* in company strategy; the use of outsiders is a special aspect of the fundamental make-or-buy issue; and overall limits on R & D take their cue from strategy for the inevitable rationing of scarce resources. By interlacing strategy and R & D policy, we harness the potential of modern science to the management of an enterprise.

QUESTIONS FOR CLASS DISCUSSION

1. Fourteen years ago Xerox Corporation established its Palo Alto Research Center with a handsome budget and a promise to leave its talented researchers very much alone. The primary mission was to create the automated office of the future. Xerox wanted an integrated package capable of data storage, retrieval, and manipulation, including word processors, letter writers, graphics generators, intercoms, and duplicators (Xerox's established strength) that would revolutionize office work. The emphasis was to be on a total system, not just bits and pieces.

   The investment to date has been $150 million, and an array of innovative bits and pieces has emerged. Xerox is using a few of these—ideas for laser printers, custom chips, computer-aided design; most of the other concepts are being used by upstart companies often founded by former Xerox engineers who became impatient with the corporation's desire for a complete system. The industry as a whole has gained a lot more from the research effort than has Xerox. A total automated office system is proving to be both complex and costly. If and when Xerox does have such a system to sell, it would have a strong differential advantage in large offices. Meanwhile, returns on the R & D investment have been modest.

   Do you think Xerox is following a wise policy at its Palo Alto Research Center?

2. More people in the United States are engaged in service industries than in "production" industries (manufacturing, mining, and agriculture). (a) Do you believe as many opportunities exist for innovation in services as in "production"? Give illustra-

tions. (b) What does your answer imply regarding the nature and the directions of R & D work in service industries?

3. Five key R & D issues have been discussed in this chapter (see the list on page 173). Do similar policy issues arise with respect to *marketing* research done by a company?

4. Wendy's International, Inc. sells hamburgers, chili, baked potatoes, salads, and assorted drinks in competition with McDonald's, Burger King, and other fast-food chains. It regularly measures consumer taste preferences, and it used this data in a suit that eventually compelled Burger King to drop its advertised claim that Burger King's broiled hamburgers tasted better than the fried hamburgers sold by McDonald's and Wendy's. Should Wendy's pursue a research and development policy that does more than evaluate consumer taste preferences?

5. The Strategic Planning Institute finds in its analysis of the experience of over 1000 business-units that high R & D spending hurts profitability when the business has a relatively low market share. More specifically, the return on investment (before interest and income taxes) for firms with a high R & D-to-sales ratio is 30 percent if the firm has a high market share; but it drops to 4 percent for firms with a low market share. The drop in return on investment which is associated with market share is much less severe for firms which have a low R & D-to-sales return: 27 percent for high market-share firms and 17 percent for low market-share firms. (a) What do you think is the explanation for this impact of R & D spending? (b) What are the implications for R & D policy?

6. Several of the more innovative companies in the mobile home industry are subsidiaries of lumber concerns or metal producers. Assume that you are president of one of these subsidiaries and have been given a free hand to develop your company as you think best. In what ways, if any, would you want your affiliation with a materials supplier to influence your R & D effort?

7. The Less Developed Countries (LDCs) complain bitterly at the United Nations and elsewhere that multinational corporations do not transfer the latest production expertise to the LDCs. "Because the multinational corporations can afford large R & D investments they will continue to have a large advantage in production. That means that the big nations will continue to exploit our natural resources, and we will fall behind instead of catching up in national income per capita." How would you respond to such an argument?

8. A U.S. manufacturer of small turbine and jet engines was falling back in the race to sell engines designed for executive and commuter aircraft. Company executives believed that it had high-quality engines, but that it was losing out to the Garrett Corporation because its salesforce, its service facilities, its ability to sell on extended credit, and it supply of parts were limited since it did not have the financial strength to fund these needs. The firm sold some engines to Cessna and Beech aircraft companies, one British manufacturer, and a German-French consortium, but prospects

abroad were not good for the future—even in Europe. The company has been approached by one of the huge Japanese manufacturing and financial conglomerates with an offer to buy its unissued stock. The offer will give the Japanese firm owner-ship of 35 percent of the U.S. company's common stock and will provide all the capi-tal needed for continued engine development work as well as the manufacturing and marketing requirements. The Japanese also insist that the U.S. firm license its patents and expertise to a newly-formed Japanese company, at a royalty rate of 2 percent of the costs of goods manufactured. But the Japanese refuse to engage in a joint venture to make engines in Japan even though they foresee (as does the U.S. company) the rapid development of a Japanese aerospace industry. The U.S. firm prefers to manu-facture and ship goods because that is where it creates the value added. But it esti-mates that the probability of exporting engines to Japan will be very small. Import restrictions will prevent such sales. (a) Does the proposal have any advantage for the U.S. firm? Drawbacks? (b) Will the proposal contribute to technological develop-ment in the U.S. and Japan? (c) What stages of the processes of technological innova-tion are involved in the proposed arrangement? (d) As an executive of the U.S. firm, what is your attitude toward the proposal?

9. A small group of scientists and engineers have formed a company to design, manu-facture, and sell an atomic-powered heart pacer. Thousands of people already have battery-powered heart pacers in their chests; use of atomic energy will reduce the size of the pacer and avoid biannual operations to replace the batteries. To date the company has focused entirely on the very exacting design problems and on obtaining FDA (government) approval of the device. (a) Assuming this effort is successful, what major problems will the company face? (b) What are the pros and cons of con-tinuing the manufacture and sale of the device as an independent company versus selling or licensing the device to a large established firm already serving the medical profession? (c) If the company decides to undertake the manufacture and sale of the heart pacer, should it also continue R & D effort on other complex health devices?

10. "Tomato processors would like a wooden tomato if they could breed one, and the big canning companies want a square tomato with lots of pulp and little water. So, should we get into this business by trying to turn a wild tomato plant from the Andean mountains into a cold-resistant, domesticated edible tomato?" This is the question for Alpine Engineering Company, a regular player in the biotechnology and genetic engineering game. Altering the genetic structure of the bacteria that are har-bored by soybeans and alfalfa and that fix nitrogen from the air and turn it into food for the plants is the regular business of Alpine Engineering. The firm hopes that, within the next ten years, it can change the bacteria to be more efficient and thus improve the yield per acre of soybeans. This yield held steady over the last decade. But it is a long, long step from single-celled bacteria on which research has concen-trated so far to vastly more complicated plants. "Should we leave tomato research up to the regular plant pathologists and geneticists who work by crossing breeds through conventional cross-pollination methods? Eventually, in perhaps fifty years, they will develop a square, pulpy, wooden tomato." Alpine would need to proceed in steps: first understanding plant biochemistry, then finding ways to identify and isolate the exact gene or genes carrying a desired plant trait, then finding a way to

transmit a gene from one cell to another, then growing the plant, then getting rid of undesired effects—and so forth. Alpine, a subsidiary of a major chemical firm, can do some of this work on its own, seek government funds for some projects, attempt to persuade researchers in universities to carry out other projects, follow the work of competitors and keep up with the world of plant genetics to see how conventional approaches are succeeding. "Should we stick to legumes and then move toward self-fertilizing corn or wheat or should we start in on tomatoes? We can't do both and results in either case will be both uncertain and decades away. Much basic research will be needed in either case. One problem is just as interesting to science as the other—but maybe not to the consumer or farmer or agricultural company. Who knows what the future will bring? But to be a substantial player in either game, we have to start now, shoulder our responsibility, and stick to the task." Is there an answer for Alpine Engineering? How can it be found?

Case 8
COATED OPTICS, INC.

A lull in military orders has led to a debate about what assignments to give available engineers. "Experienced engineers are our most precious asset," says C. Barnard, president of Coated Optics, Inc. "The way we use them comes close to determining where the company will be five years from now." Alternatives being considered include frontier research for COI's own account, product refinements likely to lead to orders from customers in the near future, or study of manufacturing processes which would prepare COI to mass produce one or more of the products it now makes in small batch lots.

E. Fermi, technical director, explains: "Our company is a leader in a field of great potential. We know how to deposit an extremely thin coating of a metal or dielectric material on a surface such as glass. Such coatings are vital for lenses and mirrors in optical instruments, color filters in television cameras, solar energy collectors, laser applications, fiber optics, and many other situations involving the transfer of light or heat.

"The production process involves placing the workpiece to be coated into a vacuum chamber and allowing vaporized materials to condense on the surface. Vacuums equivalent to the vacuum in space outside the earth's atmosphere are often required, as well as temperatures which will change, say, silver or silica (sand) into vapor. By controlling these conditions, we can deposit a uniform film only a few atoms thick.

"COI was established about fifteen years ago, just when coated optics and lasers really began to take off. We have always had very able people, and have stayed at the forefront of the technology—learning as we went along. Consequently, we have a reputation of being able to do difficult, high-quality jobs for both military and civilian customers. Advanced technology is our forte.

"Normally, our customers pay us to do our R & D work. For example, NASA may give us an order for an unusual lens that they want to try in satellite communication. In a sense the customers also do our market research because they know how the surfaces we create will be used.

"Now, when there is a temporary lull in orders, as at present, I think we should experiment with new combinations. We know pretty well the new performance characteristics that will intrigue customers, so if we have some promising results to point to we can improve our chances of getting some customer to underwrite further development. I doubt that we could discover an entirely new process which could give us an exclusive patent. Trying that would be very risky and expensive. Instead, my thought is to stay a bit ahead of what our competitors can do."

E. Caruso, marketing director, says: "COI must decide what part of the action it wants. Sure, we're a good-sized duck in our pond, but it's a limited pond. My guess is that we did almost 20 percent of the $200 million total contracted coating work done last year. A few big users like Bausch & Lomb, Kodak, and Perkin-Elmer have internal departments which do most of their own work. Then we have about 100 competitors ranging from garage operators to a couple of outfits about our size. That's a lot of competitors and the number is increasing.

"Over half our work goes indirectly to the military—for lasers on tanks, infrared spotting scopes, high-power night-viewing instruments for satellites, and the like. Most of these orders are for prototypes or pilot operations, so there is a small number of any one thing. The civilian part of our business is also mostly small orders–special filters, coating of telescope lenses, mirrors for lasers, special coatings of glass tubes used in fiber optics, and so forth. There is some good repeat business here, but we are not set for the big play.

"The biggest prospect right now is the use of glass fiber optics to replace copper telephone cables. Stretched very fine (five-thousandths of an inch), a hairlike glass fiber can carry communications on a beam of light. Its capacity is thousands of times that of copper wire. Both GTE and AT&T are installing such cable, especially to carry color TV programs and computer 'conversations.' No one knows how many *miles* of such cable will be wanted soon. Also, fiber optics can greatly simplify photocopying machines, and these sell by the thousands. Owens-Illinois has a glass-coated tube which is unusually efficient in catching solar energy and might be used in hundreds of thousands of homes.

"These are just examples of big volume applications of the coating processes we know so well. The question is whether COI is going to sit on the sidelines and watch other companies take the tremendous growth which lies ahead. We should put our engineers to work figuring out where we can cut into this large-volume business. With all our know-how, it is criminal not to stake out a position where the big growth lies."

G. Atlas, production director, has a different perspective. "In the early days our organization was quite informal. Each new order would be assigned to an engineer and a few appropriate technicians to help. They would work out the necessary processing and then get the shop to run the order. If it was a pioneering job, the engineer would call on colleagues for their help and hover over actual production. On the other hand, repeat business could be quickly turned over to technicians. Our small size made it easy to work as a team.

"However, when we reached thirty engineers and maybe two hundred employees in all—half our present size—priorities on the use of equipment became real headaches, and marketing had to have more reliable information about delivery dates. So we reorganized. We now have what we call a civilian plant and a government plant (based on the kind of jobs they run). Each is fully equipped, and has its own production scheduling and cost control. Also, engineering has been split up and placed under the plant managers.

"Cost control, as well as scheduling, was a reason for this reorganization. For example, ten years ago when lasers were just getting into industrial processing, we could sell a set (2) of half-inch laser mirrors for $25. Now competition has driven that price down to $5. Sure, our costs have dropped, but not proportionately. Our margin on that kind of business is quite narrow. More and more of our orders have moved from frontier or experimental projects where price is secondary to components that a purchasing agent puts out for bids. This means the engineer on such jobs must think more in terms of lowering processing costs than making a unique product; and, the total amount of engineering charged to the job has to be low.

"If we should move into mass production, processing costs would become even more critical. Mechanical conveyors, electronically controlled pressures and temperatures, and very sensitive speeds are essential for an efficient production line. This would be a new ballgame for us. Also, at present our customers ship materials to be coated to our plant. Maybe coating—our contribution— should be done at the same place the substrate material is made. Does that mean COI should start making glass fibers or ceramics? If we are going to move into long production runs, I recommend that we do it in a separate plant with a separate group of people devoted to making it a success. And, before we make that leap, we need some solid research on production processes to know just what we are getting into."

J. Addams, personnel director, is concerned about morale of the present engineers. "We have to develop our own corps of optical coating engineers. Only two schools in the country, U. of Rochester and U. of Arizona, give specific courses in optics and they graduate only one or two coating experts a year. So we recruit physicists and chemists and help them learn on the job.

"These people are intrigued with moving molecules around, and also with working on the frontiers of technologies in optics, lasers, radar, and other fields. Sure, they also like to live in Arizona and we pay what good engineers generally are earning. But the excitement and pride in being an important contributor to a wave of new products is also rewarding. We have attracted capable people because of the prestige of being associated with COI.

"As COI grows, it is difficult to maintain the morale of the past. The reorgnization didn't help because the engineers were separated organizationally and physically. On many jobs they now feel more pressure to keep expenses down, and more time must be devoted to fitting into the production planning and control system. As a result, we have had more turnover of 'free spirits.' They often go to small competitors.

"An R & D policy which gives the engineers more chance to experiment with frontier problems would help overcome the somewhat negative reaction to the steps being taken to control costs and deliveries. If we could rotate our imaginative people onto projects where they think breakthroughs might be made, I'm sure we'd stir up enthusiasm.

"Of course, such a policy would not do much toward cutting costs or moving into what we loosely call mass production. If these latter skills are to be our aim, we need people with different interests. The focus shifts from new coating techniques to designing a system—involving machines and people—that can apply known techniques in a reliable and economical way. In such a system materials handling is just as important as coating. A few of our engineers may be able to shift their interests to system design, but that has not been their reason for joining COI. We would have to bring in some new, experienced people to spark such a development. Also our whole company thinks in terms of *physical* processes. We do use a lot of technicians, but we have never thought about the interface between machines and people in a production system."

Question

What R & D policy do you recommend for Coated Optics, Inc.?

9 PRODUCTION POLICY

Company strategy, as we saw in Chapter 5, involves effective integration of the supply of goods (or services) with their marketing. Somehow, someplace, the goods must be procured. In the preceding chapter we discussed the creation of *new* products and processes. Now we turn to key issues in buying or making all the products that a company sells.

Many firms have separate departments of purchasing and production, but the basic problems that demand attention of central management are so entwined that it is simpler to consider production policy and purchasing policy together. This chapter and the next chapter should be considered as a unit.

Although our discussion of production will deal primarily with manufacturing (the physical fabrication of products), a comparable set of problems arises in the creation of intangible services. Banks, brokerage houses, consulting firms, and retail stores, for instance, face issues of capacity, technology, make-or-buy, and purchasing that are just as vital as production problems in a factory. With relatively minor adjustments, the points raised can be applied to intangible as well as tangible "production.".

Historical Changes in Procurement Problems

For many years procurement of merchandise was the primary problem of business people. The rounding of the Cape of Good Hope and the discovery of America were actually attempts to find new trade routes. The enterprising merchants of those days were seeking products of the Far East because these products had a ready market in European nations. For centuries thereafter merchants searched the four corners of the earth for goods that they might bring back to sell in their home markets. These early merchants had some sales problems, but their major task was that of finding goods to bring to the markets.

Following the Industrial Revolution in the latter half of the Eighteenth Century, with its application of power and large-scale production methods to the processing of goods, more attention was given to the production than to the buying of goods. In the United States particularly, businesses gave their energy to exploiting natural resources, developing more efficient methods of production, and harnessing steam and electric power. Nevertheless, the dominant issue remained one of securing goods that could be offered for sale.

During the last fifty years problems confronting central management have shown a still further change in emphasis. The great increase in variety of goods produced and the improvements in transportation have compelled businesses to give added attention to marketing their wares. This increasing attention required by the marketing end of business has changed procurement problems in some respects but cannot be said to have diminished them. The production department had to move fast to keep up with the latest fads in marketing. Timely production, low costs, and quality standards had to be shifted to support new product and marketing mix strategies.

Now, the tables are turning again. Several U.S. (and European) industries are sick because their former supremacy in production is being seriously challenged. The great American automobile, steel, and electronics companies, for instance, are being underpriced by foreign competitors even in their home markets. The difficulty is not just the high cost of labor; the technology and equipment may be obsolete as well. An ability to produce competitively may again become the dominant influence in strategy and policy.

As to the future, world shortages of basic resources will raise the strategic importance of production. The supply of energy, mineral deposits, fresh water, even fresh air cannot expand to meet the accelerating rates of use. And these restraints will create other shortages. Moreover, environmental protection will slow up readjustments. In our opinion, the industrial system will not collapse, as some environmentalists predict, but resource availability and efficient use will certainly command closer attention.

Issues Requiring Central Management Attention

Production and purchasing, like other phases of a business enterprise, involve a myriad of detailed problems. At this point, however, we will focus on broad policy issues that need the attention of central management. Many, if not all, of these issues have a profound effect on the destiny of virtually every firm.

We will discuss these major production and purchasing policy issues under the following headings:

1. deciding the extent to which vertical integration is strategic
2. selecting the general processes to be used in production
3. setting total capacity and facility balance
4. providing basic guides for maintenance and replacement
5. resolving make-or-buy questions regarding services and supplies
6. selecting vendors from whom purchases should be made
7. correlating purchasing, production, and sales

We will look at the first four in this chapter and the last three in the next chapter.

EXTENT OF VERTICAL INTEGRATION

"Should we manufacture what we sell or should we buy it? If we manufacture, should we just assemble purchased parts or should we make the parts?

Should we make or buy raw materials for the parts? Should we produce the supplies needed to make the raw materials?" These are questions of vertical integration. Every firm faces them, and for many firms a sound answer is the key to long-run success.

Vertical Integration in the Aircraft Industry

The problem of whether to make or buy products is well illustrated in the aircraft industry. Clearly, Boeing will design and assemble its planes. Just as clearly, it will buy engines and navigation equipment from suppliers who specialize in those products. In between is a whole array of landing gear, subassemblies, galleys, and other equipment which Boeing could manufacture itself but typically does not. In fact, to simplify its production tasks and to draw on the most advanced ideas of suppliers, seventy percent of Boeing's material costs is likely to be outside purchases.

The Air Force, to move back one step, buys all its planes. However, the Air Force does have its own designers and testing capabilities, so it plays a more active role in overall design than, say, Boeing does in engine design. In this way, the Air Force promotes competition among suppliers and retains a high degree of flexibility in what and when it will buy.

Combining Publishing, Printing, and Paper Making

The sharp differences in vertical integration in the publishing field throw more light on the issue. Most book publishers do not print or bind their products themselves. Their printing needs fluctuate in volume; one week they may have six printers working for them and the next week none at all. Also, being free to get printing done anywhere gives them greater flexibility in the design of their books. On the other hand, contract printing is expensive. The former president of the company publishing this book, for example, often said as he passed the plant that did most of his printing, "My business made the owner of that company wealthy. But, I have enough worries already."

In contrast to book publishing, larger newspapers always do their own composing and printing. Probably this saves them money. The dominant consideration, however, is the need for very close coordination—literally down to a few minutes—between writing copy, setting it in type, proofreading, headlining, layout, and printing. And when a hot story breaks, much of the work may be redone in an hour or two. Such fast coordination can be best supervised by a single management.

Also newspapers own paper mills and timberlands. The big papers and the chains have a large, fairly steady need of a single product. Production economies are a natural result. To be sure, these same economies might be obtained by an independent supplier under a long-term contract, but some risk would remain for both newsprint producer and newspaper. So, at least those papers that predict a long-term rise in newsprint prices and that have capital for investment try to reduce supply risks by integrating clear back to the forest.

To Farm or Not To Farm

Still unsettled is the extent to which frozen food companies should raise their own vegetables and fruits. Several orange juice firms, for instance, raise most of the oranges that they use. Most firms, however, rely on local independent farmers. Farmers tilling their own land conform to the centuries-old cultural pattern; and reliance on independent growers presumes that the resourceful, close supervision of farmers over their crops will be more effective than hired management. But the frozen food packers must be assured of a supply of quality produce suitable for freezing. So they sign annual contracts with farmers well in advance of planting, provide selected seed, and offer advice. We see here, not vertical integration in the usual sense, but an arrangement with supply sources that accomplishes several of its benefits.

For poultry, however, the advent of "factories" which often process a million birds a season has led to substantial vertical integration, including genetic design, chick production, scientific feeding, and automated processing. Only the actual rearing of the birds is contracted out.

Key Factors in Vertical Integration

The examples just discussed show that a variety of factors may influence a decision on when to integrate. Among the many possible considerations, the following are likely to be key ones.

Possible Benefits Resulting from Coordination. If a company manufactures the products or the materials it needs, the promptness of delivery and adjustment to emergencies may be easier to achieve. When the parts have to fit together into a complex balance, the engineering may be more easily coordinated. Unusual quality requirements may be easier to meet. A firm knowing its own needs and being assured of continued use of equipment may develop more specialized machinery than is feasible for an outside supplier. Also, it avoids the selling expenses of an outside vendor.

Lower Supply Risks. If there is reason to doubt that raw materials will be readily available, then a company may acquire its own sources as a means of protection. For example, virtually all the basic metal processors mine their own ore, and the leading oil companies want a controlled supply of at least part of their crude oil requirements.

Mobility Barriers. Company mobility within the supplying industry affects the attractiveness of entering it—as we saw in Chapter 2. If the industry is easy to enter, its products should be readily available (or new suppliers could be encouraged); then, the incentive for a consuming company to integrate into that industry would be low. Contrarily, high entry barriers and a few dominant suppliers in an industry might create conditions where the consuming company would try to get out from under the power of those suppliers by supplying itself.

Exit barriers would become important if a company wished to abandon its integration—for example, Botany clothing giving up its woolen textile mills. High exit barriers would tend to delay such a switch, whereas low exit barriers would make withdrawal easy. Obviously, the ease or difficulty of exit affects the potential inflexibility associated with vertical integration.

Flexibility. Vertical integration tends to limit flexibility in product design. Heavy investment in plant or raw material sources hampers the shift to completely new designs or materials, whereas the firm (or Air Force) that buys its requirements is not so concerned with making a large investment obsolete.

In the short run, too, the nonintegrated firm may cut down its purchases or shift to another supplier, whereas the integrated firm must recognize the effect of such action on unabsorbed overhead. To guard against such a stultifying effect, General Motors has a longstanding policy that none of its divisions is required to buy from another division if the profit or the long-run development of the first division would suffer from doing so.

Volume Required for Economic Production. Many small companies simply cannot consider backward integration because the volume of their requirements for any one part or material is too small to keep an efficient plant busy. Also, the requirements may be so irregular that a plant (like a college football stadium) would be kept busy only part of a year. Occasionally a company builds a plant larger than needed for its own use and then sells the balance of the output to other users. Such an arrangement, however, does divert both financial resources and managerial attention from the major activity of the firm.

Financial Status of the Company. Many firms have only enough capital to operate their principal line of business and may not be in a position to acquire new capital under favorable conditions. This precludes substantial investments in manufacturing facilities for the production of parts or raw materials. On the other hand, financially strong companies may undertake vertical expansion because their suppliers are financially weak. In such circumstances, the added financial strength may permit substantial improvements in the manufacturing operation.

Capacity of Management to Supervise Additional Activities. In a great many instances, a decision to produce products that formerly were purchased means that the executives of the company are undertaking activities of a distinctly different nature from those with which they are familiar. While they can employ an executive from that industry, central management cannot escape giving some attention to the new undertaking and bearing responsibility for making final decisions regarding it. Sometimes central management becomes so absorbed in directing the new activity that it fails to give adequate guidance to the older part of the business where it has demonstrated competence.

On the other hand, if inadequate managerial attention is given to the new venture, expected savings may not be realized. Perhaps low cost will exist when production is first started because the new plant will have new equipment and the latest methods; but with only secondary attention by central management and the opiate of an assured market, there is real danger that the plant will fail to keep up with other concerns.

General Conclusion. Vertical integration decisions of the type that we have been considering in this section are of substantial significance. Each proposal should, therefore, be thoroughly examined in terms of the key factors listed, estimated ratio of savings to investment, and unique considerations such as idle plant or lack of technical knowledge. But underlying such a detailed analysis—and guiding a decision to devote time and energy to the study in the first place—should be a consciously determined disposition (policy) to move toward vertical integration or to stay away from it. Such a general policy should be based on an appraisal of what is required for success in our basic industry, the distinctive competence and resources of our company, desire for diversifying economic risks, and similar factors reviewed in Part 1. Few policies are more crucial to the long-run development of a company.

PRODUCTION PROCESSES

Closely related to decisions on what production activities the company itself will perform are choices of processes to be used. Broad issues in this area are:

1. choice of technology
2. extent of division of labor
3. degree of automation
4. size and decentralization of plants

Choice of Technology

In the production of many products the manager has no choice regarding the process to be used. For instance, a company that manufactures wallboard, using fiber of sugar cane as its primary raw material, need be in no quandary about the process to be employed in removing the small quantity of sugar remaining in the cane after it passes through a sugar mill. The only commercially practical method is fermentation. By allowing the sugar to ferment, it can be almost completely removed and the remaining fibers are than in a light and workable state. Since this is the only feasible process, the manufacturer promptly turns attention to the detailed methods and facilities for carrying out the process.

Not all manufacturers can solve their production process problems as readily as the wallboard company. For instance, small airlines that provide local feeder service to major cities must decide whether to use jet or prop planes. In the same way a company manufacturing steel must decide upon the extent to which it will use electric furnaces, open-hearth furnaces, or oxygen inverters. Stemming from such basic decisions will come a whole array of plans for equipment, personnel, methods, and organization.

Technology is not confined to physical processes. Universities, engineering firms, and mental hospitals—to mention only a sample—face similar choices. A management consulting firm, for instance, can either design standard solutions (statistical quality control, sales compensation plans, budget procedures, and the like) and adapt them to each client, or it can make a fresh analysis of each situation with no preconceived ideas about the solution. The choice here does not involve large investment in facilities, but it does affect personnel, organization, sales appeals, and other facets of the business.

A recurring issue of "production technology" in a business school revolves around the use of cases versus lecture-discussion. And in elementary education the busing of white children to black neighborhoods and vice versa is even more controversial. These examples suggest that when output and processes become more human and less physical, choice of technology has a lot of subjective value overtones.

Extent of Division-of-Labor

Practice differs among manufacturers of inexpensive dresses as to the use of the "section system." Sewing constitutes a major part of production activity, and under the older system each sewing machine operator did a whole series of operations on either the blouse, the skirt, or the other parts of the dress. The newer system has each operator do a much smaller piece of the work and then pass the garment to the next operator for another small seam. Thus, when work can be standardized and secured in sufficient volume, the idea of line production is applied. While not so called by people in industry, students of economics will recognize this as an example of the *extent of division-of-labor*.

Fine division-of-labor has been a common, and usually productive, policy in business operations since the establishment of pin factories in the early days of the Industrial Revolution. Recently it has faced two challenges—mechanization and automation of routine work, and "job enlargement" in which the duties of workers are deliberately diversified to give them more nearly a "whole" operation. In deciding how much emphasis to give division-of-labor, then, managers should weigh their policies regarding standardization of products, mechanization, type of labor to be employed, and style of motivation.

Degree of Automation

Automation is widely proposed as a way to increase productivity. The drudgery of our factories and the slowdowns in our offices, the argument says, can be removed by letting computers do the work.

In manufacturing there are degrees of automation extending from simple repetition of an operation after a machine is "set up" to an entire automated factory that is still only a dream. Among the fascinating possibilities are the following.

- *Robots* direct and control the action of a machine, telling it, for example, to pick up and position a blank, cut it to size, drill three holes in different directions, clean the part, and place it in a box. A modern robot can go beyond such multiple directions; it can change these directions for *each part*.
- *Integrated material handling and inspection* extends the robot concept to include moving selected materials to the machine, inspecting the finished part, and conveying that part to the next work station. Again, the control device has flexibility, being able to change directions as often as desired. Both the robots and materials handling can work at high speeds, with a minimum of waiting times.
- *Computer-integrated manufacturing* is a grand concept that starts with the number and description of end products desired, calls up the equivalent of engineering drawings, schedules the flow of work, and instructs the robots and the materials handling equipment. Of course, an occasional person has to drift by to pat the computer and admire the finished products sitting on the shipping platform already addressed to a specific customer who ordered thirteen of size 5, each painted fire-engine red.
- *CAD* (Computer-Assisted Design) simplifies and speeds up the designing of complex products. The computer keeps track of size and stress restraints, the design of a previous similar product, tentative decisions already made, and displays all or part of the plan on a screen in three dimensions. After successive refinements by the designer, the machine converts the plan into appropriate drawings (or tapes). These specifications can then be sent to the manufacturing system.

Flexibility is featured in all these new systems. Previously, automated production required large volumes of identical products to justify the heavy investment in special-purpose equipment. In the new systems change is computerized and available almost instantaneously, and this permits short production runs and low inventory—even though customers want individualized variations in their purchases.

Examples of all these forms of automation are in use. So the concepts are not blue-sky theory, but they still are very small clouds in the sky.

Automation is not confined to the factory. In southern United States, for instance, crop-dusting from the air, flame-throwers for killing weeds, mechanical harvesting equipment, and other power-driven machines are creating changes that alter the plantation more than the Thirteenth Amendment did.

There is a sharp distinction, however, between automation that is technically possible and automation that is wise for a specific company. The evidence on mechanization, of which automation is a part, suggests caution.

Figure 9-1 shows that high mechanization, which results in a high investment per dollar of sales, does not lead to high profits. Just the reverse occurs! Further analysis of these data by the Strategic Planning Institute suggests that mechanization usually does lower costs, as expected, but that the associated high fixed overhead creates such strong pressure to obtain volume that the savings are passed on to consumers in the form of lower prices. The competitive pressure to lower prices and obtain volume is especially severe for firms having low market share.

Consequently, any policy to highly mechanize should be accompanied by other plans which will assure the company that it will be able to retain enough of the benefits to pay for the costs of mechanizing.

Size and Decentralization of Operating Units

Large manufacturing companies have considerable choice in the size and the location of their plants. For many years, most of them assumed that the larger the plant, the more economies would be possible; transportation costs of raw materials or finished products were usually considered the limiting factors on the size of a plant. Present thinking challenges these assumptions. At least the advantages of large plants are not taken for granted.

A firm in the clothing industry has a clear-cut policy toward separation of production into several operating units. Production technology does not require large-scale operations, and the company believes the optimum size plant is one just large enough to support specialized service divisions such as accounting, personnel, and maintenance. In this case, plant location is determined primarily by nearness of consuming markets and availability of women workers—but again, not in a big city.

In some industries, such as the chemical industry, technology requires a large-scale plant. However, once a plant is large enough to use economical processes and to support specialized service divisions, there is a question whether expansion should be at the same plant or at a new location. Smaller plants, especially those in smaller communities, have advantages of closer and friendlier relations among all employees (operators and executives), easier identification of the worker with the product being produced, less bureaucracy, more face-to-face contacts in place of expensive and impersonal communication systems, executives who have first-hand knowledge of what is going on, less commuting

FIGURE 9-1.

RELATION OF DEGREE OF MECHANIZATION TO RETURN ON INVESTMENT OF TYPICAL COMPANY

(Bars on chart within each degree of mechanization show, in addition, the influence of company's market share)

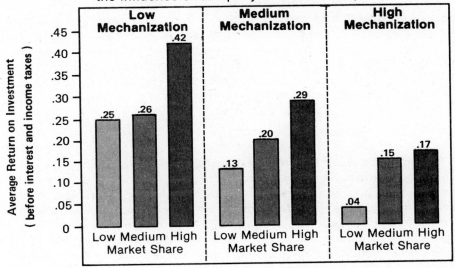

Source: Strategic Planning Institute.

time and expense for employees, and so forth. Moreover, modern means of communication and transportation have reduced the disadvantages of having several plants separated from the home office.

The dispersion of plants and offices out of urban centers contributes to unemployment difficulties in depressed areas. Recognizing the seriousness of the urban crisis, several companies are experimenting with a policy of locating some production operations in city slum areas. Initially such plants usually are high-cost units, but the hope is that the new ways of training and supervision will turn the plants into economically sound ventures. Again, small-sized plants are better suited to this policy.

A similar challenge to size of operating unit is occurring in the retail field. Most department stores now rely heavily on suburban branches for sales volume. Wide differences exist, however, in policy regarding the number and size of branches and in the range of inventory carried in each branch.

For multinational companies, the location and size of branch plants raises a fundamental issue about sourcing of production and relationships with host countries. This important topic is discussed in Chapter 23, "Managing Multinational Enterprises."

HOW MUCH CAPACITY?

Data from a variety of sources must be brought together to estimate the productive capacity a company needs. Sales forecasts of physical volume, policy decisions on what will be purchased instead of made, engineering estimates of machine productivity, and production plans on how equipment will be used all contribute to projections on size of plant needed. In addition and overriding such data are several central management policies regarding capacity desired. These policies deal with provisions for peak versus normal requirements, backward taper of capacity, provision for growth, and balance of facilities.

Peak Versus Normal Load

A completely stable level of operations is virtually impossible. All types of business activity are affected by cyclical fluctuations, and most industries experience seasonal, daily, or even hourly variations in volume of business. In addition, the demand for a company's product may increase or decrease because of wars, government regulations, inventions, floods, changing fancies of the consumer, and many other influences. Moreover, mere random distribution will lead to peaks and valleys. Management must decide whether it will provide capacity large enough to satisfy all demands during peak periods, knowing that some of this capacity must remain idle during slack periods, or whether it will maintain a smaller capacity and hope that failure to render service during peak requirements will not have unbearable consequences.

A leading example of a company that tries to meet peak requirements is found in the electric utility industry. On dark winter evenings or hot summer days, we hope to have current available at the flip of a switch. Utilities have a policy of building capacity to meet such peak demands (occasionally there are some restrictions on industrial customers). Fortunately, the demand is predictable; nevertheless, the investment made for peak needs is tremendous.

Most companies follow a policy of letting the customer bear part of the peak load burden. This is obvious to the subway or bus commuter during rush hours and to the Christmas shopper on December 24. Neither the bus company nor the retail store is indifferent to crowds of customers. They provide capacity several times their volume during slack periods. The problem is one of balancing the amount of delay and inconvenience of X percent of the customers versus the cost of providing the increment of capacity to meet the peak. Perhaps the policy will be to meet 90 percent of the requirements without delay. (When peaks occur in random fashion, queuing up theory is useful to estimate customer inconvenience.)

Other means of meeting peak capacity will, of course, be incorporated in the policy regarding maximum capacity. (1) Manufacturers of standard, durable products may manufacture stock during slack periods. This arrangement is explored in the next chapter. (2) Overtime work may be feasible for operations not already run twenty-four hours a day. (3) Obsolete or high-cost equipment may be maintained on a standby basis and placed in service just during the peak. (4) Some of the work may be subcontracted, although this is often difficult because potential subcontractors are likely to be busy during the same peak period. (5) Off-peak discounts, "mail early" campaigns, and other measures may be used to induce customers to avoid peak periods. These devices also involve extra expense and may be more or less satisfactory to customers. Clearly, policy guidance is needed to indicate the reliance on these various ways of responding to peak needs.

Backward Taper of Capacity

Vertically integrated companies may deliberately follow a policy of backward taper of capacity. Such firms normally perform final operations on all their finished products, but they manufacture only parts of their material requirements. A tire manufacturer may have its own textile mill in the south to weave tire fabric. This mill will probably have the capacity to supply only the minimum needs of the tire manufacturer. Additional fabric for peak requirements will be purchased from outside concerns. Such an arrangement has the obvious advantage of keeping the units in the earlier stages of production operating near their productive capacity. The feasibility of this policy depends on the presence of potential suppliers who are willing to supply fluctuating amounts of material.

Provision for Growth

Experience indicates that a business enterprise does not stand still. In economies or industries enjoying strong growth, time rescues executives who overestimate the capacity they need. But with a slowdown in overall growth rates, excess capacity becomes a continuing burden.

The serious consequences of too much or too little capacity have already been discussed in Chapter 2 in connection with mobility. Also, the possibility of using an expansion move as a strategic positioning device was suggested at the close of Chapter 3.

It is both expensive and inconvenient to customers and employees to have additions to facilities made at frequent intervals in piecemeal fashion. On the other hand, the financial downfall of many firms can be traced to the construction of excessive facilities, construction which absorbed a large part of the company's liquid capital and entailed annual charges that further depleted the company's resources.

Again, some middle ground is desirable if it can be arranged. Often provision for expansion may be included in the amount of land purchased and the shell of the building, while only part of the equipment is purchased initially and a work force is hired as needed. Perhaps the original plant can be used for both manufacturing and warehousing, and then a warehouse may be added later. Offices may be treated in a similar fashion. Whatever the specific scheme, the basic decision to be made by central management is how much growth to anticipate and the extent to which investment will be made now in anticipation of that growth.

Balancing Capacity

Each phase of an operation—materials handling, office processing, warehousing, selling, and the like, along with their subdivisions—has its own capacity. A recurring task is trying to keep the volume of business that each subdivision can perform about equal.

Lack of balance shows up quickly in a cafeteria line when customers stack up at the sandwich counter or the cash register. The difficulty here—and on a larger scale in hospitals, plants, and offices—is that the optimum size unit for various activities differs. Several stock brokerage firms, for instance, got into serious trouble because their optimum size selling activity was larger than the conventional "back office" (paper processing) could match. Deliveries were slow, accounts were not posted daily, and errors could not be located. To avoid catastrophe, sales had to be restricted until a new system permitted enlarged capacity of the back office.

Even if balance is achieved through careful planning, it is hard to maintain. Over time, the character of work may change, small modifications will be made in the techniques employed, and people will move about. With such shifts, some one operation becomes the bottleneck. Consequently, there seems to be a never-ending task of overcoming one bottleneck after another. On the other hand, there is the task of trying to reduce the expenses in those phases of operations where the workload has dropped off.

Most of the examples of problems with capacity have been in terms of physical facilities. Nevertheless, similar issues arise in stores, offices, and firms dealing with intangibles. How to deal with peak requirements, what provision to make for growth, and how to balance capacity are questions likely to arise in any kind of enterprise.

Integrated Systems

Often process, capacity, and make-or-buy choices are interrelated. We must look at the total system. At McDonald's and most other fast-food restaurants, for instance, the amount of work done on the premises, the way the food is prepared, and the size and location of each outlet all fit into a whole system. Similarly, in branch banking the optimum size of a branch depends partly on the technology used, and the best technology depends on how self-sufficient the branch is to be.

A specific production system is good only when it supports company strategy. McDonald's system would be a disaster in Maxime's in New Orleans.

New systems can be devised by combining the elements in fresh patterns, of course, but time is required to discover and learn the new harmony. For example, one-room schools, regional graded schools, and open-classroom schools each fit particular needs. However, if we decide to switch from one to another, pupils, teachers, and facilities all have to adjust or be adjusted. So in each situation we need a well-conceived policy for general guidelines and consistency of action.

MAINTENANCE AND REPLACEMENT

Closely associated with issues of how much capacity should be provided and the design of an integrated system are questions of maintaining and replacing existing capacity.

Levels of Maintenance

The statement "Captain Svenson runs a tight ship" conveys meaning to any sailor. It refers to much more than caulking the hull; everything throughout the vessel—engines, galleys, winches, and whistle—is kept in excellent running condition. Sloppiness and procrastination are not tolerated.

Similarly, a tourist driving through Kansas can easily tell when he or she is in a Mennonite section. The fences are mended, the barns are painted, the fence rows are weeded, and the crops look good.

Plants and offices, likewise, may be run like a "tight ship" or in a more casual and relaxed fashion. The level of maintenance results partly from the personal preferences of key executives, perhaps reflecting a cultural value inherited from their forebears. It may also reflect a calculated decision on the kind of maintenance that will most effectively support the other objectives and policies of the particular company.

Maintenance involves expense (the Mennonite farmer in Kansas works hard and long). And the "tight ship" approach may be unwarranted in, say, a sawmill located on a tract that has just been cut over. Railroads appropriately vary the level of track and right-of-way maintenance on their main lines compared with a branch line soon to be abandoned. Incidentally, railroads also accelerate or hold back on deferrable maintenance depending upon their financial condition from year to year.

Preventive Maintenance

In atomic energy plants, avoiding accidents through preventive maintenance is even more important than keeping the equipment running. In fact, the accident at the Three Mile Island plant, while involving no immediate casualties, so frightened the general public that the use of atomic energy to generate electricity was set back at least five to ten years.

Preventive maintenance has many applications, though most are less dramatic than in atomic energy or air travel. We are all familiar with this approach in the care of an automobile—regular greasing and oil changes, driving within prescribed limits, 5,000-mile checkups, prompt inspection of unusual noises or performance, and replacing tires when they are worn. Observing such practices enables us to depend on the automobile instead of wondering when we will have a flat tire or whether the motor will start.

Proper care, regular inspections, and scheduled repairs—all are designed to avoid unexpected breakdowns. The same general concept can be applied to a sales organization or an accounting office, except that here we deal with people, social relationships, paper forms, and procedures.

Again, there are questions of degree. The attention given a fire engine should differ from that given a wheelbarrow; an integrated chemical plant, from that given a roller rink. If a breakdown can be repaired quickly without serious interruption, the intensity of preventive maintenance can be relaxed.

Timing of Replacement

Routine replacement of parts of an established facility can be done on a scheduled basis. The typical trouble-free life of electric bulbs, autos, water meters, and airplane engines can be measured and replacements made regardless of the apparent condition of a specific piece of equipment. Compulsory retirement of air pilots at age 60—or professors at age 70—is based on the same logic. The replaced item may be rebuilt, but the aim is to make the change before performance falters.

Much more crucial is replacement to keep pace with modern technology— or perhaps with economic location for a revised strategy. A major cause of the current plight of the U.S. steel industry is a failure of the steel companies to keep their plants up-to-date. Japan has modernized its steel mills far more rapidly. Only the new "mini-mills" appear to have the flexibility and cost structure to effectively match foreign competition. Several other basic industries have similar difficulties.

Apparently U.S. firms should depreciate equipment more rapidly and build replacements sooner than has been general practice in the past. Doing so would raise problems of income taxes, short-run profits, and possibly cash flow. The fundamental issue is how much sacrifice of short-run gain a company should make to keep itself in top condition to meet competition in the future. It is like a baseball player keeping in good shape over the winter.

When setting its replacement policy, central management is reflecting the value it attaches to being a top performer next year and the year after.

QUESTIONS FOR CLASS DISCUSSION

1. Vertical integration has had only limited success in the men's suit industry. After several unsuccessful attempts at integration between cloth manufacturing and suit making (e.g., Palm Beach, Botany, United Merchants & Manufacturers), today no major suit producer owns—or is owned by—its sources of cloth. Experience with forward integration is mixed. Hart, Schaffner & Marx, the largest manufacturer of medium- to top-quality suits in the industry, controls about 250 men's clothing stores; these are operated under a variety of local names and they do not limit their suit inventory to goods supplied by Hart, Schaffner & Marx. In low-priced suits, however, where volume is the largest, integration of manufacturing and retailing has been a disaster. The once successful chains of stores of Robert Hall, Bonds, and Richman Brothers have all been liquidated. "Direct from the factory to you" does not seem to work in the 1980s. How do you explain this inability to integrate manufacturing and retailing of lower priced men's suits?

2. Legislation requiring tighter control on air, water, and other forms of pollution has limited processing options and added over 40 percent to the investment and operating costs of numerous manufacturing processes. New safety laws have the same effect. (a) Do you think this kind of regulation will be a more serious obstacle to large or small businesses? (b) Who will ultimately bear the added cost? (c) Under what conditions is such regulation likely to lead to significant modification in a company's strategy?

3. Among the possible ways to improve the ratio of actual operation to theoretical maximum capacity are: (a) not accepting peak business, (b) manufacturing to stock, and (c) buying goods or otherwise using idle capacity of another company in the same industry. To what extent can these three ways of reducing necessary capacity be used by: (a) a legitimate theater in which plays are presented by both a resident company and traveling companies, (b) an hotel near a major convention center, (c) a cement-block plant, and (d) a bank?

4. (a) According to the president of the Campbell Soup Company, the firm contracts for its vegetables by giving a farmer the plants and fertilizer and then setting a price

in advance for his "farming act." This is as true in Taiwan and Israel as in the United States. The farmer then performs "the farming act, not the gambling act."

(b) The president also said that the company should keep and expand its restaurant chains because they will keep the company alive. "Restaurants react to consumers tomorrow morning. If you feed them a bad dinner tonight, they don't come back tomorrow. If you give them a bad can of soup, you find out about it nine months later." He also explained that a high-priced consulting firm and the vice president responsible for retailing operations both recommended that Campbell's divest itself of restaurants because they are and had been money-losers.

Vertical integration appears to be beneficial one way, but not the other. Explain.

5. The new autos coming out of Detroit have an increasing number of electronic controls. If one of these controls breaks down, the local auto mechanic will simply replace it—if the source of the trouble can be found—because the mechanic will be unable to fix it. Assume that Ford Motor Company has asked you to devise a general plan to minimize complaints from Ford owners about electronic maintenance problems. What do you recommend?

6. Does a trend toward increasing freedom of trade among nations add to or detract from the attractiveness of vertical integration? Illustrate in terms of a company dealing (a) in shoes, (b) in lumber and building materials, and (c) in loans to commercial and industrial companies.

7. (a) The robot that is best known to the general population of the U.S. is the automated cash register used in many food supermarkets. It sees, calculates, records, and explains the bill to each customer. Does, or will, the use of this robot fundamentally alter food retailing? (b) Does, or will, the use of automated bank tellers fundamentally alter retail banking? (c) In general, what impact do you think robotics will have on retailing during the next ten years? (d) Select one or more local retail firms known to most members of your class, and explain how important you believe it is for that retailer to move quickly to the use of robots.

8. Midwest State University rarely has the capacity of its facilities in balance. One year it increases its dormitories so that it can admit more students. A couple of years later inadequate classroom space is the basis for a plea to the state legislature for new classroom buildings. When these are in place, the laboratories, library, even the gym are too small for first-class education. Is this bad planning? Should expansion take place by, say, biannual increments to all types of facilities? Is the concept of tapered capacity applicable to a university?

9. The good news is that Ultra Hydro and Machinery Company has concluded an agreement with Toygo Manufacturing of Osaka. The Japanese company is to license one of Ultra's patents and some proprietary information about making parts for hydraulic equipment for an immediate $2 million payment and then a 7 percent royalty on sales of these parts. The $2 million can be used to expand the plant of Ultra's Spanish subsidiary, which then can supply all of the parts needs of Ultra's French

and British subsidiaries and can also send some parts to the U.S. The bad news is that productivity in Ultra's Eureka plant has declined for the twelfth straight year (while productivity has been rising in Spain) to the point that the Eureka plant no longer has any cost advantage over German, Japanese, and Spanish parts manufacturers. It also has some quality deficiencies because the older machinery there cannot always hold to the tolerances required. Ultra's vice president for production is contemplating using the Spanish plant to supply all of the parts needed by the two European machinery manufacturers (rather than 50 percent as before) and using a combination of supply from the Spanish plant and the Japanese licensee to bring in parts needed in the La Jolla, Mackinack Island, Bar Harbor, and Hilton Head assembly operations in the U.S. Backward taper would be given up in Europe, but introduced in the U.S. The future of productivity gains in Spain and Japan indicates some promise of dropping the cost of parts for the U.S. plants. Shutting down the Eureka plant would decrease the maintenance expense account in the company's consolidated statement of profits and losses. Should these proposed changes in production facilities be made?

CASE 9
Black Opal Coal Company

In their long-range planning for Black Opal Coal Company, executives are considering (1) ways to meet the increase in demand expected over the next ten years, and (2) ways that will help resolve a major problem for the country as well as for the industry and the company—declining productivity. Output per worker hour in bituminous coal mining is now 70 percent of its 1972 average. Costs have risen substantially as a result. Black Opal Coal Company, like other major competitors, has lost markets and customers to both imported coal or coke and to nonunion, U.S. mines.

The Industry. Bituminous coal has, it is generally believed, a sound future in the long run. This is based upon its economic advantage in generating power over competing fossil and nuclear fuels. Total operating, fuel, and overhead costs of a utility company burning coal and using the very best pollution-control gear are about 3 mills a kilowatt hour, while the total costs of burning oil amount to about 4 mills a kilowatt hour.

The President of the United States urged public utilities to convert power plants from oil to coal. New technologies, such as fluidized-bed burning, show considerable promise in removing sulfur, ash, and other pollutants from coal as it is burned, thus preventing their escape into the air.

In the short run, there is an excess of coal supply over demand—about 75 million tons excess capacity in a market using about 760 million tons per year.

With the expected rate of growth of demand for coal at 5 to 7 percent a year and with the expected withdrawal of marginal mines from the market, the excess of supply is commonly predicted to disappear within two to three years. Tighter regulation through the strip-mine law will have an effect by eventually wiping out 50 million tons per year of Appalachian coal production.

The Company. Black Opal Coal Company (B.O.C.) has three operating divisions: Eastern (West Virginia, Pennsylvania, and Kentucky), Midwestern (Indiana, Illinois, and Iowa), and Western (Wyoming and Montana). The Western Division, at present, operates one large strip mine in Montana and has leased land in Wyoming for possible future mines. The other two Divisions operate both underground and surface (strip) mines.

An old, established firm with a long history of paying steady dividends to its stockholders, B.O.C. has these financial results: A current ratio of 1.6 to 1; long-term debt is 60 percent of total long-term debt and equity; the next profit-to-sales ratio is 5 percent (a bit better than the industry average); the turnover of total assets is 1.7 times; depreciation charged is $33 million; the current, post-tax rate of return on equity is 28 percent; and stockholders' equity is $150 million. Financial analysts call B.O.C. "very liquid, a solid performer, not likely to go up in smoke."

The company has a market share in its operating regions of 5 percent in the East, 6.5 percent in the Midwest, and less than 1 percent in the West. It has enough unmined coal in the ground to hold these market shares for 200 years.

The Opportunity. Reaching its first goal of maintaining market share east of the Mississippi River means a 35 percent increase in output over the next five years. The long-run goal is to produce 30 million tons of coal per year, one-fifth of it in the West. This will about double the present output and increase total market share by 3 percentage points.

Executives see three possible ways to increase output and productivity: (1) changing compensation of the miners to an incentive plan, (2) continually improving equipment, machinery, and production methods, and (3) expanding only by opening strip mines in the West. These three possibilities are explained in the following highlights from presentations by the personnel vice-president, the labor relations vice-president, and the West Regional operations vice-president.

The Personnel Vice-President: "We have 8 percent more people in the mines than we need just because of absenteeism.

"Eighty percent of the total tons we can produce at current productivity levels is already sold and committed for 1989. One hundred percent is committed for the coming two years.

"Nonunion mines of comparable situations to ours and whose market share has increased in five years from 20 percent to 35 percent of total production, have a 20 to 30 percent higher rate of output per worker hour.

"Tons per worker day are now 69 percent of the rate we had six years ago. Our productivity is dropping steadily. The industry was down 24 percent over the same period.

"Under the next union contract we now have an opportunity to install an incentive payment plan.

"Data from the Strategic Planning Institute (see the text, page 203) show that improving our market share and improving our capital utilization should improve our profits and return on investment.

"This is a major departure from all our past union-management relations policies and practices, so the board of directors will want to consider it. Three months after the Board's approval we can get the plan going in one mine. After one year, and necessary adjustments, it can be expanded to five mines. Then, in another year, it can be used in an entire region.

"The formula is technical but it will pay off for the miners in three ways. (1) A bonus of one percent of the hourly rate will be paid for each one percent of increase in output per worker above present standards—up to 20 percent maximum. (2) An added amount will be paid for reductions in lost-time accidents. (3) The bonus will be reduced by one percent for each percent of absenteeism—to a limit of ten percent.

"The effect on profits will be a 43 percent improvement since overhead will not increase. The bonus can be taken in cash—three weeks later—or by buying shares in any one of three different investment and savings opportunities, including the company's common stock.

"The plan is not traditional for hourly wage earners. But it will improve productivity and safety and lessen absenteeism at the mines because the workers will be aware, for the first time, of the effect of actual output results in their pay. With this plan we do not risk any investment; the only risks are lost operating time and perhaps a changed state of union-management relations."

The Labor Relations Vice-President: "My plan is to continue what we have been doing—making continual improvements in our technology which will, eventually, increase productivity. These process improvements should be focused on underground mining where the problem is. Output per worker may increase slowly, but it will be up and it will allow us to keep up with the predicted rate of growth for the industry. This method is tried and true. It has no time delay. In the near future we can extend the use of high-pressure water to cut the coal and go to emerald nozzles on the high-pressure hoses. We can complete testing of an hydraulic haulage system which uses a slurry to move the coal. We can extend further the use of the long-wall technology in the Eastern underground mines. The increasing use of machinery and the specialization and complex jobs which result match the kind of miner who now works for us—young, better educated, and very mobile. The average age is becoming much younger. These people do not want pick-and-shovel jobs. The yearly investment required will be no more than our present capital budget—depreciation plus one-third of profits.

"Our safety record is already good—9.9 lost-time accidents per million worker hours. The industry is at 37.3.

"An incentive pay plan is not traditional for hourly wage earners. The union is against it. Inventive plans were one of the major reasons behind the 1978 110-day industry-wide walkout. That cost us $150 million in lost sales and $11 million in lost profits. A strike means lost market share, damaged employee relations, and damaged plant and equipment.

"This is a high-risk area. Since the '78 strike we have had at least three wild-cat walkouts each year—one for eleven days. And fifty grievances have been taken to arbitration in one state in which even Peabody and Big Ben had no more than twenty. Strikes cost. We have to ask what will happen when we reach the output limits of our present technology and bonuses no longer rise.

"Grievances under an incentive plan will be numerous. Other problems will be numerous. The president will have to spend a lot of time deciding who is to administer the plan since both the personnel department and the mine superintendents will have to make it work. Any conflicts between the mine management and personnel will go to the president for resolution.

"I cannot see making negative investments in an incentive plan which will inevitably mean wildcat walkouts like the big one in 1978."

West Regional Operations Vice-President: "The answers to our concerns about output, appropriate technology, and productivity can be found in Wyoming, Montana, and Utah. Demand that is increasing more rapidly than it is in the East, plenty of non-polluting coal, and high productivity in surface mines are the factors that make it wise for us to open more strip mines as rapidly as possible.

"Output in our Montana mine is two to three times more productive than it is in the eastern undergrounds—35 to 40 tons per worker-day as compared to 14 tons per worker-day at best. The technology is different. Strip mines in the West resemble huge construction sites. They are capital-intensive rather than labor-intensive and use huge draglines to remove the cover and dig the coal. Transporting by truck and rail, sorting plants, and cleaning plants are all highly automated.

"Population growth and industry moves to the Sun Belt—the Southwest and the West—lie behind the increases in demand. Will these trends slow and die? No.

"Bringing in a mine in Wyoming will take no more than two to three years on land on which we now have leases. Annual output can be anywhere from one to three million tons per year, depending on how much we invest. Additional surface mines can be opened in five to six years from the time we start to negotiate leases.

"We can finance the investment of $70 per annual ton of production by using the present cash flow. In two years that would double the output of our West Region."

Questions

1. What are the strengths and weaknesses of the three proposals?
2. What goals of Black Opal Coal Company can be attained by the various alternatives?
3. As a director, what proposal do you favor?

10 PROCUREMENT POLICY

MAKE-OR-BUY SUPPLIES AND SERVICES

Every company uses a variety of supplies and services—heat, power, packaging, transportation in and out, telephone, electronic computing, and many other items. Time and again the question arises of whether to make or buy these supplies and services. The following examples suggest the nature of the problem.

Production of Containers and Printed Forms

All firms must decide whether to purchase or manufacture printing and packing supplies such as plastic containers, cartons, and seals. Large insurance companies, for instance, often have a shop in which they print their own forms, circulars, and notices, and do other job printing. While this practice is convenient, few firms have enough actual printing (not just photocopies) of a similar type to justify the most economical machine methods. Consequently, the wiser policy usually is to have such printing done by an outside firm which serves many customers.

A similar situation exists in connection with packing boxes. For example, the Taft Pharmaceutical Company, which had its own box shop, needed boxes in a considerable range of shapes and sizes for the packing of its various products. Because of the variety, several different machines were needed; however, most of these machines were used only part of the time. While the boxes made in the local shop were satisfactory, an independent check showed that it would be less expensive for the company to purchase boxes from a manufacturer specializing in this type of work. This also gave the company more flexibility to shift to plastic containers.

On the other hand, a leading manufacturer of prepared breakfast foods concluded, after an exhaustive study of the relative costs of manufacturing and of buying packages and cartons, that a considerable saving would result from its own manufacture of these products. In this instance, large quantities of identical boxes and cartons were required, and the cereal company was able to install machinery as efficient as the independent box companies'. Furthermore, under this arrangement the company was able to exercise direct control over all phases of production and to coordinate under the same roof the manufacture of the packing boxes with the packing of the final product. This same company, however, decided that its job printing could be done more economically by an outside concern.

Company Power Plants

Larger companies must decide whether they will produce their own power and light or buy all their electric current from a public utility. The policy sometimes followed in this case is to manufacture the minimum load and to purchase from the public utility only for the purpose of meeting peak requirements. Thus, the company plant can be operated continuously and the burden of fluctuating demand can be shifted to the public utility. The feasibility of such a plan depends, of course, upon the rates charged by the public utility. If the peak demand for a particular company occurs at the same time that other utility customers have peak demands, the rates charged are likely to be high.

Emergency power supply for hospitals, alarm systems, dairy farms, and the like is quite a different issue. For safety, in-house generators or batteries are needed.

Guides to Make-or-Buy Policy

The following line of analysis provides an answer to most make-or-buy questions relating to supplies and services.

1. Does a dependable outside source exist? If the answer is "no," then we presume that our own production is best unless unforeseen obstacles arise. For instance, a cement plant in Chile has its own foundry and machine shop because no reliable source of repair parts is within reach. Similarly, most large industrial plants in Argentina have their own power plants because public power is unreliable.
2. When a dependable outside source does exist, we will use it unless a strong case can be made for not doing so. The reasons for this preference include simplifying the total managerial burden, focusing executive attention where major opportunities lie, reducing capital investment, retaining flexibility regarding sources, and—in competitive markets—gaining some of the economies that suppliers serving several customers will obtain.
3. Possible reasons for making exceptions to the preference for buying, just stated in (2), are: (a) Coordination with outside sources would be very cumbersome. For example, although office buildings frequently contract for janitor service and window washing, industrial plants rarely do so because cleaning up is intimately related to plant operations. (b) A large volume of a uniform item would result in unusually low costs. (c) The supply source is unwilling to provide special services (for example, speedy delivery or unusual sizes) we desire.

This approach at least puts the burden of proof on the executive who suggests deviating from the main activities on which the firm is staking its success.

SELECTION OF VENDORS

Regardless of how a company resolves its problems of vertical integration and of make-or-buy supplies, some sorts of goods must be purchased. The manufacturer must buy raw materials and factory supplies, the retailer must buy finished goods, even the professional firm must buy office supplies. In most businesses, a number of vendors, local or perhaps foreign, are available to fill these needs. This raises the question of whether purchasing from several vendors is wiser than concentrating the business on only one or two. Even after this policy is settled, the type of vendor that will be the most satisfactory source has to be resolved.

Number of Vendors

The number of suppliers of at least the essential products purchased by a firm should receive careful attention. Entire operations of the firm can be jeopardized if this issue is not wisely handled.

Allocating Buying To Secure Vendor's Services. A school supply jobber, for instance, followed the practice for a number of years of buying from as many different manufacturers as possible so that the firm name might be widely known. The company later became involved in financial difficulties and regretted its policy of using a large number of vendors. The purchases it made from any one manufacturer were not important enough to that manufacturer to justify granting special credit terms, and each vendor sought to collect bills promptly. Had this firm concentrated its purchases to a greater extent, it might have induced its vendors to be more lenient in making collections during the period of financial stress.

Advantages and Dangers of Concentration. A few companies that buy large quantities of merchandise concentrate their purchases to such an extent that they buy the entire output of the supplier. By doing so, they are able to secure favorable prices because the manufacturer is relieved of all selling cost and is able to concentrate its production operations on just those commodities desired by its one customer. A danger in this practice is that the manufacturer may fail to make delivery because of labor troubles, lack of capital, fire, or some other catastrophe, thus leaving the company deprived of its supply of products at a time when they are sorely needed.

Also, relative power—as discussed in Chapter 4—is involved. If there is a single supplier of a vital part or material, that supplier may have a lot of power. A threat—implied or explicit—to shut off the flow of a needed resource can force the buyer to pay a high price or to accept irregular delivery. The potency of such a threat depends, of course, on the availability of alternative sources of supply.

A large mail-order house that was buying the entire output of a refrigerator plant guarded against these dangers to some degree by having at the plant its own representative who watched accounting records and was familiar with plant operations. Such a representative could warn the mail-order house of any impending difficulties. Another large firm followed the policy of buying no more than 25 percent of its requirements of any one product from the same manufacturer. If for any reason something happened to one of these sources of supply, the company would be able to continue to get at least 75 percent of its requirements from its other vendors. When buying abroad, use of several sources gives protection against political interruptions—as petroleum companies using Middle East crude oil well know.

Many firms follow a policy that seeks to gain the advantages of both concentration of purchases and multiple vendors. They find that buying most of their needs of a particular material from one source is desirable; the quality, price, delivery service, or some other factor makes concentration clearly the best arrangement. So, they give 70 to 80 percent of their business to one vendor. The remaining part of the business is divided among several other suppliers. In this manner, business relations are established, specification problems are met and resolved, and the way is prepared for much larger purchases at a later date. Placing these small orders with several vendors is probably more expensive than buying all requirements from the chief source, but it serves two important purposes: (1) If a strike, fire, or other catastrophe hits the main supplier, the firm can shift to other suppliers much more quickly than it could if no relationship had been established; and (2) the main supplier is "kept on its toes" because the buyer is in close touch with the market and in a position to shift to other suppliers if the price, quality, or service from the main source does not continue to be the best.

Buying Distress Merchandise. Some retail stores appeal to their customers primarily on the basis of price, and in order to make a profit they continually seek to buy merchandise at "distress" prices. These stores usually offer to pay cash for merchandise, and they ar not particularly concerned about being able to secure additional products from the same company. Such stores will deal with any vendor who has merchandise to offer for sale at a reasonable price, and they are continually "shopping around" for more favorable terms. Although such a policy appears to be good for companies operating on a purely price or cut-rate basis, most concerns have learned by experience that it is preferable to cooperate with vendors. A cooperative relationship will not be disrupted by either party because of apparent temporary advantages that may be obtained from time to time under special conditions.

Factors Determining Number of Vendors. These illustrations show that there are both advantages and disadvantages to limiting the number of vendors from whom purchases are made. It is often necessary to balance the advantages of better service and quantity discounts that can be secured by concentrating business with a few vendors against the disadvantages of possible failure of supply and the passing up of occasional bargain merchandise. The problem often resolves itself into the following questions:

1. Can a limited number of vendors supply the variety of products required?
2. How much special service and price concession will result from concentration?
3. How important is such service to the purchaser?
4. Is the company too dependent upon any one company for materials?

Type of Vendors

The type of vendors selected by a company will depend on the company's requirements in regard to quality, service, reciprocity, and price.

Importance Attached to Quality. Selection of vendors by a company will be influenced, in part, by the quality of the products that it wishes. Thus a publishing house, desiring all its books to be made of a high-quality material, buys only from mills that make paper of dependable quality. Although paper is purchased according to detailed specifications, every paper mill has some difficulty controlling quality. The publishing house therefore prefers to pay somewhat higher prices to those mills that have a reputation for exercising care in maintaining the quality of their products.

Even a product that is highly standardized and that has a recognized market price may be purchased from one vendor rather than another in order to secure certain intangible qualities. Operators of textile mills, for instance, point out that considerable variation occurs in the way raw cotton of identical staple and grade will work up in cloth. Consequently, when a textile mill discovers that cotton coming from one region through a given broker is more easily handled on its equipment, that mill will try to concentrate its future purchases on cotton coming from that particular section.

Service of Vendors. Vendors may be selected because of the service they render their customers. For example, companies manufacturing computers, duplicators, and other types of office equipment often give their customers a great deal of aid in designing office forms and in establishing new systems. Most of these companies also maintain an extensive repair service; if a machine should break down, it can be quickly repaired without serious interruption in the work of the office using the equipment.

The importance of such service became striking in Brazil when that market was flooded with relatively inexpensive office equipment of German manufacture. The machines had entered Brazil under a barter agreement in which Brazil exchanged coffee and other raw materials for a specified quantity of machinery from Germany. Inadequate provision had been made for servicing the German machines, however. Consequently, when one of these machines broke down, it was both expensive and time-consuming to get it back into working order. As a result, many of the office managers were turning to more expensive American machines because of the repair service maintained by the American manufacturers.

Under some conditions promptness of delivery is a controlling factor in the selection of vendors. This has been one of the primary reasons why small steel companies have been able to secure in their local territories business that otherwise might have gone to the big steel companies. With standardized products and uniform prices prevailing in the industry, such special services as delivery often become controlling influences. The large companies have recently given more recognition to this factor and have spent substantial funds in an effort to expedite the handling of customers' orders.

Reciprocity. Under special circumstances vendors are selected on the basis of reciprocity. Thus, railroads are careful to place orders with concerns that are in a position to route a large quantity of freight over their lines. Sometimes the reciprocity may be a three-cornered deal. For instance, a Great Lakes steamship company decided to place a large order for motors with a particular manufacturer as a favor to a pig-iron producer. The pig-iron producer shipped large quantities of ore and could therefore demand favors from the steamship company in exchange for a contract to transport ore. To complete the circle, the pig-iron producer used its controls over the order for motors in selling pig-iron to the motor manufacturer. Hence, each of the three concerns selected vendors with an eye to the indirect effect such selection would have on sales.

Formal reciprocity agreements have been challenged legally as a restraint of trade, but this aspect is very cloudy. Much more common is the objection of "professional" purchasing agents. In fact, a policy on reciprocity is often necessary to keep peace between the purchasing department and the sales department.

Role of Price. Thus far, no mention has been made of price in connection with the type of vendors. Prices for many products are uniform, and for other products the differences are not of sufficient importance to offset such factors as quality and special service. It should be clear, however, that price is an ever-present consideration, and if for some reason one vendor charges higher prices than another, the former is automatically eliminated unless there is some special reason for dealing with that particular vendor. As already noted, the significance of differences in prices depends partly upon the emphasis that the company buying the material gives to price in reselling the material and also upon the importance of that particular product to the total cost of the company.

Gifts and Friendship. Especially when large purchases are to be made, gifts and lavish entertainment may be offered to the person who selects the vendor. In its gross form this is clearly bribery. But the line is hard to draw; for instance, is a free lunch unacceptable? While not so strict as government on rules regarding favors, most companies do have a clear-cut policy forbidding the acceptance of any significant gifts from vendors.

PART 2   Defining Major Policy

More subtle is the question of friendship. Business relationships naturally lead to numerous contacts and mutual dependence—as we noted in Chapter 1. Friendship often grows out of such contacts. And cooperation between friends typically flows in both directions. The principle that we assume should guide business relations between friends is clear enough: cooperate to the hilt as long as the interests of the two companies are compatible (and such action is legal), but when interests conflict always give one's own company uncompromising priority. This norm is so widely understood it is rarely stated as a policy.

Summary Regarding Selection of Vendors

In selecting vendors a company is responding to the *sales appeal* of the numerous companies desiring to sell merchandise of the type used by the company. The point of view, however, is essentially different because the purchasing company is concerned only with its own specific problems and has no interest in the sales activities of the vendor unless these activities are of some value to it. There are also a number of questions, such as the number of vendors that do not have an exact counterpart for the seller. The more important factors that should be considered in making vendor selections are indicated in Table 10-1.

TABLE 10-1.
FACTORS INFLUENCING VENDOR SELECTION

Capacity and Willingness of Vendor to Meet Company Needs	General Characteristics of Desirable Vendors	Factors Limiting the Choice
Quality of Product: Specifications Dependability	Size of vendor: Interest in our business Financial stability	Reciprocity Time and expense of locating and dealing with new vendors
Services offered: Delivery Technical aid Repair Credit terms Guarantees Adjustments	Geographic location: Support of "local" industry Dispersion of risks Manufacturer *vs.* jobber	Habit and conservatism; potential "headaches" in new relationship Friendship and loyalty
Price: Competitive level Inclination to squeeze Protection on changes	Maintenance of alternative sources: Divide equally One main source, others minor	Willingness of using departments to try new vendors

Company policy determines which of these factors should be given primary consideration and which should be disregarded.

COORDINATION OF PRODUCTION, PURCHASING, AND SALES

Even after policies regarding integration, capacity, processes, procurement of supplies, and selection of vendors are clear, a cluster of problems on *timing* of purchasing and production remains. We are concerned here not with specific programs—a topic explored in Chapter 20—but with several underlying guides that must be established before programs can be built. As a basis for coordination of purchasing and production with sales, central management should set policies regarding:

1. procurement "to order" or for stock
2. minimum inventories
3. size of production run or purchase order
4. stabilization of production operations
5. adjustments in inflationary periods

Procurement "to Order" or for Stock

The Made-to-Order Policy. Coordination or procurement with sales is accomplished in some industries by buying or making goods only if the customer's order is already received. The purchase of raw materials and supplies is not undertaken and production is not started until the order is actually in hand. Manufacturers of heavy machinery almost always follow such a make-to-order policy.

Other companies, such as producers of radio and television broadcasting equipment, make finished products only "on order"; but, in fact, they produce many parts and even subassemblies for stock. Then when an order is received, only the final assembly operation has to be done according to customer specification.

Firms that manufacture high-class upholstered furniture may follow the same policy to even a lesser extent. In this industry, it is customary to manufacture the furniture up to the point where the upholstery is to be put on. This final covering is not applied until a specific order is received from a customer designating the kind of cover desired.

While a policy of making-to-order does reduce inventory risks and gives customers just what they want, it also has serious drawbacks. Delivery is inevitably slow and costs tend to be high because mass production techniques cannot be fully utilized.

Carrying Stock. The majority of products are purchased or produced long before the customer's order is received. Orders are filled from inventory already on hand. This is true of most of the products that we, as consumers, purchase, and it is also true of a great many products purchased by industrial concerns.

A compromise policy is followed by some firms that carry only standard products in stock. If their customers want an article that is not standard, the merchandise will be purchased or produced according to the customer's choice. For example, a shop dealing in dinnerware and glassware may carry an open stock of certain popular patterns. Should a customer wish other patterns, the manager of the shop will be glad to order them from the factory.

Since there are various degrees of making-to-order and of carrying stock— as the preceding examples show—and the degree affects purchasing, production, and selling activities, management should provide policy guidance. This is not a decision to be made from the viewpoint of any one department alone.

Minimum Inventory

If stock is to be carried, a company must establish some general guide to assist the purchasing and production departments in determining how much inventory to have on hand at any one time. Let us look first at the more mechanistic aspects of the problem—ordering points, size of production runs, and purchase quantities—and then note two main reasons for further adjustments, namely, stabilization and speculation on price changes.

How low should inventories be permitted to go before they are reordered? Each retail store in a modern grocery chain, for instance, is expected to maintain a minimum of all items regularly sold. Since the store gets frequent deliveries of additional merchandise, the minimum may be only a week's supply. In contrast, because of slow turnover the minimum inventory carried by many independent furniture stores is equal to a full year's sales.

Manufacturing firms must establish some general policy for minimum inventory for both finished goods and raw materials. Thus, a company manufacturing rugs had a policy of carrying finished merchandise only at the beginning of each selling season and gave no assurance to its customers that it would carry an inventory throughout the year. On the other hand, it did wish to carry a minimum stock of raw materials so as to avoid possible delay in production operations. Here the policy was to carry approximately three months' supply of yarn and other raw materials.

A general rule for finished merchandise is that the stock level at which replacements will be ordered should approximately equal the sales of that merchandise during the period required for replenishment. Thus, for stock that can be replenished within two weeks, the reordering point would be approximatly two weeks' sales. If it takes three months to procure new inventory, then the minimum at which orders should be placed would be correspondingly higher.

The same general idea can be carried back into the inventory of raw materials. Of course the rule does require estimates of future sales and of the speed of procurement, and these may be quite unstable.

Since the sale or the use of stock on hand will continue during the period of replenishment, it is customary to add a reasonable margin of safety to any such reordering point as a protection against contingencies. The size of the safety margin will depend upon the likelihood of delays in getting replacements and the seriousness of the delay to production operations or customer service. These considerations lead many firms to follow a policy of carrying a minimum inventory much higher than strict interpretation of the replenishment rule requires.

An intriguing mix of these factors affecting minimum inventory is the Japanese concept of "just in time." Here, parts or subassemblies are delivered to a plant that uses them just when they are needed for operations—but no sooner. In a few plants, deliveries are made two or three times a day—timed almost like waiters serving a five-course meal at the Waldorf-Astoria Hotel. The obvious beauty of this scheme is that investment in raw materials is almost zero. A more subtle benefit is the discipline necessary to make the plan succeed; the pace of work at the plant must be predictable, the quality of delivered parts must be very reliable, the ability of suppliers to deliver exactly what is needed *just in time* must be assured. This kind of disciplined behavior tolerates no sloppiness; it is likely to be efficient. But note that most of the headaches—and inventory cushions—are pushed back onto suppliers. The suppliers' costs probably rise, and who actually pays this bill depends on the relative bargaining power of the using plant and the supplier.

Size of Production Run or Purchase Order

When reordering is necessary, how much should be ordered? Primary considerations are the cost of carrying inventory—just noted—and economical production runs in a company's own plant or quantity discounts offered by vendors due to economic production runs in the vendor's plant or warehouse.

A company producing printed plastic bags for bakeries and candy companies, for example, found that the cost of preparing plates, setting up plates in the printing presses, threading the proper weight of plastic film through the presses, and making other preparations necessary for actual printing was often a substantial part of the total expense incurred on small orders. It was found that labor and idle machine charges were often $200 per order, and when this cost had to be charged to a few hundred bags, the cost per unit was quite high. If the order was for several thousand, the expense could be spread over the entire order and thus the cost per unit could be lowered.

To meet this situation, the company often printed more bags than were actually on order by the customer, thereby securing a low production cost per unit. The extra stock was then held until the customer placed a reorder. This policy substantially increased the company's inventory but was the only way that the company could secure satisfactory production costs.

Policy regarding size of purchase orders, like policy regarding size of production runs, may be stated in total quantities or in so many weeks' or months' supply. Then order standards for specific items may be computed, giving effect to economy of large lots, cost of storage, perishability and obsolescence, and related factors.

The judgment of central management is needed to establish safety margins on receipt of goods and to evaluate the seriousness of disappointing a customer. These judgments are often stated as policies. Moreover, management may choose to modify statistically optimum schedules (1) to stabilize production or (2) to adjust to price changes.

Stabilization of Production

The business of every company fluctuates by seasons and by cycles. For example, a firm manufacturing electric blankets may find that it sells two thirds of its products in the last half of each calendar year, and a company manufacturing gloves may find that it sells 45 percent of its products in the last three months of the year. Even articles in daily use, such as cosmetics, have a seasonal fluctuation.

Production for Stock. Faced with such a seasonal fluctuation, a company may decide to synchronize procurement with its sales volume so that it will not carry inventory in excess of its sales needs at any time. Most women's shoe manufacturers, for instance, do not attempt to produce very far ahead of the season in which they will sell their shoes. Style changes may make shoes produced in advance of a season unsalable or salable only at a reduced price. But, unfortunately, seasonal production means unstable employment.

Other firms produce at approximately a level rate throughout the year. This means that they accumulate during the seasons of slack sales an inventory to satisfy demand during the peak periods. One of the leading manufacturers of skis follows this policy to avoid having an idle plant during part of the year and to keep a group of efficient workers employed the entire year.

Theoretically, a similar policy of production stabilization could be applied to cyclical fluctuations. But few companies have financial strength to do more than stretch out a product for a few months while looking for a prompt recovery in sales. (The massive stabilization programs undertaken by the federal government for agricultural products involve resources far greater than any company possesses.)

Any company that considers producing during slack periods for sales in later boom times must reckon with obsolescence, deterioration, storage costs, and financing. Fully as important is the ability to forecast the duration and the amplitudes of downswings and upswings. Even seasonal drops are difficult to interpret during the downswing because a manager usually cannot tell *at the time* how much of the change is random, trend, or seasonal. So, an important aspect of a policy to stabilize production is how long production will be maintained above sales—or how large an inventory will be built up—in the face of below-normal sales.

Other Ways of Dealing with Fluctuations. Production in excess of demand during slack seasons is not the only way companies have sought to adjust to fluctuations in sales volume. Making products that have complementary seasonal fluctuations is one possibility. The combination of motorcycles and snowmobiles is an illustration.

Subcontracting at times of peak demand has been used by some companies in place of a temporary expansion in their own work force. This is not always practical, however, since subcontractors are likely to be busy just at the times when the prime contractor has a peak load.

The automobile industry changed the date for bringing out new annual models from the spring to the fall in an effort to level out seasonal fluctuations. A large number of people prefer to buy new cars in the spring of the year. When the new models were brought out at this time, there was a double incentive to buy during the months of March through June. By changing the time of introducing the new models to the fall, the companies shifted some volume from spring to fall.

These methods, like almost all stabilization devices available to private enterprise, apply best to seasonal fluctuations and have only limited application to cyclical changes.

Adjustment in Inflationary Periods

Many companies adjust their purchasing and production schedules in anticipation of changes in prices of raw materials and finished products. When price increases are anticipated, goods will be procured in excess of immediate requirements; when declines are forecast, inventories will be reduced. In this way the companies hope to secure additional profits. This practice is so hazardous—and yet in inflationary periods so necessary—that the elements involved should be separately evaluated.

Total Inventory Position. Exposure to inventory price risks involves commitments as well as physical goods in the warehouse. Firm orders to purchase entail just as much price risk as goods in-house. On the other hand, firm orders from customers with fixed prices are an offset against goods on hand. The amount of exposure is the net total of these commitments and goods on hand. In fact, a company making products such as aircraft, which are ordered several years in advance, may have a negative inventory exposure. When we establish policy regarding inventory price risk, the focus should be on net exposure.

Case Against Speculation. There are three main reasons why merchandising, manufacturing, and nonprofit enterprises should not vary the size of their inventory in an attempt to buy-low-and-sell-high. First, it detracts from the primary function of the enterprise, and most managements have all they can do to accomplish their primary mission. Second, every enterprise is exposed to a wide variety of risks that cannot be avoided; it is desirable to try to minimize these risks rather than add others. Third, someone within the company who has exceptional price forecasting ability should resign and concentrate all his or her talent on speculation. Perhaps this person can join a trading firm where speculation is part of the mission.

This injunction against speculation is generally accepted. But it applies to the more extreme situations, and it leaves unresolved a lot of inventory variation that most managers insist is not "speculation." These remaining price risks arise directly from performing the regular business. The question is how to deal with them prudently.

Assuring Uninterrupted Operations. Availability of goods often fluctuates with price. At times of rising prices, demand is brisk and it may take twice as long to get delivery as is necessary when business is dull. Consequently, purchasing agents who are responsible for having an adequate supply of inventory on hand may buy ahead in boom times just to make sure that they get goods on time. On the downswing, prompt deliveries are easier to get and the purchasing agents may safely cut back their inventory.

Thus, in times of material shortages—and these are likely to occur during a period of general inflation—a company quite properly protects itself by building inventory. However, there are practical limits because some inventory may become obsolete—due to changes in style or engineering specifications—or may deteriorate as do many food products and sensitive chemicals. Also storage and other carrying costs may be quite high. These factors place an outer limit on the physical supply it is practical to hold. But within these limits, inventory accumulation is desirable if it is needed to assure uninterrupted operation.

This kind of inventory buildup is not really an anticipation of price changes. The underlying reasons for expansion and contraction are so entwined with price fluctuations, however, that they are difficult to separate. The motive is availability of supply, but an accompanying side effect is exposure to inventory price fluctuation.

Known Risks of Not Buying. Interwoven with problems of having inventory when needed are adjustments to "known" price changes. Sometimes suppliers announce price increases in advance of an effective date. Clearly, when this occurs, a company should buy its future requirements as far ahead as it is practical to store goods.

More common are situations where the odds are, say, 80 percent that prices will rise in the near future. For instance, the supply may be known to be tight, a labor contract providing higher wages has just been signed, prices of competing products have already gone up, or the world price may have firmed. And there is certainty the price will not fall in the near future. Under these conditions a firm is assuming greater inventory price risks from not buying than from buying.

Limits on Exposure. Inventory buildup for the two reasons just discussed— assurance of uninterrupted operations and reduction of "known" risks—should be subjected to one other influence. A company's total risk posture may place constraints on the amount of inventory risk assumed. Overall business uncertainties usually set a time span beyond which it is dangerous for a company to cover its specific needs. Just as we consumers don't buy an oil filter replacement that our car is likely to need two years hence, there are limits on how far ahead a company has full confidence in its detailed projections. In turbulent periods the possibilities of an international monetary crisis, war, overthrow of the government, drastic government intervention, or comparable events may make firm commitments beyond six months unwise. Under more favorable conditions management may feel reasonably confident about the shape of events for a year or more ahead. Regardless, then, of specific expectations about a particular material or part, management often sets a general horizon beyond which commitments should not go.

Likewise, as we shall see in Chapter 12, the scarcity of capital may require a company to set some limits on the total sums tied up in inventory.

Summary. A strong case can be made against out-and-out speculation on inventories—except for a trading company organized for such a purpose. Nevertheless, especially in periods of inflation, adjustment of inventories in anticipation of external shortages and price shifts may be prudent. An approach to this troublesome issue is (1) to focus on inventory necessary to assure uninterrupted operations—within the practical limits of holding such inventory. In addition, (2) inventory may be built up when the price outlook makes the risk of not doing so quite high. Here, again, the inventory is confined to future operating needs. Finally, (3) the accumulations for either 1 and/or 2 should be restricted to a general commitment horizon and financial allocation set by central management.

Conclusion Regarding Timing of Procurement

In producing and in buying, wide differences exist in anticipating customers' actions or waiting until orders are in hand. Many companies carry larger stocks than are required for customer service to secure economic production runs or to obtain discounts from vendors. Sometimes the procurement of merchandise is adjusted in an effort to stabilize production operations, but more frequently it is adjusted in anticipation of price changes or to assure adequate supply.

The more important factors that an executive should consider in dealing with such timing issues include:

1. customer requirements for specially designed merchandise or for prompt deliveries of standard merchandise
2. economies possible from larger production runs
3. economies that may be secured from level production, including maintenance of a well-trained labor force, more complete utilization of facilities, and possible reductions in tax burdens
4. expenses of carrying goods in inventory, including the storage charges, the financial cost, the insurance expense, and the possible deterioration or obsolescence of merchandise
5. accuracy with which price changes may be predicted
6. accuracy of prediction of the volume and nature of products demanded at a subsequent period of time

This list, though incomplete, does indicate that the timing of procurement is a complex problem. Central management should provide policy guidance in this area because actions will affect the company's ability to render good customer service, influence its operating costs, change its circulating capital requirements, and bring about special losses due to adjustment in inventory valuation.

SUMMARY

Every business enterprise will face many of the production and procurement issues discussed in the last two chapter. There is the inevitable question of "make-or-buy," and this applies to the whole range of finished products, parts, supplies, and raw materials used.

Production processes must be selected, and here policy regarding division of labor, automation, size of plant, and process research is needed.

Then comes the issue of how much capacity. Plans for meeting peak loads should be set up. Provision for growth, balance between departments, and backward taper of capacity also have to be fitted into the general scheme. Guidance on the level of maintenance and on replacement should be correlated with product line, customer service, and financial policy.

For goods to be purchased, policy dealing with the number and the types of vendors is necessary. And there are basic issues of when and how much to buy and to produce.

In this array of issues we are concerned with the company's basic strategy for generating the goods and the services that its marketing strategy requires. Each part of the total production plan should support the other and also should be consistent with personnel and financial policy—to which we now turn our attention.

QUESTIONS FOR CLASS DISCUSSION

1. Ed Tripp and Oscar Stone became good friends long ago when Ed, a paper salesman, helped Oscar get his first job in a book printing shop. Their families spent vacations together, and recently Oscar's son married Ed's daughter. Oscar is now superintendent of the greatly enlarged printing plant. Ed is retired but his daughter is an active, successful sales representative for the same paper company. A year ago the printing plant was acquired by a multidivision corporation which has a centralized purchasing department. Now the purchasing department is challenging Oscar Stone's practice of buying over half of his paper requirements through his daughter-in-law. They say, "Buying from close relatives is contrary to corporation policy. Besides, you are too dependent on a single source." Stone responds, "Our long association with the paper company is an asset. They have gone out of their way to fill our needs in good times and bad. It makes no sense for you to start shopping around among unknown and even foreign sources just because of the marital choice of the sales rep of our long-standing supplier." Should the corporation's policy prevail?

2. In several Far Eastern countries, the local culture calls for the sending of substantial gifts to individuals (often part owners) who place large orders with a company. These are regarded as expressions of friendship and tokens of appreciation. What should be the policy of a U.S. company with a branch in such countries (a) if it is buying goods or services? (b) if it is selling goods or services?

3. Which of the factors listed in Table 10-1 do you think should carry the most weight in the selection of vendors by (a) a men's clothing store, (b) a franchised steakhouse, (c) the buying agent at the headquarters of Hospital Corporation of America, which owns and manages scores of small and medium-sized hospitals throughout the United States, (d) a computer store, and (e) your city government's buying agent for desks, files, typing paper, and pens?

4. Most discussions of stabilization of production, including that in this chapter, accept fluctuations in sales and consider ways of adjusting production to those sales. An alternative approach would be to set the production volume—at a stabilized level—and consider ways of adjusting sales to production. The second approach (widely used in Japan and in Chile and Zambia in the copper mines) enables companies to provide stable employment and helps maintain the gross national product. Would such a practice be socially desirable in the United States? What would companies have to do to operate in this manner?

5. Shortly before its collapse, W. T. Grant Company—a nationwide retail chain selling clothing, housewares, toys, luggage, and related items—put two pressures on its store managers: (a) increase annual profits, (b) keep the inventory-to-sales ratio low. One way store managers avoided reducing their profits was not to write down the book value of unsold merchandise carried over into the new year. A secondary result of this practice was to increase the proportion of old (carried-over) merchandise available for sale during the new year. The restraint on total inventory meant that the more dollars that were tied up in old inventory the less fresh inventory could be purchased. With a limited array of fresh merchandise, sales volume tended to drop. Do you think W. T. Grant was following a good inventory policy? If not, what should have been done?

6. (a) At what point should company policy bar the acceptance of gifts and entertainment from vendors: lunch at a local restaurant, golf game at an exclusive club, three-day technical seminar at a comfortable inn, Christmas calendar, bottle of Scotch, electronic watch, theater tickets, mink coat, opportunity to invest in Florida real estate, assistance in getting son a seat on a booked-up plane flight, employment for Uncle Ben, $10,000 to a pet charity, $50 bet at favorable odds, or you name it? (b) Should the company policy be the same with respect to company bankers? union leaders? advertising agents? customers?

7. (a) A Wall Street analyst says: "During a period of inflation the smart person owns things, even if it means going into debt to do so. A company has an even better built-in opportunity to own things and should buy inventory to the extent of its financial capacity." Do you agree? Why? (b) How should a company take advantage of inflation?

8. At one time, universities often operated their own farms to provide vegetables and dairy products to their dining halls for students. (Students often had part-time jobs on these farms.) Why do you think a "make" (instead of a buy) policy of this sort has largely disappeared?

9. A student organization run by the dairy management specialists in the College of Agriculture of a large, Western university sells ice cream and cheeses once a month to raise money. The students make their own ice cream but buy the cheeses from vendors in the state of Wisconsin—almost 2,000 miles away. Why would the students do this? Why not buy cheese locally, or from vendors in the state of Washington or from Switzerland and Holland? Why not make the cheese themselves?

10. One of the Big Three automobile producers in the United States buys about 50 percent of its auto parts from outside suppliers. Its purchasing policy includes manufacturing almost every part it uses in its own plants but only to the extent of about 50 percent of the volume of items needed by its assembly divisions. The costs of manufacturing these parts are checked carefully against suppliers' prices. The company buys from no more than two outside suppliers of each part and attempts to see that its purchases make up at least 25 percent (and preferably 50 percent) of the suppliers' sales volume. The automobile company also insists on daily delivery of its purchases

and, in a few instances, on delivery three times each day. It also insists that its quality assurance inspectors be allowed to visit suppliers' plants at any time unannounced and that quality inspectors from the suppliers visit the automobile company's assembly plants regularly. (a) Explain the purpose(s) of these policies and practices. (b) Explain the relative power of the buyer and supplier. (c) Relate your explanations to Figure 4-1 on page 73. (d) Do these practices lead toward cooperation, trust, and cordiality or toward competition, suspicion, and adversary relations?

CASE 10
McFadden's

Chris McFadden must decide soon how much reliance to place on a single source of men's suits. He has just signed a lease that will more than double the selling space of his menswear shop in the Park Plaza Shopping Center, so the time for "exploring" is rapidly coming to an end.

"I'm the third generation of McFaddens in menswear. Working weekends in the family shop on Peach Tree Boulevard taught me about the merchandise. Then my six years with Cluett Peabody, mostly on the road selling shirts to retail stores, opened my eyes to recent trends in retailing and taught me what to do and what not to do in buying inventory and designing displays. That experience is invaluable for running my own shop, but this move into suits is different and tough—and frankly I'm a bit scared."

The McFadden family business had always been in men's furnishings—shirts, ties, socks, sweaters, belts, rainwear, and sports clothing for golf, tennis, swimming, and the like. For years that shop has had a good middle-class clientele in its suburban area. However, the suburb is now mature, with the population shifting to lower income classes, and sales in real terms are slipping.

When Chris decided that he wanted to run his own business, he and his father agreed that the Peach Tree location had limited growth possibilities. In contrast, the new shopping center about five miles away was flourishing. While the shopping center draws people from a much wider area, the McFadden name still could be some help to a shop there.

The new McFadden's in the shopping center belongs to Chris. It is his creation and it reflects his flair for merchandising. In effect, he has two boutiques—one featuring ties and dress shirts and a second featuring sports ensembles. The rest of the merchandise—a line similar to his father's—is displayed along the opposite side and the rear. Something seasonable is used to generate interest at all times.

For a newly established men's furnishings store, the shop is doing quite well. The displays in the boutiques convey a feeling of zest and liveliness. Shoppers do drop in, and repeaters are building up. But competition in the shopping center comes from the two department stores, a general clothing store, a large store that sells Hart, Schaffner & Marx suits, and two specialty shops. With all this company, Chris is earning only a modest income.

Suits are a normal addition to the lines of goods Chris now carries. A full range of men's clothing has the possibility of synergy in advertising and of selling more to customers once they are in the shop. Unexpected availability of space adjacent to the present good location forced the issue. After talking to suit manufacturers—and considerable agonizing—Chris signed up for more space, which will make the addition of suits possible (and necessary).

Chris explains, "Not many customers who stop in for a tie will buy a suit, but we do expect benefits the other way. People who look at suits are good prospects for furnishings. Besides, more people will know about McFadden's and that always helps.

"I don't want to stress the overlap too much. The suit business is a big jump for us. It will double our overhead and should be fully self-supporting. My hesitation comes from not knowing the suit business as well as I know furnishings, which I grew up with.

"Fortunately, there are plenty of suppliers to buy suits from. Overcapacity is high in manufacturing. Actually, because of a change in living styles and a population drop in first-suit-buyer age range, the production of suits in the United States is declining—down from 19 million in 1960 to 15 million in 1980 or something close to that. Several big manufacturers have gone bankrupt. The industry is quite volatile; entry and exit is easy, and today very few producers try to do their own retailing. All these trials and tribulations of the manufacturers make them very courteous to guys like me; they'll even buy me a free lunch.

"My policy choice really boils down to this: shopping the market each season or signing up with a big supplier who will treat me as a special customer. On the second alternative, Rapid-American looks like the best bet. They have several well known brands—MacGregor, Botany, Worsted-Tex, Stein Bloch, and others. If I agree to be what they loosely call a 'franchise' they will give me exclusive use in this and the nearby shopping center of any two of their brands. Also, they promise help in selecting a balanced inventory, preferred treatment on deliveries, a coop advertising plan (rather limited), and an attractive deal on seasonal credit, especially during the first year.

"The reason for Rapid-American's interest in me is to give Hart, Schaffner & Marx some more competition in the Park Plaza Shopping Center. Hart, Schaffner & Marx indirectly owns our leading apparel store, and the department stores here sell mostly private brands. This makes it difficult for Rapid-American to get any representation. Of course, I'm still an unknown in the suit business and would have to show results, but Rapid-American is full of enthusiasm about the combination of my merchandising with their products.

"Now, everything is fine and dandy during the courtship; the real question is how will we get along after two years of marriage? Will Rapid-American give me the help I need, or will they load me up with merchandise that will have to be sacrificed at the end of each season? Will they put so much pressure on me to increase the sale of suits that the furnishings business suffers? How sure am I that their styling will be as appealing as Hart, Schaffner & Marx's in this locality? What happens to me if my turnover is low and they pull out after two years?

"A more cautious approach for me is to make the rounds each season of, say, a dozen manufacturers in New York. I could find out what everyone was pushing, and then make my own judgment about the colors, hues, weight, weaves, and styling that would sell in our location. Experimentation would be easier.

"Because McFadden's is new in suits, we do need at least some known brands on the racks. Otherwise, I have to take on the Hart, Schaffner & Marx boys on a price basis, and that doesn't fit with our present image. Fortunately, competition is keen enough so I can get suits with good brand names even when I shop around, though not the 'reserved' patterns.

"This shopping around is the way I buy many of my present lines, and it helps give the shop a bit of distinction."

Question

What purchasing policy for suits do you recommend for Chris McFadden?

11 HUMAN RESOURCES POLICY

Every enterprise requires labor inputs. Survival depends upon continuing cooperation of the men and women who convert resources into services. Moreover, any strategic redirection of a company's mission is possible only if human resources can be focused on the new tasks.

When central management turns its attention to mobilizing human resources, three underlying issues are always present:

1. Will the necessary labor force be available? More specifically, what must the company do to develop the number and type of workers needed to carry out its proposed strategy?
2. Can the company afford the cost? Are the satisfactions—monetary and others—that may be necessary to attract and retain such a workforce within the company's ability to provide?
3. Can viable relationships with unions representing the workers be maintained?

In addition, an array of problems bearing on the effective use of labor must be confronted: organization design, motivation, informal relations are examples. But these are largely internal matters. We will deal with them briefly in Part 4, and a large body of "organization behavior" literature is available on various aspects of internal relationships. Our focus here is on the company's boundary looking outward, on mobilizing human talent suited to the specific strategy that a company hopes to pursue.

Because of its importance, executive personnel is discussed separately in Chapter 19. Here we will deal with policy guides covering personnel as a total resource.

SELECTING AND DEVELOPING PERSONNEL

Each person has distinct abilities. Each job has particular duties. One must fit the other. For convenience, we often talk of labor in general, but within that broad resource highly individualistic matches with jobs are essential.

Skills Matched to Strategic Requirements

Are Suitable People Available? A large labor pool is only a start. During the Great Depression, for instance, millions of people were looking for work. However, it was a very unusual group of refugees from Nazi Germany who had the exceptional intellectual skills and training which enabled them to become the founding nucleus of the New School for Social Research, an unusual graduate school in New York City. Or, to note another educational example, the Nigerian government has both funds and desire to build a full-fledged medical school in the northern city of Kano. But there are not yet enough trained medical professors available to make more than a small start. In each example, suitable personnel became a key to the execution of strategy.

Finding Pools of Talent. A company may have to move to find qualified workers at competitive wages. The scarcity of laboratory personnel in the U.S. has forced several pharmaceutical firms to shift parts of their research work to Europe. The movement of textile firms to Korea and Taiwan reflects a search for cheap, though dexterous, labor. Publishers have located part-time editorial staff in middle-class suburbs.

This searching for more favorable sources of labor is similar to marketing executives looking for attractive niches for products. The aim is to establish a strong position before competition becomes tough.

Adjusting to a Changing Labor Market. Of course, sometimes it is practical to modify company operations to fit available labor. For example, for years a drug wholesale company followed a policy of hiring high-school graduates to staff its large warehousing operations. These people stacked, marked, and kept track of the thousands of different items involved; assembled orders for prompt delivery to retail druggists, priced the order, and computed the bill; kept track of back orders; and helped maintain records needed for buying new stocks. High-school graduates were found to have the accuracy and the dependability required, and at the same time they did not find the highly standardized operations offensive. The more energetic employees became supervisors, sales representatives, buyers, and sometimes, branch managers.

The company now finds that most of the more able and energetic high-school graduates go to college. Efforts to use men and women who want a full-time job while working their way through school have shown unsatisfactory results because many of these people become bored with their routine work. So, some modification in hiring policy clearly was called for.

A modification in the *structure of jobs* was the first move. Instead of assuming that everyone would have a basic competence to perform a variety of tasks, the work has been more sharply graded in terms of reading, writing, and arithmetic skills. This permits relaxation of the high-school graduation requirement. Also, more minorities have been hired even though some are weak in desired basic skills at the time of employment. This new type of employee is given intensive training on limited tasks. Turnover is high during the early months of employment, but out of the group come a significant number who can do the simpler tasks well and quite a few who quickly move on to the more skilled jobs.

In addition, provision has been made for hiring a few college graduates and moving them rather quickly through various operations with the expectation that they will qualify for buying, selling, or supervisory jobs.

The revised policy has some disadvantages. It is more difficult to move people from task to task to meet peak requirements. More significant, lost is the feeling that everyone starts out on an equal basis and progresses to more difficult positions on the basis of demonstrated merit. Even though it is now possible to move up through the hierarchy, and some people do, new employees enter the company at different levels. This generates an undercurrent that some people—because they are lucky enough to get more education—continue to receive favored treatment.

How Much Provision for Growth? Communications Systems, Inc., is a growth company centered around some patented devices that transmit and receive multiple electronic messages. These devices are particularly well suited to handle communications between branch offices and a centralized computer. The company founder and president, however, regards the equipment merely as the base from which all communications systems can grow. Among the possibilities already worked on are central inventory control of multiple warehouses, central payroll records for all branches of a state government, logistic systems for the Air Force, a nationwide bidding system for commodity exchanges, and complete integrated data processing systems for business firms.

With these possibilities in mind, the firm expanded rapidly. Its stated personnel policy was "to attract the best brains in the country." The glamour of the company's objectives enabled it to hire both theoretical and applied experts in systems design, communications equipment, computer technology, and in the activities to which the systems might be applied.

The match between the mission conceived for the company and the kinds of people employed was excellent. But serious difficulty developed in terms of the rate of growth. Communications Systems was employed to make a variety of pilot studies, but full-scale applications proved to be complex and costly. Concepts such as national bidding on commodities require legal and institutional changes that probably are decades away. The result was that many members of the high-powered staff became frustrated. The high morale in the early stages turned to internal criticism and disappointment with lack of personal advancement. Since many of the people employed were indeed very capable, they began taking other jobs. Turnover accelerated. Hiring mistakes during the intitial expansion became conspicuous because these individuals were less able to find other jobs and so tended to stay with Communications Systems. The company is still in business, but it now has a poor name rather than a good name in its particular labor market.

Hiring policy has a quantitative as well as a qualitative aspect, as we clearly see in the preceding example. While it was an extreme case, other companies have discovered they moved too fast in the right direction. (It *is* possible to have too many bright MBAs.) Excess inventory of talented human resources is both hard and expensive to keep in storage.

Constraints on Selection

In addition to policy guides regarding types, sources, and numbers of employees it intends to attract, each company must decide how it will cope with "thou shalt not" laws.

Hiring, promotion, and discharge of employees are surrounded by increasing government regulation. Equal opportunity for blacks has been extended to other minority groups. Women likewise are guaranteed explicit rights. Discrimination on the basis of age and compulsory retirement ages have been outlawed. And the list is increasing.

In each of these areas there are past injustices to be corrected and worthy social goals to be achieved. The perplexing challenge for managers is that the new laws, and regulations supporting them, are inconsistent, and no consensus exists on how rapidly the "equal opportunity" norms are to be evident in various occupations and levels of organization. Preferential treatment must be given to blacks, women, and other under-represented segments of society; but such preferential treatment may involve reverse discrimination against other individual workers. Or to cite another example, jobs retained by elderly white males block the promotions of younger women or blacks.

Broadly speaking, companies can respond to these—and similar—issues in one of three ways. *Minimum compliance* just to stay within the law is a short-run option. Meanwhile, several of the inconsistencies and uncertainties may be resolved. Conscientiously carrying out the *underlying intent* of laws is the second alternative. Here a company seeks to move with changing social norms. It recognizes that changes are appropriate and tries to be a good citizen. *Pioneering* is a third possibility. This involves being a leader in social reform, perhaps to the extent that favorable ties to particular segments of the labor market will become a "differential advantage."

Reliance on Internal Development

Interwoven with decisions on who and where to hire are questions about "promotion from within." One source of specialized talent is to "raise your own." This is like the "make" option in make-or-buy policy regarding materials.

Companies vary in the degree that they expect to fill better jobs and managerial positions by promotion. General Motors, like the wholesale drug company referred to earlier in this chapter, relies almost entirely on internal sources. Such a policy, of course, requires a company to do a lot of training if people are to be fully prepared for new assignments. And in fact, General Motors has the equivalent of a college, the General Motors Institute, for this purpose. Training on the job and horizontal transfers are even more important. A major hurdle in such internal development of personnel is the lack of opportunity for injecting new ideas, especially when a company's external environment is turbulent.

The primary factors in choosing between "raising your own" versus "hiring seasoned workers" include, first, the probable length of employment. Industries such as construction or the theater, which work on relatively short projects, typically assemble the talent needed for immediate purposes and leave the task of training to the individual worker and to other institutions. Staffing of government contracts in the space and defense industries largely falls into this category. Of course, any company that undertakes to enter a difficult industry on a large scale lacks time to do very much training. Second, the existence of well-established skills or professions affects the need for in-company training. Thus, printers, doctors, and welders are usually hired as experienced individuals. By comparison, if the work of a particular company is primarily unique, internal training is necessary to assure the skills required.

Companies that are technological leaders in their field are always faced with a problem of training people who then go to work for competitors. A substantial number of engineers and sales representatives in the computer industry, for instance, have been trained at IBM expense. If a company's strategy is to be a leader, it should anticipate not only the cost of overcoming the pitfalls of a new product or process, but also a personnel development cost. Moreover, the company will probably have to be a leader in compensation and supplemental benefits in order to keep its turnover low.

DESIGNING A REALISTIC COMPENSATION PACKAGE

Recruiting and developing personnel, as we just saw, focuses on the inflow of a vital resource to the company. The other side of the coin is an outflow of compensation that will retain this talent. And as noted in Chapter 1, this outflow must be of a size and nature that the company can afford to pay.

An attractive job includes a whole set of factors: the work itself, future opportunities, security, status, hours and working conditions, fringe benefits, as well as monetary compensation. The ability of a company to provide most of these attractions depends especially on two conditions we have already stressed: (1) An economically strong business is crucial. No personnel policy or government regulation can be a substitute. Security, growth opportunities, status, and many other benefits are possible only when a company has a sound strategy well executed. (2) People must be well matched to the jobs they hold. Individuals vary and jobs vary. Unless a good fit is achieved, the employment situation will be unstable and probably unsatisfactory.

Assuming that these preconditions are met, there will still remain important issues about both direct compensation and supplemental benefits.

Level of Pay

Relation to Prevailing Rates. Many firms simply decide that they will pay "going rates" for each occupation or level of job. Such a policy seeks to neutralize pay as a competitive factor. Employees will have to be attracted and motivated in some other way.

Paying above the market is an alternative that has popular appeal. Here a firm may seek to get the "cream of the crop," to give customers distinctive service, or perhaps to reduce turnover. Of course, if too many companies are prepared to pay above the average, the policy loses its distinctiveness (and the actual average being paid keeps moving up). Moreover, unless the company's technology gives it low labor expenses relative to the total, or unless it has some offsetting cost advantage, a high wage policy cuts into the company's ability to attract other kinds of resources.

Few firms admit that they consistently try to pay less than market average, but it is an option which suits some situations. A small, remote firm drawing from a local labor pool is a convenient place to work; commuting time and expense are low. Or the enterprise may offer offsetting attractions, such as prestige (working for the leading bank in town) or service opportunities (hospitals). Also, if a company does not need high skills its wage rates may look low when, in fact, it is paying reasonably well for what it needs.

Keeping up with Inflation. Pay rates are not viewed just in terms of comparable jobs elsewhere. They also have a history. What is good pay today depends on what was paid last year. Especially during inflation these historical comparisons loom large.

Periodically raising wages to match increases in living costs is a straightforward basic policy. Its application, however, raises prickly problems. Accurate and acceptable measurement of of relevant price increases is not easy. Leads and lags become important; in Brazil, for example, real wages fell during a period of 50 percent inflation per year simply because the indexed adjustments lagged a couple of months behind actual price raises. By no means least important, a company's selling prices and hence ability to pay often does not rise as fast as living costs. Commitment in advance to match cost of living increases could (and has) forced companies to shut down. A popular compromise is to commit to matching cost of living increases only up to a maximum percentage per year; this is widely known as a *cap* on cost of living adjustments.

Internal Alignment. Workers—from janitor to president—are also sensitive to how their pay compares with their fellow workers. Because internal alignment is such an emotional issue, most companies have an explicit method for setting differentials in pay within the organization. The usual technique involves job evaluation to place jobs into standard pay grades, and establishing a fixed relationship between grades.

A serious drawback to such schemes for internal alignment is inevitable inflexibility in recognizing outstanding performance of specific individuals. Attention to equity—equity that can be proven objectively in this age of government regulation and union surveillance—tends to stifle recognition of individual merit. So in setting a policy of maintaining fair internal alignment, each company must also consider how it will reward its stars.

As with other policy issues, central management should attempt to find a compensation policy that gives positive support to company strategy. Just the opposite effect is all too common. The combination of trying to keep payscales in line with external rates, make some but not catastrophic adjustments for inflation, maintain acceptable internal alignment yet reward outstanding performance, observe government regulations regarding discrimination, maintain maximum permissible increases, and keep those fast-track MBAs happy—all becomes so complicated that compensation can be a hindrance rather than a help in pushing for selected goals.

Supplemental Benefits

In today's labor market every company must offer supplemental benefits that are at least in line with general business practice. These benefits typically provide for (1) paid vacations and holidays; (2) protection against risks of illness, unemployment, premature death, and old age; and (3) social and recreational activities. Incidentally, the cost of these benefits plus the company share of social security taxes often exceed 25 percent of an employee's base pay.

The basic policy question is whether merely to follow general practice as it develops or to take the lead in one or more of the various areas we noted above.

Sharing the Costs of Pioneering. The company that pioneers in liberal pensions, early retirement, or guaranteed annual wage may find itself at a competitive disadvantage because of high costs.

One policy is to have the employee share the cost of a new benefit. This has been done for medical insurance, pensions, and even recreational activities. In addition to cutting cost, an advantage of this arrangement is that most of us prize those things for which we have made some sacrifice. Thus, employees may appreciate major medical insurance more if they contribute to its cost.

Employee Expectations. Not so long ago all regular employees expected to work at least half a day on Saturday. Now, an employee who doesn't get a 2-day weekend feels abused. The attitudes toward other supplemental benefits follow this same pattern. Consequently, if a company expects to generate strong employee enthusiasm because of its supplemental benefits, it must be prepared to keep adding new ones.

Also, what interests an employee shifts over time. The automobile and television have radically changed the social structure and the recreational patterns at the place of employment. Suburban living segments a person's life. Added purchasing power permits diversified and dispersed recreation. Living patterns diminish the feasibility of mutual family assistance. Government aid reduces the tradition of self-dependence. Because of such changes as these, a supplemental benefit that was heralded a generation ago may generate little excitement today. Consequently, leadership must be sensitive and imaginative.

Showing Genuine Concern. Mayo found in his famous Hawthorne studies that the employee's belief that the company was concerned about him or her as an individual was more important than the particular actions the company took. This insight suggests that supplemental benefits cannot be passed out with the assumption that the employees will be grateful. A policy of pioneering in this area must be accompanied by other demonstrations of genuine concern about the employee as an individual. Organization, personnel development, and supervision—discussed elsewhere in this book—are all part of the picture. In the proper combinations they give synergistic effects.

Coordinating Supplemental Benefits with Operations. For reasons just outlined, central management must carefully analyze the particular operations of its company when deciding which supplemental benefits to stress. Generally speaking, companies that want to hold their employees over long periods and have low turnover will probably find their employees more responsive to supplemental benefits. In contrast, companies that use many part-time employees or have wide fluctuations in employment, as in the space industry, are more likely to find their employees saying, "Put it in the pay envelope." Location in or outside a big city will also affect the social and recreational activities that are attractive to employees. The general age of employees is still another factor. In personnel, as in marketing or research, being a successful pioneer requires keen discernment.

INDUSTRIAL RELATIONS

For managers and employees to work together to accomplish the objectives of an enterprise, they must agree on wages, hours, and other conditions of employment. For many years these agreements were made primarily between managers and individual employees. Even today, over two-thirds of the employees in the United States bargain individually with their employers. However, negotiations with powerful labor unions often receive wide publicity, and agreements reached with such unions set the pattern for many of the individual agreements.

Some people contend that the existence of a union makes the objective consideration of human resource policy futile. The assumption is that if management is not entirely free to make final decisions on such matters, the alternative is an irrational patchwork of agreements based on the bargaining surrounding

each issue. Such a view is both unrealistic and unproductive. The manager
designs products in terms of what customers will buy, sets prices on the basis of
competition and within the limits permitted by law, and buys materials and borrows money under terms negotiated with the supplier. The views and strength of
the union will, of course, influence the personnel policy finally established, just
as the operating situations influence other policies. But the fact that the decisions
are not made by the manager alone does not remove the desirability of a workable, integrated plan of action. The need for unemotional, careful analysis
remains unchanged.

Policy regarding the selection and the development of a work force, compensation, and supplemental benefits has already been discussed; consequently,
we will concentrate here on the way relations with unions are conducted. In this
connection, a company should establish its policy regarding:

1. character of union relations
2. scope of bargaining
3. recourse to outside agencies

Character of Union Relations

A key aspect of all union relations is the underlying approach of a company
to its relations with the union. The following examples illustrate the wide choice
and the importance of this policy.

Belligerent Policy Towards Unions. Companies engaged in interstate commerce
are required by federal law to bargain with unions that represent a majority of
their employees. Similar state laws require collective bargaining by most local
businesses. Nevertheless, some employers balk at union activities whenever possible and do anything in their power to weaken the union.

Such a policy usually stems from a conviction that unions are antisocial. It
may be supported by experiences with corrupt union officials, or communist-led
unions, or unions that fail to live up to their contracts. Whatever the causes,
there is strong dislike and mistrust of the union by the company executives.
They try to conduct themselves so as to discredit the union in the eyes of the
employees. They hope that sooner or later the employees will repudiate the
union and it will no longer have to be recognized as the bargaining agent.

Obviously such a militant policy keeps the union stirred up; it will probably
continue to use defiant tactics in its organization efforts. At best there will be
only an armed truce between the two factions.

The Horse-trading Approach. Another view accepts the union as being inevitable but anticipates that relations will be conducted along horse-trading lines. The
union is assumed to be unreliable and conniving; consequently, negotiations are
conducted in an air of suspicion and sharp bargains are quite in order. In keeping with this approach deals are made that resolve immediate difficulties but that

violate sound principles of human relations. As one advocate of this policy said, "It is just a question if you can outsmart the other guy."

Follow the Leader. Often smaller companies try to establish an understanding with the union that the company will grant any wage increase or fringe benefits that have been agreed to by the leading companies of the industry or in the local market. These firms feel that they are too small and weak to stand out against the union. The most they hope for is to be no worse off than their large competitors.

This is undoubtedly a practical policy in some circumstances. It does, of course, have the weaknesses of any policy of appeasement. Naturally, the union is going to ask for, and probably get, the most favorable clauses that are granted by any of the leading companies. Having won these points, the union leaders may ask for even more, particularly if they face political problems within the union and feel they must win further concessions to strengthen their own position. Moreover, one important way a small company competes with a large one is by making special adaptations to the local situation. The follow-the-leader policy sacrifices this potential strength insofar as industrial relations are concerned.

Straight Business Relationship. When both company executives and union leaders take a mature view of their relations, a company may approach union negotiations as a straight business proposition. This can occur only after union recognition has been accepted and the bitterness so often associated with such activities has passed into the background. There is mutual confidence, respect, and trust, just as there should be between the company and its major suppliers of raw materials.

This sort of business relationship does not mean that there will be no disagreements. The company may take a firm, even tough, position on certain matters; but the positions it takes are based on long-run business considerations, and there is a strong undercurrent of sound human relations.

Company executives must recognize that union leaders hold elected offices and that at times they must press grievances simply in response to pressure from some of their constituents. Under the straight business policy, this does not create a strong emotional reaction but is regarded simply as a normal part of the relationship. This type of relationship is often found in industries that have been organized for several years by a union which itself is stable and follows a bread-and-butter philosophy.

Union-Management Cooperation. Still another policy is to regard the union as an ally in improving the efficiency of the business. One of the best examples of union-management cooperation is the agreement developed over a generation ago between Hart, Schaffner & Marx and the union representing its factory employees. The union recognized that the company was in a highly competitive industry; consequently, it helped make improvements in labor productivity. On the other hand, the company acceded to demands for higher wages and better hours.

From the start there was emphasis on settling disputes by arbitration. The arbitrators have been highly respected individuals and always insist that questions regarding interpretation of an agreement be examined objectively. Even more important than wise administration of fixed agreements, however, are the methods developed to deal with technological and economic changes in new agreements. The actual operation of the plan has required a great deal of patience. Nevertheless, there is substantial evidence that employer and employees alike have benefited by the spirit of cooperation and tolerance created by working together under such circumstances.

Union-management cooperation has taken different forms in the steel industry and in other places where it has been tried. In some cases a sharp distinction has been made between cooperative activities at the plant and bargaining over a new contract. In other instances, as in some agreements in the hosiery and ladies' garment industries, plans for improving productivity have become part and parcel of the basic contracts. Whatever the form, the important point here is that the company followed a basic policy of union-management cooperation.

The foregoing illustrations, ranging from a belligerent policy to union-management cooperation, are among the more common policies followed in union relations. Of course, many other variations are possible. Until a company formulates some kind of policy on the character of its union relations and gets this policy thoroughly accepted through its executive ranks, there is little hope for consistent and really effective industrial relations.

An unusual development in union-management relations is management's resort to bankruptcy as a way of abrogating its former union agreement. For example, when Continental Airlines got into serious financial difficulties in 1983 its management said that continuing operations would be possible only if employees accepted large pay cuts and larger workloads. The union disagreed. So, for this and other reasons, Continental went into voluntary bankruptcy. This move opened the way for a fresh start in union-management relations. Note, however, that Continental management immediately faced a new choice of union relations policy within the range we have just discussed. The fresh start did not remove the policy issue.

Scope of Bargaining

Recognition of a union does not, of course, indicate what activities are to be covered in the union-management relationship. By tradition and law, questions of wages, hours, and physical working conditions are normal subjects of collective bargaining. More recently, employee pensions and similar benefits have been added to this standard list. Most companies would also agree that job assignments, the use of seniority or other factors in selecting employees for layoffs or promotions, and other supervisory activities were legitimate subjects for discussion, although they might firmly oppose any written agreement as to how these matters were to be handled. As soon as discussions extend beyond these traditional subjects, questions arise as to whether the union is interfering with "management prerogatives."

Employees clearly have a real stake in the stability of their company. Their income and their economic future are strongly influenced by the prosperity of the firm for which they work. If the union function is to protect the workers' interests, is it not reasonable then that the union should participate in decisions regarding pricing, new customers, product line, and similar matters?

This line of reasoning led unions in postwar Germany to insist on membership on boards of directors and other means of codetermination. With a few exceptions, American unions have shied away from such arrangements. Union leaders have recognized that if they participated in such decisions, they would share responsibility for them. By staying away from such matters, they avoid managerial responsibility and continue to be in a position to criticize (a significant weapon in union politics).

While neither union nor management leaders want unions to become involved in the entire managerial process, it is likely that an increasing number of topics will fall within the orbit of union-management relations. Unions can be helpful on such matters as absenteeism, productivity, and installation of new processes. They are concerned about changes in plant locations and mechanization.

Some firms follow a policy of keeping unions as far away from such matters as possible. In other cases, such as union-management agreements on mechanization of hosiery mills and contracting in the garment industry, union contracts deal with what typically are regarded as management matters. A more common and more flexible policy is to restrict the formal collective bargaining process to conditions of employment and to work out other matters of mutual interest in a much more informal manner.

Recourse to Outside Agencies

Union-management relations are not confined to an individual company and the unions representing its employees. Other parties may enter the picture, and a company will do well to clarify its policy on recourse to outside agencies.

Impartial Arbitration. Most union contracts provide for arbitration of disputes over the interpretation and the application of the contract. Typically, a dispute follows a grievance procedure moving up from the worker and the first-line supervisor through several administrative levels. If the matter cannot be settled by management and union representatives, an impartial arbitrator is called in to make a decision that becomes binding on all parties concerned.

Some such provision is necessary if strikes are to be avoided during the period of the contract. Where a single impartial arbitrator has been used over a period of years, a sort of "common law" develops. Once this common law becomes accepted, many potential disputes are settled without reaching the arbitrator. Many companies take the position that minor disagreements can be worked out best by the parties directly concerned, and they follow a policy of minimum use of outside arbitrators.

Group Bargaining. The negotiation of a new labor contract is quite a different matter than its interpretation, which has just been discussed. The distinction is like that between the legislative and the judicial branches of the government. Usually the company itself works out the new agreement with its employees. To an increasing extent, however, employers are joining together in groups to negotiate new contracts with labor unions. Roughly a tenth of all contracts in effect are negotiated through employer groups, and these cover approximately a fourth of all workers under union agreements.

Industry-wide bargaining is used in a few industries, such as coal mining and glassmaking. More often, group bargaining covers employers in a city or a region. A company might want to join such a group for several reasons. The executives in small firms lack the time typically consumed in negotiations. In many instances they are not as skilled in the process as the professional union representatives with whom they must deal. Even the larger companies that have full-time industrial relations staffs may join an employer group in an effort to increase their bargaining strength. Moreover, the union has less opportunity to play one company against the other, pushing for different concessions with the several companies and then requesting everyone to agree to the most favorable concessions any competitor made.

On the other hand, such group bargaining makes it much more difficult to adapt the agreements to the particular situation of a given company. Also, at times the company may find itself being pushed into agreements that it would not make had it bargained alone. Consequently, companies whose industrial relations policy differs significantly from others in the industry, or whose economic position is distinctive, are often reluctant to participate in group bargaining.

Government Mediation and Arbitration. When a company and a union cannot agree upon a new contract and a strike threatens or actually begins, it is possible to call for the assistance of a government *mediator*. This person explores the dispute and tries to find some basis on which the two sides may agree. The company will determine in part when a mediator should be called in and how effective the mediator is likely to be. Some companies believe that this type of mediation is very helpful, while others resent the intrusion of an outsider.

If the impending strike is of sufficient importance to the public interest, the company may face other forms of outside assistance. Public utilities and basic industries are subject to fact-finding boards and impartial commissions of various kinds, depending upon the state or federal laws under which they fall. In this country we have not yet adopted *compulsory arbitration,* in which parties to such a disagreement have to submit the dispute to an arbitrator whose decision is binding. But government seizure and other forms of pressure bring us pretty close to that point.

Each dispute has its own unique problems, and a general policy governing the way a company will conduct itself in this type of negotiation is difficult to establish. Nevertheless, some companies very carefully steer away from government intervention, whereas other firms either are willing to submit to government decision or they permit themselves to be jockeyed into that kind of position. The reason why the general policy of resorting to government intervention has detrimental value is that the whole preliminary bargaining process tends to break down if it is assumed that the dispute will be carried to mediators, political bodies, and public opinion. Strong pressure for the negotiators to arrive at an agreement is lacking if they feel that a final settlement will not be reached at their level. On the other hand, if the feeling is that some type of an agreement must be hammered out without recourse to outsiders, the local negotiations can be carried on in an atmosphere where results are likely to be achieved.

SUMMARY

The resource converter model of a company, sketched in Chapter 1, shows labor as one of the essential resources. If a company's strategy is to be carried out, personnel suited to that strategy must be available on a continuing basis. In this chapter we have looked at three broad issues involved in obtaining such an adequate flow.

Selecting and developing a workforce that fits company needs raises several questions. Policy is needed regarding the main sources to be tapped, the size of the staff to be assembled, the way "equal opportunity" constraints will be dealt with, and the extent of reliance on promotion from within.

At the same time consideration must be given to how the company will attract and retain the personnel it desires. Fair compensation is vital. Here policy must deal with (1) an optimum alignment with what other companies are paying, (2) provision to keep up with inflation, and (3) reasonable internal alignment that permits individual merit to be recognized.

In addition to financial remuneration, every company must decide how far it wishes to go with supplemental benefits. Vacations, holidays, recreational activities, and an array of protections against economic risks such as sickness, old age, and unemployment should be appraised. Few companies dare lag behind general practice in such matters, so the major issue is in what ways a company wishes to be a leader in granting special benefits.

Finally, relations with unions must be considered. The underlying approach of a company, which may be anywhere from militant to cooperative, will permeate all union contracts. Within this general policy, more specific guidelines regarding support to existing union organizations, the scope of topics that will be discussed with the union, and the extent to which the company will join in group bargaining and use outside arbitrators need to be clarified.

Just as viable, continuing relationships with customers and suppliers are essential to a firm's existence, so, too, are its relations with its employees. The ritual of collective bargaining in no way diminishes the value of objective analysis in formulating a pattern of relationships with employees that are suited to the mission and the technology selected by central management.

Having discussed policy issues in three areas vital to every business enterprise—marketing, production, and personnel—we turn in the next chapters to a fourth inherent dimension: finance.

QUESTIONS FOR CLASS DISCUSSIONS

1. For years all U.S. automobile manufacturers paid approximately the same wage rates. When Chrysler got into a very difficult financial situation survival of the company and of jobs was doubtful. To help save the company, the union and its members agreed to a sweetheart contract that provides for wages significantly lower than those paid by General Motors and Ford. What *quid pro quo* do you think the Chrysler workers should get for such a concession: (a) a union-designated member on Chrysler's board of directors? (b) a profit-sharing plan providing for, say, 20 percent of Chrysler's net profits (if any) to be paid as an annual bonus? or (c) some other consideration? Do you advocate the practice of making similar concessions to workers of any company in which workers receive less than prevailing wages because the company is in financial difficulty?

2. For the following positions do you recommend a hiring policy giving preference to women, giving preference to men, or being based solely on objective measurements: (a) taxicab driver? (b) hospital dietitian? (c) coal mine superintendent? (d) office secretary? (e) army officer?

3. For two generations Springfield Hardware Store gave personalized service to its customers. Salespeople had a wealth of knowledge about using tools and hardware products, and they gave friendly advice to do-it-yourself customers as well as to professionals. The pay and year-end bonus for the salespeople reflected this expertise to some extent. But competition has become increasingly tough for Springfield Hardware, and the third generation of owners has finally sold the store to a chain which operates on a self-service basis. The primary task of the few employees in the expanded store area is to keep the shelves stocked with prepackaged merchandise.

Do you recommend that the new owner retain the former Springfield Hardware sales personnel? If so, will retraining be desirable? How should the compensation of these people compare with their former pay? with that of newly hired workers?

4. In selecting an employer after you graduate, will you give preference to a firm that has a strong policy of promotion from within? Explain your answer.

5. Equal Pay for Comparable Worth—should a company accept this when it is proposed by a union? This is not equal pay for equal work, which has long been required by The Equal Pay Act of 1963, but equal pay for jobs rated by industrial engineers with the same number of total points for skill, effort, responsibility, and working conditions. For instance, in a California plant, assistant supervisors—all men—earned $11.28 per hour for a job rated at 1,528 points, while the company's three librarians and five telephone supervisors—all women—earned $9.45 an hour for jobs rated at 1,520 points. The telephone supervisors complained that the engineers failed to recognize the stress factor in their work which resulted from working in a computerized environment and from having no control over the flow of work. The industrial engineers noted that the men all had 20 years or more of seniority while the women had no more than 10 years of seniority because some of them had quit their jobs early to be married and had only recently returned to the workforce. (a) What compensation policy do you recommend for jobs rated close to the same number of points? (b) What should be done about the pay for the librarians and telephone supervisors in the Califonia plant?

6. A regional manager of the drug wholesale company described on pages 000–00 has an explicit policy regarding the training of new college graduates in his region. " Those young people will never be good managers for us unless they can effectively supervise the less educated people we are now hiring. Therefore, their first assignment is to work in our basic tasks as lead persons and trainees. And they will stay there until we are completely assured that they can communicate both ways, up as well as down, can understand the feelings and attitudes of their associates, and can win cooperation and otherwise motivate their fellow employees. They have to overcome the stigma of being college graduates." Do you think this is a wise policy?

7. Should unions, as representatives of employees, have more, or less, participation in company discussions regarding expansion, product lines, mechanization, location, and vertical integration than representatives of (a) customers, (b) major suppliers of materials, (c) government, (d) bondholders, and (e) stockholders?

8. A three-year international survey commissioned by the Public Agenda Foundation revealed that many American job-holders are giving less than their maximum effort. Only 22 percent of the workers interviewed said that they were performing to their full capacity while 44 percent said they do not put a great deal of effort into their jobs over and above the minimum requirement. Has the great American work ethic disappeared? No, report the researchers. "People still say their jobs mean more to them than just a paycheck and that doing a good job is important to their self-respect. But pay is a different matter. About 50 percent of the workforce believes

there is no relationship between how well they do a job and how much they are paid. The workplace does not reward or recognize people who put in extra effort," the researchers said. (a) What kind of reward systems might overcome this effect? (b) Can management do anything at all to increase worker productivity? (c) Does company strategy have any influence on worker productivity? Should it?

9. (a) Home and Business Finance Corporation has had a steady growth of about 5 percent per year for the past twenty years, when measured in real sales volume or real dollars of profit. "This underlying growth has meant both happiness and problems for the company," said a personnel director. "Much of the growth has come about because we have been buying out smaller firms that were family-owned or that were financially troubled and were turnaround situations for us. We have had to absorb family members and some executives in ways that have caused trouble with our middle-level managers. Outsiders have been brought in for positions that blocked promotion chances for insiders and many insiders have had to move to new (for them) regions and cities if they wanted promotions. Surprisingly enough, many did not want to move. Either their spouses had good jobs and would not change locations or their children were at the wrong age to move. One thing we are thinking of doing is to introduce a package of perquisites: company-paid life insurance; health, hospital and dental care programs for the entire family; executive dining privileges; company cars; and personal financial counseling. These perquisites are perfectly legal and would cost the company at most $5,000 in after-tax income but the executive would have to generate at least $20,000 in pre-tax earnings to duplicate what is provided in the company's package. A middle-level executive earning $50,000 a year might be induced to move by this package when he or she would not be enticed by a 20 percent salary increase, all of which would go right out in taxes. Do you think this will be effective?

(b) "Also, a group of middle managers has been promoting the idea that we retain an executive recruiting firm to assist in out-placing some executives and in finding others for the turnaround situations. Their point is that our promotion-from-within policy will be made meaningful at last if the acquired family members can be well placed elsewhere and those few insiders who might want to look elsewhere be given help so that channels can be freed for promotion of loyal, long-term employees.

"We have approached a couple of executive recruiting firms informally and one has given us an idea. It is to promote line managers from the inside and bring in outsiders to fill staff functions. Attorneys, human resources vice presidents, public relations executives, and computer science managers have a particular expertise that cannot be developed quickly even through training. They have transferable skills. Would this be a way to clean up some of our troubles?"

CASE 11
JENNINGS & LOWE

As a step toward reducing the cost of legal services, Jennings & Lowe is experimenting with the use of "legal assistants." Neither the managing partners nor the legal assistants themselves are satisfied with results to date.

Need for Restraints on Legal Costs

In the United States total outlays for legal fees have increased dramatically—almost as fast as medical costs— during the last decade. Much of this increase reflects a social trend toward suing somebody whenever a loss is suffered. The widening net of governmental regulation adds further to the burden.

In addition to more suits and more reports, the cost per hour (or per case) for a lawyer's time has jumped. This rising "cost per unit" is closely correlated with higher salaries paid to lawyers, especially by the large law firms, and to the higher overhead of these firms (rent in new buildings, price for word processors, and the like).

The widespread professional practice of law firms is to charge each client a fee based on the hours devoted to work for that client. Each member of the firm has a "billing rate," and the fee normally is hours worked multiplied by the appropriate billing rate—plus direct expenses such as travel. So, when law firms must pay high salaries to attract the cream of the crop from leading law schools and to retain outstanding individuals on their staff, the billing rates for these individuals are increased, and this in turn leads to higher fees charged to clients.

Jennings & Lowe, one of the largest and most prestigious law firms in Chicago, is concerned about the impact of this rise in cost of legal services. Although Jennings & Lowe benefits from higher income in the short run, the managing partners are keenly aware that many of their clients are considering ways to hold their legal expenses in check. Greater use of an in-house legal staff, instead of an outside firm, is only one of the various moves that clients are weighing. Moreover, the managing partners feel that they have a professional obligation to keep their fees no higher than necessary to provide first-class legal counsel.

The Legal Assistant Concept

In 1970 the American Bar Association endorsed, amid much dissent, the use of paraprofessionals. This new stratum of workers, often called "legal assistants" or " assistant attorneys," perform routine and standardized legal activities under the direction of a professional lawyer (a person who has completed law school, passed state bar examinations, and otherwise qualified for a license). Such legal assistants can do such work as index and file documents, summarize testimony, prepare wills and tax returns, and prepare copyright and trademark applications. Many of these activities have increased in volume as government regulations have become more complex, and they can consume a lot of time of fully trained (and high-priced) professionals.

The basic concept is that persons with at least two and preferably four years of college education will take an intensive three- to six-month course specially designed for paralegals. Such a course gives students extensive exposure to legal terminology and methods and then requires a concentration in one field of law: Probate-Estates, Tax, Labor Litigation, Insurance, Criminal Law, Corporate Law, Trademark and Patents, or the like. A few special schools have built a reputation for giving such training. However, state certification standards and examinations have not yet been established, and consequently ambiguity exists about who is entitled to perform paralegal work.

The use of legal assistants can provide some relief on the pressure to lower legal costs. Salaries for legal assistants are only 40 percent or less of salaries for newly-minted, lowly lawyers who are brought into law firms as "junior associates." The hourly billing rates to clients is also much lower, typically half of the rate for junior associates. (The ratio of billing rate to salary is larger for beginning personnel than for senior personnel because more time is devoted to training and supervising the less experienced persons.)

At first, the new profession of legal assistant mostly attracted single women with bachelor degrees in liberal arts who were having difficulty finding socially acceptable jobs. Others included those who were thinking of or could not get into law school and felt that being a legal assistant was the next best job. More recently, junior colleges have introduced paralegal programs and there has been an influx of 20-year-olds. This influx has tended to lower both the salaries and status of legal assistants. In general, the role and position of legal assistants has not yet stabilized; for example, how legal assistants might compare with trained nurses or other paramedics is far from clear.

Legal Assistants at Jennings & Lowe

The managing partners at Jennings & Lowe have to decide how the concept of legal assistants can best be fitted into their activities. Indeed, Jennings & Lowe is sufficiently influential in the Midwest to help shape developments in the entire profession.

Founded in 1880, Jennings & Lowe has a long history of successful practice. Its partners over the years have included a presidential candidate, a United Nations Ambassador, an Atomic Energy Commissioner, and an ex-president of the American Bar Association. It has represented many top corporations, railroads, and public utilities, and through its unoffical lobbying it has written many pieces of federal legislation.

The firm now consists of about 250 attorneys, half of whom are junior or senior partners. In addition, there is a staff of 150 secretaries and 75 other supporting personnel. The firm occupies five floors of a very modern office building. It is clearly a prestigious place to work.

Because of Jennings & Lowe's age, size, and traditions, internal relationships tend to be formal and stuffy. The hierarchy among managing partners, senior partners, junior partners, senior associates, and junior associates is well recognized, and orderly procedures are carefully observed.

Offically, management of the firm is exercised through a series of committees of partners. However, the partners are deeply involved in client problems, and daily administration of the supporting staff is performed by an office manager who reports directly to the chairman of the executive committee (which is composed of 17 managing partners).

Recent growth of Jennings & Lowe has created minor strains. Several of the newly hired associates are known to take their coats off while in the office! In an effort to hold rising overhead in check, limits on salaries of the supporting staff have been set—with the result that Jennings & Lowe pay is only average for the city and well below that paid by other top law firms. Turnover of the supporting staff is high.

Five years ago the executive committee decided that Jennings & Lowe should try using legal assistants. The firm now has 30 (27 women and 3 men); see Table 1 for the amount of education, length of service, salary, and other information about each legal assistant. They were hired by the office manager but are assigned to work under lawyers who deal with their respective specialties. These legal assistants are kept busy, and most of the associates —who are the ones that give them most of their assignments—find their help quite satisfactory. The chief drawback is that the newly hired legal assistants do require quite a bit of supervision—"and then they quit." The average employment span of legal assistants who have come and gone is under three years.

Reasons for Turnover

In exit interviews with legal assistants who have left Jennings & Lowe, low pay is mentioned as a reason in ninety percent of the cases. However, other sources of dissatisfaction loom large.

"It's a dead-end job. Without a law degree there is simply no chance I can ever do much more than I'm already doing."

"I feel like a flunky. The lawyers are very secretive, especially the older ones. They don't tell us what a case is all about or what they wish to prove. That's supposed to be part of 'Jennings & Lowe tradition.' They talk about being assigned to a team, but we aren't treated that way. How can you be part of a team if you don't even know what play has been called?"

TABLE 1.
LEGAL ASSISTANTS AT JENNINGS & LOWE

Specialty	Age	Education	Prior Experience	Starting Salary	Years at J & L	Current Salary	Billing Rate/hr.
Docket							
Coordinator	31	High School*	Salesman	$12,000	5	$20,700	$45
1	26	B.S. History*	—	11,200	4	15,300	37
2	25	B.S. Business†	—	12,600	3	16,500	33
3	25	B.S. Business‡	—	12,700	2	16,000	33
4	22	High School*	Legal Secretary	12,700	-½	12,700	30
Probate							
Coordinator	47	2 yrs. College	Banking	8,000	14	25,500	52
1	42	B.S. Home Econ.	Banking	12,000	5	20,700	45
2	26	B.S. English*	Accounting	12,000	2½	15,200	37
3	27	B.S. Philosophy*	Accounting	11,700	2	14,100	33
4	25	B.S. Psychology*	—	11,200	2	13,800	33
5	51	High School*	Banking	13,800	1	15,000	37
Litigation							
Coordinator	37	B. S. Pol. Sci.*	Paralegal	18,000	1	19,500	40
1	25	B.S. Psychology*	—	12,300	3	14,700	37
2	24	B.S. Sociology	Congressional Aide	12,700	3	15,000	37
3	24	B.S. Psychology	—	12,400	2½	14,100	33
4	23	B.S. Rhetoric	—	12,000	1½	13,600	33
5	24	B.S. French	—	12,300	1½	13,500	33
6	25	B.S. History	—	12,700	1½	13,600	33
7	25	B.S. Psychology*	Real Estate	13,500	1½	15,700	30
8	21	High School*	—	12,300	1¼	13,500	30
9	23	B.S. Art History	—	12,900	1	13,900	30
10	20	High School*	—	12,300	1	13,800	30
11	20	High School*	—	12,700	-½	12,700	30
12	19	High School	—	12,700	-½	12,700	30
Real Estate							
1	23	B.S. Sociology*	—	12,700	1	14,400	40
2	22	B.S. History	—	13,000	1	13,900	37
Environmental Law							
1	28	B.S. Chemistry*	E.P.A.	13,000	3¾	18,000	50
Corporate							
1	27	B.S. Teaching*	—	12,000	3¾	15,700	45
2	23	B.S. Psychology*	—	12,700	1	14,100	37
Marketing							
1	25	B.S. Advertising*	Advertising	13,000	2½	14,700	37
2	22	B.S. Marketing	Advertising	13,500	1½	14,200	30

* Also has certificate from paralegal school.
† Also has 2 years of law school.
‡ Also has 1 year of law school.

"At the office we live in 'no man's land.' We are not accepted as professionals because we don't have a law degree. On the other hand, many of the secretaries resent the fact that we are supposed to be different from ordinary staff and that our time is billed to clients in the same way as a fullfledged lawyer's. Actually the experienced secretaries make more money than we do, but we're younger and they act like they wish we'd blow away."

"The office manager is a Scrooge. Like the lawyers, our pay is reviewed on employment anniversaries. But they set a maximum percentage on our increases and don't include us in annual bonuses that the lawyers get. As paraprofessionals, we aren't paid for overtime work. The lawyers I worked for—who are great—asked Scrooge to give me a raise, but he said he had to follow firm policy."

"I'm tired of being exploited. I take home only a small fraction of what Jennings & Lowe collects for my services."

A recent incident stirred up the legal assistants. An across-the-board 5 percent "inflation adjustment" pay increase was announced for all supporting staff. The wording of the announcement could be interpreted to include the legal assistants, but a few hours later a notice was distributed to legal assistants saying that any adjustments in their salaries—like that of the lawyers—would be considered at the time of anniversary reviews. Several legal assistants decided to organize a meeting of paraprofessionals, and this was called off only when the office manager issued a further clarifying notice to the legal assistants stating that they would receive at least a 5 percent raise at their anniversary date.

Management Viewpoint

For the older partners who have been skeptical from the beginning about the use of legal assistants, the high turnover is regarded as evidence that the paraprofessional concept does not fit into a high-class legal firm.

The office manager disagrees. "Paraprofessionals make sense. Using them saves money for our clients. The quality of work does not suffer. We make a normal profit. The legal assistants have a nice job in excellent surroundings. Everybody gains.

"Of course there will be turnover. Most of them are not ready to settle down. 'Relationships,' not lifetime commitments, are fashionable these days, and the legal assistant has a relationship with the firm for a few years and then moves on to something else. Oh, there will be a few who are content with the low level of responsibility and will stay on, but the legal assistant position is not a career for most of the people we hire for that spot.

" Remember that a law firm is built around its legal staff. We devote a great deal of effort recruiting young lawyers; *they* will be the future of the firm. We select carefully, pay well, and hope they will stay for a long, long time. That's where we put our money—not on paralegals.

"It's not difficult to replace the legal assistants, given a little time. Most who leave their first job go into some other kind of work, so we depend on the schools for replacements. As we learn to use them, I think we should increase the number substantially."

Questions

1. Do you think the use of paralegals, as the practice is described in this case, is desirable from the social point of view? Would your answer be the same for the use of paraprofessionals in the medical field?
2. What policy do you recommend that Jennings & Lowe follow with respect to the use and treatment of legal assistants?

INTEGRATING CASES

Strategy and the Creating of Goods and Services

DOVER APPAREL COMPANY

"The apparel industry is a critical source of jobs in the United States—over a million of them," explains an industry representative. "Traditionally poor immigrants, today many garment workers are women and minorities. They are on the borderline; for most of them, if they lose their jobs, unemployment and welfare are their only alternatives.

"In fact, the industry has already lost about 200,000 jobs—from a peak of 1,400,000 in 1973—because of foreign imports, and the trend will continue unless steps are taken to stop it. Apparel imports mean more unemployment. The country can't stand more unemployment. So from an economic, as well as humanitarian, view imports should be reduced."

The issue expressed in the above quotation is only one of the factors Dover Apparel Company must weigh in deciding whether to go abroad for expanded production capacity.

Need for Expansion

Dover Apparel Company is a successful producer of children's clothing, especially girls' dresses. Under the leadership of Irving Perlman, son of the founder, Dover has become a recognized leader in higher-quality girls' dresses and related outer garments. Its Princess line is regularly carried by better stores throughout the country. Styling is good; also, stores have learned to depend on consistently high-quality products and dependable deliveries. In a volatile industry, this kind of dependability is a basis for repeat business.

Dover's reputation is no accident. Twenty-five years ago, Irving Perlman (now 58) convinced his father to shift emphasis from women's to girls' dresses, and they were fortunate in hiring a very good designer. Irving then switched his attention to production. Hoping to get a relative cost advantage, Dover opened a new plant close to Atlanta, Georgia. And as the relative sales of girls' dresses grew, the Georgia plant was expanded. Production in New York City was stopped completely by Dover in the early 70s.

Actually, the expected low southern labor costs were not obtained. To ward off unionization, Dover kept its wage rates and benefits almost equal to those in New York City. And to maintain quality and assure delivery, Dover employed technical staff and bought new equipment. Within the last few years the company went even further into "modernization." It has invested over $1 million in recently devised electronic pattern-making equipment and electronic cutting equipment. This equipment greatly speeds up the making of patterns for various sizes of a basic design; it speeds up and probably improves the laying out of the patterns on stacks of cloth so as to reduce waste, and the actual cutting is also faster and more precise. Only large and financially sound manufacturers can afford such equipment.

In addition, Dover has fully computerized its production scheduling and inventory control. While adding to overhead, this computer set-up aids in stabilizing the sewing operations, and it is especially valuable in helping the company meet its delivery promises.

As a result of these and related moves, Dover is on the leading edge of production technology. But its costs are not low. Assuming good volume, it can match New York City costs for comparable quality. However, other southern shops which keep overhead and labor costs low, can produce for 5 percent less.

Last year, profits were just over 2 percent of sales. On $51 million sales, net profits were $1.1 million. The condensed balance sheet, shown in Table 1, at year-end was (000's omitted):

TABLE 1.

Cash	$1,350	Accounts payable	$6,040
Accounts receivable	6,580	Other Current Liabilities	1,100
Inventories	7,260	Long-term debt	3,040
Fixed assets (net)	3,090	Equity	8,100
Total assets	$18,280		$18,280

A third generation Perlman, Joseph (age 32), is being groomed for management and he is spearheading an expansion. Dover does not now sell knit slacks, knit skirts, shorts, or sportswear. Joe has convinced his father that this is a natural expansion of the present line. Although such products are often sold at low, highly competitive prices, the Perlmans believe that well-styled, color-coordinated numbers could be a good complement to their Princess line—and might be extended to boys' wear. Even when treated as a supplement to the Princess line, knitwear sales could add 10 to 20 percent to total sales. And the potential knitwear market is much larger than the niche Dover now serves.

The main difficulty with this expansion is production costs. Typical children's knit clothing does not have clear quality differentiation. Production is simpler than for dresses. So low-cost products provide keen competition. Foreign competition is especially severe. More than one-third of children's knitwear clothing is imported, chiefly from Korea, Taiwan, and Hong Kong. Although

Dover hopes to sell its knitwear at premium prices (because of styling and company reputation for quality) a wide margin above prevailing prices could severely limit the volume of sales. Success of the new line requires, among other things, production costs which are no higher than costs which other dependable suppliers will have in the future.

Sourcing Options

Joe Perlman has explored alternative locations for the production of the proposed knitwear products. He summarizes his present thinking as follows.

1. U.S. Production "Wherever we go we want to take advantage of our modern pattern-making equipment and our computerized production scheduling and inventory control. We're ahead of our competitors and must reap the benefit of the investment we have made. There is ample capacity in these operations.

"On the other hand, we are short of space in sewing. Besides, sewing knit goods takes different machines and somewhat different skills. So we do not plan to sew the new products in the present plant.

"The simplest arrangement, especially when the volume is still small, is to subcontract sewing of all knitwear and do everything else in the present plant. Or, if we found the right subcontractor, he could also finish and pack. We have subcontracted girls' coats with good results, and there are even more shops looking for knit goods contracts.

"An alternative is to set up a separate knit goods plant of our own. It's just a question of where to send the cut pieces for sewing and finishing.

"The obvious trouble with either subcontracting in the U.S. or opening our own shop here is high labor costs. Labor rates in developing countries are a fifth to a tenth of what we pay. In the U.S., labor is about 30 percent of total costs, so foreign producers have a 25 percent overall f.o.b. cost advantage. Of course, there is freight, tariff, and time to consider. Nevertheless, for as long as we can see, smart foreign competitors will be able to sell in U.S. markets with lower costs than we will have if we manufacture domestically."

2. Latin American Production "How about subcontracting in Latin America instead of in the U.S.? Incidentally, we have reluctantly dropped Puerto Rico from consideration because their cost advantage is narrowing. If we go into a non-English speaking country, we might as well go where the labor differential probably will continue to be substantial.

"The political climate in most Central and South American countries is not attractive for new investment. Governments are unstable, inflation is causing unrest, socialism if not communism is becoming common, and Yankee business is a popular target for nationalistic politicians. I think Colombia has one of the least troublesome situations right now, and that country seems interested in more textile business.

"We have been advised that using a local subcontractor in Colombia would involve much less political risk than setting up our own subsidiary. But that raises other problems. The prospective subcontractors we have contacted so far do not have a long record of dependable, quality work. And if the one we selected got into difficulties, we would be in a poor position to step in to help. We hesitate to be so dependent for a supply of products which we are just launching into the market."

3. Far Eastern Production "Of course, most apparel imports come from the Far East. Japan is no longer competitive; its labor rates have risen so that it is importing products like knitwear much as the U.S. is doing. And the costs in Hong Kong—long an apparel center—are beginning to rise. Taiwan and Korea are now the major sources of low-cost products imported into this country. In the U.S., we can't come even close to their costs.

"Frankly, I'm leery of both Taiwan and Korea on political grounds. Both countries need strong U.S. support to prevent a communist takeover. As we build closer ties with China, our commitment to these buffer-states could diminish.

"There is an interesting alternative. Sri Lanka (formerly Ceylon) has unused capacity and is highly interested in establishing new foreign markets. This island, about the size of West Virginia, lies to the southeast of India. Known for centuries as a source of tea, spices, gems, and rubber, industrialization has passed it by. Its 16 million population has a very low average income, and because much food is imported, the country often has an unfavorable balance of trade.

"A study by the World Bank recommended establishing a textile industry, and the Bank advanced funds for training and for equipment. Apparel cut and sewn in Sri Lanka soon flooded the European markets. However, at just this time an 'orderly marketing agreement' was negotiated (under GATT auspices) which sets quotas for textile imports into Western Europe. These quotas are based on historical trade and sharply restricted permissible imports from newcomers like Sri Lanka. As a result, textile plants which started with high hopes and grew rapidly for two or three years now are closed or cut way back.

"Dover Apparel Company could easily form a joint venture with a Sri Lanka mill. I know of two enterprises eager to join with us, and the government is encouraging such a scheme. We could lease existing plants and equipment (though additional machines would be needed for our specific requirements) and have low taxes. Probably $200,000 is all we would have to invest in the joint venture.

"Air freight makes production in a country on the opposite side of the world possible. Only three or four days, either way, are necessary for transportation. We might cut cloth here in the U.S. and ship pieces out for sewing—as mentioned for Columbia. The import duty on such work applies only to the value added abroad. More likely, however, we would purchase fabric on the world market (possibly in the U.S.) and have it both cut and sewn in Sri Lanka. They have facilities for cutting and would use the patterns we supply.

"Wages of three dollars a day look attractive to many Sri Lanka workers. In fact, that additional cash income can raise an entire family out of poverty. However, a direct comparison with U.S. rates of four dollars an hour is not warranted because of differences in the social structure and in productivity. Most Sri Lankans are Buddhists, and I understand they have even more holidays than we do! Nevertheless, at present exchange rates, preliminary estimates do indicate that after paying freight and import duties garments made in Sri Lanka would cost us 15 to 20 percent less than comparable products made entirely in the U.S. Estimates for sewing in Columbia show a 10 percent saving.

"The government of Sri Lanka, formed with a new constitution in 1972, is still developing its traditions and institutions. However, the country was ruled by Great Britian from 1796 (as a self-governing dominion of the Commonwealth from 1948). English is commonly spoken and it should be as easy for Yankees to do business there as in India. As governments of developing nations go, Sri Lanka is reasonably stable.

"Incidentally, the U.S. government has negotiated some bilateral 'orderly marketing agreements' for textiles with Korea, Taiwan, Hong Kong—like those restricting imports into Europe. However, Sri Lanka has been such a minor source of textile imports into the U.S. there is currently no prospect of quota restrictions between these two countries."

Other Views

Dover's production vice president is skeptical about foreign production. "I have to admit that I can't get costs down to match foreign competition. But I'm afraid we are heading for trouble. We have to work hard to keep on schedule with good quality right here in our own plant. How can Joe or anyone else do that thousands of miles away?

" Even more serious is what may happen to our labor relations. Our workers aren't dumb. They know that importing means fewer jobs here in the U.S. When Dover starts importing even knit garments, some workers will start thinking that their jobs might come next. And that's the kind of issue which labor organizers can exploit—no matter how much we deny it. I'm sure we could learn to live with the ILGWU, but we would have had a rough time installing our new pattern-making and cutting equipment if each move had to be negotiated with a union. We have good relations now. Is it wise to rock the boat? "

Irving Perlman is more venturesome. "When I came into the business my father gave me a chance to try something new. And it succeeded. Now I've told Joe that he should develop a way that we can live with foreign competition. He will have to make whatever plan we adopt work—even if that means spending months abroad every year. We now have many more dollars at stake than I did, but it is much the same. Now, as then, the company might be ruined or it can position itself to be strong for the next couple of decades."

Questions

1. What is Dover Apparel Company's social responsibility in this situation?
2. Assuming that Dover does add knitwear to its line, what procurement policy should it follow? If you wish, consider variations or additions to the alternatives discussed in the case.
3. On the basis of the information that you have and your answers to questions (1) and (2), do you recommend that Dover add knitwear to its line?

WARDWELL VINYL COATINGS, INC. (R-2)

" I think that there are four strategic issues we face about which you will want to make up your own mind. The first is the product-market mix. Do we have a tenable domain—a particular part of the market—to work in? The second is our differential advantage. Harleton Rowe thinks that we can do some things better than our competitors—especially the big things. But my cousin is not so sure and wants to change how we operate. We need to understand these first two issues very clearly. The third strategic issue includes the returns we make and the risks we run. How do we look from the standpoint of return on equity and return on sales? Does our financial position seem sound or are we running a big risk? Financially, where will we be years from now? Are we in a position to borrow a healthy amount of money? How much? The fourth issue is the one the Board hired you to make a recommendation about: Do we have programs in place that will keep the company moving in the way we want it to go and is the organization in such a shape that I can step aside as president and turn over the operating responsibilities?

"I'll take you around to introduce you to our people so that you can start your investigation."

In this manner Beckley Wardwell, president of Wardwell Vinyl Coatings, Inc., helped me get started on the project for which the directors of this firm had engaged the consulting firm in which I am one of many senior investigators.* We work internationally on the problems and projects of many organizations. One matter that I have learned to be careful about and needed to pursue in this company was to find out just how the organization was tied together. A functioning organization is more than just the sum of its parts and I needed to see how the parts were put together. Or, in other words, I had to see how integration of the specialized activities was brought about.

In a short time I have developed the information that follows.

---

* The questions at the end of this case put *you* in the position of this senior investigator.

Nature of Company

Wardwell Vinyl Coatings, Inc., of Charleston, West Virginia, designs and makes vinyl-coated fabrics for the automobile, luggage, shoe, and furniture industries. Wardwell's fabrics cover interior panels of some of Ford and Cadillac's more expensive models, and they grace Knoll Associates' line of Saarinen-designed chairs.

Wardwell Vinyl Coatings is directed by Beckley Wardwell, the president, who started in the firm as a salesperson on house accounts. Even though his duties in the organization have since changed, Beckley has continued to sell to some customers; in fact, at present he still does all the sales work with the two largest customers whose purchases are now $2,950,000 annually. Under Beckley Wardwell's supervision, the company's sales have grown and profits are at such an all-time high that he is thinking about a political career. With some satisfaction, he contemplates reducing his operating responsibilities, changing his position to chair of the board of directors, and beginning an effort toward a higher post in the state legislature. Occasionally Mr. Wardwell muses: "If Winthrop, Nelson and Jay Rockefeller can be state governors, why not a Wardwell?"

The family-owned firm has competed successfully for years in the fabric coating industry with subsidiaries of B. F. Goodrich, and the other major rubber companies, with divisions of General Motors and Ford Motor Company, with departments of E. I. du Pont de Nemours, Monsanto, Eastman Kodak, and Dow Chemical Company, and with a host of smaller competitors.

Within the past month, the firm has received a proposal from a European company that provides a chance to broaden and diversify Wardwell's product lines.

Marketing

Harleton Rowe, the sales manager, came to Charleston four years ago after a fifteen-year career as salesperson and product manager with eight garment manufacturers and textile producers. His first move was to add a person who specialized in sales to the furniture industry. Earlier, Wardwell Vinyl Coatings, Inc., had sold only through manufacturer's representatives whose total compensation was an 8 percent commission.

Half of the manufacturer's representatives have now been replaced by six company salespeople who specialize by industry. They are guaranteed an annual draw of $30,000 and are then paid by commission at an increasing rate when their sales exceed $1,000,000 to a maximum rate of 8 percent.

Beckley Wardwell approved the changes in sales representatives and their compensation as being consonant with his belief in putting great trust in his senior managers and in allowing them all the responsibility they are willing to take. Harleton Rowe had come highly recommended by some old family friends of the Wardwells who were associated with the J. P. Stevens Company.

Mr. Rowe commented that he attempted to give some direction to the selling effort. "In the past, for the most part, we took any order that came along. We did well because of the quality of our products. I don't reject orders that come in, of course, but I believe that it is also possible to define certain industry groups that will naturally want to buy what a small firm like this can best sell— fast delivery, a short order cycle, design help, and a quality product. It did not take any particular marketing skill to figure this out, just look at those customers whose buying characteristics and buying decision-making fitted our demonstrated skills.

"I did this on my own. Beckley Wardwell does not question what you are doing and lets you alone so long as you keep him informed. On any scheduling problems with new orders I talk directly with him. Leon Torbit, the plant manager, listens to Beckley but runs around the factory so much that I have found it difficult to reach him, let alone work out a decision with him."

Products of the vinyl resin coated fabric industry are upholstery for vehicles, coverings for luggage, engine, and equipment covers, baby carriages, casings for typewriters, yard goods sold by mail-order houses and department stores, shoe materials, furniture upholstery materials. shower curtains, wall coverings, surgical tape, ribbons, and other applications. Major producers in the industry include rubber and chemical companies that specialize in organic and polymer chemistry and a large number of smaller producers who purchase their resin in bulk from a major supplier and concentrate their efforts on the production process of coating fabrics at the lowest possible cost.

Buyers want their color, finish, and durability needs met carefully. Successful selling also depends on preconsultation with designers about the various fabrics needed in the customer's line. Frequently a Wardwell salesperson works for several days, at various intervals, with a customer's designer. A supplier is also expected to furnish samples rapidly—even of new materials—when new items are being considered for a customer's line.

Automobile manufacturers and the consumer divisions of the rubber companies, which do not necessarily buy from producing divisions of the same firm, generally place large orders. Furniture, shoe, and luggage manufacturers tend to place small orders and to repeat them frequently if sales of the item for which the coated fabric is used catch on. A customer's pressure for a low price is related to the number of yards of coated fabric bought and to the ultimate price line at which the product—be it baby carriages or washable wall covering—is offered to the great consuming public.

Harleton Rowe said that Wardwell succeeds by marketing a high-quality product to a large number of customers who desire fast and accurate service. Individual orders are often small, but they are repeated eight to ten times a year.

Manufacturing

Wardwell coats the cloth it purchases from textile producers with a resinous liquid. The mixtures can be sprayed on, as is common practice in the industry, but Wardwell uses a calendering process to control the amount of liquid applied, its spread-rate, and its penetration.

Fabric is bleached, stretched, and then run between calenders (large steel rollers) to dry it and smooth it before coating. Vinyl resin, in combination with color pigments and solvents, is applied on the coating machine as the cloth is pulled through to a drying oven at the end of the coater. Coated cloth is later finished by stamping or by rolling it on embossing machines to impart a grain, a raised surface (such as pigskin texture), or any other finish desired. Until recently, each of these three processes—bleaching and smoothing, coating, and then finishing—has been done in batches on separate pieces of equipment.

Coating is the crucial production department. Resin ingredients are prepared and applied under closely controlled conditions. Tensile strength of the resin has to be related closely to the speed of coating machines. Both temperature and the concentration of chemicals have to be held within exact tolerances. Stains left by the rollers or rips in the fabric cause spoilage losses or reduce fabric quality. Close attention by the plant workers to the fabric belt as it is calendered and rolled is required for a satisfactory product.

The process is dangerous to unskilled or careless employees. Machinery is heavy and runs at high speeds. Chemical odors are strong and cannot all be removed from the building even by the best of ventilating and solvent extraction processes. While the equipment is kept in the best repair, the rest of the plant is old and facilities are rundown.

Worker turnover is high. Experienced workers can be hired from the glass factory or the chemical plants near the city. When absolutely necessary, new workers are taken on from the large pool of migrants from the hill country and are trained at some cost in lost productivity or rapid turnover.

Last year a Teamster's Union local was voted in to replace an AFL craft union. After one month, the company settled a strike for higher wages for 85 percent of the union's demand.

Leon Torbit, the plant manager, rose through the ranks. He knows the process and the equipment and he demands careful attention to plant activities by his supervisors, who spend most of their time closely overseeing production runs to minimize spoilage and waste. Leon Torbit also spends at least half of his time touring the plant, checking on the status of individual orders, and questioning various machine operators. He knows most of the two hundred plant employees by sight, but few by name. Hiring, firing, and discipline are entirely the responsibility of the various supervisors—subject to negotiation on some disciplinary matters with union stewards.

Chemical Research and Development

Chemical research and development is directed by John Minton, who earned an advanced degree in organic chemistry years ago and has since followed the old tradition of experimentation. He has six assistants with university training in chemistry, but they basically "engineer" his suggestions. Professional conflicts arise occasionally because John diverges in some instances from currently accepted laboratory and analysis techniques, but his methods are often quite ingenious. Chemical research at Wardwell is really "mixing and brewing" and relies but little on modern quantitative polymer theory. John Minton firmly believes in using "art" and experience in his formulations. However, if manufacturing difficulties arise, he will modify his processes, and he constantly checks the application of his new product ideas to make sure they work out in the plant.

The present vinyl resin resulted from "rational" trial and error that converged on the successful mixture. Knowing the desired properties of the finished compound and the characteristics of the component chemicals, John Minton exhausted many combinations of reactants, allowing for fine differences among different brands of the same product. The result is Wardwell's vinyl resin which has advantages over its competitor's products. The coating is less likely to crack, has better tensile strength, absorbs dye more easily, and can be applied at lower temperatures. It is a quality product demanded for more expensive applications, yet its production cost is not much higher than that of common vinyls.

John Minton has also adapted other processes to vinyl manufacturing. For example, the dyeing process used at Wardwell came from an industrial magazine article about coloring fabrics in the garment industry.

John has over thirty years of experience in working with vinyl and finding a replacement for him will be difficult; nevertheless he plans to retire within the next year. "I'll be seventy years old soon, and threescore and ten is enough for anyone." Any replacement as director would probably be accustomed to using more sophisticated equipment; new methods might be incompatible with the existing staff of technical people, who must then be retrained. The greatest incompatability to a modern researcher would be the responsibility for watching after the production process; any new person might be surprised with the autonomy given in order to perform the development activities.

Engineering

Process development—the improvement of equipment used in manufacturing—is carried on by Spencer Wardwell, the president's cousin and a mechanical engineer trained at California Institute of Technology. Spencer joined the company to carry out some recommendations by his consulting firm. He devotes his time to machine design, to some outside consulting work, and to a complete factory redesign now in process. The goal of this change is a factory that will produce fewer defects while utilizing much less labor.

On Spencer's recommendation, a wall was knocked out and the factory floor space was extended by about a third. The result was a longer, more efficient linear series of rollers that made each run easier to mount, process, and finish. This improvement was beneficial since Wardwell depends on a manufacturing process that has little down-time and that can handle orders in a very short time. Increases in roller speed have reduced the crucial turnaround time, but on the very oldest equipment, they have also led to increased defects as tension overcomes the fabric's tensile strength. Workers cannot follow the process at very high speeds. Even at lower rates a marred roller that leaves a mark with each revolution is difficult to detect. Now a pilot model of a new coating machine is under test to prove out its design characteristics of a 50 percent reduction in labor hours and a 10 percent increase in fabric output. Discretionary settings have been reduced substantially, mechanical handling has been substituted for manual, and tension controlling devices have been added to reduce tearing.

Engineers seldom stay with the company more than three years. As one said, " I learned a great deal from Spencer about both mechanical engineering and consulting and put up with him to get this knowledge. In a weak moment he once told me that company policy was to kick the worker when he didn't produce and to reward him as little as possible when he did. Of course, that was only Spencer's idea of it. I don't know how Torbit carries out company policy."

Spencer Wardwell said: " We have efficient competitors. Although their manufacturing cost is, as a percent of sales, about the same as ours, their average length of run is 48,000 yards, while ours is more like 12,000. The number of items they carry in inventory is one-fourth our number. But dollar totals are about the same. If we used their methods we could drop our manufacturing cost to 55 percent of sales. Then we could really afford to drop our prices somewhat, undercut them, and shoot up the volume. This would give us a hefty return on the new equipment we need.

" For a near term investment of $12,000,000 over two and one-half years, I calculate that we can cut our labor force by 30 percent and thus reduce our labor cost by $1,400,000 annually. After that, another investment of $3,000,000 per year for five years will eventually allow us to cut our labor force to 50 percent of what it is now and save another $800,000 per year. This is investment in machinery only—the only kind we really need.

" We need to do this because the Teamsters are now really at our throats. The last contract we signed jumped wage costs 25 percent over two years. They are surely going to ask for more next time. The only way to fight them is to get them out of the plant.

"Our policy should be to triple the length of each run, cut the setup and changeover time by two-thirds, reduce the number of employees, and pay them enough so that they won't quit to work at Union Carbide. Just give me seven years and twenty-five million dollars."

General Management

Beckley Wardwell believes in getting expert outside advice. One consulting firm recommended the recent plant expansion. Another firm recommended increased coordination among the managerial group and attempts at cooperation through dinner meetings and general discussion. Dinners were held for awhile and then discontinued when Spencer Wardwell had to be out of town. Meetings led by Leon Torbit for the plant supervisors were discontinued when the bleaching, coating, and finishing supervisors argued at length over technical matters.

Beckley Wardwell spend 20 percent of his time with two customers and, at times, assists individual salespersons with difficult relationships with other customers or accompanies them on visits to celebrate unusually large orders. But the balance of his work is mainly on financial matters. He analyzes cash balances and cash flows each day with the treasurer. He looks at actual and predicted budget comparisons for previous and succeeding months. He, the treasurer, and the purchasing agent check the investment in inventory each month—both in total dollars and by reviewing summary tally sheets prepared from the detailed records.

With the purchasing agent, Roy Ascoli, Beckley Wardwell reviews individual purchase orders amounting to more than $2,000 and analyzes alternative sources of supply for new items. Beckley Wardwell says: "Clay Weston, the treasurer, and Ascoli are perfectly competent executives. They can perform all the duties asked of them, and they do careful work. I spend time with them to keep myself informed. I need the data to press for increased revenues and decreased costs. In my view, a chief executive's major role is to establish the rate of return on investment and the rate of sales growth that he wants and then push continuously for these. Secondly, I need it to keep the family happy.

"Spencer Wardwell is the only family member in the firm. I was lucky to attract him away from his full-time consulting business with the help of a special stock option arrangement. No one member or one branch of the family has controlling stock interest, but they all have a personal interest. One or two of them are in the investment business and are convinced they know as much about coated fabrics as anyone else. A few of the others I would call professional Monday morning quarterbacks; this is not something I have not told them directly.

" While a few nephews, cousins, uncles, and aunts have asked for jobs here, I have refused to hire them—except for Spencer. I can't see that they would be any more competent than the people we already have, and none of them seems to want to start in the coating room.

" Judge our managerial methods by our results. Sales are now $45,000,000 a year, whereas they were $9,000,000 ten years ago. Our manufacturing cost is 65 percent of sales—4 percentage points lower over the same period. We now spend 7 percent rather than 9 percent of sales on our total marketing effort. Research and engineering cost us 9 percent of sales. That compares well with any of the big chemical companies. After taxes, we net out 9 percent of sales, which is even better than General Motors. A dividend payout ratio of 60 percent takes better than adeqaute care of the three branches of the family.

"Look at our balance sheet (Table 1) and I think you will have to agree that I can begin to satisfy all those impulses I have had toward politics in recent years. I'll give up my sales work and that will free up a lot of time. Harleton Rowe can handle all our marketing effort. School board membership, chairman of local welfare organizations, and two terms in the state legislature have not been enough. I've traveled this state —and the country—widely over the past two decades, and have gotten to know a fair number of people. I think I can contribute politically."

TABLE 1.
WARDWELL VINYL COATINGS, INC.
CURRENT BALANCE SHEET
(In Thousands of Dollars)

Cash	$ 4,800	Accounts Payable	$ 2,500
Receivables, Net	7,500	Accruals	2,000
Inventory	7,200	Long-Term Debt*	2,000
Marketable Securities	4,000	Common Stock and Retained Earnings	27,5000
Plant and Equipment, Net	10,500		
Total Assets	$34,000	Total Liabilities & Equity	$34,000

*Debt due in equal amounts over a five-year period.
Current amount carried as an accrued item.

New Opportunity

A month ago Harleton Rowe learned that a European manufacturer was looking for U. S. firms to produce and sell a poromeric leather that the European manufacturer has developed and introduced successfully in some regions of the European Common Market. Beckley Wardwell, in his characteristic manner, encouraged Harleton Rowe to "follow up on any idea that looks promising."

The following information has been assembled by Harleton Rowe, and now he feels ready to report back to Beckley Wardwell.

The European manufacturer is seeking two U.S. licensees for its product. To date, this artificial leather has been used primarily for shoe uppers and to a lesser extent for lightweight shoe innersoles. It can be given the appearance of any kind of leather; it is more durable and it has some of the same "breathing" characteristics of leather.

Poromeric leather (of which du Pont's Corfam was the first sold on any scale in the U. S.) is not an animal product but a synthetic leather made by coating a nonwoven substrate with either a polyurethane or vinyl finish. In the case of Corfam, the substrate had three layers, including one of a woven polyester. When sales did not reach the expected volume, du Pont sold its process and remaining inventory to a Polish company.

The proposal by the Common Market firm is that each licensee should manufacture the substrate (one layer of nonwoven material) and coat it with polyurethane in its own plants and then sell the product primarily to shoe manufacturers, using a specialized salesforce. The European company wants the U.S. affiliate to carry out the entire process for both quality control and process security reasons.

The European developer seeks two U. S. licensees because a tariff of $.12 per pound plus 15 percent ad valorem effectively rules out exports to the U. S. from Western European and Eastern European manufacturers. European technology is widely thought to be 2 to 3 years ahead of U.S. technology in its development stage. The European firm expects to continue its development work and would keep the U. S. licensees fully advised of any process and product advances as a part of the licensing agreement. The license fee would average about 1 percent of net sales.

Current U.S. efforts to manufacture an acceptable leather substitute have failed on the three desirable properties of the substrate (strength, absorbability, breathability). The European firm claims that it has exported one million square yards of its substrate to U. S. coating firms and has had good acceptance from them. Preliminary checks by Harleton Rowe with three of his present competitors (the coating firms) have substantiated this claim.

Several market studies by the European manufacturer indicate the information shown in Table 2.

TABLE 2.
U.S. SALES AND POTENTIAL SALES OF LEATHER
AND LEATHER SUBSTITUTES FOR SHOE UPPERS
AND INNERSOLES
(Millions of Square Yards)

Product	Current year	5 years hence	10 years hence
Leather shoe uppers	75	58	35
Nonleather shoe uppers	5	20	35
Leather shoe innersoles	75	n.a.	n.a
Nonleather shoe innersoles	1	15	20

The market study was carried out using an assumed U. S. price of $23.50 per square yard as contrasted with the shoe upper leather price of $47.50 per square yard.

Harleton Rowe is enthusiastic about seeking a license. His arguments are: (1) the firm would have an early entry into a rapidly expanding market and thus could capture a major market share; (2)the proposed selling price makes the synthetic leather highly competitive; (3) neither du Pont nor Monsanto Chemical is now interested in the product (du Pont's plant for making Corfam had been built to produce 100 million square yards annually, but its total sales in two years were only 35 million square yards); and (4) the proposed product would have only two layers and this would tend to stretch and adapt itself to the wearer's foot, whereas Corfam did not.

In a short conversation Rowe had with Spencer Wardwell about the proposal, Spencer Wardwell said, "It's not worth serious attention. I'm having enough difficulty getting money for the new plant, so why bother with something in addition? We don't have the extra $20,000,000 for the initial poromeric leather investment."

Clay Weston said, " Well, we can probably finance the investment by borrowing since, based on preliminary figures, it promises a rate of return close to what we are now earning. But what is the risk? What will the competition be? Will sales of our present products be affected? If sales turn out to be half the amount predicted, will the fixed overhead bankrupt the rest of the company, since the pattern of costs of this venture will be about average for the industry?"

Questions

Assume that you are the senior investigator making the study of Wardwell Vinyl Coatings, Inc.

1. How would you answer Beckley Wardwell with respect to the four issues that he raises in the first paragraph of the case?
2. What strategy do you recommend that the company adopt? Include in your answer (but do not limit yourself to) recommendations on the poromeric leather license and on Spencer Wardwell's proposed new plant. Also cover the strategic thrusts that should be started within the next six months.

12 FINANCIAL POLICY—ALLOCATING CAPITAL

Need for Capital

Capital, like personnel, is an essential resource for every enterprise. Equipment must be obtained, materials purchased, employees paid, sales and administrative expenses met—all before goods are available for sale. Then a month or more may elapse before customers pay for purchases. Even a law firm selling only services will incur payroll expenses and have accounts receivable. Capital fills the gap between the time outlays are made and revenues flow back in.

In formulating policy regarding uses and sources of capital, *cash flows* require primary attention. Capital already invested in fixed assets or debts already incurred become active when they affect the inflow or the outflow of cash. Occasionally direct exchanges are made of, say, company stock for land, but these are exceptional shortcuts. Most pressing problems relate to (1) getting capital in the form of cash and (2) allocating cash (liquid capital) to the most propitious uses.[1]

In this chapter we discuss central management's guidance of capital allocation for fixed assets and current assets, the use of cash for dividends, and the related issue of calculation of profits. Then we examine the acquisition of new capital in the following chapter.

Relation of Strategy to Capital Allocation

In a sense, financial policy concerning the use of capital does not stipulate the *specific* uses of capital; these are determined by other management decisions. Plans for sales—such as products to be sold, sales appeals to be stressed, plans for production and purchasing, decisions to "make" rather than "buy," heavy use of automation, and other comparable plans—dictate the uses of capital. Nevertheless, capital plays an essential supporting, facilitating role.

---

[1]Remember that accounting profit or loss does not refer to cash. A profitable company may be short of cash when expanding sales call for additional inventory and accounts receivable; likewise it is quite possible for a losing company to liquidate assets (turn them into cash) at a faster rate than losses occur and thereby increase its cash position. Of course, profits should sooner or later generate cash; the question for financial management is when this cash will be available and whether the flow is large enough to meet cash requirements.

Strategy lays out the positive direction a company will take. Executives throughout the company then create plans for carrying out their respective parts of strategy. And from these plans come specific requests for capital and other resources. Specific allocations of capital can be made only after the creative planning process has generated alternative proposals.

In a well-managed company, however, planning is not done in isolated bits. Instead, tentative ideas are passed back and forth among departments, alternatives are suggested, rough estimates are provided, and objections are raised while plans are still being formed. A vital part of this give-and-take process is checking on the availability of capital and other resources that each alternative would need. And as we have already seen, often a resource—people, plant capacity, vendors' cooperation, capital—can be provided only if certain conditions are met. Bargaining and trade-offs occur. Eventually, specific requests for capital emerge out of this discussion.

Financial considerations enter into this planning process in two highly important ways: (1) Financial policies are set that provide guidelines in advance on how capital may or may not be used and how recurring needs will typically be met. The availability of such guidelines expedites the planning process described in the previous paragraph. (2) Targets for financial results are one dimension of company strategy (see pages 101–103). These targets and subgoals derived from them serve as standards to evaluate various proposals.

REGULATING INVESTMENT IN FIXED ASSETS

General Restrictions

In every active enterprise, from landscape gardening to generating electricity, all sorts of proposals are made for additions to facilities. Executives concerned with a particular operation naturally think of new equipment that would enable them to do their job better or at lower operating expense. Long-term development programs are also proposed. One way to regulate such proposals is to subject them to a series of tests or screens, as indicated in Figure 12-1.

Consistency with Long-Range Plans. Company strategy often stipulates the markets to be sought or the production technology to be used. Such aspects of strategy can be translated into more specific policy guides.

A paper company with a mill in the northern United States, for example, became concerned about the increasing costs of its pulpwood. Careful study showed that on many of the types of paper it was making, southern mills using southern pine enjoyed a cost advantage. While shifting to specialty papers was a possibility, the company concluded that the best strategy was to move closer to large raw material sources.

Consequently, a policy of making no major investment in fixed assets in its

FIGURE 12-1.
FINANCIAL SCREENING OF CAPITAL EXPENDITURE PROPOSALS

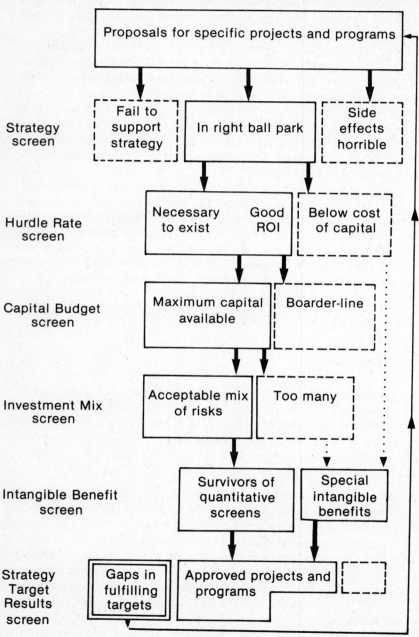

northern mill was adopted. Only the purchase of miscellaneous equipment necessary to operate existing machines would be permitted, and installation of new machines or substantial expenditures on the existing building would be postponed at least until the outlook for a northern mill improved.

Another firm announced a similar policy because the probable shift in demand for its product would make its present plant somewhat obsolete. If new processes had to be adopted, then the firm wanted to move into a new building in a suburban location. In the meantime it chose to keep itself in a flexible position and made only essential investments in fixed assets.

A policy that places definite limits on the use of capital for fixed assets must be administered with discretion. A change in technology may necessitate installing new equipment if a company is to continue to compete in a particular industry. If the concern wishes to render distinctive service to its customers, investments in fixed assets may be essential. Nevertheless, investment policy should be disregarded only in unusual circumstances.

"Hurdle" Rate of Return. The policy just illustrated stipulates a type of fixed asset to be avoided or encouraged. A different kind of investment guide is a minimum rate of return that must be anticipated if capital is to be assigned to a proposal. For example, the policy might be that any new investment in fixed assets must earn at least 15 percent annually on the initial investment after provision for depreciation and taxes. Then, a proposal to buy an accounting machine costing $10,000 that was expected to result in an average net saving of $1,200 per year during its life would be rejected because the 12 percent return falls below the acceptable minimum.

For such a policy to be useful, the method of calculating the rate of return should be defined. Depreciation, taxes, interest, net investment, and several other items can be treated in different ways. So, to avoid ambiguity, the policy should indicate the formula that was assumed when the minimum was set.[2]

Theoretically, the minimum permissible rate of return should be the average cost of capital to the company (a weighted average of the company's long-term borrowing rate and the price/earnings ratio of the company's common stock). In practice, desire for expansion, willingness to sell more stock, funds already available, judgment about future risks, and similar considerations affect management's choice of the minimum rate. Since most executives who propose new investment in fixed assets tend to be optimistic in predicting the benefit of the action, central management of many companies counter by setting the "hurdle" rate higher than the theoretical minimum.

---

[2]For most situations the estimated rate of return in a typical year or average year is as precise as the underlying data warrant. However, for proposals involving long time periods in which the cash outflows and cash inflows will occur at sharply different and irregular dates, the estimated rate of return should be made by the discounted cash flow method.

Risk Classifications. Many investments are so risky that they should have an expected return higher than the basic hurdle rate. Uncertainty surrounds every investment: The activity made possible by the investment may not work as predicted; workers may like the change or they may sabotage it; materials and energy inputs may cost more than expected or be unavailable; customers' tastes may shift; competitors may react vigorously; pollution controls may be more severe than predicted. Since one investment often is subject to many more such uncertainties than another investment, we cannot compare them without making an adjustment for differences in risk.

One way to deal with differences in risk is to place proposals into classifications reflecting the odds for success. Table 12-1 illustrates simple classifications.

TABLE 12-1.
RISK CLASSIFICATIONS.

Risk class	Extra discount factor for risk	Representative investment
High risk	0.2 or more	Exploratory oil well
Medium risk	0.5	R & D on disposable oil can
Low risk	0.8	Expansion of frozen food display cases
Minimum risk	1.0	Replacement of 40-year-old elevators

A company can either set a minimum acceptable return for each risk class, or the predicted result of an investment can be multiplied by the appropriate discount factor to obtain an "expected return." If the classification and the discount factor are accurate, the "expected returns" for all investments have been adjusted for risk and can be compared with one another.

In theory, discounting for risk can be greatly elaborated. A whole array of possible outcomes with probabilities for each can be projected. Successive contingencies can be recognized in a "decision-tree" computation. Risk discounts can be combined with time (interest) discounts. Rarely in practice do the underlying data warrant actual computations of this sort, but the concepts nay help clarify the degree of risk involved. More signifcant and subtle is the absorption of risk by people making various estimates. Central managers should know how much allowance for risk their subordinates have already made in the figures submitted before they do their own classifying or discounting.

The simplest way to use risk classifications is to establish a hurdle rate for investments in each class—say, 15 percent for minimum risk investments and 30 percent for medium risk investments. The " expected return" computations give synthetic figures which are best suited to capital budgeting.

Capital Budgeting

Frequently, a company has many more possible investments in fixed assets than it can prudently finance. The issue then becomes which projects to endorse and which to reject. *Capital budgeting* is a method for making this selection.

First, all major proposals for additions to fixed assets are described and analyzed and predictions are made of the amount of the investment and the resulting benefits of each proposal. Obviously, this analysis and prediction must be carefully done because the soundness of all subsequent steps can be no better than the data fed into the process. The whole task will be simplified by promptly screening out all proposals not consistent with marketing, production, purchasing, and personnel policy and with the general investment policy just discussed.

Next, the predicted investment and results of each proposal should be expressed in dollars insofar as possible. The figures that are pertinent are *additional outlays* the company will make if the project is undertaken and *additional receipts* (or reduced expenditures) that will result from the project. (If outlays are widely separated in time from receipts, they can be made comparable by reducing each to its "present value.") Intangibles should also be recognized, both intangible costs and intangible benefits; for example, flexibility or strategic advantage of entering a new market. These intangibles must be listed because the budgeting process deals only with dollar figures and time; it tends to deemphasize intangibles and strategic considerations.[3]

Then, proposals should be ranked, with those showing the highest rate of return-to-outlay at the top and those with the lowest return at the bottom.

Finally, management can proceed down the ranked projects until (1) the capital available is exhausted, assuming overriding reasons exist for keeping the total within a fixed amount, or (2) the rate of return falls below the minimum acceptable rate. Before projects below the cutoff point are rejected, intangible benefits should be appraised to decide whether the added advantages are important enough to move a project up into the acceptable list. Similarly, intangible

---

[3]Theoretically the dollar estimates can include contributions to strategic moves or detractions from them. In practice, these broader effects are difficult to estimate (and may not be fully understood by people making the specific proposal), so they are normally treated as "intangibles."

The scope of each proposal determines which intangible factors should be weighed. If the proposal deals only with, say, replacing autos used by sales representatives, we disregard many intangibles because all alternatives assume the same people doing the same work. However, if closing a branch or dropping a product line is at issue, then many questions about employee morale, competitors' reaction, and the like must be included.

Note that the rate of return based on incremental results and incremental investment differs from the overall average. For instance, assuming we stay in business, the incremental value of a telephone vs. no telephone will be very high. One of the major reasons for prior screening of capital proposals against strategy criteria, suggested above, is to clarify the assumptions and to narrow the factors to be weighed for a particular proposal.

costs of projects above the cutoff point should be assessed with an eye for projects that might be dropped.

Investment Mix

Every firm makes some high-risk investments and some low-risk investments. The proportions, however, among the high-, medium-, and low-risk commitments can vary a lot. Just as the "marketing mix" (see Chapter 8) used by a company should be adapted to its strategy, so also should the "investment mix." A company that makes only high-risk investments would be too unstable; all minimum risk forces liquidation. A healthy arrangement is some mixture, like a healthy human diet provides a mixture of nutrients and energy.

Risk Profile of a Small Firm. Alain Ribout, the owner-manager of a successful motel in the Laurentian mountain region of Canada, faces several attractive propositions: enlarge and improve his present kitchen and parking facilities, add a large wing to his present building, build a new motel thirty miles away at a site of a proposed new ski lift, and invest in a new ski lift. Both the uncertainty and the potential rate of return rise in the order in which the four alternatives are listed.

Selection of any one investment will affect Ribout's interest in making other investments. For instance, commitments to both the new motel and the ski lift, Ribout feels, would be risking too much on the success of one development. Likewise, if he embarks on a new wing expansion, he hesitates to also start a second motel. But he does want to share in the growth of the area. So to keep his overall risk exposure in balance, Ribout is now inclined to make two moves: (1) ensure continuation of his present success by improving the kitchen and parking, and (2) take a high risk by investing in the ski lift.

A Missouri farmer, to cite another case, is being encouraged by a poultry processor to double his capacity to raise broilers from chicks. This would involve a $100,000 investment in highly mechanized facilities, which could be recovered in four or five years *if* the demand for broilers continues to grow. The farmer actually spends most of his time raising corn, but with present equipment this is not profitable. A shift to large-scale mechanized methods for raising corn would require changing fences and fields and buying new equipment worth $85,000. An alternative is to use fields for grazing beef cattle and to take a job that will provide cash income for current expenses. Since the family can easily muster the small additional labor to care for the expanded broiler activity, the farmer could handle both the broiler and the new corn venture. But he hesitates to take both risks at once. He prefers a choice between (1) the new corn operation plus present broiler activity or (2) expanded broiler activity plus cattle grazing and cash income from an outside job.

A mixture of high-risk and low-risk investments with an eye on dependable cash flow is needed in both of these examples. Since a choice of any one alternative modifies the attractiveness of the others, a policy dealing with the total mix is desirable.

The concept of investment mix has application beyond the particular examples for small and large firms just cited. Single-product firms face questions of acquiring raw material sources or mechanization: an art museum must select the kinds of art and the kinds of services it will provide, and even universities venture forth in some directions and hold back in others. The investment policy on such matters is midway between broad stategic directions and specific projects. It identifies, for all persons involved, areas where investments will be encouraged and other areas where investments will rarely be made. Clearly, the investment mix approach is less mechanistic and more sophisticated than capital budgeting.

An additional risk arises from investment intensity. Data on many businesses analyzed by the Strategic Planning Institute show clearly that heavy investment in mechanization and in inventory and accounts receivable tend to reduce profitability. More capital tied up per dollar of sales increases the risk of low profits. (See Figure 12-2.) The risk is especially great for companies with low market shares.

Summary. Policy guiding the use of capital in fixed assets takes several forms. First, we set up general restrictions that screen out many proposals. These restrictions often state the kind of activity that will, or will not, be supported— based on company strategy. Also, hurdle rates-of-return, perhaps refined for different risk classifications, narrow the projects that receive serious consideration. Then, to select among remaining proposals, we can either employ capital budgeting or seek a balanced mixture of high- and low-risk ventures.

Leasing Versus Purchase of Fixed Assets

Analysis of investment proposals may reveal more attractive opportunities than can be absorbed by a company's normal financial structure. When this occurs, long-term leasing instead of buying the fixed assets should be considered.

Of course, reasons other than financing may make leasing attractive. The outlook may be so uncertain that owning your own building is imprudent, or prospects of rapid expansion and relocation may suggest flexibility in asset commitments. However, in the present discussion we are concerned with leasing as a way of reducing the need for tying up capital in fixed assets. Here is the way it works. An investor, perhaps an estate or an insurance company, with funds for long-term investment buys a building we want to use and at the same time leases it to us for a long period. The rental payments are high enough to cover real estate taxes, depreciation, and repairs, as well as interest on the capital tied up. Note that these are all expenses we would have to pay if we owned the building.

If the asset to be leased has to be constructed for our own peculiar require-

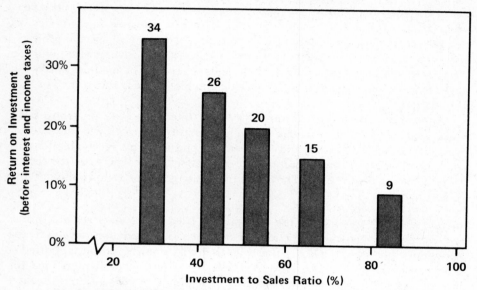

FIGURE 12-2.
AS INVESTMENT RELATIVE TO SALES RISES
PROFITABILITY DECLINES

Source: Strategic Planning Institute.
"Investment" is fixed assets at book value plus working capital. The
sharp drop in profitability is largely due to two very different reasons:
(a) arithmetic — investment intensity enlarges the denominator of
ROI; (b) intensity of competition — high investments and fixed costs
cause anxiety to obtain sales.

ments, we may actually build and equip the structure and then *sell and lease
back*. Also, we may have the option to buy the asset when the lease expires, ten
or twenty years hence, at a depreciated value. Both these provisions make leasing even more like owning. The investor, in turn, is in much the same position
as a mortgage holder because the investor relies on our contract for interest and
the return of the investment. (In some circumstances, the investor may be able
to postpone paying income tax.)

A few companies have a *policy* to lease rather than buy certain types of
assets. For example, oil companies and retail chain stores may regularly use such
an arrangement for their many retail outlets. Most firms resort to leasing only
occasionally for some large asset. Whatever the frequency, the operating cost
and the tax implication should be carefully studied because a long-term lease

obligation is just as binding as mortgage or debenture bond obligations.

Since a long-term lease creates a continuing financial burden in many respects comparable to owning fixed assets, it must not be used promiscuously. The general policy of a company regarding its investment in fixed assets and capital budgeting comparisons of alternative uses of company resources should normally apply to property leased for a long term as well as property that is purchased.

POLICY RESTRAINTS ON CURRENT ASSETS

Operating Needs for Inventory

The size and the composition of inventory should be determined primarily by operating needs. As we explained in Chapter 10, the following factors should be considered: minimum inventory necessary for uninterrupted operations, economical size of purchase orders and of production runs, production for inventory to stabilize employment, advance purchases to get seasonal discounts, and anticipation of price changes and shortages of supply. Inventory policy blending all these considerations is one of the main issues in wise procurement. Financial limitations are a different and additional constraint.

Budgetary Limits on Inventory

Inventory absorbs capital. The cash spent for finished goods, work in process, and raw materials is not available for other uses as long as these stocks remain on hand. Consequently, financial policy dealing with the allocation of capital to competing uses frequently places an overall limit on the size of inventories.

A common way to limit inventory is to budget the total size month by month. Each time the budget is revised, the use of capital for inventory is weighed against other needs. This establishes a mechanism for seeking the optimum use of capital throughout the company. Of course, since inventory serves as a buffer between purchasing, production, and sales, the actual inventory may deviate from the budgeted amount, but the guide to desired inventory levels is clear.

Budgetary control of inventories is particularly well suited to companies that have wide seasonal fluctuations. In the automobile industry, for example, cutting-back of production and disposing of inventory of one model while scheduling startup on production of next year's model is a tactical problem of considerable significance. Similarly, the buildup and disposition of Christmas merchandise and agricultural supplies calls for short-run adjustments.

Policy on Inventory Turnover

A second way to limit inventory is in terms of turnover ratios. Thus, a retail shop may aim for an inventory in relation to sales of 25 percent, or four turns per year. The turnover standard creates pressure to dispose of slow-moving, obsolete stock; accumulation of such stock is likely to lead to future losses. Moreover, high inventory relative to sales increases the company's exposure to price fluctuations. And, since inventory turnover is frequently used by outside credit analysts, a company's credit standing can be improved by fast inventory turnover in relation to industry averages.

For internal administration, separate turnover ratios for raw materials and for finished goods, perhaps broken down by type of product, are more useful than a total composite figure. Often the turnover will be stated in terms of months of supply to avoid arguments about values to be used. A primary purpose of this kind of policy is to induce inventory managers to decide what kind of stock is worth holding and to clean out past mistakes.

Note that as inventory policy becomes more specific, it shifts from a general financial guide to an operating control. This fuzzy dividing line between finance and operations is characteristic of many financial issues and unless adroitly handled becomes a source of jurisdictional dispute.

Investment in Accounts Receivable

Central management's concern with accounts receivable is similar to inventory. First, the company's credit policy should aid the execution of strategy. This means that liberality in granting credit to customers and in making collections should be consistent with stress placed on credit as a sales appeal. Defining the function (service) that it is to perform is primary. Second, budgetary limits may then be set for the total capital allocated to accounts receivable. These limits will arise from the capital-allocating process and will reflect a balancing of alternative uses of capital. And third, turnover ratios can be set to check the soundness of accounts and to avoid further losses from an accumulation of uncollectible accounts. As with inventory, even more detailed constraints, such as "aging" the accounts receivable (that is, listing those thirty days overdue, sixty days overdue, etc.), move from general financial limitations into operations. The basic task of central management in the area of accounts receivable, then, is to set policy regarding (1) purpose, (2) allocation of capital among competing uses, and (3) maintenance of the quality of the asset.

A special issue is the *use of outside financial institutions*—banks, credit companies, and factors—to provide customer credit. Outside firms will be glad to extend installment credit because this is profitable business by itself. For help in carrying regular commercial accounts receivable, the company must pay a fee, the size of the fee depending on who makes the credit investigation, who collects the accounts when due, and who bears the risk of bad accounts. The basic question that central management must resolve is whether to reduce capital needs for accounts receivable by turning to outside firms. The answer hinges on two factors: (1) How important to the company is close customer contact and integration of credit with other services provided to the customer? (2) How does the cost of outside service (the fee paid or the installment profit foregone) compare with income that can be earned by using the capital saved for other purposes?

CALCULATION OF PROFITS

Allocating capital among fixed and current assets, the problem we have just been discussing, is part of a broader task of guiding the flow of capital in, around, and out of the company. Clearly the allocation of cash for dividends is another part, and we explore that question at the end of this chapter. Before doing so, we need to look at a subtle issue that bears on dividends and a whole array of financial matters—policy affecting the calculation of profit.

Management has significant discretion in how profit is calculated. And, more than protection against unwarranted dividends is at stake. Income taxes, reputation in the financial community and hence ability to raise new capital, perhaps executive bonuses—all are affected by this calculation. The three main areas where policy guidance is needed on this matter are:

1. accounting reserves
2. capitalization of disbursements
3. inventory valuation

Accounting Reserves

The extent to which accounting reserves are set up may affect company profits significantly. The issue is what expenses to anticipate in accounting reserves and what decline in asset value to show in such reserves.

Expenses that involve an immediate outlay of cash or those for which there there is written evidence, such as a bill from a vendor of raw materials, are easily recognized. On the other hand, expenses that require no immediate outlay of cash but that must be met eventually are subject to greater error or manipulation. Depreciation of equipment and buildings, provision for uncollectible accounts, and anticipated expenses such as unassessed taxes or contingent losses are examples of this latter type. Often the amount of the expense is not known accurately, and opinion may differ as to how much should be charged against the operations of a particular year.

The customary way of handling such items is to make a reasonable estimate of the amount to be charged against operations each year, and then to include this figure along with other expenses as a deduction from gross income in the calculation of net profit. At the same time a so-called "reserve" is set up on the accounting books in anticipation of the time when the cash payment or the discarding of assets will take place. It should be remembered that this reserve is not a special cash fund put aside to meet an anticipated cash payment. Such an account does, however, perform an important function in preventing the overstatement of profits.

A conservative policy is to create large reserves even though this cuts stated earnings. Conversely, a company wanting to show immediate profits may build accounting reserves slowly. For example, a steel company may depreciate equipment that will not wear out with twenty years of continuous use at a rate of 10 percent a year because improved methods of operation will probably make this equipment obsolete in ten years' time. In contrast, a large resort hotel depreciated its equipment at an average rate that would have taken fifty years to cover the original cost, even though this hotel catered to upper-income customers who expected up-to-date service and modern equipment.

Capitalization of Disbursements

A similar issue arises in the treatment of product development expenses and improvements of fixed assets. Here the cash has been paid out, but the question is whether to treat the disbursement as an expense in the current year, and thereby reduce profits, or to *capitalize* it.

The treatment of patents illustrates the problem. If a company buys a patent, it clearly has an asset the cost of which should be charged as an expense, not all at once, but year-by-year during the life of the patent. But when a patent comes out of the company's research laboratory, the situation is not so clear. How much research cost should be attached to that patent, treated as an asset, and written off year-by-year? The more cost that is capitalized as an asset, the higher the profits in the current year.

Likewise, when a wooden floor in the plant is replaced with a concrete one, should the cost be treated as a repair expense or should at least part of the outlay be shown as an asset? Disbursements for intangibles like training or advertising a new product are regularly treated as expenses, but what of the cost of an elaborate demonstration model which while built for a World's Fair will be used for several additional years?

Inventory Valuation

Still another fuzzy area in the computation of profits is valuing inventory. Judgment has to be exercised in deciding what is obsolete, damaged beyond its point of usefulness, or missing an essential bearing. Value depends on future demand as well as on physical condition of the inventory; but future need in the company for repair parts, or demand by customers, often is uncertain. Someone has to say that a specific item is still a good asset or that it should be written off (or down). Here, again, the higher the value attached to inventory carried as an asset, the higher the current profit.

Inflation adds further questions on inventory valuation. If inflation causes a specific item to rise in value while it is held in inventory, the company can sell that item at attractive nominal profit. But the cost of replacing the item has also risen; so much or all of the nominal profit is used up just getting the physical inventory back to the starting size. Real profits have been overstated in such a situation. One way to reduce such a misleading statement of profits is to compute cost on a LIFO (last-in-first-out) basis. Here the price of the most recently purchased item (during inflation this will be the highest priced item) is used to compute profits; the remaining inventory is valued at the earlier and lower profits. Thus the use of LIFO helps to cut down overstating of profits during inflation, but inventory will probably be undervalued in terms of current price levels.

Many companies now use LIFO, and then report in a footnote on their balance sheets how much their inventories are undervalued in terms of the current prices.

Policy Issues in Profit Determination

Limitations surround the size of reserves, the capitalization of costs, and the valuation of inventories. The public accounting profession has devoted much effort to establishing "acceptable practice" in these and related areas. Federal tax regulations of what may be treated as an expense on income tax returns (and hence not taxed) are comprehensive and complex. Securities and Exchange Commission stipulations stress full disclosure in annual financial reports. Nevertheless, a substantial latitude for management action in these areas remains.

Central management does not, of course, deal with the numerous specific entries involved in profit computation. Instead, it should set general policy indicating the degree of conservatism to be followed throughout the company. When room for judgment is present, should it be resolved in favor of low value of assets, large reserves, and, to the extent that these entries are acceptable to the Internal Revenue Service, low taxes? Or will the policy be to show as high a profit as is legitimate within the area of judgment?

A related policy issue is *when* guides for profit computation should be changed. If a given method for computing profits is followed consistently year after year, the effect of the method chosen tends to balance out. Profits postponed from last year show up this year and largely offset this year's potential profits that have been deferred until next year. However, if a conservative policy is followed one year and then a liberal policy the next, the effect on results reported for any one year can be much greater. Consequently, many prudently run companies stress *consistency* fully as much as the particular valuation methods employed. Other companies have a policy to postpone and *minimize income taxes* in any legitimate way, including a shift in treatment of matters of judgment if such should be propitious.

Like so many other policy problems we have examined, calculation of profits is interrelated with several aspects of central management. Protection of capital calls for conservative estimation of profits; but income taxes, executive incentives, and ease in raising new capital also should be considered. In addition to these explicit factors, the policy should reflect the kind of company envisaged in its strategy. A risk-taking, fast-growth, volatile firm needs a public image quite different from a dependable, steady-growth, stable enterprise.

DISTRIBUTION OF EARNINGS

Net profits of a company after income taxes belong to the stockholders. This does not mean that stockholders will receive a cash dividend equal to their share of the profits, because the board of directors may decide that part or all of the profits should be kept in the company. Policy regarding the disposition of profits varies widely.

Plowing Back Profits

A very common practice in American business is to use profits as a source of additional capital. Profitable enterprises typically are growing concerns, and additional capital is required to finance this expansion. Rather than distribute profits in the form of dividends and then seek new capital from other sources, many managements believe that it is wiser to use their earnings to meet this need.

One prominent company manufacturing office equipment has relied exclusively on profits to finance its expansion. The founder of this company had an idea but no capital. A loan from a bank was therefore sought to launch this enterprise. The unsympathetic treatment that the founder received at the hands of the bankers made him resolve never to seek their aid again. Finally a partnership was formed with a person who had some capital. The partnership soon became successful enough to finance further expansion from its earnings. This meant, however, that the original partners could not withdraw any profits from the business and that the use of this single source for additonal capital would not permit a rapid expansion or exploitation of the market. On the other hand, it did permit a healthy growth of the company, which now enjoys freedom from any long-term financial obligations.

The process of plowing earnings back into a business rather than distributing them in the form of dividends has proved to be such a desirable practice in the past that some authorities advocate a standard policy of distributing no more than half of the profits to the owners in the form of dividends. Such a policy certainly contributes to the financial strength of a company, but it may lead to the accumulation of unnecessary capital if the company is not expanding the scope of its operations. One small company, for example, kept about 20 percent more capital than it needed for over ten years simply because the board of directors thought it was "sound" to plow back half of the earnings.

Inflation and Dividends

Except in special circumstances, traditional attitude frowns upon the payment of dividends in excess of current earnings. For instance, one company seeking the aid of investment bankers in the public sale of a large block of its stock was required to make a detailed explanation of its dividend policy because it had paid out more money in dividends during the preceding year than it had earned. Without a good explanation, this was regarded as a blot on the record of the company and a handicap to the sale of its securities.

This tie between current earnings and dividends is especially sensitive during inflation. Inflation leads to an overstatement of earnings because:

1. The cost of materials taken out of inventory is usually understated relative to replacement costs—as explained above in connection with LIFO.
2. The cost of fixed assets (depreciation) is likewise understated. In fact, because the fixed assets often have been purchased a long time ago, the difference between original cost and replacement cost may be large indeed.

These overstated earnings are insidious for three reasons. They give a false guide to the real profitability of the business. They are subject to income tax and thus a drain of capital out of the company. And they mislead management in pricing and other competitive moves. The combined result is likely to be a shortage of cash simply to maintain the productive capability of the business.

Consequently, during inflation it is particularly important to consider whether current earnings are adequate to warrant paying dividends, or whether an even higher than usual percentage of stated earnings should be plowed back into the business.

Stable Dividends

Another dividend policy, and one that is sometimes contradictory to the idea of plowing back at least part of the profits, is the payment to stockholders of a regular amount of dividends each year. Of course, the payment of regular dividends on cumulative preferred stock is not uncommon, because companies wish to avoid large accumulations of back dividends that must be paid before any dividends can be paid to common stockholders. Common stock and preferred stock on which dividends are paid regularly tend to have a better market and are more likely to be regarded by purchasers as an investment rather than a speculation.

To maintain a stable dividend rate, it is often necessary to retain part of the profits earned in prosperous years, irrespective of the present need of the company for additional capital, so that dividends in less prosperous years can be assured. Thus, a company may pay dividends of $2 a year over a 10-year period rather than pay dividends of $4 a year for the first 5 years and no dividends for the next 5 years. This policy, however, is likely to lead to the payment of dividends in excess of earnings during depression years. If it is clear that a company has refrained from paying large dividends in prosperous years in order to be in a position to continue the stable dividend rate in lean years, then payment of dividends in excess of earnings need not be condemned. On the other hand, if profits are retained in order to provide needed capital, then the payment of dividends in excess of earnings may lead to an inadequacy of circulating capital.

Inflation also bears on dividend policy. The issue is whether the profits that companies report are partly fictitious and, as a result, whether dividends based on such profits are actually cutting into capital which should be retained in the business. Here is the argument: If a company depreciates its fixed assets on historical cost (not replacement costs), it is failing to recoup its real costs. Such low costs lead to high stated profits and high dividends. Then, when the company must replace worn-out assets there is insufficient capital to pay the inflated prices of new equipment. This line of reasoning suggests that dividend policy should always be tied to "real" profits.

Need for Adequate Retained Earnings

Net profits within a company are generally shown in a surplus account, which is more aptly called "earnings retained in business."[4] It is illegal to pay dividends that wipe out the retained earnings account and create a capital deficit; in fact, most companies prefer to show a surplus that is much larger than current dividend payments. A relatively large retained earnings account is desired because any operating losses or dividends in excess of profits may be charged against this account without impairing the original capital invested.

Before leaving this topic, one distinction should be made clear. The condition of the retained earnings account may be a restraining factor on the payment of dividends if the account is not as large as the management believes it should be. On the other hand, a large retained earnings account does not mean that the company is in a position to pay dividends. The capital represented by this account may be tied up in buildings or inventory, and dividends are paid in cash—not bricks or commodities. In addition to adequate retained earnings, there must be adequate cash in order to pay dividends. This goes back to the

---

[4]Surplus may, of course, be created in other ways, such as by purchasing bonds at less than par value and retiring them or by reducing the par or stated value of the stock.

need for additional capital that has already been discussed in connection with plowing back earnings.

Conclusion Regarding Dividend Policy

Major factors to be considered in the distribution of profits are:

1. present cash position and need for additional capital, especially during inflation,
2. desire to maintain a stable rate of return to stockholders, and
3. adequacy of the retained earnings account to meet present and future reductions due to dividends and losses.

In establishing a dividend policy, the attitudes of people outside the company should be considered as well as those inside. A stable dividend payment, for instance, will affect not only the income of present stockholders but also the marketability of stock to new holders. Likewise, care to maintain a strong cash and retained earnings position will influence the credit rating of the company and its ability to borrow long-term capital. In addition, the effect of high income taxes on large individual stockholders should be kept in mind when the dividend policy is set.

SUMMARY

Policy guiding allocation of capital cuts across and intertwines with almost all other policy of the enterprise. (1) Restrictions on inventory are directly involved in the coordination of procurement and sales. (2) Credit limitations tie in with customer service policy. (3) Fixed asset controls will affect, to some extent, almost all divisions of the business.

Financial policy should not attempt to stipulate the *specific* uses of capital, as this would extend the financial arm too far into the responsibilities of other departments. Instead, policy on use of capital is primarily concerned with general soundness, total size, and balance between various types of assets.

Capital allocation is not a mechanistic activity based on numerical estimates alone. Instead, allocations are made within the boundaries of service aims specified in company strategy. Judgment about acceptable degrees of risk are introduced either by varying the hurdle rate-of-return or by reducing estimated income to an "expected value." Moreover, the total risk exposure—and the prospective drain on cash—is brought into balance through policy on the investment risk.

The use of cash for dividends should be done on a policy basis because stockholders and creditors develop expectations as to a high but fluctuating payout, a stable rate, or a 100 percent plowback for future growth. The dividend policy combined with announced strategy enables investors to characterize the company in terms of growth rate, capital gains, current income, and so forth.

Related to this whole cash flow picture is the calculation of profits. Management can emphasize current earnings versus future earnings by the policy it follows on accounting reserves, capitalization of disbursements, and inventory valuation. The result has bearing on earnings available for dividends and also on the company's ability to attract new capital—a major consideration that we discuss in the next chapter.

QUESTIONS FOR CLASS DISCUSSION

1. The Worldwide Hotel Corp. and the China Transit Bureau have a joint venture to build a luxury hotel in Shanghai. The agreement says that the new hotel will provide service at international quality standards and prices will be the same as Worldwide charges at its luxury hotels in other countries. (a) During the final planning Worldwide urged that a separate electric generating plant be included to assure uninterrupted power for lights, elevators, kitchen equipment, etc. This would add $300,000 to the investment but would not change prices. Worldwide said that the hotel could not be considered in the luxury classification without such backup power. (A change in classification would have doomed the entire deal.) Even with the power plant, estimates showed a 30 percent net profit per year on the total investment. (Worldwide would also earn a management fee.)

   (b) A second issue was the inclusion of some automatic message, paging, and wakeup-call equipment. Such equipment would add another $100,000 to the investment. Based on room rates it charged elsewhere, Worldwide reported that the rates in Shanghai could be increased about $7,000 per year if the equipment were installed. However, the overall return would still be close to the 30 percent estimate.

   Would you advise (a) installing the generating plant? (b) installing the automatic communication equipment?

2. Bill Norris, the new treasurer of the Norris Paper Company and nephew of the chairperson of the board, hoped to quickly put to work the theories and ideas he had learned from studying corporate finance at his university. An inventory turn of four times and thirty days outstanding for accounts receivable were goals that he was convinced were both useful and desirable. When he pushed the credit manager to tighten up on terms and the purchasing manager to cut back purchases, he was surprised to find that they resisted firmly. A complaint to his uncle only drew the response that this Chigaco-based wholesaler and distributor of coarse and fine papers and folding boxes had done well for years with sixty to ninety days outstanding receivables and an inventory turn that, at times, dropped below two. "But," said Bill to his sales manager cousin, "if we cut receivables outstanding to thirty days and increase the inventory turn, we will have enough assets to support a sales increase of

at least 20 percent. Don't you want that?" "No," said the cousin, "sales are hard enough to make against my competition without requiring that the bankers, grocers, and stationery stores pay cash. If you want to get cash out of receivables, sell them to Atlantic Factors. We have done this before. They will buy 80 percent of the receivables right away." As Bill Norris, (a) what is your response? (b) What are suitable goals for and constraints over investment in receivables and inventory?

3. Assume that Alain Ribout sold his motel to an aggressive, financially strong motel chain and that he is now a district manager for that company. (a) How should he decide which of the investment alternatives listed on (page 000) to recommend to his new employer? (b) If you think he should recommend more investment than he would have made as owner, do you conclude that big firms do and should take more risks than small firms?

4. Steve Svenson has just inherited Morris County Tire, Inc. The business is the leading dealer in farm equipment tires and heavy-duty truck tires in the county. It has supported both Steve and his young family as well as his parents. Steve says, "Frankly, I'm a bit weary of six-day weeks in the tire business. Sure, it will provide a good living for the rest of my life, but twenty years from now I'll be tied down just as I am now. Before I invest in another truck bay, I want to look at alternatives. My cousin in Western Australia has located an undeveloped vein of gold ore near Kalgoorlie. Maybe I should sell out and join him. With gold over $400 an ounce that's real attractive. My wife says I always was a bit crazy. She suggests hiring someone to run the tire business for us, buying a camper, and taking a good look at mining in Colorado and Idaho—working while we do so." Does the concept of "investment mix" have anything to say to Steve?

5. According to economic theory, managers and others with capital to invest will (should?) seek out the maximum rate of return—with due allowance for risk. This theory implies that capital allocations to foreign vs. domestic purposes will be determined by a financial calculation of future incremental return and risk. In this chapter several financial policies have been suggested which may encourage or discourage foreign investment. (a) List and briefly explain examples of such policies. (b) How do you reconcile each item in your list with the economic theory noted above?

6. For twenty years the Beta Gamma Retailing Co. has paid a dividend to its shareholders amounting to 60 percent of after-taxes earnings. A vocal minority of shareholders have said over the years that they prefer to receive their earnings in the form of cash dividends rather than capital gains. Their belief is that high dividend payouts are important for high market values. But the treasurer of Beta Gamma Retailing has seen three studies during the past year in various academic financial journals that conclude that the stock market as a whole shows a strong preference for capital gains. In these studies the measure of correlation ($R^2 = 0.80$) is much higher than is the correlation of high dividend yields and high stock prices ($R^2 = 0.30$). So the treasurer wonders if he should try to persuade the directors of the company that, given the present tax laws, Beta Gamma Retailing should either cut the dividend payout in half or reduce it to nothing. The company has several investment opportu-

nities that will widen its market coverage and reduce its business risk even though they are borderline when their possible returns are compared with his best guess as to the company's cost of capital.

7. A successful fertilizer manufacturer says: "We are definitely pushing foreign production and sales because our industry can serve a great need in many areas of the world. At the same time, our policy is to invest no more dollars abroad than we have to." (a) What reasons do you think lie behind the policy to keep foreign investments low? (b) How can a company such as this avoid tying up U.S. dollars? (c) Should the amount of hunger in different countries be a factor in selecting countries in which to invest?

8. The directors of General and Standard Machines, Inc., have decided to imitate the General Electric Company and move into the domain of natural resources (see page 413). The first proposal that has come to them is an opportunity to buy shares (35 percent of the total) in a newly-formed Australian firm that owns proven reserves of zinc, copper, molybdenum, gold and silver ores. This proposal carries with it a predicted return on the investment of 24 percent before U.S. income taxes and an explanation that this rate will hold for at least twenty years because "ore does not get out of date as does machinery, the mines are easy to shut down and reopen because the costs are mainly variable, and the world's needs for metals will increase." The board's longstanding hurdle rate for capital investments abroad has been a pre-tax return of 30 percent on the investment. The board has been assured that the Belgian part-owner will proceed no matter what but that the Japanese group will not put up its third of the money unless the Americans do. As a director, would you accept the lower "hurdle rate"? Explain.

9. Pruitt Materials Co., successor firm to Asbestos Brake Linings, Inc., has been advised by legal counsel to establish a $200 million reserve to cover potential costs and possible judgments against the firm that will result from pending and potential law suits by persons exposed in the past to its asbestos. Manville Corporation has put itself into voluntary bankruptcy to protect against such suits, but the directors of Pruitt Materials do not wish to follow the Manville example. The reserve can be established in two ways: one, by charging against the Retained Earnings account one-half of the total amount this year and charging the other half against retained earnings over five successive years; or second, by not paying dividends for as long as is necessary to set up the reserve. A third possible course of action is not to establish a reserve; instead, Pruitt Materials would simply wait until the law suits begin to be settled and then make payments as required by the courts at some unspecified future times. Previous policy has been to pay out 20 percent of each year's earnings as a cash dividend. The present net worth of the company includes three accounts: Common stock—$25,000,000; Additional paid-in capital—$75,000,000; and Retained Earnings—$100,000,000. This year's net profit is expected to be $20,000,000 after taxes.

    An immediate $100 million charge against retained earnings will mean that no dividends can be paid this year and that expenditures for research and development work will have to be reduced so that the cash can be turned to paying off long-term debt more rapidly. The company's present long-term debt-to-equity ratio of 0.5/1 means, in effect, that no more borrowing can take place and the loan covenant restricts the company's use of cash. What action do you recommend that Pruitt Materials Co. take with respect to the recommended $200 million reserve?

CASE 12
HEALTH PROFESSIONS INVESTMENT COMPANY, INC.

With a rocky and largely unprofitable history of twenty years of operations behind it, Health Professions Investment Company (HPIC) has a clean balance sheet, a new manager, and a fair sum of money to utilize. Douglas Asher, a young friend of the man who had by considerable effort brought the company through and out of a period of large losses and then low profits, has signed a five-year management contract and has become immediately concerned with what investments and uses of funds to undertake for the good of the company and of its shareholders.

History

The company was started by three promoters who sold stock in the firm to nurses, dental assistants, and counselors through local and regional professional associations of people who worked in what were called, by the promoters, "health professions." Officers of the associations helped promote the stock to their members and, in return, received stock at a discount and a sales fee which went to the treasuries of the associations. The stock was offered as a long-term investment with possible capital gains and dividends for the buyers. The promoters cited their many years of previous experience with investments that had turned out well and sold the stock only in one state so that registration with the SEC was not necessary.

One million shares of stock were sold at $2.50 per share and Health Professions Investment Company, Inc., was capitalized with a stockholder's equity of $2,000,000 (one million shares at $1 par and the balance was stated as "additional paid-in capital"). Promotional and organizational expenses accounted for the rest of the funds from the original sales. The promoters did their work within one year and then turned the firm over to the board of directors. Members of the board were officers of the various professional associations.

The directors, largely unskilled in investment management, hired two people recommended by the promoters to run the firm for them. The original $2,000,000 was invested in an apartment building, an office building, some land in a resort area in another state, a small insurance company, and a medium-sized firm which made and sold electrical and electronic components. One hundred thousand shares were immediately repurchased due to a misunderstanding about the conditions of sale.

The insurance company specialized in high-risk automobile policies. It went bankrupt within two years. The loss reduced Health Professions Investment Company's net worth by $250,000. The manufacturing firm lost out in its attempt to develop microelectronic components and also went bankrupt. The resulting loss of $500,000 to HPIC was a combination of an original stock purchase and subsequent loans to finance development work in electronics.

When occupancy in the apartment and office buildings lagged because of over-building in the area, the two managers were fired. In desperation, the directors turned to Mr. John Newly, who had bought a considerable number of shares of Health Professions Investment Company on the local over-the-counter market from disgruntled original shareholders. Mr. Newly, a retired financial executive, agreed to manage the firm with the aid of the one full-time employee who remained—Mrs. Worthington, the bookkeeper and office manager.

In an attempt to diversify the firm's holdings and to gain some liquidity, Mr. Newly tried to sell the apartment building. He quickly found that its book value overstated the market value for several reasons and then decided to write down the assets to a reasonable market value so that he could know where the company really stood. After an appraisal, the write-downs, plus accumulated operating losses of $90,000 over six years, reduced Health Professions Investment Company's net worth to $800,000.

During the succeeding years, Mr. Newly struggled to keep operating expenses of the buildings and the company less than revenues and waited for the real estate market to improve so that he could sell the buildings and invest the funds in stocks and bonds with which he was more familiar and much more comfortable. Eventually his efforts succeeded and the results can be seen in Tables 1 and 2.

During all this time, no dividends were paid to the stockholders. Those who became desperate to sell their shares did so on the local over-the-counter market at twenty to thirty cents on the dollar.

At age 80, Mr. Newly decided that he had had enough. He gave Douglas Asher—a younger neighbor and close friend—control over 15 percent of the shares of Health Professions Investment Company and then persuaded the directors to hire Mr. Asher as manager. Mr. Asher, a lawyer with a sepcialty in real estate law, had grown tired of the legal profession and was glad to move into this new endeavor. The directors approved his hiring, added him to the board, and authorized options for his purchase of some unissued stock. With shares or proxies for the shares amounting to seventy-five percent of the total outstanding in the hands of the directors, these decisions were readily passed.

TABLE 1.
CURRENT BALANCE SHEET.

Assets		Liabilities	
Cash	$ 30,000	Current Portion—Mortgage	$ 25,000
Money Market Funds	90,000		
Notes Receivable	45,000	Accrued Taxes	40,000
Industrial Bonds	400,000		
Total Current	$ 565,000	Total Current	$ 65,000
Installment Mortgages		Retirement Agreement	26,000
Receivable	546,000	Real Estate Mortgage	100,000
Real Estate—Pine Lands	200,000	Deferred Gain on Real Estate	
Furniture and Fixtures	10,000	Sale	250,000
Leasehold Improvements		Common Stock (900,000 shares)	
—Net of Depreciation	20,000	Outstanding, $1 par value	900,000
Other	4,000	Earned Surplus	4,000
Total Assets	$1,345,000	Total Liabilities	$1,345,000

Note A: Payment for real estate sold in past year was made in part by installment notes, with interest, due over the next ten years.

Cash reveived from the sale	$200,000
Installment Mortgage Notes Receivable	600,000
Total Price at which sold	$800,000
Total Price of Real Estate	$800,000
Depreciated Cost of the Real Estate	525,000
Gain on Sale	$275,000

The gain on the sale, $275,000, is being taken up into income as the payments on the installment mortgage are made. The monthly payments on the notes have been made on time. The gain, which is income, and the monthly payments which convert the asset, Installment Mortgages Receivable, into cash are, of course, not the same.

Douglas Asher then worked out a projection of the firm's results based on maintaining its assets about as they were with some minimal changes in the portfolio of stocks and bonds. His forecast is shown in Table 3. He was not entirely satisfied with what he saw, since it did not appear to justify much in the way of dividends to the stockholders nor an opportunity to repurchase significant amounts of outstanding stock.

It then occurred to Mr. Asher that the undeveloped resort land might be sold and the funds used for other purposes. He visited the area to become more acquainted with the property and then talked to several developers with whom he was acquainted. None of them were particularly interested in the property, but one did put him in touch with a Canadian group which specialized in resort development. After much negotiation, this group offered $300,000 for the land in its raw, undeveloped state. Mr. Asher thought this was a fair price.

The Canadian group then suggested that Health Professions Investment

TABLE 2.
INCOME STATEMENT FOR THE YEAR JUST COMPLETED.

Revenue
Interest Income—Securities	$ 51,200
Interest Income—Mortgage Notes	72,000
Realized Gain—Sale of Real Estate	25,000
Total Revenue	$148,200

Expenses
Rental Expense	10,000
Insurance	2,500
Interest Paid	10,000
Real Estate Taxes	800
Office Salary	12,000
Retirement Payment	3,000
Depreciation	4,000
Supplies and Expenses	3,000
Fees and Expenses—Professional Services	18,000
Miscellaneous Expenses	4,000
Total Expenses	$67,300

Net Income Before Income Taxes	$80,900
Income Taxes	15,064
Net Income for the Year	$65,836

Company not sell the land, but enter into a partnership with it to develop it and sell off either developed lots or lots with cabins built upon them. The land was not far from both ski and lake country and promised an opportunity for both summer and winter recreational usage. HPIC's contribution to the project would be the land. The Canadians estimated that the developed project could be completely sold to individuals within sixteen years and that the total returns from the project to HPIC would come to about $750,000 (this includes a return of the original capital). The revenue to HPIC would not be evenly spread over the years, but would undoubtedly begin in twelve to eighteeen months and would be at least three times as much in the final year as in the first. Mr. Asher thought this to be a conservative figure and a low rate of return, but the project seemed to him reasonable and not very risky since the Canadians had an excellent reputation with the other builders. The resort area was a few hours drive from a major city with a population of about 1,750,000.

Mr. Asher could, of course, accept the $300,000 and then invest it in the portfolio of stocks and bonds. He does not consider himself an expert in this kind of investment, but can lean upon the advice of brokers in any one of several major stockbrokerage firms. Preliminary talks with two brokers indicate an expected return of about 20 percent per year from the combination of dividends and capital gains. This would be an average return over a ten-year cycle, they believe, is their advice were followed. Mr. Asher then noted that Standard &

TABLE 3.
PREDICTED INCOME STATEMENT SHOWING
A MINIMAL CHANGE IN OPERATIONS

Revenue		
Interest Income—Securities		$ 55,000
Interest Income—Mortgage Notes		72,000
Realized Gain—Sale of Real Estate		25,000
Total Revenue		$152,000
Expenses		
Rent	$ 10,000	
Insurance	2,200	
Interest	10,000	
Real Estate Taxes	800	
Office Salary	14,000	
Retirement Payment	3,000	
Depreciation	4,000	
Supplies and Expenses	2,500	
Professional Fees	9,000	
Manager's Salary and Benefits	40,000	
Miscellaneous Expenses	3,600	
Total Expenses		$ 99,100
Net Income Before Taxes		$52,900
Income Taxes		8,817
Net Income for the Year		$ 44,083

Poor's index of 500 common stocks had about doubled over a previous ten-year period—this meant an average capital gain of seven to seven and one-half percent per year—and that the dividend yield had been about five and one-half percent per year during this time. This left him somewhat uncertain as to the wisdom of investing in common stocks.

While talking with the brokers, Mr. Asher had also been in touch with a local inventor and several associates who were about ready to put a security system on the market. The people were specialists in remote sensing and had all worked for large firms in the fields of radar, measurement of atmospheric pressure, optics, fragrances, and microelectronics. During the past eighteen months, using funds supplied by a venture capitalist, they had developed an electronic, computer-based security system which they thought could be used to protect hotels, garden-apartment complexes, walled-in housing developments, industrial plants, and offices. One prototype was currently in operation at a nearby resort-hotel complex owned by the venture capitalist. It appeared to have been working satisfactorily in the three months since its installation.

Financial statements for the inventor's firm indicated a net loss for the past year of $150,000 with sales of computer and communication systems for $92,000. Expenses for research and development work amounted to $90,000 for the year. The balance sheet shows a current ratio of 1:1, a long-term debt equal to the par value of the common stock and an accumulated deficit of $230,000.

Health Professions Investment Company is asked to invest $300,000 in this firm. Half will be for cumulative preferred stock paying a 12 percent dividend, but with no voting rights. The other half will be for 150,000 shares of common stock of which 1,000,000 shares are authorized and 40,000 shares are outstanding. The inventor and the venture capitalist have plans to hire a marketing and public relations consulting firm for about $100,000 to develop an advertising and promotional program and to attend conventions of builders and architects to show videotapes of the security system. The rest of HPIC's investment would be used to improve the balance sheet so as to justify further borrowing. With commercial construction on the upswing and crime and arson on everyone's mind, the entrepreneurs confidently expect sales of $5,000,000 in two years and $10,000,000 in five. Profits predicted are 10 percent and then 20 percent of sales, respectively.

The entrepreneurs know of only one competitor—a small subsidiary of Dictograph Corporation.

As soon as it became known that Mr. Asher was managing Health Professions Investment Company, stockholders began to call to request dividends and repurchase their shares. Two relatives of the former manager, Mr. Newly, who had each inherited shares amounting to 10 percent of the number outstanding, were particularly insistent. Not a week goes by that Mr. Asher does not receive a telephone call or letter from each of them. They believe that their shares should be redeemed for $2.50 each—the original sales price. Mr. Asher finds this pressure burdensome.

He does believe that the firm should begin to pay a regular dividend, if at all possible. The final idea which has come to Mr. Asher in moments of duress is to liquidate the firm. This might well result in a payout to the shareholders of considerably more than the thirty cents per share at which the stock is quoted on a local market. The present notes receivable could probably be sold readily at a five percent discount.

Question

What policy do you recommend to Mr. Asher for use of capital in the Health Professions Investment Company?

13

FINANCIAL POLICY—SOURCES OF CAPITAL

The cultivation of adequate sources of capital is of prime concern to central management. Other aspects of company operations may be just as crucial to success, but none is more relentless in insisting on proper attention. For small and medium-sized firms especially, the supply of capital is frequently a restraint on the successful execution of their preferred strategy.

The principal sources of capital available to most companies are:

1. owners,
2. long-term creditors, and
3. short-term creditors.

We shall first review the typical ways capital is obtained from each of these sources and shall then consider how a management can combine the use of various sources to form a financial structure suited to the strengths and the needs of its specific enterprise.

INSTRUMENTS USED TO OBTAIN CAPITAL

Owners

Some cash for investment is generated within a company, if it is at least breaking even financially. Much of this results from a bookkeeping reduction in the value of assets, called depreciation, which is an "expense" but involves no disbursement of cash. Sooner or later, however, cash from such depreciation charges will be needed just to maintain existing capacity.

A second internal source of cash is *retained earnings*. As noted in our discussion of dividend policy, owners normally leave a large portion of the company profits in the enterprise to finance expansion. This flow of funds depends upon the profitability of the company. A dramatic example occurred in Japan during its boom in the early 1970s, as Table 13-1 indicates. The companies with high market share and correspondingly high earnings were able to finance almost three-fourths of their rapid growth from retained earnings and reserves. During the period they actually reduced their debt-to-equity ratio. In contrast, the less profitable companies could not finance their somewhat more modest growth from earnings and had to rely heavily on increased debt. Their debt-to-equity ratio increased sharply, leaving them vulnerable to a downturn in business.

TABLE 13-1.
RELATIVE IMPORTANCE OF VARIOUS SOURCES OF GROWTH
CAPITAL IN LEADING JAPANESE COMPANIES[*]

	High Market Share Companies	Low Market Share Companies
Retained Earnings	60%	18%
Reserves	14	9
Equity	3	2
Debt	23	71
Total	100%	100%
Annual sales growth	17.2%	11.2%
Annual return on equity	14.4%	9.3%

Source: Boston Consulting Group
[*]Data cover growth period 1970–1975 for two prominent companies in each of thirteen industries, one company with high market share and one with low market share.

The amount of additional direct contributions from owners will depend upon the legal form of organization and the particular rights granted to each class of owner. In a sole proprietorship the amount of capital is limited by the personal resources of the proprietor. Partnerships expand the potential resources, but the instability of partnerships limits their usefulness. So, as soon as capital needs of an enterprise exceed the wealth of one or two persons, a corporation usually is created. Then, raising ownership capital becomes a matter of selling stock.

Common Stock. A share of common stock is simply a small percentage of the ownership of a company. So, when we raise capital by selling stock, we are trading a bit of ownership for cash. If 100,000 shares are outstanding, each share represents 1/100,000 of the owner's claim on profits, and on assets if the corporation is liquidated. When additional shares are sold, profits have to be divided into more pieces, which the original shareholders will not like unless the total earnings increase faster than the number of shares, giving them a smaller portion of what they hope will be a bigger pie. The new stockholders pay in capital primarily for the right to a piece of this bigger pie, usually expressed as "earnings per share."

If the common stock is *split* (several new shares issued to holders of each old share), the earnings per share go down. The individual shareholders retain their percentage claim on the total, however, since they now own more shares.

Preferred Stock. Some investors are willing to buy stock having a limit on the dividend they will receive if they also get assurance that special effort will be made to pay such dividends. More specifically, if a company issues $7 preferred stock, a $7 dividend must be paid on each share before any dividend can be paid on common stock. In addition, preferred stock dividends are usually cumulative. Thus, if no dividends are paid on the preferred stock just mentioned for two years, $14 for back dividends and $7 for current dividends would have to be paid on each share of preferred stock in the third year before any dividend could be declared on common stock. Less significant, a preferred stock typically has prior claim on, say, $100 of assets if liquidation should occur.

Normally, after the preferred dividend has been paid on preferred stock, all remaining dividends are divided among common stockholders. In exceptional situations the preferred stock *can* be made "participating," which means that both the preferred stock and the common stock will share in dividends after a stipulated amount has been paid on each type of security. Participating preferred stock may be issued, for example, to some stockholders who are reluctant to approve an expansion program; they get preferred treatment if any dividends are paid at all, and if the expansion proves successful they also share in the profits from growth.

Frequent Use of Stock To Raise Capital. The sale of additional stock is often used to raise money for expansion. To attract particular types of investors, the rights of an issue may be specially tailored. Different issues of preferred stock will have priority in rank and often will vary in the amount of the preferred dividend; voting rights will vary; occasionally preferred stock will be convertible into common stock; and so forth. A package of preferred and common may be sold as a unit. Sometimes *warrants* entitling the bearer to purchase common stock at a stated price are included with a share of preferred stock or common stock, thus giving the holder of the warrant an opportunity to benefit from a price rise. Or, to ensure that a new issue of common stock will be sold, present stockholders may be given *rights* to buy stock at slightly less than the prevailing market price. These special provisions, however, do not modify the basic transaction of securing additional capital through the sale of additional shares of ownership.

Long-Term Creditors

In additon to investments by owners, capital may be secured by borrowing it from long-term or short-term creditors. Let us look first at reasons why a company may seek funds through long-term borrowing.

Trading on the Equity. The advantages and the disadvantages of obtaining capital from long-term creditors are illustrated in the situation facing the Red River Power Company. This local electric company, with assets of about $40 million, wished to finance an expansion program that would cost $9 million. The new expansion might have been financed by the sale of additional stock. The present common stockholders, however, did not wish to use this source of capital because (1) high income taxes make earning of net profits more difficult than earning money to pay bond interest, and (2) all profits would have to be shared with the new stockholders.

Interest on borrowed capital is an expense deducted from income *before* income tax is computed. Profits available for stockholders are net income *after* income tax has been paid. Consequently, a corporation in the 48 percent income tax bracket has to earn almost $2 for each dollar available to stockholders. If capial is borrowed, less earnings are needed to pay for the use of capital because the tax collector has not taken a toll.

The effect of these factors on the Red River Power Company can be seen by comparing the disposition of operating profits (before paying bond interest) under bond and stock financing. The Red River Company already had outstanding $14,000,000 of 9 3/4 percent bonds, $9,000,000 of 10 percent preferred stock, and $9,000,000 of common stock. It was estimated that an average annual operating profit of $5,500,000 would be earned when the expansion was completed. The effects of borrowing the necessary $9,000,000 at 9 3/4 percent or selling stock at par are shown in Table 13-2.

TABLE 13-2.

	Borrowing $9,000,000 at 9¾ %	Selling $9,000,000 of Common Stock
Estimated annual operating profit	$5,500,000	$5,500,000
Less bond interest	2,242,500	1,365,000
Net profit before income tax	$3,257,500	$4,135,000
Income tax @ 48%	1,563,600	1,984,800
Net profit	$1,693,900	$2,150,200
Less preferred stock dividends	900,000	900,000
Available for common stockholders	$793,900	$1,250,000
Rate of return on par value of common stock outstanding	8.8%	6.9%

The present stockholders would profit by borrowing because a larger rate of return would be earned on capital than would be required for interest. If for some reason, however, the operating profit of the company should fall to $4,700,000 or $3,900,000, the earnings on common stock would have been altered as illustrated in Table 13-3.

Thus, by borrowing, the common stockholders increase their possibilities for profits but also incur a greater risk of loss. Such use of bonds for raising capital is referred to as *trading on the equity.*

Instruments for Long-Term Borrowing. Trading on the equity may be accomplished through the use of any of the following instruments:

TABLE 13-3.
RATE OF RETURN ON COMMON
STOCK OUTSTANDING

Annual Operating Profit	Borrowing $9,000,000 at 9¾%	Selling $9,000,000 of Common Stock
$5,500,000	8.8%	6.9%
4,700,000	4.2	4.6
3,900,000	-.4	2.3

Mortgages. To attract long-term capital, a mortgage on real estate or other assets may be given as security. If the interest and the principal of the loan are not paid on schedule, the lender may force the sale of the mortgaged property and use the proceeds to repay the debt. If the proceeds do not cover the entire debt, the borrower is still liable for the remaining balance.

Bonds. To borrow large amounts, the total can be divided into a series of identical bonds that can be sold to as many lenders as necessary to secure the sum desired. The bonds may be *secured* by a mortgage or other pledged asset, or they may be *debentures* that rely only on the financial strength of the borrower. Typically, a borrower who issues bonds must continue to meet stipulated requirements such as maintaining minimum working capital, having no senior debt, paying conservative dividends. Also, most bonds either call for *serial* repayment year by year or have a *sinking fund* in which money to repay the debt is accumulated. Bonds usually are *callable* by the borrower if the borrower is willing to pay a premium. These provisions are stated in the *bond indenture* and are administered by a trustee.

Long-term Notes. Increasingly, large sums can be borrowed from a single financial institution like a life insurance company or a trust company. Here, dividing the loan into bonds in unecessary. Instead, 10-,15-, or 20-year promissory notes are used. There is, however, an agreement similar to a bond indenture stipulating various protective measures and the repayment schedule. Such *private placements* avoid underwriting costs. Their use depends largely on the total to be borrowed and the comparative interest expense.

In addition, as with preferred stock, numerous variations can be used to tailor long-term securities to attract particular groups of lenders. In addition to the interest rate, maturity date, and protective features mentioned above, some loans are *convertible* into common stock. If the stock price rises above the specified conversion rate, the lender has the option to switch to an equity security at a low cost. Thus, convertible bonds give the investor the security of fixed debts plus the possibility of benefiting from a rise in stock prices. Another variation is to issue warrants along with bonds. In tight money markets, offering a security that appeals to special classes of lenders can reduce interest expense significantly.

Anyone who lends money for a long term is concerned about the continuing ability of the borrower to meet obligations. Hence, new companies lacking a record of demonstrated ability and companies in risky industries may be unable to borrow for long terms. In contrast, loans will be easier to obtain by an established firm that over the previous ten years has earned at least twice the interest on proposed new debt and in no year has failed to at least equal the fixed payments. Although future earnings are what really matter, past earnings are often used to decide a company's credit worthiness.

Short-Term Creditors

The sources discussed thus far provide capital for a long period. Short-term creditors, however, are better adapted to supply funds for seasonal requirements or other temporary needs. The most common short-term creditors are commercial banks and merchandise vendors.

Commercial Banks. The most desirable way to borrow from a commercial bank is to establish a *credit line.* Under this arrangement, the company anticipates its needs for temporary cash and works out an understanding with the bank, prior to the time the cash is required, that credit up to a certain maximum will be available. This gives the bank ample time to make its customary credit investigation, and it also enables the company to plan on the bank as a temporary source of capital. The bank wants to feel confident that the company will pay off the loan within a year; consequently, it checks the character of the people running the company, the nature of its existing assets, use to be made of the money borrowed, obligations already incurred, and the earning record of the company. The bank is also interested in the company's budget of monthly cash receipts and disbursements during the coming year. The aim of the bank is to avoid embarrassing bad debt problems by not making dubious loans in the first place.

For some types of business a commercial bank makes loans that are secured by collateral. For example, an investment house pledges stocks and bonds as security for its bank loans, and a dealer in commodities backs up its loans by means of warehouse receipts or bills of lading. When such security is provided, the preliminary investigation by the bank is less rigorous.

Commercial banks also make some mortgage loans and buy marketable bonds, but these are not primary services they render to business firms.

Merchandise Creditors. Companies normally purchase products and services "on account"; that is, they make payment thirty to sixty days after the products are shipped. With a continuing flow of purchases, some bills will always be unpaid. In effect, the vendors are supplying part of the capital needed to carry on operations. If a company is slow in paying its bills, it may have accounts payable equal to two months of its purchases.

Extensive use of such trade credit is usually unwise. Vendors often offer substantial discounts for prompt payment of bills, which means that this is an expensive source of capital. Furthermore, a company with a reputation for slow payment will not receive favorable treatment from vendors when there is a shortage of merchandise or when closeouts are being offered at low prices.

Buying on trade credit is but a counterpart of the use of capital to finance accounts receivable from customers.

Other Short-Term Credit. Selling on the installment plan clearly increases a company's need for working capital. As we noted in the preceding chapter, special arrangements can be made with finance companies either to take over or to lend money on such accounts receivable.

Postponing payment of taxes, installment payments on machinery, loans against inventory placed in a bonded warehouse, and even advance payments by customers can be resorted to in periods of stringency. Few companies care to have a continuing policy of obtaining short-term capital from such sources.

With this summary view of possible souces of capital in mind, we can now turn to this issue of how to combine their use in a sound financial structure.

FINANCIAL STRUCTURE

Meaning of Financial Structure

The various sources of capital used by a company make up its financial structure. In establishing policy for obtaining capital, the overall general structure must be considered because the relative importance of one source will affect the desirability of others.

The size of the company, the nature of its assets, the amount and the stability of its earnings, and the condition existing in the financial market at the time the capital is raised—all have an influence on the sources of capital used by the company. From time to time, changes will be made, either because capital can be secured more advantageously from another source or because some lender decides to withdraw its capital. Expansion or contraction of the total amount of capital used also will affect the relative importance of the sources.

At any given time the right-hand side of the balance sheet of a company will reflect its financial structure. So, to review the policy followed by three different companies, we will examine briefly their condensed balance sheets.

Financial Structure of Schultz Electronic Controls, Inc.

The balance sheet of Schultz Electronic Controls, Inc., shown in Table 13-4, is typical of many comparatively small manufacturing companies.

Almost three-fourths of the total capital of $2,685,000 was supplied by owners of this company. Par value of preferred and common stock is

$1,600,000, and earnings retained in the business have increased the stockholders' investment by another third of a million dollars. Limited use of long-term notes is shown. These notes are only about one-third of the depreciated value of fixed assets and thus appear to be protected by an ample margin of assets. The serial feature provides for a regular reduction in the amount of the long-term debt.

TABLE 13-4.
SCHULTZ ELECTRONIC CONTROLS, INC.
BALANCE SHEET
DECEMBER 31, 19—

Assets		Liabilities and Stockholders' Equity	
Cash	$140,000	Accounts payable	$117,000
Accounts receivable (net)	410,000	Accrued liabilities	84,000
Finished inventory	196,000	Long-term serial notes	550,000
Materials and in-process		Preferred stock, 11%	600,000
inventory	439,000	Common stock	1,000,000
Fixed assets (net after		Earnings retained in	
depreciation)	1,500,000	business	334,000
		Total liabilities and	
Total Assets	$2,685,000	stockholder's equity	$2,685,000

The short-term debt of the company at the time of this balance sheet was comparatively small, the accounts payable to trade creditors being only a fraction of the total assets and actually less than the cash on hand. The company did, however, have a bank line and normally used bank credit to finance a seasonal peak in inventories and receivables from March through August.

Financial Structure of the Red River Power Company

The sources of capital used by the Red River Power Company reflect the difference in the nature of the operations of an electric utility company compared with a manufacturing company like Schultz Electronic Controls, Inc. The balance sheet in Table 13-5 shows the financial condition of Red River Power Company after its expansion program was completed.

Perhaps the most striking feature of the financial structure of this company is the large bond issue that represents almost 50 percent of the total assets. This company could obtain such a large bond issue at favorable rates because of the stable earning records of utility companies and also because of the large amount of fixed assets that the company could pledge under a mortgage issue. This company has also issued both common and preferred stock. Earnings retained in the business instead of being paid out as dividends amount to about 27 percent of its total proprietorship.

TABLE 13-5.
RED RIVER POWER COMPANY
BALANCE SHEET
DECEMBER 31, 19—

Assets			Liabilities and Stockholders' Equity	
Cash		$ 600,000	Accounts payable	$ 600,000
Other current assets		400,000	Accrued taxes, etc.	200,000
Fixed Assets	$55,100,000		Mortgage bonds, 9¾%	23,000,000
Less allow-			Preferred stock, 12%	9,000,000
ance for de-			Common stock	9,000,000
preciation	7,600,000	47,500,000	Retained earnings	6,700,000
			Total liabilities and stock-	
Total assets		$48,500,000	holders' equity	$48,500,000

Inasmuch as there is no such thing as inventories of finished goods in a utility company and accounts receivable can be collected from customers promptly, the assets of this company are virtually all in the form of fixed assets. The company has used bank loans to finance temporarily the expansion of its facilities.

Financial Structure of The Long-Shot Printing Company

The balance sheet of a company financed on the proverbial shoestring offers an interesting contrast to those already considered. At the end of its first year of operation, the financial condition of The Long-Shot Printing Company is shown in Table 13-6.

The owners of this company have actually contributed less than 22 percent of the total capital and are relying heavily on both long-term and short-term creditors. Machinery, which is the principal fixed asset of the company, was purchased on time payments, and the vendor, in order to protect its claim, still holds a first mortgage on the machinery amounting to almost two-thirds of its book value. It is doubtful, however, whether even the book value could be realized if it became necessary to sell the machinery at a forced sale. Credit from material suppliers has been used to a point where it exceeds the value of the inventory actually on hand. This means that the vendors are not only financing the entire inventory of the company but other assets as well.

Fortunately, the notes payable are due to an affiliate company that will probably not force their collection at maturity but will accept new short-term promissory notes in exchange for the old ones. Nevertheless, the current ratio is approximately 1 to 1, and any shrinkage in the value of current assets would probably cause immediate financial complications. The company has no bank loan and has been unsuccessful in securing a line of bank credit that it may use in an emergency. It is doubtful if new capital can be attracted to correct the existing weak cash position, with the possible exception that the company might offer a new investor the speculative possibility of sharing in future profits if they are earned. Under such a plan, however, the present management would probably be required to give up part of its control over affairs on the company.

In this situation the company must adopt a strategy of improving short-term earnings with existing assets—a very different strategy from that of Red River Power Company where the physical expansion financed by debt with a fixed interest cost was the strategic direction to higher earnings per share. In fact, The Long-Shot Printing Company decided to operate on a three-shift basis, cutting its prices close to incremental cost if necessary to keep the plant busy.

The close interrelation between overall strategy and financial structure is evident in all three of these examples.

TABLE 13-6.
THE LONG-SHOT PRINTING COMPANY
BALANCE SHEET
DECEMBER 31, 19—

Assets		Liabilities and Stockholder's Equity	
Cash	$5,200	Trade accounts payable	$61,600
Accounts receivable—net	28,400	Notes payable	18,000
Inventories	52,500	Accrued liabilities	7,600
Total current assets	$86,100	Total current liabilities	$87,200
Deferred charges	3,000	Mortgage on equipment	72,500
Machinery and other fixed		Common stock	40,000
assets—net	115,300	Retained earnings	40,000
		Total liabilities and stock-	
Total assets	$204,400	holders' equity	$204,400

SELECTING CAPITAL SOURCES

Industry Patterns

Typical financial structures of other companies in its industry will give management a lead on what the financial community will accept as satisfactory. More often than not, however, wide variations in assets, in earnings, and in existing capital structures, in addition to the differences in management, make reliance upon typical industry patterns both unsatisfactory and even dangerous. The policy adopted should suit a particular company and the conditions existing at the time plans for the financial structure are made. Important factors to consider are:

1. use to be made of the capital,
2. cost of this capital, and
3. rights granted to persons or concerns from whom capital is secured.

Use of Capital

Funds to finance seasonal peaks or other temporary needs can probably best be obtained from short-term creditors, such as commercial banks. This is a comparatively inexpensive way of raising capital and permits an immediate reduction in the total amount owed after the peak requirements are over. On the other hand, capital for fixed assets or for circulating capital that will be permanently retained in the business calls for a different solution. Because the company cannot expect to have cash to return to the lender for several years, owners or long-term creditors present a more logical source for such funds.

The use of capital will also affect the ability of the company to offer the lender some special security for its loan. As an effective guarantee that a loan will be repaid, a company may pledge as security one or more of the following assets: inventories that can be readily sold on the market, machinery that is standard in design and that can be easily moved from one plant to another, buildings located and designed so that they are suitable for use by other companies, or marketable securities. If valuable collateral can be given to the lender, borrowing will be much easier. If the funds are to be used for purposes that cannot be made to yield cash readily, the raising of capital from owners is indicated.

Cost of Capital

To ascertain the cost of capital, consideration should be given to the original cost of obtaining it and also to the compensation to be paid for its use. In sole proprietorships and partnerships, capital is usually secured by negotiations between the owners and those with whom they are intimately acquainted. Other concerns or persons not acquainted with the owners are unlikely to provide capital to such organizations. Therefore, the cost of procuring such capital, if it can be obtained at all, will usually be nominal.

Underwriting and Registration. In the case of a corporation, securing capital by issuing bonds or selling stock to the public often involves a considerable expenditure. Frequently these securities are sold through an investment banker, who is equipped to reach prospective purchasers of securities, and in most instances substantial commissions must be paid to the investment bankers for these services. Also, complicated legal requirements must be complied with before such securities can be sold. Federal legislation requires the registration of all widely distributed securities with the Securities and Exchange Commission, and the expense involved in preparing the detailed statements required for registration is quite large. In fact, the minimum cost of registration is so large that it makes public offering of less than $1,000,000 of securities uneconomical.

Private placement of bonds and long-term notes also entails legal and accounting fees and perhaps a fee to a consultant who helps arrange the loan, but the total expense of procuring capital in this manner is normally less than half the expense of a public sale.

Use of Rights. Some companies are able to sell securities directly to present stockholders. This applies particularly to the sale of additional stock similar to that already outstanding. The charters of many corporations require that when additional stock is sold, it must first be offered to the present stockholders; and if the new stock is offered for sale at a price somewhat lower than the current market price, the present stockholders will probably exercise their right to buy the new issue. When this procedure is possible, the cost of securing additional capital may be reduced substantially. If, however, there is any doubt about stockholders exercising all of their rights, it may be necessary to employ an investment banker to underwrite the issue, in which case many of the expenses incident to an initial public sale of securities must be incurred.

Adjusting Sources to Prevailing Interest Rates. The compensation, or interest, that must be paid for the use of capital not only varies according to the use to be made of the capital, but also is often affected materially by the state of the financial market. Interest rates reflect the anticipated level of inflation during the period of a loan and also the efforts of the Federal Reserve Board to control inflation. During the early 1980s, for instance, these pressures drove interest rates to unprecedented levels. The resulting changes in corporate financing costs in recent years are shown in Figure 13-1.

When interest rates are high, a company may choose short-term obligations, with the exception that these can be paid off from the proceeds of long-term bonds that will be sold at a later date when interest rates are lower. The success of such a plan depends, of course, upon the accuracy with which movement in interest rates is forecast. There is always the danger that the interest rate on the long-term obligation will be even higher when the short-term notes mature, or other changes may occur that will make it difficult for the company to sell its long-term obligations as planned. Income taxes play such an important part in corporate profits that the timing of changes in capital structure may be based on an attempt to get the most favorable tax status.

Return Paid on New Stock. When common stock is sold to obtain additional capital, the company does not agree to pay a specific amount of interest for the use of the new capital. Nevertheless, the new stockholders will share in any dividends paid, which will reduce the amount of dividends available for former stockholders. This sharing of dividends is a cost of capital so far as the former stockholders are concerned.

Many companies prefer to secure capital from the sale of stock, even

FIGURE 13-1

CHANGES IN CORPORATE FINANCING COSTS

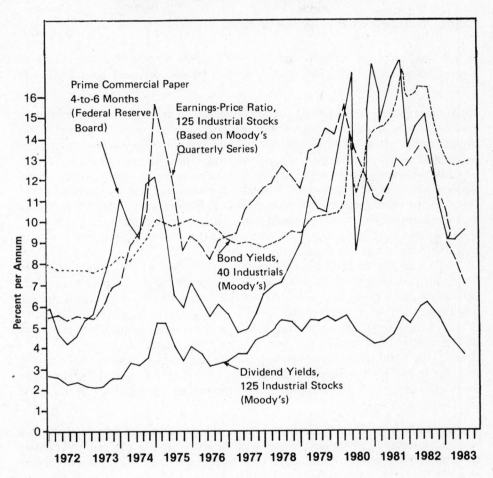

though it is anticipated that earnings necessary to support this stock will exceed the interest that would have to be paid on the bonds. Their willingness to pay this larger cost lies in the fact that dividends do not have to be paid when there is not a sufficient amount of earnings or cash to justify their declaration. Conversely, interest on bonds must be paid regardless of the amount of earnings and the cash on hand. If this interest is not paid on time, the stockholders run the risk of losing control of their company and perhaps their investment in it.

We have assumed that capital can be secured from any source at any time provided the compensation offered for its use is high enough. As a practical mat-

ter, the sale of bonds or stock becomes so difficult in some phases of the business
cycle that new capital is virtually unobtainable from these sources.

Rights Granted with New Securities

A final factor to be considered in selecting the source from which capital
should be secured is the authority exercised by the different contributors of
capital.

Rights Granted to Creditors. If capital is obtained from short-term creditors,
they usually have no control over the affairs of the company. Of course, if the
obligations of these creditors are not paid at maturity, they have the right to
bring legal action against the company to enforce their claims.

Likewise, long-term creditors ordinarily have no voice in the current operations of the company, although a bond indenture may impose certain restrictions on the management. For example, the indenture may restrict the amount
that the company can invest in fixed assets, it may restrict the future debts that
the company can incur, or it may require that the ratio of current assets to current liabilities be not less than 2 to 1.

The loan agreement may also restrict the freedom of the company to pay
dividends. Some agreements provide that dividends cannot be paid if the ratio
between various types of assets is below the standards established or if there is
any default in the payment of interest or principal on the long-term obligations.
If any of these requirements are not met or if any interest or principal payments
on the bonds are not made, the company may be declared in default. In case of
default, the bond trustee has the right to take legal action against the company
in order to enforce the payment of the *total* amount of the bonds. These restrictions may become so burdensome that the management prefers to seek capital
from other sources.

Rights Granted to Stockholders. If capital is secured by the sale of stock, the
new stockholders have certain rights with reference to the company. The new
stockholders frequently have full voting rights, and they thus become participants in the future management and control of the corporation. Sometimes present stockholders wish to retain a balance of control of the company and do not
care to grant participation to others outside their group. The possibility that the
sale of stock will change the balance of power in the board of directors depends,
of course, on the relative size of the new issue as compared with the stock
already outstanding, the amount of stock held by those already in power, and
the extent to which the present stockholders exercise their right to purchase the
new issue.

Preferred stockholders normally do not exercise control over company
operations. Usually, though not always, they have the right to vote for directors

just as do the common stockholders. The par value of a share of preferred stock, however, is typically higher than that of common stock (often $100 and $10 respectively), so a given investment in preferred stock gives considerably fewer votes than an equal investment in common stock. The common stockholder usually runs a risk of losing control to preferred stockholders only if preferred dividends are unpaid for several years and if the charter provides that voting powers of the preferred stockholders are increased under such circumstances.

SUMMARY

An important task of central management is to see that capital necessary to execute the company strategy is provided at a reasonable cost and with a minimum of risk. Short-term creditors, such as commercial banks and suppliers of materials, can be used to cover seasonal needs and other temporary requirements. It is risky, however, to place too much reliance on short-term loans because the capital might be withdrawn when business conditions become unsettled. If used to the maximum for continuing needs, short-term credit will be unavailable for temporary increases in capital requirements.

Long-term loans in the form of bonds or long-term notes are a natural source of capital for companies with relatively stable incomes. Since the credit is extended for a period of years, various types of protection may have to be granted to the lender, such as mortgage liens, regular reduction of the debt, and limits on additional debts. The greater the stability of a company's earnings and the greater the protections offered, the easier long-term loans will be to obtain and the lower the interest rate. Conversely, unless a company can meet these conditions, few, if any, lenders will extend long-term credit. And, from the viewpoint of the company, heavy fixed interest and debt retirement charges may cause financial disaster for concerns with volatile earnings.

Owners' contributions of capital may take the form of either preferred or common stock. The special provisions of preferred stock, like those of bonds, should be tailored in terms of conditions prevailing at the time of issue. Moreover, the total owners' contribution should be a large enough part of the whole financial structure to be able to absorb shocks and losses of bad times. Typically, the owners' capital is increased by retention of earnings as a company grows, as discussed in the last chapter.

Company strategy influences many of the factors that shape financial policy, for example, movement into risky ventures, building new plants to cut production costs, emphasis on keeping a steady flow of standard business, or limiting R & D expense to enhance current earnings. These kinds of decisions affect the earning base, the kind of assets available for security, and the degree of uncerainty around which a financial structure must be designed. And because of this interdependence of strategy and financial policy, a major change in strategy usually necessitates an adjustment in company financing.

CONCLUSION TO PART 2

A brief re-emphasis of the role of policy in the total management process is desirable here at the close of Part 2, "Defining Major Policy."Three basic points should be kept in mind.

A. Policy amplifies and clarifies strategy. We have seen this in our exploration of product lines, customers, and product mix in the marketing area; in R & D, production, and procurement in the service creating area; in selection, development, compensation, and industrial relations in the human resource area; and in capital allocation and capital sources in the financial area. In these, a variety of questions keep bobbing up that should be answered in a way that reinforces company strategy. Policy provides these needed guidelines and the bridge back to strategy.

Strategy quite appropriately stresses major directions and criteria. Its strength arises partly from its selectivity in emphasis. To specify all the ramifications would cloud the central theme. Instead, strategy leaves this amplification to policy. What is the implication here? What should be done there? How does strategy limit action in this field? What priorities are implied? These are legitimate questions that management should answer, and it does so largely through policy.

B. Establishing policy, in fact, is more complex and disorderly than we have implied. By stressing the way policy grows out of strategy, we inevitably give an impression that policy formulation is a neat, deductive process. "First pick the strategy, then figure out the necessary policy"is the implied formula. To a substantial degree this is what should be done. But it is an oversimplification. Three important elaborations help to round out the process.

1. *Not all policy is deduced from strategy.* Policy may arise from at least two other sources. First, managers and the decision-makers respond directly to pressures from the environment. For instance, employing more blacks, reducing oil imports from the Middle East, posting interest charges made on installment accounts—all are probably direct reactions to external events rather than interpretations of strategy. Second, a series of similar actions in specific situations may become a custom, and then this custom becomes so established that it is treated as a policy. Overtime work or customer discounts may be guided by policy that arose in this way. It is hoped that these policies originating in the field of action are compatible with company strategy even though they were not initiated to execute strategy.

2. *To some extent existing policy influences future strategy, rather than the reverse.* Strategy, we have said, is designed to take advantage of company strengths and to minimize the effect of company weaknesses. In other words, when mapping out a new strategy, the company is treated as an established institution with recognized characterisitics. And one of the elements that gives a company its "strengths" and "weaknesses" is its policy. The existing policy may be so ingrained that it is treated as fixed when new strategy is drawn up.

3. *Most important, revisions and restructuring of policy occur frequently.* Change—in the company environment, in the action of competitors, and in the company's own size and resources—requires adaptation. As time marches on, the strategy may be revised, policies may be modified, organization may be restructured, resources may be shifted, and systems of motivation and control may be revamped. If we were to take an annual picture of the total management structure, each year would differ from the preceding one. Just as an automobile company is designing a new model before this year's model reaches the market, so central management is continually predicting and responding to change. The dynamic company, like a growing city, seems always to be under construction. So, forming policy is a never-ending process responding to influences in addition to strategy.

C. This untidiness in policy formulation increases the value of a conceptual framework. In a situation where pressures push in opposite directions and where people differ on priorities and values, a mental framework that puts facts and ideas into some kind of order is a great help. Granted that the convenient sequence of industry analysis → company strength → strategy → policy → organization → execution does not always work in just that order. Nevertheless, the model does enable us (1) to sort out and arrange the pieces into familiar categories, and (2) to have a set of logical relationships between the categories that suggests priorities and dependencies. The power of the model is its contribution to both orderly and comprehensive thinking in bewildering, complex situations.

QUESTIONS FOR CLASS DISCUSSION

1. The Abdu brothers own two-thirds of the common stock of Lakeside Real Estate Company. The company is expanding and needs more capital. Instead of investing in additional common stock, the Abdu brothers have made a five-year renewable loan to the company. The interest rate is 12 percent per year; however, both interest and repayment of principal are *subordinated* to any other current liabilities and mortgage loans that Lakeside Real Estate Company may make—that is, these other obligations must be met before any payments are made on the Abdu loan. Why do you think that the Abdu brothers made a loan to Lakeside instead of investing in more common stock? Consider the viewpoints of the company, the Abdu brothers as individuals, and persons doing business with Lakeside.

2. Atwood Oceanics, Inc. is in the offshore well-drilling business. It owns and operates several large drilling rigs, and works as a contractor for oil companies. In 1982 it had

drilling rigs operating in the coastal waters of India, Indonesia, Australia, Nigeria, and Mexico. From 1978 to 1982, Atwood shared in the high level of industry activity with its operating revenues rising from $44 million to $95 million and its net income going from a $7 million loss to $24 million profit. No dividends have been paid by the company; instead, net earnings have been retained in the business—increasing stockholders equity more than threefold.

As the figures in Table 1 show, these retained earnings have been used primarily to reduce long-term debt. The company has not enlarged its fleet of rigs, but it has bought and sold some rigs and has reinvested depreciation of about $11 million per year in modernization. It now is as efficient a driller as any of its many competitors.

TABLE 1.
(figures in millions)

	1982	1978		1982	1978
Current assets	$ 34	$ 22	Current liabilities	$ 8	$ 6
Rigs & other equip-			Long term	43	101
ment (net)	116	108	Deferred income tax	18	—
Other assets	1	1	Stockholders equity		
			Total liabilities		
Total assets	$151	$131	& equity	$151	$131

What reasons do you think explain Atwood's policy to significantly reduce its "trading on the equity"? Is this a wise policy in this situation?

3. McGregor and Casey own a successful filling station which does a relatively large service and repair business as well as gasoline business. McGregor, age 50, is an excellent auto mechanic and runs the repair business; Casey, age 35, takes care of financial matters, gasoline sales, public relations, etc. Currently they have a 50-50 partnership. Casey believes large stations will have a competitive advantage in the future, and he wants to almost double the size of the present station with self-service pumps and a larger line of tires and accessories. McGregor likes things the way they are, and he doesn't like the big debts with which Casey proposes to finance the expansion. So Casey suggests that they form a corporation with various kinds of stocks and/or bonds that could be tailored to fit the respective preferences of the two persons.

Assume the total assets of the enlarged station will be $375,000, with a long-term mortgage of $125,000 and short-term liabilities of $50,000. Recommend a financial structure for the remaining $200,000 which could be allocated between McGregor and Casey in a way that reflects their respective preferences.

4. "Inflation should not affect a company's choice of a capital structure because all the factors tend to move up or down together—the inflation rate, interest rates, company costs, selling prices, profits, etc." Do you agree with this quotation? If not, how do you think inflation is likely to influence the choice of a capital structure? Will such a change in sources of capital influence company strategy?

5. Many shifts are taking place in the financial services industry—commercial banks are selling insurance and stocks, insurance companies are in the brokerage business, stockbrokers are offering checking accounts, and on and on. What effect, if any, do you think this reshuffling will have on the "financial structure" of business firms? (For this question, focus on customers of financial service firms, not on financial firms themselves.) For instance, will the reshuffling affect the financial structures of firms like Schultz Electronic Controls, Red River Power, or Long-Shot Printing?

6. Look up the current interest rates on bank loans and on high-grade bonds and the dividend yields on utility stocks. On the basis of this information and your forecast for the future, how do you recommend that Red River Power Company raise $4,000,000 which it needs for transmission lines to tie into a multistate power grid? Assume the existing financial structure of Red River Power Company is as shown in Table 13-5, that it can obtain funds at prevailing rates, and that the transmission line must be built to maintain service (estimates show a 12 percent return on the investment after income taxes).

7. "Pollution controls are killing us," says Gerald Cox, the owner of a small iron foundry. Sales have been dropping and a new government requirement for a $40,000 exhaust control would add expense but no income. Joe and Dawn Sandusky, a husband-wife team, have a growing precision alloy casting business and need a larger building. Cox's building is very well suited to their requirements, so Cox proposes to sell out to the Sanduskys. Cox wants $120,000 for his total business—plant, equipment, accounts receivable, inventory. The Sanduskys can scrape up only $20,000 cash; they already have $30,000 in their business. An insurance company is willing to buy the plant for $85,000 and lease it to the Sanduskys. If the Sanduskys gradually liquidate the iron casting inventory and receivables, they might realize $65,000; a quick sale of these assets would yield only $15,000. But they would have to install the exhaust control if they continue to run the iron foundry. Cox recommends that the Sanduskys continue both businesses and indicates that he will accept one-fifth of the stock in such a venture in place of $35,000 of his sales price. The supplier of the exhaust control equipment will take 25 percent down and a 5-year installment mortgage note for the balance. What do you recommend the Sanduskys do?

8. Fast-growing High Temp, Inc., which makes boilers, is doing good business worldwide in the energy equipment and chemical process plants field. Stockholders will be asked at the next meeting to authorize a four-for-one stock split and a tripling of the number of common shares from 10 million to 30 million. Current earnings are $27 million, or $2.99 per share outstanding. The company has no preferred stock. A split is estimated by some to increase the number of registered shareholders by 24 percent. Directors doubled the total amount of dividends paid over the past year to a 60 percent payout ratio. High Temp has heavily publicized its order backlog of $1.7 billion and its recent increases in market share. Can you explain why the directors have approved and put through these undertakings?

9. Specialty Chemicals, Inc., has been growing rapidly and now needs more and more capital because both inventories and accounts receivable are rising at the same rate

as sales. But the owners can put no more equity into the business since their personal financing has been strained to the hilt. Their friends at the First National Bank will not lend any more money because the funds are needed for working capital and not for fixed assets. The long-term bond market has been shut off because very high interest rates—especially after the inflation rate is taken out—mean an excessive strain on company earnings and cash when the sinking fund provisions are considered. The owners of Specialty Chemicals like to believe that sales will grow forever because the firm sells to only one-third of the North American market and not to the rest of the world. Some financial service companies will make loans secured by inventory up to 80 percent of the LIFO value at an interest rate that is five percentage points above the prime rate. Should the owners slow the growth of the company until profits will provide the working capital that is needed—which means no more than a 5 percent growth rate per year for the next five years—or borrow from a financial service company and continue the 25 percent per year increase in sales? (For every dollar of increased sales, current assets have to increase by one dollar. The current ratio must stay at 2/1 so trade creditors cannot furnish more than 50 cents. Net profits after tax are a very respectable 5 percent of sales.)

CASE 13
CLEANING CHEMICALS, INC.

William "Bill" Herbert, president, once again contemplated last year's sales and net profits as he thought about future financing for his company and the three possible ways of providing capital for his family-owned firm.

"I'm feeling desperate. We're up against it once again. We've reached the limit of our ability to finance both plant expansion and increased inventories so that we can make the sales that I know are out there. The small recession that hit our industry last year hurt us badly. Now, what should we do—stay as we are, take on a major stockholder and move to Dallas, or borrow more money to expand in Salt Lake City?"

Bill Herbert's company, Cleaning Chemicals, Inc., processed, mixed, and packaged various chemicals, soaps, detergents, and surfactants for sale to janitorial supply, plant and office cleaning, and the maintenance supply industries. It dealt only with large institutions (hospitals, real estate management companies, industrial plants, and large office buildings) and with state, local, and federal governments. To these customers it sold cleaners, cleaning equipment, algicides, acrylic sealers, degreasing chemicals, insecticides, shampoos, liquid and powdered soaps, disinfectants, stain removers, soap dispensers, gasket removers, lubricants, steam cleaners, deodorants, liquid bacteria, rust removers, and many other products in fifty-five-gallon drums and barrels or by the truckload.

The company, with plants in Oakland, California, and Salt Lake City (and headquarters in Salt Lake), marketed its products along the Pacific Coast and in the area west of Omaha and north of Oklahoma City. While in competition with hundreds of other large and small companies, Cleaning Chemicals has grown rapidly and profitably during the past ten years. (See Tables 1 and 2.) Bill Herbert envisions extending operations across the United States, following expansion into the Middle West, Texas, and the South. His vision of expansion, however, has been limited by recent financial realities.

TABLE 1.
INCOME STATEMENTS
(in 000's)

Account	Last Year	Previous Year	Previous Year	Previous Year	Previous Year
Sales	$6,010	$5,500	$4,510	$3,700	$3,101
Cost of Goods Sold	4,400*	3,570	2,760	2,230	1,860
Gross Margin	1,610	1,930	1,750	1,470	1,241
Selling and Promotional Expense	920	660	560	505	430
General and Administrative Expense	690	568	484	435	360
Taxes	-0-	312	330	250	210
Profit After Taxes	$ -0-	$ 390	$ 376	$ 280	$ 241

*Depreciation expense, included in the cost of goods sold, was $100,000.

"Although our plants perform simple operations, such as diluting, mixing, and packaging chemicals that we buy in bulk, our specialized equipment and low labor costs allow us to sell a good product at a relatively low price and thus provide effectiveness, satisfaction, and value to our customers. Last year we had to reduce prices and increase our sales effort in order to keep volume up, the plants filled with orders, and the employees busy. But that is behind us now and I am looking forward to further growth. We are operating the plants six days per week for fifty weeks out of the year. Working this close to absolute capacity makes cost control difficult. I think that it would be highly desirable to get a larger plant and somehow reduce shipping costs so that we can sell in the Midwest. Chicago is a great market.

"After we looked around at various cities for a new plant and headquarters location, we were approached by the city of Dallas and an investor from there with a promise of a leased plant close to highways and to the Dallas-Fort Worth International Airport. The city would provide whatever space we needed for now and for the next ten years on favorable lease terms and the investor would provide capital by buying stock in our company.

TABLE 2.
BALANCE SHEET
(in 000's)

Assets		Liabilities	
Cash	$ 102	Notes Payable	$ 300
Accounts Receivable	912	Current Portion of	
Inventories	876	debt due	100
Prepaid Expenses	10	Accounts Payable	600
		Accrued Expenses	200
Total Current		Total Current	
Assets	$1,900	Liabilities	$1,200
Equipment		Long-term Debt*	1,000
(net of depreci-		Common Stock†	250
ation reserve)	1,510	Retained Earnings	960
Total Assets	$3,410	Total Liabilities &	
		Net Worth	$3,410

* 14 percent Senior Notes.
† 1,000,000 shares authorized; 250,000 shares outstanding. Two hundred thousand shares were owned by Bill Herbert and his wife. Executives and supervisors owned the rest—acquired through stock bonus plan.

"The deal we finally worked out was that we would issue an additional 200,000 shares of common stock which the investor would purchase for $1,200,000. This would provide funds to pay off most of our long-term debt, increase cash by $100,000 to improve our current ratio, and provide $300,000 to pay for the move and for expanded equipment needs for the 20 percent increase in sales which I expect will come along when we have the added capacity and the new region for sales of our products.

"After we settle in at Dallas, the balance sheet should look much better and it should provide plenty of debt capacity for further borrowing as sales volume goes up.

"If you look at last year's figures, we need fifty-seven cents in assets to support each dollar of sales. But our working capital was excessively low. Whether we stay here or move, we should improve our net working capital (current assets minus current liabilities) to about $900,000 so we'll need another $200,000 in assets. This will run up our total assets to sales ratio to about 0.60 or sixty cents for each dollar of sales (3,610 ÷ 6,010).

"When the word got out that we were planning to move both the Salt Lake plant and our headquarters, some local people swung into action. The mayor and a county supervisor called on us, and the president of a local bank came to see me with an offer. The banker and the mayor both promised us space in a plant that we could lease on favorable terms and that would allow us to expand physical volume by about 50 percent. The banker was not particularly happy with our balance sheet, but she proposed that we combine the notes payable and the long-term debt into another loan which her bank would make at a reduction in interest of two percentage points and with a fifteen-year term. The total loan would amount to $1,500,000 so that we could acquire enough equipment to let sales grow. Repayment would be in equal amounts each year over the term. The bank would require that we pay no dividends for five years and that the current ratio be kept to a minimum of 1.7 to 1. It also wants accounts receivable and inventories reduced by $100,000 each since the banker believes that collections were a bit slow (about fifty-five days outstanding) and that the inventory turnover of five times per year should be increased to about six times.

"We can, in fact, stay where we are and continue with our present level of production and unit sales. My wife wants to do this. If we follow this idea, sales will probably go up about 5 percent in dollar volume because we will be able to raise our prices since economic conditions are improving. We can stay in the present plant and not incur the costs of moving. With more experience in producing at close to capacity we can probably drop our cost of goods sold back toward the percentage of sales that we used to enjoy. And perhaps all this will get us back to a net return on sales after taxes of 4 percent. That's not a bad figure since it is about the average for all U.S. industrial companies but it is certainly a smaller rate of return on sales than we were accustomed to earning in the past.

"Life would be a lot easier if we didn't move. And we would be solidly established in the West. Selling expenses would not increase more than 5 percent and we could hold general and administrative costs to about what they are. Yes, I think I can see a 4 percent return on sales. Our interest costs went way up with the increase in debt we took on last year, but that will be a little less next year."

Question

What course of action do you recommend to Mr. Herbert?

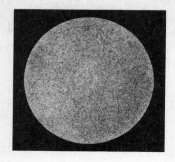

INTEGRATING CASES

Strategy and Financing

POWDERED METALS, INC.

"During our first eight years we had to take large risks," said Mr. Hubler, president of Powdered Metals, Inc. "Bankruptcy was always a threat, but we had no choice. We simply proceeded on faith that our small company would master the art of making high-precision parts out of powdered metal, and then the leading companies of the nation would be glad to do business with us. Now we have mastered the art, at least to some extent, and we are doing business with the Xeroxes and the IBMs. But the risk problem has become tougher because we now have choices. We can use our profits to pay off debts and remove the threat of bankruptcy—or we can seize the opportunity we worked so hard to create and help push powdered metal parts into every sophisticated machine that's made—or we can decide to do something in between."

options for profit

Product/Market Target

The company makes an array of specially shaped gears, bearings, and other machine parts. Instead of starting with the usual casting or forging process, the new metallurgy injects a finely powdered form of iron, steel, or other alloy into a mold and packs the powder together under high pressure. The "raw" part is then placed in a furnace where high temperature unites the fine particles into a solid form.

distinctive advantage

It is the combination of (1) high-pressure molding in very precise molds with (2) heat treatment ("sintering") that makes the company's products distinctive. The molding process enables the company to make oddly shaped parts that are difficult or impossible to produce by ordinary machining. And the sintering process imparts strength and hardness matching or exceeding conventionally formed metal parts. Moreover, the process significantly reduces unit costs, virtually eliminates waste and scrap, and can be used for rapid mass production.

Actually, the technique of producing metal parts by compacting powders has been in use for many years. Early applications were limited to small, relatively crude parts not subjected to heavy bearing or shock loads. The process gained acceptance by providing lower costs than were available through conventional machining or forging methods and by providing unique compositions not readily obtained through conventional melt-alloying methods.

324

As powder-compacting techniques were refined and improved, the competitive advantage broadened dramatically. It is common practice today for engineers to design components specifically for production by the powdered metal process. Load-bearing characteristics, density, dimensional and shape conformity, and ease of machining can now meet a wide range of requirements once considered available only from wrought materials.

The powdered metal industry is generally expected to continue to expand at its current rapid rate because the competitive capabililty of the process is gaining wider acceptance in all sorts of uses. The largest *tonnage* consumer is and will continue to be the automotive industry: bearings, gears, oil pump vanes, etc. However, the largest *number* of parts, requiring a high degree of precision, are being consumed in home appliances, business machines, recreational products, and the electrical and electronics industries. It is to this latter segment of the market that Powdered Metals, Inc., has directed its efforts.

Some of the more intricate precision parts made by this latter segment of the industry cannot be directly compacted to exact finished dimensions and contours and thus require secondary or finishing operations, generally by machining. Powdered Metals, Inc. has a unique capability in this area, shared with only four or five other of the ninety noncaptive powdered metal parts-makers in the country. The success it has attained in becoming a primary vendor to IBM and Xerox is testimony of Powdered Metals' competence in the high value-added portion of the market. The company has the expertise to continue to penetrate premium markets where its proven competence and its highest-grade tools and equipment are demanded.

Four years ago, total industry sales of powdered metal parts was $108 million. By last year the sales had risen to $217 million, more than doubling in three years' time. About $120 million of last year's total went to the automotive industry, the balance to the more specialized markets. And this second part of the industry grew somewhat faster than the total, almost 30 percent per year. This rate of growth may not be maintained but industry speakers predict an average increase over the next decade of 20 to 25 percent per annum.

Powdered Metals hopes to increase the number of customers it serves; it is now somewhat vulnerable because two large firms account for over half of its business. However, because of the cost of making precision molds, reorders of specific parts are likely to be placed with the company that produces the original run. An industry rule-of-thumb is that, on the average, a machine part will continue to be used by a customer in making new machines for seven years. Powdered Metals has not yet had much experience with such reorders.

The company is well equipped to seek orders for complex parts. It has a very good machine shop where molds are made, its compacting presses and sintering furnaces are new, and it has equipment for secondary machining if this is required. Both Mr. Hubler and Mr. Chang, the chief engineer, are recognized for their specialized knowledge, and the company has established a reputation for high-quality output.

Progress to Date

Mr. A. B. Hubler dropped out of engineering school, became a machinist in the Navy, and later worked at this trade while completing his engineering training at night. He was a partner in several small firms, and in one of these he hired a bright young engineer, J. K. Chang. These two men soon developed the idea of a new firm in the powdered metals field. Four years later, Mr. Hubler had assembled the initial capital and Mr. Chang had studied the latest technological developments. The new firm was launched in a suburb of Columbus, Ohio.

The early years proved to be even more difficult than anticipated. Learning how to get dependable quality from new equipment, training personnel, obtaining test orders from customers and waiting while they evaluated the products in their own shops—all took time and money. But now, eight years later, Powdered Metals, Inc., is a profitable business.

The plant is running on a two-shift basis. The margin between prices and costs is improving, reflecting both an ability to get more attractive orders and improved efficiency in the plant. And the company has a four-month backlog of orders. Table 1 shows the improvement in income over the last five years, from a staggering deficit to a 19 percent return on the book value of stockholders' equity.

TABLE 1.
INCOME STATEMENT
(in thousands)

	Last year	2 years ago	3 years ago	4 years ago	5 years ago
Net sales	$3,732	$3,019	$1,778	$ 821	$ 316
Cost of sales	2,631	2,262	1,325	644	530
Gross profit............	$1,101	$ 757	$ 453	$ 177	$−214
Selling, general & administrative expenses..	797	484	386	294	189
Net income	$ 304*	$ 273*	$ 67*	$−117	$−403

*No income tax has been paid because of loss carryovers for preceding years. At the beginning of the present year the remaining loss carryover was $370,000.

Present Financing

Obtaining the capital necessary to finance Powdered Metals has been a strain. During its early years the company relied on equity investments by Mr. Hubler and his friends. Equipment, especially compacting presses obtained from a Japanese manufacturer, was usually purchased at least in part with chattel mortgages, and other loans were secured.

About three years ago the company was successful in a significant recapitalization: (1) 50,000 shares of common stock were sold to the public at $10 per share by a local investment banker; (2) the Buckeye SBIC made a $2,000,000 mortgage loan to the company[1]; (3) debts outstanding at that time were either paid off or converted to common stock. The Buckeye SBIC loan runs for ten years with $50,000 maturing quarterly ($200,00 per year); the interest rate is 8½ percent per annum. As part of the deal, Buckeye received warrants (rights to buy) for 50,000 shares at $8 per share, which can be exercised any time during the ten years that the loan is outstanding.

recap.

This injection of capital, helpful though it was, has not been adequate to support expanding production. New equipment to expand capacity has been financed with chattel mortgages; $300,000 of such mortgages were outstanding a year ago, and an additional $600,000 were issued during the past year. These chattel mortgages mature at the rate of $100,000 per year and bear 10 percent interest. Incidentally, the Buckeye SBIC was willing to subordinate its claim on this new equipment because the added capacity increases the chance that its warrants will become valuable.

$900,000 chattell mort.

The present financial structure of the company, reflecting these capital inputs, is shown in Table 2.

Future Opportunities

"At long last," Mr. Hubler observes, "we have the opportunity to have a balance sheet look the way the bankers like it. Assuming earnings just stay steady, our cash gain from operations each year will be:

Net Income.........	$304,000
Depreciation	216,000
Available	$520,000

"With that amount of cash we can make our annual debt repayments of $300,000 and still increase current assets $220,000. In two years our current ratio would be 2:1 and our long-term debt would be only 82 percent of the stockholders' equity. For anyone who has been squeezed for capital for eight years, that kind of a picture is very attractive. And maybe the equipment people would stop insisting on my personal guarantee of those mortgage notes.

"But we didn't enter the powdered metal business to stay even. We believe the industry will continue to grow rapidly, and naturally we'd like to benefit from that growth. The future is never certain, of course; too many competitors may enter the business or some new technique may replace powdered metals. But powdered metals have grown much faster than the industries we serve—

---

[1]SBICs (Small Business Investment Corporations) are private lending organizations that are granted federal tax advantages because they concentrate on lending money to small firms that are having difficulty obtaining long-term capital.

TABLE 2.
BALANCE SHEET—END OF YEAR
(in Thousands)

	Last Year		Preceding Year	
Assets				
Current assets:				
Cash	$ 199		$ 89	
Accounts receivable, net	650		651	
Inventories	637		308	
Prepaid and deferred items	89		61	
Total current assets...........		$1,575		$1,109
Plant and equipment:				
Land and buildings	$ 941		$ 909	
Machinery and equipment	2,853		2,244	
Furniture and fixtures	260		230	
	$4,054		$3,383	
Less depreciation reserve	−747		−531	
Net plant and equipment		3,307		2,852
Research and deferred charges.......		74		83
Total assets....................		$4,956		$4,044
Liabilities				
Current Liabilities:				
Current portion of long-term debt .	$ 300		$ 200	
Accounts payable	517		345	
Accrued liabilities	109		73	
Total current liabilities		$ 926		$ 618
Long-term debt:				
Long-term loan	$1,600		$1,800	
Equipment mortgages	800		300	
Total debt due after 1 year......		2,400		2,100
Stockholders' equity:				
200,000 shares outstanding, par value $1	$ 200		$ 200	
Capital in excess of par value	1,800		1,800	
Retained earnings (deficit)	(370)		(674)	
Total equity		1,630		1,326
Total liabilities and equity		$4,956		$4,044

business machines, electronics, home appliances, and the like—and Powdered Metals has been growing faster than its competitors. So I feel that 20 percent increase per year for us is very conservative. We should be able to do that and at the same time be more choosy about the orders we take, which will help our profit margin. Of course, if a real recession descends on us, it's a new ball game.

"The main catch is that fast growth takes more capital—capital we do not have. With an additional $500,000 in equipment we could produce a volume of $5,000,000 in sales. The building is big enough to handle $7,000,000—with a bit of squeezing. But as we move beyond $5,000,000, all kinds of machinery will be needed, on the average of $.80 per every additional dollar of sales or $1,600,000 of new equipment for the expansion from $5,000,000 to $7,000,000.

"In addition, more sales require more working capital. Inventory, accounts receivable, accounts payable, and accrued items all go up. My rough estimate is that the net increase in working capital would be about one-sixth of the annual sales. Where is all that money coming from? Retained earnings will help, but in any one year during the growth period the profit on the added volume (say, 9 percent) doesn't provide necessary working capital (17 percent).

"I've asked our treasurer, P. L. Jablonski, to explore all the different ways we might finance the business that I'm sure we can get during the next four years. With all these alternatives before us, we can sit down and figure out whether it is wise to go plunging ahead."

Alternative Sources of Capital

Ms. Jablonski summarized the various potential ways Powdered Metals, Inc., might finance its growth as follows:

1. The company's commercial bank suggests no growth this year and cutting inventories $100,000. These actions will allow the company to significantly improve its working capital position. Then the bank would make a short-term loan of $500,000 (perhaps requiring the pledging of accounts receivable if the inventory reduction was not feasible). The interest cost would be prime rate plus 1½ percent and maintenance of a bank balance of 20 percent of the loan.[2]
2. The investment banker who helped sell company stock three years ago thinks that improved company performance would create an interest in an additional issue, in spite of the present depressed condition of stocks generally. However, the selling price to the public would be only $7.50 per share, and after underwriting charges and other costs the company would receive $6.70 per share. Thus an issue of 75,000 shares would yield $502,000. Such an issue would improve debt/equity ratios. It would be "expensive" for present stockholders; for example, after such an issue, the people who invested $500,000 three years ago when risks were greater would hold only 18 percent of the total equity whereas the new stockholders would have 27 percent of the total equity.
3. An investment broker, recommended by the commercial bank, suggests a "sale and leaseback" of the company's land and buildings (for $800,000) plus the new equipment (costing $500,000). The $800,000 would be used to pay off existing chattel mortgages on equipment. The company would pay an annual rental equivalent to 9½ percent on money advanced (a total initially of

---

[2]The minimum balance requirement, a customary banking practice, means that the company would get only $400,000 for other uses. Assuming an 8 percent prime rate, the interest cost would be 9½ percent of $500,000, or $47,500 per year. On $400,000 this is equivalent to almost 12 percent per annum.

$1,300,000) plus 5 percent depreciation on the building and equipment. The lease would run for 20 years, at which time the company would have an option to repurchase the land, buildings, and equipment at 20 percent of the total $1,300,000 advanced.[3]

4. Mr. Bender, a Cleveland financier and president of Empire Investment Co., proposes a merger with another small firm that he controls. The firm, a profitable truck-leasing operation, would be merged into Powdered Metals so that the profits from the trucking operation would be offset by the tax loss carryforward of Powdered Metals. Empire Investment Co. owns the trucking firm and would get 75 percent of the shares of the merged companies. Mr. Bender says he can always find capital for profitable investments, and he would be able to devise some scheme to provide whatever capital the powdered metal activities can use effectively.

5. Buckeye SBIC is willing to advance more capital if the total debt structure is improved. It proposes a combined package: (a) a $500,000 loan for the new equipment on the same terms as its present loan, plus (b) purchase of 80,000 shares of stock at $6 per share. The $480,000 from the stock sale, $100,000 from reduction of inventories, and current earnings are to be used to retire the equipment mortgages.

Ms. Jablonski notes, "All five of the proposals focus primarily on raising $500,000 to expand production facilities. This will enable Powdered Metals to increase its sales to $5,000,000. At the projected rise in sales, that takes care of us for only about eighteen months. Consequently, any plan adopted must also consider the ability of the company at that time to raise further growth capital."

Questions

1. Do you recommend that Powdered Metals, Inc., buy the $500,000 worth of new equipment at this time? If so, how should the expansion be financed?

2. Assuming that your recommendation is accepted and that you have $5,000 available for investment, what price per share would you be willing to pay for Powdered Metals common stock?

2. Assuming you're an outside corp. looking to acquire this Co., how much do you think this company is worth? And why?

ESSEX CREEK DISPOSAL CO.

Essex Creek Disposal Co. faces difficult questions about who should take the initiative and who should bear the cost of "environmental protection." Company officers are subject to several conflicting pressures.

---

[3]The company would continue to pay real estate and property taxes and insurance just as though it owned the property. The interest portion of the rent would drop as the depreciation portion retired the loan. Broadly speaking, the company would be getting a 20-year loan at 9½ percent, except that it would have to pay 20 percent to retrieve its property at the end of the period. There also would be a book loss on the land and buildings at the time of the transaction ($941,000 minus $800,000), but this is not a real loss since the property could eventually be recovered on the basis of the $800,000 figure. Presently, depreciation on the buildings is about $25,000 per year. It is anticipated that Buckeye SBIC will waive its mortgage lien on the land and buildings because it will obtain a first lien on equipment when the $800,000 chattel mortgages are paid off and because its warrants become more attractive.

The company itself was born an unwanted child of an outlying housing development. The builders of Essex Manor, a 300-unit garden apartment and home development, had to include sewage disposal in their plans for converting a large farm into a modern housing complex. Lewis Township[1] has no general sewage system—other than septic tanks for individual homes—but insisted on a biochemical plant for a population concentration like Essex Manor. To meet this need, Essex Creek Disposal Co. was formed.

Essex Creek Disposal Co. is a small, privately owned public utility, chartered to serve Essex Manor. It owns collecting lines, pumping equipment, and a treatment plant two miles from Essex Manor. Its effluent (which is potable) is discharged into Essex Creek. Initially the company was owned and operated by the promoter of Essex Manor. The promoter donated to the company about two-thirds of the original investment and also set service charges low enough— $20 per quarter—to appear minor to prospective buyers of homes and apartments.

After the Essex Manor development was completed, the promoter wanted to move on to new ventures, and therefore sold all the common stock of Essex Creek Disposal Co. to a group of investors for a nominal amount. These special stockholders have diverse experience with local public utilities, and they bought the company with the belief that the state Public Utility Commission (which must approve changes in utility rates) would agree that the heavy investment justifies some increase in service charges. Mr. Boynton Boyd, Jr., president of Essex Creek Disposal Co., says, "The $600,000 invested in this company entitles the owners to roughly $36,000 income per year, even under the very limited profits allowed public utilities."

During its six years of operation the company has never made a profit. Costs of chemicals, power, and labor have risen while service charges remained constant—with a resulting increase in annual deficits. (The condensed balance sheet and income statement for the past year are shown in Tables 1 and 2.)

Obtaining approval to increase the service charges has proved to be more difficult than the present owners anticipated. Two current complications are new antipollution equipment and possible plant expansion to serve a new high school.

Who Pays What for Cleanliness?

Detergents used in homes for washing clothes and dishes have sullied our natural environment. First, in the 1960s high-foaming detergents that do not break down in the earth through biological action began accumulating at alarm-

TABLE 1.
CONDENSED BALANCE SHEET

Assets			Liabilities and Equity	
Cash	$	540	Accounts payable	$34,170*
Accounts receivable		2,268	Accrued items	9,606
Total current assets	$	2,808	Total current liabilities	$43,776
Utility plant & equipment:			Long-term debt	75,000
Cost	$596,777		Contribution to aid	
Depr	71,613	525,164	construction	379,752
			Common stock	100,000
			Retained earnings	(70,556)
			Total liabilities and	
Total assets		$527,972	equity	$527,972

*$30,000 of notes due to company officers are subordinated to other claims.

TABLE 2.
CONDENSED INCOME STATEMENT

Total revenue	$ 25,920
Operating deductions from revenue:	
Operating expense	$ 22,495
Maintenance expense	4,382
Depreciation expense	11,377
Taxes other than income taxes	3,855
Total operating deductions	$ 42,109
Interest expense	$ 4,930
Total deductions	$ 47,039
Net (loss)	$(21,119)

ing rates; surface wells in some areas produced sudsy water! To correct this problem, detergent manufacturers substituted phosphates. Phosphates do a good job of cleaning and they foam only a little. But they do remain in disposed wash water, and this creates a different kind of pollution. Phosphates are excellent plant food—as their use in fertilizer attests. In water, phosphates stimulate the growth of algae and other plants, especially in warm shallow ponds and lakes. The algae die, rot, and use up the oxygen in the water, the fish die, and the whole body of water becomes a stinking mess. The more phosphates in the water, the greater the mess.

Phosphates in our lakes and streams were identified as a villain just as public concern with ecology accelerated. Since then, state health boards and others have demanded a reduction in the inflow of phosphates. One route is to ban the use of phosphates in detergents, but there is no convenient substitute that does not have its own polluting effects. (Besides, public authorities are embarrassed to ask detergent manufacturers to stop using an ingredient they were forced to adopt a few years earlier.) Another route is to remove the phosphate from the waste water before it is released back into the environment. It is this latter approach that complicates life for Essex Creek Disposal Co.

In response to the public outcry about polluted waters, the state Department of Health is urgently seeking ways to reduce the discharge of phosphates. And, the effluent from the Essex Creek Disposal plant is clearly high in phosphates (as are discharges from most other sewage treatment plants). An engineering firm, the Chemical Equipment Company, has invented a chemical process for removing phosphates from sewage, and the Department of Health is pressing Essex Creek Disposal Co. to install the process even though it is still in the development stage. Company executives feel that the company is being used as an experimental guinea pig, perhaps because the company is small, but state officials deny this.

Following negotiations with Chemical Equipment Company, Essex Creek Disposal Co. decided to pursue the plan urged by the Department of Health, provided the cost of doing so could be recovered in service charges to its customers. Toward this end, the company petitioned the Public Utility Commission for permission to increase its basic rate for each living unit, or equivalent, from $20 to $75 per quarter. The requested increase explicitly included both an adjustment to overcome past deficits and projected costs of the new phosphate removal process. The key information supporting the request is summarized in the pro forma statements shown in Tables 3 and 4.

This proposed rate increase of 275 percent was greeted by howls of protest from residents of Essex Manor, many of whom had already strained their financial resources when moving into the new development. The Public Utility Commission's hearing on the proposal was a stormy session. Shortly thereafter, the Commission ruled the company was not entitled to relief for phosphate removal since the equipment was not installed and working properly. However, the Commission did authorize an interim rate increase from $20 to $31.25 per quarter to overcome current cash deficits. The ruling also indicated that if and when the company had a phosphate removal system installed and operating properly,[2] and had experience with additional costs, a request for further increase would be appropriate. Of course, no commitment was made as to the amount that might be allowed under such conditions.

Now, the company must decide what to do about phosphate removal. (1) It can proceed as the Department of Health is urging—i.e., invest $78,000 in new equipment, hoping that the system will be effective, and then go back to the Public Utility Commission for a further rate increase. Or (2) It can stall. Under

---

[2] Proper functioning is defined by the Department of Health as removal of at least 95 percent of the phosphate coming into the treatment plant and less than one part per million in its discharge.

TABLE 3.
PRO FORMA ANNUAL INCOME STATEMENT
SHOWING EFFECT OF PROPOSED RATES AND PHOSPHATE REMOVAL

	Present	Projected
Total Revenue		
(324 residential units, at $80 and $300)	$ 25,920	$97,200
Operating expenses:		
Operating Labor	$ 3,052	$15,600[a]
Power and fuel.	3,633	5,433
Chemical expense	1,754	7,154
Miscellaneous supplies and expense	438	3,138
Administrative expense	8,458	8,458[b]
Office supplies and expense	2,385	2,385
Professional services	2,275	588
Property insurance	500	945
Maintenance of plant and equipment	4,382	4,382
Transportation.	—	750[c]
Depreciation.	11,377	14,892[d]
Taxes—payroll, gross receipts, franchise, excise	3,855	15,242
Income taxes @ 22%.	—	2,927
Total operating expenses	$ 42,109	$81,894
Operating income or (loss).	$(16,189)	$15,306
Interest charges:		
Interest on long-term debt	4,500	4,500
Other interest.	430	430
Total income deductions.	$ 4,930	$ 4,930
Net income or (loss)	$(21,119)	$10,376

[a]Addition of full-time operator stipulated by Department of Health.
[b]Administrative expense includes part-time salaries of all officers.
[c]Station wagon for operating personnel.
[d]All depreciation charged at 2 percent per year, except 33 percent on station wagon and 20 percent on new laboratory equipment.

this second alternative, the Department of Health will probably obtain a court order compelling the company to remove the phosphates. (The company could argue that a statewide or national prohibition of the sale of detergents containing phosphates would be more effective, but such action is unlikely because it would be unpopular with detergent users and opposed by manufacturers.)

The second alternative differs from the first primarily in four aspects. (1) Essex Creek Disposal Co. will be regarded as uncooperative by the Department of Health, Lewis Township officials, and ecology buffs. (2) There is a possibility, though very small, that the order compelling Essex Creek Disposal Co. to install the new equipment will not be issued. (3) The need for action will be postponed

TABLE 4.
PRO FORMA ESTIMATE OF RETURN ON INVESTMENT

Rate base:

Present plant and equipment, depreciated		$525,164
Add: New investment in phosphate removal		
Plant and equipment	$70,745	
Transporation equipment	4,500	
Laboratory equipment	3,000	78,245
		$603,409
Less: Contribution to aid construction		379,752
New rate base		$233,657
Return on investment at proposed rates:		
Projected operating income		$ 15,306
Divided by new rate base		$223,657
Equals rate of return on investment		6.84%

for about six months. (4) The Company's posture in appealing for a rate increase will differ, but whether the Public Utility Commission will be more—or less—considerate of the company if it is acting under court order rather than its own initiative is unknown.[3]

Either alternative is risky for the company. The process may not work satisfactorily; the company would then be stuck with ineffective equipment with no one to pay the bill. The Department of Health has much enthusiasm but no money to underwrite experiments. Even if the equipment works properly, there is no assurance that the Public Utility Commission will permit the company to pass off the entire operating and capital cost to users of its services. Yet everyone agrees that phosphate pollution of waters should be reduced.

New Customer on the Horizon

Essex Creek Disposal Co. has another opportunity that is related to its action on phosphate removal. Lewis Township is building a new high school close to the company's sewer line and clearly will need arrangements for disposal of sanitary sewage.

When plans to build the school—to provide for a growing population—were first announced, Mr. Boyd recognized that a large potential customer would be created. However, he decided not to seek a tie-in of the school with company facilities for the following reasons: (1) The treatment plant would have

---

[3]The Public Utility Commission is an independent body with its own due process procedures. There is no possibility of a working agreement between the Commission and the Department of Health, especially on a very small case such as this.

to be expanded. Although some excess capacity exists, the addition of the high school would create a risk that the existing processing tanks might overflow into Essex Creek before treatment was completed. To maintain a comfortable safety margin, a 25 percent increase in capacity would be necessary. (2) The service charge to support this additional plant would look high to school and township officials. More than half of the construction cost of present facilities was donated by the developer of Essex Manor, and prevailing residential rates do not provide reasonable earnings even on the residual investment. So, charges that would provide a reasonable return on the added investment needed to serve the new school would appear high in comparison to residential rates.

The company charter does not require the company to serve new customers such as a high school. Since the company was created explicitly to solve a problem related to the Essex Manor development, it is not part of a scheme to serve the total township or county. In fact, the company has accepted about thirty residential customers located outside Essex Manor, but these could be easily handled with existing capacity.

Recently Mr. Boyd discovered that the school architect assumed that sanitary sewage would flow into Essex Creek Disposal Co.'s line. Contracts have been let and construction is under way based on this assumption.

Thus, the company is in an unusually favorable bargaining position. For the school to build its own treating plant would cost more than the addition to Essex Creek Disposal Co. plant. Moreover, planning and construction of a separate plant would delay opening the school for perhaps a year, whereas no delay (though perhaps a short-run pollution risk) will be involved in a tie to company facilities.

The relation of the new school to phosphate removal is explained by Mr. Boyd as follows: "If Essex Creek Disposal Co. has already embarked on a phosphate removal program when school officials approach us—as they undoubtedly will—the school can be expected to bear a reasonable share of that expense. On the other hand, if we are still arguing with the Department of Health, then the school people will focus on our present costs and rates, and phosphate removal will come as a separate issue on top of that.

Mr. Boyd continued, "I wish the high school problem had not come up, because I doubt that we can make a decent return on the necessary investment. It complicates our picture, and we'll end up having another group—the Board of Education—trying to tell us how to run our business."

Questions

1. What should Mr. Boyd do to resolve his phosphate problem?
2. How do you recommend that such a solution be financed?
3. Explain how your recommendations relate to social responsibility and to a longer-run strategy for Essex Creek Disposal Co.

Part 3

COMBINING
BUISNESS-UNITS
IN A DIVERSIFIED
CORPORATION

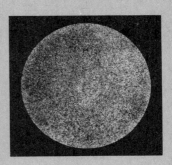

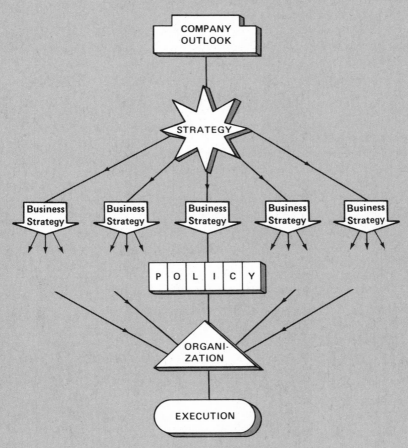

14 PORTFOLIO STRATEGY

Business-Unit Versus Corporate Strategy

Strategy and policy for a *single business-unit* has been our focus thus far, in both Parts 1 and 2. These single product line, self-contained companies are the dynamic building blocks of our economic society. Each requires individualized attention. Our prime attention on the creation of strong business-units is more than a convenient analytical approach; it reflects the cardinal importance of these units.

Nevertheless, successful business-units often outgrow their original mission. Their market may have matured; they may have strengths that can be applied to related businesses. Or, a broader base may be needed to match competition or spread risk; assurance of supplies may become critical; perhaps an irresistible deal may present itself. For such reasons as these, many companies find themselves engaged in several different businesses.

Sooner or later the benefits of combining the collection of business-units within a corporation must be assessed. Potentially, the federation of units will be stronger than the sum of each business operating independently. But this does not happen automatically. We need a *corporate strategy* which focuses on the selection and the interrelation of units that will, in fact, yield the benefits of union. In addition, the corporate strategy should identify the resources that the corporation will supply to its business-units to give them a distinctive competitive advantage.

Corporate strategy, in contrast to business-unit strategy, applies to a different level of organization and it differs in content. It is primarily concerned with building an effective collection of business-units. This requires (1) thoughtful investment (allocation) of resources. Some units will be built up, others liquidated; perhaps new units will be acquired. Because this allocation process is similar to that of a financial investment manager changing the composition of securities in his or her portfolio, the term "portfolio problem" is widely used to identify this part of corporate strategy. (2) Then, to buttress the business-units, the corporation should provide "resource inputs" which give the businesses added strength.

A basic approach to formulating corporate strategy is indicated in Figure 14-1. A careful appraisal of the business-units presently owned is the first step. For each unit, the results to date, the standing relative to competitors, threats and opportunities in its environment, and projected future results based on existing plans should be studied. Moreover, the projections for all business-units should be combined into a consolidated picture of what the corporation will be and do if the staus quo is maintained.

FIGURE 14-1.
CORPORATE STRATEGY FORMULATION

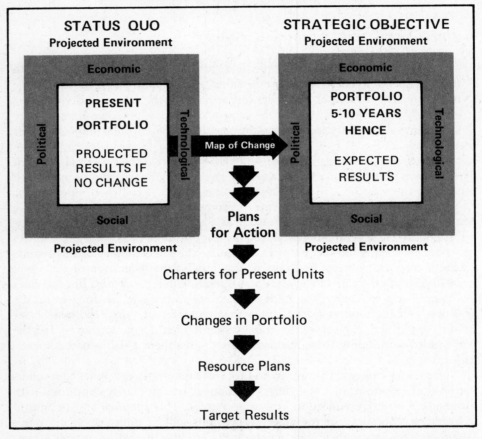

If this combined picture is not entirely satisfactory, then the second broad step is to decide what changes, executed within the projected environment, would put the corporation in the best balanced position. This becomes the strategic objective. It stipulates the desired portfolio of business-units five to ten years hence, their relative competitive positions, the key corporate resources, the individual unit results, and the combined results for the corporation as a whole.

To move from the status quo to the strategic objective will require some supporting changes along the way. The main features of these planned changes, which become part of the corporate strategy, deal with charters for present units (domains, expectations, constraints), changes in the portfolio, resource plans including sources and allocation of capital, and target results at intervals along the course.

The main elements in a corporate strategy, then, include:

1. The desired portfolio of business-units five to ten years hence.
2. The distinctive corporate resources that will add power and luster to these business-units.
3. Major moves (thrusts) needed to get from the present situation to the holdings pictured in l above:
   a. charters for business-units to be retained;
   b. additions or deletions of business-units, including desired acquisitions;
   c. consolidated resource mobilization and allocation plans.
4. Target results.

The chief issues and hurdles in developing the portfolio of business-units are discussed in this chapter. The inputs of corporate resources are considered in the next chapter, and the process of acquiring a new firm is explored in Chapter 16.

PORTFOLIO DESIGN

A good portfolio has several dimensions. Four are always significant: (1) growth and profitability of the business-units considered separately, (2) synergy among the units, (3) risk and profit balance, and (4) cash-flow balance.

1st Dimension: Attractive Business-Units.

The business-units within a diversified corporation will naturally vary in attractiveness. Industry growth rates change, competitors expand capacity, risks assumed turn out well or poorly, and so forth. So an initial step in reviewing portfolio strategy is to compare the relative attractiveness of present units, especially in terms of their *future* prospects for growth and profitability. Corporation resources will be limited, especially with respect to central management time and perhaps capital. Consequently, guidance is needed on where to place the "bets."

A useful way to highlight such a comparison of business-units is on an evaluation matrix. One such matrix, adapted from layouts used by General Electric and Royal Dutch Shell, is shown in Figure 14-2.[1] Here each business-unit is eval-

---

[1]This matrix is a significant refinement of the more familiar 2 x 2 matrix stressed by The Boston Consulting Group. The earlier B.C.G. version focused only on cash flow and simply looked at industry growth versus company market position. The resulting four boxes were designated: 1:1 stars, 1:2 wildcats or problem children, 2:1 cash cows, and 2:2 dogs.

uated on the basis of its industry attractiveness and its competitive position in that industry.

Placing a business-unit on such a matrix involves many subjective judgments. Both the subfactors to be included and the outlook for each factor have to be decided. Among the subfactors which determine an industry's attractiveness are: market growth rate, stability of demand, availability of resources, product and process volatility, number of customers and suppliers and the ease of entry, governmental support/regulation, gross and net margins, inflation vulnerability. A similar set of subfactors bear on the competitive position of a business-unit. These include: relative market share, product and service quality and reputation, favorable access to resources, R & D strength, relative productivity and costs, community and government relations. (See Chapters 2 and 3 for discussion of industry and business-unit subfactors.)

The matrix is designed to provoke strategic thinking. For instance, in the example shown, business-unit D clearly should be divested, and A, the corporation's original business, has such poor prospects that it should be used to generate cash as it is phased out. In contrast, units E and G may warrant significant resource inputs because they are in attractive industries.

This sizing up of the business-units separately, of course, builds upon the thorough strategic planning done within the respective units. Each business-unit should have its own plans which, if successful, may change its location on the evaluation matrix. At the corporate level harsher judgments about their *relative* prospects are needed as a basis for allocating scarce resources.

2nd Dimension: Synergy Among Businesses

A good portfolio is more than a collection of attractive business-units. The fact that the units are associated under a single central management should add extra value. Often a unit when viewed separately has only medium appeal, but when combined with other holdings it may add unusual strength. Synergy and balance are both involved.

Four potential sources of synergy deserve attention. (1) First is the ability of corporate executives to manage (serve as "outside director") various kinds of businesses with acumen. Historical data show that the more successful diversified companies stick to "related" businesses. In its diversification, Federated Department Stores stays with retailing because its central managers understand that type of activity. In contrast, in its initial growth phase, Teledyne concentrated on new high-technology businesses. The rationale is that the experience gained and the competence needed in guiding one part of the portfolio will be especially valuable to *other business-units* in related fields.[2]

---

[2]This argument also has negative connotations. As we shall see, considerations of balance may suggest that unrelated businesses be assembled, but if this is done part of the cost will be added complexity in management.

FIGURE 14-2.

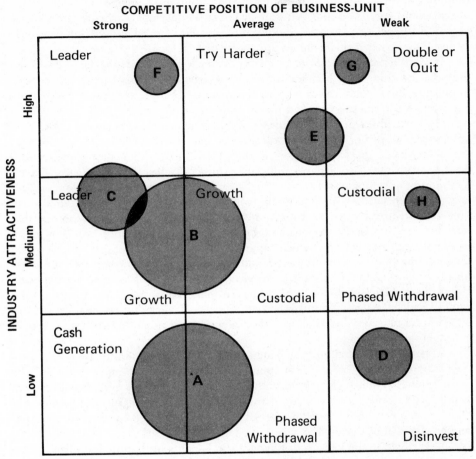

COMPETITIVE POSITION OF BUSINESS-UNIT

EVALUATION MATRIX
Area within circles indicates relative size of business-units

By no means rare are companies with managements that dislike decisive action. The president of a medical supply company had placed close friends in charge of branch operations and was unwilling to replace these executives in spite of submarginal performances. Nevertheless, this company was attractive for merger because the elimination of two losing units and the change of one additional executive made the remaining activities a successful venture. Quite clearly, objective managers, introduced following the merger, were all that was needed.

(2) Synergy may be possible from the broader use of a particular strength of

one of the business-units. The Campbell Soup Company provides a well-known example. Over the years this company has built up a strong national selling organization for its soups. When it acquired Pepperidge Farm, an East Coast producer of specialty breads, cookies, etc., it used its marketing strength to give Pepperidge Farm products national distribution.

In another case, the R & D capability of a production systems company helped a machine tool business develop electronic controls for its equipment. Similarly, the national repair service organization of a printing press company is a great boost to the sale of Swiss-made auxiliary equipment.

(3) Vertical integration is another potential source of synergy. For instance, an assured supply of paper periodically becomes critical for magazine publishers. Time, Inc. has its own paper subsidiaries which provide supply protection. At the same time, Time's paper mills are assured of a large steady customer with a minimum of selling effort.

(4) When business-units are relatively small, the parent may be able to provide a centralized resource more efficiently than the units could obtain that resource independently. A prime example, of course, is raising capital in major financial markets on terms which separate units could not command alone. But there are many other possibilities. Small commercial banks, when they are combined, find substantial economies in electronic processing of checks, deposits, billings, etc. (The local unit is also able to make larger loans because the total capital which sets size limits is larger.) The central room reservation service which hotel and motel chains provide is a significant advantage to local units in maintaining occupancy.

Care must be exercised in seeking synergies. Some possibilities run into antitrust barriers. Also, obtaining a synergistic benefit clearly implies that two or more business-units will operate within certain constraints; and over time that requirement may become a serious drag. Many vertical integration schemes, for instance, tend to limit flexibility, as rubber companies tied to obsolete national rubber plantations discovered.

Nevertheless, the prospect of synergistic benefits may influence decisions of which business-units to retain—or add—in a total portfolio. The potential impact of ability to manage, use of special strengths, vertical integration, and central resource pools should be considered at least.

3rd Dimension: Risk and Profit Balance

A third consideration in portfolio strategy is the degree of risk and the resulting fluctuation in profits that is acceptable. The mix of businesses selected clearly affects the overall uncertainty about the stability and size of sales and profits.

An issue here is whether to reduce risk by diversifying even with some sacrifice of profits, or to support risky ventures with potentially high profits. Similarly, there may be a trade-off between liquidation with a known payout versus continuing in business with an uncertain future.

Prevailing norms provide two portfolio guides. (1) Companies in mature businesses are expected to shift investment to new lines of business in order to provide continuity even though the new businesses are more risky than the present ones. For example, Handy & Harman's traditional activity of processing silver and gold is "mature", because major new uses of these venerable metals are unlikely, and rising metal prices dampen much increase in the physical volume of present uses. So Handy & Harman has adopted a long-run objective of deriving half its future profits outside the precious metal area. It is steadily adding business-units in other high value-added industrial processes. This is an explicit strategy of reducing the risk associated with remaining in its primary field.

(2) Another indication of the importance attached to survival is the concept that a corporation should not bet its existence on a single, risky venture. No publicly owned firm relies entirely upon the success of drilling a particular offshore oil well; it gets other investors to share the risk on that well, and then it "diversifies" to part ownership in other wells, probably in other geographical areas.

Hedging against cyclical risks is often proposed. If you are in the construction business, the idea is to also enter a business that goes up when construction goes down. In practice, cyclical hedges are very difficult to find. A corporation supplying auto manufacturers, for example, may enter the replacement-parts market because this has a much steadier demand; but the replacement-parts industry is at most stable, not contra-cyclical, so the combined result is only a dampening of the auto production fluctuations. To return to the Handy & Harman example, that corporation does have a large refinery for secondary recovery of precious metals, so when metal prices rise, the refinery is busy even though the processing mill is slack.

In the shorter term, some revenue stabilization can be achieved by balancing *seasonal* products. The nostalgic "coal and ice" business is now reflected in Head's production of skis and tennis rackets, of ski clothing and shorts.

In each of these examples, one specific risk is offset (to some extent) by another with counterbalancing characteristics. The aim is greater stability of revenue and profits, even though the average result may be lower than the "expected" returns from one of the ventures alone. Carried to the extreme, this averaging of risks leads to a conglomerate where a catch-all collection of businesses is assembled with no special effort to match one against another. (Full diversification gives a corporation an average growth about the same as the GNP, a growth rate unacceptable to many managers and investors.) However, even the high-flying conglomerates rarely admit to such indiscriminate averaging. Instead, some other rationale dominates portfolio selection—such as synergy—and risk balancing is a constraint bring total exposure down to a level acceptable to major stockholders.

4th Dimension: Cash Flow Balance

Growing businesses typically absorb cash—for working capital as well as for plant and equipment—even when they are highly profitable. In fact, companies do fail because their cash resources cannot support a very successful "take-off" of their product. Mature and declining businesses, in contrast, often generate cash, as assets are gradually being liquidated. Such net investment flows vary widely by kind of business, having a high early cash requirement in mining, for example, and the reverse in magazine publishing where consumers pay in advance for subscriptions.

One additional dimension in building a portfolio, then, is balancing cash flow. *Internal* generation of needed cash is the aim. Of course, this is not the only potential source of cash; new equity and loans can be secured for profitable ventures. (Declining ventures rarely need or justify new infusions.) Nevertheless, our tax system makes internal generation of cash a significant advantage. Cash paid to stockholders as dividends is subject to personal income tax; even if the stockholders are willing to reinvest it in the corporation, they have much less— maybe only 50 percent—to so invest. However, if the corporation itself makes the reinvestment directly, the personal income tax bite is avoided. (Underwriting expenses are also avoided.) Moreover, if a new business-unit is showing a loss which can be offset against a profit of some other unit, then to that extent can also be avoided until the loss carry-over is used up.

Since internally generated cash is a comparatively inexpensive and convenient way to finance growing business-units, one or more "cash-cows," as cash generating units are often called, are attractive segments in a portfolio even when their long-run prospects are poor. This ability to shift cash flows from cash-cows to stars and wildcats can provide a corporation with immortality— Ponce de Leon's fountain of youth!

Summary: The design of a desired portfolio considers several different factors, including: attractiveness of the business-units separately, synergy, balanced risk and profits, and cash flow. The weight attached to each factor depends upon the strengths that the corporation already possesses, environmental opportunities, and personal values of its key executives.

MAJOR MOVES TO ATTAIN DESIRED PORTFOLIO

Charters for Present Business-Units

The portfolio strategy for a diversified corporation blends several different considerations, as we have just seen. The long-run strength and direction of the consolidated group is the dominant criterion. The various business-units are assigned roles in terms of what is good for the *family as a whole*.

In this composite plan, some business-units are destined to grow rapidly; others have to modify their emphasis, overcome particular weaknesses, or demonstrate improved capability before they will be strongly supported; a few may be encouraged to take high risks because the potential gains are great; several have the role of cash-cows; one or two may be retained largely for the protection or strength they give one of the "stars"; and so on.

With this overall concept in mind, it is possible to negotiate a "charter" for each business-unit. This charter will be an agreement between corporate executives and the senior management of the business-unit regarding:

1. The *domain*—the product/service/market scope—in which the business-unit will operate.
2. The *expected results,* including sales and growth, competitive position, productivity, profitability after interest and taxes, cash generation, R & D output, community leadership, and perhaps other objectives. Some of these will be numerical and sharp, others may be intangible and "soft."
3. *Constraints* regarding expected interaction with other business-units of the company, external behavior norms, required management systems, and the like. These, too, may be quantitative or qualitative.
4. *Resources* which will be made available from the corporation and those which the unit is free to acquire itself.

Such charters are the bridges, the connecting links, between corporate strategy and the strategies of the various business-units. They define the mission of each unit insofar as that mission is shaped by corporation-wide considerations. As with all strategy, the content is selective, focusing on vital issues while deliberately excluding procedural and personal relationships. For each business-unit, its charter sets the scope and broad objectives of its activities. And for the corporate office, each charter provides the major guidelines for approving or disapproving various proposals for specific actions.

We should note that business-unit charters are not holy words passed down from omniscient corporate officials. Rather, they emerge from recurring give-and-take discussions between executives at the corporate and business-unit levels. Business-unit executives must be active participants because they know most about possibilities and problems of the business and because psychologically they must accept the challenge that the charter provides. At the same time, a location within a family of business-units inherently creates needs which must be fitted into the more specific strategies of the respective units.

Changes in the Portfolio

In addition to providing a basis for charters for existing business-units, corporate portfolio analysis flags the need for additions and deletions in the portfolio. Which of the present units are irrelevant and a drag? What gaps need to be filled with split-offs or acquisitions? And if acquisitions are called for, what characteristics should they have?

Opportunities for new synergy or improved balance may stand out during the careful portfolio analysis outlined above. *Or* proposals from internal entrepreneurs or outsiders may call attention to ways the overall portfolio could be strengthened. Once recognized, such potential additions become "opportunity gaps" for strategic planning to fill.

The next question is whether to try to fill the opportunity gaps by *internal growth or by acquisitions.* Sometimes there is little choice. For example, when Pan Am recognized that its international bookings were being jeopardized by lack of coordinated domestic flights, merger with an existing domestic airline was the only realistic alternative. To start its own domestic flights was neither legally feasible nor economic. So a tie-up with someone like National Airlines was the direction in which to move.

In other circumstances, gap-filling by acquisition is impractical. Proctor & Gamble learned that antitrust barriers prevented it from getting a running start in the bleach business through an acquisition of Clorox. For legal reasons, the bigger the parent company, the more it will have to rely on internal growth in new businesses which are closely related to its existing businesses. Moreover, in a brand new industry, acquisition candidates may not exist. When Western Union moved into satellite communications, for example, the necessary satellites were not yet in orbit.

Between these extremes, however, a choice often exists. In many states, for example, commercial banks can increase their geographic coverage either by opening branches or by acquiring existing banks in the desired locations. Acquisitions provide faster entry and some resources (such as people, market position, trademarks, or patents) that might be difficult or time-consuming to assemble. On the other hand, acquisitions often bring with them unwanted assets or traditions; they may foreclose taking other attractive steps; they may be more difficult to meld into the family; and they may be expensive.

During the late 'sixties and early 'seventies, many corporate planners fell in love with acquisitions. Corporate strategy and acquisition plans were treated as almost synonymous. Now a more balanced view prevails. A total portfolio strategy is developed, as outlined in this chapter, and acquisition criteria and opportunities grow out of this broader picture. Acquisitions often are a significant facet of corporate strategy, but they are only a part.

Divestments are the other side of the coin, hence also a part of strategy. The matrix analysis suggested at the beginning of the chapter identifies business-units which both now and in the future make little contribution to corporate goals. Further, study of synergy and of risk and of cash flow balance refine this diagnosis. In any turbulent environment, some business-units will be either a continuing drain on resources or at least a drag on energies that could be better directed elsewhere.

In practice, divestments are usually made too slowly. Even outstanding companies are reluctant to get rid of—in Boston Consulting Group language—their "dogs." RCA held on to its venture in computers until losses were in the hundreds of millions; General Foods dabbled first in gourmet delicacies, then in the fast-food business well beyond the point of no return; Johnson & Johnson kept TEK brushes long after that unit failed to serve the evolving corporate strategy. Such tardiness is explained partly by waiting for a propitious opportunity to sell or liquidate the unit. The primary cause, however, is personal. There is no inside champion for disposal, as there will be typically for an acquisition; some people will lose their jobs; and senior executives are reluctant to admit that they cannot make a success of everything they direct.

Without clear strategic direction, these normal pressures for inaction are likely to dominate. To avoid the high cost of inaction, both corporate strategy and effective execution are needed.

Resource Plans and Target Results

A well-conceived corporate strategy provides several kinds of guides. It leads to coordinated charters for existing business-units, and also to plans for additions to and deletions from the present lineup, as we have just seen. In addition, two other forms of guidance should be developed.

The projected courses for various business-units will generally call for *resources* from the central corporate pool, notably capital and perhaps executives or central services. To help assure that these resources will be available when needed, a summary program of the expected flows to and from the business-units should be prepared. Such a program will (1) alert corporate officers to any prospective need for obtaining new resources. A revision in capital structure may be involved, and, if so, groundwork for the issuance of new securities should be laid. Contingency plans reflecting shifts in capital markets may be advisable.

Also, (2) the resource plans will show in approximate numbers how much will be allocated annually to each business-unit for what purposes. These allocations will probably be revised as wants unfold. Nevertheless, the strategy provides guideposts, and any major deviation in resources needed will call for a review of the continuing wisdom of the strategy. Meanwhile, the various business-units can proceed with their planning on the working assumption that the projected resource allocations will be made available to them over the next several years. We explore possibilities for strategic uses of corporate resources in the next chapter.

A final set of guides tied in with strategy are the *target results.* Every strategy is designed to reach certain goals by given dates. These are the expected consequences of the stipulated actions. Some of these target results will be *financial*: perhaps sales, profits, return on investment, or earnings per share. Other targets may be more *qualitative*: market position in selected industries, community endorsement, product leadership, resource base, and the like. Such targets are good for keeping on course, motivation, and control, as we shall see in Part 5.

MODIFICATIONS DURING EXECUTION

Portfolio strategy is a powerful tool. It pulls together the actions of the various business-units into a balanced synergistic program; it channels scarce resources; it endorses missions for operating managers; and it sets targets for results. But it is a difficult tool to use.

The Lure of Exceptions

Cynics say that most corporate portfolio "strategy" is merely a high-sounding rationalization of acquisitions already made. Somehow, the argument runs, between risk balance, cash flows, and synergy you can justify any combination. And it is true that many promoters who are guided by little or no consistent strategy do dress up their actions with the language of strategic management. However, the possibility of such sophistry does not reduce the strength of strategic management for those who sincerely use it as a way of harnessing their own behavior. We don't forego medical treatment just because a few quacks exist.

The real difficulties in practice are more subtle. A common problem is the temptation of "a good deal." For example, a proposed acquisition may offer attractive short-run financial benefits. One company may have a large tax loss carry-over, and if a profitable unit can be merged into that company the taxes that the profitable unit would otherwise have to pay can be avoided.

Acquisition of companies for far less than their replacement cost is also tempting, even though replacement would be a serious mistake.

Or, mergers may be suggested solely because of differences in price-earnings ratios. Suppose the stock of the Apple Company is selling at twenty times its earnings per share and the stock of the less glamorous Orange Company at ten times its earnings. Then if Apple acquires Orange and its price-earnings ratio stays at twenty, the capitalized (market) value of Orange's earnings has doubled.

The acquisition of privately held businesses may be focused primarily on inheritance and estate taxes. Or, a proposal may pivot around the predilections of a few key individuals. Indeed, the resourcefulness of matchmakers is an impressive display of human ingenuity.

"Good deals" are fine *provided* they also are compatible with corporate strategy. The danger is that managerial energies and other resources will be side-tracked into ventures that are alluring at the moment but do not contribute to a strong, balanced portfolio. In contrast, if a corporation has thought through its strategy, then it already has a screening mechanism to quickly decide which proposed deals warrant further attention. Too often the strategy is fuzzy and the "good deal" is embraced as an exception.

The reverse also occurs. Actions that should be taken are postponed—as exceptions. Here the common examples are sick business-units where drastic action in unpleasant. A *Fortune* 500 corporation turned down an opportunity to sell (at a loss) one of its oldest business-units which was clearly in a declining industry; because of its long affiliation, an exception to the recognized strategy was made. Losses increased and three years later the division was liquidated because no buyer could be found. In another corporation, an ailing division with dim prospects was nursed along for seven years, as a "special case." The serious cost in this instance was the required time and attention of senior management which could have been much more productive if it had been spent on growing businesses.

Because exceptions to beautifully designed plans are sometimes warranted, the tough judgment to make is what special benefits are great enough to justify intentionally going off course. Our observation is that exceptions too often win the day.

Baffling Uncertainties

In designing portfolio strategy, many uncertainties must be resolved. Somehow, through some combination of facts, expert opinion, and intuition, forecasts of business conditions, industry outlooks, and business-unit success must be made. Of course, revisions and contingency plans may be included. But without agreed-upon forecasts a full-blown strategy cannot be formulated.

Many forecasts can be made with reasonable confidence, at least within the time and tolerance limits necessary for strategic planning. Other factors, such as international political developments or finding a cure for cancer, are baffling. And when several key factors are interdependent, scenario forecasting is often the best we can do. For example, the attractiveness of a company planning to produce manganese from modules laying deep on the ocean floor depends upon technological advances, world price of manganese, and international agreements on a law of the sea—to name only three related uncertainties. Forecasting in such areas is hazardous. And when a parent corporation is largely dependent upon a naturally biased business-unit for assessment data, the evaluation becomes even tougher.

Two dimensions which are increasingly frustrating for international investment are rates of inflation and foreign exchange rates. Inflation is pushing long-range planning away from profits based on conventional accounting and toward annual cash flows. Then the cash flow estimates have varying value due to shifts in exchange rates, if we assume that transfer of the money will be permitted. The cumulative uncertainty in such computations may well exceed the tolerance of practical planning.

In such circumstances, some parts of a corporate strategic plan may have to retreat to "prepared opportunism." The future is seen too dimly to lay out market positions and other expected results. Yet a conviction remains that truly attractive opportunities will develop, and those firms ready to serve such opportunities will benefit from an early start. So the corporate strategy seeks to position one or more business-units where they can move promptly as the prospects become clearer. As we noted in Chapter 3, such a strategic position may involve frontier technology; local marketing and distribution systems, staffed with indigenous personnel; transportation facilities; skill and favorable reputation in managing joint enterprises; ties to world markets; or access to raw materials.

Under prepared opportunism a particular business-unit may be encouraged—its charter may provide—to develop along certain lines which the unit acting alone would shun. Within the parent corporation's total portfolio may be several such business-units, each building strength on particular front. Then as events unfold, those strengths that prove to be valuable can be forged into a more specific plan. Rarely will all the specially directed units find a significant role in the final program, and to this extent effort and investment will have to be discarded. The hope, of course, is that the strengths actually used will be sufficiently valuable to offset losses on the others.

Such a strategy lacks the completeness, neatness, and efficiency of a fully developed plan. However, it does have the virtue of feasibility in the face of baffling uncertainties.

Workability Test

No strategy is well conceived until its workability is weighed. If the chances of its being carried out are remote or the cost of doing so are very high, then the strategy itself should be at least reassessed.

Two implementation issues are directly created by corporate portfolio choices. Since they can be serious enough to lead to a modification of portfolio strategy, they should be noted here.

Sometimes corporate strategy makes demands of a business-unit that are inconsistent with the strategy the unit would follow if it were independent. For example, the business-unit may wish to expand whereas the corporate strategy wants it to be a cash-cow. It is natural for unit executives to feel that they should be permitted to use the cash they generate to strengthen their own position, instead of denying themselves for the benefit of a small upstart activity.

In other cases, business-units are asked to incur risks (or avoid risks) because doing so helps corporate balance. Synergy may require that a business-unit refrain from developing its own raw materials. Or prepared opportunism may call for a form of expansion that is very expensive from the unit viewpoint. Such corporate demands seem especially onerous to managers of the business-unit when they arise unexpectedly because of some other activities of the corporation and the cause is therefore unrelated to their own situation.

Now, in a decentralized corporation the commitment of local executives to their assigned role is very important for successful corporate results. If the business-unit executives think that the corporate guides "don't make sense," foot-dragging or misleading information or other maneuvering is likely to occur.

A conviction of unit executives that a corporate-imposed strategy "will never work" can very easily become a self-fulfilling prophecy! The basic point is that there is a practical limit to which the business-units can be "pushed around." And this limit is a constraint on what corporate strategy is workable.

Portfolio strategy may create a second kind of workability strain. Each business-unit strategy calls for a managerial system (planning, organizing, leading, and controlling) which is suited to that strategy. A large "cash-cow" unit needs a different management system than a unit experimenting with coal gasification. The desirable management system for a commercial bank differs from that for an aircraft manufacturer. The more diverse the units within a portfolio, the more heterogeneous will be their management systems.

Few corporation managements have the capability of understanding, melding, and skillfully directing widely diverse management systems. Such diversity raises issues of tempermental and management style as well as difficulties of intellectual grasp. "We just don't know how to run that kind of business" is a frank and perceptive comment often heard.

Here again is a practical constraint on corporate portfolios. Cash flows and risk balance may appear desirable, but not beyond the point where effectively administering the diversity of units is no longer feasible.

SUMMARY

This chapter shifts attention from business-units, which have been the focus up to this point, to the assembly of such units by a diversified corporation.

At the corporate level, prime consideration goes to developing a strategic portfolio of business-units. Four criteria are important in this portfolio design: (1) attractive business-units each considered separately in terms of its industry and its competitive position; (2) synergy that will arise from having a particular mix of business-units within a single corporate group; (3) the combined balance of risk and of short- and long-term profitability; and (4) the prospects of internal generation of cash by some business-units that will help finance projected expansion of other business-units.

Several types of additional strategic plans should be derived from the portfolio design. (1) For each business-unit which is to be retained, a charter can be negotiated covering domain, expected results, constraints, and resource support from the corporate pool. (2) Desirable acquisitions, spinoffs, and divestments of business-units will be indicated. (3) The total financial, critical personnel, and other corporate resource pools required can be estimated. (4) When these business-unit needs are combined with corporate resource plans—to be discussed in the next chapter—consolidated results can be set for intermediate and longer-range periods. Such supporting plans, coupled with the portfolio design, constitute the corporate strategy package.

Carrying out such a corporate strategy calls for unusual persistence. In addition to the array of unexpected events affecting the several business-units, alluring opportunities to make acquisitions which deviate from the portfolio design may arise. Also, the business-units cannot be treated like pawns on a chess board; the morale and responsiveness of managers within the business-units may significantly affect what can be done with those units. Consequently, compromises and adjustments in corporate strategy are likely. Nevertheless, some integrated and consistent direction is far better than mere opportunism or passive drift.

QUESTIONS FOR CLASS DISCUSSION

1. The disclosure by the new president of Gulf and Western Industries, Inc. (60th in sales in *Fortune's* list of 500 industrial companies and 17th in profitability in *Forbes'* list of conglomerates) that he intended to see that G & W sold off most of its $750 million stock portfolio and divested itself of some (unspecified) operating subsidiaries led to an immediate 35 percent increase in the price of its common stock. G & W announced that it would use the money to pay off its long-term debt and reduce its debt-to-equity ratio far below 0.8. This move will cut off G & W's opportunities to trade on its equity and also decrease considerably the number of industries in which its subsidiaries operate. Why would the stockmarket suddenly revalue G & W's stock and why would these changes win G & W many new friends?

2. IC Industries was for years the Illinois Central Railroad, and half of its $3 billion assets are still related to transportation. Recently the corporation has been diversifying. Among other companies, it acquired Abex, a prominent manufacturer of railroad brake shoes and wheels, castings, automotive parts, etc.; Midas, with its chain of muffler and related auto repair shops; Pet (Milk), which has a line of nationally advertised grocery products; and several soft-drink bottling companies. It is also active in real estate development. Now 41 percent of its operating profits come from commercial products, 44 percent from consumer products, 14 percent from real estate, and only 1 percent from transportation. (a) In terms of portfolio strategy, what role do you think the railroad company is assigned? Where would you place the railroad on the "evaluation matrix"? (b) What rationale do you think explains the corporation's choice of diversification moves? Do you think the apparent portfolio strategy is wise?

3. In the medical field, both hospitals and nursing homes are trying to find the optimum scope of their services. (a) What advantages do you see in a merger of a community hospital with one or more nearby nursing homes? What disadvantages? (b) What guidelines for mergers of other kinds of enterprises does this analysis suggest?

4. Several universities have established a "corporation" to finance and manage a variety of student enterprises. The primary purpose is to create jobs for students, but each enterprise is expected to be self-supporting. In effect, the corporation has a portfolio of small business. At one university, these businesses include refreshment stands at the football stadium and gym, programs for football games, student laundry service, sale and delivery of sandwiches to dormitory rooms in the evening, a secondhand bookstore, a concert series, and the daily student paper. Also, the corporation's new ventures include a literary magazine, a tutoring service, and a babysitting service. (a) Use the four "dimensions" discussed in this chapter to make a preliminary evaluation of this portfolio. (b) Do the basic ideas presented in the sections on "Major Moves To Attain Desired Portfolio" and on "Workability Test" have any application to this student enterprises corporation?

5. Cleartone Laboratories, a privately owned manufacturer of hearing aids, would like to be acquired by a financially strong corporation. In addition to capital to finance growth, Cleartone is seeking affiliation which can provide synergy. Cleartone is in the fastest growing segment of the market, the in-the-ear or canal device, which now accounts for about 45 percent of the one million units sold annually. The canal hearing aids are very small with amplifiers only four-hundredths of an inch wide. That miniaturization makes quality control in production difficult, but it also permits a device which is scarcely visible when worn. Actually only about 12 percent of the nation's 20 million hearing impaired people wear hearing aids. Past drawbacks have included the obviousness of behind-the-ear and similar devices, and a retail price ranging from $350 to $600. Cleartone is looking for an interested buyer in several different fields: an electronics firm with experience in producing miniaturized products; an eyeglass lens or frame distributor with a strong reputation among opticians (who often also sell hearing aids); or a distributor of medical supplies. With what kind of corporation do you think Cleartone will find the best synergistic fit?

6. Individuals vary widely in the way they balance risk and potential profit. A few endure great hardship and risk their lives for a chance to discover gold. Others take telephone operator's jobs in their home town and put their savings into government guaranteed savings accounts. (a) Assume *you* just inherited $100,000 with the proviso that you invest it in any of four places in any proportion you choose: residential real estate, U.S. government short-term bonds, exploratory drilling for oil in northern Canada, your own business. How would you allocate the $100,000? (b) Assume you inherited $1,000,000 with the same conditions; how would you allocate it? (c) Assume a corporation has $10,000,000 cash not needed for present operations; how should it decide what to do with the cash?

7. What are the chief differences in scope and content of a business-unit strategy as described in Chapter 5 and a charter described in this chapter for a business-unit which is part of a diversified corporation? What *reasons* lead to these differences?

8. Sears, Roebuck & Co. has recently bought a controlling interest in Dean Witter Reynolds, Inc., a well-known and successful U.S. stockbrokerage firm.
    A Sears official explains: " We do not intend to hold Dean Witter Reynolds as a

passive investment. Rather, it is a major step in our move into financial services. Sears has a reputation for reliability and good values with millions of Americans, and we believe that reputation will be helpful in financial services. We are experimenting with placing Dean Witter offices in several of our stores to give our customers an opportunity to use their services."

One long-term Sears customer, when seeing such an office, said: "What are those guys doing in a Sears store? When I want to buy a good hammer I don't go to a bank. And when I have saved a few dollars, I don't ask Sears to keep them for me. . . .Now I'm not a betting man, but if I were I'd go to the racetrack."

An executive of Dean Witter Reynolds comments: "We are pleased with the new accounts opened at our offices in the Sears stores. The typical size is OK, about like many of our suburban branches. And most of these clients are people we've never known before. We are tapping a new market.

Do you think Sears will find, or develop, a significant synergy between a Dean Witter Reynolds office and a typical Sears retail store operating in the same building? Are there any other major advantages or disadvantages for Sears in adding Dean Witter to its portfolio?"

9. The president of the consulting subsidiary of a major New York City bank said: "Premiums above the existing market price paid by corporate acquirers merely for the purposes of diversification are equivalent to charitable contributions to random passersby. They may even subtract from the value of the shares of the buyer. For shareholders, the inescapable conclusion is that true diversification is almost always a bad deal. The shareholder can gain the same diversification by buying the potential seller's shares on the stock market at only the going price. The shareholder need not pay the premium." Why, then, do companies diversify? How can the shareholder gain?

Case 14
RCA'S PORTFOLIO

To overcome a shortage of cash in 1983, RCA was considering the sale of one or more of its major operating divisions. RCA's problems, however, ran deeper than a temporary cash squeeze. A basic issue was what kinds of businesses this $8 billion, highly prestigious corporation should be in during the 1980s.

RCA held strong market positions in a variety of business niches—ranging from satellite communications to financial services—and its new CEO, Thornton F. Bradshaw, had to decide which of these would provide the best foundation for reversing RCA's lackluster performance of the preceding decade.

CORPORATION HISTORY

Birth of an Industry

RCA is a direct descendant of two outstanding technological successes: wireless telegraphy and home talking machines. Under General David Sarnoff's guidance, the U.S. interests of Marconi (inventor of wireless communication) and the Victor Talking Machine Company were merged in the 1920s into the Radio Corporation of America. Many of the present activities of RCA can be traced back to these early activities (see Figure 1).

Figure 1.

Simplified Diagram

Evolution of RCA Product Lines
from "Internal Development"*

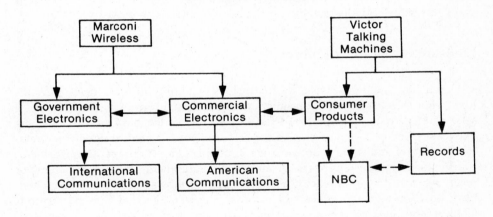

* Not shown are product lines, such as computers, which have been discontinued,
nor product lines based on recent acquisitions of established businesses.

The development of the "wireless" led RCA in two broad directions—electronics and radio communications. The design and manufacture of broadcasting equipment, aviation radios, microwave equipment, and a variety of related products were the forerunners of today's *commercial electronics* division. Parallel work for the U.S. government on radio communication, radar, sonar, fire control, and the like led to RCA's present *government electronics* division.

RCA also ventured into the commercial use of such equipment in its *communications* divisions. Its international communications division competed with transcontinental ocean cables, and its domestic communications subsidiary sought ways to supplant U.S. telephone and telegraph services. Marconi himself had sponsored such developments. But today's satellite communication, in which RCA plays an active role, is beyond even Marconi's dream.

General Sarnoff carried integration of RCA's communications activities one step further. He fostered the development of the first national radio network—what is now the National Broadcasting Company (NBC).

NBC is also related to RCA's second kind of business—*home entertainment*. The Victor Talking Machine Co. had won a dominant position in the phonograph business by the time that company was acquired by RCA. In fact, the name Victrola almost became a generic name for phonographs. In an associated development, RCA became a leading producer of phonograph records. The production of home radio receiving sets, then, was a natural move for RCA, both because home radios competed with Victrolas for home entertainment and because RCA was already manufacturing commercial braodcasting equipment.

Thus, NBC provided a double synergy. By supplying outstanding radio programs and a national news coverage, RCA increased the revenues of radio stations—its customers for broadcasting equipment. Simultaneously, these same programs helped build a demand for home radio sets—also made by RCA!

Division of the RCA Empire

Actually, the ties between RCA's various activities during General Sarnoff's long reign were not close. Consumers who purchased radio sets (and later, TV sets) neither knew or cared that RCA owned one of the national broadcasting networks. Nor was membership in the NBC network related to decisions of station engineers about the source of their equipment. Keen competition existed at every stage—among suppliers of broadcast equipment, among suppliers of receiving sets, among broadcast networks, among shows that the stations scheduled, and among the producers of records. The FCC (Federal Communications Commission) insured that a common basic technology eased entry of competitors.

A second reason General Sarnoff kept the RCA divisions separate was because of the divergence in their technology. The commercial and government equipment divisions have a high R & D input and make a small number of large and specially designed products for sophisticated customers. The communication service activities are regulated utilities. The consumer products, in contrast, must be mass-produced and marketed to nontechnical buyers. And NBC is in show business—intuitive, temperamental, and fickle—calling for skills sharply different from each of the foregoing businesses.

Still another reason for the traditional independence of RCA divisions was General Sarnoff's disinterest in the managerial process. He treated managing more like show business than a subject for R & D. He relished dramatic moves and sought increases in volume of sales by exploiting new frontiers. At least, careful planning and control was an option for each division rather than a corporate input.

Diversifications Under Robert Sarnoff

When Robert Sarnoff succeeded his father in 1966 as head of RCA, he was under the normal pressure to find new ways to match the impressive record of his parent. Diversification was then in fashion and RCA joined the fray. In addition to supporting existing lines—notably, pushing the expansion into color television—RCA entered several different businesses. RCA took on IBM in the mainframe computer business, building a new organization from within. It acquired the Hertz Rental Car business. It entered the information industry by buying the publisher, Random House. Other acquisitions included Banquet Foods and Oriel Foods, Coronet Industries (manufacturer of high-grade carpeting), Cushman and Wakefield (a leading real estate management firm), and the Alaskan Telephone Co. (Alascom).

Each of the acquired companies already had a strong position in its industry. Thus, they added to both RCA sales and its total net profits. On the other hand, the industries they represented had no higher growth prospects than the industries RCA was already in. And it was unclear what managerial skills or other differential advantage RCA brought to these diversified companies that could not have been applied to advantage in its traditional business.

Robert Sarnoff had perhaps even less interest in professional management than did his father. A widespread feeling developed within the corporation that promotions were based more on friendship than on merit.

This diversification had a serious impact on the financial structure of RCA. Acquisitions were funded to a significant extent by "leveraging"—that is, increasing RCA's debt. By 1976 the consolidated balance sheet showed a total debt of double the stockholders' equity. Moreover, the earnings of the new businesses rarely justified their high purchase price. Outstanding companies commanded outstanding prices. Also, the venture into computers was a disaster, resulting in a $490 million write-off in 1971. Meanwhile, the earnings on RCA core business had flattened out.

So, in 1975, Robert Sarnoff became a consultant to RCA at $75,000 per year.

Bottom-Line Management of Ed Griffiths

To trim the accumulated fat, RCA directors appointed Edgar H. Griffiths president. Griffiths, a thirty-one year veteran of RCA, had spent much of his career as a controller. He applied a tough, bottom-line approach; expenses were cut, profit goals set, and unsuccessful managers removed. In addition, Griffiths set out to sell off divisions that were not currently earning an attractive return on investment.

During the first few years of Griffiths' administration, earnings per share of common stock improved. This improvement partly reflected better operating profits and partly, fortuitous tax breaks or one-time capital gains on the sale of assets.

Griffiths, too, had a short temper. One observer noted that "his favorite way to solve a problem is to fire somebody." Even some successful managers, such as the president of Hertz Corporation, got the axe. And not all replacements were improvements, notably Fred Silverman as the new president of NBC.

Finally, the RCA board of directors concluded that short-run, bottom-line management was taking a toll of longer-run improvements. Morale among top executives was low, and even quarterly earnings per share of common stock began to slide. So in mid-1981 Griffiths was retired.

Current Challenge to T. F. Bradshaw

Griffiths' replacement is Thornton F. Bradshaw who, at the time of his appointment, was the highly successful president of Atlantic Richfield (Petroleum) Company and had been an RCA director for ten years. Bradshaw's task is not easy. The internal disarray left by Griffiths is complicated by an externallly imposed cash squeeze. High interest rates make RCA's large debt especially burdensome just at the time a recession has reduced current earnings. The cash flow is inadequate to support rebuilding of key divisions, such as NBC; to maintain the long dividend record; and to pay current interest.

Temporary relief might be secured by selling off one of RCA's large divisions. Bradshaw announced his preference for this purpose is the Hertz Corporation—an RCA subsidiary since 1967—if a buyer can be found who is willing to pay a good price in spite of the currently depressed condition of the automobile industry. But there are other possibilities. The critical issue is which remaining businesses (or new ones) provide RCA the best prospects of recapturing its vitality in the 1980s.

A. F. Ehrbar, writing in *Fortune* (March 22, 1982), suggests: "Bradshaw and the board ought to give serious thought to a radical alternative—splitting up the company and courting a takeover. They could accomplish that by spinning off NBC to shareholders in the form of a dividend, and the surviving RCA would be available to the highest bidder. . . . They probably ought to spin off NBC in any event. The stockmarket is likely to put a much higher value on NBC once it is certain that the network's profits won't be used to subsidize poor investments in RCA."

FINANCIAL DATA

Information on the sales and profits of various segments of RCA from 1977 to 1982 are given in Table 1 on page 362. These figures should be interpreted in the light of the brief description of each business segment appearing in the Appendix. Other financial information for the corporation as a whole is included at the bottom of Table 1.

Consolidated balance sheets for RCA at the opening and close of the period of 1977 through 1982 are presented in Table 2 on page 363. Information on assets employed in each business segment is given in Table 3 on page 364.

Question

What strategy do you recommend to Mr. Bradshaw?

APPENDIX: RCA PRODUCT SEGMENTS

Electronics: Consumer Products and Services

RCA's current efforts in consumer products are focused in three areas: (1)TV sets, (2)video disc players, and (3)phonograph records and recorded tapes and discs.

In U.S. sales of TV sets, RCA is in a very close race for leadership with Zenith. Each brand has about a 20 percent market share in color receiving sets and about a 16 percent market share in black-and-white receiving sets. Next in ranking are General Electric, Sears, SONY, and Magnavox—each with about 7 percent of the color set market—and there are at least a dozen other active competitors. Because of this competition, high quality and frequent improvements in design are essential. Industry-wide operating profits are only about 2 percent of dollar sales.

RCA is making a major effort to sell video disc players. Its Selecta Vision players—which attach to almost any television receiving set—were introduced in March 1981 after fifteen years of development work. The investment in Selecta Vision has been substantial; it had a negative impact on profits of $109 million in 1981, $55 million in 1980, and $21 million in 1979. Market response to the new product was much less enthusiastic than expected—with final sales to consumers in 1981 of about 65,000 players compared with projections of 150,000. Sales in 1982 were about 130,000 units.

Video discs compete with video tapes—which have been on the market longer. Disc players are less expensive than tape players, but the usual tape sets can record television programs for subsequent playback. (Such home-recording is subject to copyright litigation.) The recorded discs are also less expensive than recorded tapes. Technology is still volatile, with some companies using a laser

TABLE 1.
RCA SALES AND PROFIT (OR LOSS), BY BUSINESS SEGMENTS, 1982–1977 (in millions, except per share)

	1982	1981	1980	1979	1978	1977
Sales by Business Segments						
Electronics:						
Consumer Products and Services	$2,102	$2,318	$1,916	$1,756	$1,589	$1,363
Commercial Products and Services	1,204	1,196	1,281	1,113	966	881
Government Systems and Services	1,048	896	768	660	522	440
Total Electronics	4,354	4,410	3,964	3,529	3,077	2,685
Broadcasting	1,786	1,619	1,522	1,368	1,213	1,097
Transportation Services (Hertz)	1,555	1,428	1,290	1,122	938	837
Communcications	319	270	254	282	323	287
Financial Services (C.I.T.)[a]	-	-	-	-	-	-
Other Products and Services	223	278	982	1,154	1,050	975
Total Sales	$8,237	$8,005	$8,011	$7,455	$6,601	$5,881
RCA Profit (or Loss)						
Electronics:						
Consumer Products and Services	$ 87	$ 132	$ 100	$ 97	$ 145	$ 143
Commercial Products and Services	17	(56)	96	97	103	84
Government Systems and Services	80	65	51	40	25	21
Total Electronics	184	141	246	234	274	248
Broadcasting	108	48	75	106	122	153
Transportation Services (Hertz)	66	36	127	147	154	131
Communications	143	83	91	68	66	50
Financial Services (C.I.T.)[a]	192	168	177	9	-	-
Other Products and Services	(6)	10	33	63	78	60
Business Segments Total	687	486	750	627	693	641
Corporate Research Costs	(108)	(104)	(93)	(77)	(63)	(52)
Corporate Administrative Expenses	(77)	(82)	(73)	(63)	(59)	(55)
Interest Expense (other than Hertz & C.I.T.)	(181)	(217)	(164)	(87)	(64)	(58)
Other Income	-	14	87	71	7	(6)
Profit before taxes on Income	321	98	507	472	515	470
Provision for Taxes on Income	(98)	(44)	(192)	(188)	(236)	
Net Profit (or Loss)	$ 223	$ 54	$ 315	$ 284	$ 278	$ 247
Dividends on Preferred & Preference Stock	$ (69)	$ (69)	$ (64)	$ (5)	$ (5)	$ (5)
Net Profit (or Loss) Applicable to Common Stock	154	(15)	252	278	273	242
Per Share of Common Stock:						
Net Profit Applicable	$2.00	$(.19)	$3.35	3.72	$3.65	$3.23
Dividends	.90	1.80	1.80	1.60	1.40	1.20
Price Range: High	24⅛	32¼	33	28¼	33⅞	32½
Low	15¾	16¾	18½	21⅛	22⅝	24⅜

C.I.T. was acquired in December 1979 and January 1980. Only data on RCA's equity in C.I.T. are included in the above figures.

Note: Columns may not add exactly, due to rounding.

TABLE 2.
RCA BALANCE SHEET
(as of December 31, in millions)

	1982	1976
Cash and Equivalent	$ 76	$ 178
Accounts Receivable (net)	1,274	763
Inventories	615	521
Rental Automobiles of Hertz	851	277
Prepaid expenses and TV Program Costs	574	299
Total current assets	3,390	2,038
Other Equipment of Hertz (net)	865	333
Investment in C.I.T.	1,341	115
Long-Term Receivables (net)	161	70
Plant and Equipment (net)	1,652	1,281
Other Assets	334	—
Total Assets	$7,743	$3,838
Notes Payable	$ 303	48
Hertz Debt Payable in One Year	487	154
Accounts Payable	631	918
Accrued Wages and Salaries	236	
Accrued Taxes on Income	165	119
Other Accrued Liabilities	1,071	21
Total current liabilities	2,893	1,261
Long-Term Debt of Hertz	872	290
Other Long-Term Debt	1,014	654
Deferred Taxes and Other Non-Current		
Liabilities	522	355
Total liabilities	5,301	2,560
Preference Stock	552	—
Preferred Stock	10	12
Common Stock (75,000,000+ shares)	54	50
Capital Surplus	586	447
Reinvested Earnings	1,284	768
Translation Adjustment	(44)	—
Total equity	2,442	1,278
Total liabilities and stockholders' equity	$7,743	$3,838

Note: Columns may not add exactly, due to rounding.

beam to read discs instead of the RCA "needle" system. To help establish its system and its discs, RCA has licensed most U.S. manufacturers to use its patents; also, RCA and CBS have made commitments to assure an ample supply of new recordings.

TABLE 3.
RCA EMPLOYMENT OF ASSETS
(in millions)

	Assets Identified with Business Seg-	Capital Expenditures in 1982	Depreciation Expense in 1982
Electronics:			
Consumer Products and Services	$ 986	$ 46	$ 34
Commercial Products and Services	576	49	32
Government Systems and Services	266	26	12
Total	1,828	121	78
Broadcasting	823	57	21
Transportation Services (Hertz)	2,424	57	397
Communications	781	190	62
Other Products and Services	109	5	7
Financial Services (RCA investment in C.I.T.)	1,341	—	—
Corporate	438	6	14
Total assets or changes	$7,743	$436	$578

Note: Columns may not add exactly, due to rounding.

RCA has been a major supplier of phonograph records for many years, and more recently of audio tapes. In 1980, sales of such products were about $600 million, with operating profits (before corporate expenses and taxes) of about $50 million. The income from record sales, however, fluctuates from year to year—depending upon the ability to discover new talent to produce "hits." Competition is keen.

Although a strong leader in the areas just discussed, RCA has withdrawn from most other consumer electronic products. It sells no home or auto radios, no audio systems. Its video cassette recorders are made abroad by other suppliers. A premature venture into video games was abandoned in the mid-1970s. Nevertheless, consumer products continue to be RCA's largest business segment.

Electronics: Commercial Products and Services

RCA is a leader among the ten large producers of color television picture tubes. These tubes are sold to other manufacturers of receiving sets and used for RCA's own purposes. The competition in this niche of the industry has resulted in sharp price-cutting, and in 1981 RCA withdrew from European joint ventures—writing off $130 million of assets at that time.

For years, RCA has made equipment for broadcasting radio and then television. It also produces equipment for cable television companies. Moreover,

RCA makes receiving and rebroadcasting equipment for communication satellites. This is a specialized and obviously limited market.

Electronics: Government Systems and Services

Government sales focus on military and space equipment for the Armed Services, NASA, and related agencies. For example, RCA made the UHF radios and closed-circuit televisions for the space shuttle Columbia—and comparable equipment for the Apollo moon landing.

Military sales include the radar-based, computer-controlled weapon system AEGIS. RCA does not design or manufacture space craft, but is a prominent subcontractor for communications equipment used on such craft. Participation in this government market helps RCA keep on the technological forefront of commercial space communications. This expertise enables RCA to build the communication mechanisms—the payload—of its own satellites (which we discuss in the later section on Communications).

As Table 1 shows, sales to the government account for only about 13 percent of RCA's total sales. Thus, while RCA plays an important role in particular niches, it has not become a major prime contractor for military hardware.

Broadcasting

RCA is vertically integrated. It owns NBC and five television and four radio broadcasting stations. However, the equipment used in these operations is a necessary but minor factor in their success. The production of popular programs is the crucial variable.

NBC-TV regularly serves about 200 affiliated stations, and NBC-Radio serves 300 affiliated stations. NBC was the first broadcasting network and for years had the largest audience. During the late '70s and early '80s, however, it fell significantly behind both CBS and ABC in the audience it attracted. This drop in comparative rating had a serious adverse effect on the prices it—and affiliated stations—could charge for commercial advertising interspersed with the programs.

In an attempt to revive NBC, Mr. Griffiths hired ABC's highly successful programmer—Fred Silverman—to become president of NBC. The results of this move were disastrous. NBC's ratings dropped further; morale slipped; $34 million of unpopular programs were written off in 1981. NBC now has a new management team, and its ratings have turned up; but even if NBC continues winning audiences from ABC and CBS it will take two years to rebuild advertising revenues.

The long-term outlook for the large national broadcasting chains such as NBC is uncertain. Cable TV enables millions of homes to get excellent reception from a much larger number of stations. And, broadcasting via satellites enables local stations to economically obtain a much larger number of programs. The combined effect of these two developments could diminish the size of network audiences—and their advertising revenues as a result.

An added unknown, is the possibility of interactive links between home TVs (or computers) and broadcasting stations. Such links could be used for retail selling, banking, games, library reference, etc. To date, RCA has not been an active experimenter in this arena.

Communications

RCA now has two subsidiaries that provide communication services: Global Communications and American Communications.

A direct descendant of Marconi wireless ventures, RCA Global Communications provides overseas voice and record communication services via radio, cable, and satellites. These services take the form of telex, telegrams, private (leased) lines, teleprinter circuits, data transmission, and variations thereof.

RCA American Communications owns and operates satellites and a number of earth stations in the United States. These are similar to a public utility, and are subject to regulation by the FCC. They are used for private-line voice, television, and data services, which are sold to cable TV companies, broadcasting organizations, large business companies, and the federal government. These services expanded significantly in 1982.

Satellite communication is growing and competitive. Western Union, which also owns and operates satellites, is seeking permission to enter the overseas market while RCA-American is encroaching on Western Union's domestic turf. AT&T Long-Lines is affected both domestically and overseas, and is responding to this new competition through a joint venture with IBM, Aetna Life, and Comsat. Other companies are entering the field, either as operators of satellites or as "retailers" of services to users who are not large enough to lease their own channel to a satellite. Western Union had four satellites in orbit in 1981—more than any other commercial firm. By that date, the FCC had approved the launching by various companies of twenty more within the next few years.

RCA did own a third communications subsidiary for a few years—the Alaska Telephone Co. This was sold in 1979 as part of Mr. Griffiths' housecleaning. (Sales in 1978 were $134 million.) However, in 1981 RCA entered an agreement with Alaska Telephone to sell the company a satellite (for $29 million) and maintain and service it and related earth-stations for eight and a half years (for $150 million). So the association with Alaska Telephone remains close.

Transportation Services

The "transportation services" segment of RCA is really the Hertz Corporation. Acquired by RCA in 1967, Hertz continues to be the largest automobile leasing company in the world. In addition to being "Number 1" in the United States, Hertz operates in one hundred foreign countries.

In addition to automobile leasing, Hertz is the second largest truck-leasing company in the United States. Most of these trucks are leased for three to five years on a full-service basis. This business, which serves a market quite distinct from auto leasing, is very competitive. In 1981 RCA wrote off $59 million of assets devoted to Hertz truck-leasing activities.

After a decade of growth in sales and profits, the auto leasing turned down in profitability (possibly because Mr. Griffiths changed Hertz presidents at this juncture). And in 1981 with the decline in airline passengers—who are primary customers for rental autos—earnings dipped even more.

Largely because of cash flow and related financial problems, RCA has announced that it would like to sell the Hertz Corporation. Such a sale would remove $1.4 billion of debt from RCA's consolidated balance sheet. Moreover, if the Hertz Corporation could be sold for between $500 million and $600 million—a price RCA is believed to be seeking—RCA would pick up a capital gain over book value of around $200 million before income tax. Such a transaction would improve the RCA balance sheet ratios and provide some cash (assuming the sale was for cash); but a market leader would have to be sold for less than five times its 1980 pre-tax earnings.

Financial Services

The "financial services" segment of RCA is really the C.I.T. Financial Corporation. C.I.T. is one of the largest industrial financing and leasing organizations in the United States. It borrows money "wholesale" at relatively favorable rates and then reloans that money "retail" at somewhat higher rates. C.I.T. customers use the loans to finance installment purchases of railroad cars, aircraft, medical equipment, marine tankers, data processing equipment and the like. (These loans may take the form of a purchase and lease-back.) Also C.I.T. makes loans to manufacturers and distributors to finance their inventories and accounts receivable.

In support of such loans, a subsidiary of C.I.T. sells life insurance on key executives in borrowing companies. And this insurance business is being extended to other persons.

C.I.T. is treated as an investment on the RCA financial reports; its figures are not consolidated like those of other subsidiaries. This separation is done for two reasons. (1) C.I.T. does it own fund-raising. Indeed, it borrows at more favorable rates than can its parent. And to protect C.I.T.'s financial standing, restrictions exist on the dividends and loans C.I.T. can make to RCA. Thus C.I.T. is prevented from being a cash cow for RCA. Showing C.I.T. only as an investment on RCA financial statements emphasizes C.I.T.'s independent financial status. (2) The asset and capital structure of a financing company such as

C.I.T. differs so much from that of an industrial concern like RCA that consolidating the accounts would create confusion rather than light. The condensed balance sheet for C.I.T. on December 31, 1981, is shown in Table 4.

TABLE 4.
C.I.T. BALANCE SHEET
(in millions)

Receivables, net	$5,723	Payables and accruals	$ 842
Prepaid expenses	208	Deferred taxes	270
Investments	398	Debt	4,492
Investments in Canadian		Shareholders' equity	1,008
subsidiaries	283	Total Liabilities	
Total Assets	$6,612	and Equity	$6,612

RCA paid a substantial premium to acquire the stock of C.I.T. The purchase price of $1.22 billion exceeded the fair value of the net assets of C.I.T. by $315 million. C.I.T. has not yet shown results that justify this premium. In the currently changing financial industry, C.I.T. has stayed with its traditional business. So if RCA were to sell C.I.T. today with its retained earning for the last two years, the selling price would be at least $200 million below RCA's purchase price.

The C.I.T. purchase both helped and hurt RCA's financial picture. About half of the purchase price consisted of $552 million of RCA preference stock. Since dividends on this stock are not an "expense," the income received from C.I.T. increases RCA net profit by a small amount. However, dividends on the preference stock must be subtracted from net profit to arrive at profit available to common stockholders, and when this adjustment is made it is clear that the earnings per share on RCA common stock have thus far been lowered by the C.I.T. purchase.

Other Products and Services

This segment includes several product lines which have been sold during that last five years. Consequently, the sales and operating figures are not comparable from year to year.

Presently the chief remaining product line is tufted carpeting made and sold by a subsidiary, Coronet Industries. Coronet is a leader among 200 competitors in this business.

RCA Laboratories

Although not treated as a profit center, RCA Laboratories are a large, semi-independent part of the corporation. The bulk of RCA technical research is done in the Laboratories. The work ranges from classified research for the armed services to development of products such as Selecta Vision. The Laboratories are known primarily for their success in communications electronics; product development is sometimes too remote from the operating divisions.

This corporate service plays an important role in keeping RCA abreast of technology in electronic communications and related fields. In 1982, for example, RCA spent $504 million on research, development, and engineering activities. Contract research for the U.S. government accounted for $309 million of this total.

15 CORPORATE INPUT STRATEGY

The preceding chapter focused on the choice of a good portfolio of business-units. Indeed, that is the only aspect of corporate strategy which most writers—in professional journals and the public press—consider. The implied assumption in the typical discussion is that corporate managers merely pick winners, or some preferred mix of investments that provides a balanced risk and cash flow and then passively await results.

Second Pivot of Corporate Strategy

Developing an attractive portfolio is vital, but it is an incomplete view of good corporate strategy. A second crucial dimension deals with *inputs* which the corporation makes to strengthen its various businesses. The progressive corporation *does* "bring something to the party." The aim is to provide most—if not all—of its business-units with some differential advantage that they could not muster if they operated independently.

Wide variation exists in the kind of inputs diversified corporations furnish to their business-units. Familiar inputs include low-cost capital, a supply of outstanding managers, or assured access to markets. More unusual is product and process knowledge that, for example, a pharmaceutical firm can supply to its veterinary affiliate or a central room-reservation service that a motel chain furnishes to its members.

Corporate inputs are any kind of resources—tangible or intangible—that a corporation obtains or generates and provides to its business-units.

Our focus here is on *major* inputs. Every corporation provides minor services for its operating units—such as stockholder relations, filing consolidated reports with governmental agencies, a logo to place on the letterhead. But these minor, usually necessary, activities do not significantly affect the fate of the business-units. Even such work as central purchasing or institutional advertising is typically helpful but does not govern the growth or death of specific business-units. Corporate input strategy concentrates on major actions which are fundamental to success. It adds yeast, not just seasoning.

The central issues of corporate input strategy are:

Reprinted with permission of The Free Press, a Division of Macmillan, Inc., from *Strategy In Action: The Execution, Politics, and Payoff of Business Planning* by Boris Yavitz and William H. Newman. Copyright © 1982 by The Free Press.

1. selecting a few kinds of contributions which the corporation will make to its business-units—contributions of such quality and value that the business-units gain a significant advantage over their competitors
2. finding ways to develop a differential advantage in the "production" or "delivery" of such services
3. integrating these strengths into portfolio selection and corporate mission and into the design of charters for business-units

Note that this view supports the concept, already stressed, that business-units are the primary operating segments of a diversified corporation. To the extent it is practical, operating activities should be placed within these business-units. We would transfer operating activities to another division or to the corporate level only when the benefits of doing so are very high. In this sense, "corporate inputs" run counter to the basic pattern of decentralization. They are exceptions. Yet experience shows that when wisely selected and carefully administered, corporate inputs can be a powerful asset.

CORPORATE RESOURCE ARSENAL

Diversified corporations can strengthen their business-units primarily in two ways: (1) by providing one or more valuable resources on attractive terms, and/or (2) by central management of synergies among the business-units. Let us first look at the way several typical corporate inputs can serve business-units, then later in the chapter we will consider the management of synergies.

Low-Cost Capital

By far the most widely recognized aid that a parent corporation gives its operating units is growth capital. As is very clear in the cable TV arena, for example, a new business-unit often incurs losses for several years before its can build a profitable niche. Obtaining a franchise, stringing cable, signing up customers, constructing distribution gear—all require capital before income even starts to flow. And even an established venture needs working capital and fixed capital to grow.

A cash-rich parent is very convenient in such situations. Growth can proceed as rapidly as technology, markets, and environmental conditions warrant. Often it is possible to get a jump on competitors.

The parent corporation need not have cash in the bank (or flowing from owned cash-cows), if it can raise new funds at a favorable cost. If its capital structure permits more debt and it enjoys a favorable credit rating, the corporation can borrow additional capital. Interest on the loan will be a taxable expense and thus the *net* cost of capital will be relatively low compared with what a new venture would have to pay if acting alone. Or, if the parent corporation enjoys a high price/earnings (P/E) ratio on its stock, equity capital may "cost" less than the business-unit would have to pay. In this manner, financial strategy of the corporation builds a resource that strengthens the business-units.

Of course, not all diversified corporations are in such enviable condition. They may already be saddled with debt and have a low P/E ratio. Indeed, a large and well-known business-unit with an exciting new product or with extensive collateral may be able to raise capital on better terms than its parent. Many recent mergers of large corporations which create newspaper headlines actually provide no financial benefits to the merged firms. For small firms, however, the cost of capital may be significantly lowered.

So, the crux is whether the diversified corporation can and will give its operating units a differential advantage with respect to the supply of capital.

Outstanding Executives

Other corporate inputs may be as invigorating. For instance, a few corporations go to great lengths to develop a pool of unusually well-qualified managers. The pompous expression, "Our greatest strength is our people" may be accurate. Selection, training, and shared expertise are designed to give managers in such corporations a competitive edge.

To cite two examples, both General Electric and IBM give high priority to executive development. General Electric's training center at Crotonville, New York, is like a college for adults. IBM devotes even more effort and money to improving the capability of its upper-level as well as its lower-level managers. The clear aim is to have outstanding managers who can be moved into various business-units—with the expectation that these managers will be able to run their units better than their competitors.

When a corporation develops enough "depth" of able general managers, it (1) can fill a strategic post immediately instead of searching for an outsider, (2) need not devote time and effort "socializing" a new executive to the corporate culture, (3) does not tip off plans to outsiders by searching for a particular kind of manager in the open market, and (4) reinforces the message that this corporation provides great opportunities for its own people.

This is an ambitious strategy. It deals with a soft asset, compared with capital. The people are mobile and competitors may seduce them. There is doubt about how transferable to other kinds of business some of the skills and expertise will be. Nevertheless, the potential rewards are great. If a corporation does succeed in staffing its business-units with executives who can outdistance their competitors, a whole array of other strengths may be promoted.[1]

Corporate R & D

Useful creative ideas, scientifically tested, are scarce and expensive. And for most laboratories to be effective, a "critical mass" (minimum number) is neces-

---

[1]The problems of finding executives well suited to execute a particular business-unit strategy are explored in Chapter 19.

sary. One way to seek a flow of such ideas and specialized laboratory service, without loading high costs onto each business-unit, is through a centralized R & D division.

For years the Bell Laboratories served the various operating companies of the AT & T system in this manner.[2] The worldwide pharmaceutical firms also typically centralize their research work (although separate problems may be studied at separate locations). The new products can then be sold by subsidiaries throughout the world.

Such research work is inherently risky. The results are unpredictable and even exciting developments may not fit the assigned missions of the corporation's business-units. For example, over a fifteen-year period Xerox poured close to $200 million into its Palo Alto Research Center with the primary hope that the output would give Xerox a decisive lead in "total office systems." This goal has not been achieved. The Center has done impressive work that led to a variety of useful products in the computer arena, but most (not all) of their products are being produced by other companies. The linkage between the corporate-supported R & D and Xerox's operating division has been weak.

The aim in each of these cases is to create a powerful research group which makes contributions to the operating divisions—contributions that the divisions acting alone would be unable to achieve or even unlikely to investigate.

Centralized R & D has its drawbacks, among them lack of responsiveness to operating needs, pursuit of inconsequential questions, and reluctance to piggy-back on research of competitors. The more diversified the operating divisions, the more difficult these problems become. Nevertheless, the overall success with centralized research of such corporations as DuPont indicates that this can be a viable corporate input strategy.

Centralized Marketing

The basic concept of a business-unit places control of major functions—engineering, production, marketing, etc.—within the unit. To a large extent, the unit is self-contained and autonomous; it runs its own show. Coordination between the functions and adjustments to the environment of each particular business are decentralized.

Occasionally, however, a corporation seeks to gain strength by defying the usual pattern. One such deviation is to withdraw parts of marketing from the business-units and to perform these particular activities in a corporate marketing division. In fact, this was the original strategy of General Foods Corporation.

---

[2]The future of Bell Laboratories is clouded by the split-up of AT & T. The now independent units may be unwilling to support the kind of basic research which enabled Bell Laboratories to make pioneering developments, such as, that of the transistor. In the terminology of this chapter, the corporate input strategy of the various independent pieces may down-play "basic" R & D.

Each of the several companies that were merged into General Foods—among them Post Cereals, Jell-O, and Maxwell House Coffee—continued to buy, manufacture, package, price, and ship products as they had done previously. The key contribution of the new corporation was nationwide promotion and selling for all products. By combining selling and promotion into a single division, the corporation provided the several operating companies much more complete coverage and skillful promotion than any of the companies could muster when acting separately.

The large Japanese trading companies operate in a roughly similar way for the manufacturing companies they represent, although here the manufacturers maintain a more independent existence. The scope of activities performed for a manufacturer varies; often the trading company performs all the marketing functions both in Japan and abroad. Sometimes the trading company also buys raw materials, and it may provide financing as well. With this assistance, small companies can concentrate on making a specialized line of products.

The Coca-Cola Company, to cite another variation, leaves most marketing functions to its local distributors but it centralizes control over promotion of the trade name. The name is a great *corporate* resource. Distributors gain a powerful competitive benefit when they are authorized to use this resource.

Such centralized marketing activity creates numerous problems of coordination, adequate attention to each product, and accountability. And as the product-lines grow in size and diversity, the differential benefit of the pooled service diminishes. But again we observe the corporation searching for some special input it can provide so effectively to its business-units that they enjoy a comparative advantage over competitors.

Caution in Choice of Strategic Inputs

The choice of corporate inputs should be highly selective. A single corporation would rarely attempt to make inputs of strategic power in all of the areas illustrated above. And there are other possibilities that may suit particular situations. For instance, a corporation operating worldwide may realize a status level and develop contacts in various nations which give its subsidiary a distinct boost in introducing products and services in those nations. Corporations dealing in "big ticket" items such as automobiles or major appliances might create a financing scheme to assist dealers in carrying inventory and extending installment credit to consumers.

Note that in each of these examples—low-cost capital, outstanding managers, R & D capability, central marketing, or a more unusual input—the corporate strategy is to focus on just a few resources. Rarely is the development of such resources justified as a distinct business; instead, the resources have value only as they are distinctive inputs to the business-units. In effect, the corporation develops a select arsenal of exceptional resources. By drawing from that arsenal to supplement their own resources, the business-units gain strengths which they cannot muster alone.

Many diversified corporations, in fact, provide few if any strategic inputs to their business-units. This is especially true of "conglomerates"—assemblies of established firms that have little relation to each other and are merely clustered in a passive holding company. The pressure to generate short-term profits and cash flow is often so great that the parent corporation is not even a good source of capital. Moreover, the development of a truly outstanding corporate resource is difficult, time-consuming, and frequently expensive. Long-term commitment to a corporate input strategy is necessary. For these reasons, corporate management must select with care any input resources in which it undertakes to excel.

CORPORATE MANAGEMENT OF SYNERGIES

In addition to providing strategically valuable "corporate inputs," diversified corporations may seek differential advantage from synergy among their business-units.

Building synergy is a strategy of many diversified corporations. Copper firms combine mining with smelting and extend on into wire-drawing. Airlines own resort hotels (often to their regret), and newspapers form ties with local TV stations. The aim is to dovetail operations of two or more business-units in the corporation's portfolio in a way that generates extra benefits.

Of course, in selecting businesses for the portfolio, *potential* synergies are among the factors considered—as we urged in the previous chapters. However, the actual achievement of synergy usually requires strong guidance. The interaction between business-units has to be shaped so that the desired reinforcement does occur. Corporate strategy sets this direction.

A quick review of several possible sources of synergy among business-units will illustrate the role corporate strategy can play.

Vertical Integration

A corporation which published several monthly trade magazines bought out a firm which did most of its printing. The chief aim of the acquisition is to assure fast, adaptable printing service for the magazines—at normal industry prices. Under the guidance of the parent corporation CEO, this service objective is working well. The manager of the printing business, however, is not entirely happy. She is expected to obtain outside business to keep her shop busy when not printing magazines, yet she is not permitted to make major investments in equipment for that purpose unless it can also be used for the magazine. Clearly, in this simple case the corporate strategy to stress vertical integration takes priority over independent operation of the printing business. Although the printing unit is constrained, the total effect on all business-units combined is a net gain.

Marshall Field & Company's history reveals attempts at both forward and backward integration. The original company started by Mr. Field became a flourishing drygoods wholesaler. Operating out of Chicago, the firm sold a wide array of products to thousands of department stores in the entire area between the Allegheny and Rocky mountains.

The first integration was forward—a retail department store in Chicago. This venture was also very successful (and is the hub of the present Marshall Field & Company). However, the Chicago outlet quickly took on a character of its own as *the* most prestigious store in the city. Increasingly, its requirements for high quality and distinctive merchandise could not be met by the wholesale division. The retail store buyers literally traveled throughout the world searching for products that would make the store unique. With this development, the transactions between the wholesale and retail divisions became fewer and fewer; in fact, this vertical integration was of little significance.

Meanwhile, the wholesale division integrated backward into the production of several lines of its own products. Mills were built in North Carolina and Virginia to manufacture domestics (sheets, blankets, towels, bedspreads), rugs (notably the Karastan brand), woolen cloth ("piece goods"), and women's hosiery. At first the wholesale division sold the entire output of these mills. But over time the wholesale division called for less and less of the kind of products which the mills were adept at making. A classical mismatch arose: marketing selling what production could not make economically and production making what marketing was not organized to sell. And the distance between Chicago and North Carolina didn't help.

To keep their mills running and their workers employed, the mill managers in North Carolina and Virginia headed for New York and opened their own sales offices. In the beginning, these moves were undercover. By the end of ten years, however, the mills' managers were focusing their primary attention on the styles and service desired by their New York customers. "Fieldcrest Mills" became a kingdom of its own.

Corporate executives definitely *did not* manage these shifts in mill activities. Rather, the changes reflected the initiative of the managers of what became separate business-units. We should note that drygoods wholesaling was a declining industry during this period. Wisdom and courage were needed to reshape—or abandon—the original flagship business. But in this instance, corporate executives were slow to recognize that the synergies they sought from vertical integration of the wholesale division and the mills were disappearing. They permitted the situation to drift until heavy losses finally forced a drastic realignment.

Full Utilization of Raw Materials

Related to vertical integration is complete use of raw materials. To paraphrase an old meat-packing quip, synergy comes from utilizing every part of the pig but the squeal. A more recent example is found in the forest products indus-try. Peeler logs for plywood come only from the trunk of the trees, so a lumber mill is added to use the smaller pieces. Then the pulp-and paper-making is tied to lumber operations to utilize even smaller pieces, and some of the sawdust finds its way into particle board.

Each of the products—plywood, lumber, pulp and paper, and particle board—may be managed as a separate business-unit. However, the parent cor-poration is also concerned that the operations dovetail in a way that minimizes raw material costs and maximizes output of the most profitable components of the mix. The corporate task is to make the combined whole more valuable than the sum of the independent parts.

Combined Services

Offering a combination of services or of products can be a source of syn-ergy. Thus, in a household appliance industry the volume leaders have found synergies in selling or servicing a full line (refrigerators, freezers, dishwashers, disposers, ranges, washing machines, and dryers). Each product has its competi-tors—for example, Maytag in washing machines and Tappan in gas ranges—and its special design issues, but one way to compete in this mature industry is for a corporation to promote full-line service to consumers.

Such synergies are difficult to achieve. The corporate task of coordinating the actions of several business-units is burdensome, and consumers may just not care about the joint effort. Combinations of sewing machines and TV sets, for instance, are rare. Fast-food restaurants don't sell groceries. So, this kind of cor-porate strategy must be cautiously designed.

An area currently in flux is financial services: insurance companies are buy-ing investment banking firms, brokerage houses are offering checking accounts, and so on. Any corporation that hopes to benefit from such combinations needs a well-conceived strategy. One possibility is to focus on investment services for selected markets: for example, life insurance, mutual funds, stockbrokerage, commodities, and other futures contracts for the middle income individual. Although it is doubtful that a single "counselor" could provide expert advice in each kind of investment, he or she could at least draw on the many experts available within the corporation, and then balance the assets and risks for a par-ticular client. An alternative strategy might be to give full cash management and accounting service for professionals, including checking accounts, credit cards, payment of bills, income records, preparation of income and other tax returns, and personal loans on autos.

Normally, such a set of combined services must be backed up by a series of specialized business-units, each with its own technological and institutional con-straints. If these supplying organizations take the limelight or pursue strictly parochial interest, little merging of service will occur. In contrast, if the corporation manages the synchronizing of the services, the strategy has a much better chance of success.

In summary, portfolio selection of compatible business-units may make synergy possible. Realization of that synergy, however, depends on a corporate strategy requiring the separate units to integrate their activities on a few selected fronts. The synergy may be possible in vertical buy-sell relationships, in full utilization of a common raw material, in providing a synchronized set of services, or in some other reinforcing actions. But it is the corporate strategy which sets the priority to be attached to such integrated action. The strategy stipulates the thrusts which are designed to generate differential advantage in serving stakeholders. And it sets the targets for coordinated effort. Such a strategy turns independent enterprises (states) into a "federal" organization—"a more perfect union."

BEYOND THE PORTFOLIO

Corporate portfolio strategy is comparable to the "domain" in a business-unit strategy. In selecting its portfolio, a diversified corporation is picking a group of domains in which to operate. In effect, the corporation is placing, and then readjusting, its bets on attractive niches in attractive industries.

Domain, however, is just one of four parts of an action-oriented business-unit strategy—as outlined in Chapter 5. Sources of differential advantage, strategic thrusts, and target results are added elements—elements that are necessary to convert business-unit strategy from selection of a battleground into a more focused, action-prompting directive. Similarly, corporate strategy should push beyond the selection of a portfolio.

In this chapter, we have focused on corporate inputs—that is, ways corporations can help make their business-units more effective. The development of select resources is one approach. Here, the strategy of a corporation may center on low-cost capital, outstanding managers, corporate R & D, centralized marketing, or other resources that will be especially beneficial to its various businesses. As a second approach, a corporation may foster particular synergies. Like the development of select resources, fostering synergies adds potency to that of the various business-units acting independently. With imagination, corporate managers can undoubtedly devise still other inputs which will give their business-units unusual strengths.

The corporate inputs help the business-units build a differential advantage over their competitors by adding to the power the business-units acting separately could develop.

Moreover, when we think of the actions a diversified corporation should take to develop its desired portfolio and to marshal its strategic inputs, a four-part corporate strategy emerges. This four-part strategy, which parallels business-unit strategy in nature, is outlined in Figure 15-1.

Figure 15-1.
SCOPE OF ACTION-ORIENTED STRATEGY

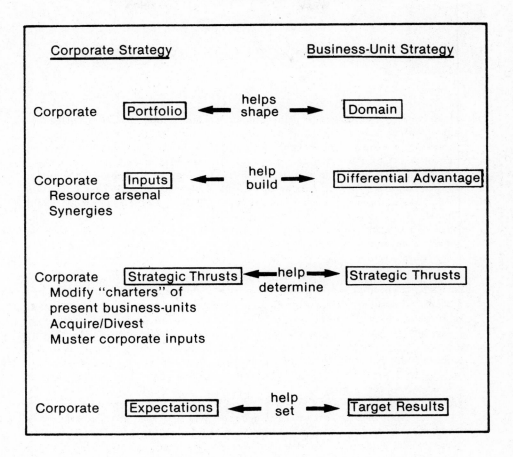

Just as a good business-unit strategy includes strategic thrusts and target results, so too does a good corporate strategy. The corporate strategic thrusts deal with (1) modifying the charters of existing business-units, (2) making acquisitions and divestments of business-units, and (3) mustering corporate inputs.

The corporate target results, or expectations, should normally include both financial and nonfinancial goals. Nonfinancial targets are often suggested by a review of the corporation's standing relative to key stakeholders. Milestone targets for specific dates will help the corporation convert the strategy into operating plans.

Clearly such a four-part strategy goes well beyond portfolio selection. It includes the elements necessary for a trajectory for the corporation.

QUESTIONS FOR CLASS DISCUSSION

1. In its various business-units, Allis Chalmers manufactures and sells agricultural equipment, bulk materials handling equipment, coal gasification systems, minerals processing systems, pollution controls, and electric utility equipment. A significant part of Allis Chalmers' sales comes from international trade, and the corporation is seeking more. One foreign market that it wants to tap is the People's Republic of China. To assist in this development, Mary Wadsworth—an expert on China with an MBA—has been hired as a corporate vice president. In the terminology of this chapter, Ms. Wadsworth's services are a potential corporate input to the operating business-units. In what ways do you think Ms. Wadsworth can serve the business-units? What should she *not* do?

2. Medalist Industries, Inc., grew into a conglomerate with sales of $139 million by acquiring a group of sporting-goods companies, which supplied equipment for professional and school sports teams, and some industrial products companies, which sold metal castings, screws, and machinery. The industrial products supplied the profits and the sporting-goods companies supplied the glamor and excitement for the founders. Growth meant the heavy use of debt for leverage and the incurring of high interest charges. Eventually even the cash-cows could not supply sufficient funds for the capital expenditures necessary to keep operations going. The parent company could not supply capital to the subsidiaries. A new president—the son of the founder—then sold fifteen of the twenty-five companies owned, and Medalist wrote off losses from the sales until the balance sheet was improved and short-term debt had been reduced to a very conservative amount. The industrial products companies were retained and continued to generate profits, but much of the excitement went out of the company as the ties with professional and school sports were broken and as the promotions and deal-making stopped.

   With a sound financial base finally realized, the son decided to push the sale of bicycles and parts by West Coast Cycle (manufacturer of high-quality Nishiki and Cycle Pro bikes)—one of his father's acquisitions. He hired a new president for the bicycle company—who had experience with cosmetics firms—and increased the advertising budget fivefold in one year. The strategy is to attempt to enter one of the two strategic groups of the U.S. bicycle business, but which group has not been decided. These groups comprise: (1) Huffy, Murray Ohio Manufacturing, AMF, and several smaller companies, which sell relatively inexpensive bikes through mass merchants, and (2) Fuji, Peugeot, Schwinn, Motobecane, and others which sell expensive bicycles through specialty shops. The first group garners about two-thirds of the industry sales. Huffy, the nation's biggest maker of bikes, has recently tried to compete in both groups by acquiring the Raleigh name and marketing Raleigh bikes through specialty shops. It "has a lot more horses going for it than Medalist does," according to a Schwinn executive.

In which strategic group do you recommend that Medalist seek to expand? What strengths can Medalist bring to bear to further the expansion of West Coast Cycle and help it succeed in the strategic group chosen? What are the key factors for success in this part of the U.S. bicycle industry? Will heavy advertising and promotional expenditures allow Medalist to hurdle the entry barriers for this industry segment?

3. All automobile manufacturers, most farm equipment manufacturers, and most manufacturers of major household appliances have a financial unit that extends installment credit to final purchasers (users) of their products. Although the retail dealers may not be owned by the manufacturer, these financing schemes are of a similar nature to a corporate input provided to a business unit. (Another difference is that these finance units are self-supporting; the interest charged covers the expenses of the service.) A few universities have a financial unit that enables the various schools of the university (the "business-units") to extend installment credit to their students (customers). (a) Do you think that all universities should have such an arrangement? (b) Should the service be self-supporting, like the automobile finance companies? (c) Do you foresee any major problems of applying the concept to universities?

4. "My family has been in the health and diet food business for years," explains Sandra Lombardo. "We have a second division that sells beauty products; our angle there is skin nutrition. I believe that we should expand into related equipment. We are working on an acquisition of a firm that makes a deluxe line of personal hair dryers. Another possibility is a firm that makes sunlamps, including heat lamps. A further possibility that fits in with the current health trend is indoor exercisers for the home—cycles, rowing exercisers, gym benches, and the like." Assuming that the Lombardo Corporation did acquire business-units in the three areas suggested, what major corporate input should it try to furnish to these operating divisions? What opportunities for synergy do you see?

5. R & D that focuses on *physical* products or processes is a well-recognized potential corporate input. In contrast, *economic* research is rarely, if ever, mentioned in this way. A corporation could set up a large central unit to make economic forecasts and to analyze various industries; presumably having use of these forecasts could give the various business-units a differential advantage over their competitors. But this does not occur. (Some corporations do have economists whose forecasts are made available to operating divisions; however, these are not expected to be so important to operating divisions that they have a differential advantage.) How do you explain the difference in strategic importance attached to physical R & D and economic research?

6. (a) In the Marshall Field and Company situation described briefly on page 376, do you feel that the mill manager of, say, rugs was justified in surreptitiously seeking orders in New York City? (b) If you had been the corporate executive in

charge of all wholesaling activities (including the mills) and learned what was going on, what would you have said to the manager of the rug mill—praise, criticism, instructions for the future?

7. At the time Joseph Flavin became president of the Singer Company, the company had the following major business-units: (a) consumer sewing machines, (b) industrial sewing machines, (c) electric power tools (drills, saw, hedge trimmers) made for Sears Roebuck, (d) furniture, (e) control products (switches, thermostats, valves) sold in large volume to home appliance and automobile manufacturers, (f) air-conditioners, (g) residential gas meters, (h) navigation systems for aircraft and marine vessels, (i) simulators for training aircraft pilots. Each of these separate business-units had sales of at least $100 million. The corporation was heavily in debt and earning low profits. What strategic corporate input, if any, do you think Singer should have provided at that time? Explain.

8. As we said in the text, "Fast-food restaurants don't sell groceries." Grocery stores, on the other hand, do sell fast-foods. In the "convenience markets" (Circle K, 7-eleven stores) you can buy milk, coffee, soft drinks, sandwiches (either cold or heated in a microwave oven) and pastries. In large supermarkets, such as Safeway and Food Giant stores, you can buy delicatessen items to be consumed on the premises or taken out—as is also the case in some convenience stores. Why would grocery stores sell fast-foods, but fast-food restaurants not sell groceries?

9. (a) Use a specific example to illustrate each of the four horizontal relationships between corporate and business-unit strategy shown in Figure 15-1 at the end of the chapter. For your example, use a corporation that you know, or one of the cases you have studied which involves a diversified corporation, or a university and one of its schools. (b) How well does a well-developed corporate input strategy affect the charter for one of the business-units in that corporation?

10. When the industry of fiber-optics (sending a signal by light through a glass or plastic fiber) was new, Corning Glass Works was fully integrated in that it manufactured a light source—a laser or light-emitting diode, the glass fiber to carry the signal, the cable that enclosed the glass fibers, a detector to convert the light signal into a video or audio signal, and connectors to hold the various parts together. But, as the industry developed, as cities were connected by glass telephone cables and office copiers used glass fibers, Corning sold off its electronic subsidiary, Signetics. Corning became less integrated and concentrated only on making the glass fibers. It formed a joint venture with the Siemens Company—a major European supplier of telephone and computer equipment—to make glass-fiber cables, but it sold the fiber to this company on exactly the same terms as it sold glass fibers to all other buyers such as A.T. & T., General Cable, G.T.E., etc. Thus vertical integration to build synergy was useful to Corning in the very early stages of the development of the industry, but it abandoned vertical integration during the take-off phase of this emerging industry. Can you explain these two different strategic thrusts?

CASE 15
White's Future?

White Consolidated Industries, Inc., needs a longer-run corporate input policy for its home appliance divisions. Results to date are far from spectacular, and forecasts indicate that a further shakedown is likely in the mature sections of the appliance industry.

White's Move into Home Appliances

Although White has significant operations in machinery and other industrial equipment, home appliances account for about two-thirds of its sales and operating income. All of these appliance divisions were acquired by White during its aggressive diversification. The acquisitions included:

1967: Hupp Corp. (for $52.7 million) with sales at that time of $195 million, mostly in its Gibson and Easy appliance lines.

1967: Franklin private label appliance business from Studebaker-Worthington Corp. (for $19.4 million), with a sales volume of $70 million.

1968: Kelvinator division of American Motors Corp. (for $24 million).

1968: Hamilton appliance division of American Hospital Supply Corp. (for $63.4 million).

1973: Athens Stove Works (for $6.2 million) from the founding family.

1975: Westinghouse Corporation's major appliance business (for about $100 million), with sales volume estimated at $600 million.

1977: From Ford Motor Co., certain tools and trademarks of Ford's Philco appliance operations, including their Bendix name, which White reintroduced with a laundry line in 1979.

1979: From General Motors Corp., the Frigidaire name, marketing organization, and central tooling and patents (estimated price $120 million), with sales of about $450 million in 1978.

With respect to these acquisitions, *Fortune* commented (July 25, 1983): White Consolidated's specialty is squeezing out fat. White built its business over the past 15 years by buying eight bleeding appliance divisions from big names like GM, Ford, and Westinghouse at fire-sale prices. Within a year of acquisition, it turned each of them around. Although it has some of the oldest factories in the industry, it has avoided big chunks of capital investment and instead has streamlined operations and slashed labor and overhead costs.

When White moves in, pink slips fly. The three unions it bargains with in various plants have had to settle for average wages of around $8.50 an hour, compared with $10 at Whirlpool. They call the company 'bloody' White. When White acquired Westinghouse's ailing appliance division it fired 40% of the workforce. . . .

Whenever possible, White has boosted efficiency by manufacturing newly acquired product lines in existing plants. When White purchased GM's Frigidaire division, for example, it bought the famous trademark, the tooling and equipment, the inventories, and a distribution and sales network—but none of the plants. Making Frigidaire refrigerators in the same plant where it was turning out Gibson, Kelvinator, and Westinghouse models, plus two private labels, improved factory utilization and, through economies of sales, reduced costs.

White sells a variety of appliances—primarily refrigerators, freezers, electric and gas ranges, clothes washers and dryers, and dishwashers. These are sold under most of the brand names that White acquired—Frigidaire, Kelvinator, Gibson, White-Westinghouse, Crosley, Bendix, etc.—and also under "private labels." Private label products carry the brands of companies which distribute them—such as Sears, Montgomery Ward, Gamble Skogmo, and other appliance manufacturers.

If we combine all of White's sales, the different brands plus the private labels, White's market position as shown in Table 1, is impressive.

TABLE 1.
WHITE'S APPLIANCES

	Shares of Total U.S. Market (%)	Position in the Industry
Refrigerators	22	3
Freezers	30	2
Clothes Washers	15	4
Electric Dryers	15	4
Gas Dryers	14	3
Electric Ranges	16	3
Gas Ranges	7	5

However, price competition in the home appliance industry is severe. Even with its cost-cutting and the economies of sale which come from being number 3 or number 4, White reports only modest profit margins and return on assets as shown in Table 2.

The major appliance industry has been a hard place to make a profit for some time—as is suggested by the availability of businesses which White acquired. From the 230 U.S. manufacturers of major appliances operating at the close of World War II fewer than 25 now survive.

TABLE 2.
HOME APPLIANCES
(in $ millions, except ratios)

	Last Year	Preceding Year	Preceding Year
Net Sales	1,347	1,470	1,355
Operating Income	77	99	69
Share of Corporate and Interest Expenses*	30	32	33
Income before Income Taxes	47	67	36
Assets Identified with Home Appliances	696	772	638
% Income before Tax to Net Sales	3.5	4.6	2.7
% Income before Tax to Assets	6.8	8.7	5.6

*Allocated on basis of sales.

Recent developments that will affect future competition in major appliances include:

1. Differences in quality and in design are narrowing. To survive at all, products must have good durability and dependability. Changes in design features are quickly copied by competitors; indeed, components often come from a common source.
2. The number of small retail outlets has shrunk. Now, most retail sales are made by small chains and independent operators that have large displays of competing brands of all sorts of appliances. Each outlet is like a supermarket filled with rows of similar-looking washing machines, dryers, ranges, etc. In such an outlet, a highly advertised brand name and/or a "bargain" price promotion is necessary to attract many customers. The second important sort of retailer is the large "mail order" chain—Sears, Montgomery Ward, etc.— which promote their own brands.
3. Most leading manufacturers are investing heavily in automated equipment in an effort to reduce production costs. General Electric, the largest producer, talks of a billion dollar program featuring robots. Even if part of this talk is competitive bluster, G.E.'s automation is clearly a major effort. Whirlpool, number two in the industry, is moving in the same direction—as are Magic Chef and others.
4. Also, the leading firms are all stressing a "full line"—a full array of appliances being sold under a single brand name. G.E. and Whirlpool already have such a line. Magic Chef, for years a well-known cooking range company, is creating full lines for both its Magic Chef and Admiral brands. Maytag, highly successful in laundry equipment, is experimenting with the use of its name on other kinds of appliances. Parts of these lines may be purchased from other (maybe competing) manufacturers; it is a full line under one brand that matters most. And the reason, in addition to some economy in national advertising, is obtaining good display space in those appliance supermarkets as noted in 2 above.

Whither White?

In this setting and with its inheritance, what should the corporate office of White Consolidated Industries do? What sort of input should the corporation make to the various businesses that White acquired to improve significantly their economic effectiveness?

Several possible courses of action are briefly outlined below. Of course, variations of these and still other courses of action might be considered.

1. *Minimize cash outlays while benefiting from investments already made.* The main corporate role here is to ferret out ways to reduce cash outlays—ways which division managers would be unlikely to develop if left alone. For instance, combining the production of a particular kind of appliance, say gas ranges, in a single plant may give that plant a more economical throughput and also permit cutting overhead at other plants.

Also, the corporate office might take a much tougher stand than the local management would undertake about cutting out division overhead and about insisting on reforms of work practices (the "bloody" White treatment). A corresponding action is to sharply curtail advertising.

Several of White's brands have a significant consumer goodwill, and will probably continue to sell in diminishing quantities even with minimal sales promotion. White could treat these brands as cash cows and proceed to milk them.

This approach is close to what White has been doing with most of its divisions. Corporate management performs the service of insisting on what it views as economical operating practice, while being careful to allow for necessary updating of design, maintenance of quality, and dependable deliveries.

2. *Build a full line of appliances under one or two brand names, supported with aggressive sales promotion.* White-Westinghouse or White-Frigidaire are possibilities.

An underlying assumption here is that most divisions would be reduced to a production plant making a single type of appliance. Since the output of such plants would be sold either by White's central marketing department or to private label customers, the overhead at each plant (division) could be greatly reduced.

In this setup the corporation would provide the centralized marketing for all of White's branded output. The featured brand would compete head-on with G.E., Whirlpool, Magic Chef, and Admiral—so some basis, not now apparent, for differentiation would be desirable.

To keep supply cost of such a line low, White could pursue two policies: (a) be a quick follower—not an initiator—in the R & D area, and (b) rely on sharp, tight cost-cutting coupled with low investment to secure production costs which would at least match the results obtained from high automation. The G.E. approach utilizing robots will require high investment, and studies of the Strategic Planning Institute (PIMS) show that relatively few businesses with high investment earn high profits.

3. *Concentrate on supplying private label products at low cost.* Reliance on customers to perform distribution functions would permit White to minimize its outlays for marketing, consumer financing, and the like. Each plant could focus on low-cost, high-quality production. Moreover, White could take the lead on importing components and subassemblies from foreign sources. The corporate office would be the selling agent for all the plants.

Private-label selling is a widespread practice in major appliances. For example, Whirlpool grew up as a supplier to Sears, and it still sells almost half of its output to Sears. Admiral (now owned by Magic Chef) sells refrigerators and freezers to ten other companies with their labels. Design & Manufacturing, a manufacturer unknown to most consumers, sells dishwashers to eleven other companies to be marketed under their own names.

As full-line marketing becomes more common, companies that manufacture only two or three kinds of appliances are filling out their line by buying other appliances from companies already established in that business. Such cross-selling contributes to a larger volume of production in each specialized plant. Usually these private-label supply relationships continue over several years.

Question

As an outside consultant, what corporate input policy do you recommend for White Consolidated Industries' appliance divisions?

16 MERGERS AND ACQUISITIONS

Mergers are exciting. They make headlines; new thrusts into growth areas are foreshadowed; realignments of supply are imminent; the status, security, and social relationships of many people are affected; large blocks of capital are involved; government agencies gird for action.

For managers of a specific enterprise, however, the excitement of a merger is only the tip of the iceberg; a merger with another company is a major event in the life of an enterprise; it may be the key to success or failure. And like the marriage of a man and a woman, it has deep emotional as well as economic effects. Consequently, mergers should be approached with care.

Corporate strategy, discussed in the two preceding chapters, indicates the kind of new business-units desired. Now we turn to three related issues:

1. Should the new unit be developed within the corporation or be an acquisition of an existing outside company?
2. If it is to be acquired, how should the acquisition be financed?
3. What steps need to be taken to assure that the anticipated benefits will be realized after the merger takes place?

These questions apply to both mergers and acquisitions. Formerly, the term "merger" applied to the consolidation of two companies about equal in size, whereas "acquisition" involved a larger firm taking over a smaller one. Since this distinction is no longer consistently observed and is not significant to our analysis here, we use the words interchangeably.

ACQUISITION VERSUS INTERNAL DEVELOPMENT

Why Look Outside?

Every merger involves complicated financial negotiations, revamping organizations, and career adjustments. Physical moves might be necessitated. A central manager could avoid most of the burdens by expanding from within instead of merging with a stranger. Consequently, a merger must offer strong advantages over internal expansion. Typically, a sound merger must provide major benefits in terms of time, expense, or physical possibility.

The mergers of local banks to take advantage of new technology, provide the needed volume of activity quickly; slower internal growth would postpone the use of new methods for years. Similarly, when DuPont Laboratories was successful in discovering several new drugs, a marketing organization capable of contacting doctors throughout the country was needed immediately. Building such an organization from scratch would have taken a long time, so DuPont acquired Endo Laboratories with its established marketing expertise and contacts in the ethical pharmaceutical field. Incidentally, this was the first exception in twenty-four years to DuPont's general policy of expansion from within rather than via mergers.

Expense as well as time is often critical. Creating a "going concern," especially in a field already keenly competitive, can be costly in terms of intitial investment and losses during the buildup period. In the insurance industry, for example, finding a significant number of new policy holders requires a substantial input of time and expense. So if a corporation wishes to have an insurance division—and many do because of the cash flow advantages—acquiring an existing firm is much simpler.

Likewise, if rare assets are needed, say a Coca-Cola franchise in Miami, or the talent of an outstanding entrepreneur, a merger may be the only feasible way to obtain the resource.

Antitrust Restrictions

Many potential mergers that would improve productivity are illegal. So before management spends much time exploring a possible acquisition, it should "see its lawyer."

To protect the free enterprise system, the United States government has a battery of antitrust laws and regulations. Unfortunately, much uncertainty and disagreement exists regarding the application of these laws; each new U.S. Attorney General brings a different viewpoint, and court decisions provide no clear-cut guidelines.

It is helpful to recognize the basic premise of antitrust effort—broadly, that competition is best protected by having many small, viable, locally owned competitors in each industry. Of course, competitors cannot be created by the passage of a law; instead, the antitrust laws try to prevent actions that reduce the number of effective competitors.

More specifically, the Antitrust Division is likely to challenge the acquisition of a competitor (a horizontal merger) if (1) only a few companies already dominate the relevant market, (2) either of the merging companies already serves over 20 percent of the market, (3) the merger decreases the number of companies in an expanding market, or (4) the merger makes entry of other companies quite difficult. So, except for very small firms, horizontal mergers are forbidden. The chief ambiguity arises in defining "industry" and "market." For instance, are skis just a small part of the sporting goods industry or an industry of their own? Is a major milk distributor in Los Angeles within or outside its market if it acquires a milk distributor in San Francisco? On such questions as these, see your lawyer.

A vertical merger (acquisition of a supplier or customer) gets into trouble when a new supplier would have difficulty entering the market or a new customer would have difficulty obtaining supplies, because the merger forecloses part of the market. Here again, the bigger the company, the more likely the objection. Recently, further uncertainty was added when the wording of the Clayton Act was amended to cover mergers that *may* substantially lessen competition or *tend* to create monopoly. Under this revision, the effects of a merger on potential, as well as existing, competition must be considered.

These expanding legal constraints have forced many companies to sharply alter their merger policy. Especially the larger companies are placing increasing reliance for growth on their own research and development because antitrust considerations virtually preclude expansion within their existing industries via mergers. Except for sharp diversification, mergers must be a highly selective aspect of corporate strategy.

FINANCING THE MERGER

Once a potential merger is identified that seems to be the best available way to move ahead with the corporate strategy, the second major question is, "What financial arrangements will be attractive to both companies?"

Every merger has its unique features, and the financial arrangements must reflect these. Nevertheless, we can suggest an approach to the main issues that arise in most mergers. Think of a merger as a swap. The company being acquired is trading a business for cash or securities of the surviving company. Involved in this trade are two packages of assets and two sets of owners; *each* set of owners attaches its own value to the assets it is giving up and to the assets it receives. The crux of negotiating the swap is to devise an arrangement that leaves each set of owners with a new package of assets that it prefers over the assets it has parted with.

To apply this approach, we must understand (1) the value both parties attach to the business being traded and (2) the value to both parties of the payments to be made. Figure 16-1 indicates the main elements involved in a merger and the value assigned to these elements by each party.

Value of Business Traded

In valuing the business being traded, agreement must be reached on what is to be traded and the value to be attached to it.

FIGURE 16-1.
Main Elements in Negotiating a Merger

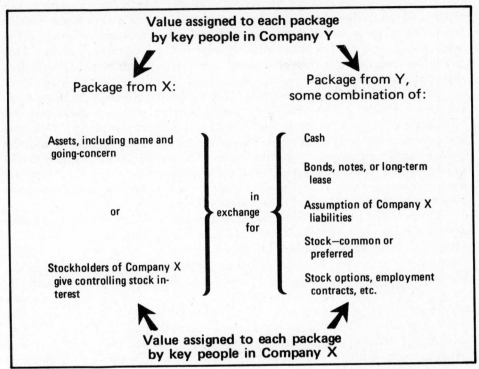

**Value assigned to each package
by key people in Company Y**

Package from X:

Package from Y,
some combination of:

Assets, including name and
going-concern

or

Stockholders of Company X
give controlling stock interest

in
exchange
for

Cash

Bonds, notes, or long-term
lease

Assumption of Company X
liabilities

Stock—common or
preferred

Stock options, employment
contracts, etc.

**Value assigned to each package
by key people in Company X**

What Is Included. A company may be acquired either by taking over ownership of the corporation stock or by purchasing the assets. When stock ownership is the mechanism, the entire legal entity with its intangible assets and liabilities is acquired. Later the corporation may be dissolved and a complete melding may occur, but at the time of the merger we think in terms of the complete enterprise. (If minority blocks of stock remain outstanding, clearly only a percentage of the ownership is traded, but it is still a percentage of the total concern.)

Sometimes a corporation owns assets that the acquiring firm does not want, for example, a large tract of land or a company store. Or there may be serious disagreement over the values attached to a separable asset or liability. In such cases, most but not all of the tangible and intangible assets along with current liabilities and mortgages are transferred. This leaves the old corporation with the same set of stockholders still, but the corporation now holds the cash or securities received in the trade instead of its former operating business, plus assets excluded from the trade.

Basis of Evaluation. With agreement on what is to be traded, attention shifts to the subjective values each party attaches to its business. Obviously, subjective values differ. People and companies vary in their needs, opportunities, and resources. So, no bookkeeping figures or simple formula can produce a value acceptable to everyone. Historical costs, book value, and market price (if the stock does have a market price) may influence the evaluation, but usually each individual feels that a particular package of assets is worth more, or less, than these conventional measures show.

A rational basis for setting a value is to estimate the incomes that the company (or its assets) will provide over a period of years, including the disposition of the assets at the end of the period; to adjust these annual estimates of income for uncertainty (for example, cut the figures in half if there is only a 50-50 chance that the estimated net income will arise in the specified year); and finally to reduce each of the adjusted or "expected"incomes to present values by allowing for alternative uses of the resources that are being committed to the venture in question. This gives a discounted present value of future incomes.[1]

But note that present owners and the acquiring company will come out with quite different answers even if they use the same "rational" approach. The acquiring company will manage the assets differently and it expects to obtain synergistic benefits from the consolidation; consequently, its estimated incomes, uncertainties, and alternatives are unlike those of present owners if the merger is not consummated. In any economically sound merger the minimum the owners will accept (their value of the property if the merger is not completed) should be well below the maximum the acquiring company might pay (the present value of all incomes including the expected benefits arising from the merger). The spread between these two figures leaves a wide margin for bargaining. These outer limits are rarely revealed in the negotiations because both parties seek a substantial part of the margin and because they also attach different values to the payment package.

Other Considerations

Present value of future company income, just discussed, is not a complete picture, especially to the owner of a family business. People who have devoted their lives to building an enterprise normally have deep concern about perpetuating the company name and reputation; their interest is in the future welfare of their employees; they want the company to continue to give support to the community in which they live. Also, in selling the company, these individuals may be sacrificing an attractive salary and a prestigious position.

---

[1]We have deliberately used more general wording here than is found in the typical "discounted cash flow" procedure because company owners usually have personal values that are broader than the strictly financial figures commonly used in cash flow analysis.

The acquiring company has no such emotional attachments to the firm being absorbed, but it does know that such considerations cannot be ignored. To a large extent, the combined company can meet the social obligations to the community; in fact, it may make substantially larger community contributions than would be made if the companies continued separate existences. Brand names and perhaps company names are often continued because of the goodwill attached to them. Employment may actually increase, although some individuals might suffer. The acquiring company may have a more liberal pension plan (and if past-service credits are large, the final merger arrangement may be adjusted to cover them). Often key executives are given an employment contract for three to five years, and the senior exectutive may be elected to the board of directors of the combined company.

Unless the executives of the company to be absorbed feel that these "other considerations" will be reasonably met, serious negotiations may never start.

Value of Payment to Be Made

The second half of a merger trade is a package of cash or securities exchanged for the acquired business. This *quid pro quo* must be attractive to the buyer and at the same time must not involve too high a sacrifice for the seller. Here, again, we must consider what is being traded and the value each party attaches to that package.

Form of Payment. The most common type of payment in mergers is stock of the surviving corporation. For example, R.C.A. gave 3,450,000 shares of its common stock for the F. M. Stamper Company, a privately held frozen food concern. RCA stock with a quoted market value was attractive to Stamper stockholders; on the other hand, it was newly issued stock, so existing RCA operations were not hampered by the acquisition.

Payment in the form of common stock is especially likely when that stock has a high price-earnings ratio. Thus, Electronics Company A with a price-earnings ratio of 20 would find it advantageous to use its stock to acquire Company B having a price-earnings ratio of only 8. In the simplified illustration shown in Table 16-1, the market value of the shares of the combined company has increased $6 million as a result of using Company A's price-earnings ratio on Company B's earnings. In the example, two-thirds of this increase goes to Company A stockholders and one-third to Company B stockholders.

Cash is, of course, the simplest form of payment. It is used when the acquiring company is highly liquid and sellers are not confronted with high capital gains taxes.

Many other forms of payment are used to meet particular circumstances. Preferred stock gives the sellers greater assurance of dividends. Debenture bonds or notes provide even greater security but are less favorable from a tax standpoint. Bonds or preferred stock may be made more attractive by having them

TABLE 16-1.
ILLUSTRATION OF
EFFECT OF PRICE-EARNING RATIOS
(Assume one share of A is exchanged for two shares of B, and
A's price-earnings ratio remains constant)

	Shares Outstanding	Total Earnings	Earnings per Share	Market Price per Share	Imputed Total Market Value
			Before Merger		
Company A	1,000,000	$1,000,000	$1	$20	$20,000,000
Company B	500,000	500,000	$1	$ 8	4,000,000
					$24,000,000
			After Merger		
Company A	1,250,000	$1,500,000	$1.20	$24	$30,000,000
Former Owners of Company B	—	—	—	($\frac{24}{2} = \$12$)	($6,000,000)

convertible into common stock. Or stock options (rights to purchase common stock at a fixed price) may be used to give the seller an opportunity to benefit from company growth.

Frequently, a combination of several forms of payment is used. The Ingram Company, for example, received cash for its net current assets, twenty-year mortgage bonds for its fixed assets, and a large block of stock options that gave it an opportunity to share in any synergistic gains that might grow out of merged operations.

Tax on Payment. Sellers are concerned about the income tax they will have to pay on the package of cash and/or securities they receive. If they get only voting stock in the surviving company, as in the RCA example on page 393, the transaction is tax-free. The stockholders are merely exchanging one form of equity for another; no capital gains have been realized, and hence there is no basis for levying an income tax. (Of course, if stockholders subsequently sell their stock, any appreciation over their original cost is taxable.)

In contrast, payment in the form of cash or bonds that have a fixed value does establish a capial gain that is taxable. And some stockholders may find such a tax quite onerous. One way to avoid the tax pressure on stockholders is the sale of assets by the corporation. If a corporation exchanges its assets for cash and/or bonds, *it* will be subject to capital gains tax on any appreciation over its "cost," but the stockholders incur no tax obligation since they simply continue to hold the same stock in the same corporation.

Market Liquidity. In addition to tax implications, the response of a seller will be influenced by liquidity. Stockholders of corporations whose stock is closely held often have difficulty selling their stock quickly. Family-held companies are the prime example, especially when cash is needed to pay inheritance tax. So, in appraising any merger proposal, the stockholders will be concerned about the salability of the securities they receive. Stock in a large corporation that is actively traded on a major stock exchange is attractive because it is liquid. Of course, the significance attached to liquidity, or to a tax-free exchange, depends upon the financial postion of each stockholder.

Financial Structure of Acquiring Company.   The acquiring company, likewise, evaluates the alternative forms of payment in terms of its particular situation. Cash may be readily available or extremely scarce. Long-term debt of the company may already be so high that the issuance of additional bonds would be imprudent. Of course, if the assets acquired can support more debt, then a loan from a third party may supply cash to use in partial payment to the seller. (A sale-and-leaseback of the fixed assets can be used in the same way.) But normally the acquiring company must guarantee repayment of the loan, and this becomes a contingent liability even though it does not show on the balance sheet.

Perhaps convertible preferred stock will appeal to the owners of the prospective acquisition, but a relatively small issue of an additional form of stock would interfere with larger financing by the surviving company in the future. In other words, both debt and equity payments should be appraised in terms of their effect on the total financial structure of the acquiring company.

Loss of Control.   When common stock is used for a large acquisition, one or two of the new stockholders may become the largest owners of stock in the surviving corporation. They are then in a strategic position to gain control. This prospect may be unattractive to the executives in charge of the acquiring corporation.

Dilution.   Stockholders of an acquiring company will also be concerned about "dilution." Usually dilution refers to a reduction in earnings per share. For example, assume that Company A with 100,000 shares of stock outstanding gives an additional 10,000 shares to acquire Company B. If Company A's previous earnings of $500,000 are increased to only $535,000 when A and B are combined, then Company A's stockholders will see their earnings per share drop from $5.00 to $4.86. Although the management of Company A can enthusiastically report increased sales and higher total profits, the picture on a per-share basis is the reverse. Presumably such dilution is only temporary; a sound merger should help increase earnings proportionately more than the increase in shares outstanding. Nevertheless, any merger proposal that shows short-run dilution will require strong justification.

Negotiating a "Good" Merger

Clearly, a variety of considerations enter into a good merger. We start with a potential combination of businesses that will generate productivity gains and perhaps financial benefits. Our task then turns to devising and winning acceptance of a trade that is attractive to the management and the stockholders of both the acquiring firm and the acquired firm. The following brief case illustrates the adaptation that may be necessary.

The Enid Corporation of Ohio was highly successful in manufacturing and selling indoor-outdoor acrylic carpeting in Midwest and Eastern United States. It had annual sales of over $50,000,000 and profits of around $3,500,000 or $1.75 per share of common stock. The stock was listed on the American Stock Exchange and had been selling at the $26–$35 range. West Coast sales, however, had declined for four years following the death of Enid's original representative in Los Angeles. To correct this situation, Enid wished to acquire Thomas & Son, an aggressive wholesale floorcovering distributor in San Francisco. This firm had been earning about $200,000 per year after taxes and the senior Mr. Thomas was ready to retire. Executives of both Enid and Thomas thought the merger "made good sense."

Enid first suggested a simple exchange of stock, mentioning 100,000 shares of its stock, then selling at $30 per share. This would have given Thomas a price of 15 times its earnings while avoiding a dilution of Enid's earnings. Thomas felt the price was low because its earnings did not reflect two pieces of undeveloped land that Thomas believed could be sold for as much as a million dollars. Also, the debt position of Thomas & Son was complicated by the financing of this and other real estate.

The discussion then shifted to the purchase of all assets except real estate, which would remove the threat of a capital gains tax on stockholders. Thomas then said the corporation would rather have cash than stock. Enid next proposed a package consisting of $500,000 cash; $1,800,000 in 6 percent notes, maturing $100,000 per year over 18 years; a "consulting" contract with Mr. Thomas, Sr., of $35,000 per year for 10 years; and an employment contract with Mr. Thomas, Jr., for $30,000 per year (his present salary) for 10 years. Later, to recognize goodwill and growth potential, Enid added stock options giving Thomas & Son the option to buy 100,000 shares of Enid common stock at $33 per share any time during the next 5 years. And on these terms the deal was made.

Both sides were happy. Mr. Thomas, Sr., said: "We keep all our real estate, get a steady flow of cash into the corporation, I'm on a liberal pension, and Tom has a good job. All these incomes add up to $2,950,000 or about Enid's original offer. Then top it off with an option that should be worth another million in five years."

Enid's president was equally pleased. He reasoned: "Our major gain is strong distribution on the West Coast, with young Thomas committed to stay on the job. Mr. Thomas, Sr., has been drawing big bonuses, so much of his pension can come out of a reduction in executive compensation. Any way we figure it, the $400,000 pre-tax earnings will more than cover the interest, capital cost, and other charges. So we expect to get an immediate improvement in net profit. True, the book value of the assets we acquired is a bit under the $2,300,000 we paid, but within a few years our profit from West Coast operations should be at least $500,000."

Note that each executive used different criteria to place a value on the business being transferred and the package of payments being received. Both packages of assets had been tailored to fit the particular situation. The swap was good. Nevertheless, the long-run soundness of the merger remains to be demonstrated in the profitable growth of Enid's West Coast business.

MAKING MERGERS SUCCESSFUL

Many mergers fail. Often the anticipated benefits do not develop, at least to the degree predicted, and unforeseen problems arise. Some of these failures are due to poorly conceived combinations—the marriages of convenience that never were thought through. Others are high-risk ventures that turn up in the losing column. Rarely can managerial skill save such ill-fated mergers.

More disturbing are the well-conceived matches that do not work out. Such results usually can be avoided by proper managerial action. Experience with successful mergers suggests a twofold approach: (1) perceptive, careful management and (2) special attention to communication and motivation.

Perceptive Management

The first step in making mergers successful is a *specific program* to bring about the projected results. This requires spelling out the necessary changes and the resources—new engineering, new equipment, hiring and training people, advertising, etc.—and then setting a timetable. Probably the program will need adjustment, but this adaptation will be easier if the various moves have been delineated in advance. In addition, changes needed to reconcile the policies and the procedures of the merged companies should be identified and scheduled. Such programming demands a lot of time and thought by key people (one of the reasons it is often neglected), but it pays off because in the merger process individuals who have never worked together before are expected to do new work.

A second step is realignment of and staffing the *organization* needed to execute the program. Every merger upsets the subtle understandings of status and power in the two companies; the jockeying for new positions is inevitable. Although the situations may be too fluid to define detailed relationships, placing responsibility and providing a prompt means for resolving differences of opinion are essential for positive action. The new mixture of personalities in every merger makes this reorganizing a very delicate task.

Installing dependable *controls* is a third essential element. Cash controls and accounting reports usually are quickly adapted to a format familiar to central executives. However, meaningful cost data and information on market development, research and development effort, management development, and other intangibles are rare. Many a merger has floundered because executives lack a means of knowing what was really happening in their new operation.

Communication and Motivation

Cutting across the more explicit management actions just described is a critical need for communication and motivation. A merger signals change. Just what will be changed is unknown, so anxiety builds up in many people whose jobs might be affected. Rumors substitute for facts and spread rapidly.

In such circumstances, key executives should make their plans known just as soon as possible. If some matters are unsettled, they can at least indicate how and when these will be resolved. The communication should be two-way, giving employees an opportunity to ask questions and hear frank answers. New executives have low *credibility* in the early stages of a merger, and they need to explain what will be done and then see that it happens. Suspicion of motives is apt to flare up at any time during the first year or two, and executives need to be available to make personal explanations of actions they take.

An aspect of communication is when to discuss problems and with whom. One successful pattern is to explore what changes are necessary and how merged operations will be organized *before* the agreement is final. Usually these discussions include all key executives who will have to work together. If a merger does take place after such a frank exchange, its chances of success are high. The chief drawback is that the airing of problems may cause one party to withdraw. But if these early stages cannot survive frank recognition of what working together involves, then major personnel and morale difficulties should be anticipated.

Coupled with the frankest communication possible should be positive reinforcement—tangible or intangible rewards—of desired behavior. By emphasizing the achievements of a merger and rewarding them, management builds a new morale. Employee attention shifts from concern with the past to interest in the future.

We shall examine programming, organizing, communicating, and controlling more fully in later parts of this book. As indicated, mergers generate some especially difficult tasks of execution. Unless these receive their full share of attention, the entire merger effort may be futile.

MERGER VIA TAKEOVER

The vast majority of mergers are "friendly," that is, they are recommended by the directors of both companies. But recently the business world has been dazzled by a rash of "takeovers" in which the acquiring company gains control of another concern without the cooperation of its existing management. Here the "raider" gets control of the majority of the stock, ousts the existing management, and then arranges a favorable merger.

Use of Tender Offers

A raider may gain control of the desired merger partner in several ways: (1) by joining forces with key stockholders not supporting the management (for example, Hilton acquired the Statler Hotel chain in this manner); (2) by acquiring stock on the open market (for example, James Hill's classic fight for the Burlington Railroad); and (3) by soliciting proxies of stockholders (Young used this route to gain control of the New York Central Railroad). Today, these methods are becoming very expensive.

Currently, the popular path to control is a "tender offer." Here the raider makes a public offer to buy or exchange stock. The terms may be any one of the alternatives we have already discussed under friendly mergers—cash, common stock, convertible preferred stock, and so forth. However, the offer must have a value well above the prevailing price of the stock being sought, typically 25 to 30 percent higher than the market price under the present management. In other words, the raider bypasses company management and appeals directly to stockholders.

Prior to the passage of new laws regulating tenders, this was a cloak-and-dagger game. Surprise offers, secret deals, extra commissions to brokers, counterattacks, splitting stock, and legal injunctions were all employed in a manner reminiscent of the battles between the industrial barons of the 19th century. Slowly the process is becoming more open and orderly.

Who is Vulnerable?

No company will attempt a takeover unless it sees an opportunity to substantially improve the return to its stockholders by better management and/or synergistic benefits of the merger. Consequently, a firm is vulnerable to takeover: (1) when it shows poor performance relative to other firms in its industry—especially when its dividends are declining more than those of its competitors; (2) when it has surplus liquid assets or large unused borrowing capacity; (3) when it holds assets that could be sold for more than their market value; or (4) when potential synergistic benefits are being disregarded.

The best defense against a takeover is, of course, managing a company so that its assets are wisely deployed, its earnings record creates a good price for its stock, and synergistic benefits are aggressively exploited. Under these conditions, a stockholder gains little or nothing by transferring the stock to a raider.

Such a sound defense against a takeover takes time. If a company is really vulnerable and finds itself being raided before it has time to put its house in order, the management can, and often does, seek a friendly merger with some other company on terms as attractive as those of the tender. Management casualties are usually lower in a friendly merger!

Economic Effects

The immediate effects on a company of a takeover are costly. Anxiety is at a peak, personal hostilities are generated, and none of the perceptive management steps discussed in the previous section can occur in advance. Nevertheless, a takeover does serve as one way of deposing a stodgy management. More important, the possibility of a takeover lurking in the background serves as a spur to management. No longer can executives be complacent just because company stock is dispersed among so many stockholders that no one can make a significant complaint.

From the point of view of society and of a stockholder, then, the potential threat of a takeover stimulates good management. All parties—stockholders, society, *and* management—will be better off if the company is administered so that the costly process of takeover is impractical.

SUMMARY

Merging with another company can be a major step in carrying out a desired strategy. The acquired company may provide a much needed resource, give access to a new market, extend company operations back into earlier stages of production, provide a scale of operation that will support improved technology, or improve company services and productivity.

Not all mergers are so well conceived. Some are opportunistic, taking advantage of short-run fiancial gain. Ideal, of course, is a partner that both pushes us forward on basic strategy and provides a financial advantage.

Whatever the fit, the "price" paid must also be weighed. A heavy debt burden, troublesome stock options, and exhaustion of cash reserves can result, and this unhealthy financial condition can seriously deter execution of other facets of company strategy. Or the package given to owners of the acquired company, say common stock, may create no strain. Since we know that a strong financial structure is closely related to future growth, both the *quid* and the *quo* of the merger deal require close scrutiny in terms of their impact on the master strategic plan.

Even soundly conceived mergers fail if the two institutions are not melded by good follow-up action. Numerous internal adjustments in both companies need careful planning, organizing, and controlling; new motivations and communication flows have to be established. These are problems that we examine more fully in the next two parts of this book.

QUESTIONS FOR CLASS DISCUSSION

1. El Paso Company's directors and management opposed a tender offer from Burlington Northern, Inc. of $24 a share for El Paso's common stock. Burlington Northern went ahead, however, and then made a "hostile" offer direct to the shareholders by offering to buy 51 percent of the common stock of El Paso, which was then selling at about $16 per share, with a deadline of fifteen days after the offer was made. (Burlington Northern is a large railroad and natural resources company. El Paso produces and sells natural gas and owns several natural gas pipelines.) Within ten days 25.1 million shares (51 percent) were tendered to Burlington Northern by, as it turned out, stockmarket professionals and arbitragers. The overwhelming majority of El Paso's 111,000 shareholders were not represented in the original pool of the tender offers—nor were El Paso's management and directors. Recognizing this, and being unable to find a rescuing company to make a better offer and keep the El Paso management on the job, the management proposed a deal to Burlington Northern. The deal included a withdrawal of the first offer and its deadline, a new offer of $24 a share for 21 million El Paso shares (about 43 percent), an extended deadline and takeover-triggered "golden parachute" employment agreements for four top officers. Burlington Northern expected that about 80 percent of El Paso's shares would be tendered under the new offer and that it would purchase half of these. Thus the Wall Street professionals and arbitragers would sell less than half of their shares, and El Paso's other shareholders would get an opportunity to share in the Burlington Northern offer. Burlington Northern executives believed that El Paso had a bleak near-term (three years) earnings outlook and that it would have to keep enough funds in reserve to tide El Paso over these hard times. Some arbitragers alleged that Burlington Northern and its investment advisers (Merrill Lynch, White Weld, and Shearson/American Express) would be double-crossing those El Paso stockholders who had originally tendered control of the company if it accepted the new deal.

    Do you recommend that Burlington Northern accept the deal proposed by El Paso's management?

2. Executives of Dean Corp., a large U.S. paper company, recognize that the paper industry is mature and they have been seeking diversification ventures. Four years ago, Dean acquired B.B. Laboratories "to become our internal source of new ventures." B.B. Laboratories was owned and run by two creative engineers, Bob Brown and Boris Bohr, who had developed several new products related to aerial photography. Brown especially was well known in aviation and space engineering. Brown and Bohr each received common stock in Dean Corp. worth about $1 million along

with a five-year employment contract. Brown commented at the time, "Since we will continue to run our own shop this is a case of having our cake and eating it, too."

Although informally organized, B.B. Laboratories actually had three sections: (a) Service contracts with the Air Force were the cash cow that paid the rent and provided a base for R & D activities. (b) Project Q was a secret military activity in a separate part of the plant. (c) The research lab worked on whatever ideas Brown or Bohr thought were promising. After the acquisition, Dean Corp. formalized the research division and added to section (b) a military development project it had purchased a year earlier.

The acquisition did not work out. Within a year Brown resigned to take a prestigious job in Washington. "Just can't turn it down—now that I don't have to worry about where the next meal is coming from." Eighteen months later Bohr left. His reasons were less sharp. "I was spending almost two days a week going to dull meetings. As the in-house expert on new inventions, I was called in every time an executive heard of a new way to walk on water. Then there were budget presentations, budget reviews, personnel evaluations, and a lot more red tape. Those things have their place, but the Dean Corp. system just did not fit us; budgeting R & D doesn't make much sense to me, and the controller at Dean can't understand contract work for the government. Whatever the reason, we weren't getting anywhere; so I pulled out."

With both Brown and Bohr gone, Dean Corp. decided to close the B.B. lab. The service contract did not meet Dean Corp.'s profit target rates and it was sold recently to another company. Project Q is still there, but nobody ever presumed that it alone would be worth the price Dean had paid for B.B. Laboratories.

What do you suggest might have been done to avoid this unhappy marriage?

3. Not long ago the chairperson of the Securities and Exchange Commission warned board directors, lawyers, and accountants of unfortunate results from continuing emphasis on acquisitions and mergers. "Unfortunately . . . most discussions of tender offers seem to center on . . . various devices to comply with or avoid the application of the federal securities laws and the state antitakeover requirements. . . . The most unsettling aspect . . .is the legitimacy which hostile tender offers have come to enjoy. It has become acceptable to treat corporations as the sum of their properties and to assume that corporate control may change hands with no greater concerns of the consequences than accompanies an exchange of property deeds in a game of Monopoly." The chairperson also took issue with the speculators, arbitragers, and lawyers who benefit from the takeovers and can then easily walk away once the transaction is completed. "The corporation is more than the aggregate if its tangible assets." (a) What did the chairperson mean by the phrase "the most unsettling aspects"? (b) What might the corporation be other than the sum of its assets? (c) Why might the lawyers and accountants be especially interested in devices to avoid the application of various laws? (d) Is this social responsibility on the part of the specialists?

4. In the Enid-Thomas merger described on pages 396 and 397, *assume* that the following difficulties arose after the merger was completed: (a) anxiety and communication difficulties during the first year reduced the effectiveness of the Thomas employees;

(b) the Thomas product line needed trimming and more emphasis was put on Enid products—a switch that was not readily accepted by the Thomas group; and (c) Thomas, Jr. wanted to take independent action on a variety of matters and was "too rich to be motivated from Ohio" so he resigned after three years. What action might Enid executives have taken to minimize or forestall these difficulties?

5. Many "developing countries" now want companies located and operating within their boundaries to be at least 51 percent owned by local citizens. Assume that you, as international manager for Scripto, Inc., wish to acquire an office supply firm in such a country for the purpose of setting up a local assembly plant. Would you agree to the acquisition if you could obtain only 49 percent of stock ownership? Is there any alternative that you think might be acceptable to you, the local government, and the manager of the local firm? Aside from ownership, are there other conditions related to the acquisition that you believe are especially important?

6. The reverse of a merger is a "spin-off"—the separation of a single company into two or more independent concerns. In practice, relatively few spin-offs or divestments occur, and most of these arise from antitrust activity of the federal government. (a) How do you account for the much larger number of mergers than spin-offs? Are the economic advantages predominantly in favor of increased size? What of other social considerations? (b) Assume that, as president, you concluded that dividing up your company made good sense. What problems do you foresee in accomplishing the split-up? (c) Do your answers to (a) and (b) apply to profit decentralization, that is, to establishing semiautonomous self-contained divisions?

7. Financial policy seeks a good adjustment of the company to suppliers of capital; personnel policy, a good adjustment to suppliers of labor; purchasing policy, a good adjustment to vendors; marketing policy, a good adjustment to suppliers of outlets. And the list can be extended to other important resource groups. (a) How does social responsibility fit into this array of policy? (b) Does the answer to (a) differ for small vs. large companies?

8. "Vic, how would you like to be a millionaire?" Joe Javitz, the president of Roadwise Carburetor Co. asked his friend, Victor Savas. "As you know, Roadwise Carburetor is building a nationwide distribution system and Savas Auto Parts Co. could be the Northwest part of that system. So we might be persuaded to give you $1 million of Roadwise stock for your company."

"That millionaire stuff sure has a nice ring to it, Joe, but your suggestion is a bit too simple. What would I live on? You told me last month that your expansion was soaking up all the cash you have, and that dividends on your stock had to wait. Also, what about my partner, Tim Lyle? He owns 25 percent of Savas Auto Parts Co. Does he get a million, too?"

Roadwise Carburetor Co. sells *replacement* carburetors to automobile repair shops. Some are new and some of the recent complex ones are rebuilt. Roadwise's goal is to have carburetors for any car available anywhere in the United States. To achieve this, Roadwise needs distribution branches throughout the country, one or two plants, and four or five rebuilding shops. Savas Auto Parts has distribution branches in Washington and Oregon and does rebuilding in its Portland plant. Currently, Savas gets most (not all) of its carburetors from Roadwise. At one time Savas made replacement carburetors; but as carburetors became more complex, Savas confined production to a few older, simpler models and bought the others from firms like Roadwise. Savas is still a very strong distributor in the Northwest. Vic Savas believes that as carburetors become more sophisticated Roadwise is likely to become one of the leading independent suppliers in the replacement field.

Two weeks after the conversation above, the controller for Roadwise visited Savas Auto Parts Co. and reported the following back to Javitz. (a) The Savas plant is old but is on a valuable piece of land. Under Lyle's direction the plant is doing subcontracting, mostly aircraft parts and some "cages," which space the balls in ball bearings. The land, plant, and equipment, plus working capital not associated with carburetors, have a book value of $150,000 and could be sold for about $250,000. (b) Lyle said that if he had the money he'd like to buy the plant himself. (c) Accounts payable are high, so net working capital in the carburetor business is only $300,000. (d) Last year Vic Savas paid himself a salary of $65,000. Apparently he does use this money to live on, and he expects to continue to work.

At the next meeting of Javitz and Savas, Javitz suggested, "(a) You would work full time running our Northwest operations at least until you are sixty-five (four years) at a base salary of $65,000 per year. Upon retirement you would continue as director and consultant to Roadwise for life with a compensation of $30,000 per year. Assuming that your life expectancy is age seventy-five, that adds up to $560,000. That's over half your million. (b) In exchange for all your inventory, receivables, and goodwill associated with carburetors we will give Savas Auto Parts Co. common stock in Roadwise Carburetor Co. The book value could be low for tax purposes, but the future value would be $500,000. If you personally take that, and I hope you will, then you'll have your million. (c) Your land is indeed valuable, but frankly we are not interested in investing in land at this time. Our suggestion to you is that Lyle get all the assets not associated with carburetors. One simple way to achieve this is to spin-off everything associated with carburetors into a subsidiary which you would take (and then sell to us); Lyle would own the old corporation and all that's left (with *no* taxes to pay)."

Use the factors discussed in this chapter to appraise Javitz's proposal. Is it likely to be accepted by the key parties? Do you have a better plan?

9. *A* corporation offered to buy *B* Corporation and when *C* Corporation heard about the proposal it also offered to buy *B*. Two directors wondered about which offer to recommend to the shareholders. The *B* family, including the two directors, owned a little more than 40 percent of *B*'s common stock. The *B* company had no preferred stock. The common stock of both *A* and *C* was traded actively on public exchanges. The price per share offered by *A* and *C* for *B*'s shares was almost the same, but *A* offered a choice of cash for half the amount and its common stock for the balance *or* its common stock for the entire amount. The choice was left up to each person who owned *B*'s stock. Corporation *C* offered a new class of its cumulative preferred stock with a dividend 25 percent per share more than *B* had been paying in the recent past to its shareholders. The new preferred had no voting rights unless dividends had been omitted for three years. Both *A* and *C* were about three times the size of *B*. *A* company planned to move all central offices and staff divisions to its own headquar-

ters in a different state but offered to set up a subsidiary named for the *B* family and to keep open one plant and the *B* Country Club in *B*'s former headquarters city. *C* planned to combine all operations in various parts of its plants in the city in which both it and *B* were located. It also planned to sell off all the real estate holdings of *B* in that city to help to increase its working capital. The two directors, like other executives in the industry and the city, respected *C* company for its excellent products, modern plants, and first-rate human resource policies and practices. They also respected *A* company for its excellent products, rapid growth through successful acquisitions, and high standing in the financial and investment communities.

Which offer should the two directors of *B* Corporation recommend to their shareholders?

10. (a) Companies that stress long-range planning often become involved in mergers. This is especially so when the long-range planning focuses on strategy rather than on budgeting. How do you explain this tendency? (b) Review the key elements of strategy outlined in Chapter 5 and identify the areas where a merger is likely to be an attractive way to proceed.

CASE 16
T&T Acquisition

Background of Acquisition Proposal

Executives in Davis Data, Inc. are looking for ways to benefit from their ownership of several diverse businesses. One possibility is to develop a computerized reference service; that is, build a large data bank that can be queried via computer to provide information on specific questions. Two existing divisions of Davis Data might sire such a service. One division designs and sells computer software programs for a variety of purposes, including library reference and catalog systems. The publishing division deals mostly in technical books, but it also has acquired several "yearbooks" for various industries. The yearbooks contain a lot of industry statistics and related matter which are updated annually.

With all the talk about having vast quantities of reference material available to people who have personal computers, Davis Data sees an opportunity to create a new service utilizing the industry data that its publishing division already compiles. Personnel in the software division could design a system for accessing this information; then subscribers could tap into the data banks quickly from any location having a personal computer and a telephone.

Since the publishing division puts out yearbooks for the hotel/motel industry and the resort industry, a computerized reference service for managers in those industries is being considered by Davis Data, Inc. Such a service would also be valuable to firms selling supplies and services to hotels, motels, and resorts. To be successful, the reference service will have to be responsive to the interests and problems of its users. And at present Davis Data, Inc. does not have personnel "who think like a resort manager." Executives in Davis Data, Inc., believe that kind of perspective is needed in order to be positioned to move quickly into the new service.

As Davis executives were looking for a young, imaginative person already familiar with the hotel/motel and resort industries, the name of Willis White surfaced. White is well respected for his trade association work. A follow-up check revealed, however, that White has recently become editor of two trade papers in this field. And thus the trail leads to the T&T Publishing Company, where White is now part owner and managing editor. To get White, Davis Data, Inc., may have to acquire T&T, and even then he could move to another job.

Present Situation at T&T

T&T has been in the printing and publishing business for a long time. When Mr. Tilson died a few years ago, all the printing equipment and business went to Tilson's heirs. The building, the two monthly trade papers, and the name went to Mr. Taussig. However, most of the building is under long-term lease to the printing firm, providing Taussig with about $40,000 yearly income from that source.

Taussig wants to retire, but having recently remarried he needs an additional $20,000 per year to live on. He expects to get this sum from the trade papers. A managing editor hired three years ago to take over the running of the papers left after the first year due to a clash in personalities. Then, following extended negotiations, Taussig "sold out" to White and his wife.

The expression "sold out" overstates the arrangement. Taussig has an employment contract with T&T to remain as "publisher" for twelve years, when he will be eighty, at a salary of $20,000 per year. (This salary is subordinated to the normal obligations of T&T so as not to impinge on T&T's credit standing.) Taussig sold the Whites 4,500 shares of the 10,000 shares of T&T common stock outstanding for a "nominal" $5 per share, and gave the Whites an option to buy the remaining shares at the same price when his employment at T&T ends.

This arrangement appeals to the Whites for several reasons. It gives the Whites a business of their own where they can work as a team. They now own part of the company and will eventually buy the rest at a price already fixed. Thus, they can reap the benefits of improvements they make in the business. Taussig assured them that they will have a free hand since he wishes to withdraw, and that he is retaining voting control only to safeguard his salary which is really what he is being paid for the company.

Acquisition Proposal

As Davis Data, Inc. enters the picture, then, it will either have to persuade White to give up the T&T venture just described, or it can try to buy the stock of both Taussig and the Whites. In fact, acquisition of T&T as a going concern might serve Davis Data's purpose very well. (1) The trade papers will probably pay all or most of White's salary. This is advantageous because the *time* when it will be wise to start the contemplated reference service is uncertain. Davis Data will probably rely on some distributor or TV channel to handle the physical transmission, and that activity in turn depends on widespread development of the whole reference service concept. It is quite possible that Davis Data could be unable to proceed for several years. (2) Mrs. White, who is twenty-eight, complements the talents of her husband, who is thirty-two. She has a degree in operations research and would be very useful in building bridges between data bases, managers' needs, and computer programs.

The acquisition expert at Davis Data (vice-president for Corporate Planning) has been trying to design a "package" that is attractive to both Taussig and the Whites. Taussig is easy to satisfy. He'll probably sell out at $5 per share if Davis Data will take over his employment contract. Or, Taussig will rent to Davis Data the space in his building that the trade papers now use at an increased rental of $20,000 per year for twelve years—an arrangement Taussig prefers because the rent would continue to flow to his young wife even if he dies in the twelve-year interval.

For the Whites, the proposal is: (1) Davis Data, Inc., will purchase their shares at $5 each, and the stock option on Taussig's shares will be canceled. (2) The Whites will continue to have full reign in running the trade papers—there is no one else in Davis Data who understands that kind of business. (3) At the same time, the Whites will work with other people in Davis Data on the development of a computerized reference service for the hotel   otel and resort industries. Future net income—before tax (but not losses)—from the sale of such service will be included with the income from the trade papers in the calculation of the White's options and bonuses. (4) For each of twelve years, starting three years hence, the Whites will receive an option to buy one share of Davis Data, Inc., stock at $20 per share for each $100 increase in the annual income-before-tax earned by T&T trade papers and the reference service. Such increases will be computed against last year's income-before-tax. (5) The Whites will be given an employment contract for five years at their present salaries (combined total $50,000 per year) plus any cost-of-living adjustments made generally by Davis Data, Inc. Of course, the Whites may be employed by Davis Data beyond the five years by mutual agreement.

The purpose of the possible options on Davis Data, Inc., stock is to compensate the Whites for giving up their existing ownership and options on T&T stock. The reason for deferring the dates of computation is to encourage a longer-run viewpoint.

The T&T trade papers are now barely breaking even financially, after paying Taussig his salary. Subscriptions have been declining, due in part to consolidations of motels; also, Taussig has become quite conservative and opinionated about the way the papers are run. Of course, it is possible that under the White's direction income from the papers could be increased $100,000 and maintained at that level for ten years—giving the Whites options on 10,000 shares of Davis Data, Inc., stock. An improvement well below that level is more likely. The price of Davis Data stock, which is sold frequently in the over-the-counter market, will probably move up and down at about the same percentage as Standard & Poor's 500 stock index moves. Davis Data stock is now selling at $20 per share, or ten times earnings.

The assets and liabilities of T&T are not a significant consideration is the proposed acquisition. There are virtually no fixed assets (printing and mailing are contracted out, following industry practice). The current assets are quite liquid, but this is offset by the inherently large liability for prepaid subscriptions. Because prepaid subscriptions provide most of the capital needed for growth, it is customary to distribute most of the net profits of trade papers to stockholders in the form of dividends.

Questions

Do you recommend acceptance of the vice-president's proposals by: (1) Davis Data, Inc., (2) Taussig, (3) the Whites? If not, what changes do you think would be more likely to be acceptable to all three parties?

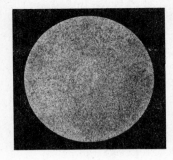

INTEGRATING CASES

Diversified Corporation Strategy

PHILLIPS FIBRE DIVISION[1]

Lee Roberts, vice-president of The Woods Corporation and general manager of its Phillips Fibre Division, is uncertain as to just how to state his reply to a letter and telephone call from James Herbert, executive vice-president of the parent corporation in charge of all its operations. Herbert has reminded Lee Roberts of the conclusion reached at the last meeting of the parent corporation's operating committee that it probably would be beneficial to the entire firm for the Phillips Fibre Division to attempt to increase its sales revenue markedly by widening its present product line, by selling in new geographical areas, and by developing new products. Lee Roberts is not a member of The Woods Corporation's operating committee but his boss, group vice-president Halyard is. Halyard has acquainted Lee Roberts with the general sense of the committee meeting and has told Roberts that he would hear from James Herbert who heads the operating committee.

Lee Roberts knows that his reply will be that he does not agree with the suggestions about his division's products but he has held off making a reply until he has devised a positive action that he could recommend to the committee.

The Woods Corporation is a conglomerate with sales revenue last year of $800 million, post-tax profits of $20 million, and a return on the stockholder equity of about 8 percent. These results can be compared with the average results for all conglomerates of a 3.6 percent return on sales and a 10 percent return on common equity. All industry composite averages were about 4.5 percent and 12 percent, respectively.

The corporation's operating organization consists of four product groups, each reporting to a group vice-president who, in turn, reports to James Herbert. The four product groups are made up of various divisions.

In general, the divisions operate as strategic business-units with careful attention paid to some of them by central management as their fortunes vary.

The corporation is now about 20 percent smaller than it was several years ago and its retained earnings account has been reduced as various divisions have

---

[1]Phillips Fibre sells fiberglass reinforced panels for use in building construction as skylights and translucent panels.

Group	Sales Revenue (approximate)	Divisions
1. Paints, coatings, and abrasives	$300 million	4 paint companies, 2 specialty chemical companies, and 1 abrasive firm
2. Metal buildings, siding, and outdoor furniture	$175 million	1 metal building and siding company and 1 outdoor furniture firm
3. Automotive and garden equipment	$220 million	6 automotive parts suppliers and 1 garden and farm equipment company
4. Miscellaneous products	$105 million	1 wine division, 1 liquor division, 3 textile companies, and Phillips Fibre Division

been sold off at a capital loss.[2] These changes have taken place subsequent to the promotion to chair of the board and chief executive officer of Thomas Roberts who had long been the executive vice-president of the parent corporation. Thomas Roberts replaced his uncle, William Roberts, who had built the firm from a small, family-owned, metal-working shop to somewhat more than its present size. William retired at age 70 and immediately set out on a three-year, around-the-world trip in his 80-foot schooner. He has successfully navigated the Atlantic and Indian Oceans and, at last report, was somewhere in the South Pacific, near the Fiji Islands. Lee Roberts is his grandson and the nephew of Thomas Roberts. Lee's father, Thomas' brother, is the skipper of his father's schooner. At last count, the Roberts family owned about 12 percent of The Woods Corporation's voting stock with the shares equally split among ten family members. The balance of the shares are publicly owned. Two mutual fund investment companies own about 9 percent each of this stock. No other public holding amounts to more than 0.5 percent of the stock.

The financial community has generally approved the efforts undertaken on Thomas Roberts' initiative. The price/earnings ratio of the common stock has climbed steadily to its current reporting of 10 which can be contrasted with its level of 5 a little over two years ago.

As part of its effort to revitalize the corporation, central management is now turning its attention to the more profitable divisions in the hopes that sales and profits can be increased further. Phillips Fibre is a profitable division. Over the past five years its sales have increased at 2 percent per year in real terms (2 percentage points above annual inflation rates), its pre-tax contribution to parent corporation overhead and financial expense is now 25 percent of its sales,

---

[2] Including a paper tape manufacturer, a mattress maker and distributor, a tableware company, and a bicycle maker.

and its return on net assets has grown from 20 to 30 percent.[3] The Woods Corporation's "par" for return on net assets is 20 percent—a figure attained by only a few of its divisions.

Lee Roberts believes that his division's strategy is well known throughout the corporation. Phillips Fibre concentrates on sales to only two of the various market segments that make up the FRP (fibre-reinforced plastic) market.[4] It does this because it has well-established positions in these segments based on its contacts through the metal buildings division of The Woods Corporation and its product quality which is especially adapted to corrosive atmospheres.

In his reply to James Herbert, Lee Roberts plans to state that the division's favorable results have come about through his constant attention to customer service problems, through minimizing the number of salespersons so that sales per individual is about 20 percent higher than that of principal competitors, through keeping the division's overhead expense low, through dropping the cost of goods sold account to 55 percent of sales (an unusually low amount for manufacturing companies), and through his spending all the time he has available on his supervisory and planning work.

Halyard told Lee Roberts that the operating committee considered the following four ideas at its meeting.

1. Phillips Fibre's panels are suitable for the liner panel segment of the market as the result of their corrosion resistance and their potentially large size which will be allowed by some new equipment recently installed.

2. The high quality polyester resins used by Phillips Fibre to coat, mesh with, and adhere to the glass mats can be made by one of the specialty chemical firms after some equipment is added. Vertical integration has proven to be profitable to The Woods Corporation, as in the case of the aluminum rolling and shaping machinery purchased by the metal siding division so that it could make its product directly from aluminum ingot and no longer buy the shapes from outside suppliers.

3. Investment in equipment will turn some of the parent corporation's excess cash into working assets. As a result of selling off various divisions, the firm has excess cash of about $50 million.

4. Lee Roberts has proven his ability as a division manager and so could clearly manage a larger division.

Roberts' reaction is that the chemical company's ability to make the polyester resin of the quality that is necessary is only a dream at the moment. The firm

---

[3] The return on net assets is calculated as profits after expenses, but before interest and taxes, divided by net assets. Since the net asset figure typically is a larger amount than the stockholder's equity, the return on net assets will ordinarily be reported as less than the return on stockholder's equity. Net assets equal working capital plus the book value of fixed assets.

[4] See the Alpha Pyro Glass, Inc. integrating case on pages 157–64 for an analysis of this market and the various competitors.

has no experience in making a similar resin. He also likes his job just the way it is and his location in northern Indiana on the shore of Lake Michigan.

Further, if central management is interested in improving its position with the fibre-reinforced plastics panel trade, it should attempt to buy out Alpha Pyro Glass.[5] Several years ago, according to various industry sources, the large oil company which owns APG decided that it would sell off APG because the firm did not fit with the oil company's basic strategy of finding, mining, and selling basic minerals and energy products. The oil company also wishes to decrease its position in petrochemicals and petroleum-based fibres and resins because the Saudis will soon expand the world's supply of petrochemicals greatly when their huge plant on the Red Sea comes onstream. The sale of APG has not yet taken place because it has been a consistently profitable division with steadily increasing sales.

From his knowledge of the market and competitors, Lee Roberts has concluded that APG has first-rate marketing which has overcome the disadvantage of a high-cost manufacturing process and an out-of-date production system. A new manufacturing manager has recently taken over production at APG at the insistence of the parent company. The central manager of the division is something of an enigma because the high costs and the out-of-date production system have been tolerated for many years. He is also known as something of a maverick when it comes to complying with the forecasting, planning, and budgeting requirements of the parent company. This Texas-based company also has a plant in South Carolina.

Phillips Fibre buys its polyester resins from the same firm that supplies Alpha Pyro Glass so Lee Roberts has an indirect contact with his competitor. From his knowledge of the market, he estimates that APG's sales are somewhere in the range of $22 to $27 million. He also suspects that its operating profit before any allocation of parent company overhead is in the range of 12 to 15 percent of sales.

Questions

1. What is your opinion as to the wisdom of an acquisition of Alpha Pyro Glass, Inc., by The Woods Corporation? What price seems right to you? How will the acquired firm be managed and directed?
2. What and how should Lee Roberts reply to James Herbert?
3. As James Herbert, what would you like to see done about the Phillips Fibre Division? As group vice-president Halyard, what would you do?

---

[5] A detailed description of this company is given in the case on pages 157–64.

GENERAL ELECTRIC-UTAH INTERNATIONAL MERGER

The merging of the General Electric Company and Utah International, Inc., raises a variety of issues. What benefits accrue from combining two dissimilar giants? Where is the synergy? Will traditional U.S. doctrines of competition be violated? Will General Electric's outstanding managerial savvy suit mining ventures? How is a $2 billion acquisition financed? Who will reap resulting financial gains—and personal glory?

To help answer these questions, the scope of each company's activities at the time of the merger is briefly sketched and the key financial data summarized. Then we present a more detailed analysis of this landmark event, as seen by *Fortune.*

The General Electric Company has become one of the largest manufacturing concerns in the world. Table 1 shows the contributions in 1976 of its major categories of operations to sales and net income.

TABLE 1.
G.E.'s SALES AND INCOME

	Sales		Net Income	
	(millions)	share (%)	(millions)	share (%)
Aerospace	$ 2,099	14	$ 95	13
Consumer goods	3,307	22	198	26
Industrial components and systems	4,787	32	266	35
Industrial power equipment	3,074	21	72	10
International	4,024	28	196	26
General Electric Credit Corporation	—	—	59	8
Corporate eliminations	-2,595	-17	-136	-18
Total company (before Utah)	$14,696	100	$750	100

In recent years, almost all of G.E.'s growth and diversification has come from its own initiative; it is not a conglomerate built via acquisitions. A significant part of its success arises from sophisticated management processes.

Utah International is not a manufacturing enterprise like G.E. had always been. Its major venture is the mining of coking coal in Australia. In addition, it mines steam coal, notably in the Four Corners area in New Mexico; iron ore, primarily in Brazil; uranium, and copper. To support the foreign mining, Utah International also is in ocean shipping. These mining and related activities account for 95 percent of its sales and earnings; the remainder comes mostly from oil and gas production. Eighty-three percent of its sales and 86 percent of its earnings in 1976 originated outside the United States.

The growth of Utah International and of G.E. prior to the merger is reflected in the financial data in Table 2, and the financial structure of the two companies is shown in Table 3 at the end of the case.

A few months after the merger was complete, Louis Kraar of *Fortune* wrote an article on the courting and marriage process. Mr. Kraar's description of these events is as follows.[1]

The combination of these great enterprises created the largest corporate merger in U.S. history. More than anything else, the merger served to fulfill the needs and ambitions of the two men who conceived it—Reginald Jones, Chairman of General Electric, and Edmund Littlefield, Chairman of Utah International.

Utah, though highly profitable, was also very risky—90 percent of its earnings came from a single commodity in a single country, metallurgical coal from Australia. Littlefield, now approaching retirement, was eager to obtain greater security for Utah's shareholders and was willing to trade off some of his company's fantastic growth to get it. The most prominent of all those stockholders was Littlefield himself; when his talks with Jones began, he, his wife, and their children held shares worth about $50 million.

For his part, Jones wanted to make a lasting imprint on his corporation by providing a new source of earnings growth and creating what he likes to call "the new G.E." Utah provided him with a means to make that concept credible. When the opportunity arose, he relied not on his hallowed planning staff, but rather seized the chance to personally lead his company into the biggest move in many years.

Littlefield, a director of G.E. for the past dozen years, and Jones were on friendly terms. Both served on the Business Council, and espoused a conservative political philosophy. The possibility of a merger was broached by Littlefield in an informal conversation late one evening in May 1975.

Victimized by Good Fortune

As they talked, Jones complimented Littlefield on the great job he had done with Utah. The G.E. chairman, who constantly refers to "the bottom line," was well aware of Utah's spectacular earnings growth, then 24 percent a year, compounded, for the prior decade, compared with 5 percent for his own corporation. Jones' recent experience with rising prices had made him keenly aware of the value of raw materials, for they seemed to be the best hedge. But he most admired the way Littlefield prudently minimized his own risks by signing up customers for coal, iron ore, and uranium to long-term contracts (with escalation clauses) before developing a new mine.

Though Jones had no way of knowing it at the time, Littlefield had been waiting for just such a moment as this. He eagerly told Jones the tale of a company that was being "victimized by our own good fortune." While Utah's min-

---

[1]Louis Kraar, "General Electric's Very Personal Merger," *Fortune* (August, 1977). Reprinted by permission. Copyright by Time, Inc.

eral interests were highly varied, its disproportionately large investment in Australia greatly concentrated the risks. To make the situation worse, Utah's continued growth required plunging more capital into Australia to expand both its metallurgical-coal and iron-ore operations.

Littlefield urgently wanted to diversify. His yearning to spread the risks was heightened because Utah's iron mine in Peru was about to be expropriated, which, he says "drove home to me what a big blow that could be." Even in Australia, where similar risks seemed remote, he had grown wary. The Labor government worried investors by increasing taxes and talking up economic nationalism.

Secondarily, Littlefield was concerned about capital. Utah had plenty of its own, but he felt it would be comforting to have access to a great deal more. The company's significant stakes in everything from steam coal in the U.S. to iron ore in Brazil would require substantial funds to exploit in the years ahead.

The Utah chairman carried a much heavier burden than most C.E.O.'s because he was tied to the company by blood. He belongs to one of "the families," the innumerable descendants of Utah International's founders, who still owned collectively 40 percent of the stock.

For nearly half a century, Utah was a heavy-construction company, first a leading builder of railroads in the West, then a major contractor for such dams as Hoover, Bonneville, and Grand Coulee. By the end of World War II, though, the company had lost much of its early vigor—until Littlefield came along.

Littlefield had avoided employment in the construction business because of feuding among the families. But in 1951, the chairman, Marriner Eccles, prevailed upon him to come in as vice-president and treasurer. He accepted the job only on the condition that he did not have to hire anyone's relations. Soon he was running the corporation in ways that yielded the profit record which Jones so admired.

Littlefield had his own game plan for the construction business, which was then unprofitable. By carefully selecting its work, he put that part of the company into the black and then sold it to Fluor Corp. in 1969.[2]

Littlefield poured Utah's capital completely into mining. The company's able geologists located valuable minerals in the U.S., Canada, and ultimately Australia. Utah became one of the first American mining companies to anticipate and feed Japan's hunger for raw materials, and Littlefield took care to develop a mutually beneficial two-way trade. To control the cost of transportation, Utah's biggest single operating expense, the company ordered large ore-carrying vessels from Japan, which was then desperate for foreign exchange and sold them at relatively low prices. Thus Littlefield helped cultivate an early relationship with the Japanese trading companies and steel mills that proved to be of

---

[2]This was a major divestment. At the time, construction activities accounted for 60% of Utah's gross revenues and 69% of its employees.

enormous, continuing benefit. By the time he sat telling his "troubles" to Jones, a decade of steady expansion had increased sales eight times, to $686 million, and multiplied the share price fourteenfold.

For several years, Littlefield explained to the G.E. chairman, he had hoped to diversify by acquisition. But Utah's lean management team, superb as it was at mining, knew practically nothing about other industries. Much of the business world was totally ignorant of Utah, which had never bothered with advertising or public relations. Littlefield had meager means for evaluating possible acquisitions and the executives who would come with them. Utah's assets totaled about $1 billion, and he figured he would have to buy $1 billion more "to get the risks down to 50 percent, which I thought was tolerable." As he recalls with characteristic modesty: "Frankly, I didn't think I was that good."

Consequently, he decided to look for a company that would acquire Utah. For months prior to his New York trip, he sat alone in his office poring over Moody's *Handbook of Common Stocks* in search of an appropriate corporation. It had to be one that offered broad diversification, could afford the $2 billion he was thinking about asking for Utah, and could get by the Justice Department's antitrust monitors. That last prerequisite, he felt, ruled out the major oil companies.

After turning many pages, he chose three corporations "that we could seriously look at." And G.E. was one of these.

The Boss Liquidates Empires

Jones had his own reasons for liking what he heard. He felt that his company had "fumbled around and missed the computer industry" after a costly, abortive effort. His well-reasoned arguments for abandoning that business, in fact, had helped propel him from financial vice-president to the chairmanship in December, 1972. Though he rarely said so, Jones believed that G.E. had also made other "terrible mistakes." During the rapid inflation of the early Seventies, for instance, the company got caught selling power-generation and transmission equipment under long-term contracts with inadequate escalation provisions. Now he wanted to make his own batting average better than those of his predecessors by expanding G.E. into faster-growing fields while doing everything he could "to limit downside risk."

Until Utah came along, Jones had carefully selected businesses inside the company that seemed to offer exceptional potential, feeding them capital while relentlessly weeding out the losers. Quite naturally, as Jones put it, "no one wanted to liquidate his empire," so he simply told the managers of fading products: "You have no money to continue." Gradually, G.E. stopped making vacuum cleaners, fans, phonographs, heart pacemakers, an industrial X-ray system, and numerous other products that failed to deliver the returns that Jones demanded.

These executions were far more visible than the birth of exciting new ventures. G.E.'s hottest prospects were such businesses as engineering plastics, carbide cutting tools, apparatus service shops, and the company's financial subsidiary, General Electric Credit Corp. Indeed, synthetic materials and various services were becoming the fast-growth standouts in a corporation long known for its mastery of electrical products.

The traditional mainstays no longer provided a dynamic expansion of earnings. Sales of equipment to the public utilities had fallen off as these companies came under financial pressure, and Jones figured that they were unlikely ever to regain their relative importance for G.E. Nuclear power plants, one of his great hopes, were losing money, causing a drain that was sure to continue for some years. Even G.E.'s more solid position in jet engines partly hinged on the uncertain fate of military programs, such as the controversial B-1 bomber. Plainly, G.E. needed something more.

As Jones listened to Littlefield's proposition, he recalled some of the basic economic trends that his planners had spotted. Manufacturing, G.E.'s main activity, seemed to be declining in its importance to the economy. Thinking in his usual broad-gauged manner, Jones saw himself "fighting to gain a diminishing share of G.N.P." The rapid rise in prices of raw materials had encouraged him to consider finding assured supplies and perhaps integrating backward. The light-bulb managers, for instance, toyed with the notion of mining tungsten. But nothing much had happened yet. Because of its sheer size, G.E. tends to move at a deliberate pace.

As an important part of his concept for "the new G.E.," Jones wanted to beef up the company's position overseas. Its share of most foreign markets was still quite small, less than 5% for most products. In "the G.E. culture," some managers still tended to think in terms of domestic product lines, rather than of the opportunities awaiting around the world. To shake domestic executives out of their provincial mind-sets, Jones had gone so far as to team them up in internal joint ventures with G.E.'s international units. As Littlefield described a corporation that sold mainly abroad, Jones sensed a fresh means for G.E. to become the "worldwide company" he envisioned.

Before mentioning the idea to anyone, however, Jones and Littlefield decided to continue exploratory conversations in private, which they did through the next six and a half months. Littlefield wanted what he calls "maximum understanding before proceeding," and he refrained from drawing in his only confidant, Utah's financial vice-president, James Curry, until late October. Jones did confide in only one person, Alva Way, his own successor as chief financial officer. All these individuals went to great lengths to camouflage the purpose of their investigations and meetings.

Disturbing the Ostriches and Emus

While the figures looked great to Jones, he realized that their validity depended heavily on Australia's economic climate. To get a better feel for the country and Utah's operations, he and Way flew out there in November. In the Bowen Basin of Western Australia, he saw that Utah's situation was indeed fabulous. Most of the company's coking-coal reserves lie close to the surface of this flat, sparsely populated area. The ecological problems are minimal, largely because the Australians are relatively relaxed about the impact a few miners have on a vast frontier. As Jones toured the area, he mused: "Here, you only disturb ostriches, emus, wallabies, and kangaroos."

Utah's facilities are so highly mechanized that each of its four mines is run by only 500 people, including clerks. Huge draglines take off a hundred feet or so of overburden to reveal a seam of what Jones calls "pure black gold." "My God," Jones exclaimed when he saw it, "you just scoop it out." In an around-the-clock operation, the coal is crushed and cleaned, then loaded on five 140-car trains to be hauled to the sea for shipment to Japan and Europe.

Over the Thanksgiving weekend, Jones dispatched Way to Brazil, where Utah owns 49 percent of the Samarco iron mine. Carved out of the brush, the mine has reserves of at least 300 million metric tons. Its output travels 246 miles through a slurry pipeline—the longest iron-ore line in the world—to the Atlantic coast, where it is pelletized and loaded aboard ships. The pipeline assures many years of relatively stable transportation costs from mine to seaport. And Utah has negotiated long-term contracts to deliver the pellets to steel mills in the U.S. and Europe.

Their firsthand impressions convinced Jones and Way that the risks were quite manageable. Clearly, Utah was an efficient, low-cost producer. And from their talks with Australian businesspersons and government officals, they anticipated a new conservative government that would be more hospitable to foreign investment.

Finally, Jones was ready to act. In early December when he and Littlefield were in Washington for a Business Council meeting, they reached the terms that would go to their boards. G.E. would issue 41 million new shares to purchase the company, but Utah's ample earnings would more than compensate for the dilution, allowing Jones to promise that the merger would increase G.E.'s earnings per share "from the very first day." Littlefield's stockholders would get a premium, 1.3 shares of G.E. (worth $68.74 on the closing day) for each Utah share (worth $47 when the deal was announced).[3] Just two days before the boards met, Australia elected a conservative government, and everything seemed to be going well.

Enter the Department of Justice

Then the scene turned to Washington. As Jones put it, the marriage arrangements stipulated that "we had better be damned sure that the deal would

---

[3] During 1976, the market price of General Electric stock ranged from $46 to $59 1/4. The dividend payout was also attractive to Utah International's stockholders. In fiscal 1976, Utah International paid $1.15 per share. General Electric was then paying $1.80 on each of its shares, which if continued on the 1.3 shares exchange for each Utah International share would yield $2.43—more than double what Littlefield's shareholders had been receiving.

not present substantial problems on the antitrust front." In a letter that G.E. hand-delivered to the Justice Department, Jones asked for a business advisory clearance, basically a review of the merger and assurance that the government did not plan to fight it. He also decided against lobbying Congress or the executive branch, reasoning that any signs of an attempt to influence Washington would only cause trouble.

He hoped to complete the merger in about five months, by May, 1976, but as things turned out, Robert Morse, the attorney who headed the Justice Department investigation, was ready to give it quite a bit more of his time. Morse felt that he was playing a role in a drama—"the most important merger ever"—whose denouement could affect the future of the nation's energy supplies.

Initially, Morse examined three areas that seemed to have some antitrust potential. Utah mines copper, and G.E. is one of the largest American users of that metal, a circumstance that prompted fears that the merger might foreclose other copper suppliers from selling to G.E. Steam coal posed other questions for Morse: "Who buys steam coal? Utilities. Who sells to utilities? G.E." His concern here was whether G.E. could use Utah's steam coal to unduly influence equipment-purchasing decisions of the utilities. Finally, he investigated whether G.E. might be able to force its suppliers of steel to make reciprocal purchases of Utah's coking coal. Ultimately, none of these issues provided grounds for a challenge.

A Reaction to Uranium

What caused more concern was Utah's uranium business. Westinghouse had promised to supply uranium to the purchasers of its reactors, but ran into trouble when it couldn't lay its hands on enough to cover its contracts. If G.E. controlled a uranium producer, it would have a captive supply and could gain an insurmountable competitive advantage. Thus Justice's initial antitrust review came out opposed to the merger. Soon G.E. lawyers were phoning Morse to ask how they could modify the deal to make it acceptable. He replied: "You have enough high-priced attorneys to come up with an idea."

Eventually, they worked out a new arrangement. G.E. and Utah relinquished control of the uranium assets until the year 2000. The subsidiary, Lucky Mc (named for the amateur prospector, Neil McNeice, who found its first lode in Wyoming), has been spun off into a separate company run by an independent board of trustees. G.E. retains ownership and will get most of the profits, but has agreed not to buy Lucky Mc's uranium and cannot influence its choice of customers.

Finally, on October 1st, after some prodding by Jones, Justice announced that it did not "presently intend to bring action to enjoin the proposed merger." The way was now clear. In December stockholders of both companies approved the fusion, and the joining together was consummated on December 20th.

Avoiding the Heavy Hand

But the marriage was just beginning. The surprise announcement had shocked and disappointed many of Utah's employees. "We dropped a bomb on them," Jones now acknowledges. The mining company's managers had come up together within Utah, like one another, and relished the informality and opportunities available in a lean, fast-growing corporation. Some of the Utah's 5,500 employees worried about being submerged in G.E.'s 380,000. Even as well placed an executive as Keith Wallace, a senior vice-president of Utah, concedes he had felt "some concern" about suddenly being "in a big company, where your future is not as certain."

The last thing that Jones wanted was a disruption of Utah's management team or an overlay of bureaucracy that would impair its ability to make quick decisions. He reassured Utah's management that G.E. would be a gentle mate. The mining company kept its own board, which includes five descendants of the founders; G.E. simply added Jones, Way, Vice Chairman Jack Parker, and Utah's financial vice-president, Curry. And, in what he calls "a signal to both companies," Jones made it plain that no one in his organization may so much as approach Utah's management without going through Jones, Way, or Parker—who have largely left Utah alone.

Preserving relative independence seems important to Utah's continued vitality, though how long this freedom will last remains to be seen. G.E. prides itself on strong financial controls and conformity to its own culture. But it does not know the mining business, so Littlefield expects Utah to remain autonomous "as long as it gives a good account of itself." Under G.E.'s rules, Littlefield will have to retire as Utah's chairman within two years, but he can remain on the board for yet another six, until his seventy-first birthday. He still acts in the interests of "the families," which now own about 5 percent of G.E.—more than any single institutional investor or individual.

Just as Jones had promised, the merger pumped up G.E.'s earnings (by 7 cents a share last year), but it also stirred more imaginative visions. Among other things, Jones claims that Utah's business relationships in Australia, Brazil, and Japan will increase "customer acceptance" of G.E.'s other products in those markets. But neither he nor any of his senior executives can clearly explain how a Japanese steel mill that buys Australian coal, for instance, will be made more receptive to the purchase of G.E. equipment. To be sure, the business relationship will help open doors. But the Japanese buy from Utah's mines because the prices are attractive, and for the same reason they purchase most of their capital equipment at home rather than getting it from suppliers in the U.S. In short, it's difficult to see G.E.'s selling job getting any easier.

As the Justice Department learned, G.E. does not actually "control" Utah's raw materials, for most of them are committed under long-term contracts. But the company still gains a degree of price protection from Utah's natural resources. Eventually, of course, Utah could develop fresh sources of copper, tungsten, and other minerals for G.E.'s own use. In addition, G.E. might one day be able to market a coal-gasification system along with steam coal from Utah's mines. But any push too far, too fast toward such tie-ins could well provoke antitrust action. For the foreseeable future, Utah's output will go mainly to its usual customers, mostly abroad.

On balance, the arrangement wrought by the two chairmen has given each essentially what he wanted. Jones has made an indelible mark on his corporation, which now looks more like "a new G.E.," with its completely fresh source of earnings. Littlefield has given the Utah families and other owners a greater sense of security with a tax-free exchange of stock. He also did very well for himself. The Littlefields' recently acquired G.E. holdings are now worth $19 million more than the Utah International shares they held when the merger was first announced.

Questions

1. Do you believe that the General Electric-Utah International merger is desirable from a broad social viewpoint?
2. (a) Aside from the personal interest of Jones, is the merger wise for General Electric in the long run? Explain. (b) Aside from the personal interest of Littlefield, is the merger wise for Utah International in the long run? Explain.
3. In view of General Electric's acclaimed management skills, do you recommend continuation of the "hands-off" relations between General Electric's headquarters and Utah International?

TABLE 2.
UTAH INTERNATIONAL, INC.
CONSOLIDATED BALANCE SHEET - OCT. 31, 1976
(in millions)

Assets		Liabilities & Equity	
Cash	$ 37	Current liabilities	$ 237
Accounts & notes		Long term liabilities	223
receivable	80	Other liabilities	119
Inventories	113		
Other current assets	11		
Total current assets	241	Total liabilities	579
Investments	302	Common stock, @$2 share	63
Property, plant & equip-		Additional paid-in capital	91
ment, net	720	Retained earnings	529
		Total equity	684
	$1,263		$1,263

TABLE 3.
GENERAL ELECTRIC COMPANY
BALANCE SHEET—DECEMBER 31, 1976 AND 1975
(in millions)

Assets	1976 (Includes Utah)	1975 (Excludes Utah)
Cash	$ 1,613	$ 853
Current receivables	2,717	2,597
Inventories	2,355	2,115
Total current assets	6,685	5,565
Investments	1,286	1,050
Property, plant & equipment, net	3,357	2,562
Other assets	722	586
	$12,050	$ 9,763

Liabilities & Equity	1976 (Includes Utah)	1975 (Excludes Utah)
Current Liabilities	$ 4,605	$ 3,964
Long-term liabilities	2,073	1,646
Total liabilities	6,678	5,610
Minority interests	119	84
Common stock, @$2.50 shr.	576	469
Additional paid-in cap.	618	483
Less: treasury stock	−192	−171
Total equity	5,253	4,069
	$12,050	$ 9,763

Part 4

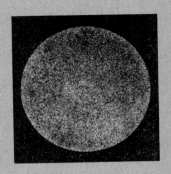

ORGANIZING THE ENTERPRISE

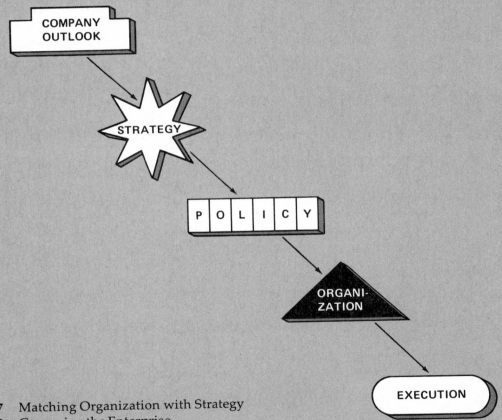

COMPANY OUTLOOK

STRATEGY

POLICY

ORGANI-ZATION

EXECUTION

17 MATCHING ORGANIZATION WITH STRATEGY

Organizing for Growth

A change in a company's strategy and policy usually leads to realignment of its organization. Some activities will be expanded, others curtailed; new priorities will determine which divisions report directly to senior executives. Unless these adjustments are aligned with the shift in objectives, the anticipated growth may never materialize.

In designing an organization we are concerned with (1) the way the myriad of activities required to operate any firm are assigned to people. To be effective, each person has to focus on particular segments of the total task. At the same time, (2) each person's work must be coordinated with the work of others. All sorts of grouping of activities and of interconnecting links are possible—just as letters of the alphabet can be combined in numerous ways—but the particular combination into subgroups and these subgroups into larger divisions has a profound impact on the successful execution of any strategy.

Central management must frequently review the interaction between strategy/policy and organization structure. This matching of strategy and structure shows up most dramatically as a firm moves through different stages of growth. So this chapter deals especially with issues arising in the shift from one stage to another. Two further issues—the organization of central management itself and the staffing of positions created in the organization design—are the foci of the following chapters.

Need for Activity Analysis

Just as the selected strategy and its implementation policy are unique for each enterprise, so too is the organization design: organizing calls for perception of subtle differences, imagination in devising special combinations, judgment in balancing benefits and drawbacks, and human understanding in turning an intellectual concept into a social reality. Although common patterns exist, we can't jump from a particular strategy to a predetermined form of organization.

The link between strategy and organization design is activity analysis. What work—planning, operating, controlling, and so forth—must be performed to execute a specific strategy and its associated policy? We need this transformation into work or activities because at least the formal aspects of organization deal with who does what work.

When the J. C. Penney Company, for example, gave up its long-standing "cash sales only" policy and started to grant credit, an array of new activities arose in the accounting, customer credit, and financial control sections of each store as well as in the home office. Likewise, Dole Pineapple Company's decision to make rather than buy its tin cans in Hawaii added activities ranging from purchase of tinplate to running a conveyor from the can shop to the warehouse. It is these new activities that are the grist for any organizational change that may be needed.

When thinking about organizing a large department or an entire company, as central managers must do, a comprehensive review of *all* activities necessary for successful operations is desirable. To examine only a part—the "squeaky wheel"—is likely to lead to a remedy that creates as many new problems as it removes old ones.

The degree of detail to which this analysis should be carried depends upon the scope of organization being considered. When an executive is studying broad, overall organization structure, a listing of major activities is usually adequate. However, when the organization of individual jobs is the aim, listing minute details may be useful. In either case, a lot more detail is analyzed in the design process than appears in the final conclusions because (1) the organizer must be sure to have a complete and realistic grasp of the work involved, and (2) novel and strategic combinations of duties are apt to be missed if the organizer thinks only in terms of large customary groups of work. Also, greater detail should be considered in those areas that are new, that are especially crucial to success, or that have been sources of trouble.

With the activities in mind, our next step is to decide how they can best be grouped together into manageable divisions, departments, sections, or other units. In management circles, this grouping is called *departmentation* even though the final units are not necessarily named departments.

STAGE I—ONE DOMINANT INDIVIDUAL

The simplest form of organization is one key individual with a group of helpers as depicted in Figure 17-1. The central figure is aware of the details of what is happening and personally gives instructions to the helpers as to what they should do. Of course, the helpers learn the routines of repetitive activities and can proceed with minimum guidance. And they may become specialized in their normal assignments: for example, accounting, dealing with customers, making repairs. But the boss decides any changes from customary patterns and provides the initiative to move in new directions.

FIGURE 17-1.
STAGE I ORGANIZATION

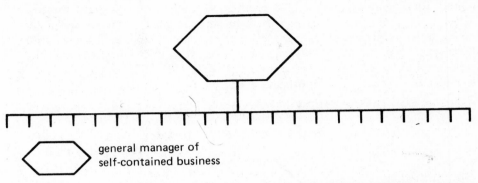

general manager of
self-contained business

Many small businesses (dress shops, drugstores, filling stations, etc.) are operated in this fashion, often with remarkable success. The key individual normally has high energy and skill, doing part of the work as necessary. Even though the business may be legally a corporation, action pivots around the moving spirit. One such self-made businessperson, for instance, left a budget discussion at a director's meeting to help repair a broken air-compressor that had brought the shop to a standstill.

Organizations dominated by one individual can change strategy quickly *if* the change is within the capacity and the interests of the central person. A lawyer can easily decide to enter the real estate business, or the TV repair shop can add home alarm systems to its line. A few more helpers with technical knowledge will suffice. The key uncertainty is the central person. Thus, an expansion of a Canadian motel, described briefly in Chapter 12, depended on whether Alain Ribout was prepared to supervise the building and running of a nearby unit. Too often the necessary adjustment in managerial organization is overlooked; an energetic entrepreneur pushes ahead on an attractive expansion without analyzing the nature and the volume of new activities, only then discovering the difference in Stage I and Stage II organizations.

STAGE II—FUNCTIONAL DEPARTMENTS

Dividing the Managerial Load

Functional departments become necessary when the entrepreneur alone can no longer keep track of all of the operating activities. As the business expands, there are just too many people to be seen, quotations to check, letters to answer, inventory to watch, even for the most energetic manager. Especially when the business involves nonroutine activities and frequent emergencies, the manager must be free of normal day-to-day operations. Otherwise, mistakes are made, opportunities are passed by, and the work of helpers is slowed down waiting to see the boss.

The normal remedy is to appoint functional managers—one for selling, another for accounting, a third for production, and so on—as diagrammed in Figure 17-2. These people (or *their* helpers) answer most of the questions that bubble up from activities; they check on progress and expedite lagging action. Being specialists, they are likely to be more expert in their particular field than the general manager. And because they focus on a narrower array of work they become more sensitive to its particular needs and opportunities.

FIGURE 17-2.
STAGE II ORGANIZATION

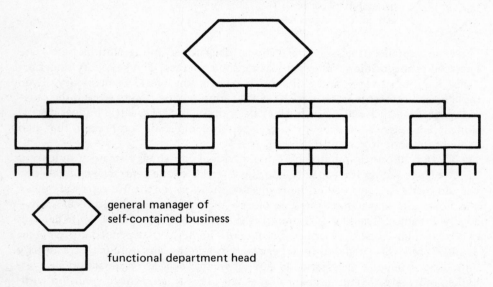

general manager of
self-contained business

functional department head

With such help, the behavior of the general manager should differ sharply from that of the dominant individual in a Stage 1 organization. The general manager has to be willing to delegate. This means knowing no longer exactly what is happening day-to-day and accepting decisions that are not quite the way the general manager would have made them. A cardinal purpose of creating functional departments is to give the general manager time to focus on interdepartmental coordination and on policy and strategy issues. Many executives whose success as Stage I managers makes possible a Stage II organization find this required change in their personal behavior very difficult and sometimes impossible.

An organization made up of functional departments is well suited for companies which have only a single "business-unit." For example, firms concentrating on automobile insurance typically have departments for sales-underwriting, claims, finance, investment-treasury, and legal matters. Similarly, a stereo equipment manufacturer will probably have R & D, production, marketing, and finance as basic departments. With only a single line, coordination between departments can be handled through procedures, meetings, and mediation by the general manager. Each department continues to render the same kind of service, so neglect of parts of the business is unlikely. The general manager concentrates on maintaining effective teamwork.

A strategy of a "full line" of services to a single set of customers also matches a functional setup reasonably well. In "one-stop banking," for instance, a customer contact (branch office) department will be aided by headquarters departments dealing with checking and special accounts, small loans, commercial loans, brokerage, safe deposit, trust, and other services. Here the relationships overlap more and competition may arise for the concentrated attention of the customer contact personnel, but customer service provides the mediating objective.

Defining the Scope of a "Function"

The use of functional departments creates some problems of its own. We need to answer (1) what constitutes a function—how shall the boundaries be set? (2) How should activities within a function be organized? Until we have at least a way to approach these questions, the concept of a Stage II organization is difficult to apply to any enterprise.

Functions singled out for separate status as a department often reflect the differential advantage emphasized in the strategy. A department store that places great reliance on advertising, for instance, treats advertising as a major function and not as a subordinate part of marketing. Companies that seek to lead in product design will treat R & D as a major department. Purchasing might be separated from other operations to give it strong emphasis.

In addition to such strategic functions, every firm has a variety of activities that do not neatly fit into a limited number of major departments. Two general guides are helpful in this respect:

1. Place in the same department those activities that have the same immediate objectives. For example, activities as diverse as running a cafeteria, performing medical service, and administering a pension plan may be placed in the personnel department because all of these contribute to the objective of building an efficient work force. In the same manner, the management of salespeople and of advertising may be placed under the sales manager, because the objectives of both these activities is the same—to procure sales orders.
2. Place in the same department activities that require a similar type of ability and experience for their efficient management. For example, in pharmaceutical companies quality control is often placed in the research department. Control of the quality of pharmaceuticals requires someone who is objective, analytical, and expert in laboratory techniques. These similarities with research seem to warrant combined supervision even though the mission of the two activities differs significantly. Budgeting and finance might be placed in the same department for similar reasons.

Advantages of functional departments depend partly upon the integrating theme for the particular unit. Among the benefits often secured are (1) expertise with a similar type of problem, (2) adequate attention to an activity that otherwise might be given hurried treatment, (3) consistent action in such matters as price concessions, and (4) easy coordination of activities having a common purpose.

Except in unusual circumstances, the number of major functional departments (not counting staff and services) in a Stage II organization should not exceed about six.

Organizational Options within Departments

Although a small functional department can be organized on the one-dominant-individual basis, its own size and the need for systematic relations with other departments soon call for orderly grouping of internal activities. Among the common bases for further subdivision are products, processes, territories, and customers.

Products. In the typical department store, the buyer was "king" for many years. There would be separate buyers for hosiery, jewelry, gloves, shoes, millinery, and dozens of other products. Normally, each buyer was responsible for the purchase of the merchandise, its pricing and display, and its sale. Of course, there were storewide departments for such activities as building operations, delivery, finance, accounting, advertising, and personnel. Nevertheless, the very crucial trading function remained the domain of the respective product buyers. This provided close coordination of buying and selling each product, and it aided control by localizing responsibility.

With the substantial expansion of suburban branches, the role of the department store buyer has been changing. Because of the distance factor, buyers cannot directly supervise the people selling their products in the several outlets and they have difficulty maintaining their former close observation of display and proper maintenance of stocks. Buyers are becoming providers of merchandise and sales promotion planners. Nevertheless, divisions by product line remain very important.

Product subunits are also often introduced in engineering and production. And we shall see, building around products is a key feature of Stage III organizations.

Processes. Manufacturers—and government offices—often perform several distinct processes that may serve as the basis for organizational units. For example, in steel production typically we find separate shops for coke ovens, blast furnaces, open-hearth furnaces, hot-rolling mills, and cold-rolling mills. Each process is performed in a separate location and involves a distinct technology. Even if the company shifts its basic technology from blast furnaces to oxygen converters, the plant will be divided organizationally into process units.

Libraries, to cite another field, normally divide their work into units dealing with book acquisitions, cataloging, circulation, and reference. There may also be separation by type of "customer" such as children and adults.

The grouping of activities by process tends to promote efficiency through specialization. All the key people in each department become expert in dealing with their particular phase of the business. On the other hand, process classification increases problems of coordination; scheduling the movement of work from department to department on each order becomes somewhat complex. Also, since no department has full responsibility for the order, a department may not be as diligent in meeting time requirements and other specifications as a group of people who think in terms of the total finished product and their customers.

The organization issue just posed—product versus process grouping—has additional ramifications. It ties in with the desirability of subcontracting, extent of mechanization, and of course the characteristics of executives needed.

The conflict between the desire to increase skill in performance through specialization and mechanization, and the need for coordination to secure balanced efforts recurs time and again in organization studies. Insurance companies, hospitals, and even consulting firms face the same issue.

Territories. Companies with sales representatives who travel over a large area always use territorial organization. Large companies will have several regions, each subdivided into districts, with a further breakdown of territories for individual sales representatives. Airlines, finance companies with local offices, and motel chains all by their very nature have widely dispersed activities and consequently use territorial organization to some degree.

There are three primary issues with territorial organization:

1. What related activity should be physically dispersed along with those which by their nature are local? For example, should a company with a national salesforce also have local warehousing, local assembling, local advertising, local credit and accounting, and local personnel? And how far should the dispersion occur—to the regional level or to the district level? Typically, whenever such related activities are dispersed, they are all combined into a territorial organization unit.
2. How much authority to make decisions should be decentralized to these various territorial units? In other words, how much of the planning and control work should go along with the actual performance?
3. What will be the relations between the home office service and staff units and these various territorial divisions?

The major advantage of territorial organization is that it provides supervision near the point of performance. Local conditions vary and emergencies do occur. Persons located a long distance away will have difficulty grasping the true nature of the situation, and valuable time is often lost before an adjustment can be made. Consequently, when adjustment to local conditons and quick decisions are important, territorial organization is desirable. On the other hand, if a lot of local units are established, some of the benefits of large-scale operation may be lost. The local unit will probably be comparatively small, and consequently the degree of specialization and mechanization will be correspondingly limited.

Customers. A company that sells to customers of distinctly different types may establish a separate unit of organization for selling and servicing each. A manufacturer of men's shoes, for instance, sells to both independent retail stores and chain stores. The chain-store buyers are very sophisticated and may prepare their own specifications; consequently, any salespeople calling on them must have an intimate knowledge of shoe construction and of the capacity of their company's plant. In contrast, sales representatives who call on retailers must be able to think in terms of retailing problems and be able to show how their products will fit into the customer's business. Few sales representatives can work effectively with both large chain-store and independent retail customers; consequently, the shoe manufacturer has a separate division in sales organization for each group.

Commercial banks, to cite another example, often have different vice-presidents for differing types of customers—airlines, manufacturing concerns, stockbrokers, consumer loans. These people recognize the needs of their particular group of customers; also, they are in a good position to appraise the credit worthiness.

Ordinarily, customer groups include only selling and direct service activities. Anyone who has been shunted around to five or six offices trying to get an adjustment on a bill or a promise on a delivery date will appreciate the satisfaction of dealing with a single individual who understands the problem and knows how to get action within the company. On the other hand, this form of organization may be expensive, and a customer-oriented employee may commit the company to actions that other departments find hard to carry out.

Summary. This short review of product, process, territory, and customer departmentation indicates the many variations that are possible in organizing within a major department. A full analysis of the various options would go beyond our main focus on central management. However, even this brief discussion does indicate the necessity of clearly relating central organization to basic operations "where the real work is done." Also a by-product of this review is to mention alternatives to functional departments. In special circumstances we may decide that, say, an international department or a government contract department fits a company strategy better than a functional department.

This elaboration of a Stage II organization does not change its basic features. We start with a sharply focused domain and differential advantage mission, and then we establish specialized departments each of which has a different though important contribution to make to that mission. The work of these departments is interdependent, so the entire operation has to be managed as an integrated whole. The role of the general manager of such an organization is to find department managers who will be responsible for day-to-day operations while the general manager concentrates on integration and longer-run strategy and policy issues.[1]

STAGE III—SELF-CONTAINED PRODUCT OR REGIONAL DIVISIONS

Most successful enterprises outgrow a Stage II organization. They become too large or too diversified. As a Stage II company grows from less than a hundred to over a thousand employees, communications become more formal, standard procedures prevent quick adjustments, the convenience of each department receives more consideration than company goals, and people feel insignificant in terms of total results. Careful management can diminish these tendencies, but sooner or later sheer size saps vigor and effectiveness.

In addition, successful companies take advantage of opportunites to diversify product lines, to develop new sources of materials, and to provide new services in response to changing social needs. This adds complexity. But large functional departments often give secondary attention to such opportunites; they are busy doing their established tasks well. So the new developments fail to receive the attention and the coordinated effort they deserve.

Unless a company makes a deliberate strategic decision to stay relatively small and clearly focused on a particular mission—a strategic option few U.S. companies elect—a shift in organization becomes necessary.

Concept of Semi-Independent Divisions

The basic remedy for oversize is to split up into several Stage I or Stage II divisions. A series of separate business-units is created within the larger corporation, as diagrammed in Figure 17-3.

Establishing Manageable "Businesses." Ordinarily these divisions are built around product lines. That part of marketing dealing with a particular product is transferred from the marketing department to the product division. And likewise with production, engineering, and perhaps other functions. Ideally each division has within it all the key activities necessary to run independently—it is *self-sufficient.* Moreover, the management of the newly created division is given a high degree of authority, making the division *semiautonomous.* The general manager of such a division then has virtually the same resources and freedom of action as the president of an independent company and is expected to take whatever steps are necessary to make the "little business" successful.

---

[1]The department managers should participate in strategy and policy formulation, as we will point out in Chapter 18. Their primary duty, however, and the viewpoint they are expected to bring to central management deliberations, is that of running a specialized department very well.

FIGURE 17-3.
STAGE III ORGANIZATION

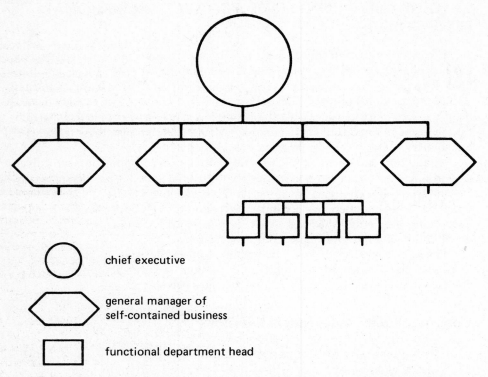

chief executive

general manager of
self-contained business

functional department head

Even when it is practical to place within a division all of its own marketing
and production activities, some central services are retained. Obtaining capital,
exploratory research, and staff assistance on labor relations, law, and market
research, for example, usually can be performed more economically in one place
for all divisions of the corporation. Such central assistance gives operating divisions an advantage over fully independent companies.

Typically, self-contained divisions are built around product lines. A company may have anywhere from two to (for G.E.) a hundred such product divisions. The same idea, however, has been applied by department store chains on
a territorial basis. And large metal fabricators place their mining and transportation activities ("process" units) in self-contained divisions.

Advantages. Breaking a large firm into several self-sufficient, semiautonomous
divisions has several managerial advantages:

1. Morale is improved because people see the results of their own efforts and feel
   the importance of their action.

2. Communication is faster, often face-to-face, and the significance of information is easier to recognize.
3. Adequate attention can be given to individual customers, product adjustments, and other matters that may be brushed over in a larger organization.
4. Coordination of production with sales, costs with income, personnel training with needs, and other interfunctional adjustments are improved.
5. Control can be exercised more promptly and with fuller appreciation of the total circumstances.

With more manageable and sharply focused divisions, changes in strategy can be put into effect more rapidly.

Difficulties with Optimum Size

In applying the concept of small, self-contained divisions we soon discover that functional departments often cannot be neatly divided. Technology and other forces dictate an *optimum size* for various activities. For instance, an oil refinery to serve only Spokane, Washington, would be much too small to be efficient. On the other hand, the task of increasing employment of minorities can readily be divided and assigned to separate divisions.

The optimum size issue is complicated because optimum volume is not the same for each function. A men's clothing firm, for instance, found that plants with two to three hundred employees could achieve virtually all economies of scale in production and that larger plants generated more personnel problems. However, the output of one such plant would be far too small for marketing purposes. National advertising and promotion were the key to the firm's marketing success, and the sales volume needed to support national distribution was six times the output of a single plant.

The optimum size of an elementary school, to cite a very different industry, would be small—less than fifty pupils—if we think of travel time for pupils, and large—over a thousand—if we focus on the cost of heating and maintaining the buildings. Professionals in the key function—education—have still a third view of optimum size; they want classes of about twenty-five, which yields a typical school of about two hundred.

These differences in optimum size affect the number of self-contained divisions we establish. In a steel company, for instance, marketing considerations call for twenty or thirty separate divisions, each focused on a product arket target. Production technology, however, dictates that almost all the end-products come out of a few large plants. These plants can't be split up by product lines. So twenty or thirty self-sufficient product divisions are impractical. The best we can do is break out a few products, such as oil-field pipe or barbed wire, that have separate plants for their final stages of manufacture.

In fact, a review of self-contained divisions in a wide variety of industries indicates that most of them have a volume of work that is below the optimum size for one or two functions and above the optimum size for other functions.

The aim, of course, is to build divisions that are *optimum in size for critically important functions*, even though this results in some diseconomies in other areas.

Compromise Arrangements

Companies often try to get most of the benefits of self-contained divisions and also keep functional operations at optimum levels. For instance, one paper company leaves production in a single functional department, but it breaks product engineering and marketing down into product divisions. The division managers are expected to act like "independent businesspersons" except that they must contract for their supply of products from the production division.

A comparable arrangement is used by a food processor, except that in this instance it is selling rather than production that is centralized in one department. Each product division does its own product design, engineering, buying, production, merchandising, and pricing, but it utilizes the sales department to contact customers. The rationale here is that a single field organization can cover the country more effectively for all divisions than they could do separately.

Whenever a product division has to rely on an outside department for a key activity, problems of adequate attention, coordination, and control become more difficult. Occasions for bickering jump dramatically. Central management has to judge whether the harm done by restricting self-sufficiency is offset by the benefits of the larger-scale activities in the functional department.

All sorts of compromise arrangements are found in practice. Sometimes the product division has the option to buy services from outside companies instead of using the inside department if it can obtain better service at less cost. This clearly puts pressure on the central department to be responsive to the needs of the divisions. In other cases, the centralized department merely notifies the divisions what capacity it has available, and the divisions must live within this limit. Understandings are needed on planning, transfer prices, emergency changes, quality of service, risky experiments, and the like. Basically such issues should be resolved in terms of what contributes most to company strategy, and this interpretation usually must be made by central management.

The compromises just discussed all presume self-contained product or regional divisions will be the primary organizational form of the corporation with an exception being made for some one functional department. Two other kinds of modifications, midway between Stage II and Stage III formats, are also used. One leaves the functional departments intact and merely establishes a "product manager"—really a staff person who keeps track of his or her products in the various departments and attempts to negotiate adjustments that will aid the line. As with any staff, the strength of a "product manager's" influence can range from merely raising questions to suggestions that carry weight of commands.

The second kind of modification, found in the space industry, construction companies, and consulting firms, is "project management" (sometimes called matrix organization). Here competent individuals are temporarily assigned by the functional departments to a project team. This team, usually with its own manager, runs the project somewhat like a product division might; but when the project is completed, members of the team return to their functional base.

Organizing for Strategic Benefits

The difficulties of achieving a smoothly running set of self-contained operating divisions, just discussed, naturally raise the question of when a shift from a Stage II to a Stage III organization is worth the effort.

Recently, more and more attention is being focused on business-unit strategy and policy, as discussed in Parts 1 and 2 of this book. This emphasis encourages the use of a Stage III organization. Ideally, whenever a distinct business-unit strategy is warranted, we would create an organization division to match the strategy in its scope. Then a set of division executives can easily combine strategic planning with execution of that plan.

However, as already noted in our discussion of optimum size, the business-unit needs a minimum volume of activity to support its own marketing organization, its own production, and so forth. Until the volume reaches this level some kind of compromise arrangement may be necessary.

If central managers feel confident that a business-unit will attain in a year or two sufficient volume to support its own organization, they may create the self-contained organization immediately. High expenses will not be covered by income during the start-up period. But the expectation is that these initial losses will be offset by the benefits of an aggressive strategic thrust.

A women's shoe company, for example, decided to integrate forward into selected retail outlets. This marketing thrust might have been assigned to the existing sales department. However, management decided on a separate retail division because analysis showed that adjusting store inventory to local tastes was vital; a separate division was expected to be more objective and to act more quickly in this critical area.

A conservative alternative is to delay splitting off the activities covered by the strategy. Instead, these activities are left in functional departments, or in a division with a different strategic mission. The managers of these multiple-mission operations—perhaps with the aid of a product manager—have to cooperate in getting the fledgling business-unit started. They test the market; they experiment with production; they watch responses of competitors; they feel their way. And only after these initial probes signal promising results will a separate division dedicated to the strategic domain be created. Of course, a danger in this conservative approach is that the managers who are involved with several different strategies will not provide the energetic, coordinated effort required to make each strategy successful.

A decision *not* to set up a separate carton division was reached by a paper company. Here investigation revealed that this segment of the industry was already mature and that low cost was crucial to success. So the company strategy was to operate only its most efficient plants as near capacity as possible. Although a separate carton division would have provided more intensive marketing effort, it would have contributed little toward cost reduction. Consequently, the proposal to form a self-contained carton division separated from the larger container branch was turned down.

We see in these examples that organization changes are intimately connected with the strategy selected.

STAGE IV—CONGLOMERATE ORGANIZATION

Conglomerate organization differs from a Stage III organization of self-contained divisions primarily in the absence at headquarters of service and staff units and the limited attempt to secure synergistic benefits among its components. Typically, conglomerates are built from previously independent companies, each with its own traditions and a full complement of central services. Moreover, these companies are not expected to contribute to each other's business. So there is little to be gained from "coordination" and from overall service units. A conglomerate truly is a collection of disassociated businesses.

Primary Attention to Investment Portfolio

The main benefits of conglomerates are financial. Operating companies are brought into the corporate structure mainly to diversify risks or to provide cash flow balance, as outlined in Chapter 14. In the majority of conglomerates, "corporate planning" consists entirely of looking for attractive acquisitions and does not deal with businesses already in the fold. The presumption is that each operating unit will do its own strategic planning, except for major questions on sources and uses of capital.

Since the interactions between the central office and the operating companies in a conglomerate are largely limited to the financial, the basic organization structure can be simple. The chief executive in each operating company reports to the president or a group vice-president in the central office. In addition, there will be the usual transfer of funds and upward flow of financial reports. That is all that's needed.

Of course, each operating company has its own organization; this may be a Stage I, II, or III organization or any variation that best suits the needs of the particular company. Incidentally, the legal status of the operating company is not significant from the viewpoint of managerial organization. Each operating unit will be treated as a separate company even though its corporate identity may be washed out for financial reasons.

Role as "Outside" Member of Board of Directors

Although the organization may be simple, the role that the supervising executive from the central office plays in the management of an operating company can be extremely valuable. This executive should be an ideal "outisde director."

FIGURE 17-4.
STAGE IV ORGANIZATION

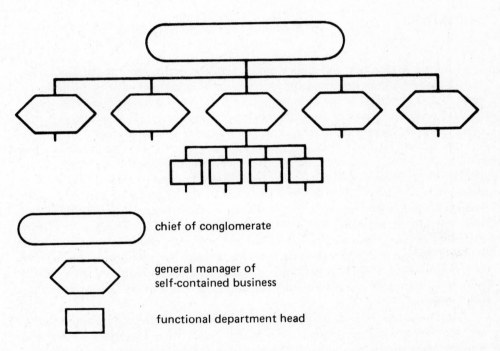

chief of conglomerate

general manager of
self-contained business

functional department head

Every company needs objective senior counsel to its chief executives, as we will explain in Chapter 18. Presumably this independent counseling is the main job of an outside member of the board of directors. Unfortunately, all corporations face severe difficulties in attracting to their boards of directors individuals who are (1) wise, courageous, and well informed and also (2) sufficiently concerned to devote energy and initiative to the affairs of that particular company. Obtaining good outside directors is a chronic and serious problem.

A conglomerate, however, can overcome this difficulty. It has sufficient stake in the success of its operating companies to locate and employ individuals who are fully qualifed to be good "outside directors." Such a person should devote full time to serving as a member or head of the board of, perhaps, half a dozen operating companies. By assuring that major decisions are wisely made, insisting that unpleasant action be taken promptly, and counseling on future possibilities, a strong director can stimulate operating executives.

By aiding with finance and by providing able outside directors, then, conglomerates help make their operating companies strong. Most of the central management functions, however, should be left to fully staffed operating companies.

SUMMARY

Company strategy and policy set directions, limits, and goals. But these broad plans must be matched by a corresponding managerial organization to carry out the implied array of activities. In this first chapter of Part 4 we have focused on basic structure. Two themes keep reappearing: (1) structure depends upon size and complexity, and (2) structure should reinforce strategy.

As a company succeeds and grows, it must change its organization. Four quite distinct stages are clear. Stage I represents the small budding enterprise, in which *one dominant individual* does both long-range planning and day-to-day managing. Sooner or later the business exceeds the capacity of even the most energetic single manager, and a shift must be made to Stage II, in which day-to-day operations are delegated to *functional departments.* Then as the firm expands and diversifies, the functional departments become too large and bureaucratic, so a further shift is necessary to a Stage III organization, composed of *self-contained product or regional divisions.* In a final possible stage, a collection of independent companies may be combined into a Stage IV *conglomerate organization.*

Many variations and compromises are essential to fit the organization to the specific technology, optimum size, resources, and other features of a specific firm. A cardinal aim in making such variations should be to strengthen the company in those areas in which it has chosen to build strategic distinction. In this way, the organization gives potency to the unique services the company wants to provide.

To complement the basic organization design, two other aspects of central management organization are crucial. First, the central management tasks themselves need organizing if they are to be performed effectively, and second, individuals must be found to fill the various positions in the formal organization structure. These important subjects are examined in the next two chapters.

QUESTIONS FOR CLASS DISCUSSION

1. The Mercury Bicycle Company is doing a flourishing business with its "Syncro-Shift" and "Mountain King" models sold out of its Indianapolis plant through mass merchandisers (Sears, Penney's) and discount stores (K-Mart, Zayre, Korvette's) to children and parents who purchase them for hard-riding, bumping over curbs, "popping wheelies," and general touring. Now it proposes to add a new line by trading up into 10- , 12- , and 15-speed bicycles sold through specialized bicycle shops to customers who race or who ride seriously for exercise. Parts (wheels, derailers, brakes, and lightweight frames) will be purchased from Taiwanese, Japanese, Italian, and French sources, assembled in a plant in the United States and then sold in the U.S. and Canada. Should Mercury combine the two manufacturing operations in one location? (Parts for the traditional bikes are made and assembled in Indianapolis.) Should the firm organize into two product divisions while maintaining centralized finance and accounting departments and a centralized engineering group doing product and process development work?

2. The Kentucky Fried Chicken chain has a subsidiary in Japan. Do you suggest that the Japanese subsidiary be treated as an operating unit in a Type III organization or as an operating unit in a Type IV organization? Give your reasons.

3. Sr. Gomez, president and part-owner of Tubora, S.A., is concerned and decidedly unhappy because his company, manufacturer of tubes and plastic bottles used to contain cosmetics, seems to be on a profit plateau. Sales are up nicely; profits are not. He explains: "So that I could concentrate on our rapidly growing sales and on my general responsibility to hold the company together, I brought in a production manager, a chief mechanic, an accountant, and a personnel manager. But our profits show the added expense of all these managers.

   "I still have to walk through the plant several times a day to check on quality and on the settings of the machines. The slightest deviation can throw off the colors and the printing. I like to come in early and leave late so I can talk with the second-shift supervisor and see the results of the night's work. The personnel manager hasn't yet shown that she can get the people on the line to stop talking and work harder. I really should spend almost all of my time out of the office making sales, but troubles with machine settings and arguments between operators and mechanics seem to come to me for settlement. And the new accountant has not helped us to cut costs. What can I do with an organization like this one?"

4. Jean Stevens is the owner-manager of a very successful restaurant. Located on a main highway in an attractive setting about 20 miles outside of Atlanta, it is the favorite place to have "a really good dinner" both for people in the area and from the city. There are tables for 200 people, in addition to the bar and a large terrace. The restaurant reflects Ms. Stevens' personality and ability, and it has grown as a Stage I organization. (a) Now Ms. Stevens wants to reduce the burden of day-to-day operations. Do you recommend a Stage II organization? If so, define the functional departments. (b) What problems would occur if Ms. Stevens, or new owners, tried to expand to several other locations? Would you recommend a Stage II or a Stage III organization for the expanded operations?

5. A successful TV set manufacturer with a Stage II organization has just completed arrangements to take over a small electronics plant in England as a first move in international expansion. The English plant will become a production base for the British market. A major anticipated gain will be use of American engineering and production expertise in the newly acquired plant. Should the manager of the British plant report to the production vice-president in the home office? If so, what happens to marketing and finance of the British operation?

6. Several astute observers of organization note that a management crisis is usually necessary before companies change from a Stage I to a Stage II structure and also from a Stage II to a Stage III structure. Explain the typical nature of the crisis in each of the two transitions. Why do you think a basic change in organization design is so often postponed until crisis pressures develop?

7. (a) Many executives regard acquisition of their company by a conglomerate with fear. The idea of being "taken over" comes as a great psychological blow. How do you account for this feeling? (b) Do executives have more, or less, opportunity if the company they work for becomes part of a conglomerate? (c) Is there any reason to presume that the conglomerate executives will push for actions contrary to healthy growth and good service of the operating unit?

8. Basically, the 7-Eleven convenience stores—over 7,000 of them—are run by a Stage II organization. They stay open twenty-four hours a day to sell some 3,000 food and other convenience items. One of the fastest growing products handled by about 2,700 of the 7-Eleven stores is gasoline. This is sold on a self-service basis from pumps located in the parking lot in front of a store. There is no attendant because the whole transaction is handled by the store cashier, who never leaves the counter. She or he collects the money and turns the pumps on or off by remote control. Over a billion gallons of gasoline flow through 7-Eleven pumps each year. Do you think this $1 billion volume should just be fitted into the existing Stage II organization? Or, in view of its size, should gasoline be separated out into a more or less self-contained division as in Stage III organizations?

9. (a) A university could be organized so that each course ran as a separate self-contained unit (the students would sign up, use equipment, and pay for each course just as is done for private flying lessons). Or each department might be so organized—or each division. What are the key factors that determine which separations, if

any, of this type should be made? (b) Should any of the following be se
sufficient divisions: Dormitories? Bookstore? Intercollegiate athletics? Ea
Should they at least be expected to break even financially?

10. Allied Manufacturing, International, recently paid $534 million (25 percent over book value) for Sunrise Electric Co., whose divisions make and sell small appliances to households and small electric products to industrial buyers. Sunrise has six product divisions all of which, save one, are losing market share and are looking at a 7 percent per annum post-tax return on investment. Loss in market share is attributed to out-of-date and "me too" products while return on investment is heavily influenced by very large inventories. One proposal for Allied is to centralize and focus manufacturing (small motors for all products made in one factory, electrical cords only made in another, all consumer appliances assembled in a third plant, and industrial products in a fourth), use venture teams to design, manufacture, and test-market new or updated consumer appliances; and to leave only the selling effort to what used to be the product divisions. Also, regroup the product divisions into kitchen appliance, bedroom appliance (electric blankets and sheets, specialized lighting and electric space-heaters), dining room appliance, and hobby room appliance divisions. In your opinion, will this reorganization improve the selling effort, the products' market share, and the return on investment? Does organization structure have anything to do with effectiveness and efficiency of the business firm?

CASE 17
Milano Enterprises[3]

Mr. Milano is concerned about the long-run future of the group of enter- *concern* prises he personally has built into a flourishing establishment. Located in a Latin American country, Milano Enterprises is recognized as a dynamic factor in the private sector of the nation's economy. In fact, the success of the business complicates its continuation.

Scope of Activities

Mr. Milano, son of Italian immigrants, started in business forty-five years ago in a small but growing city. He anticipated a building boom and left the family grocery store to enter the building-supply business. Several of Mr.

[3]Newman/Summer/Warren, *The Process of Management: Concepts, Behavior and Practice,* 2nd Ed., © 1967, pp. 144-51. Reprinted by permission of Prentice-Hall, Inc., Englewood Cliffs, NJ.

Milano's present companies are a direct outgrowth of this early start. He still owns two regional wholesale companies dealing in building supplies. A separate company imports specialty plumbing items, and another is the national representative of a worldwide electric elevator manufacturer that sells, installs, and services elevators for apartment buildings, offices, and warehouses. Currently, the largest company in the building field is a plant of his that manufactures boilers and other heating equipment. Still another plant manufactures electric fixtures.

Mr. Milano's activities in other fields followed a somewhat similar pattern. Foreseeing needs arising out of urbanization and industrialization, he sought to become the import representative for products serving these needs. Because imports were sharply restricted for economic and political reasons, he undertook the manufacture of selected items. For example, in the automotive field he has been the Ford representative for many years. One company does the importing of Ford cars, trucks, and parts. In addition, Milano Enterprises owns a controlling interest in several large dealerships. It also represents the British and German Ford affiliates. Quotas and tariffs place severe restrictions on the number of vehicles that can be imported, and legislation encourages local manufacture. Consequently a separate company has been established for truck assembly and body manufacture. Also in the automotive area, Milano Enterprises owns a chain of filling stations.

In the office equipment area, Milano Enterprises has separate companies for the importation of duplicating equipment and of typewriters. In addition there is a substantial and growing unit that manufactures metal furniture for offices.

About ten years ago, a new company was established to manufacture electric refrigerators locally. Compressors are imported but the cabinets are manufactured in a plant adjacent to the furniture plant. Other Milano units include a large textile plant that weaves and finishes cotton fabrics, a prominent hotel, a soft-drink bottling company, and a small mining-exploration venture.

In total, there are twenty-five active operating companies ranging in size from twenty to five hundred employees. The textile plant and the boiler plant are the largest units in terms of employment. Milano Enterprises owns all or at least a majority of stock in each of these operating companies. In several instances, the manager of a company owns a minority interest, but he in under contract to Milano Enterprises to sell back his stock at current book value when he retires.

Obviously, a man who can put together such an array of companies in a single lifetime possesses unusual ability. Part of Mr. Milano's success arises from working in growth areas. Within these areas, Mr. Milano has been willing to invest risk capital, but he has been unusually adept in picking particular spots where growth was strong and at adjusting his operations as the economic environment shifted. Also, once an investment has been made, it has been carefully nurtured and controlled. Mr. Milano is modest in manner, eagerly seeks advice wherever he can find it, and works hard in a well-disciplined manner. His per-

sonal integrity is widely respected throughout the business community. He is a
religious man and is highly devoted to his family.

Present Organization

Each of the twenty-five companies has its manager and, with minor exceptions, each has its own offices and other facilities. As might be expected, the central organization reflects its evolutionary background and is not sharply defined.
Six people, in addition to Mr. Milano, share in the general direction of Milano
Enterprises.

Mr. Lopez has been closely associated with Mr. Milano during most of his
business career. Both men are the same age and , like Mr. Milano, Mr. Lopez
has had only elementary school education. In general, Mr. Lopez is more concerned with the operation of existing enterprises than with the starting of new
ones. He acts as troubleshooter for Mr. Milano, takes care of labor problems
when any arise, and represents the Enterprises at various public functions. Managers of the various companies often find that Mr. Lopez is available for consultation when Mr. Milano is concentrating on some new negotiations.

Mr. Peche has been chief accountant for Milano Enterprises for over twenty
years. He has an intimate knowledge of the accounting system of each company
even though great variation exists in the way records are kept. Mr. Peche keeps
a close eye on profits, liquidity, expense ratios, and other key figures for each of
the companies and calls Mr. Milano's attention to any significant deviations.
Mr. Peche works up estimated projections for Mr. Milano's use in negotiations
and in arranging financing, and he takes care of tax matters.

Mr. Gaffney has been Mr. Milano's chief associate in the automotive end of
the business, although he is twelve years younger than Milano. Mr. Gaffney
serves as manager of the automotive import company and exercises supervision
over European imports, all distributors, and the filling stations. He spends about
two-thirds of his time with this group of companies but is available for general
consultation on other matters. In several new ventures, Mr. Milano has asked
Mr. Gaffney to make the preliminary investigation.

Mr. Bolivar is the official representative of Milano Enterprises to the government, obtaining import licenses, which often involve protracted negotiation.
Numerous changes in regulations, often without much warning, require Milano
Enterprises to maintain an able representative in close contact with administrative and legislative personnel. Also involved is a certain amount of "lobbying"
when new legislation is being discussed in the legislature. Mr. Bolivar devotes
his full time to this government work and does not get involved in operating
problems of the companies.

Mr. Juan Milano is the thirty-two-year-old son of the company's founder.
He has been educated abroad. He now works with his father and with Mr. Lopez
on special projects, such as several consumer studies (for the hotel, bottling com-

pany, gasoline filling stations, and electric refrigerator plant). Because of his education, he often meets with foreign visitors.

Mrs. Rodriques, who has an M.B.A. from a leading American university, serves a dual role. She is a personal assistant and interpreter for Mr. Milano, and as such she has a keen interest in learning the lastest developments and management thought of companies abroad. In this capacity, she not only presents the ideas but discusses with Mr. Milano the way they might be related to the Enterprises. Mrs. Rodriques' more formal assignment deals with executive and technical personnel. A few general conferences have been held, but thus far most of the work in the senior personnel field is still in the planning stage. Competent executives are scarce, and even though Milano Enterprises has an excellent reputation, executive selection and development has been more opportunistic than programmed.

All of these people are very busy and there rarely is a time when two or three of them are not working on some pressing current problem. The board of directors of Milano Enterprises is composed of Mr. Milano, his wife, Juan Milano, Mr. Lopez, and Mr. Gaffney. Because most of these people are in frequent informal contact, formal meetings of the board are held only when some official business must be transacted.

Concern for the Future

Even though Milano Enterprises has been successful and is highly regarded in business circles, Mr. Milano is concerned about the future. For one thing, Mr. Milano recognizes that the central organization lacks system and is too dependent upon him personally. He says, "I'm not proud of our organization. All I can say is that thus far it has proved to be adequate."

More pressing is what will happen after Mr. Milano's death. He is in good health, but he is already sixty-five and wishes to take steps now for the perpetuation of the Enterprises. He would like any reorganization to provide for three objectives:

1. Modern, effective management that will be flexible enough to meet changing conditions as he has done during his lifetime.
2. Continuing contribution to the economy of the country, particularly with respect to the initiative and adaptability that free enterprise can provide better than government bureaus.
3. Continuing family ownership of a controlling block of stock. This does not mean that some of the stock may not be sold publicly, as local capital markets develop, nor does it mean that members of the family will always hold top executive positions unless they are fully qualified to do so.

A banker with whom Mr. Milano has thoroughly discussed this matter urges "decentralization." He advises:

No one can keep track of all of your companies that way you have, because only you have the background that comes from founding and working with these companies and their executives over a long period of years. Consequently, you should follow the practice of the leading United States companies by appointing able people as the chief executive of each of your operating units and then decentralizing authority to each of them. You already have this general form, but too many decisions are made in the central office. You should immediately decentralize and find out which of your managers are competent and which ones have to be replaced. The sooner you start, the better, because it will be some time before all twenty-five of the companies can stand on their own feet.

The idea of having strong managers in each operating company appeals to Mr. Milano, but he is dubious about the long-run effect of such a decentralization. He fears that Milano Enterprises will become primarily a passive holder of investments, and this certainly has not been the key to success in his personal experience. He anticipates that local managements may continue to do well what they are now doing but is not sure whether they will adapt to changing conditions, seek out new opportunities, and provide the kind of control that spots difficulties early and ensures vigorous remedial action.

Because so much is at stake, Mr. Milano decided to call in an international management consultant. On the basis of advice from companies with whom the Milano Enterprises does business and several personal interviews, Mr. Eberhardt Stempel was selected to make a thorough organization study of the Milano Enterprises. Mr. Stempel presented his recommendations orally and then wrote the following summary report.

Recommendations of Management Consultant

INTERNATIONAL CONSULTANTS, INC.
New York - London - Frankfurt - Caracas

Dear Mr. Milano:

You have asked that we briefly summarize the recommendations we discussed in your office a week ago. In the original assignment you requested we focus our attention on the central management of the Milano Enterprises, and our investigation confirms your diagnosis that major problems of the future lie in this area.

No report on Milano Enterprises can be made without first recognizing past achievements. Milano Enterprises occupies a unique position in the national economy. Highly respected for its growth, financial strength, willingness to back new ventures, and alertness of management—this group of companies has become a recognized leader in the private business sector. The Milano name carries a high and well-deserved prestige throughout the business community.

The crucial question now facing Milano is not immediate. Instead, it is how to prepare for the time when you, Mr. Milano, can no longer serve as the guiding force of the combined group. Note, the problem is greater than the continuing direction of present enterprises. In addition, the future management of Milano Enterprises must have wisdom and courage to expand or contract in various lines as economic opportunities change. Any true perpetuation of your leadership must be dynamic, not static.

We beleive the best way to perpetuate Milano Enterprises is to build a strong central organization. The present organization is able to cope with the problems it faces only because of long experience in the field and the exceptional talents of the senior executives. To ensure maintenance of present success and to provide for growth, a variety of high-grade specialists should be added to the central organization so that expert talent is readily available to help each of the operating companies meet their respective problems. The organization that we believe will best meet the future needs is shown in Figure 1. This organization is patterned after several of the most successful companies in the world and it embraces features we have found to be helpful to many of our other clients.

FIGURE 1.

PROPOSED ORGANIZATION, MILANO ENTERPRISES

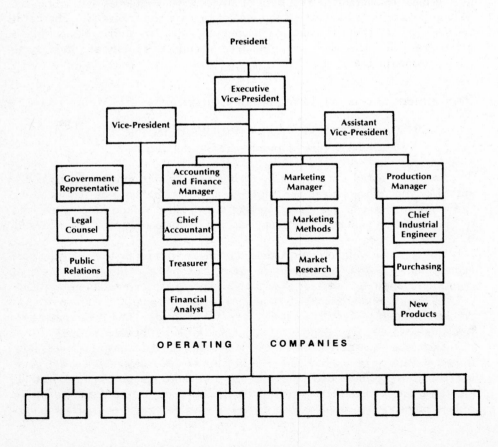

After you have had an opportunity to study this organization carefully, we will be glad to prepare job descriptions and manpower specifications for each of the positions shown. Before doing so, however, you should be clear in your own mind that this is the direction you wish to follow. We would like to again stress the advantages of this form of organization to Milano Enterprises:

1. A strong central office is provided, including experts in marketing, production, and finance. Every company, large or small, must perform these basic functions well. Consequently, you should have the strength to deal with the problems in these areas.
2. Provision is made for current effectiveness. Subsections are provided for industrial engineering, purchasing, marketing methods, accounting, finance, legal advice, and government representation. When these sections are properly staffed, the central office will have talent to help streamline the operations of any existing and newly acquired operating company.
3. In addition, provision is made for growth. The sections on market research, new product development, financial analysis, and public relations will be primarily concerned with finding opportunities for expansion.
4. Senior executives of Milano Enterprises are given titles and recognition commensurate with the important roles they play in the group itself and in the nation.

We fully recognize that time will be required to find the proper indivduals to fill these posts and to get the entire group working together effectively as a team. We believe that you can best serve Milano Enterprises by devoting most of your time toward this end. You should anticipate that it may take three or four years before the transition can be completed. It is important that the change be made while you are still able to give it your personal attention and endorsement.

It has been a pleasure to serve you and we shall be happy to be of any further assistance that we can.

Sincerely yours,
(s)Eberhardt Stempel, on behalf of
International Consultants, Inc.

Attachment

Reactions to Mr. Stempel's Recommendations

The central management group had heard Mr. Stempel's oral report, and as soon as they had an opportunity to review the written summary, Mr. Milano called a meeting for a frank discussion of the recommendations.

Both Mr. Lopez and Mr. Peche expressed grave concern about the heavy overhead expense that the proposed organization would entail. It was far more elaborate than anything they had contemplated, and they felt the central office would be so big that personal contacts with one another would become even more difficult than they already were. Mr. Gaffney said that from the point of view of the automotive unit, he would much prefer to add staff under his immediate direction than be charged for a share of a central office staff that probably would have only superficial understanding of his particular problems. Mrs. Rodriques expressed disappointment that the report was not specifically adapted to the needs of Milano Enterprises. "Except for the special emphasis given government representation, the organization looks as if it was designed for General Electric or Unilever." Juan Milano endorsed this point of view, saying that he did not see how the particular organization would fit the hotel business or the filling station business.

To close the meeting, Mr. Milano made a general statement of his feeling:

"All of us, I'm sure, have been startled by the recommendations. I confess considerable sympathy with most points that have been made. And yet I ask myself whether I am rejecting recommendations because they are new and because they cast some reflection on the way I personally have been running the business. We asked Mr. Stempel to come here because we face a grave problem, the most serious problem of my entire life. I personally want to be sure before I reject these recommendations that it is not because they will require a great change in my own behavior, but because I have a better plan for the future of Milano Enterprises. One of the reasons for the success of many of our companies has been a willingness to recognize a need for change and then to move in that direction aggressively. I would like to think that I am strong enough to apply that same doctrine to my behavior as the head of the Enterprises. Unless we come up with a better plan, I intend to start to put Mr. Stempel's ideas into effect because time does not permit us to stand still on this issue."

Questions

1. Do you agree with Stempel's recommendations? If so, how would you respond to criticisms by members of central management? If not, what do you recommend and why?
2. Some of the operating companies have Stage I organizations and some have Stage II organizations. In your opinion, would Stempel's plan be more suitable for either Stage I or Stage II companies?

18 GOVERNING THE ENTERPRISE

Vital to the success of every enterprise is the organization for central management itself. A small group of key people decides on—or at least endorses—company strategy, policy, organization structure, and related matters. To assure positive, consistent direction there is obviously a need for a workable understanding among this group as to "who is to do what."

More than internal organization is involved. Just who wields power in modern society is also at stake. Currently the debate focuses on boards of directors, but inevitably the relation between boards and senior managers is also questioned. The primary issues—from the viewpoint of making business enterprises more effective—include:

1. How can the board of directors be maintained as an independent, strong check on senior managers?
2. Should the board be composed of representatives of special interest groups, or should it be dedicated to the well-being of the enterprise?
3. How should the full-time senior managers be organized to assure that central management tasks are done well?
4. How should those in power be ousted if they are doing a poor job? (We discuss this in Chapter 19.)

INDEPENDENT CHECK ON SENIOR MANAGEMENT

Within a company we can trace formal authority up to the "chief executive officer." But where does the C.E.O. get power and who checks up on performance?

Legal Theory

Stockholders of a corporation are not expected to perform management functions, and typically they are even more passive than they need be. Except for rare insurrections, stockholders do little more than vote for directors, approve recommendations submitted by management, and, they hope, collect dividends. Normally they simply sell their stock if they do not like the way the corporation is run.

A large stockholder may be active, to be sure, but this is almost always done as a director or perhaps as an officer of the corporation. Once in a while, when a corporation is badly mismanaged, a group of dissident stockholders will wrest control from the existing management. However, they too pass management responsibility to a "new" board of directors. So, the stockholders *per se* do not provide central management.

According to legal documents, the board of directors establishes objectives, sets policy, selects officers, approves major contracts, and performs many other functions. Unquestionably the board has authority to do these things. The practical questions is: Can we expect the board to perform these functions well or should most of the initiative and activity be delegated to executives of the corporation?

An Inactive Board

The activities performed by boards of directors vary widely. Until recently, most boards left the entire administration of the firm to executives.

The rationale for such an arrangement was that operating problems can be settled best by people who have an intimate acquaintance and long years of association with the company. These people can dispose of problems in their normal daily contacts without bothering with a meeting of the directors. The directors then confine their attention to formal action on dividends; to the election of officers; to the approval of any public reports; and to decisions on various minor matters, such as the approval of a given bank to be used as depository for company funds or the granting of a power of attorney to some trusted employee. Most of these actions are taken upon recommendation of the senior executives, and consequently the meetings of the board of directors have been perfunctory affairs.

However, a sharp change is taking place. Especially for corporations whose stock is owned by many people, boards of directors are becoming much more active. Underlying this switch are: (1) a restiveness about "the establishment" and a general challenge to anyone in a position of power; and (2) a series of social reform movements dealing with ecology, women's rights, consumer protection, aid to developing nations, human rights, questionable payments, nuclear power, and the like—all of which put pressure on the conduct of business. Organizations such as the New York Stock Exchange are sensitive to these social attitudes, and they are insisting on reforms in the ways companies are governed.

Incidentally, this challenge to the way corporations have been run is worldwide. In Europe and many developing countries, numerous efforts are being made to enlarge participation in board activities.

Far from clear, however, is just what these reactivated boards should do. A closely related question is who should be board members.

Inside Versus Outside Boards

An Inside Board. In the past, a board of directors often consisted largely, if not entirely, of executives of the company. Such directors are well informed about internal operations, the success of the company is of great importance to them, and they are readily available for discussion when critical issues arise.

Unfortunately, operating executives have difficulty taking a long-run objective view of their company. They are inevitably immersed in day-to-day problems and they are emotionally committed to making certain programs succeed. Moreover, they cannot disassociate themselves from the social pressure of their colleagues and particularly their bosses; they are naturally concerned with maintaining the goodwill of these persons who can make life easy or hard for them. To assume that these operating executives can change their perspective and their loyalties when they walk into an occasional board meeting is unrealistic.

Rarely can an unaided inside board develop an objective, independent, and tough-minded view of the company as a whole.

An Outside Board. As the name implies, an outside board of directors is composed of people whose principal interest is in some other company or profession. A banker, a prominent attorney, and senior executives of companies in other industries are commonly chosen as outside directors.

The advantages and disadvantages of outside directors are just the opposite of those for inside directors. The persons coming from the outside have independence of judgment and objectivity; they can see the company from a different point of view, and they are not wrapped up in short-run problems. On the other hand, they lack an intimate knowledge of the company's operations and its relations with outside groups. More serious, they lack the time to become fully informed; having major commitments in their principal line of activity, they cannot be expected to devote more than a few hours a month for the small directors' fee that is customarily paid. All too often people accept a directorship for the prestige attached or as a friendly gesture. They are willing to give advice, but they cannot be expected to exercise initiative in seeking directions for the company's expansion.

Since the aim is to secure an objective appraisal and independent check on senior managers, widespread opinion now favors a *majority* of outside directors. And an increasing number of publicly owned corporations are moving toward at least two-thirds outside directors. A recent survey of about a thousand *large* corporations by the American Association of Corporate Secretaries found that almost 80 percent had at least a majority of outsiders.

These figures apply to corporations in which management and ownership are already clearly separated. In closely held corporations, however, a tight association of a few owners-directors-managers continues mostly in the traditional pattern. There is little basis for assuming that larger corporations need objective review more than smaller ones. So, the contrast in board membership reflects sensitivity to external pressures rather than need for guidance.

Extent of Board Participation

Election of outside board members only sets the stage. What are such directors expected to do? Their independence also means that they lack knowledge and time to deal with day-to-day operations. And their interference with supervisory relationships would certainly lead to internal confusion. To cite an analogy, a U.S. senator should not try to steer a battleship.

Who Takes the Lead? Furthermore, it is doubtful that outside boards—acting as a group (or committee)—can be expected to exercise active leadership. Again, limitations on knowledge, time, and the process of arriving at decisions stand in the way. In unusual circumstances the board may grasp the initiative. But most of the time the creative proposals and well designed programs will come from the full-time executives. The primary role of the board will be to make sure that senior managers do, in fact, provide the active leadership. Board members can prod, help, evaluate, occasionally veto, stimulate, or request action—all of which are aids to central management.

Realistic Role for Board of Directors. A feasible assignment for a board of directors, then, would normally include at least the following duties:

1. *Approve major changes in strategy, policy, organization structure, and large commitments.* This assumes that carefully prepared recommendations on such matters will flow up from the senior executives. Even if the board approves a large majority of the recommendations made, the necessity for developing a thoughtful justification of the proposals stimulates executives to think through such changes from all angles. This careful preparation of a recommendation by executives may be as valuable as the combined judgment of the board of directors.
2. *Select top executives, approve promotions of key personnel, and set salaries for this top group of executives.* This assignment is both delicate and highly important. It requires independent and yet informed judgments. The board of directors is in a better position to perform this task than anyone else.
3. *Share predictions of future developments, crucial factors, and responses to possible actions.* Here the board is contributing to planning in the formulative stage. The benefits of the broad experience and the diverse points of view are made available to the executive group. Outside members of the board can provide this sort of counsel without unrealistic demands on their time.
4. *Evaluate results and ask discerning questions.* The board should appraise operating results both for prudent control and to obtain background information. This evaluation process should include the asking of a variety of penetrating questions. Most of these questions will be readily answered, but a few may set off a line of thought previously overlooked. Both directors and executives should recognize that the prime purpose here is to see problems from new and useful angles.

5. *Provide personal advice informally.* Already familiar with the company, a director may be an excellent source of advice to executives. The treasurer may call a banker-director about a recent change in the money market, or the marketing vice-president may call another company executive about a new advertising agency. Or the president may want to test out an idea before a formal recommendation is presented to the board as a whole. The informality of these contacts encourages a free exchange of tentative ideas and intuitive feelings.

A board performing the functions just described is particularly valuable because such a check and an independent viewpoint can rarely be developed within the executive group. This is a facilitating role, however. It assumes a harmony of values and objectives which, as we will see later, may not exist.

Maintaining Independence

In the role just outlined for a board of directors, the initiative on most matters is assigned to the chief exectuive officer. There is danger that this full-time manager may choose to consult the board only in a perfunctory manner. This is inevitable when outside board members do not "get into the act" until after important decisions are already made.

Several devices are available to help assure that outside board members do take an active part in at least two or three areas. The board may appoint standing committees composed of a majority, if not all, outside board members. The increase in this practice in a ten-year period is indicated in Figure 18-1. Subjects most often covered are:

1. *Audit.* With the outside auditor, this committee reviews both the auditing process and the findings. Ninety-eight percent of the large companies surveyed by Korn/Ferry International had such a committee. All of those were composed entirely of outside directors.
2. *Senior management compensation.* Both salaries and bonuses for officers and other senior executives are approved by this committee. About 86 percent of the large companies surveyed by Korn/Ferry International had such a committee. They were composed entirely of outside directors.
3. *Nomination of new board members and senior executives.* This committee focuses on composition of the board and on management succession; it transfers the power of picking successors from the chief executive officer to a more broadly based group. Over 55 percent of the large companies surveyed by Korn/Ferry International had such a committee. The typical nominating committee had one inside director and four outside directors as members.

A more potent possibility, though not yet widely used, is an agenda committee. This device enables outside directors to select the subjects to which they will give most attention. Thus, trouble is more difficult to "brush under the rug," and new opportunities can be assured of full study.

Since many smaller companies and not-for-profit enterprises are organized as corporations, they, too, face the question of just what their boards of directors should do. Managers of not-for-profit hospitals and smaller organizations

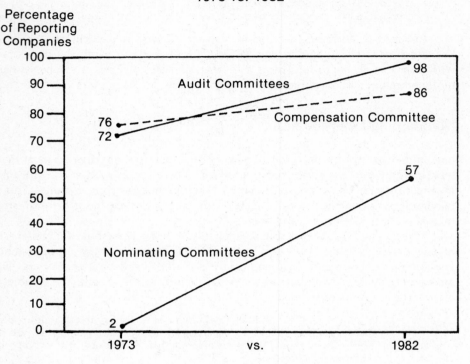

FIGURE 18-1
INCREASE IN NUMBER OF AUDIT
COMPENSATION, NOMINATING COMMITTEES
1973 vs. 1982

Source: Korn/Ferry International, *Tenth Annual Survey, Board of Directors.* Based on responses
from 611 large U.S. industrial and financial companies.

often look to their boards for money-raising and wish only a minimum of interference with running the institution. Nevertheless, the issue of basic responsibility for direction of the institution is, at least legally, within the scope of the
board. How it carries out this assignment is unclear.

DEDICATED VERSUS WATCH-DOG BOARD

Who should the outside directors be? This question is closely linked with
the duties assigned to the board. For instance, if a director is to help set the
monthly agenda, than a resident of Saudi Arabia would be an unsatisfactory
choice, no matter how much stock the person owned.

Interest Group Representation

One proposal repeatedly heard is that various interest groups should be represented on the board. According to this thesis, each major resource contributor (see resource converter model in Chapter 1) might expect to designate a representative. Indeed, for years it was customary to invite an investment banker or commercial banker whose firm helped finance the company to "sit on the board." Another example is the co-determination movement in Europe which provides for labor representatives to be board members. (The Chrysler Corporation in the United States also has labor representatives on its board.)

Community representatives or a consumer representative are often proposed, but their selection and relation to their constituency has no traditional pattern. Even more ambiguous as to representation status is "a woman on the board" or "a black on the board." Nevertheless, pressure is mounting for selections based on such criteria.

The advantage of having interest group representatives as directors is also its weakness. The chances of continuing cooperation from the resource represented are improved. To some extent the resource has been "co-opted." But the very fact that such directors are obligated to promote the interests of their particular groups undermines their loyalty and objectivity toward the company itself. A major customer, for instance, can advise regarding the market and may be inclined to buy from the company of which he or she is a director; however, inside knowledge of the company will also put him or her in an advantageous bargaining position. And when a choice has to be made, the customer's first loyalty is to the major employer.

Of course, having two or more related jobs is not unusual, and an individual may be scrupulously careful to withdraw from one or both roles when a conflict of interest arises. Most professional bankers feel that they conduct themselves in this manner. On the other hand, open and frank discussion is unlikely among persons who may find themselves on opposite sides of the table tomorrow.

If a board of directors consists largely of interest representatives—like a little United Nations—the potential usefulness of the board shifts. It might become a forum in which commitments to a program are developed. The boards of some not-for-profit institutions function in this way. For business corporations, however, much more flexible and extensive negotiations for resources are needed (as the key actor analysis described in Chapter 4 implies). Moreover, if the necessary corporations are joined together in a single board, the antitrust prosecutors would raise a storm.

Alternatively, if the board is to perform as suggested in the preceding section of this chapter, then watch-dog directors are inappropriate. Instead, directors unquestionably committed to the company are required. Such directors may well have diverse backgrounds. But each is selected, like a Supreme Court

Justice, for his or her capability rather than as a representative of an interest group.

Conflicting Interests

When John Doe sells a large block of land to a company of which he is a director we say there is a potential conflict of interest. The danger is that Doe will use his internal influence to promote a deal which is not optimum for the company but is very beneficial to him personally. There are other sorts of conflicts of interest, as with all group representatives discussed above, but it is the personal gain problem that rears its ugly head most often.

The dividing line is fuzzy. A director may recommend the employment of a neighbor's son, but if that son is married to the director's daughter, the qualifications of the young man better be outstanding. The head of a very large corporation almost lost his job because by some coincidence his nephew was writing much of the company's casualty insurance. The eminent president of a large life insurance company did resign when there was public criticism about a long-term loan by his company to a firm in which the president was a significant stockholder.

It is unfair to condemn all such relationships. The normal protection is (1) to make one's connections clearly known, and (2) to insist that an objective, independent assessment is made of the benefits to the company of any transaction. However, the mores of what is an unethical divided interest have been changing over time, and they vary from country to country.

On the borderline now is the question whether a company's investment banker or a partner in its outside legal counsel should serve on the board of directors. There have been two traditonal sources of well informed outside directors, and there has been virtually no scandal associated with the practice. Nevertheless, the presence of such individuals on the board probably does affect where the company does its banking and where it turns for legal advice.

Obtaining Good Directors

Good directors will be increasingly hard to recruit. We have already presented a case for (1) raising the number of outside directors, and (2) significantly increasing the amount of work they will be expected to do. On the other hand, we have (3) cautioned against using "watch-dogs," and (4) raised the question about the propriety of directors who may gain personally from their part-time association. Where, then, are suitable directors to be found?

As in the past, some senior executives of leading companies will serve on each other's boards. Prestige, useful contacts, and some general knowledge comes from such posts. But as the workload gets heavier and the legal constraints more annoying, this will not be an expanding source of outside directors. Professional outside directors probably will increase, though slowly. There are usually people with broad experience, either as former executives or as consultants, who devote a significant amount of time to any directorship they accept. In return, they are paid a fee—often $10,000 to $20,000 per year. University presidents and business school deans will continue to be a source.

In addition, companies will probably move down a status level to tap a larger pool of talent. Top vice-presidents of other companies are often very well qualified. They (and their main employers) probably would welcome the exposure to another corporation. Likewise, some professors may supplement administrators as an academic source. A few lawyers and financiers may find a directorship intriguing even though there is an understanding that it will not lead directly to professional engagements. Even with these additional sources many companies will have to search to find a full complement of good directors.

Because good directors will be scarce, the development of boards as strong independent arms of corporate government may be slow.

"Outside Directors" Within Diversified Corporations

Each business-unit within a diversified corporation needs the same kind of independent check on its activities as we have been advocating for separate companies. Someone outside the unit itself should approve major changes in strategy and organization, select top executives and set their compensation, share vital forecasts, evaluate results, insist that unpleasant problems be confronted, provide personal counsel. This is the "outside director" role noted in Chapter 15.

A unique strength of a diversified corporation (using a Stage III or Stage IV organization) is its ability to provide people to act as "outide director" for each self-contained business. At least one corporate executive should be so designated for each business-unit; the dilemma of obtaining good outside directors is thereby avoided. The person appointed can be given the time and resources necessary to be well-informed and concerned about the unit as a total undertaking. Contacts with other units and with external developments give the individual broad perspective; at the same time, he or she is not protecting a particular department within the business-unit, nor is beholden to the general manager for his or her job.

Because the parent corporation has such a large stake in each business-unit, it can afford to recruit and pay able individuals to fill this role—typically one person will serve, say, half a dozen units. Along with finance, this "outside director" service is a primary contribution that parent corporations can make to strong operating divisions.

ORGANIZING FOR CENTRAL MANAGEMENT

Although the board of directors has an essential role, the major burden of central management must be carried by full-time senior executives.

They are the persons who must work out operational definitions of strategy and policy based on a careful appraisal of trends, company strengths, obstacles to be overcome, impact on the rest of the company, and the like. The executives, with rare exceptions, negotiate major agreements for the company. They are the ones who represent the firm before congressional committees. A review of the annual budget with an understanding of its implications is an assignment senior executives are best able to perform.

An active outside board does not reduce the demands on the time of senior executives. Instead, preparing presentations for the board and responding to their questions adds another dimension in getting plans approved. The decisions should be wiser, but participation by an independent board complicates rather than simplifies the process.

Legal Titles

Officers of the corporation—president, vice-presidents, treasurer, secretary, and others—are formally elected by the board of directors in accordance with provisions of the company's bylaws. Occasionally, the bylaws also contain a realistic job description for these officers; but typically the bylaws simply make some sweeping statements about the duties of the president and the treasurer and say little or nothing about other officers. Often a senior executive such as a general manager is not a legal officer at all, whereas an individual performing perfunctory duties in the secretary's office may be formally elected by the board. Common practice is to leave the legal authorization quite general, because this is difficult to change; instead, the actual working relationships are developed orally, by exchange of memoranda, or in a company's organization manual. Legal titles, then, give us only vague clues about how a top management actually functions.

THE CHIEF EXECUTIVE

Normally, the chief operating officer also serves as the focal point for central management. This individual usually holds the title of "president" but for diplomatic reasons may be named chairperson of the board, executive vice-president, or perhaps general manager. Ideally, this individual has vision, laying plans for five, ten, or twenty years ahead; is a master of strategy and negotiation; has the ability to pick able personnel; stimulates and leads both immediate subordinates and employees throughout the company; is a popular and effective leader in civic and industry affairs; expects high standards of achievement by subordinates; and courageously takes remedial action when all is not well.

Again, realism forces us to admit that no single person can excel is all these respects. Even if one had the ability, that individual would not have the time to do all these things personally. Consequently, wise chief executives try to see that important activities they cannot perform themselves are done by someone else in the company. This conclusion leads us to the question of how the chief executive's "office" can be organized.

A "President's Office"

Dual Executive. The most common way to relieve the central management burden on the president is to share the job with another senior executive. Various combinations of titles are used; chairperson of the board and president, president and executive vice-president, or president and general manager are examples. Whatever the titles, the two individuals have to develop their own way of splitting the total task. The division is likely to reflect the particular interests and abilities of the two individuals. One person may handle most external relations, while the other works with executives within the company. One may focus on long-range development, and the second may deal with current problems. Sometimes the division is along functional or product lines. Perhaps no continuing pattern exists; each works on whatever seems most pressing at the moment. Regardless of how the work is shared, an intimate and frequent interchange is desirable so that the two individuals function as a closely integrated partnership.

Occasionally, three people work together as peers, but the integration of their thoughts and activities into a single president's office view is difficult.

The dual executive arrangement works better in the top job than in other executive positions—probably because a higher proportion of the total work involves planning and deliberation and less time is involved in supervising daily activities. Nevertheless, it is a delicate arrangement and depends on getting the right combination of personalities.

Group Vice-Presidents. Diversified corporations with a Stage III or Stage IV organization often extend the "president's office" in another way. Group vice-presidents are added to take over relationships with clusters of business-units. These senior executives share frequently and informally in the thinking and planning for the entire corporation. However, typically they are designated as the main contact for four to eight business-units, and they keep track of these units more closely than is possible for other senior executives. These are the people who perform the "outside director" role for their assigned units.

Group vice-presidents usually have no staff of their own. Instead, they rely on staff which serves the entire "president's office." Like the dual executive, they are members of a partnership right at the peak of the executive pyramid.

Management Committee

A further sharing device is the management committee, perhaps called policy committee or planning committee. Here all top level managers serve on a committee that deals with several central management tasks. Establishing strategy and policy, building long-range programs, appraising capital expenditures, and reviewing annual budgets are typical activities.

A top management committee has all the inherent advantages and limitations of any committee. It clearly is a good coordinating mechanism; but if it is just an added assignment for executives who are already fully occupied with managing their respective departments, not much creative central management work will be accomplished. The firms with best success with a genuine central management committee have deliberately relieved their members of a significant part of their supervisory burdens, often by placing a single deputy under each member. The members are then expected to devote a quarter to half their total time to central management problems assigned to them by the president.

Central Management Staff

Another well-recognized way to assist the chief executive with central management tasks is the use of a staff. Several leading companies, for instance, have a staff group working on *long-range planning*. These people study future trends, explore possible additions to the product line, project requirements for buildings and for training personnel, and prepare similar data and recommendations for consideration by the president. The organization for long-range planning is a special problem in itself because central staff should tap the ideas of thinking people throughout the company. A few firms rotate young executives in and out of the longe-range planning group for this purpose. Decentralized companies may select a long-range planning person in each operating division; the ideas of these persons are then funneled up to a coordinating staff, the chief executive, or the management committee.

The use of an *organization planning* staff reporting to the president is becoming more common. Such a unit assists in adapting the company organization structure to changing needs. A related task sometimes combined with organization planning is *executive personnel development*. Executive development may simply be a part of the training activity of the company; but in some cases the personnel staff advisor to the president shares in the selection, development, and compensation planning for senior executives.

The role of the *business economist* is often confined to making cyclical forecasts of volume and prices in the industry; however, in a few instances the business economist has become an active participant in central management discussions. Similarly, *financial analysts* occasionally become advisers on central management issues.

These are merely illustrations of the kinds of problems the top staff might handle. Such people do more than assemble information specifically requested by the president, helpful though this may be. To be a really significant member of the team that assures that central management tasks are performed well, a staff member must be a respected, intimate adviser of the senior executive. Such staff members are hard to find, and not all chief executives know how to use staff effectively on difficult, intangible problems.

The particular combination of staff, multiple executives in the president's office, or committees obviously must be fitted to the needs of the each company and to the personalities holding top positions. But whatever the design, provision for getting the central management tasks done well is crucial.

Socially Responsible Governance

Central management of corporations can be considered from at least two viewpoints. The managerial view, which we take in this book, assumes that we are working from the inside of the enterprise trying to make it more effective. The viewpoint of society in general is different. Here results and impact on society are all that matter. From this outside viewpoint, if corporations serve society well, they should be encouraged. If they do not, then the institution should be modified or even abolished.

As corporations become larger and more powerful, their impact comes under closer scrutiny. Also, as our society becomes more interdependent and sensitive to the health of each part, more people are deeply concerned about the behavior of each wheel in the complex machine. For these reasons, corporations are in the limelight. The very success of our business enterprises makes them the target for investigation and criticism.

With a lot of people wishing the world were different, any institution as powerful as our business enterprise system is sure to get a share of the blame. Inevitably, suggestions for altering the system will be advocated.

A popular point of attack is the board of directors. The board is presumed to have the ability to change the behavior of the corporation. Therefore, reformers propose changes in the composition of the board, or in the legal liability of board members, or in the way a board operates. The shift to more outside directors, discussed above, and pressure for special interest representation on boards reflect in part this public concern. Business corporations (and powerful not-for-profit corporations) can disregard this challenge to past board practices only at their peril.

Basically, the response proposed in this chapter is (1) that corporations should indeed make sure that they strengthen their boards and use them for a continuing objective check on the direction and results. But (2) each board should be committed to serve its company with undivided interest.

As a general scheme, we do not expect the board to be the place where agreements with various resource contributors are negotiated. If the board becomes a meeting place for special interest groups, or a device to induce cooperation, then it cannot effectively serve the function of constructive, objective "advice and consent."

In a pluralistic society with many different enterprises, each looking for new niches to serve, competition for resources and customers determines who will survive and grow. Each enterprise—resource converter in the language of Chapter 1—is continually looking for new and more acceptable relationships with key actors. And an important function of the board of directors is to see that this process of dynamic interaction with the changing environment is wisely pursued. However, the board should not be turned into a town meeting for interest representatives. Instead, each board has the important task of assuring that its enterprise is an alert, responsive, effective participant in the competitive system.

Each board should do its utmost to create a strong, virile company, a company which performs its particular mission with distinction. Society is served by such effective "resource converters."

QUESTIONS FOR CLASS DISCUSSION

1. A recent major and thorough study of what directors of companies actually do in fact found that boards followed an unwritten set of rules. Among these were (a) keep your distance from subordinate company executives; (b) be prepared to counsel individually the chief executive officer, both at his or her request and on your own initiative; (c) don't set strategy; and (d) keep up the pretense that the board is present to act in the shareholders' interests. What is the functionality of these rules; that is, what do you think is their usefulness to the board, to the executives of the company, and to the financial community? Explain why each rule is often found in actual practice.

2. (a) Does a Stage I enterprise—one dominant individual—face the kinds of problems described in this chapter? (b) To what extent does such an enterprise need a separate check on the chief executive to perform at least the duties listed on pages 454–55? (c) How do you recommend that a small, privately owned enterprise obtain the kind of guidance you suggested in answering (a) and (b)?

3. Look up the background and experience of the trustees (directors) of your college or university. On the basis of this information, what do you surmise are the kinds of issues each trustee is qualified to deal with? Also make a list of the kinds of issues that the board of trustees *should* consider. How do the qualifications of the board members match with the issues and other matters to which the board should be giving its attention?

4. (a) Do you recommend that corporations make special efforts to find women to appoint as directors? Should they give preference to women over men in such appointments? (b) Answer the same questions with regard to blacks. (c) Answer the same question with regard to American Indians.

5. At the last annual stockholders meeting of the Metropole News, a question was asked about the fees paid to the paper's legal counsel, Plaistead & McCoy, and a possible conflict of interest because Mr. McCoy is a member of the board of directors of Metropole News. The president replied that, "Plaistead & McCoy have been our legal counsel for many years and we pay them the normal legal fees for the work we ask them to do for us. The total amount paid last year is stated in the proxy statement." At a subsequent board meeting, Mrs. Driver pursued the question. "How do we know that Plaistead & McCoy's bill is correct?" Mr. McCoy explained, "We keep track of the time each member of our firm spends on Metropole News work and bill this at our regular per diem rates." Later the president thought to himself, *Mrs. Driver, who is an officer of half a dozen women's organizations, has aggressively pushed for the employment and the promotion of women. Also, "Tiny" Kelly once was president and is still an officer of the printers' union, and he sure looks out for our printers. These two both are board members, yet we make no public report about how their outside interests are served. In fact, the question has never been raised.* Is there a significant difference in the potential *conflict of interest* of these three directors? What should be done to protect other stakeholders against such conflicts of interest?

6. According to recent law in West Germany, a corporation with more than 2,000 employees has one-half of its board of directors elected by its employees; the other half are elected by stockholders, as in the U.S. The theory underlying this "co-determination" is that employees have as vital an interest in company operations as do stockholders. (a) What effect do you think such co-determination is likely to have on (i) the way the board functions, (ii)the decisions the board makes on strategy, policy, etc., and (iii) the long-run strength of the company? (b) Why has the co-determination concept received little support thus far in the United States?

7. Assume that you are Assistant to the Administrator of a nearby hospital. Nominations for the Board of Directors must be made soon, and the Administrator asks you: "What should our directors really do? And what kind of people should we seek to do those tasks?" While thinking how to reply you recall the problems which the Administrator has confronted recently; some, but probably not all, should go to the Board. His problems included union demands, federal ceilings on Medicaid payments, negotiations with Blue Cross, public outcry about high medical costs, use of doctors trained outside the U.S., increase in out-patient service, annual deficit, fund raising, regional plan (restrictions) on specialized facilities, large liability suits against the hospital by disgruntled patients, relations with community chest, developing a computer system for patient records, puchasing a three-dimensional laser scanner, maintaining professional ethics of staff, and replacing the chief of medical staff. What would you reply to the questions addressed to you by the Administrator?

8. Almost all not-for-profit enterprises are governed by a *board* of directors (or trustees). This applies to hospitals, universities, museums, professional orchestras, unions, coops, etc. As in profit-seeking companies, the boards typically appoint full-time executives to actually manage the enterprise. (a) How do you explain such widespread use of boards (instead of an individual) to be the top governing management? (b) Who should select the boards of hospitals? universities? orchestras? mutual insurance companies? Why? (c) If a board is inactive and its enterprise declines, who if anyone should initiate corrective action?

9. Envirometrics, Inc. is a small part of the solid-waste disposal industry. It designs, makes, and sells trash compactors to residential and apartment-building owners and managers. Sales opportunities exist in all major cities in the U.S. The first four years were tough and Envirometrics' owners and managers had to scramble hard to survive and grow. But now a fortunate sale of stock to the general public at a price that was very favorable to the company has brought in about $1,500,000, allowed the company to pay off its debts, enriched the original shareholders, and provided opportunities about which the directors differ. The directors are: (1) *Mike Morris, President,* who devotes 8 hours a day to his electrical contracting business and then comes to Envirometrics at 4 P.M. to discuss problems and provide incentives to push the work along, (2) *David Baruch, Vice President,* who is active on the Board of Directors, takes no part in day-to-day operations and spends his time running the Baruch Steel Works and his other business and public affairs (Baruch Steel supplies 75 percent of the parts bought by Envirometrics for assembly into the compactors. Baruch prices the parts at cost plus and provides excellent service). (3) *A. B. Morris* is a passive stockholder who relies on his brother to represent him. (4) *Carl Curtis,* a successful real estate developer, who was an early shareholder and was invited to join the board "to help with finances." He attends and works hard at board meetings but never gets involved in daily affairs. (5) *Pat Seymour, Marketing Vice-President,* has had substantial experience in several aspects of the housing market. He likes personal selling and "closing a deal" but gladly leaves the production and operating activities to other executives. He devotes his entire time to building sales in the metropolitan New York area. "What this company needs is volume, and it's my job to provide it." He did raise a question about the prices paid for parts recently when costs rose, but the board decided not to consider the issue. Ideas differ among the directors as to a future direction for the company. Pat Seymour pushes national sales and company-owned branches. David Baruch says, "Let's raise prices and also get into the contracting work to install our compactors. This will increase our value-added and also our profits." Carl Curtis deplores the failure to use leverage. "With no long-term debt and a current ratio of almost 5 to 1, we are losing opportunities daily. Suppose we make the unheard of ratio of net profit to sales of 13 percent; even then, after taxes, our stockholders are going to be earning about 3 percent on their personal investment. They bought at the top of the market for a very high price per share. Let's lease, borrow, and franchise so that we can cover solid-waste with a system—from the trashcan to the sale of recycled raw materials." Mike Morris believes that "we should keep up with product development, keep pushing in several directions and see where that leads us. We are now in a good position to feel out other markets and look for new products without running a deficit."

(a) What do these comments tell you about the future direction of this company with this board? (b) What is your appraisal of the composition of the board? Are the right kinds of people on it? (c) What important topics should the board be considering? Is it now taking these up? (d) Is the board carrying out a realistic role? (e) Who checks on management? Which directors?

CASE 18
Columbia Bell Telephone Co. (R)[1]

Maybe I should resign, thought Gene Williams. *We don't agree on what the board of directors should do and I'm not interested in being merely a show-piece director.* Williams, a political science professor at the state university, has been active in the civil rights movement and is an articulate spokesperson for the black community. Six months ago he was elected a director of Columbia Bell—the first college professor and first black to serve on that board.

The monthly board meetings which Williams has attended have all been well planned, friendly sessions. Routine legal actions—approval to file documents, signature authorizations, bank loan agreements, and the like—take up some time. Operating results and short-term projections are reviewed. At this stage, board members typically exchange views on the economic and political outlook. Then a vice-president or department head makes a brief presentation of current problems and plans for his or her division of the company. These presentations are intended to inform the board, not seek its advice. By this time, several directors have to leave for other appointments, and the meeting is adjourned.

At the close of the last meeting Williams asked, "Does Columbia Bell have any basic problems which the board should be digging into?" Another director responded, "That's what we pay the management to do."

The president took the question more seriously. "We have lots of problems and want all the help we can get. Perhaps you are thinking of our 'equal opportunity' posture, and I'd be grateful if you had the time to take a thorough look at what we are doing on that front. Or if there is any other area which concerns you, I'll be glad to arrange for you to talk with our people."

---

[1]Columbia Bell Telephone Co. operates as a state-regulated utility in two large states. Although it is a subsidiary of Ameritech (formerly part of A.T. & T.), it has an impressive outside board of directors and is fully responsible for operations in its territory. The present organization of the company is indicated in Figure 1. Its assets are over $3 billion and it has almost 30,000 employees.

Williams did find the time to visit with nine Columbia Bell executives and staff people, and came to two conclusions. (1) The company is actively pushing equal opportunity for blacks and women. In fact, to increase its percentage of black and women employees in areas where they are under-represented, reverse discrimination occurs. The number of blacks and women in middle management is still low, and almost nonexistent in upper management. However, there is strong evidence that time is needed for minorities to gain experience and for vacancies to occur. Williams' conclusion was just to keep the pressure on.

(2) The chief problem confronting Columbia Bell is labeled "marketing" but is even more fundamental. Williams has sorted his notes into three piles (see attached): (a) Threats, (b) Inertia, (c) Possible Actions. This is where the board of directors should be active, Williams believes.

Williams has talked on the phone with several other outside directors about the importance of "marketing" to the future of Columbia Bell, and has received a cool response. One said, "Our job is to keep the company financially sound, like it is now. The utility commissions will never accept extra marketing expense as a necessary outlay, so we can't recover the expense in income. It would simply cut net earnings." Another commented, "Let's let Ameritech worry about the future competition. They ought to do something to earn their overhead charge." A third said, "As directors we should not interfere with internal organization. That is a managerial job. We can't know enough about the specifics to tell the president how to run the shop. We come from a wide range of companies and are appointed to assure that the stockholders and customers both get fair treatment, also the employees."

Questions

1. To what extent and in what ways should the board of directors of Columbia Bell involve themselves in the "marketing" issue?
2. How do you recommend Columbia Bell be organized to deal with future competition and "marketing"? Should other steps, in addition to organization, be taken?

Notes Based on Interviews—Threats

1. Columbia Bell now must permit customers to hook up their *own* equipment to company lines. Many new competitors sell phones, PBX equipment (in-house exchanges), etc. to customers. Columbia must now sell, as well as lease, such equipment to meet competition. We have some advantage in repair service. But field is now open to computer companies and many others.
2. Cable TV may move into interacting systems. Customers will then shop, buy, pay bills, select news on their initiative. Meter reading in customers' houses— electricity, water, gas—is also a possibility. Columbia Bell would merely lease lines— maybe glass fiber optics—to customer's home or business; routine, low-profit end of business. Millions in revenue at stake.

3. Other big companies have headstart in satellite communications. Already used for TV and radio. Large future market for national business hookups—computer data, picture-phone and conferences (complete with airplane business travel), instant photocopies of documents and drawings. IBM and Xerox getting into this, including software. Mostly competes with Long Lines. * Maybe will use Columbia Bell's local connections, but as routine service—see #2 and #1. Again, multimillions involved.
4. Competitors will design, sell or lease, train employees, and maintain entire communication systems for major users—including software. Customer-oriented systems vs. hardware which Columbia Bell stresses.
5. Small satellite receiving—and maybe transmitting—stations at plants and company headquarters are being engineered. These could bypass the Bell system entirely. We would not get even routine business.

Inertia

1. Columbia Bell, like A.T. & T., very *service* oriented. Pride in being best telephone system in the world. Feel like stewards, *not entrepreneurs.*
2. Bell Labs and Western Electric (subsidiaries of A.T. & T.) generate new products. Excellent engineering. Technically, not customer, oriented. Think in terms of products. Columbia Bell relies on them for new sources of income.
3. Engineering and Operations are dominant departments in Columbia Bell. They produce the good service. Have most influence on budget allocations. Commercial Department "necessary"—second-class citizen. Local push for news services is weak.
4. Promotion from within very common. Heavy internal training; therefore executives rise through ranks. Believe in present company values.
5. State Public Utility Commissions regulate service, approve rates. Must serve all customers, so Columbia Bell may be saddled with uneconomic customers (like Postal Service). Good service helps rate increase. Expenses must be in line to get reasonable return on investment. So, more attention to expense control than profit. Commissions indifferent to *who* provides future services.

Possible Actions

1. Add staff to the Commercial Department. Specialize by type of business—chain stores, banks, interstate trucking companies, stockbrokers, etc. Each group designs and promotes communications systems suited to its business. Work with departments to give each business what it needs.
2. Reorganize Commercial Department along industry and business lines, not geography unless industry section needs local reps. Rename Marketing. Do staff job in plus. Act like competitors whose survival depends on creating better total communication systems suited to new technology. Maybe transfer some installation and maintenance from Operations Department to new industry sections. Rate setting?

---

* Long Lines is a separate division of A.T. & T., operating the long-distance connections between regional companies like Columbia Bell.

3. Bring in experienced marketing executives. Put in key spots, maybe next president.
4. Tie all approval of capital expenditure projects to new kind of service listed in #2. Use ROI standards by kind of business.
5. Reward "entrepreneurs" with bonuses; never done in Columbia Bell.
6. Call in A.T. & T. or Ameritech industry experts. Maybe hire management consultants.
7. Possibly organize national companies to give full service to particular industries. Use regional companies like Columbia Bell for local operations only. Bypass state utility commissions. Meet competitors head-on.

FIGURE 1.
ORGANIZATION OF OPERATING ACTIVITIES

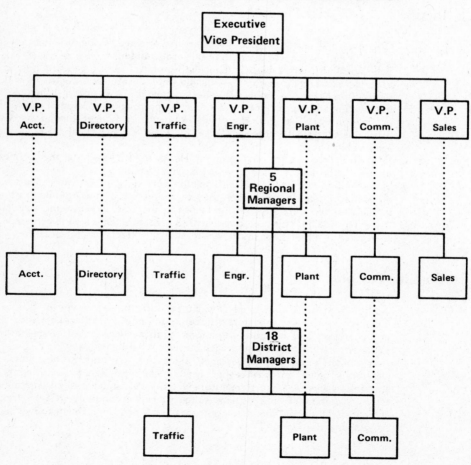

Supplement to Organization Chart. Main Functions of Each Department

Engineering (design of facilities): customer equipment; outside plant; switching equipment; transmission.

Plant (installation and maintenance of facilities): construction, installation, and maintenance of local switching, trunk lines, outside plant, etc.; connections to network; response to trouble reports.

Traffic (running the plant): operators—toll calls, number assistance, etc.; assign lines and numbers; supervise use of circuits and trunk lines; service evaluation, future usage.

Commercial (interface with residential and other small customers): sales, negotiation and coordination of service for small customers; coin service; annoyance call bureau; teller and cashier service; community relations.

Accounting: customer billing; payroll processing; supplier payment; corporate accounting; banking activities; financial planning.

Directory: directory compilation and production; sale of Yellow Page advertising and special listing; directory delivery.

Sales: planning, negotiation, and administration of sales to large business customers and sales of data (nonoral) communications; special services.

19 EXECUTIVE PERSONNEL

Without suitable executive personnel in a company, sound strategy, effective policy, and a clear organization plan soon become unrealistic aspirations; with good executive personnel, they provide the guidance and the structure for purposeful enterprise.

Developing Executive Personnel

The development of a competent group of immediate subordinates is a duty that can never be fully delegated. Larger companies may have a service unit that provides assistance in dealing with human resource problems, but each executive still carries primary responsibility for having competent people in key positions under his or her direction.

The typical executive is concerned with only a relatively few executives and other key personnel. These are likely to be people he or she has worked with over a period of years; they may well include close friends. An executive is expected to see that they perform today's tasks effectively and also develop so that they can assume the larger responsibilities of tomorrow. This development may take years and involves habits, attitudes, and skills. Except for filling unexpected vacancies caused by death or resignation, executive personnel is a long-run problem. Because of these *personal*, *intangible*, and *long-run* characteristics of executive personnel development, general policy is inadequate to deal with specific situations. In addition to using policy, the manager should give personal attention to the delicate and highly personal situations in the company or department.

Wide Variation in Company Practice

Since executive personnel involves personal relationships, considerable difference occurs in the way executive selection and development is handled in various companies.

A President Who Evaded Responsibility. In one relatively small company with eight key executives, the president had been for many years the key figure in coordinating operations. The subordinates were given considerable latitude within their own departments, but they were expected to concentrate their attention in their own areas. The executives were very friendly with one another, and the president had a personal interest in and a deep loyalty to each of the members of the group. There was a general understanding that the sales manager would probably be the next president, and beyond that the matter of executive succession was given little thought.

The cold facts of the situation were that the sales manager was an excellent salesperson but not an effective executive. The manager was indecisive and preferred not to assume administrative responsibility. As long as the president was active, these traits were not a serious handicap to the company. The sales representatives were experienced individuals who were glad to accept the kindly suggestions of the sales manager and who were able to proceed with a minimum of supervision.

When the president died and was succeeded by the sales manager, the latter's lack of executive ability created an acute problem. The other executives found it difficult to get positive decisions from the new president, who in an effort to please everyone, was likely to reverse decisions. Coordination, or lack of it, was largely a result of the voluntary contacts between the several executives. The new president could not adjust to the responsibilities of the job and suffered a nervous breakdown within three years. The person who was next appointed as president had considerably more ability but had been given virtually no training for the job as chief executive. Six to eight years elapsed before the company really recovered from the shock of the death of the president who failed to provide adequately for a replacement.

Note also that the president made no provision for change in the scope of company activities.

Looking back on this case, one wonders why a successful president for so many years failed to anticipate the difficulties upon his withdrawal from the company. Perhaps he never faced the question squarely. More likely, he recognized the limitations of the sales manager but could not bring himself to take the drastic action that would have been involved in the selection and training of another executive to be his successor. This would have created strain and upset personal friendship. Since no immediate action was necessary, he probably evaded the issue and hoped it would work out all right somehow. Had he taken the necessary action when he was still president, the company would certainly have been better off and the sales manager spared a nervous breakdown. This would have taken considerable courage, however, because there was no assurance that all the people concerned would have recognized the need for action.

Informal Development Program. More thought is given executive development in many companies than appears on the surface. Frequently these concerns have no announced program or procedure but do give the matter of executive personnel regular attention. One company, for example, has a "little green seedbox" that contains a card for each key person who is a present or potential manager of one of the concern's principal operations. Each year the work of these people is reviewed by a senior executive along with the individual's supervisor, and when a person is assigned to a new position his or her performance is watched closely. Then, as opportunities open, people are moved into positions of increasing executive importance. If it is decided, after watching a person for several years, that the individual has reached maximum, his or her card will be removed from the file.

Wide variations exist in this type of approach. Typically, the cards or the pages of a loose-leaf notebook contain little information other than a record of the positions a person has held, the salary, and perhaps notations on any outside civic or educational work done. If the president or a senior vice-president is the one who directs the activity and makes sure that each person's performance is reviewed at least once a year (though not necessarily in a formal review session), then it is likely that considerable executive development work will take place and that the selection of people for promotion will be based on a broad view of the person's experience.

Where the activity is treated more casually or where the reviews are sponsored by an individual who lacks prestige with other executives, the attention given to executive development will probably be substantially less. In any event, the kind of training on the job that occurs depends almost entirely upon the interest and the ability of the supervising executive. Given the proper company tradition, backed by the necessary inspiration and guidance of the chief executive, such informal plans for executive development have worked remarkably well in some companies.

These informal approaches to executive development have two basic weaknesses: (1) little thought is given to preparing for growth or major changes in strategy, and (2) executive development receives low priority in the plans of most executives. To overcome these limitations, highly formalized programs of executive appraisal and replacement schedules have been created, especially in multinational concerns where lack of qualified executives may be a major restraint on expansion.

Essential Elements for a Sound Formal Program

Even though substantial disagreement exists on how formalized executive development should be, we can identify several basic elements that every manager should keep in mind when dealing with executive personnel problems. Whatever the forms and the procedures used, the manager's thinking should embrace the following steps:

1. a prediction of the types and number of executives the company (or department) will need for successful operations in the future
2. a review, or inventory, of the executive talent now available
3. a tentative promotion schedule, based on the two preceding steps, that provides for filling each of the positons in the anticipated organization and, inso-

far as possible, provides for a potential replacement for each of the key executives

4. a plan for the individual development of each person slated for promotion, so that each may be fully qualified for the responsibilities

5. compensation arrangements that will attract and hold the executives covered in the foregoing program and provide incentives for them to put forth their best efforts

The significance and the nature of each of these steps will be considered in the following sections. A detailed analysis of techniques, however, is beyond the scope of this book.

ANTICIPATING EXECUTIVE REQUIREMENTS

The basis for any long-range planning for executive personnel is a prediction of the kind of people that will be needed. Surprisingly, this obvious first step is sometimes overlooked. In one company, for example, the top administrator held the view that "we always have room for good people around here" and on several occasions had hired competent people with no clear-cut idea of what they were to do. These individuals either got bored waiting for a significant assignment or created friction by interfering with activities of other executives.

A more common failure is to assume that a title provides an adequate guide to the kind of person needed. A hard-driving, enthusiastic sales supervisor is quite a different individual from an analytical and imaginative planner of merchandising campaigns, and yet either of these persons might have the identical title of product sales manager. Before sound executive development can be done, a clear understanding is needed of (1) the jobs to be filled and (2) the characteristics of the persons needed for these jobs.

Jobs to be Filled

A study of strategy and future organization, along the lines indicated earlier in this book, will result in a long-range organization plan with descriptions of each key position needed. These position descriptions are not necessarily put in writing, but there must be an understanding of the duties and the relationships of each executive position. If plans for the future administrative organization have not already been clarified, then organization analysis becomes a first step in the executive personnel program.[1]

---

[1]We clearly are recommending that organization design *precede* executive selection. Of course, in the short run a company must be managed by the executive talent available, and since the available executives may not fully match the ideal organization, the only practical action is to adjust the organization so that optimum results will be obtained. Executive development, however, should continue to be aimed toward the best future organization we can realisitically expect to achieve.

Position descriptions prepared to clarify organizational relationships differ in emphasis from those used in an executive development program. The more ticklish aspects of organization involve defining the borderlines between the various units and spelling out interactions when activities must be closely coordinated. Such refinements of responsibility are not so important for executive development purposes. Here, interest centers on the major duties to be performed, the degree of decentralization and hence the judgment that must be exercised, the importance of initiative and enthusiasm, and similar matters. In other words, we need to sense the role the person in the executive position will play.

Characteristics of Persons Needed for These Jobs

The second phase of this analysis of executive requirements is to translate the duties into *person specifications*, that is, the personal qualities an individual needs to fill a given position effectively. We can describe the duties of a football quarterback or a plant superintendent, but it is another matter to set up a list of qualifications that a person should have to fill such a position successfully.

These person specifications may be stated in terms of knowledge, supervisory skill, emotional stability, judgment, dependability, ability to deal with outsiders, social attitudes. Unfortunately, it is difficult to define requirements for positions in such terms because experience shows that people with quite different makeups may be successful in the same kind of a job.

Another way to draw up person specifications is to list the principal things they will be expected to do, such as build customer goodwill, control expenses, plan for future expansion, or stimulate and develop their subordinates. This kind of a list is easier to prepare but its application still may require subjective judgments when an individual is being selected for work that is quite different from what he or she has already done. Your being a crack salesperson, for instance, does not tell us how good you might be as branch manager.

One additional point should be emphasized. Much executive development work cannot be expected to show results in less than three to five years and some of it may take much longer. Consequently, the organization structure five years hence is more important than the present one. The outlook and the strategy for the company must be studied to forecast the volume and nature of activities. These will throw light on the organization structure that will be needed and hence on the requirements for executive personnel. Moreover, the existing organization may be far from ideal. A logical time to realign duties and correct organizational weaknesses is when executive personnel is being shifted. If this is to be done, plans for executive development should, of course, be based on the new, rather than the old, organization structure.

INVENTORY OF EXECUTIVE TALENT

The second basic step in planning an executive personnel program is appraising the executives already in the organization. The organization and position analysis just discussed predicts what executive talent will be needed; the appraisal of executives, considered in this section, shows what talent is available to meet these requirements.

Generally an inventory of executive talent is taken to discover weak spots in the normal flow of executives through the promotion channel. It indicates where additional development work is needed to assure that satisfactory replacements are available when necessary.

A good inventory will also bring to light the competent executives who are not being used to their fullest capacity. For example, the president of a pharmaceutical company was shocked when her nephew resigned, along with two key salespeople, and established a competing firm. Evidence clearly indicated that these people had not been assigned to challenging positions and they considered their prospects for promotion so remote that they preferred to take the risk of establishing a new enterprise. A good plan of executive appraisal would have shown the president that these people were prepared for additional responsibilities. She should then have tried to find positions that would more fully utilize their ability, and if this was not possible, she should at least have openly examined the situation with each individual. In other words, an executive inventory would have been useful even though there was no immediate need for replacing key personnel.

Different Uses of Executive Appraisals

We may use executive appraisals in several different ways, and their value will be improved if we recognize these uses at the outset.

1. The primary purpose of executive review may be to *select* a person for an existing or anticipated vacancy. For this purpose an objective appraisal of the person's future potential is needed.
2. Executive appraisal may point to the need for development when abilities of executives are matched against the person specifications for a given position. Individual *development programs* can be built to remedy deficiencies. When the emphasis is on personal development, the appraiser can identify much more closely with the individual being reviewed and together they can seek out opportunities for improvement.
3. Executive appraisal may be used to establish bonuses and to pay increases or other forms of *compensation*. Here attention centers on past achievements rather than future potential. Objectivity is needed here, as it is when considering individuals for promotion.

Be prepared to reinterpret an appraisal designed for a purpose that differs from your current interest.

Informal Appraisal of Executives

No systematic appraisal, or inventory taking, of executive ability is made in many companies. Nevertheless, considerable informal appraisal typically takes place. This was the method followed in a financial company, for example, that had thirty-two senior and junior officers and approximately eighty-five first-line supervisors and other key employees. The size of the company permitted each senior officer to know personally all of the executives as well as some of the outstanding operating persons.

The president and the senior vice-president made it a practice to "keep their eyes on the staff." They asked questions and otherwise followed the work of the various executives closely enough to have a clear impression of what most of the people were doing. In addition, they occasionally talked with the individual officers about the people under their supervision and what might be done to assist in their development. The officers felt that more formal ways of inventorying executive talent were unnecessary in their situation.

Informal executive appraisal, such as that just described, is a natural and continuing process that should be used by everyone in a managerial position. The more formal appraisal techniques, discussed in the next paragraphs, supplement rather than substitute for this type of evaluation. The informal appraisal is done at convenient times, in connection with other work; consequently, it creates no special burden on executives.

Limitations of this method are: (1) some executives who are primarily interested in technical problems may fail to assess the complete personalities of those they come in contact with; (2) the appraisals may be incomplete, with emphasis on past performance and little attention to future potential; and (3) in larger concerns where no one executive can know personally all of the present and potential managers, it is extremely difficult to compare candidates in one department with those in another and to exercise guidance over an executive development program.

Systematic Evaluation of Executives

To overcome the limitations of informal appraisals, several companies have definite procedures for executive personnel reviews. In their simplest form these evaluations consist of only an annual memorandum written by the supervisor of each key person outlining the person's outstanding accomplishments and failures during the year, steps taken for development, and future potential.

At the other extreme are rather elaborate evaluation forms that record an overall appraisal of the person's work during the past year, a rating of personal qualities, promotion possibilities, and plans for individual development. The Armed Services use a similar technique; in fact, the file of fitness reports is the primary basis on which Navy officers are selected for promotion.

These formal evaluation plans build up a record covering each executive, which is very helpful when he or she is being considered for transfer or promotion. Usually several different people have submitted appraisals and the total record is not dominated by some single event, as may happen when sole reliance is placed upon informal appraisal. Moreover, the formal procedure tends to make the evaluation more thorough and consistent.

On the other hand, standard forms and procedures by no means insure that appraisals will be made carefully and honestly. Unless the executives making the appraisals believe that the whole process is worthwhile, they may fill in the form hastily and with answers that they think will lead to the promotions and transfers they would like to see made. Also, the standard forms emphasize factors that the designers of the forms think are important; for some jobs these factors may not match the actual operating requirements.

Recent antidiscrimination laws have increased the importance of appraisal records. Suing someone has become a national pastime, and employers must be careful (1) not to discriminate on the basis of race, religion, sex, age, etc., and (2) to have evidence that they did not discriminate. Consequently, fair but tough evaluations have to be made—regardless of their impact on individual egos.

PLANS FOR FILLING EXECUTIVE POSITIONS

Development of executive personnel, as already noted, is largely a long-run problem. Individuals need time to develop the knowledge, skills, and judgment required in most executive posts.

Need for Planned Executive Progression

The treasurer of a medium-sized company wished to retire within a year and recently told the president. In the discussion at the next meeting of the board of directors, two facts emerged: (1) the assistant to the treasurer, specially selected two years earlier, had displayed more energy than judgment and clearly was not qualified to replace the treasurer, and (2) there was wide misunderstanding about how vital a role the new treasurer should play in overall company operations (some board members wanted a senior executive, whereas the president thought in terms of a cashier). Two years elapsed before a satisfactory, strong person could be found.

Having the right person in the right position at the right time is of supreme importance, especially when expanding or shifting into a new field. Here is an area, then, where long-range planning is of vital importance—even though human behavior is hard to measure and to predict, and results may not turn out just as planned.

Staffing-Plan Approach

Transfer and promotion of executives is a normal occurrence in a typical business concern. Deaths, retirements, firings, and resignations create vacancies. New positions, resulting from expansion, have a similar effect. If these positions are filled by promotions, additional vacancies are created in the lower ranks. In fact, one vacancy at the vice-president level may result in shifts of half a dozen people at lower levels. The problem is how a company can plan to meet such changes.

The staffing-plan approach rests on three ideas that we have already discussed. The first is anticipating executive requirements in terms of positions to be filled and the person specifications of executives needed in such positions. The second is a policy of promotion from within. The third, assuming promotion from within, is the inventory of executive talent discussed in the preceding section, which provides the personnel data needed for concrete planning. Staffing tables are simply a device for weaving this information into a tentative plan.

Staffing plans, such as the one in Table 19-1, show for each executive position (and anticipated position) one or more persons who might be moved into that spot. The preparation of such plans requires that the person specifications for each position be used to select the best candidate available within the company. Some companies distinguish between candidates who are already qualified and those who need a year or more training before they would be prepared to take on the new duties. To be useful, such a chart should be realistic. Thus, if some contemplated positions are now vacant, they should be shown in this way. If there are no real candidates for a given position, this too should be frankly revealed. Of course, one individual may be considered as a candidate for two or more positions.

Ideally, every senior post in the company should have one or more potential replacements listed. Some people contend that there should be a replacement for every executive throughout the organization. Such an ideal is often very difficult to achieve in practice, and there is serious question as to how much money and effort a company should spend training a replacement for a person who, in all probability, will stay in the present position for ten or more years. On the other hand, having replacements for executives who are likely to retire or to be promoted to other positions is highly important. Some staffing plans attempt to show this timing; but more often the likelihood of a shift, and consequently the need for a fully prepared replacement, is left to the judgment of the people reviewing the plan.

Such staffing plans are subject to frequent revision. Unexpected changes in company operations or in the personal lives of executives may shift requirements. Some people will develop faster and others slower than anticipated; in fact, in time, some persons will be added and others will be dropped as candidates for particular positions. Not infrequently, an understudy is moved to still another position and a new understudy must be found. Nevertheless, prepara-

TABLE 19-1.
SAMPLE STAFFING PLAN[1]

Job Title	Job Incumbent	Age	Senior Candidate	Age	Junior Candidate	Age
Management Level Group "A"						
Service Manager	K. L. Foster	47			G. E. George C	38
					A. A. Day C+	35
Sales Engineer	B. C. Johnson	65	C. D. Dewey C	42	L. M. Mason D+	38
Const. Manager	E. E. Bryant	49	No Senior		E. F. Burnes C+	37
Accountant	F. G. Bray	55	No Senior		No Junior	
"B" Office Managers						
Loc.	G. H. Miller	63	)		)E. D. Hill C	42
Loc.	A. A. Day	35	)G. E. George C	38	)M. N. Johns C+	35
Loc.	C. D. Dewey	42	)L. M. Mason D+	38	)W. X. Hobbs C	33
Local Service Managers "A" & "B" Offices						
"A" Office	R. R. Colby	62	)			
Loc.	G. E. George	38	)M. N. Johns C+	35	X. Y. Bell C+	37
Loc.	R. S. Williams	41	)M. X. Hobbs C	33	E. D. Hill C	42
Loc.	S. T. Fuller	57	)			
Zone Maint. Prom.	T. U. Webster	51			R.S. Williams D+	41
					X. Y. Bell C+	37
Zone Modern. Prom.	"Vacancy"		No Senior		T. V. Dodge D+	32
Zone Maint. Super.	V. W. Gary	58	F. E. Hyde C+	39	No Junior	
Zone Field Eng.	P. T. Monroe	39			T. U. Olson D+	48
					U. V. Larsen C	41

[1] Sample sheet from staffing plan of Otis Elevator Company. "Senior candidates" are qualified to take over positions without further training other than normal job indoctrination; "junior candidates" need one to five years more training. Letters after names tie in to annual executive appraisals. Note that some individuals, such as Hobbs and George, are listed as candidates for more than one position.

tion of staffing plans serves a very useful purpose in pointing up where available replacements or candidates for new positions are lacking. Moreover, it forces realistic review of the persons who are likely to be promoted; if they need further development, immediate steps may be taken to start the necessary training.

Staffing plans are, of course, confidential documents because they reflect highly tentative promotion plans that may have to be revised later. For this reason, some executives prefer never to put their ideas down in writing. For smaller companies or for a single department this may be satisfactory, *provided* the same basic thinking takes place. The chart is merely a device to help an executive think through a very "iffy" subject. It is the systematic analysis of executive placement, rather than the particular pieces of paper, that is important.

Methods of Selection

Planned placement of executives modifies, but by no means eliminates, the need for wise selection of individuals to fill executive positions. Possible candidates must first be identified; later, one of these may be designated as an understudy; and when the vacancy occurs, the final selection must be made. This shifting process should improve the selection because judgments are made at different times, often several years apart, and this provides opportunity to reconsider earlier impressions. In addition, there will, of course, be unexpected vacancies for which final selections must be made quickly.

The use of periodic appraisals to provide data on individuals and the matching of such data against position descriptions and person specifications have already been recommended. The surprising thing is how often these basic steps in selection are disregarded. Many executives are inclined to substitute their intuitive likes and dislikes of individuals for the analytical approach suggested.

Selection will also be improved generally if *group judgment* is used. The appraisal of individuals involves so many intangibles and personal bias is so difficult to remove that the views of at least two or three people should be considered in making executive decisions. The final decision usually rests with the immediate supervisor, subject to the approval by the boss. In addition, the views of other executives who have worked with the candidate, and of the central personnel advisor who has studied all available candidates, should be considered. Often the views of all these people will confirm the wisdom of the proposed selection. If there is a difference of opinion, then a warning has been raised and further observation on the points in question can be made. Probably in no other phase of business administration is group judgment more valuable than in executive selection.

When tentative selections of one or more candidates for a position are made several years before the actual vacancies occur, *trial on the job* may be possible. A candidate may pinch-hit in the job when the present incumbent if off on vacation or on special assignment. This is not an adequate test because usually the interval is too short for the candidate to exercise much initiative, but it may throw some light on that person's capabilities.

A more likely arrangement is to assign the candidates to work in a department or a branch where they can demonstrate ability to do certain phases of the work. Such assignments typically serve the purpose of both training and selection. If time permits, people may be tried out in several different positions.

What people have done in the past is no definite assurance of what they will do in the future, but it is probably the best evidence we can obtain.

To avoid raising expectations of a promotion that later is not made—for any of a variety of reasons—most companies do not tell a person about tentative plans for his or her promotion. Nevertheless, alert candidates are well aware of being assigned to positions which provide good training and testing.

No mention has been made of psychological tests for selecting executives. When a quick selection has to be made from individuals outside the company, test data may be a useful supplement to other sources of information. However, when careful appraisals of people already in the company are possible and group judgement and trial on a series of different jobs can be utilized, psychological tests in their present state of development rarely add much that is useful.

Removing Ineffective Executives

Strong performances in each executive position is vital to company effectiveness. More than salary expense is at stake. A weak incumbent blocks the possibility for a more capable person to do that job well.

Removing ineffective executives is always painful. As we have already noted, legal complications are increasing. A company must be wary of charges of discrimination based on race, religion, or sex. Now, even the use of normal retirement *age* may be illegal. Instead, clear evidence of inadequate performance is necessary to remove an executive who wishes to stay in the job.

This need for clear evidence will force companies to maintain more elaborate, explicit (and expensive) performance evaluations—and evaluation of future usefulness. Instead of merely treating old Bill kindly until he finally reaches compulsory retirement age, records which he sees will have to spell out bluntly how obsolete he has become.

These evaluations should have a future focus, covering among other things:

1. ability to contribute to projected new activities of the company—for example, willingness to move, capacity to learn new technology or language, health and energy
2. commitment to the company versus outside interests and tendency to take jobs with competitors
3. effectiveness in securing cooperation of people in other departments and outside the company

Unless senior managers have the courage to make unpleasant personnel decisions, and also develop the tools which enable them to act wisely, their company can become choked with mediocre performers.

DEVELOPMENT OF EXECUTIVE TALENT

Executive training cannot be accomplished well *en masse.* As already noted, executive training deals with a relatively few individuals, each of whom is typically in a different stage of development and is preparing for a different job. Consequently, executive training should be approached on an individual basis.

Plans Center on Individuals

The planning for executive progression, already described, points to the area where each individual needs further development. Any gap between the specifications for a position and the abilities already possessed by the candidate should receive attention in the development plan. Likewise, if a person's performance on the present job does not measure up to what is desired, these weaknesses should be corrected.

One company asks the questions in designing a development program for each executive.[2]

1. WHAT IS THE PERSON? What are the candidate's executive qualifications, strengths, and weaknesses?
2. WHAT MAY THE PERSON BECOME? What are the candidate's possibilities and growth potential?
3. WHAT DOES THE PERSON NEED TO GET THERE? What experience does the candidate still need for the position aspired to?
4. WHAT PLANNED COURSE OF ACTION SHOULD BE TAKEN? What action is needed to fill the gaps in the candidate's experience?

One aspect of individual development plans deserves emphasis. Most of the initiative and the work must come from the individuals themselves. To be sure, the company has a vital stake in the matter and typically does a number of things to assist in the process. Nevertheless, good executives cannot be developed unless the people do a large share of the work. Since in this chapter we are concerned with company action, our discussion necessarily focuses on what managers can do to guide and aid the process.

Training on the Job

By far the most important and lasting training an executive receives is on-the-job experience. In all types of work, there is no adequate substitute for actually doing the operation; this applies to executive planning, direction, and control fully as much as it does to selling or operating a machine.

Supervisors and other executives close to operations can make work experience much more valuable if they will *coach* the people being trained. Just as athletic coaches make suggestions, watch performance, point out weaknesses, and encourage athletes to do better, so may executives help their subordinates to learn on the job. Good coaches need to understand the emotional as well as the

---

[2]Formulated by George B. Corless, Exxon Corporation.

intellectual makeup of their proteges and to use discretion in the time and the manner in which they make suggestions. They need to cultivate mutual respect and a desire for improvement. Conceived in this manner, the combination of work experience plus coaching can become a powerful tool for executive development.

When an individual is a candidate for the position of an immediate boss, the *understudy* method may be employed. The subordinate takes every available opportunity to think through what action he or she would take if given responsibility and put in the boss's situation. The senior, in turn, welcomes suggestions and wherever practical, permits the understudy to participate in action or even carry out particular projects on his or her own responsibility.

Often an executive cannot get all the needed training on a single job. For example, in preparing for the position of sales manager, the person may spend several years as a sales representative, two or three years in the sales promotion division, five years as a branch manager, and at least three or four years as an assistant sales manager. Many companies make a regular practice of such *job rotation* for purposes of executive training. The staffing plans described previously may provide for transfers that do not immediately put the best person available in each vacancy; instead they use some of these vacancies as training spots for individuals who are thought to have high executive potentials.

Job rotation for executive development normally assumes that a person will fill a given position for a few years and will show the ability to handle that job well before being moved on to the next position.

Training off the Job

A variety of activities are useful supplements to training on the job. The following list, while by no means complete, indicates some of the possibilities.

Committees. Committees are rarely established for the sole purpose of training. Nevertheless, they often provide a fine opportunity to sense the viewpoints of other departments and to become acquainted with problems outside the normal scope of one's position. Consequently, people may be assigned to committees partly for the training they will get from participation.

Company Conferences and Courses. When a company undertakes a new activity or a new approach to some function, such as computer programming or management-by-results, conferences or perhaps even a whole course on that subject may be desirable. The difficulty of finding a subject and a time when enough executives can attend such courses places a definite limit on how far this type of training can be carried.

Industry Contacts. Literally thousands of trade associations hold meetings amd make studies on various problems relating to their particular industries. Work with such trade associations, or with professional associations, provides a range of new ideas and an opportunity to explore problems with persons who are not indoctrinated with the same company approach. Trips to other offices or plants often have the same broadening effect.

University Courses. Universities are giving increasing attention to executive education and often provide a variety of courses on business subjects. Many companies encourage their executives to take courses in areas where they have limited background. Also, several universities are offering intensive four- to twelve-week courses in top-management problems; these are particularly valuable for persons who are moving from departmental positions to jobs demanding wider perspective.

Individual Reading. Few executives have the time or the energy, after a busy day, to study long and difficult books. They often gain much information, however, from the regular reading of trade periodicals and professional journals. Also, if they are assigned a special project, they may have to do considerable outside reading.

Adaptation of off-the-job training to individual needs is particularly important because the executive has only limited time to devote to such purposes. The executive has a major job to perform and, in trying to get the maximum benefit from on-the-job training, does not want to slight this major assignment. Consequently, the off-the-job training should have real significance for the individual to justify the additional effort it entails.

EXECUTIVE COMPENSATION

Plans for executive selection, promotion, and development will lead to limited success unless the executives believe that their compensation is reasonable. To round out the picture, then, we need to take a brief look at such issues as base salaries and pensions, executive bonuses, stock options, and nonfinancial compensation for executives.

Base Salaries and Pensions

Basically, setting salaries for executives may be approached in the same way as pay for lower-level employees.

1. The different positions are compared with one another in order to establish a reasonable internal alignment. Usually salary grades are not necessary, but the several positions should be at least ranked and some means used to determine the approximate spread between the different positions.
2. Executive salaries are related to outside compensation. This is difficult, because comparable jobs in different companies are hard to find. Usually it is possible, however, to set the president's salary in some reasonable relationship to companies of similar size in the same industry. Also, salaries of junior executives frequently tie into, or overlap, those established under the employees' salary

administration plan. With both ends of the "salary curve" established, a general curve for the entire group can be drawn.

3. Allowances for individual differences are made by establishing a range from starting salary to maximum for each position.

This approach to executive salaries is far from exact. The relative importance of positions is hard to measure and is likely to be colored by the efficiency or the inefficiency of the particular incumbent. Nevertheless, a decision as to salary has to be made, and this approach is as fair as anything yet devised.

Because of the uncertainty in evaluating individual positions, and also because there can be a wide difference in the individual performance of persons holding similar positions, a wide salary range, often with a 50 percent spread from the miniumum to the maximum, for a given job is customary. For example, it might be determined that the president should be paid somewhere between $100,000 and $150,000 per year, whereas the sales manager should be paid between $60,000 and $90,000 per year. This still leaves room for considerable judgment regarding the specific salaries, but there are at least some general guides within which to work.

Executive Bonuses

Many companies use bonuses for their executives. In fact, one recent study shows that approximately 50 percent of all companies use this method of compensation in one form or another. Bonuses enable the company to vary executive compensation in good and bad times, and they serve as an important incentive.

The use of a bonus plan is illustrated by a lumbering concern that recently received stockholder approval for an executive bonus fund. A 6 percent return on the total stockholder investment is first set aside from the net profit; then 20 percent of any profit in excess of this amount is put into the executive bonus fund. The division of the fund among the several executives is determined by the board of directors. Actually, percentage shares amounting to approximately three-fourths of the total fund are assigned at the beginning of the year, at the same time that base pay for the executives is set. The remainder of the fund is kept in a "kitty" and is used to reward special performance during the year.

Variations on this general pattern can be made with respect to the size of the total fund and also to the division of the fund among the several executives. But the general idea of a fund somehow related to profits is fairly common practice. Of course, many special bonus arrangements are designed to meet particular situations. For example, a sales manager may receive a bonus on total sales volume. Whenever such special arrangements are made, care must be taken to make sure the executive works as a member of the total management team, even though the bonus is determined by only one or two factors.

When executives have an opportunity to earn a large bonus, the size of their base salaries is usually cut. In general, the base salary plus the average bonus that will be earned over a period of years should about equal the total amount that would have been paid a comparable executive earning salary alone.

Stock Options

Executives may be given an opportunity to buy stock in their company for several reasons. Some people believe that stock ownership will significantly increase an executive's interest in company welfare. In other cases, the company may not be able to pay executives a cash salary and bonus large enough to retain their services, and some form of stock bonus or stock option is used to supplement the cash compensation. By no means the least important reason for using stock options and similar schemes is an attempt to help executives meet their personal income tax problems.

Since income taxes rise sharply as the amount of the annual income increases, many executives find that a large portion of their bonus has to be paid to Uncle Sam. Consequently, executives would prefer to have their income relatively stable, rather than large in some years and small in others. Even better, they would like some arrangement to have their financial returns from the company classified as a capital gain on which the income tax is substantially less than on current income. Stock option plans, which give an employee the privilege of purchasing the company stock at some stipulated figure, may help an executive meet these personal income tax problems.

The laws and rulings on such matters are highly technical, but in general they provide that if executives buy stock below the current market value, they have to consider the difference between their purchase price and the market value as current income. Under special circumstances, they may be given an option to buy stock at close to the market price prevailing when the option is granted, then wait for the price rise before exercising the option, and still count their profit as capital gains. If executives hold their stock over a period of years and the market value rises in the meantime, they can, of course, sell the stock at the higher price and treat the rise in value as a capital gain. In general, then, stock options do not enable executives to avoid personal income tax. They may, however, give executives more flexibility in adjusting the time when the income is considered to be earned. Also, within limits, the income from a stock option may be treated as a capital gain.

Nonfinancial Compensation

In thinking about executive compensation, we should recognize that virtually all managers are motivated by nonfinancial considerations as well as the cash payment for their services. In fact, after salaries enable them to live comfortably, the nonfinancial factors become increasingly important. For example, some persons respond to the urge for power, others desire social prestige, and some will sacrifice additional income for security. Improving the company's position in its industry or otherwise "winning the game" is often a strong spur, and the desire to create something and to render social service is a more common motive than is generally realized.

The ability of a company to provide such nonfinancial compensations usually is not a matter of deliberate decision by the board of directors; nevertheless, they are vital forces in enabling the company to attract and retain competent executives, and they should be recognized when decisions are being made regarding financial compensation.

SUMMARY

An able corps of executives is crucial for the execution of any strategy. The selection and the development of executive talent often is given inadequate attention, however, because problems are not diagnosed far enough in advance and because personal relationships may make an administrator reluctant to take the necessary action.

A systematic approach to building the needed corps of executives includes: (1) anticipating executive requirements through advance organization planning and forecasts of the positions to be filled along with specifications for persons needed to fill them; (2) taking an inventory of executive talent available within a company; (3) developing tentative plans for using the available talent to fill the anticipated positions and noting needs for further training or additions; (4) helping individuals meet their current and planned future responsibilities through on-the-job and off-the-job training; and (5) providing compensation that will attract the quality of executives required and keep their morale high.

Larger companies may find printed forms and standarized procedures helpful, whereas the central managers in smaller firms may use the same method of attack with no formal paper work. In fact, there is always danger that the use of forms will become a substitute, rather than an aid, for the careful thought that development of good executive personnel demands.

Flexibility in the use of this systematic approach is necessary to adapt it to individuals. Executive development is always a personalized matter, and no standard approach will fit all situations exactly. Application to a particular group of persons, or to a single department within a company, calls for ingenuity, especially in preparation for major changes.

QUESTIONS FOR CLASS DISCUSSION

1. Most executive compensation plans are based on either past performance or short-run (annual) improvements. Strategy, however, focuses on longer term moves, the

results of which may not show up for five to ten years or even longer. How can executive incentive plans be geared, at least in part, to strategy formulation and execution?

2. An increasing number of women are embarking on lifetime careers in business with job aspirations just as high as their male counterparts. And we are seeing more and more marriages of two career-oriented people. These dual career families complicate executive development, especially in the movement of individuals to new locations as a step in career advancement. Such a move may interfere with the career of the spouse. What can companies do to lower this strain and yet make optimum use of their executive talent? If the couple must make a choice, whose career should be interrupted or constrained?

3. "Our policy is to search out retirees or semiretirees whom we think can help the bank," said the personnel director, a vice-president of a growing and successful medium-sized bank in a very large urban area. "Earnings last year were excellent because net income increased substantially, because expense was controlled rigidly, and because effective income tax rates decreased. Other operating expense (which includes all personnel costs) as a percentage of average total resources decreased to 2.93 percent and one reason is that retirees are more interested in the work than in high pay so they earn about the minimum for each job category. Another measure of efficiency in which we take great pride is total resources per staff member which was $1.49 million at the year end." Do you think that hiring older people who are nearing the end of their working life leads to efficiency? Explain.

4. How do executive personnel problems and the practical ways of dealing with such problems differ in Stage I, Stage II, Stage III, and Stage IV companies (described in Chapter 17)?

5. The typical stock option plan is designed for companies whose stock is listed on some stock exchange; this listing helps establish a known market value and also adds to the liquidity (salability) of the stock. Small companies and not-for-profit organizations don't fit into this pattern. (a) What can a small firm do to provide its managers with an incentive something like a stock option plan? (b) Is any comparable incentive available for not-for-profit organizations?

6. Most business forecasters accept the premise that the U.S. economic growth rate is slowing down—that we have become a mature economy. One implication of that forecast is fewer new management jobs and slower promotions. Nevertheless, more people are graduating from business school, most of them with high job aspirations (encouraged by studying books like this one!). One consequence of these two developments, assuming that they occur as predicted, will be more frustrated lower-level managers who aren't being promoted as fast as they wish. What can a company do, if anything, in its executive development activities to relieve this frustration?

7. Multinational corporations increasingly are using local citizens of a country in managerial positions. And, several developing countries have laws requiring the use of

their citizens in managerial positions of subsidiaries located in their country. (a) Do you think this strong emphasis on the use of local "nationals" is desirable? Explain the pros and cons. (b) If foreigners are permitted to hold only one or two positions should the multinational parent fill with outsiders? (c) If a foreigner is placed in a subsidiary, should he or she be paid the same salary that a "national" would receive in that position? (d) From what countries should a multinational corporation recruit its regional and headquarters managers? How should such managers gain adequate understanding of conditions in the several countries that they supervise?

8. (a) When should executives be brought in from other companies? (b) How can this be done with the least disruption to the morale of individuals already working for the company? (c) Does such action indicate a failure on someone's part in executive development duties? (d) How does the concept of a dynamic strategy, emphasized earlier in this book, relate to the preceding questions?

9. If a diversified corporation decides to use a particular division as a cash-cow (see Chapter 14), what can it do to retain and motivate highly competent executives?

10. In considering the next year's compensation package for the five top executives of Muller Tool and Hardware Company, the compensation committee of the board of directors had before it a recommendation from the company's auditors that the salary of Robert Wallace, president, be increased by 21 percent to $430,000 and that the salaries of four vice-presidents be raised by 28 percent "to bring them into line with the average salaries in comparable firms." Mr. Wallace had been chairman and chief executive officer of this once family-controlled company for the past year and was credited by the board with keeping the company's decline in sales to only 5 percent and the decline in profits to 10 percent during a year of general recession in which there had been an average drop in sales for capital-equipment suppliers of about 15 percent. Control by the Muller family had passed over to all stockholders two years before when large primary and secondary stock offerings had been successful. Members of the compensation committee and their years of service with the board were: Herbert Muller (15 years, now retired, and former president); Jean Weber (6 months, dean of a local school of business); Marvin Fortman (4 years, legal counsel); Thomas Moses (2 years, investment banker); and William Horne (4 years, retired executive of a large nonelectrical machinery company). The auditors recommended no changes in stock-option plans, in profit-sharing bonuses, or in an insurance, health, and recreation package available to the executives. Sales of the company had shown an average yearly increase of about 4 percent for the past twenty years. The ratio of net profits to sales for the past year was 3 percent and the return on equity was 8 percent. Mr. Muller and Mr. Horne were primarily responsible for attracting Mr. Wallace to the company and for asking the auditors to study the issue of executive compensation. Do the stockholders' interests appear primary to you in this affair? Is an accounting firm the appropriate place to seek advice on compensation of an executive for the performance of his duties? Is "the average salary in a comparable firm" a suitable norm? Are the directors mentioned suitable, by virtue of their positions, to constitute the compensation committee?

CASE 19
Hoosier Bank and Trust Company

personell problem

In August of 1984, Charles Sims, personnel vice-president, went into Lew Winters' office to complain about the high turnover in the Mortgage Loan Division. "I thought we had finally solved our personnel problem in that division when we still had Dan Davis and Ed Smith a year after they were hired. After firing Davis two weeks ago and finding out today that Ed plans to take another job, I am back where I started from eighteen months ago." Mr. Winters looked up from his work, sneered, and declared, "As long as we have the 'ol man's nephew running that division, the situation will never improve. How in hell does he expect to run this bank when the old man hands over the reins if he can't even keep one division operating smoothly?"

Background

description for reasons for growth

Hoosier Bank and Trust is a medium-sized, full-service bank in Indiana. In recent years, Hoosier Bank and Trust Company, HBTC for short, has experienced a rapid growth in assets. Part of this growth has resulted from an increase in the tri-county population. Forty percent of HBTC's business comes from two adjacent counties, so bank officers consider the tri-county area as their territory. Between 1972 and 1982, the population of the tri-county area grew from 310,000 to over 430,000. Continuing industrialization is expected to result in a 5–10 percent annual increase in population for the next five years.

population increases 5 to 10%

A second force behind HBTC's growth was the adoption of more aggressive strategies. In the past, HBTC had avoided the use of branch locations. It was estimated that a branch location would require a capital outlay of between $100,00 and $200,000, depending on the cost of the land. In addition, John Curry, chairman of the board, did not like the idea of having three or four employees running an HBTC branch with no senior officers around to supervise. Hoosier's first and, until recently, only branch was created when HBTC moved into a newly constructed main office in 1975 and the old main office was retained as a branch.

1st branch

During 1982, Irwin Spears was able to convince his uncle that if HBTC did not provide branches for its customers, it would eventually lose customers to its competition. HBTC opened its second branch in early 1983 in the fashionable western end of the county. Since its opening, the branch has been very successful at attracting new customers.

2nd branch

During 1983, Mr. Spears developed a master plan for branch development which called for the addition of two new branches each year for the next five years. Two branches, which are to open next year, are presently under construction. One is in each of the adjacent counties. Table 1 compares the assets of banks and savings and loans with the number of branches each has. As can be seen, competing banks are well established in the tri-county area.

TABLE 1.
ASSETS OF TRI-COUNTY BANKS AND SAVINGS & LOANS AND NUMBER OF OFFICES 12/31/83
(ten largest institutions in millions)

Institution	Total Assets 12/31/81	12/31/82	12/31/83	Number Offices 12/31/83
American Bank and Trust	$229	$251	$286	7
Citizens Trust Bank	227	257	295	5
Farmers Federal Savings and Loan	126	137	150	1
First National Bank	594	631	716	12
First Federal Savings and Loan	139	193	262	13
Hoosier Bank and Trust Company	145	154	170	3
Merchants and Investors Bank	118	129	136	4
Peoples State Bank	74	89	86	2
Pioneer Federal Savings & Loan	87	102	116	3
Second National Bank	581	615	654	10

growth due to TV adv.

A second newly adopted strategy that has contributed to HBTC's growth is the use of TV as an advertising medium. In the past, HBTC advertised exclusively in the financial section of the *News-Reporter*, a regional newspaper. These ads emphasized to the depositor that he or she could always depend on HBTC because it offered a wide range of banking opportunities (Passbook Saving, Money Market CD's, Now Accounts, and Super-Now Accounts, and others). Mr. Curry considered TV advertising a waste of money.

With the help of Richard Holland, HBTC's President, Mr. Spears prepared a very persuasive presentation early in 1983 that convinced Mr. Curry and the board of directors to try a TV campaign on a trial basis. Mr. Spears, working with HBTC's advertising agency, then developed a campaign for the fall of 1983. After reviewing the campaign's success, Mr. Curry agreed to adopt TV as HBTC's principal advertising media.

John Curry

Hoosier Bank and Trust is managed by John Curry, chairman of the board of directors. It is said that a Curry has been affiliated with Hoosier Bank and

Trust ever since it was established in 1899. Mr. Curry is a respected member of the financial community, and he personally makes all of the commercial loans of the bank. He is regarded by the officers of HBTC as an expert banker.

However, he is an autocratic individual. He believes there are two ways of doing things: his way and the wrong way. If he believes in a new idea, it is implemented. If he does not like an idea, it is abandoned.

One case where his autocracy cost the bank a large sum of money was in the purchase of data processing services. In 1982, HBTC had to decide whether to modernize its existing data processing system or buy computer services from an outside source. After listening to a sales presentation by representatives of the Time Share Corp., Mr. Curry decided to rent time from TSC. No outside experts were consulted to determine what HBTC's needs actually were or whether TSC could handle these needs. Several of the bank's officers expressed skepticism of TSC's promises, but they were ignored.

As it turned out, the Time Share Corp. did not fulfill its promises. Only half of HBTC's needs were handled by the TSC and the service was very poor. As a result, HBTC finds itself paying for the use of two data processing systems. HBTC is now making plans to modernize its own system.

In addition to making all of the major decisions, Mr. Curry also believes in maintaining absolute control over the board of directors. Mr. Curry handpicks the board in order to guarantee his control over the bank. The average age of the board is 67. All of the directors are respected businesspeople in the county, most of whom have retired from full-time positions at firms in the area. The board meets once a month.

A major complaint by the loan officers is the number of loans that have to be taken to the board for approval. The guidelines placed on the loan committee are very tight and inflexible. Any loans that do not meet the guidelines have to be approved by the board. This situation has required each loan officer, during peak loan demand, to prepare fifteen to twenty loans for the board.

Another example of the board's inflexibility is in purchasing. Mr. Sims, who is in charge of purchasing, has to get the board's approval before spending over $150 for any nonroutine item.

Mr. Holland

Mr. Holland holds the title of president and supervises daily operations of the bank. In the past, this did not require a great deal of responsibility. As Mr. Curry nears retirement, however, more of the actual decision-making is being done by Mr. Holland. Mr. Curry plans to retire on January 1, 1987, at the age of 70.

Mr. Holland has a degree in Agriculture from Purdue University. He worked as a branch manager for another bank for ten years, prior to joining HBTC in 1975. Mr. Holland began his career at HBTC as a mortgage loan officer. He was made a vice-president in 1978 and was promoted to executive vice-president in 1981. In 1983, when Mr. Curry assumed the titles of chairman of the board and chief executive officer, Mr. Holland was made president.

Mr. Holland's personality is the opposite of Mr. Curry's. Mr. Holland is very friendly with everyone and never loses his temper with employees. He is open-minded and can be persuaded to adopt new methods if their worth is substantiated by convincing data. He has been instrumental in carrying the banner of change in the board of director's meetings. Mr. Holland and Mr. Curry are the only officers of HBTC who are members of the board.

Mr. Holland rose through the ranks of HBTC largely as a result of his personality. He has worked closely with Mr. Curry and knows when to keep quiet on an issue.

Mr. Holland recognizes that Mr. Curry has been grooming his nephew to eventually assume the leadership of HBTC. This does not bother Mr. Holland, however, because he will be ready to retire in four years. Mr. Holland does not feel Mr. Spears will have enough experience to take control before then.

The worst situation Mr. Holland has handled in his tenure as president was the dismissal of Mr. Breedlove. Mr. Breedlove was an assistant vice-president and had worked at HBTC for fifteen years in the mortgage lending area. A crotchety yet amiable man, he was fifty-seven years old when he was terminated. It disturbed Mr. Holland a great deal to dismiss a man he had worked with when he was a mortgage loan officer.

The Mortgage Loan Division

The Mortgage Loan Division, which is typical of HBTC, lends money that is brought in primarily by the Savings Division. Each loan officer is responsible for a loan from the time of application until it is closed and a permanent file is made.

The Mortgage Loan Division is headed by Mr. Spears. He has a B.A. from Butler University and an MBA from Indiana State University. After graduation, he served two years in the Peace Corps before joining HBTC in 1981. He began his career at HBTC working in a number of different departments before becoming a loan officer in the Mortgage Loan Division.

Soon after Mr. Spears was assigned to the Mortgage Loan Division, conflicts between him and the other loan officers developed. The other loan officers resented the fact that Mr. Spears sometimes left work early to play golf or would take extra long lunch hours with friends at the Riverview Country Club. Mr. Holland justified Mr. Spears' activities to the other loan officers by pointing out that he worked late several nights a week.

In January of 1983, Mr. Spears was made vice-president in charge of the Loan Division. One of his first actions after his promotion was the dismissal of a loan officer. Prior to his dismissal, the loan officer had indicated that he could not make ends meet with the salary he was receiving. Two months after that dismissal, Mr. Spears was the driving force behind the termination of Mr. Breedlove. Mr. Breedlove was assistant vice-president in charge of Mortgage Lending prior to Mr. Spears' promotion. After his promotion, Mr. Spears had indicated to Mr. Holland that he could not gain complete control over the Loan Division unless Mr. Breedlove was removed.

During the fall of 1983, Mr. Spears set out to develop an efficient Mortgage Loan Division for the 1984 lending season, especially for the normal seasonal peak in spring and summer. A new phone system was installed that allowed the secretaries to answer the phones of the loan officers. Two new secretaries were hired so that each loan officer would have his own secretary. Electronic calculators were purchased for the loan officers to avoid the time of doing calculations by hand. Plans were also made to bring a branch manager and management trainees into the Division during peak periods to help out the two new loan officers. Underwriting standards were raised; to avoid risky loans on low-quality housing, a house had to sell for at least $25,000 and be located outside a declining neighborhood before it would qualify for a loan.

In addition to these changes in the Mortgage Loan Division's operations, Mr. Spears attempted to improve HBTC's image among the realtors and builders in the area. He encouraged the bank's appraisal firm to be more generous and set values on houses at their selling prices, and he started a monthly newsletter which informed realtors and builders about mortgage interest rates and similar matters. The response from the builders and realtors was very favorable.

The addition in August of the two new loan officers helped improve the efficiency of the Mortgage Loan Division. Both Mr. Davis and Mr. Smith were young and aggressive individuals. Mr. Davis had completed two years of college and worked at a small savings and loan in Chicago for three years prior to joining HBTC. Mr. Smith, on the other hand, was a spring 1983 graduate of the Ohio State University with a major in Finance and did not have any previous business experience. Both individuals were hard workers and took pride in doing their best.

Mr. Spears adheres to the philosophy that competition increases productivity. With this in mind, he established two teams made up of a loan officer and secretary. Data was kept on each team's performance and a total of the loans closed by each loan officer was announced at the end of the month.

The team system worked out better than had been expected. During May of 1984, Mr. Smith and Mr. Davis closed $48 million of loans and took a total of 370 loan applications. This was an alltime record for the division and Mr. Spears was very satisfied.

The competition had its price, however. Anxious to impress bank officers, both Mr. Davis and Mr. Smith worked 70 to 80 hours a week during June (without extra compensation). In a sample check, Mr. Spears discovered that Mr. Davis had made serious errors in three of ten loans that he closed. Also, Mr. Sims reported that Mr. Davis was turning off his phone at the switchboard; as a

result, Mr. Smith had to bear the brunt of incoming calls. Mr. Smith was espe- *comp. created havoc*
cially upset when he discovered that Mr. Davis had instructed the company
which examined land titles to process his (Davis') titles first. This maneuver,
which Mr. Smith reported to Mr. Sims, enabled Mr. Davis to close more loans
than Mr. Smith during May.

To overcome these difficulties and to provide for further growth, Mr.
Spears hired another loan officer in July. He also replaced two secretaries for not- *Davis term. Smith resigned*
performing their duties. The lowering of workloads was only temporary, how-
ever. Mr. Davis was terminated in August, after he had argued with Mr. Spears
over the quality of his work. Two weeks later, Mr. Smith resigned to take a job
with a larger bank in Indianapolis.

Outside of the turnover problem in the Mortgage Loan Division, Mr.
Spears had compiled an impressive track record during his short tenure at
HBTC. As noted above, he had developed a program to establish branches and
was instrumental in establishing more effective advertising campaigns.

Treasurer's Division

The Treasurer's Division is headed by Lew Winters, a 1962 graduate of the
University of West Virginia. Prior to joining HBTC in 1975, Mr. Winters
worked as a C.P.A. for one of the Big Eight accounting firms. Mr. Winters occupies the position of vice-president and treasurer of HBTC and is responsible for
the accounting function and cash planning in the bank. As treasurer, he handles
the bank's investments in government securities.

The Accounting Division at HBTC is very efficient. Mr. Winters trains people in his deaprtment to do two or three different jobs to avoid any disruption if
an employee decides to quit. In the last two years the Accounting Division has
lost only one employee.

The employees in the Accounting Division are very loyal to Mr. Winters.
He had also developed good relationships with Mr. Davis and Mr. Smith. Outside of the Accounting Division, Mr. Winters is considered to be short-tem-
pered. He is not above swearing at employees who make mistakes, and he insists *disliked because he is "watchdog"*
that all tellers stay at the bank until they balance their cash—even though this
may require working four hours beyond normal closing time. Mr. Winters is disliked by a large number of employees in the other divisions, largely because Mr.
Winters' position is the "watchdog" for the bank.

During 1979, Mr. Winters was concerned about the liquidity position of
HBTC and discussed his concerns with Mr. Curry. However, Mr. Curry ignored
the suggestion, and he continued to allow the Mortgage Loan Division to operate at full capacity. A few months later the outside bank examiners strongly recommended that HBTC strictly curtail its loan activity until its liquidity
improved. Mr. Winters was very disturbed that the situation had reached the
point where bank examiners were dictating to HBTC what they should do.

Personnel Division

Mr. Sims is vice-president in charge of the Personnel Division. He joined HBTC in 1974 following his graduation from Western Michigan University where he majored in psychology. Mr. Sims is a dedicated employee who is very conscientious about doing a good job.

Mr. Sims is responsible for hiring new employees and terminating those who do not work out. He is also responsible for resolving all personnel problems that arise in the bank, except for those that occur in the Mortgage Loan Division. Mr. Spears does not feel he can be an effective manager unless he has complete control over the employees under him.

This situation has resulted in conflicts between Mr. Sims and Mr. Spears. Mr. Spears believes that if an employee is not doing a good job, he or she should be terminated and a new employee hired. Mr. Sims, on the other hand, believes it is necessary to work with the employee in an effort to resolve the problem. Mr. Sims feels termination should be used only when all other steps fail.

One of HBTC's long-standing personnel policies is to start new employees off at relatively low salary—actually between 10 and 15 percent lower than salaries at other financial institutions in the tri-county area. Mr. Curry is proud that HBTC has been able to maintain proportionately lower salary expenses than other banks in the area.

Mr. Sims is pleased with HBTC's accomplishments in the area of equal opportunity employment and advancement of women. The assistant savings division officer, a branch manager, and two assistant branch managers are women. All four of these employees started their careers as tellers and worked their way up. HBTC has a higher percentage of women in middle management positions than any other bank in the area.

Mr. Sims also takes pride in two personnel development programs which he instituted. Under the bank's employee education program, HBTC will pay tuition for any employee who enrolls in and completes courses sponsored by The American Institute of Banking. A total of twenty employees, thirty percent of HBTC's labor force, participated in this program during the last five years. The second program Mr. Sims developed is a management training program in which trainees are rotated through the different divisions to give them a broad exposure to HBTC's various operations. In the future, he hopes new loan officers and branch managers will be chosen from the individuals who have completed this program.

Savings Division

David Burris, who is in charge of the Savings Division, has been with HBTC since he graduated from Ohio State University in 1960. Mr. Burris has worked in a variety of positions and has just recently been placed in charge of the Savings Division. He is quiet and does not lose his temper very often. These *quiet* qualities are essential to a good Savings Officer who is in constant contact with the public and has to resolve conflicts between what the customer wants and what HBTC can give.

Mr. Burris, in conjunction with Mr. Holland and Mr. Spears, established two new programs in 1983 which have been quite successful. One is a save-by-mail plan in which HBTC pays postage both ways for the customers. This feature is attractive to savers in rural areas who are not able to obtain an equally high return on their savings at an institution in their locality.

The second innovative program is a "dial-a-check" savings plan. Under this plan, a customer can authorize a transfer from his or her savings account to a checking account by phone. This enables customers to avoid large balances in a noninterest-bearing checking account.

Mr. Burris is looking forward to the opening of new branches. Savings that *new branch* come in through branch locations have a lower interest cost than savings enter- *expansion* ing through the main office—because there is a greater proportion of low-inter- *means lower* est passbook accounts at a branch. The main office has a much larger propor- *int. rates* tion of savings certificates that call for a higher interest rate.

Loan and Trust Servicing Division

The Servicing Division is run by Wally Saunders. Mr. Saunders completed a two-year course in computer programming at United Electronics Institute before joining HBTC in 1978. He was promoted into his present position in 1981 after spending three years in Data Processing. Mr. Saunders' division is responsible for loans after they are closed and a file on each one has been assembled. This involves paying property tax bills, adjusting escrow accounts, sending out bills to customers, and the like. The Servicing Division also performs the routine administration of Trust accounts. The establishment of trusts is handled by an outside attorney who is on a retainer by HBTC for this type of business. Mr. Holland assists in dealing with trust customers when necessary.

The operations of the Servicing Division usually proceed quite smoothly. In the summer of 1984, however, when Mr. Saunders was preparing to pay the property tax bills, he discovered his department did not have information on over 200 mortgage loans. Upon investigation, he found that the Mortgage Loan Division had been closing loans and then failing to prepare a file. After talking to Mr. Curry about the problems this practice created for Servicing, Mr. Curry assigned several people to assembling files.

The only other disruptions that occurred in this division during the year *turnover* were the departures of three employees. At the end of July, three of the seven *problem* clerks were new. Of the clerks replaced, two of them had quit and the third was *high* fired. The majority of the clerks, tellers, and secretaries at HBTC are younger than twenty-five.

feels inferior to Spears

Mr. Saunders is happy with his position at HBTC. However, he does worry about his future since he is not a college graduate. He feels that Mr. Spears looks down on him because of this. Mr. Saunders knows that Mr. Spears and Mr. Holland would prefer to have college graduates in upper management positions. This preference is emphasized by the present group of three 1985 management trainees, all of whom are college graduates.

In Review

As HBTC enters the fall of 1984, Mr. Holland is contemplating what steps to take regarding the problems which cropped up over the summer. He also realizes that he has to look to 1985 and map out the needs of HBTC in the future. Among the key issues he recognizes must be addressed are:

1. The turnover problem, both at management level and among the staff employees.
2. How to deal with Irwin Spears who in some respects had made some very positive contributions but whose actions on other fronts had been disastrous.
3. The whole idea of growth. The additional branches which were planned over the next five years offer some exciting possibilities for HBTC, but he is not convinced the organization is ready for this expansion.

Question

What advice would you give Mr. Holland regarding these key issues?

[Handwritten notes:]

$\text{acid-test} = \frac{CA - INV}{CL}$

$\text{current} = CA/CL$

$\text{inventory t/o} = COGS/\text{ave. inv.}$

$\text{debt} = TD/TA$

$\text{debt-n.w} = TD/NW$

$\text{R. on Assets} = \text{net } PAT/TA$

$EPS = \frac{EARNINGS}{\# \text{ of shares out.}}$

$\text{GP margin} = \text{sales} - COGS/\text{sales}$

$\text{NP margin} = \text{net } PAT/\text{sales}$

$\text{A/R T/O} = \text{net sales}/\text{ave. rec. (net)}$

$\text{asset t/o} = \text{net sales}/\text{ave. total assets}$

$\text{PE ratio} = \text{mkt price of stock}/EPS$

$\text{Payout ratio} = \text{cash dv}/\text{net income}$

$\text{BV per share} = \text{c. stkdrs equity}/\text{out. shares}$

$\text{cash flow per share} = \frac{\text{income} + \text{noncash adj.}}{\text{out. shares}}$

$\text{RoR on assets} = n.i./\text{ave TA}$

$\text{RoR on c/stock equity} = \frac{n.i. - \text{pref dv.}}{\text{ave. c stock equity}}$

$BV = TA - TL = NW$

INTEGRATING CASES

Strategy & Organization Structure

QRS, INCORPORATED

Nature of Industry

QRS[1] is among the top twenty companies producing space-age equipment. Although much of its output is airborne military equipment, QRS also produces communication equipment for commercial satellites. The work involves complex, sophisticated designs; frontier technologies; and often uncertainty about both cost and performance.

Often an order calls only for a single expensive product, perhaps a tracking missile or a communication satellite. And for military items, a first contract usually covers only the design. When the design is finally approved by the customer (for example, NASA or the Air Force), several companies will bid for the construction contract. Subcontracting for major components is also common, so if a company misses out on a prime contract it still may obtain a piece of the business as a subcontractor.

The learning curve is important in this industry, and companies develop distinct abilities to design and make particular kinds of products or to utilize particular technologies. Such expertise helps a company obtain further contracts, if its strengths relate to popular technologies. The right expertise enables companies (1) to bid more wisely for new contracts, and (2) to efficiently produce designs or products. Moreover, (3) customers may give preference to companies that they think will be able to fulfill contract specifications. Because of the inherent uncertainties in frontier technologies, actual results often vary from plan—so much so that renegotiation as the work proceeds is not uncommon.

Companies that wish to enter a growing area may bid low or accept considerable risk so as to learn particular techniques. They hope that their newly acquired skill will help them obtain more profitable business in the future. Millions of dollars and even company survival may be involved in such maneuvers.

---

[1] Disguised name.

QRS Management Structure

Like other companies in the industry, QRS stresses a project form of management to deal with the business characteristics just described. Four features are crucial.

(1) Short-range planning focuses on projects. Because each new order is unique and large, it becomes a unit of planning, or a "project." Specific plans are made for the end results, the timing, the resources, and the costs for each project (like building a house). There are no continuing flows, as in a chemical plant, or regular repeating business, as in a school; annual accounting reports are merely snapshots taken to conform to conventional financial practice. Most QRS projects last from six months to four years, and cost from $500,000 to $50,000,000.

(2) The work necessary to carry out a contract is also organized around the project. A temporary unit of organization is established with its own managers, engineers, and other operating personnel; separate offices; budget allocations; reports and controls. This group works as a semi-independent team until the project is completed. QRS does maintain centralized production plants at Quincy, Reading, and Somerville, and other central services—but these act like subcontractors responding to the requests of various project managers.

(3) To maintain and enhance QRS's ability to take on new projects, a series of resource pools (departments) are maintained. These are the home bases for specialized personnel when they are not assigned as a member of a project team. Each such department (propulsion, electronics controls, mechanical structures, and the like) also develops and trains people in state-of-the-art concepts. Thus QRS has a "matrix" organization, as shown in Figure 1. Along one dimension are resource and service pools; on the second dimension are projects. The resource pools (departments) have long-run continuity, serving a succession of projects. The projects, however, are the operating arm—that's where the action is.

(4) Two types of coordinating activities are necessary. One is the allocation of technical people and other resources from the pools to the projects. In QRS, when the combined needs of the active projects exceeds the size of the pool (including trained people that can be hired quickly or, say, money that can be borrowed), a management committee advises the Executive Vice-President about which projects should get priority. The second and more troublesome coordination is the preparation of bids for new contracts. Just as in the execution of a project, inputs from a whole team of experts is needed. In the past at QRS, if the contract sought was similar to a project currently in operation, that project team usually prepared the bid with the aid of a financial assistant. Usually, however, bids were prepared by a team of experts representing the heads of the various departments. A separate bid-preparing team was created for each bid so that the members would be qualified to assess the specific technical requirements.

QRS operates with the usual sophisticated control techniques, including accounting by projects, manpower and production scheduling, PERT networks,

FIGURE 1.
QRS MANAGEMENT STRUCTURE

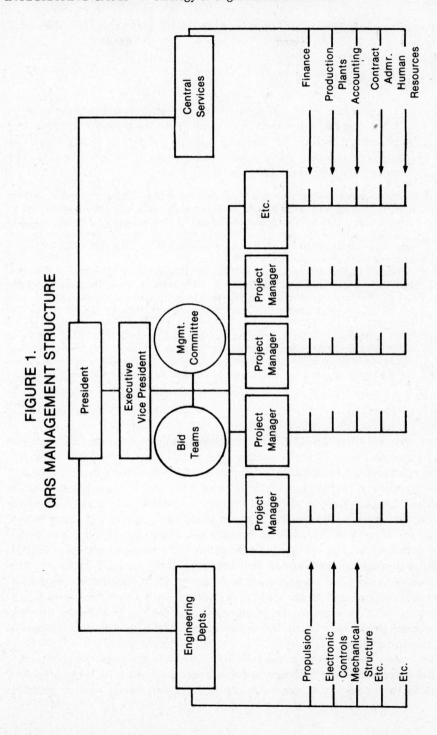

and monthly profit and loss and balance sheet estimates for the total corporation.

Operating Results

During the past ten years, QRS has been only an average performer in its industry. While it has had a few outstanding successes, in many areas it has had to accept subcontracts and try to catch up with the leaders in technology. The last three years, in particular, have yielded only mediocre financial results. The following factors have contributed to these results:

1. Project costs have often exceeded the bid price. These overruns usually occurred when engineers had to devote much more time than estimated to achieve the stipulated performance. As noted above, many tasks are new and uncertain, and the estimates proved to be overly optimistic. Less often, the bid was deliberately set low so as to win a contract in an area that QRS wished to upgrade its skills.
2. A related difficulty was failure to meet the delivery date objective (a common problem in this industry). Such delays often increase costs because of (a) the use of overtime to catch up, (b) interference with scheduled use of people and plants on other projects, and occasionally, (c) penalty payments in the contracts.
3. QRS appeared to have a declining number of areas where it could win large continuing contracts for further design work or actual production. These are the kinds of contracts where profit estimates are more reliable and companies have a better opportunity to recoup losses often suffered on pioneering work.

A Shift at the Top

The board of directors finally decided that a change in top management was called for. A year ago, B. H. Spaulding was brought in from a large computer company as the new president. R. B. Zimmer, a QRS director who strongly supported the change, explains, "We concluded that the old system had to be shaken up. And we wanted someone who would take a fresh, hard look at the traditional practices in the space equipment industry. Too many industry people assume that somehow the government will bail them out. I must admit that results under Spaulding don't show much immediate improvement, but it is probably too soon to see the results of his changes in the financial figures."

After reviewing the management structure at QRS, Spaulding concluded: "The matrix organization is probably necessary in this industry. However, it has been used as an excuse for a lack of discipline and clear responsibility. We will correct these weaknesses by adopting three simple, though basic, principles of profit accountability.

"First, we need *integrity in the bidding process.* In the past, the engineering department provided the technical estimates upon which bids were prepared, but it was the project managers—not the departments—who were responsible for fulfilling contracts which we won. The department could be optimistic while failure to perform was blamed on the project managers. To correct this in the future, we are going to have the (prospective) project manager commit to the cost and completion dates in each bid. The departments will continue to give their opinions of what can be done, but this will be treated as advice.

"Second, after a project manager has agreed to the provisions of a bid, then we will hold him or her to it if we win the contract. The manager has taken on a *commitment* and will be held accountable to make that happen. Of course, occasionally external events may lead to an overrun or (preferably) to renegotiation; as a normal matter, we must get rid of overruns.

"Third, in addition to dubious estimates, we have been making bids which we knew in advance would hurt our earnings. The potential profit ratio to sales was very low, and that almost always meant that the *return on investment* (ROI) was also low. You can't earn a necessary profit for the stockholder unless you start out that aim at the beginning. So following the practice of every well-run company that I know, we will set a minimum ROI hurdle-rate. All bids must at least meet that standard.

"If we build a reasonable ROI into our bids, and have the project managers committed to those numbers, the basis for improved profits will be laid."

Results of Spaulding's Changes

During the eight months since Spaulding's changes went into effect, the QRS boat has been rocking. Because of the long time-cycle of several major contracts, it is too early to measure the full impact. Nevertheless, several clues are available.

Overruns on new contracts have not yet appeared. Both the accounting office and the project managers continue to predict, on the basis of PERT feedback, that final results will be close to estimates. This is in line with Spaulding's aim.

The number of new contracts won has declined from the preceding year. This is more apparent in design contracts than in production contracts. Although many factors enter into winning a contract, in at least three important cases that QRS lost, QRS's bids were substantially higher than its competitors.

The drop in new contracts along with some cuts which Spaulding made in overhead expenses, created a nervousness and anxiety throughout QRS. The feeling is mixed, however, partly because the space equipment industry is always volatile and people in it have learned to live with uncertainty.

More specifically, the morale of project managers is generally good. They like the opportunity to make a commitment to what they consider are realistic goals. And they say privately that the clipping of department heads' wings was long overdue. Several project managers have expressed concern about losing design contracts. For instance, one said, "I like an occasional way-out design project. In production work, there is less room for imagination and much more of just running a tight ship. Besides, design contracts are the basis of our bread-and-butter five years hence."

The mood of department heads is somber. They don't like their lower influence on bidding and think the ROI standard is unworkable. One twenty-year veteran says, "Frankly, I'm looking for another job. Any project manager in his right mind will commit only to high-priced, low-risk bids. That means we will be confined to standard work. And the ROI rate will prevent us from buying our way into new developments. Spaulding ought to go back to an industry that he understands." Another department head is more patient, "I've been training engineers and project managers for a decade, and now it looks like I'll have to start training our new president."

Question

Assume that R. B. Zimmer asks for your advice on what should be done now in QRS, Incorporated. What would you tell him?

SOLARTRON ELECTRONICS[1]

With its new ownership, Solartron again faces questions of basic organization design. Its impressive history has created both strengths and weaknesses which must be weighed in making these design decisions.

Original Mission of the Company

The company was founded in southern England by two engineers, first to repair but soon to manufacture laboratory instruments. Oscilloscopes, amplifiers, and a variety of testing equipment were developed during this early period. Within two years, funds were badly needed for expansion. John Bolton then joined the firm, providing capital and becoming managing director. He continues to be the leading personality in overall management.

Bolton quickly observed that customers expected Solartron to carry inventory for prompt shipment and to grant credit. This tied up capital. And since the company sold only in the British Isles, inventory turnover tended to be slow.

Electronic systems, which were just becoming popular at that time, offered attractive diversification. By building systems only on customers' orders, inven-

---

[1]This case is based on three much longer cases prepared by Peter Brengel under the supervision of Professor Kenneth R. Andrews for l'Institut des Methodes de Direction de l'Enterprise (IMEDE), Lausanne, Switzerland.

tory turnover could be increased. Moreover, the potential growth was high, and opportunities for creative innovation were great. At this early stage, Solartron chose a strategy of focusing on electronic systems for customers who had relatively little sophistication about the equipment. Thus, Solartron would perform a service in system design as well as equipment manufacture.

From that time to the present, laboratory instruments have been the bread-and-butter line (the cash-cow), while electronic systems have provided the excitement and the high growth prospects.

Solartron works on several different kinds of systems. Among the more important are (1) radar simulators, used by several governments to train air pilots; (2) electronic cash registers, to be used by a chain of drug stores—Boots—to compile data for prompt sales analysis and for perpetual inventory control; (3) high-speed checkweighers, to be used in packaging of consumer products at speeds of up to 120 per minute; (4) cybernetic teaching machines, to be used to train punch-card operators to prepare cards accurately; (5) X-ray spectrometers, to be used to make quantitative analyses of metals and chemicals; (6) other state-of-the-art research done on contract for potential customers.

Organization To Achieve the Mission

Bolton had a conviction that the best organization to carry out Solartron's strategy would be a series of highly decentralized, democratic operating divisions. "To the greatest extent possible, managers at all levels will be given the opportunity to discharge their responsibilities as they think best within the broad framework of agreed-upon plans."

He conceived of each product line being run by a small company with a potential maximum of about 500 employees. This was to facilitate face-to-face communication and informal coordination. The organization was to be "flat" with a minimum of supervisory levels and very limited staff at headquarters. Bolton explained, "'Peaky' organizations and the 'great man' approach to management fail to reap the full potential of human ingenuity. Really, managerial needs, like vacuums, are abhorred in nature. They will ultimately be filled of their own accord—especially when competent people are readily at hand to fill them."

Actually eight separate operating companies were incorporated, with Solartron Electronics becoming a "Group." Consistent with this pattern, central research was set up as a separate company as was a production division. These latter two divisions could take on subcontracts from the product divisions, and they could (and did) accept contracts from outside the Group. The service units at headquarters were few and small—accounting, finance, personnel, and overseas sales.

With respect to people, a company document states, "Our emergent philosophy of life lays great stress not only on the importance of the individual as a person, but on the essential need to devise a 'permissive' system in which individual initiative is nurtured and encouraged to make its maximum possible contribution to the whole." Status was minimized. The lack of executive parking places and, the presence of a common lunchroom symbolized the shirt-sleeve atmosphere. However, the large number of companies created a lot of board of director positions (highly respected in British circles), so engineers at Solartron could move into prestigious jobs at a much lower age than was possible in most other companies.

The atmosphere was heady. A variety of interesting new systems to work on, welcome to innovative ideas, open discussion with anyone in the company, prestigious titles—all helped. Bolton generated enthusiasm, and he made speeches on modern management to distinguished groups. Solartron was recognized as a great place for a young engineer to work. And, in fact, Solartron attracted an unusually able group of scientifically educated people.

Company stock was made available to managers and key employees. This process continued so that Bolton held 40 percent, other executives 40 percent, and outsiders only 20 percent.

The results from a financial viewpoint were less impressive. During the years when overall employment grew from about 400 to 1,500, Solartron was barely able to break even. And this was possible only by capitalizing a lot of research and development expense. Several difficulties emerged in trying to make the organization design work effectively:

1. Bolton explained to stockholders that designing and building systems for a diverse group of unsophisiticated customers was turning out to be much more time-consuming and expensive than anticipated. Solartron has been trying to master a lot of different businesses all at the same time.
2. The volume of work in each product line has been too small and irregular to permit the product divisions to build up their own engineering and production capacity. Each division can afford specialists only for market research, general system design, and customer relations. When it receives an order, it must subcontract most of the work to the research division for detailed design and to the production division for actual fabrication. The consequence of (1) and (2) has been very high overhead for the volume of shipments.
3. With demand coming unpredictably from several product divisions, scheduling and coordination in the research and production divisions has been poor. Frequent design changes after work was started have made the situation worse. The results are slow deliveries, high costs, and very weak accountability.
4. The personnel attracted to Solartron lack production and profit orientation. And the internal procedures of the company (its deliberate informality) provide no controls to keep its high-flying engineers in line. In other words, Solartron failed to match its decentralized structure with informal and formal controls which are necessary to get work completed on time.
5. The instrument division maintained its market position during this period but it was handicapped by being treated in much the same way as the divisions focusing on new systems. The nature of its marketing and its production call for more conventional planning, organizing, and controlling.

Strategy Revision and its Consequences

During the growth phase, described above, Solartron developed an impressive public image and a variety of system-product lines in various stages of marketability. But the cash drain could not be sustained. The accumulated deficit, after eliminating capitalized R & D, was equivalent to about $2 million, and the net book value of stockholders' equity was cut to $1.25 million.

Three interrelated changes have been made: (1) emphasis is switched from seeking new system-products to making existing lines profitable; (2) the organization is centralized and streamlined; (3) overhead is sharply reduced. Figure 1 depicts these changes.

Operating activities are now in only two divisions, instruments and systems. The instrument division is virtually self-contained with its own engineering, production, and marketing—all located in a separate building. For systems, the old product line divisions have been disbanded. Now there are single, consolidated departments for R & D, production, and marketing. The two service units at headquarters are administration (accounting, finance, etc.) and personnel. Decisions for each division are made by a small group of department heads and corporate officers.

Bolton remarks, "In some respects, especially concerning our organization, we appear to have made a complete reversal, but I suppose that is all part of the process of organic growth. It appears to me that a period of decentralization of initiative and authority is necessarily followed by a period of centralization. Each phase brings its benefits and its counteracting problems."

The manager of the Instruments Division is pleased with the change in his setup. For the first time in about eight years he knows where he stands and is free to adjust all his operations to best suit the instrument business.

The new systems division is facing more problems of adjustment. These are morale problems with people who are no longer active "directors" of a company and with others who relished the atmosphere and the promise of the former structure. There is now reserved parking for executives. Some managers have resigned, but those remaining are an unusually talented group.

A longer run difficulty is that the functional departments within the Systems Division include no people with overall product responsibility. Product-line coordination—from the cultivation of a prospective customer to the delivery of a system tailored to the customer's needs—is thrust upon a busy group of senior executives.

The transition to the new organization is still in process. The hope, of course, is that the change can be made without losing too many of the past strengths. Thus far, most of the changes have been in formal organization. Revised planning and control procedures are still being worked out. Slowing that task is the fact that most of the young managers have little experience in a systematized operation.

FIGURE 1.
EARLY ORGANIZATION CONCEPT

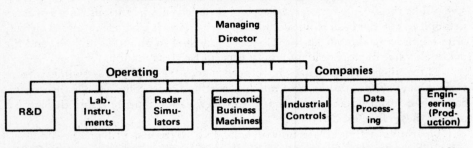

REVISED ORGANIZATION

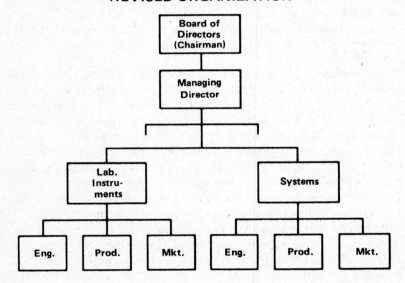

A recent financial projection anticipates that at least a year will be required to get the combined operations on a break-even basis. However, the hope is that by the third year volume will be up 35 percent and profits at a reasonable level.

New Corporate Governance

In a move to help Solartron gain access to long-term capital, its stockholders recently sold 57 percent of the outstanding shares to Schlumberger Limited for the equivalent of $4.6 million. Schlumberger is a large worldwide concern that makes geophysical studies for oil and mining companies. It pioneered in the use of seismographs, and has since expanded its services to the oil industry. Long a user of electronic equipment, Schlumberger has recently acquired several equipment manufacturing firms in Europe and U.S. This diversification, however, is quite small relative to Schlumberger's primary activities.

In commenting upon the new ownership, Bolton said, "As part of the worldwide network of electronic companies that Schlumberger is building up, Solartron can benefit from the marketing, research and development, and possibly the production activities of its sister companies; at the same time Solartron represents their major electronic interest in the U.K."

Bolton continued, "I thought it was very important to take advantage of the experience and ability of our parent company's top people. For this reason I asked Mr. Jean Riboud of Schlumberger to sit as chairperson of the Solartron Board, and our request has been accepted. Two other European executives of the Schlumberger organization will also serve on the Board. These men will contribute significantly, and not impede my freedom of action as Managing Director of Solartron."

Prior to the sale of the large block of stock, Solartron's Board consisted of six of its executives and two merchant bankers, with Bolton as chairman. Bolton used board meetings primarily to explore new ideas since operating decisions were made more frequently by the executives concerned.

Mr. Schneersohn, a director of Schlumberger European who negotiated the stock purchase, has these observations: " I wish to emphasize that money is the least important qualification that we offer. Schlumberger's primary attraction is their ability to contribute administrative management and technical skill, probably in that order of importance. In return, we are looking for a company with a good product produced in relatively small quantities, a good organization, and, most important, (a company) with one or two really good management people. Solartron seems to be a company that will fit well into the group structure that I have in mind. Looking critically, I would say that Solartron has been run a bit loosely in the past and stands in need of more effective management control. Solartron has always stressed growth. This is no longer as important a requirement as in the past. Overall, we are very pleased to have Solartron as a member of our European electronics group."

Question

What changes, if any, in (1) organization, and (2) other managerial arrangements should Schlumberger make in Solartron Electronics?

Part 5

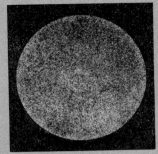

GUIDING THE EXECUTION

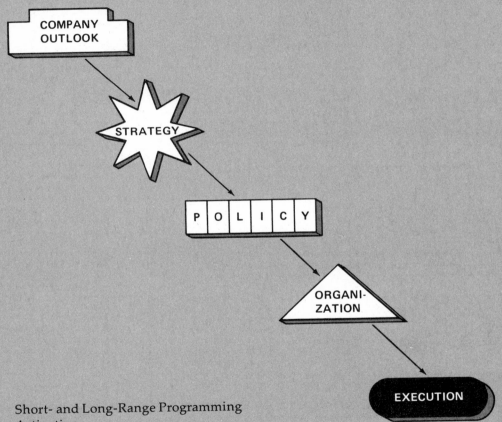

COMPANY OUTLOOK

STRATEGY

POLICY

ORGANIZATION

EXECUTION

20 SHORT-RANGE AND LONG-RANGE PROGRAMMING

Establishing strategy and policy, building organization, and developing executives are all vital to the management of any enterprise. However, there is still another group of activities that requires executive attention if the company is to achieve its goals. Steps must be taken to "get things done." This group of managerial duties we shall call *execution*, and the term is used here to cover:

1. *short-range* and *long-range programming*—which deals with what actions are to be taken when
2. *activating*—which is concerned with direction and motivation
3. *controlling*—which seeks to assure that the results actually accomplished correspond with plans

Steps in Execution

A large part of the time of junior executives is devoted to execution, that is, detailed programming, motivating, coordinating, and controlling. Central managers also must give a significant portion of their energy to getting things done. Policy formulation and organization planning set the stage, but no services are rendered and no profits are earned until action by first-line operators actually takes place.

A word of warning about these three steps in execution is appropriate. In practice, they are not watertight compartments that take place in just the order listed. Management is a continuing and complex activity in which the various phases are often mixed up. A program for putting a major policy change into effect may cut across minor policies, organization, and control procedures. Data developed in day-to-day control often are used in preparing short-range and long-range programs. Nevertheless, for purposes of understanding management, the divison of execution into phases is essential, and the outline puts these various parts into logical relationship and perspective.

Programming is discussed in this chapter. Activating and controlling are considered in the following chapters.

Nature of Programming

Our preceding discussion of managerial tasks has put primary emphasis on *what* should be done and has given little attention to deciding *how much* and *when*. Programs add this element of sequencing and timing.

515

Once an objective or "mission" has been established, the executive making the program first decides what principal steps are necessary to accomplish the objective and then sets an approximate time for each. When an entirely new activity is involved, the program may also indicate who is to undertake each of the steps.

While central management can delegate most detailed scheduling work, it should take an active part in shaping broader programs. Key issues faced in this important task will be examined in terms of:

1. short-range programming
2. critical path analysis
3. long-range programming

SHORT-RANGE PROGRAMMING

Programs for Special Purposes

Numerous short-range programs are drawn up and carried out in each department of a company. These programs deal with activities ranging from launching a sales campaign to installing word processors in an insurance office. Normally, central management delegates this kind of programming to department executives. However, when several departments are involved, a large amount of capital is committed, or when delicate external relations are at stake, central management takes an active part. Often, for such situations, the program is not neat and simple, as the following examples reveal.

Expansion Program. The operators of the hotel facilities at the Grand Canyon wished to develop an expansion program that would enable them to give better service to the many people who want to visit this scenic spot. Investigation revealed that two types of changes were needed in the physical facilities—betterments that would improve the services in the existing plant and major expansion of room and restaurant facilities. Any significant addition to total capacity, however, would have required more water; additional water could be secured only by investing $1,500,000 to run a pipeline to a spring several miles up the canyon. Pumping water from the bottom of the canyon to the brim would require additional electric power. This would probably mean bringing in a new power line. Moreover, a new sewage line would have to be laid in a ditch blasted out of rock.

The investment in these new facilities would not have been justified if they were to be used only two or three months of the year. Consequently, serious attention had to be given to attracting visitors to the canyon in the spring and the fall when, in fact, the weather is more desirable than in the summer—the prime tourist season.

There were additional factors involved, but these are enough to indicate the need for some kind of a program that would divide the total problem of expansion into logical *parts* and indicate a *sequence* in which these parts should be attacked.

In this case, a schedule probably could be established only for the first two or three steps, but the program did indicate all the steps involved and a sequence for dealing with them. Thus the program laid out a systematic approach to a very complex problem. Since the desirability of expanding facilities depended so largely on extending the tourist season and building other off-season business, changes in facilities were restricted to betterments until the practicality of the promotion program was tested.

Tax Revision Program. The desirability of a special purpose program also became apparent to a company that sought to reduce the federal excise tax on its products. The company quickly recognized that the chances of success would be materially improved if the industry as a whole presented its case rather than if each manufacturer operated independently. Clearly, the newly formed industry association should make contacts with all of the influential congressional representatives and senators. To be most effective, however, the pleas of the manufacturers needed to be backed up by significant pressure on the part of local constituents. This meant that the retailers and, to the extent possible, the consumers should be enlisted in the overall campaign.

If the efforts of all these people were to be most effective, there was need for a common program in which the role of each group could be clarified and some attention could be given to the timing of the several efforts. In a situation such as this, involving many independent enterprises and people, a detailed program and schedule covering an extended period probably would be of little value; but at least a general program was essential to get coordinated effort. Since the program basically concerned public opinion, there was great need for personal leadership and flexibility as the work proceeded.

Programs for special purposes, such as the two just discussed, are often difficult the project very far into the future. Forecasts of future needs and of operating conditions may be unreliable because the activity is so new and different. This unreliability of forecasts makes it hard to set dates and to estimate volume of work. Moreover, strategy in meeting competition or winning support of people often plays a key part in such programs, and it is difficult to decide on strategy very long in advance.

Basic Steps in Programming

The examples of programming given here indicate that skill is needed in fitting the general concept to specific situations. Nevertheless, six elements or steps are found in the majority of instances. Managers will do a better job of programming if they are fully aware of the nature and the importance of each of these steps.

1. Divide the total operations necessary to achieve the objective into parts. The division of an operation into parts is useful for planning, organization, and control. Planning is improved because concentrated attention can be given to one part at a time. Organization is facilitated because these parts or projects can be assigned to separate individuals, if this will give speedier or more efficient action. Such division also aids control because the executive can watch each part and determine whether progress is satisfactory as the work is carried on without waiting for final results.

If the division into parts or projects is to be most effective, the purpose of each step should be clearly defined. The kind of work, the quality, and the quantity should all be indicated.

Often a single part of a large program is itself again subdivided; in fact, this process of subdivision may be continued for three or four stages. For example, an anniversary program of a department store may include as one of its parts a sale of men's suits. This sale in turn may be divided into buying, advertising, displaying, selling, etc. The advertising project may be divided up into selection of merchandise to be featured, writing the copy, preparing illustrations, scheduling the days and the newspapers in which the ad will appear, and integrating the suit sale ads with other advertisements of the store. Thus the concept of programming is applicable to situations ranging from large operations down to the work of a single individual.

2. Note the necessary sequence and the relationship between each of these parts. Usually the parts of a program are quite dependent on each other. The amount of work, the specifications, and the time of action of one step often affect the ease or the difficulty of performing the next step. Unless these relationships are recognized and watched closely, the very process of subdividing the work may cause more inefficiency than it corrects.

Any necessary sequences are particularly significant. For example, a motel chain had to complete refinancing its debt before embarking on a West Coast expansion. These necessary sequences have an important bearing upon scheduling. They tend to lengthen the overall time required for the operation and, since a shorter cycle gives a company more flexibility, the necessity of delaying one action until another is completed should be carefully evaluated.

3. Decide who is to be responsible for doing each part. If the operation being programmed is a normal activity for the company, the assignment of responsibility may already be covered by the existing organization. In an airline, for instance, the opening of a new route involves sales promotion, personnel, traffic, air operations, maintenance, and finance, and assignment of each of these activities is already set by the established structure. However, if the program covers a new operation, then careful attention should be given to the question of who is responsible for each part. These special assignments do not necessarily follow regular organization relationships and create only a temporary set of authorizations and obligations. In a very real sense, a special team is formed to carry out the program.

4. Decide how each part will be done and the resources that will be needed. The amount of attention that must be given to each step in setting up a program will depend upon the circumstances. Sometimes standing methods and procedures will cover almost all of the activities (as is true of military programming), and in other situations, questions of "how" will be fully delegated to the persons responsible for each part. Nevertheless, the executive building the program must have enough understanding of how each part will be performed to appreciate the difficulties in the assignment and the obstacles that may be encountered. In particular, the executive needs some understanding of the *resources* that will be necessary to carry out each part of the program.

For realistic programming, the need for materials and supplies, facilities, and people must be recognized. Then the availability of these necessary resources should be appraised. If any of them is not available, another project to obtain the resource should be set up; this may be treated either as an additional part of the original program or as a subdivision of the project needing the resource. For example, if necessary personnel are unavailable, then plans shold be made for hiring and training new employees. Many programs break down because the executive preparing them does not have a practical understanding of how each part will be carried out and the resources that will be needed.

5. Estimate the time required for each part. This step is, of course, closely related with Steps 3 and 4 above and really involves two aspects: the date or hour when the part will begin and the time required to complete the operation once it is started. The possible starting time will depend upon the availability of the necessary resources. The time when key personnel can be transferred to a new assignment, the possibility of getting delivery of materials from suppliers, and the seasons when customers are normally in the market all have a bearing on when it is possible to begin any given part of a program.

Once the activity has begun, the processing time is typically estimated on the basis of past experience. For detailed scheduling of production operations, time-study data may permit a tight scheduling of activities. For a great many activities, more time is consumed in conveying instructions and getting people to begin the work than is required for the actual work itself. Unless this "nonproductive time" can be eliminated, however, it should be included as part of the estimated time.

6. Assign definite dates (hours) when each part is to take place. This overall schedule is, of course, based on the sequences as noted under Step 2 and the timing information assembled under Step 5. The resulting schedules should show both the starting dates and the completion dates for each part of the program.

Sometimes considerable adjusting and fitting is necessary to make the final schedule realistic. A useful procedure is to work backward and forward from some fixed date that is considered to be controlling. In promoting a new dress fabric, for example, the importance of the selling season may be so great that the retail season is taken as fixed and the schedule is extended back from these dates. In other situations, the availability of materials or of facilities may be the controlling time around which the rest of the schedule is adjusted. It is, of course, necessary to dovetail any given program with other commitments the company may have.

Another important qualification is to make some allowances for delay. It is not desirable as a general practice to have such allowances all along the line as this tends to create inefficient performance, but there should be safety allowances at various stages so that an unavoidable delay at one place will not throw off the entire schedule.

A shorthand way to label these steps is:
1. Turn big problems into smaller ones.
2. Study the linkages.
3. Pin down accountability.
4. Provide the tools.
5. Say when.
6. Integrate the schedule.

Programs may have to be revised, of course, to take account of unexpected opportunities or difficulties. If each of the six steps just outlined has been well done, however, these revisions usually can be merely adjustments of the intital planning.

Strategic Thrusts

Thrusts are identified in Chapter 5 as one of the key parts of a company strategy. These are the clear-cut moves to be started in the near term as steps toward a longer-range goal. Opening a plant in Taiwan or building a salesforce to contact retailers directly instead of relying upon wholesalers are examples.

Short-range programming is an excellent devise to assure that these thrusts receive adequate attention. The normal pressure of continuing day-to-day activities tends to push unusual work to "tomorrow." Also there may be resistance to change. Consequently, if a desired thrust is merely added to a list of things-to-be-done, it is likely to develop slowly and may be buried. In contrast, if a program including the features just outlined is prepared, action should result.

Contingency Programs

A "fire emergency plan" is a classic example of a contingency program. If the event occurs, a series of predetermined actions by assigned persons is to take place, and a special set of rules guides the behavior of all other people. The event is likely to be so serious that interruption of normal operations is warranted. And the need for prompt action justifies a standard response even though the precise location and size of the fire cannot be predicted in advance.

Most contingencies, however, do not warrant such an elaborate standby program. By far the most usual way to deal with new situations is to *revise* prevailing programs. As we will outline in Chapter 22, actual (and predicted) progress is frequently compared with the program; then whenever significant deviations are spotted, a revision of the program is at least considered. The revision technique has several advantages over contingency planning: It avoids the costly effort of preparing many plans which are never used. And the revision can be fitted much more closely to the specifics of the new situation than is possible when a plan is devised far in advance.

Contingency programs may be desirable for critical events such as a labor strike, a sudden influx in orders from customers, a major break in foreign exchange rates, or the like. The factors which justify contingency programs include: (1) the need for prompt action before the revision process can take place, (2) the likelihood that the contingency will occur about as predicted. In a company that has a well-developed planning and control system, not many contingencies meet these tests.

A secondary benefit of preparing contingency programs is training to deal with changes. Even though an alternative program may never be used, the managers who prepared it are more aware of where adjustments may be necessary and whom to consult. Psychologically, they are more receptive to change. Actually, most of this training benefit can also be obtained from fully exploring alternatives when the master program is adopted.[1] When planning skill is developed in decision analysis, the training benefit of contingency programs is reduced.

CRITICAL PATH ANALYSIS

Development of PERT

Critical path analysis is a special technique for studying and controlling complex programs. It was developed in its more elaborate form as an aid in the design and the production of Polaris missiles, and it has been used for virtually all subsequent space projects. The particular technique applied to the Polaris program was called PERT (Program Evaluation and Review Technique); many variations of the basic ideas have been used before and since PERT received wide publicity. The technique is of interest to us here because the central concepts of critical path analysis can be helpful in many programming problems.

---

[1]The term "contingency planning" is sometimes used in decision analysis. When the future is uncertain and two or more "states of nature" have to be considered, we may plan what we would do under each "contingency." Usually such projections are only concerned with estimating possible results, and they are not a commitment to a course of action, as in programming.

The design and production of Polaris missiles involved a staggering number of steps. Specifications for thousands of minute parts had to be prepared, the parts had to be manufactured to exact tolerances, and then the entire system had to be assembled into a successful operating weapon. And *time* was of the essence. The basic steps in programming, just discussed in the preceding pages, were applicable; but the complexity of the project (and the fact that many different subcontractors were involved) called for significant elaborations in the programs.

Major Features of Critical Path Analysis

The basic ideas involved in this refined programming technique are:

1. All steps and their necessary sequences are placed on a diagram (see Figure 20-1) so that the total *network* is explicitly set forth.
2. The estimated *time* required to complete each step after the preceding step has been finished is recorded.
3. Then by adding the required times for each step in any necessary sequence—or path—the path having the longest time can be identified. This is the *critical path.*
4. If desired, the difference between the total required times of the critical path and other paths can also be computed. Such differences are *slack times* or margins in which delays would not hold up the final completion.

Now, having identified the critical path, management can focus its attention on either reducing the time for certain steps in this path or at least watching closely for any delays. Also, management knows from slack time data where high pressure to meet estimated process times may be unwarranted.

The calculation of the critical path should be repeated as work progresses because some steps will be completed faster than anticipated and others will be delayed. These new data will certainly change slack time estimates, and a different critical path may arise.

With careful thought, the network of steps and sequences can usually be assembled with reasonable reliability—at least for programs dealing with physical products. The time estimates prove to be less reliable, however, especially for unique activities. To deal with this uncertainty regarding time, three estimates often are obtained from persons who will be doing the work: optimistic, most likely, and pessimistic. Then a weighted average of these three elapsed-time estimates is used.

In critical path analyses of complex programs, such as Polaris, computations are sufficiently involved to make use of a computer very helpful. In simpler programming situations, such as building construction, a computer is by no means essential.

General Applicability

The main features of critical path analysis apply to many programs that are not sufficiently complex to warrant the complete PERT treatment. Often just the

FIGURE 20-1.
CRITICAL PATH ANALYSIS

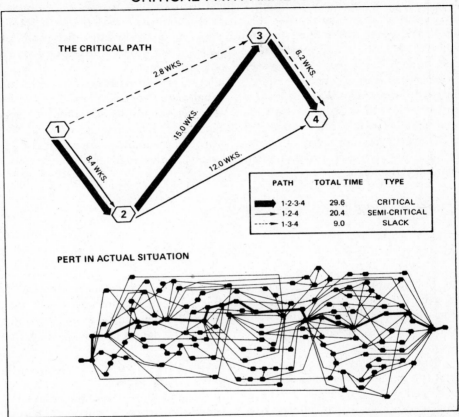

THE CRITICAL PATH

PATH	TOTAL TIME	TYPE
1-2-3-4	29.6	CRITICAL
1-2-4	20.4	SEMI-CRITICAL
1-3-4	9.0	SLACK

PERT IN ACTUAL SITUATION

The upper chart shows, for a very small segment of the total network, how the critical path is computed. The lower chart indicates how complex the networks may be.

Source: Booz, Allen, Hamilton.

preparation of a network chart of sequences of steps will clarify the interconnections between actions taken by various departments.

Moreover, the concept of a critical path can be used in many programming problems even though an entire network is not charted. In a company making nationally advertised men's shirts, for instance, the critical path runs from line-building through sales promotion to plant scheduling and on to order filling. Acquiring grey goods, training personnel, and similar steps have to be done but they are not "critical" from a timing viewpoint because of the early leads necessary in sales promotion. Programming in other companies may be geared to the erection of new facilities or perhaps the training of personnel. In all these situations, a recognition of what steps are part of the critical path will direct management efforts in "getting things done" to the crucial spots.

A word of caution is in order. Critical path analysis focuses on time, and few companies have data that enable them also to fit costs into the same framework. We would like to know how much speeding up or slowing down each step will change costs. Usually such cost estimates—even rough ones—are prepared only after critical steps are identified and an executive is trying to decide whether to make a change in plans. Similarly, critical path analysis does not deal with alternative ways of reaching a goal. The network is presumed to be settled. Of course, if the analysis identifies a serious bottleneck, then management may resort to a different method and may establish a new network.

Nevertheless, for many programming problems, timing is the major consideration. And for such programming problems, critical path analysis can be a valuable refinement.

LONG-RANGE PROGRAMMING

Nature of Long-Range Programming

Programming increases in difficulty as the time-span covered is extended, yet such extension is well worth the trouble in some circumstances. We have been discussing program cycles ranging from a few months to perhaps two years. Long-range programming seeks to extend the period covered to, say, five to ten years.

Underlying any long-range program should be a well-defined strategy. The strategy establishes the basic directions and the criteria for which the program is developed. Policy, considered in Chapters 6 through 13, provides the guides and limitations within which action is to fall. Establishing these is, of course, part of the total process of long-range planning. The *program* introduces a time schedule—the how much and when aspects—and thereby sets the intermediate objectives (which in turn become the targets for more specific and detailed short-range programs).

Applications

One of the classic examples of long-range programming is the conversion of the Bell System to dial telephones. Forecasts of telephone usage—based on population growth, higher gross national product (GNP), and telephoning habits—indicated that manual switching could not handle the load. Besides, automatic dialing would improve service and perhaps cut costs. So the goal was clear, but the magnitude of the task was tremendous. Design of equipment had to be refined for recording calls, relaying long-distance calls, tying in with independent companies, and the like. Completely new exchanges had to be built, millions of dollars of switching equipment had to be manufactured, and millions of consumer units had to be produced. Before any of this physical equipment could be installed, engineers, installers, and operators had to be trained. Incidentally, company policy dictated that the transition was to be made with only seconds of interruption in service and no layoffs of regular employees. The public had to be prepared for the switch and educated to use the new equipment; utility commissions had to be kept advised. And the multimillion dollar investment had to be financed.

This incomplete list suggests the range of elements in the program. Many of the preliminary steps were taken ten years before the conversion in that area was finished. And with new developments in technology and markets, the process is still going on.

The Bell System example is enlightening because (1) a whole series of interrelated steps were programmed years in advance, and (2) the programming was done for several elements—marketing, engineering, facilities, personnel, and finance—not just for a single element such as finance. For instance, Star Electronics, Inc., a small firm making parts for TVs and similar equipment, found its Brookline, Massachusetts, location far off from a growing number of customers in the Southwest. So a long-range plan for opening a second shop in Phoenix, Arizona, was laid out. (1) To build additional volume to justify such a shop, a sales engineer was located in Phoenix to serve customers almost as though the shop were in existence. (2) Any new equipment for Brookline was selected in anticipation of two separate manufacturing locations. (3) A year later, training of potential shop superintendent and an equipment engineer was started. (4) A cash reserve to cover startup costs was planned, and the expansion was discussed with the company banker.

These steps turned out to be especially helpful when, two and a half years after the start, an opportunity arose to buy the assets of a shop—similar to Star Electronics—that was on the brink of failure. Most of the equipment and related assets could be moved pronto to Phoenix. Without the long-range planning, Star Electronics could not possibly have seized this opportunity; it could not have developed an adequate market, a supervisory staff, or a financial plan quickly enough. Star Electronics took the plunge, earlier than it wanted and therefore risky—but with its cash outlay cut in half.

In this example, we again see (1) a series of interrelated steps extending over a period of years and (2) a plan that embraced several different elements. The timing of the various steps was subject to adjustment, as was also true in the telephone conversion, and no attempt was made to spell out detail several years in advance. But the master plan provided a definite guide for actions all along the way.

These examples may be misleading, because only a small portion of business firms actually prepare long-range programs in a clear-cut fashion. The main reason is simple. Most companies cannot, or do not, forecast the nature and the volume of their activities for three, four, or five years, let alone ten, years ahead. They may know the direction they would like to go (their objectives), but uncertainties about competition, technical developments, consumers' actions, political changes, economic changes, and the like make timing hard to nail down.

Because of the difficulty of precise long-range forecasting, we need to examine carefully the benefits the typical company can reasonably hope to obtain from long-range programming and problems that must be overcome if it undertakes this management device.

Major Benefits of Long-Range Programming

A central management that embarks on long-range programming usually seeks three advantages.

1. Long-cycle actions are started promptly. An automated plant takes at least two or three years to design, build, and get into operation. A bright idea for a new product often requires three to five years for research, development, testing, and process engineering before it is ready to be marketed. Recruiting and training salespeople for computers takes several years, assuming they cannot be hired away from established competitors. Raising a new crop of timber for lumber may consume twenty-five years.

Long-term programming indicates when such actions should be started. Opportunities will be missed or crises in servicing customers may develop unless a company takes early action. To fail to act is equivalent to a decision to postpone entry into the contemplated operation. Even though predictions of need are uncertain, there may be no feasible alternative to starting down the road.

By preparing the best program it is capable of, a company increases the probability that it will be aware of when long-cycle actions should be initiated.

2. Executives are psychologically prepared for change. Many actions embraced in a long-range program need not, and should not, be taken immediately. They can await a year or more of actual experience, and by then some modification in the original plan may be desirable.

Nevertheless, even though the program is changed, the process of preparing it aids adjustment to new conditions. As a result of preparing the program, the idea that some kind of change in response to shifts in the environment must take place is already accepted. And probably the nature of the adjustment will have been considered—for example, transfers of personnel, refunding a bond issue, or local production in a foreign country. Then, when conditions are ripe, executives are prepared to move quickly. Good news or bad news may arrive unexpectedly, and the company response may differ from the program; but the ability to recognize the opportunity, to appreciate the range of actions that are necessary, and to get in motion has been sharpened by the mental exercise of preparing (and revising) a program.

The pace of technological and economic change is quickening. Product life cycles are shorter and competitors move into profit opportunites more quickly. Consequently, the ability of a company to adjust promptly to shifts in its environment is crucial to getting ahead and staying ahead in modern competition. So this psychological preparation for change that we have been discussing is more vital to central management today than it was a generation ago.

3. Actions having long-term impact are coordinated. Often an action taken to meet an immediate problem also significantly affects the future operations of the company. For example, to get quick coverage of the West Coast territory, one firm gave exclusive distribution rights to an agent who also sold related products. The agent was successful in establishing itself as the local representative and the immediate problem was resolved. However, the firm soon expanded and diversified so that it needed a strong national sales organization of its own sales representatives; the successful independent distributor on the West Coast proved to be very difficult to supplant.

The selection of executives for key posts, the licensing of a company patent, and acceptance of a government subsidy are further examples where short-run solutions may prove troublesome in the future.

Now, if a company has a long-range program, central managers will be able to sense more easily whether current decisions do, or do not, fit into a consistent pattern of long-term development.

Note that in this list of benefits of long-range planning we do not include "a blueprint for future action." Only rarely are prediction and control of conditions several years hence sufficiently accurate to permit close adherence to a five-year plan. But such a program does help identify actions that should be initiated now, it lays a psychological base for prompt adjustment to opportunities in the future, and it provides a pattern so that action on today's problems can be compatible with long-range plans.

Problems Involved in Long-Range Programming.

Preparation of a long-range program requires guidance. Key problems are what topics and period to cover, how revisions will be made, and who will do the work of developing the plans.

Topics Covered. Too often so-called "long-range programs" are merely financial estimates conjured up by a bright young analyst in the controller's office. Such estimates take the form of annual profit and loss budgets for perhaps the next five years.

For operating purposes, dollar sales estimates have little meaning unless someone has thought in terms of the products that will be sold, the customers who will buy them, the prices obtainable in face of competition, and the selling effort necessary to obtain the orders. Similarly, the projected volume of goods must be conceived in terms of the resources necessary to produce them: plant capacity, trained workers, flow of raw materials, engineering talent, and so on.

Therefore, long-range programs should be stated in physical terms. But it is impractical to spell out such plans in full detail; instead, management should identify the crucial factors and build the program in these terms. One of the keys to successful programming is this identifying of topics to be used; omissions of vital factors will make the program unrealistic, whereas too many factors will make it unwieldy.

The long-range program should also be translated into dollar results: revenues, costs, profits, and capital requirements. Dollars are the best common denominator we have, and the financial results are an important aspect of any program. Use constant dollars first; then adjust for inflation. But the main point is that dollar figures alone are not enough.

Period Covered. Five years is the most common period covered by long-range programs. There is no magic in this figure, however. Logically, long-range plans should be based on the necessary elapsed time for such important action as product development, resource development, market development, or physical facility development. Three years may be long enough; in some cases, ten years will be needed.

In fact, the necessary time varies. Resource development may have to be started eight years before materials will become available, while two years may be adequate for market development. To deal with this variation, several companies (1) plan an action *in detail* only when a start is necessary, or (2) prepare a comprehensive program for three or four years ahead and then extend the period only for those areas requiring longer lead times.

Revisions. As results of first steps become known and new information about external conditions is learned, long-range programs need revision. The typical procedure is an annual review in which near-term actions are planned in greater detail, a new year is added on the end, and adjustments are made in plans for the interim period.

Under this scheme, programs are revised several times before the period to which they apply finally arrives. This provides flexibility in long-range programming. It also entails a lot of work, and executives may become cavalier about plans for five years hence since such plans will be revised over and over again. These disadvantages of several revisions are strong reasons for restricting the period covered and making sure the benefits listed previously are actually being obtained.

Who Prepares Long-Range Programs? Central managers will certainly participate in long-range programming. But they cannot do the job alone. They will need help obtaining ideas and specific data. Moreover, if the programs are to guide current commitments and if there is to be the desired psychological effect on executives throughout the company, all major executives should participate—research directors, plant managers, sales managers, and the like. Since these executives have other pressing duties, they may ask a staff assistant to help with long-range planning.

Altogether, then, central managers, operating executives, and their staffs probably will contribute ideas, data, judgment, or approval. This is complicated, yet necessary if the programs are to be carefully prepared and are to serve their intended purposes.

Long-Range Planning in Small Firms. Long-range planning in a small Stage I enterprise is necessarily more informal than in a large company. Executives lack the time to prepare detailed estimates; often basic historical data will not have been recorded. Nevertheless, the basic process outlined above should be followed, for the small firm has as much to gain by anticipating opportunities as a large one.

One entrepreneur with only sixteen employees has a loose-leaf notebook with alternative five-year programs based on different key assumptions. Perhaps because of his engineering training, he has spelled out steps and resources for different rates of growth in any of three directions. The estimates are his personal, subjective guesses; but when he makes a major investment or signs a long-term contract, he has a clear idea of where the action is likely to lead him.

In additon to pressure on time, small business managers have difficulty thinking objectively about events several years away. Typically, they are so immersed in day-to-day activities it is difficult to make a mental switch to a longer horizon. Preparing some estimates to present to a sympathetic board member can be a helpful discipline in this respect.

SUMMARY

Through programming, a manager formulates an integrated plan covering what, how much, when, and who.

Six basic steps should be taken: (1) divide into parts the total operations necessary to achieve the objective, (2) note the necessary sequences and relationships between each of these parts, (3) decide who is to be responsible for doing each part, (4) decide how each part will be done and the resources needed, (5) estimate the time required for each part, and (6) assign definite dates when each part will commence and end.

When faced with complex programming problems, a manager can use *critical path analysis* to identify those parts of the total activity that must be watched most closely if the final objective is to be met on time.

Long-range programming follows the same steps as any other programming. However, because of the great difficulty in forecasting accurately several years in advance, long-range programs may have to be revised several times.

Long-range programming is part of the more inclusive process of long-range planning. Establishing strategy and setting policy are also parts; they set directions, criteria, and limits. The *program* then introduces a time schedule—the how much and when—and breaks the broad plan into more specific steps.

While long-range programs must not be regarded as fixed, they do help flag actions with long lead times that should be started immediately, prepare executives to act promptly when opportunities or difficulties do arise, and provide a basis for reconciling short-run solutions with long-term plans.

QUESTIONS FOR CLASS DISCUSSION

1. "How long will my business be upset by your building that new overpass?" asks a retailer near the intersection. Assume that you are making a program for the construction project which will answer that question for the retailer and hundreds of other people affected. Follow the steps listed on page 520 in preparing the program. Don't forget the drainage, the new highway direction signs, or the grass on the shoulders. And make allowances to keep traffic moving in both directions on both highways. (a) Draw up such a program. (b) Do you recommend keeping posted on "the critical path"? (Note: the purpose of this exercise is to give you practice in preparing a program, so make any reasonable assumptions about lead times necessary to get various resources and about elapsed time to complete various steps.)

2. In Latin American and other countries, the cultural attitude toward time differs from that in the U.S. Staying on schedule is more a wish than a commitment. Even in social engagements no one expects people to arrive at the appointed hour. Explain how this attitude toward punctuality might affect programming in business. What can be done to retain as many as possible of the benefits of programming?

3. Brenda and Joe Klein are leaders of a group of citizens in Mountain View who want a community swimming pool. The village majority and council are sympathetic but say that the village cannot afford the capital costs, and they are afraid that political pressure will force them to keep admission charges so low that operating costs will not be covered. The Klein group is now considering a semiprivate swim club. A nearby village has such a club with these provisions: Capital costs are covered by an initiation fee for the 300 family members; much of this fee will be repaid by new members who replace anyone who resigns. Operating costs are covered by annual dues and fees for guests. Any citizen in Mountain View is eligible to join—first-come, first-served basis. The village leases the land (a good location owned by the

village) to the club for twenty years at a nominal charge. At the end of the lease, the village gets the pool and dressing rooms, etc. The Kleins ask you to prepare a long-range program for getting a swimming pool in Mountain View as soon as possible.

4. Assume that your university is under heavy pressure to improve its performance as an equal opportunity employer. Unless it develops an acceptable program for increasing the proportion of women in higher faculty ranks and in higher administrative positions, it may lose $28,000,000 annual research contracts funded by the federal government. What *program* do you recommend? (Be as concrete as you can—except that you may use "Xs" and "Ys" for specific numbers of people.) Does the concept of programming as outlined in this chapter fit this kind of situation? Explain.

5. Beckley Wardwell, to help make the decision about poromeric leather (see the Wardwell Vinyl Coatings case on pages 264–73), wants a program outlined for introducing the new product. The program will help to indicate the feasibility of taking on the poromeric leather license. Your analysis shows that the major steps will be:

A. Decision to accept the license
B. Engineering completed by the joint efforts of Spencer and the Belgiam firm
C. Financing arranged
D. Material purchase orders placed
E. Plant laid out and equipment in place

F. Production trials completed
G. Sales training completed and promotion program arranged
H. Initial orders received
I. Fullscale production starts
J. Initial orders shipped

Your analysis also shows that the necessary sequences among events and the estimated time required to perform the work to advance from one event to the next are as shown in Table 1.

TABLE 1.

Necessary Sequence	Estimated Time	Necessary Sequence	Estimated Time
A-B	60 days	D-E	60 days
A-C	90 days	D-I	75 days
B-E	60 days	F-I	1 day
E-F	30 days	G-H	30 days
C-D	5 days	H-I	1 day
C-G	60 days	I-J	5 days

(a) Prepare a PERT diagram. (b) Determine the critical path. (c) Do your answers to (a) and (b) suggest any action to Mr. Wardwell?

6. The expected decline in college enrollments is publicized to be about 10 percent from 1985 to 1995. During that period about 20 percent of America's 3,100 colleges and universities are expected to close their doors or merge with other institutions. Prepare a program to reduce the total number of faculty and staff members of your college or university by 10 percent to meet the anticipated decline in enrollments. What is actually happening to enrollments at your institution of higher learning?

7. C. E. Lindblom and J. B. Quinn contend that strategy is developed and carried out— not by a comprehensive program covering events from start to finish—but instead by a succession of small steps in which the manager waits until one is finished before deciding what the next step will be. This feeling-one's-way they call the *incremental* approach, or incrementalism. Incrementalism is used, they report, especially when uncertainty is high about the results of the present step or about future operating conditions; also it is used when agreement about the total picture is difficult to reach among key actors. (a) Which approach—incremental or fully programmed—should a manager use for (i) building an airplane? (ii) mining manganese modules from the ocean floor? (iii) opening a new drugstore? (iv) promoting a freeze on nuclear weapons? (b) How does incrementalism relate to strategic positioning as discussed in Chapter 3?

8. Chapter 4 recommends the analysis of key actors as part of the basis for formulating strategy. How can this concept of key-actor analysis be used in making a program for (a) introducing a new product into the market? (b) cutting energy costs for your university?

9. Your boss, the vice-president and controller of Sierra Electric Utility Company, Inc., has just given you, a new member of the Planning and Budgeting staff, these instructions: "We have direct instructions from the chair of the board to prepare a new, 8-year program for changes in the generating plant using an expected growth in peak load requirements of only 2 percent per year, and lengthening the expected time for the completion of our joint venture in the nuclear power plant two or possibly three additional years. How much new capacity—and of what kind—will we need and when must it come on-stream?"

You have the information in Table 2.

Operations at present are at capacity with no reserve. The nuclear plant under construction has been delayed by the Nuclear Regulatory Commission. Chances are 50-50 that our share will be available in the fourth or fifth years, and 95 percent probable that it will be available in the fifth or sixth years.

The vice-president for customer services stated that she had plans for a new, very low home-heating rate that would soak up idle capacity during the winter and help to meet her plans for a 4 percent growth rate in annual sales. (Air-conditioning has led to a peak demand in July.) Population increases will provide a very strong push toward meeting her plans.

The operations vice-president stated that Sierra was lucky to be able to meet demand requirements now and that, after this year, there would be no available extra power from tie-lines with other utility companies. He sees brownouts and complaints without new capacity next year. "The extra power from tie-lines (up to

TABLE 2.
PEAK LOAD REQUIREMENTS IN 1,000's OF KILOWATTS

	Last year actual	Present year	2nd year	3rd year	4th year	5th year	6th year	7th year	8th year
Peak load @ 4% growth	1,830	1,903	1,979	2,058	2,141	2,226	2,316	2,408	2,504
Added each year		73	76	79	83	85	90	92	96
Previously planned new capacity			200*	100*	50‡	50‡	150†	150†	
Peak load @ 2% growth	1,830	1,867	1,904	1,942	1,981	2,020	2,061	2,102	2,144
Added each year		37	37	38	39	39	41	41	42

*Sierra's share of a joint-venture nuclear energy plant.
†Sierra's new, natural-gas-powered, generating plant.
‡Gas turbine units.

75,000 kilowatts) is contracted for elsewhere next year. I don't see how we could get it back."

Natural-gas fueled plants require a four-year lead-time and a minimum capacity of 300,000 kilowatts. Gas turbine units can be operating in one to one-and-a-half years after ordering, and each has a minimum capacity of 25,000 kilowatts. They are 50 percent more expensive to operate than are the larger plants and purchased power (when available) is still another 15 percent more expensive.

CASE 20
Apex Internacional

The Apex Equipment Company is embarking on its first venture in foreign manufacturing. Still unsettled is how bold Apex wants to be in this new thrust.

The company has a successful record in the automobile equipment *replacement* industry. Basically it waits until the major manufacturers of its kind of product produce models which are incorporated into new autos. Then Apex very carefully duplicates each model and sells these in the replacement market. Auto supply jobbers sell Apex products to the thousands of shops, garages, and filling stations that repair autos and trucks.

Of course, the original equipment manufacturers (OEMs) also sell their products in the replacement market. However, with the passage of time there are a variety of models fitting various cars, and the volume of replacement sales on any one model is small relative to the production runs for new car use. Apex has designed its manufacturing activities to handle short production runs, and it is thus able to compete with OEMs in the replacement end of the industry.

Apex has decided mot to seek OEM business from the big U.S. auto producers (or foreign producers in their home country). The competitors are too big and entrenched, and such a move would require Apex to do much more R & D than it does at present. But the situation in developing countries which are just getting into automobile production is quite different.

In a country such as Brazil, auto production starts primarily as assembly of imported parts. However, to save foreign exchange and to provide local employment, the governments of such countries push hard to increase the use of locally produced parts; tax benefits, tariffs, and import quotas are all used. As soon as a part is available locally, barriers to imports are likely to be imposed.

Apex sees an opportunity to be an OEM supplier in Brazil—and later in other such countries. The company has demonstrated its ability to make products that work just as well as the original equipment, and it knows how to produce in relatively small quantities. One Brazilian company is already in the business but its quality is considered to be inferior. A European producer may set up a Brazilian plant. So, if Apex opens a local plant, it can promptly become a leading supplier for local OEM and replacement parts, probably with tariff protection.

Joe Androtti, Apex Production V.P. "The fastest way to get started, and with the least risk now, is to rent a small plant in the São Paulo area. Then when we are successful and know our way around—say, in three years—we would have to move, presumably to our own larger plant in Belo Horizonte (Brazil's third largest city, with a vigorous industrial development program). Production space can be rented in São Paulo—at a high price. Lead-time on the equipment delivery in the U.S. ranges from four to nine months. Then allow three months for shipping and clearing customs, and two months to get set up. That adds up to a minimum time to get started of fourteen months.

"A second alternative is to build a somewhat larger—though still small—plant in São Paulo. We would just postpone deciding what to do when we outgrow such a plant. Planning, approvals, and actual plant construction would probably take two years. But we should be able to have the equipment in and ready to go within that time. Unfortunately, São Paulo is crowded and may get worse, the smog is terrible, and the government offers no special incentives to locate there.

"In contrast, Belo is courting new industry. Maude Weaver has figures on the financial picture. It is very difficult to rent in Belo, and if we start there we would at least lay out a larger operation from the beginning. No future moves would be anticipated. The entire physical setup at Belo is more attractive than in São Paulo, but since more government approvals are involved we should figure on two and a half years to get started there."

Maude Weaver, Apex Treasurer. "If we located in Belo we can, in effect, get our new building at half-cost, have no real estate taxes for five years, and also receive a subsidy for training new workers. I know Brazilians have a reputation for being slow in taking official action, but two other U.S. firms told me that they had no major trouble. Their advice is to ask for your full needs while you are at it.

"My figures on our capital requirements boil down to this: Renting in São Paulo gives the lowest investment, but with rent expense figured in the production, costs per unit would be at least as high as those in our owned plant in São Paulo, and we would have to move in a couple of years.

"If we go to Belo immediately, we could hold back on some of the equipment until we needed it. Of course, working capital is (or should be) a function of actual volume rather than capacity. So our capital investment when sales are running $6,000,000 would not be much higher at Belo than at São Paulo—about $3,000,000 total. Production costs per unit should also be about the same. When volume moves above $6,000,000 the advantages of the larger plant at Belo would really show up.

	Sales at Capacity	Investment in Plant & Equipment	Net Working Capital
Rental plant in São Paulo	$ 3,000,000	$ 300,000	$ 750,000
Small owned plant in São Paulo	6,000,000	1,200,000	1,500,000
Full-scale plant in Belo	12,000,000	1,800,000	3,000,000

"Incidentally, Brazil has high inflation which confuses the picture a bit. But in Brazil almost everything is 'indexed,' including the amount you must repay on a loan. So we are making our estimates in constant dollars.

"Now the catch is—where do we get the $1,050,000 or the $3,000,000? Our domestic business is growing and with inflation it soaks up most of the cash it generates. We can borrow $1,000,000 from the banks on short-term loans. Above that, and certainly for $3,000,000 (which is almost 25 percent of our present assets and 50 percent of stockholder's equity), we must negotiate a long-term loan. The negotiating should start six months before we need the cash."

Paul Nichols, Apex President. "Key personnel will be our bottleneck in this Brazilian venture, in my opinion. Our present agent in São Paulo, Salvador Silvana, has done an excellent job of importing and selling our products. And he is promoting the expansion. However, like many Latin American businesspeople he has several other projects and does not want to devote his full time to Apex Internacional. He does want to handle all local sales. So, we will need a Brazilian general manager and a Brazilian production manager. I wish we had a Portuguese-speaking financial person to send down, but we don't.

"From a personnel angle, a modest start where we can test and train executives would be preferable. It is particularly difficult to select executives in a foreign country where you don't know the subtleties. I'd feel better about going the Belo route if I had full confidence in the general manager.

"The general manager should know the business backwards and forwards and preferably have a technical background. Maybe the general manager should work for Salvador for a while, as well as here in the U.S., and help plan and negotiate. It may be difficult to attract and hold a good person for two and a half years, however. I guess we should start looking and be ready to act. Who runs the project in the meantime? Production is a bit easier because we can send a couple of engineers to Brazil during the startup period.

"Another consideration is our organization here at headquarters. We have only an Export Manager who concentrates entirely on foreign sales. I'm not sure how involved our key department managers should or will get in far-off Brazil. Maybe we should be thinking in terms of an international division."

Howard Schaller, Apex Export Manager. "It is always difficult to know how hard to push in a foreign situation. There are at least two reasons for moving fast in Brazil. First, if we are going to stake out a major position we should get there before others do. There is room for only a couple of manufacturers in Brazil. If we move aggressively maybe we can discourage others from entering. Second, the government attitude about foreign investments might change quickly. I don't think it will in Brazil, but other countries have had sudden shifts in governments and in economic policy. If we are already set up inside the country our position is more secure.

"Once our production capability is established, then the more support for local production there is the more we will benefit. Silvana believes we can develop a $12,000,000 volume in our line of business within four or five years. It may be optimistic, but the potential is there. With profit margins fifty percent higher than in the U.S., this should be a real moneymaker. Meanwhile, Silvana should do everything he can to build Apex's reputation for quality."

Question

Outline a five-year program that you recommend for Apex's entry as a producer in Brazil.

ISOE (8)

apple   1. A bias for action
sLD   2. Staying close to the customer
3M   3. autonomy of entrepreneurship-break
DISNEY   4. productivity thru people
MCD   5. Hands-on, value driven
N.Amr.   6. Stick to the knitting
DANA   7. Simple form, lean staff.
IBM   8. Simultaneous loose-tight prop.

Case Format
1. Mission Statement
2. External Envir; comp., tech., soc./cul, legal/pol, economy
3. Internal; S, W, diff. adv.
4. Market Domain; T, Poss. C.
5. Key People
6. CSF
7. Key Issues
8. Goals
9. Alt.
10. Recommendation

21 ACTIVATING

The wisest strategy, policy, organization, and programs are naught until they are put into action. This need to translate ideas into action has been a recurring theme thoughout our discussion, but it warrants further recognition in a separate chapter. Central management plays an important role in activating an enterprise by:

1. creating a *focused climate*
2. *managing* major changes
3. making *MBO-type evaluations* of key executives
4. using *incentives* in a demanding way

Controlling is also necessary in achieving desired results. We will explore that aspect of central management in Chapter 22.

CREATING A FOCUSED CLIMATE

Every established organization has its own climate, or culture. The organization embodies traditional values about customer service, spending money, accepting risks, beating competitors, dealing with communist countries, taking the initiative, and many other matters. This climate affects the ease or difficulty of carrying out a specific program.

Careful Use of Executive Influence

Executives, and especially senior executives, help form the climate within their bailiwick. They cannot escape being public figures. Their behavior is closely watched for cues. The vice-president who jokingly said, "Guess I'll walk through the office in my shirt sleeves just to start a rumor," was well aware that many people would try to infer meaning from even his casual actions.

Because they are inevitably in the local spotlight, central managers should behave in a way that creates a climate favorable to the execution of company strategy. And it is actions and decisions, more than words, which convey the message. The president who is lavish with his personal expense account will have difficulty securing strong support for a cost reduction program. Likewise, the promotion of a product manager who uncovered a new market for a product will send signals throughout the organization. Specific decisions are magnified because they help generate widespread feelings and attitudes.

The importance of climate is highlighted in a study by McKinsey and Company. These management consultants carefully compared the central management practices in a set of companies with excellent performance records against a comparable set of companies whose performance has been "not outstanding." Differences in climate is closely associated with differences in results. Among their findings are the following.

Stress Selected, Simple Goals

The excellent companies all had a few well-recognized goals or themes. "Our company is built around customer service." "Growth is essential; we expect to be the largest company in our industry within five years." "Pioneers in banking. . . ." Statements such as these illustrate an overriding goal. Usually the less successful companies did not have clear-cut, integrating concepts of mission.

To an outsider these goals seem almost naive. However, they have taken on real meaning within the companies which use them, and, somewhat like a religious creed, they call forth emotional commitment.

Obviously, these overriding goal statements should be linked to company strategy. Strategy (as used in this book) has more facets; but often a tersely stated mission does capture the essence of strategy.

A second type of goal typically found in the successful companies is more immediate, short-run objectives. These are the "thrusts" in our definition of strategy; for example, "a mini-size car ready to market in 1988," or " current, error-free, computerized subscription lists by the end of the year." At any one time, a successful company singles out only a few such themes for prime attention. Usually they are simple to understand, achievable, and have a strong action focus.

Of course, the thrusts and themes change as old ones are achieved and new ones are added. The more successful climate is one that avoids a complex array of themes with varying priorities. Instead, the normal pattern is to focus on a few carefully selected thrusts. The evidence suggests that the excellent companies somehow sift through a great diversity of influences and alternatives and then select a simplified set of goals for emphasis in operations. On major issues, at least, a clear-cut value system replaces uncertainty and ambiguity.

Build Acceptance Through Symbolic Behavior

The goals and thrusts become powerful values in the company climate only when they are strongly supported by the central managers. The McKinsey study shows that the chief executive can set the tone. The way the executive allocates time and attention tells what he or she considers important. But because the C.E.O. cannot be in many places at once and personally participate in many decisions, the more effective C.E.O. takes actions which become symbols of the values he or she is advocating. Here are four kinds of useful symbols.

1. *Hands-on participation* by the key executive. Calling on customers to get their reaction to products and service, attending the closing of an important sale, personally reviewing affirmative action moves, participating in new product meetings, conducting discussions or having dinner with executive trainees are examples. Perhaps the C.E.O. gets involved only on a sampling basis—to avoid being a bottleneck—but there is no doubt about genuine concern.

2. *Positive reinforcement* of actions which are consistent with the overriding goal or selected thrusts. This includes making field visits to locations where positive action has occurred and praising participating workers; giving special awards for outstanding performance; granting immediate additional assistance to people already moving in approved directions. Some executives give such reinforcement again and again over a sustained period, driving home the central message.

3. Pointing out *role models* of desired behavior. An example of successful performance makes a goal seem real and achievable. Just as the four-minute mile is no longer a fantasy for runners, so can a pilot's on-time record or branch manager's inventory turnover be singled out for others to follow.

4. Support of *myths*. Every company has its stories of exceptional actions: the president who personally delivered a bicycle on Christmas Eve so as not to disappoint a customer; the power-line repairer who kept electricity flowing to a hospital during an ice storm; the president of Seagrams who dumped an entire batch of whiskey down the drain because the taste was not up to quality standards; the manager who was fired the day it was discovered that he had lied to a Congressional committee. Over time, the details of the stories may get distorted, but they are part of the company lore. Such stories which support the overriding goal can be repeated to help establish the mystique of the company.

Through such well-worn methods as these, the central managers of excellently performing companies make clear the selected company values. And by creating such a climate, people throughout the organization are more likely to execute their various assignments correctly and enthusiastically.

This repeated emphasis on a few selected themes builds focused behavior. By clarifying priorities, it improves performance. However, the analysis and testing which precedes the execution stage may be complex, prolonged, and sophisticated. Part of the skill in creating an effective, uncluttered climate is being most careful in selecting those goals and thrusts which are paramount.

MANAGING MAJOR CHANGES

Activating often involves change. The focused climate just described may become outdated by new opportunities. Or, within its general scope, a new product, energy-saving technology, or a new organization may be necessary. Central managers especially must be active in bringing these changes about.

A change in strategy always involves a difficult transition. Relations with suppliers and customers will be altered, people will have new jobs, priorities and power will be shifted. Typically, as Figure 21-1 suggests, years not days are required.

During the early stage, the new strategy and the accompanying policy and programs are still being worked out. Some people will be involved in this new planning, and through this participation they will understand and probably endorse the change in direction. Other people will necessarily be "minding the store" because previous activities must be continued in order to maintain company momentum while modified activities are being planned and tested. (The 1988 model automobiles must be made and sold while the 1989 and 1990 models are being developed.) Then comes a phasing-out of the old and a building of support for the new. It is during this transition and throughout the middle stage that central managers build acceptance through symbolic behavior, as described above. Finally, pressure builds for another tack, and central managers must start preparing people psychologically for fresh leaps forward.

The transition from an old strategy to a new one creates special problems in activating. Behavior previously endorsed now has to be modified. And experience clearly demonstrates that the momentum of a going concern is not redirected merely by giving an order. Central management can aid in the transition by:

1. relieving anxiety promptly
2. identifying areas where modifications in individual and group behavior are needed
3. providing time to learn new behaviors
4. giving positive reinforcement to desired behavior

Relieve Anxiety Promptly

Rumors about changes that might upset cherished relationships spread rapidly. Once the status quo is shattered, employees give attention to all sorts of idle speculation. For instance, just an announcement that the company has bought a new computer can generate stories about closing down an office, firing half the people in the accounting department, or tranferring the engineering staff to San Diego. Anxiety builds up, each minor statement or action of central management is interpreted many ways, efficiency drops, and employees begin looking for other jobs.

Much of the anxiety comes from uncertainty—not knowing what is going to happen. To be sure, some anxiety also arises because people are unsure how well they will perform under new circumstances. Only actual experience in the new setup can remove the latter insecurity, but anxiety about the unknown can be reduced by management.

Prompt communication is vital. Even though specific answers of precisely what will happen often cannot be given because plans have not yet been devel-

FIGURE 21-1.
FIVE- TO NINE-YEAR CYCLE OF STRATEGIC TRANSITION

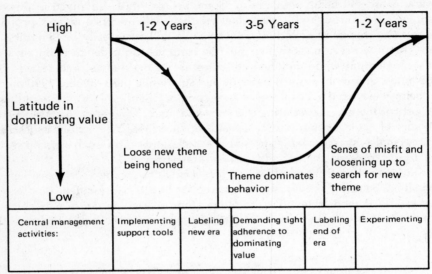

Reprinted, by permission of the publisher, from "Symbols, Patterns, and Settings: An Optimistic Case for Getting Things Done," by Thomas J. Peters, *Organizational Dynamics*, Autumn 1978, p. 21. © by AMACOM, a division of American Management Associations, New York. All right reserved.

oped in full detail, full discussion of the known facts is helpful. Publicly recognizing employee concern, presenting a positive feeling about the future, and scuttling a variety of mistaken rumors all relieve uneasiness. If decisions are not yet made, then a statement of when they will be made and how they will be communicated is much better than no news at all.

An especially sensitive period is when negotiations for, say, a merger are still in the confidential stage. Then the most that can be done is to check false rumors and to assure employees that they will be informed early of any action that will affect them. Confidence in management's credibility is important at this stage.

Identify Behavior Changes

Supplementing every formally planned organization is a host of customary though unspecified relations. Pat Lee knows whom to contact about payroll deductions, passes along advance information on big orders to the production scheduler, picks up hints on the boss's temper from her secretary, and in other ways fits into an intricate social structure. Now, when a major change in organization and activities occurs, the old social structure breaks down and for a time no one is sure (1) where to get and give bits of information, (2) who has influence in the revised power structure, and (3) whose "suggestions" to consider seriously. During this period of flux, work gets done very slowly.

By identifying the principal areas of disruption, central management can anticipate where the trouble is likely to occur. Also, by supporting selected people in disputes, by feeding information through particular channels, and by weighing and if possible accepting recommendations coming from staff or line, central management helps shape the new social structure.

Individual values and habits have to be modified, as well as the social interaction just discussed. For example, for years Tom Novello has worked closely with six southern wholesalers; he knows their buyers personally, and their goodwill has been a real asset. Now a decision to sell directly to customers makes these wholesalers insignificant customers. Novello has to stop giving them special attention; the priority goes elsewhere. Since, as is frequently the case, friendships are involved as well as personal skills or knowledge that give the wholesalers distinct worth, the new policy is tough to accept. Because emotions and habits are involved, the implications of a major change may lead Novello to unconsciously reject the general idea even while he gives verbal acceptance to it.

Provide Time to Learn New Behavior

Adjustments in behavior take time. When we first do any new task—riding a motorcycle or instructing a computer—we are clumsy and unsure how to interpret cues. The same is true of executive action. And when we *change* behavior, we may have to unlearn old habits and attitudes before picking up the new ones. Social interaction also has to be "learned"; here two or more people are involved, and they have to respond to each other as well as to their own motivations.

Management should recognize the need for this learning period. Even when employees have no reluctance to adopt new objectives, the early operations will be hard and slow. Practice is needed, and minor adjustments often have to be made. Also, in the kind of strategy changes we have been discussing in this book, some jockeying for position by energetic executives is sure to occur. Time for a "shakedown cruise" is clearly necessary; the tough question of judgment is how long to allow.

Give Positive Reinforcement

Learning the new behaviors will occur faster if management notices and strongly encourages new actions that are along the desired lines. This is the period to build acceptance through symbolic behavior, as already described. Usually the new behavior will require extra effort, and special recognition will help sustain that effort during the learning period.

Such recognition of desired behavior also helps relieve anxiety built up during the transition. People are unclear as to just what should be done in the new situation and they will welcome reassurance when they are on the right track. Some doubt is likely to exist about the feasibility of the new direction, so every opportunity to point out where it is succeeding should be used to build confidence in the plan. Role models of desired behavior should be identified.

Activating a new strategy or reorganization, then, calls for keen perception by central management of the modifications in customary behavior that will be necessary to make the revised plan succeed. By closely following the way people are responding, managers can spot the desired behavior and can encourage people to follow that course. Such positive management will reduce the learning time and will relieve anxiety.

MBO AT THE EXECUTIVE LEVEL

The activating methods discussed so far apply to everyone in the company or department involved. They create a general setting or climate for actions by individuals. Valuable as such a climate is, managers must do more. Specific direction and motivation for each subordinate is also necessary.

MBO—Management By Objectives—is an activating technique that can be easily adapted to executives at the highest level of a company. The underlying concepts of MBO are simple, and may be known by other names, such as "management by results," which is a more accurate term. Nevertheless, the use of MBO in the executive suite calls for diligence and skill.

Basic Steps

The process begins with a manager (of any rank) agreeing with an executive about the results she or he is expected to achieve during an ensuing period—three months, six months, or perhaps a year. Such an agreement on results expected should be based on a mutual understanding about several things: (1) the sphere of activities the manager is concerned with, that is, the organization; (2) the desired goals for these activities, both long-run and short-run; (3) how achievement of these goals will be measured and the level of achievement expected by the end of the period planned; (4) the help the manager may expect from the executives and others; and (5) the freedom and the restraints on how the manager pursues the goal.

Then at the end of the period the executive and the subordinate again sit down to review what actually was accomplished, to determine why deviations (both good and bad) from goals occurred, and then to agree on a new set of goals for the next period.

At each review there is grist for a new discussion because a new set of results is available for appraisal and a new set of targets and priorities need to be agreed upon. As the process proceeds, the executive has repeated opportunities for counseling the individual and for relating individual performance to company strategy, policy, organization, and programs. These discussions should be objective and frank. As a minimum, the manager should know what is expected and how his or her performance will be measured.

One of the advantages of this form of MBO is that it sets the stage for frequent dialog about goals and their achievement. In fact, when people work on distinct projects, the review may occur at the close of one project and the beginning of another. In other instances the reviews and new goal-setting sessions become a part of programming discussed in the preceding chapter. So, if a person's total job and total performance are covered in such a project or programming discussions, an additional period appraisal serves little purpose. Often, however, these discussions are sharply focused on a particular end result, and an annual examination of overall performance picks up loose ends and gives balanced direction. Whatever the timing, the important thing is that open communication takes place between each manager and the direct supervisor on the five factors listed above.

Benefits Sought

Several benefits should arise from such regular goalsetting and results review sessions.

1. Attention is focused on *achieving results*, not just being active, and these results are promptly compared to company goals. Of course, activities will be necessary to achieve results, and much of the discussion and the resource allocation will be tied to such activities. Nevertheless, if the activities are not leading to desired results—either because of internal or external events—the manager is expected to initiate revised action that will lead to the specified goal(s). In other words, the MBO system assumes considerable decentralization to and initiative by subordinates. And if results are not turning out as hoped, the person who has accepted the responsibility should be doing something about it.

2. *Personal commitment* to carry out the (agreed upon) mission is more likely. Having the opportunity to discuss both the assignment and the help needed to get it done, usually gives the junior managers a feeling that the task is achievable. Also, the goal has been endorsed by the boss as being wise and in the interests of the company. In psychological lingo, the aim is to have the goal internalized and legitimized. And if the subordinate has made the stated results a personal aim, both effort and resourcefulness are increased.

3. *Balanced goals* can be agreed upon. Especially at the upper management levels, several competing goals are almost always present. The marketing vice-president, for instance, is concerned with advertising, pricing in specific mar-

kets, new products, sales training, and branch offices, just to mention a few subjects that might arise in a single week. Some results, such as direct costs, are easily measured, while others such as community service, are intangible. Typically, short-run results steal attention from longer-run objectives even though the latter may be more significant. Senior executives are vitally concerned that goals and results be kept in an optimum balance. MBO reviews provide a forum where these balancing issues can be considered in concrete action terms.

4. *Dual accountability* can be enforced. As business operations become more complex, we often have two or more people cooperating to achieve a single result. For instance, both human resources staff and the district manager may be responsible for training recently recruited MBAs. Together, an engineer, plant manager, and accountant may be accountable for cutting the cost of product X by 15 percent. A good way to handle such joint projects is to hold *each* person accountable for the *total* result; this places a premium on cooperation to get best results. The MBO process is flexible enough to use this dual accountability concept.

5. *Interrelated support* can be provided. Meeting an air pollution regulation, for example, may call for changes in product specifications, modified manufacturing processes, some new equipment, a revised cost standard, and retraining. In an MBO review the plant manager who takes on the goal of meeting this regulation can spell out to the boss the help that will have to come from other departments. Or—as we have repeatedly stressed—strategy, policy, programs, organization, and control are interdependent; a change in one is likely to require adjustment in others. So, for example, when expansion into Mexico is undertaken, a variety of adjustments will be necessary. Ideally, these supporting adjustments will be fitted into the expansion plans from the beginning. But MBO planning and review sessions provide another occasion when the "total package" concept can be explored.

6. The MBO process is particularly well suited for activating managers of *decentralized operating units* and of units located some distance from the central office. The greater the distance between the central office and the operating unit, the fewer the opportunities for casual contacts and informal coaching. Also, when a shift in strategy has occurred, central managers need a mechanism that gives them a chance (1) to examine the interpretation of the new directions being made by subordinates, and (2) to reinterpret their intent. MBO reviews do provide such opportunities to explore the implementation of new strategy.

This list of potential benefits of MBO indicates important phases of activating individual managers. If for some reason the MBO procedure is not used, other methods of accomplishing each of the six phases should be found.

DEMANDING USE OF INCENTIVES

Important as climate and individualized goals are in activating, central management still has to create a situation in which key employees get deep personal satisfaction from achieving tough company goals. These key people—managers, top staff persons, and outstanding performers in engineering, sales, etc.—are a select group; they have ability and drive, as already indicated by the positions they hold. The challenege is to keep their vigorous efforts channeled toward the strategy that the company is pursuing.

Broadly speaking, central management can influence this eagerness to cooperate through:

1. identifying factors that motivate these persons,
2. recognizing the inherent limitations on management's capacity to use such incentives, and
3. applying incentives wisely and courageously.

Executive Motivations

The influences that spur people to exert themselves are not obvious and clearcut. Also, individuals differ in their responses. Nevertheless, we can identify several factors that are likely to motivate the kind of persons who reach key positions.

Financial Rewards. Overemphasized though it is, money does matter in our society. It is a crude symbol of success, but it is a means of achieving other ends such as security, living comforts, and independence.

We have already discussed the setting of executive salary levels in Chapter 19. The desirability of keeping pay scales (1) in line with rates being paid by other companies and (2) in equitable internal alignment was stressed. Such a salary structure enables a company to attract and to retain competent executives. But note that the base pay tends to be stable and tied to other salaries. Central management is not free to jockey the pay up and down.

The variable pay elements are merit increases, bonuses, and perhaps stock options. These are the incentives that can and should be used courageously as rewards for outstanding achievement of a strategy.

Sense of Achievement. Executives, like other people, take pride in the results of their efforts. Real satisfaction arises from knowing that telephone calls go through, homes are heated, news is timely, or test equipment improves quality. And there is satisfaction in being a good competitor in business just as there is in sports.

More subtle is an inner sense of achievement, of having a challenging assignment and doing it well. Here we are concerned with an important aspect of what the psychologists call "self-realization."

A sense of achievement is a personal matter; it depends on one's own aspirations and values. Central management cannot grant it. Instead, central management tries to create conditions in which key persons feel that they are achieving. Toward this end, winning a strong commitment to company strategy is a primary requirement. Then placing individuals in jobs matched to their abilities and aspirations is a second requirement. When both requisites are met, a strong drive toward company objectives can be realized.

Social Status and Recognition. Like all of us, executives like recognition of their accomplishments. This can come only partly from their supervisors and other respected individuals who are familiar with their work. In additon, the estimation of one's friends and the community at large carries considerable weight. Since people outside the company have no direct knowledge of what the person does, they rely on titles, the nature of an office, and other perquisites—and spending patterns that presumably reflect salary. The "symbols of office," then, can provide strong motivation.

Part of our heritage is the idea that people can raise their social status. Most of our ancestors immigrated poor and uneducated; the children and their children after them improved their station in society. Success in business has been one of the major ways of improving one's social status. So, central management can use the prospect of a promotion or assignment to a key job as an incentive.

Power and Influence. History records extreme cases of lust for power, but this motivation need not be pushed that far. There is a thrill that comes with making large purchases, watching a plant operate partly as a result of one's own guidance, seeing a new product that includes one's own choice of design, or supervising a pension plan that one piloted through to final adoption. This kind of exercise in power or influence is quite legitimate—in fact, essential psychologically. We observe it especially in government and charitable enterprises where the financial rewards are low. For some individuals it is a strong motivator.

Restraints on Use of Motivators

Awareness of motivators is only a start. Using them requires insight and skill. For example, an action intended as an incentive usually has other effects too. Thus, W. J. McGill might respond favorably to more power, but the assignment of authority to McGill will involve an array of organization issues—scope of duties, decentralization, and the like. The same is true to a lesser extent for the use of titles to give McGill status. Perhaps maintaining a sound organization is more important than the incentive effect of a special concession to please McGill. So the use of most motivators has to be dovetailed with related considerations.

Perceived fairness poses another limitation. The feeling that any reward should be fairly won is very strong in the United States. A suspicion that favoritism or casualness has been involved in a promotion or a granting of power can cause a lot of hard feeling. Therefore, central managers try to have everyone who knows about a reward feel that it was fairly granted. This need for known reasons supporting a move cannot always be met, and central management then faces a dilemma of either withholding an incentive or antagonizing a number of people who will not understand why the incentive was offered. (A misunderstood reward can have far-reaching effects. If a belief arises among employees that promotions, bonuses, and the like are made on a capricious basis—and not for supporting official strategy—then a widespread attitude of "why bother to try" may develop.)

"Calling the Shots" Courageously

Another delicate matter is to motivate particular individuals without upsetting group cooperation and morale. Incentives frequently single out one or two persons for distinctive treatment, and this inevitably creates disappointments if not hard feelings among those not chosen. Clearly, when people are promoted or given more power, their status relative to their associates rises. When several individuals aspire to the same job, say vice-presidents hoping for the presidency, the disappointment of being passed by can be acute. Good people may resign, others may lose heart and stagnate. However, such costs probably are inevitable; and the loss caused by delay or compromise might be far larger.

Going outside the organization to fill an attractive post has the same discouraging effect on those passed over. However, the message is clear. The people making the appointment will not settle for just average performance. They expect distinctive results, and are willing to make an unpopular move to get them.

Demotion or discharge of an executive is hard to do because more often than not the person has been a personal friend for several years. Procrastination is expensive, however. The main cost of a weak executive is that his or her occupancy of a key position prevents a more able person from doing that work well. A baseball team cannot afford a rightfielder who bats only .100. In addition, *if* the person's weakness is recognized by other executives, failure to clean out "dead wood" from an organization tends to undermine the determination of other people to exert themselves. A wise and courageous practice is to remove ineffective individuals from key posts; if the company has an obligation to them, they can be given early retirement or jobs better suited to their abilities.

The opposite kind of a move is pleasant all around. Moving a person who is widely recognized as able to a key spot motivates the person and colleagues as well. Individual justice and the good of the organization coincide.

Concluding this brief discussion of motivating, which is one aspect of the broader managerial function of activating, we want to emphasize that central managers have a never-ending task of sensing what impels their key people. Within the limits of their powers and without undermining other aspects of administration, they seek to tie these motivations to company strategy. At the same time they must watch the impact on the group when rewards go to one person.

SUMMARY

Central managers play a dual role in activating an enterprise, that is, "putting the show on the road." They must work with their immediate subordinates just as all other executives must initiate and stimulate action of people assigned to them. In addition, central managers strongly influence the activating process throughout the enterprise, partly by the examples they set and partly by establishing certain practices as standard procedures that all executives are expected to observe.

Important elements in this activating process are: (1) creating a focused climate by selecting overriding goal(s) and major thrusts, and then repeatedly stressing the importance of these key themes; (2) managing changes in strategy and in the focused climate; (3) within this general setting, carefully guiding and evaluating the performance of each subordinate, using a form of MBO adapted to high-level executives; and (4) assessing the incentives which are important to the key people in the organization and then, within constraints, courageously exercising power with the use of those incentives.

This discussion has concentrated on activating by central managers. Although the emphasis will differ, most of the concepts presented can also be used by lower-level managers. The emphasis on developing a clear sense of purpose, and then persistently keeping individual efforts directed toward that purpose, can be applied to even the smallest section of an organization.

QUESTIONS FOR CLASS DISCUSSION

1. Continental Air Lines was in precarious financial condition in the early 1980s and rumors were rife about cutbacks, merger, or complete shutdown. One Saturday, Continental filed for voluntary bankruptcy and reorganization; it suspended all domestic flights (foreign operations had been spun off earlier in the week) and laid off most of its 12,000 employees. The next day, the court-appointed receiver announced that flights would be resumed on Tuesday to 25 U.S. cities—compared with 78 the previous week, and 4,200 workers would be rehired at sharp cuts in salaries and benefits. (Cuts brought salaries to levels paid by nonunion competitors: from $85,000 to $43,000 for pilot-captains and from $28,000 to $15,000 for flight attendants.) Assuming that the unexpected change is carried out, do you think this "prompt relief of anxiety" will create a situation favorable to longer-run stability of employment?

2. Lesley Pond (age,53) has just been named to replace G. G. McCarthy, longtime national sales vice-president of a large consumers products company, who is retiring. Pond is one of three long-service regional managers. The other regional managers are much younger, recent appointees. Pond must decide what to do with another long-service regional manager, Alvin Dart (61). "I don't know why McCarthy put up with Dart so long. Dart hasn't had a new idea in ten years. His volume is not even keeping up with inflation, and most of his salespeople have been in their jobs longer than Dart has been in his in Atlanta. I must admit his expense ratio is low, but there is no reason to hope Al will really push the new line. The company would go down the drain if we were all like Al. Maybe I can find him a government job or cut his salary so he will quit." What do you recommend that Pond do about leadership in Atlanta?

3. Think of the various service establishments that you patronize—library, bank, stores, laundry, college, hospital, employment office, and others. Select the one which, in your observation, has the clearest "focused climate." Does this focused climate appeal to you? What other advantages might the focused elements have to the business?

4. (a) The development of a company climate—as described in this chapter—calls for continuing, vigorous, enthusiastic effort. Do you think that the kind of personality who will do this task well is likely *also* to be a good, objective, rational planner? (b) Among your classmates, which ones do you predict will be: (i) sharp, objective, analytical planners? (ii) effective climate builders? (iii) tough makers of unpleasant decisions? Now considering yourself, do you believe that you will be good in all three of the dimensions just listed?

5. Most Japanese and Chinese companies do not stress bonuses and merit pay increases for *individuals*; "fast-track" promotions are also rare. Instead, the emphasis is on *group* performance, cooperative efforts, and working for the benefit of the whole enterprise. In this Eastern culture, which of the activating concepts discussed in this chapter do you think would be effective? Which one would not fit?

6. In Chapter 4 we outlined a way to analyze competitors and other key actors in a company's environment. To what extent is a comparable approach useful in activating key actors within a company?

7. Two professors from a well-known graduate school of business recently studied in depth the actions, behavior, and reasons therefore of eight chief executives of major U.S.-based business firms. The chief executives explained that they spent the great majority of their time planning for and executing projects and actions that affected and contributed to the long-term welfare of their companies. They kept acquainted with short-term (two or fewer years) plans and results primarily to be able to answer questions from stockholders and financial analysts and to report to the employees and the general public. One reviewer of the study commented: "If this is so, why is it that middle-level executives from these, and similar, firms universally claim that their bosses are (1) interested mainly in short-term results and (2) focus time and attention strongly on the short-term?" Can both points of view possibly be correct? Are the chief executives kidding themselves? Are they stating that which is expected of them by researchers and students of business but which is, in fact, not correct?

8. Although the emphasis will vary, most executives are expected to make contributions to (a) short-run results, (b) long-run implementation of strategy, and (c) creation of innovative strategy. How do you suggest that the contributions of specific executives to each of these three areas be measured, and how can individuals be motivated to work hard on each area?

9. A consulting firm designed a new, computer-based information and control system to integrate all the departments of Southern Textiles, Inc., to cut information systems cost and plant overhead by 10 percent, and to bring about faster service to customers. These gains were secured largely by uniting sales-ordering with production scheduling in all of the processing departments of the mill (cotton cleaning, yarn manufacturing and weaving), and by tying gray goods production directly with fabric-dyeing and finishing in other plants. The president of Southern Textiles persuaded Tom Jones to leave his job as head of a consulting project and come to work as assistant to the president to supervise installation and operation of the new system. This work proceeded, but not without serious disagreements between Tom Swift, the mill manager, and Tom Jones. Swift stated that three months was too short a time for complete changeover from the old control system which covered the mill, but not sales-ordering and the dye plant. A year was really necessary, he believed, if the new system would work at all.

Installation of the new system led to employee turnover, in the first month, of about 75 percent in the production scheduling and production control departments. Ten percent of those persons leaving were not replaced. The rest came in new to the plant, although they were experienced with computer systems. The new system had broken down twice. Most of the old system had been retained as a backup for three months so one breakdown was covered—at the expense of double-overtime and weekend work for thirty employees. The second breakdown caused the entire plant to shut down for one day. Jones said that Swift was not utilizing the new system properly because the system itself allowed for one day's slack-time per month and, had it been "accessed" properly by Swift and his department managers, no shutdown would have been necessary. When Swift heard this, he forbade Jones to enter the plant at any time and said to the president: "Keep him in the front office. I won't have him out here second-guessing and double-crossing me." The president was very eager to gain the cost and service advantages which he believed would accrue once the new computer system was working properly because this would raise profits for the firm, put its earnings per share in the upper half of the textile industry, and probably raise the price of its common stock—all to the benefit of the managers through the stock option system and to the benefit of the stockholders.

What could the president do?

CASE 21
Jane Sherrill, President

Sci-Tech Associates, a small California company that makes electronic components, has just been acquired by a much larger corporation—Cyril Electronics, Inc. Cyril acquired Sci-Tech to realize two objectives: (1) to improve the quality and delivery of critical components that it buys from Sci-Tech, and (2) to sharply increase the profits of Sci-Tech by improving its management.

Sci-Tech was formed nine years ago by three middle-aged owner-managers who saw an opportunity to make large capital gains from the production of several patented, state-of-the-art components—hypersensitive unitary and interlocked-series switches and high-speed electronic-impulse transmitters. The trio ran the company like a partnership, sharing all major decisions and jumping in as current problems arose. As time passed, Connie Woodworth—a really creative scientist—ran the laboratory, focusing on novel product improvements and inventions. Bernie Ash and Mark Feldstein—who had engineering backgrounds—continued to share responsibility for production, marketing, and finance.

Sales of the company grew to $10 million but profits were too modest to justify "going public" and realizing the wealth that the partners had dreamed about. Thus the stage was set for an exchange of Sci-Tech stock for Cyril stock and the introduction of a new president. Woodworth, Ash, and Feldstein became senior vice-presidents. The Cyril stock that each man received (market value equal to one-third of Sci-Tech book equity, about $300,000 apiece) did offer the prospect of appreciation, but the main incentives were the bonuses that might be earned on large improvements in Sci-Tech's profits during five-year employment contracts that were also part of the deal.

The new president picked by Cyril Electronics to run Sci-Tech is Jane Sherrill, then marketing director for Cyril's Specialty Products division. Sherrill, 32, is an ambitious MBA who has used her formal marketing training to progress rapidly in the technical environment of Cyril Electronics. The Sci-Tech assignment, however, is her first experience as a general manager. Both Sherrill and Cyril executives recognize that her performance here will be a decisive point in her career. For the people at Sci-Tech, the outcome is even more critical.

This case focuses on Sherrill's "activating" during the first three weeks on her new job. There were many questions: What changes should she make? How fast should she move? What impression did she want to create? What anxieties would the people at Sci-Tech have? Would they try to undercut her? How would they react to a young, fast-track, female executive?

First Week on the Job

On Monday morning, Cyril's CEO came to California to introduce Woodworth, Ash, and Feldstein to their new president. After describing Sherrill's record and the confidence he had in her ability, the CEO reviewed the reasons why he believed that—with Cyril's backing—Sci-Tech could move rapidly to use the high potential that the company has. The Sci-Tech managers pledged their cooperation, and the CEO closed the meeting with a request that within a month Sherrill send him a specific plan for the future growth of Sci-Tech. All this was a necessary, though conventional, ritual. And now Sherrill was on her own.

To establish an informal, trusting relationship with the former owners of Sci-Tech, Sherrill spent a half-day with each of them talking about the history of the company, their personal interest in it, future needs, current problems, and the like. Her manner was cheerful, eager, "I have much to learn." During these visits, she toured the facilities and met a few key people. From these talks, three areas needing improvement stood out.

1. Organization at the top level is fuzzy. Both Ash and Feldstein help move product concepts from the lab to designs that customers want and Sci-Tech can produce. Although titles showed Ash as president and head of manufacturing, and Feldstein as head of marketing and finance, frequently each man follows a particular customer order across all functions.
2. The basic strategy of the company is unclear. Woodworth believes that the entire marketing and production effort should be devoted to patented products coming out of his laboratory. However, half of Sci-Tech's sales are subcontract orders which Feldstein and Ash say are essential to help carry the overhead.
3. Cyril Electronics' experience with Sci-Tech—unreliable quality and often slow deliveries—is typical for other customers also.

As soon as Sherrill moved into her office (a quickly converted conference room), she discovered that her appointment makes good local publicity. The officers' secretary said, "First, a reporter for the West Coast electronics trade paper wants to set up an interview to talk about your plans for Sci-Tech as a Cyril division. Next, the Los Angeles chapter of Women in Management wants you to talk at one of their Wednesday luncheon meetings. Third, the dean of the U.C.L.A. School of Management wants to sign you up to talk to their women students about careers for women. And fourth, a reporter for *The Los Angeles Times* wants to do a feature story on how you got to be a company president."

Sherrill's reply: "Tell them all—nicely—not right now."

Less easy to brush off were the following interruptions. First, Ash appeared at the door. "Here's something you should at least know about. I've just had a call from Pacific Thermodynamics, one of our best customers for subcontracting jobs. They're inquiring if we want to bid on a really big job, involving about a million dollars over the next nine months. A new aerospace subcontract has their plant jammed with work."

"What's the problem on our side?" she asked.

"Well, they intend to impose a firm delivery schedule, with a fat penalty for nonperformance. We could meet that deadline for sure by pushing this job ahead of a couple of orders we're producing right now. It might mean slipping their delivery by a month or two if we get in a jam. It's a big job and even if we bid close to cost it would absorb an awful lot of overhead. I'm going over right now to get the drawings and specs."

"O.K., get drawings and specs, but don't submit a bid until I've had a chance to think about it," she told him.

The next interruption came from Mark Feldstein. "Listen, Jane. The biggest problem we have right now is uncertainty among the customers for our proprietary products about what the Cyril acquisition means to our ongoing relationships with them. The merger story just hit the press last week, and I've had a half-dozen calls from present and former customers. They don't know if they're going to want us as a supplier, or if we want them as a customer. A couple of them are direct competitors of Cyril for part of their product line. This is a big slug of our business that's shook up right now. We need to put a policy statement on paper and then I think you and I should take off for a week and visit these people. You need to make their acquaintance and we have to tell our policy story. This is a top priority matter."

"Let me think about it," she told him. "In the meantime, I suggest you try your hand at drafting a policy statement and supporting rationale that I can consider."

Ivan Sunderberg, the production manager, brought the third interruption into her office. "Miss Sherrill," he began, "I think—"

"Ivan, please call me Jane," she said.

"Yes, Miss Sherrill. What I want to say is I think you ought to have a meeting this afternoon with the people in the plant. You know this merger has got a lot of them jittery. Almost half of those people out there have been with us for several years and they're used to our kind of small, informal, relaxed organization. Now Cyril suddenly takes us over, and you appear on the scene from Cyril as our new boss. There are rumors floating around that you intend to shift from salary to some kind of piecework compensation system. There's talk that if this happens there'll be a rush to sign union cards and get a representation election. I think you should assure them no such thing is going to happen. The last thing we need is a unionized plant."

"I'm not going to make such a commitment," she said, "until I have time to take a good look at our total operation, and then talk all the significant issues out with you and Bernie and Mark and Connie. Do you think we should call a meeting if I have to tell the workers that?"

Second Week on the Job

Much of Sherrill's second week was devoted to establishing a personal relationship with employees and customers—and in the process putting to rest false rumors about impending major changes.

Instead of a meeting with all the employees, she arranged to see them in groups of eight to ten. Personal introductions were the chief business, a start on Sherrill's resolve to know all 125 by name, and on the other side, an effort to be regarded as a friendly person rather than a tool of a big distant corporation. Then for each group, Sherrill briefly described existing cost and quality problems at Sci-Tech, told them that future success depended on solving these problems, and asked for their cooperation. With shop groups, she added that she had been told of their concern that a piece-rate system would be introduced and assured them (1) that she planned no immediate change in the existing compensation system, and (2) that no change would be made at any future time without advance consultation with all affected employees.

Also, Sherrill arranged to visit, as soon as possible, all eight customers buying Sci-Tech's patented products, accompanied by Sci-Tech's principal contact person with each customer. The central message at these meetings was (1) that Sci-Tech hoped to continue to be a preferred resource, and (2) that quality and delivery problems would be solved, and (3) that she wanted them to bring to her personal attention any continuing difficulties in their relations with Sci-Tech.

Sherrill instructed Bernie Ash not to submit a bid on the large subcontract job he was considering, telling him that the organization's first priority must be to resolve existing deficiencies in cost control, production and shipment, and quality control.

As time permitted between these many meetings, Sherrill studied numerous financial reports. They were not very helpful, at least to a person who had not experienced the events that the figures reflect. The absence of interpretation and analysis, Feldstein explained, was because "all three of us knew the actual facts right up to the moment decisions were made. Our practice was to deal in the present, and in this kind of business we have found that the historical accounting records are usually out-of-date."

Third Week on the Job

The experiences at Sci-Tech during her first two weeks persuaded Sherrill that she should not try to prepare a long-range plan for Sci-Tech within the month stipulated by the CEO of Cyril.

1. She lacked the necessary information and it was not readily available.
2. So many holes needed to be plugged in present operations that further changes at this time could "overload the system."
3. Plugging these holes would significantly improve short-run results, perhaps

raising profits before income tax from $117 thousand last year to $500 thousand this year.

So, using these arguments, Sherrill received the CEO's permission to postpone formulating a long-run strategy until the end of the year, eight months off.

Immediately after receiving an o.k. to defer the strategy proposal, Sherrill met with Ash, Feldstein, and Woodworth, informing them of both the postponement and her stated profit target for the present year. The vice-presidents strongly approved—a reaction Sherrill anticipated because she knew that they were concerned about drastic changes she might initiate or would be compelled by Cyril to initiate.

"You realize better than I," Sherrill continued, "that for us to achieve the goals I outlined to the CEO, we all have a hell of a lot of work to do. Bernie, within ten days I want you to let me have a detailed written plan for (1) immediately reorganizing the production scheduling system so that we meet shipment commitments most of the time rather than some of the time, (2) revising our quality control system so that product failures are reduced by at least 75 percent during the balance of the current year, and (3) cutting $300,000 out of our factory payroll and related personnel costs.

"Mark, in ten days I want you to prepare an analysis of defects and gaps in our financial and cost information and your specific proposals for a quick-fix of at least the major deficiencies so that we can promptly establish a more reliable information base that will give us reasonable measures of profit or loss by product, by customer, and by job. I want much more solid numbers than are presently available, solid enough to let us make fundamental long-range planning decisions with confidence that we know what we're doing.

"Connie, I want from you, again in ten days, a detailed evaluation of your complete ongoing research program, project by project. For each project, I want your judgment of the probability of its ultimate specific commercial application and the time required for its development from now to the stage of readiness for production. I want, that is, the kind of information that will permit us to establish R & D priorities which will help to concentrate your and your staff's effort on the most valuable and earliest-to-market payoff of all ongoing activities. In doing this, I suggest you consult with Bernie about the production implications of each product concept in your laboratory and with Mark about the financial and market implications of each product concept. I want you to reach your own conclusions, but I want you to get their suggestions and show both their and your own independent judgments in your report.

"I have an additional request with a longer deadline. Within four weeks I'd like from each of you a detailed written statement, with supporting rationale, describing what you believe to be the optimal long-range strategy for this business as a whole.

"My own assignment is to lay out an in-depth analysis of the outlook for a firm like ours.

"As soon as I have time to study the report any one of your submits, I plan to sit down with that person and establish monthly targets which will enable us to measure the progress we are making on these immediate improvements in operating practice. To keep each other informed, let's have a regular Monday morning meeting at 8:30 for coordination and suggestions.

"If we do these things, we'll have a much more effective company at year-end. The profit goal is makable. With a 15 percent increase in sales, which looks likely, we should hold the *increase* in cost-of-goods sold and other expenses to 10 percent. That in itself would put us way over the mark. This plan doesn't give us a long-run strategy, but it will put us in a much stronger position for the long-term growth that we all expect."

Privately, Sherrill has doubts about how good some of the reports that she requested will be. For instance, she is asking Woodworth to think about managing R & D in a way that runs counter to his philosophy of research. And, Feldstein has shown little grasp of how financial data can be used to analyze and control operations. So, she regards the requested reports to be as much a test of ability as a source of practical ideas.

Also, Sherrill realizes that by leaving the present organization untouched she, in effect, is endorsing it. However, going along with the status quo steers clear of a potential hassle which she would like to avoid at this early date—especially because she needs full cooperation in reaching this year's profit target to which she is committed. Besides, Sherrill rationalizes, we should have our strategy clarified before we decide what the organization should be.

Questions

1. How well do Sherrill's actions match the suggestions for activating outlined in this chapter?
2. Do you think that Sherrill has acted wisely?

22 CONTROLLING OPERATIONS

Controls are commonplace—from thermostats to speed limits. Still, in our society, what to control and how to control are often hotly debated—witness environmental control, birth control, gun control, diet control. Managers also face issues about what and how to control.

The need for some kind of managerial control is widely accepted. The aim is to ensure, insofar as possible, that plans are actually carried out. Nevertheless, the process of control is troublesome; instead of harnessing cooperation it sometimes misdirects effort and undermines morale.

Numerous controls are used in every well-managed company. Central management obviously cannot, and should not, try to follow all these detailed measurements and evaluations that occur daily. Instead central management should focus on:

1. the design of the company control structure
2. exercising control of overall results and of crucial activities
3. utilizing control data to help formulate new strategy, policy, and programs

First we need to examine the nature and the variety of applications in the basic control process.

NATURE OF THE CONTROL PROCESS

Three elements will be found in every control system:

1. Standards of acceptable performance are established.
2. Actual (or predicted) performance is appraised in terms of these standards.
3. When performance is found to be unsatisfactory, or unusually good, appropriate managerial action is initiated.

Many problems arise in using this simple sequence: what should be covered by the standards and how tough they should be; who will do the measuring of performance and how this information will get transmitted to the people who evaluate it; and what types of corrective action will lead to improved performance in the future. Often a choice must be made between post-action control, yes-no control, or steering control. Let us look at a few illustrations.

Representative Control Systems

The following examples differ not only in the activity being controlled, but also in the character of the controls being used. They show ways to adapt controls to each specific situation.

Control of Sales Volume. For many years, a chemical company had kept track of its sales in terms of dollars and physical units for each major line of products. Trends in these figures were the cause of joy or dismay, but a new sales manager felt that they did not enable her to pinpoint problem sources and to take specific corrective action. Consequently, she expanded the sales control system in two ways. First, she kept track of sales results in much greater detail; all oreders were analyzed in terms of sales representatives, type of customers, geographical areas, and products, and cross-classifications of each category were charted. Second, she tried to develop some criteria for what sales should be in each category. For this purpose, she developed an index of activity for types of customers (consumer industries), geographical regions, and long-term trends for products. From this information and data on past sales, she developed quotas for subdivisions of the sales analysis. These quotas were adjusted up or down as changes occurred in the market.

These two steps generated a mass of statistics. However, with the aid of a sales analyst, the sales manager could identify particular areas or industries where orders were falling behind quota. Often the sales representatives concerned had a good explanation for the deviation, but in other instances remedial action was obviously called for. The sales representatives grumbled about spending a great deal of their time with the new statistics. The sales manager, on the other hand, was convinced that the expanded controls brought to light difficulties that might have remained buried in the large totals formerly used. Experience also indicated that the sales representatives, who received the control data as soon as the sales manager, became more diligent about covering each part of their assigned territory.

This example raises the question of how detailed controls should be. The previous controls of the chemical company were too general to be useful for operating purposes. On the other hand, if the company had pursued the pattern of control to very small territories and fine industry divisions, the mass of statistics would have been overwhelming and the variations of doubtful significance.

Another notable feature of the system was a variable standard. If industrial activity in a particular territory was booming, the sales representative was expected to secure higher sales; but a decline in the market being served was also taken into account in appraising the sales representative's results. The assumption here is that the factors causing the expansion or the contraction in the market were beyond the sales representative's influence.

Inventory Control. One way to achieve control in sufficient detail and still not swamp executives with masses of information is to have both measurement and corrective action taken by the people who are performing the operation—or done automatically. This possiblity is illustrated by the inventory control system of an electronic cash register manufacturer. This firm has to keep on hand 65,000 different parts so that finished machines can be assembled rapidly as customers' orders are received.

Briefly, the control system involves: (1) Establishing the minimum stock for each part (the *standard*). Whenever the supply on hand falls below this minimum, a standard order for additional stock is placed. (2) Maintaining a perpetual inventory record of each item and comparing this with the minimum standard. Formerly, this record and its examination (*appraisal*) was done by stockclerks and noted on tags attached to the front of the bin containing each part. More recently, maintenance of the inventory record and comparison with the ordering point has been assigned to an electronic computer. (3) Whenever the stock on hand falls below the minimum standard, a requisition for additional materials is issued (*corrective action*). Of course, as demand and technology change, the standards have to be adjusted, and a physical inventory is taken periodically to make sure that the records are accurate.

This rather conventional inventory control system suggests two possibilities for many other controls. Once a clear-cut control is designed, it often can be operated by people close to the operation. Upper management then can limit its attention to design of the system and checking to be sure that it is being properly utilized. And when both the standards and the corrective action are clear-cut and current performance can be measured in quantitative terms, the entire control process can be automated.

Control of Large Capital Expenditures. Typically, large capital expenditures must be approved by the board of directors before they can be advanced beyond the planning stage. Often all projects contemplated for a year are assembled together in a capital expenditures budget, as explained in Chapter 12, and specific approval is given for those projects the board considers most desirable. Once approved, the project description becomes the control standard, and subsequent steps are checked against this standard.

In terms of the basic control process, this procedure differs significantly from the two controls we just examined. In the previous examples, as in many controls, measurement takes place after action is completed. So these controls fall into the broad class of *post-action* controls. In contrast, the directors' review of capital expenditures occurs during the process—after the plan is completed but before commitments are made. This control, like many in-process quality controls, is a *yes-no* control. Action may not proceed until approval is given. The board of directors reserves the function of comparing specific proposals against its standards before any damage can be done. This tight rein is in sharp contrast to a control system that operates routinely, if not automatically.

Executives maintain control over some activities by withholding permission to act until they give their approval to the specific acts. Appointing key personnel, signing large contracts, selling fixed assets, and starting a sales campaign are often treated in this manner. Progress is slowed, but the executives feel the particular subjects are of such importance that they are unwilling to rely upon such standards as they can define with appraisal after the action is completed. Obviously only a limited number of activities may be treated in this slow manner in a large, vigorous enterprise.

Strategy Control. In addition to post-action controls and yes-no controls, a third class is *steering-controls.* Control of a spacecraft headed for the moon, for instance, takes place days before the flight is finished. As soon as the craft leaves the earth, a forecast is made of where it is headed; immediate corrective action is taken based on the forecast. Post-action control, after the craft either hit or missed the moon, obviously would be too late.

Company strategy is like the flight of the spacecraft. We can't afford to wait for completed results before exercising control. Instead, we rely primarily on updated forecasts. (1) We monitor key assumptions about consumer tastes, governmental action, interest rates, competitors' actions, and the like. If new information indicates that operating conditions will differ from the original assumptions, corrective actions may be taken at once. (2) At major "milestones"—for instance, when market tests are completed or just before making a large investment—the entire strategy is reviewed, using all new information available, and an updated forecast of results is made. The forecasted result is compared with company objectives, and a decision is made whether to continue on the present course or to modify it.

Steering-controls are far from precise, but they have the great advantage of prompting an adjustment while an array of possibilities is still open. Also, people subject to this control feel that steering-controls are devices that help them reach objectives rather than judge past success or failure.

Budgetary Control. The best *comprehensive* control system is based on financial budgets. Here the already existing accounting structure is the base; the budgets are simply a prediction, or plan, of what various accounting figures should be at some future date. Income and expense accounts for, say, the next year are estimated and are summarized into a budgeted profit and loss statement. At the same time, changes in assets, liabilities, and equity are estimated and are summarized into a budgeted balance sheet for the end of the period.

For control purposes, the budgeted figures become the standards. Then when the normal accounting data come in, they are considered a measurement of actual performance and are easily compared with the budget standard. Of course this procedure can be followed for departments as well as the company and for monthly, annual, or any other periods for which regular accounting figures are compiled.

Financial budgets have several outstanding advantages: (1) The measuring process is already well established and requires no additional expense. (2) All parts of the company are covered with the same comprehensiveness of official financial reports. (3) The use of dollars as a common language permits coordination and consolidation of plans for differnt parts of the business. (4) The control mechanism is directly related to one or more typical company objectives; for example, earnings per share, return on investment, or sales growth.

Being so closely tied to conventional accounting, financial budgets also have limitations: (1) Accounting figures do not promptly reflect intangibles such as customer goodwill, employee morale, executive development, research on product and process development, equipment maintenance, or market position. (2) The annual accounting period may not match the physical production or marketing cycle, so that expenses are hard to relate to resulting income and arguments occur over allocations. (3) Early warning of trouble is usually buried; also the accuracy desirable for financial reports delays budget comparisons. These drawbacks strongly suggest that budgetary control should be accompanied by other types of control in order to achieve a balanced control structure.

In actual operations, the primary problem with financial budgets can be executives' ineffectual support of them. If executives allow budgets to be merely predictions by staff personnel or the central accounting office instead of carefully conceived plans by line managers, they will not be accepted as reasonable standards. And when the standard is not respected, the whole budgetary process is regarded as an annoying distraction. Also if central management does not insist that deviations be acted upon and that budgets be revised when changes in strategy and programs are made, budgetary control will be weak.

Control of Executive Development. The examples of control discussed thus far have dealt primarily with objective data. Many important aspects of business operation are not so clear-cut. Nevertheless, control of these intangibles may be even more crucial to long-run success than things that are easily observed and measured. Executive development falls into this intangible category.

One well-managed company measures its progress in executive development in two ways. Annually, its key executives must report executive development activities undertaken by people in their departments. The reports cover special training assignments, appraisal reviews, training meetings, civic and trade association activities, and the like. The company recognizes that such reports omit perhaps the most important training that takes place on the job. It also recognizes that the activities reported may not have resulted in any significant executive development. However, the hope is that emphasis on training activities will encourage executives and operators alike to give attention to the basic process.

The second measure of executive development used by this company is the number of people considered to be ready for promotion. Data for this purpose are assembled from an executive inventory, such as the one described in Chapter 19. Again the unreliability of the data is recognized, but they are used simply as the best information available.

Two control techniques are illustrated in the case just cited. One is the use of activities rather than end results. This is done because the company cannot afford to wait until the end of the process (perhaps as long as twenty years in the case of executive development). Moreover, actual measurement of progress is difficult if not impossible. Basic research, legal work, and public relations are further examples of business functions posing this sort of measurement problem.

The case also illustrates the use of steering-control. If the number of people classified as promotable is inadequate to meet projected requirements, a danger signal has clearly appeared. In fact, more promotable people may be present than the inventory shows, or conversely, the estimates of employees' capacity to take added on added responsibilites may be over-optimistic. Nevertheless, the warning is sufficiently serious so that more careful consideration and probably corrective action is called for. Every good control system makes wide use of steering-controls because they help to identify trouble in the early stages.

These attempts to control executive development also point to a danger. Executives can become so absorbed in making the measures look good—for example, lots of training meetings and high evaluations of subordinates—that they fail to accomplish the underlying objective. In other words, because the controls do not deal specifically with desired end-results, they may misdirect effort.

The above illustrations suggest the variations in kinds of managerial controls. Choices must be made about such characteristics as: amount of detail, level in hierarchy where evaluations are made, automatic adjustments of standards, attention to intangibles, and when in the process correction is started (yes-no, steering, post-action). Regardless of these variations, however, three basic elements are always present—setting standards, appraising results, and taking corrective action. So let us review these three elements.

Setting Standards of Performance

Some standard or guide is essential in any form of control. Even informal control requires that executives have some plan or standard in mind by which to appraise the activities they are supervising. These standards should come directly from the strategy, policy, deadlines, specifications, and other goals established in earlier stages of the management cycle.

Satisfactory performance, of course, has many aspects, and it is impractical to set control standards for all of these points. Instead, *pivotal control spots* are picked out for regular observation. Important considerations in picking these pivotal points are: (1) discovering important deviations in time to take corrective action; (2) making practical and economic observations; (3) providing some comprehensive controls that consolidate and summarize large blocks of detailed activities; and (4) securing a balance in control so that some aspects of the work, such as developing executives, will not be slighted because of close controls on other phases. What to watch is vital in every simple and effective control system.

"How good is good?" is the next question. For each control point, an *acceptable level of performance* must be set. How many sales orders per month do we expect Jean Jones to obtain? What level of absenteeism is considered dangerous? Is a labor cost of $13.95 per unit satisfactory for our deluxe model? The answers to such questions become the accepted norms—the par for the course. One of the best ways of providing flexibility in a control system is to devise acceptable and prompt ways of adjusting these norms.

Appraising Performance

Some comparison of actual performance with control standards may be done by a manager. A sales manager, for example, may occasionally travel with sales representatives to observe their performance and the attitudes of customers. Typically, however, *control observations* are made by someone other than the executive—such as an inspector, a cost analyst, or a market research person. Also, some control data are derived as a by-product of other recordkeeping. Expense data, for instance, may come from payroll records and inventory records; sales data may be gleaned from a file of customers' orders.

Such separations of measuring performance from its evaluation and corrective action necessitates *control reports*. The information must be communicated from person to person, and this raises a host of questions: What form should be used? How much detail should they contain? To whom should they be sent? How often should they go? Can reports be simplified by dealing only with exceptions to standards?

The effectiveness of a control is usually increased by *prompt reporting*. If some undesirable practice is going on, it should be corrected quickly. Moreover, the cause of trouble can be learned better if people have not had several weeks to forget the circumstances. Also employees, knowing that a prompt check on deviations from standards will be made, are more likely to be careful in their daily work. Consequently, the sooner a control report reaches a manager, the better the control will be.

Another practical issue in appraisal is whether *sampling* will provide adequate information. Perhaps refined statistical techniques, such as statistical quality control, can be used to decide the size of the sample and the inferences that can be drawn from it. In some operations—aircraft manufacturing, for example—100 percent observation is essential. And, we have already noted that for certain key actions—capital expenditures and executive appointments are typical—a manager may insist on giving personal approval before performance continues.

For activities which take a long time from start to finish, such as launching a new product or counteracting a competitor's invasion into our home market, *updated predictions* of future results may be vital. Such revised projections—based on results to date and external changes—become the basis for steering control.

The engineering term "measuring and feedback" provides another way of describing this appraisal step in the control process.

Taking Corrective Action

Real control goes beyond checking on work performed. Unless corrective action is taken when standards are not met or when new opportunities appear, the process amounts to little more than a historical record.

As soon as a deviation from standard is detected, the causes of the variation should be investigated. If the deviation is unfavorable, perhaps the difficulty will be due to a lack of supplies, a breakdown of machinery, a strike in a customer's plant, or other hinderance in *operating conditions.* In such situations, the executive will take immediate steps possible to remove any obstructions.

At other times, the difficulty will be personal in nature. Perhaps there is a simple *misunderstanding*, a failure in human communication; this may be quickly corrected. More troublesome is *inadequate training* of persons assigned to do the work. As a rule in such cases, help is provided until the person has received the training needed. Of course, if investigation reveals that the person simply does not have the necessary *basic ability* and never should have been selected for the job, transfer of the work or a replacement for the individual may be the only satisfactory remedy. All too often, the gap between performance and standard reflects a lack of effort. The person may be able to do the work and may understand what is wanted, the operating situation may be satisfactory, but the needed *incentive* is lacking. This, then, calls for additional motivation by the manager.

Corrective action sometimes leads to *revision of plans.* The check on operating conditions and on selection, training, direction, and motivation of the operators may reveal that the standards themselves are unrealistic. If control is to have any meaning in the future, such standards should be revised. Also, the delay in work may have been so serious that schedules need to be rearranged, budgets revised, or customers notified. These changes in plans should give operators and executives a new set of standards that are reasonable criteria for future actions. Or the controls may have flagged results much better than predicted, and if such results can be expected to continue, new standards should be set.

CENTRAL MANAGEMENT CONTROL TASKS

What is central management's role in all this controlling activity indicated in the preceding discussion? The answer lies in three areas: (1) design of a balanced control structure for the total company, (2) actually exercising control at selected spots, and (3) using control data to help shape new strategy and programs.

Company Control Structure

The control structure of a compnay is more than the simple aggregate of the various controls used by different executives. These controls should be examined to be sure that no important considerations are missing; balance and emphasis should be checked to be sure they are in harmony with basic company objectives; and the compatability of the controls with company planning, organization, and supervision should be assured.

Assuring Adequate Coverage. Table 22-1 suggests a way to examine a company control structure. Listed in the left-hand column are all the result areas that central management believes should be controlled by someone in the enterprise. The areas listed in the table are merely suggestive. In practice, the management of any single company will undoubtedly want to be much more specific on some points and to omit others.

With the result areas identified, senior executives can discover a great deal about control in their company by filling in the rest of the table. Usually a company will have very good controls in some areas and only vague and informal systems in others. This may be due to historical custom or to the relative ease of obtaining certain kinds of data. As a result of the analysis, central management will know where to try to devise additional controls that will fill in the missing gaps.

Relation of Controls to Decentralization. In thinking about who should set specific norms, appraise current performance, and take corrective action, organization structure should be related to control structure. The greater the decentralization of authority to make decisions, the further down the hierarchy should be the short-run control activity. It is simply inconsistent to give a manager freedom to run a division or a department and then to have some outside person make frequent detailed checks of just what is being done and suggest corrective action. In fact, control of routine activities is often performed further down the line than decision-making.

On the other hand, the manager who makes a delegation needs some reassurance that the authorization is being wisely used. Consequently, summary reports are submitted monthly or quarterly to senior executives. Also, senior executives may wish to watch a limited number of "danger signals" both for control and as a basis for future planning.

In addition, senior executives may want to be sure that adequate controls are being used by their subordinates, even though none of the reports come to them. A simple example is insistence on tight controls on cash disbursements in a branch office with no further attention (except the annual financial audit) being given by the supervising executive. Quality controls and production controls are frequently handled on the same basis. In effect, a pattern of control is stipulated when the subordinate manager is appointed, but exercise of this control is a part of the delegation made to this manager.

TABLE 22-1.
APPROACH TO COMPANY CONTROL STRUCTURE

	System Design		Exercising Controls		
Result Area to be Controlled	Control Points	Form of Measurement (Indexes)	Set Specific Norms (Pars)	Appraise and Report	Take Corrective Action
General Management					
Profitability	_____	_____	Who?	Who?	Who?
Market Position	_____	_____	"	"	"
Productivity	_____	_____	"	"	"
Technical Research	_____	_____	"	"	"
Personnel Dev.	_____	_____	"	"	"
Employee Relations	_____	_____	"	"	"
Public Attitudes	_____	_____	"	"	"
Sales:					
Output	_____	_____	"	"	"
	_____	_____	"	"	"
_____	_____	_____	"	"	"
Expenses	_____	_____	"	"	"
	_____	_____	"	"	"
_____	_____	_____	"	"	"
Resources used	_____	_____	"	"	"
	_____	_____	"	"	"
_____	_____	_____	"	"	"
Other	_____	_____	"	"	"
Production:					
Output	_____	_____	"	"	"
	_____	_____	"	"	"
_____	_____	_____	"	"	"
Expenses	_____	_____	"	"	"
	_____	_____	"	"	"
_____	_____	_____	"	"	"
Resources used	_____	_____	"	"	"
	_____	_____	"	"	"
_____	_____	_____	"	"	"
Other	_____	_____	"	"	"
Research & Eng.:					
Output	_____	_____	"	"	"
	_____	_____	"	"	"
_____	_____	_____	"	"	"
	_____	_____	"	"	"
Expenses	_____	_____	"	"	"
	_____	_____	"	"	"
_____	_____	_____	"	"	"
Resources used	_____	_____	"	"	"
	_____	_____	"	"	"
Other	_____	_____	"	"	"

Integrated Data Processing. A total view of the control structure for a company emphasizes the large number of control reports that must pass through the organization. Original data have to be compiled and then analyzed, and reports must be sent to the operator, the boss, and perhaps a staff group. In addition, summaries or reports of exceptions probably go to a senior executive. The total of these reports in a large company is staggering.

Electronic data processing equipment can speed up the analysis and the distribution of this control information—*if* it is in numerical form. Perhaps such equipment can also be used to cut the expense of report preparation, though the usual result is a substantial increase in the number of reports (better control) for, it is hoped, the same expense. However, to achieve this speedier, elaborated flow, the procedures for handling data have to be revised. Potentially, all original data will be fed into the computer, and there they become available for planning as well as control purposes. We then have integrated data processing.

This new speed and readily availability of data should be utilized in the company control structure. They make certain controls in headquarters, *or* in the field, more feasible. At the same time, a danger should be recognized—a plethora of numerical reports will increase the tendancy to overemphasize those factors that can be expressed numerically. Consequently, integrated data processing should be regarded as an aid and not as a determining factor in the design of a company control structure.

Relation of Controls to Other Phases of Managing. In stressing the desirability of having central management carefully shape the company control structure, we are not suggesting that a lot of controls be superimposed on other management activities. For example, the target dates set in the programming of normal operations or elaborated in a PERT schedule automatically become norms in the control process; quality control standards are simply the logical extension of product policy dealing with quality; and so on. Controls are the means for assuring that such plans are fulfilled.

Similarly, goal-centered performance reviews include agreeing on personal goals for the next six months or year and then comparing accomplishments with the goals at the end of the period. Many of the goals thus established will simply be norms for factors already included in the control structure, and control reports will be used in the discussion of results. Of course, additional unique goals may be agreed upon and a temporary control cycle set up. But if the company control structure deals with crucial areas, a factual basis will already exist for much of the performance appraisal discussion.

The control structure, then, should bind together the total management process.

Controls Exercised by Central Management

Design of an effective control structure is a major central management task. But even an ideal structure will not relieve cental management from exercising some controls itself. Several attempts have been made to identify a limited number of key result areas that central management should watch. The most suggestive of these is a list used by G.E. According to this approach, the effectiveness of overall management can be appraised in terms of:

1. profitability, in both percent of sales and return on investment
2. market position
3. productivity, which means improving costs as well as sales
4. leadership in technological research
5. development of future key people, both technical and managerial
6. employee attitudes and relations
7. public attitudes
8. balance of long- and short-range objectives

Note that this list places considerable emphasis on strength for future growth as well as on current profitability.

In addition, G.E. and others expect senior executives to single out crucial problems in their particular industry or function and to watch these closely. Incidentally, what is crucial shifts from time to time—union relations may be especially sensitive at one time, foreign competition at another. So, the attention of top management shifts, leaving for subordinates the task of continuing vigilance.

As emphasized in Chapter 18, central management has a particular responsibility to be alert to *new* developments that may create opportunities or obstacles. Consequently, much of the data examined by central management is not for routine control but a source of possible cues to future changes.

Using Control Data for Future Planning

Business provides a continuing flow of services. In the same day, managers are checking on final "delivery" to today's customers and also preparing for next year. Control contributes to this never-ending preparation for the future by feeding in appraisals of current successes and difficulties. For central management, inevitably removed from day-to-day action, this building for the future is certainly the most exciting facet of control.

The *replanning* that is prompted by control reports may be short-run. Often a program for raising capital or launching a new product has to be speeded up or slowed down because of success—or lack of it—in pilot plant tests. Or, a rise in production costs may precipitate a withdrawal from a marginal market or an adjustment in prices.

Likewise, control reports provide one of the main considerations in deciding what to aim for in the *next planning period*. The quality achieved, the rate of output, the expenses, and the consumer acceptance in the past period are guides to what may be expected in the next round. Care must be exercised in merely projecting the future on the basis of past experience, because conditions change and improvements are possible. Nevertheless, to disregard past performance is even greater folly. And it is control reports that provide the most readily available data on past performance.

Central management also uses control data in designing *new strategy*. Targets, we noted in Chapter 5, are one dimension of strategy; they identify the criteria by which success will be measured and indicate levels of achievement expected. So in considering strategy, one of the first steps management takes is to see how close to such targets actual performance has been. As with short-range planning, this past performance is a significant input in deciding where to set future targets.

More significant, however, are the reasons why targets have been exceeded or not achieved. Market potentials may have changed, international trade barriers may have been lowered, competitors may have exploited a new technology, or the company may have lost its distinction in key personnel. Such factors as these may show that a new operational strategy is needed. We do not mean that control reports will be the only stimulus to revising strategy; environment, industry, and key actor analyses (recommended in Chapters 2, 3, and 4) should also flag future opportunities and problems. But in a going concern, the take-off point is a careful reading of how well we are doing relative to what we set out to do. In this manner, central management used the control system as a springboard in deciding future strategy.

SUMMARY

Strategy, policy, and organization provide the broad guides and the framework for the activities of a company. Planning is then extended to detailed methods and procedures, and on to programs and schedules. The managers turn all this preparatory work into action as they issue operating instructions and motivate people to execute the plans. Even then, the task of managing is not complete; there remains the vital step of control.

Control is necessary to insure that actual performance conforms to plans. The specific measures for control should, of course, be adapted to the particular activity. Nevertheless, three basic steps must always be present: (1) Standards of satisfactory performance should be set up at strategic points—points that well provide timely, economical, comprehensive, and balanced checks—and, for each point, a norm or level of achievement should be agreed upon. (2) Actual performance should be compared with these standards by sampling, 100 percent inspection, or perhaps required confirmation, and appraisal reports should be sent to all persons directly involved. (3) When significant deviations are detected, corrective action is necessary; that is, adjusting operating conditions, improving competence of assigned operators, motivating, or perhaps modifying plans.

Central management becomes involved in controlling operations in three main ways: (1) It reviews the numerous controls that operate within a company to make sure that all key points are adequately covered and that the net emphasis of the controls is in harmony with company objectives. This is a matter of design of the total control structure. (2) Central management itself exercises control of overall company results and of a few selected activities that are especially crucial to long-run results. (3) Even more important, central management utilizes data from control reports to assess how well company strategy is being achieved. This analysis provides an important base for setting new targets and perhaps reshaping the operating strategy. Thus the controls serve as feedback into company planning, and the management cycle of planning, organizing, activating, and controlling starts anew.

QUESTIONS FOR CLASS DISCUSSION

1. "Steering-control of a strategic thrust is difficult, partly because the entire strategy is based on a set of predictions about the external world and the reactions of key actors to our moves. (See Chapters 2, 3, and 4 for typical kinds of predictions.) If these predictions are wrong, maybe our strategy should be modified. Therefore, the steering-control should include a monitoring of the continuing reliability of the main predictions." (a) Explain how this proposition would apply to control of Ford Motor Company's strategy to assemble its subcompact and compact cars in Hermosillo, Mexico, in order to reduce its costs and to be able to compete against the Toyota-General Motors assembly plant in California and the Japanese cars everywhere in the Americas. (b) Explain how this proposition would apply to control of the United States Football League's strategy to schedule its games during the spring of the year.

2. Transnational, Inc., of Houston is concerned about controlling "questionable payments" which might be made by executives of its foreign subsidiaries. Both "grease" (payments to do promptly what receiver is supposed to do) and "bribes" (payments to do what receiver is not supposed to do) are involved. Either local government officials or local business executives may be receivers. Control is complicated because local custom in some but not all countries where Transnational operates condones such payments. In contrast, U.S. law prohibits payments to government officials even where local practice endorses it. What ways do you suggest Transnational use to control questionable payments?

3. The Ascott chain of motels has a well-developed budgetary control system. In addition to monthly financial results of each motel, subdivisions of expenses for room operations and restaurant operations are budgeted. A central computer prepares

comparisons of actual results versus budget for each motel within a week after the end of each month, and these reports are distributed to central executives and each motel manager. Central staff personnel promptly investigate major deviations. In contrast, Ascott has no formal controls over employee training or morale, market position of each motel in its local area, quality of maintenance, quality of service, or changes in local reputation. What do you predict will be the long-run consequence of this control structure?

4. Pioneer Life Insurance Co. knows that several of its competitors have sold large quantities of insurance to doctors by actively soliciting and providing special service to pre-med students. These early associations lead to large policies after professional success is attained. Pioneer wishes to apply this same approach to MBA candidates, and has appointed John Bunyon vice-president in charge of the new program. Because Bunyon is in the home office, he can get a specially designed though standard type of policy approved, devise sales approaches, prepare promotional material, and the like. However, the use of such aids depends on individual salespeople who are located throughout the United States. Salespeople work under General Agents and are paid a commission on their sales. They have wide latitude in seeking clients and selecting suitable policies for each client. How do you recommend that Bunyon try to control the MBA program?

5. You are the proprietor and manager of a small, specialty restaurant near a college campus that sells excellent Greek food, wines, and beer. Hours are 11:30 a.m. to 8:30 p.m. six days each week. Revenue is satisfactory overall, although quite erratic, but profits are well below your hopes and desires and nowhere near your wildest dreams. What should you do to gain control? Think about steering-control, yes-no control, post-action control, control of activity rather than results, sampling, adjustment of norms, and corrective action. How might you apply these ideas?

6. "I've received good support from my president," explains Marianne Tierney, vice-president for corporate planning of a real estate firm that owns and operates six major shopping centers in the southeastern United States. "And the local managers usually find time to talk about future possibilities. But not much happens. I have no good control over efforts to build volume and expand beyond the next fiscal year. Our controller says that lead-times are too long to make reliable predictions, that our business is full of uncertainties, and that we must keep changing our strategy to take advantage of new opportunities—all of which, he says, makes control of results more than a year ahead impossible. There is no doubt that short-run results are what get attention around here." Do you have any suggestions for long-run strategic action in this company?

7. (a) What effect does inflation have on managerial controls? (b) What can be done to maintain effective control in periods of double-digit inflation?

8. Scientific management devotes much attention to motion and time study, production scheduling, selection and training of workers, preventive maintenance, materials specifications, and other features of shop management. What bearing, if any, does

each of these facets of scientific management have on the job of a plant superintendent in controlling operations in the plant? Should the president be concerned about the use of such techniques in designing the company control structure?

9. The Cardiz Construction Company—builders of shopping centers, offices, schools, and churches—is concerned with its public relations. Complaints about noise, dirt, upsetting ecology, workers' disregard of community customs, etc. are becoming increasingly troublesome. "We talk to our people over and over," Mr. Cardiz says, "and they correct the specific complaint. But two weeks later a group of mothers are picketing around 'the old oak tree' or a town clerk wants us to sweep up some dust in front of the mayor's house." Like other construction firms, Cardiz gets its business through competitive bidding for contracts that normally have a fixed price and penalty clauses for late completion. Each project manager is measured on how well actual performance stacks up against contract provisions. The project manager's job is complicated by the use of subcontractors for many parts of the work. How do you recommend that Mr. Cardiz get better control of public relations?

10. A large consumer goods firm specializing in food products found itself with a five-year prediction of 1 to 2 percent per year (equal to the growth rate of the U.S. population) growth in sales (in constant dollars) because its products had captured about as much of the market share as they were likely to get and because convenience foods appeared to have met almost every convenience need. Therefore, the central management proposed, and the board of directors agreed, that the firm should acquire a fast-food franchising firm and expand its locations to compete with McDonald's, Wendy's, Burger King, etc. The company had a generally accepted standard that its return to the stockholders should be 15 percent per year from a combination of dividends and stock-price increases. Central managers also desired that the company grow in real terms (after inflation) at least 4 percent per year. Acquiring a new firm would shoot sales up between 15 and 20 percent, in real dollars, in the first year. "We are experts in marketing, therefore we can market anything—including fast-foods" was the prevailing attitude at headquarters. But the acquisition might, perhaps, reduce returns to the shareholders below 15 percent per year for the first year since only companies with a less-than-average return on investment were available for sale. Company executives believed that generally it takes eighteen months to two years to turn such companies around. (a) Do the sales increase and return-on-investment goals provide adequate guidelines for company strategy? (b) Do you believe that success in marketing one kind of product will lead to success in marketing another? (c) Does a very attractive, one-year increase in sales revenue seem to you a wise idea for the company?

CASE 22
Zeus Under Control?

Zeus Corporation has eight divisions (legally wholly-owned subsidiaries).

Most divisions are manufacturing businesses related in some way to electronics. They have had varying degrees of success, but overall Zeus has been quite profitable.

Help from Headquarters

Senior managers at Zeus believe that a significant part of their success is due to their planning and control system. *Longer-run planning* focuses on developing new lines of business; it consists of (1) selecting a domain that looks promising; (2) deciding how to attack that domain, under the guidance of a Design Review Committee; and (3) preparing thrust plans and budgets, under the guidance of Project Teams. The Design Review Committees and Project Teams are drawn for these temporary assignments from anywhere in the corporation, and they are expected to cover a stipulated sequence of steps.

Annual planning for ongoing business in each division starts in September with corporate approval of the division's general plan for the following year. Then more specific plans spelling out departmental activities are prepared in October and November. These are expressed in operating budgets and capital expenditure budgets, which are approved by corporate staff and executives by the end of November. The corporate staff people feel that "making a good sales forecast is usually the heart of good annual planning."

Once its annual budgets are approved, each division is given wide latitude in carrying them out. Headquarters *control* consists largely of comparing actual performance against the budget. For capital expenditures, divisions are free to invest within the overall limit; if a division finds that it needs more funds, it requests an upward revision in the total—a process that typically takes four or more weeks.

C.D.C. Mission

One division of Zeus, the Credit Data Company (C.D.C.), provides credit information from a central data bank to lenders. Rapid information about a consumer who wants credit on a new car or wants to open a charge account anywhere in the nation is a distinctive aspect of this service.

C.D.C. offers (1) to install a "total system" in its customer's credit office, including a small computer and full procedures for using this machine to tap the huge memory of large computers at C.D.C.'s headquarters, and (2) twenty-four-hour on-line availability of currently updated credit information on many consumers. "We can tell the lender—our customer—almost immediately whether a prospective borrower does or does not pay his or her bills. It's as simple as that." Other information is often available. The bulk of its business relates to consumer credit, although recently C.D.C. has embarked on providing a similar service regarding business credit.

C.D.C. has enjoyed rapid growth, ranging from 20 to 50 percent per year. Its central computer center has capacity to store 60 billion bites of data. These files have information on 90 million consumers throughout the United States. Each month about 100 million updates are posted, and the system can handle 100,000 requests for data in a peak hour. There are already 8,000 service terminals throughout the country.

Feud Regarding Controls

Zeus managers are naturally pleased with C.D.C.'s success, but the corporate staff is unhappy with the way the control system is working.

Part of the difficulty stems from C.D.C.'s conservatism in estimating its future sales. Repeatedly C.D.C. has underestimated its actual growth, and central staff says that this shows an inability to plan. C.D.C. managers point out that their growth plans have always been ambitious, and to promise more would entail a low probability of achievement. (The use of budget fulfillment as the main criterion for annual bonuses may have some influence on this debate.) And C.D.C. managers find that explaining profits above budget is easier than profits below budget.

The squabble about "pars" for annual sales has laid the basis for difficulty regarding capial expenditures. Because sales growth has exceeded the annual budgets, C.D.C. has repeatedly sought additional funds for facilities to handle this unplanned volume. Corporate staff views this behavior as "lack of control."

Last year corporate staff made an analysis of why C.D.C. was so far off in its capital expenditure budgets. Over half of all capital outlays were found to be for computers, so attention now centers around computer purchases. "To get on top of this situation, we now have a separate capital budget for computers. Moreover, before a computer order can be sent to a supplier, it must be okayed by us (corporate staff) to be sure that it comes within the budgeted total. If it does not, C.D.C. must submit and get approval of an upward revision in its capital investment plan for computers."

Within the finance and purchasing departments of C.D.C., there is no mystery about what has been taking place. Two kinds of computers were being purchased—very large ones for central processing of data, and many small ones which were resold or leased to customers as part of the system package. The small computers are standard "shelf" models which can normally be obtained within a week. In effect, they are raw materials, and their purchase fluctuates with the number of new customers obtained.

In contrast, the large computers are indeed capital equipment. They provide capacity in the central data bank to store more information and respond to more inquiries. These large computers must be ordered eighteen to twenty-four months in advance. To be sure that it would not have to turn down new business because of lack of capacity, C.D.C. management has been placing orders on the assumption that business would grow fifty percent per year. Annual budgets typically anticipated twenty percent growth. The differnce between the optimistic and conservative assumptions is considered by C.D.C. management as a safety factor or "contingency plan." When actual growth is less than 50 percent, C.D.C. slows down delivery of the large computers—often with a penalty fee—and it may temporarily accept excess capacity which will be filled up by subsequent growth.

Until recently this ordering of large computers has not been reflected in the annual budgets. Only actual receipts of equipment are picked up in the capital expenditure account. Under the circumstances, it is not surprising that C.D.C. might be requesting an increase in its annual capital expenditure budget to pay for computers which in fact had been committed for in the previous fiscal year! When discovered, corporate staff concluded that C.D.C.'s capital expenditures were "out of control." On the other hand, C.D.C. management contends that it has been acting prudently so as to assure optimum growth, which Zeus executives urge C.D.C. to obtain.

Under the new system of a separate budget for computers, corporate staff is having difficulty reconciling orders and delivery for all kinds of computers with the current year's profit and loss budget and with next year's budget which has not yet been approved. And C.D.C. management is not inclined to simplify the confusion.

One undesirable effect of the wrangling is that toward the end of the fiscal year, C.D.C. must get approval of an upward revision of the computer budget before orders for small computers are official. This causes delays of over four weeks. Meanwhile C.D.C. is failing to provide the *prompt service* which it has been telling new customers is a hallmark of a relationship with C.D.C.

Question

Assume that you are an outside consultant. (1) What capital expenditure control system do you recommend that Zeus Corporation use for C.D.C.? (2) Are there any changes outside your recommendation for (1) which are needed to make your proposal work effectively?

INTEGRATING CASES

Strategy & Execution

SOLAR ENGINEERING SUPPLY (SES)

Company History

"For centuries the sun has been warming mankind, and it will continue to do so indefinitely. Our aim is to help harness this tremendous energy source," explains Donna Nielsen, Chairperson of Solar Engineering Supply (SES).

"My husband, Ted, and I met at an environmental protection meeting and SES is an outgrowth of our joint concern. I am still active in the movement, and I follow legislation and governmental activities very closely. Ted is an engineer who moved quickly into the practical problems of actually putting the sun to work. We tried several approaches before deciding to focus on the heating of water for residential use. That is the best place to start now.

"We soon learned that knowing the best design for water heaters is not a sufficient background to establish a business. So, we've joined forces with two very able people whose backgrounds complement ours. I. R. Resnik has an M.B.A. in accounting and is our Vice-President of Finance. P. Flannigan had ten years of experience in the sales department of a large air-conditioning firm before joining us as Vice-President of Marketing. Ted is President; he heads up engineering and also supervises production—although T. V. Florio, the Production Superintendent, actually runs the plant. It's a strong team."

Present Products

Ted Nielsen explains, "A solar hot-water heating system uses energy from sunshine to heat water. In a typical installation, the 4 X 8 foot solar collector panels which warm the water are placed on the roof of the house. The heated water is stored in a tank until the consumer draws it off through the regular hot water faucets in the house. Because the sun shines intermittently, almost all solar systems for residences are coupled with a conventional hot water heater. The solar system simply reduces the amount of fuel that has to be purchased. And of course, there are no exhaust or other potential sources of air pollution.

"SES supplies all the components needed for an installation to the local contractor who is installing the solar system. SES also advises how to do the job.

The components include solar collector panels, water tanks with heat exchangers, pumps and valves, electronic controls, mounting brackets, special fittings. SES puts its brand name on all these components, even the ones we buy from outsiders.

"The collector panels are by far the most critical and expensive components. SES assembles its own panels in accordance with carefully engineered specifications. Each panel consists of a copper absorber plate mounted on polyurethane foam insulation under a glass cover, all within an aluminum and steel frame. The absorber plate, which we buy, is a network of brazed tubing with a black chrome coating on its fins; it absorbs 95 percent of the sun's rays. Liquid is pumped through the absorber plate network to collect the heat and carry it to the water tank. The 3 X 8 or 4 X 8 foot frame must be strong enough to withstand wide variations in temperature and hurricane-force winds.

"SES also carries a less expensive plastic collector designed for heating swimming pools. Our sales emphasis, however, is on the residential product. SES does not stock the more experimental types of panels, such as the high temperature (commercial) solar panels which convert water into steam. At no time has SES dealt with photovoltaic cells which produce electricity in applications such as earth satellites."

Solar Water-Heater Industry

"Our industry is settling down from a great burst of interest which lasted over five years," Donna Nielsen observed. "Environmentalists have long noted that the use of solar energy would reduce air pollution. But it was the Middle East oil crisis that stirred up enthusiasm. Consumers wanted alternative energy and both state and federal governments tried to stimulate the industry's development. For example, as part of broad effort to develop alternative sources of energy, the federal government financed a whole series of experimental and demonstration solar projects. It also established a 40 percent income tax rebate on a consumer's cost of installing an approved solar water-heating system. The result has been a bumpy series of starts and stops as the industry took off.

"A lot of firms jumped in—both large and small. Grumman Corporation, the big aerospace firm, assigned a group of its engineers to saving energy; it came out seven years ago with a beautifully designed water-heating system and—according to industry gossip—spent more in advertising than it has made in sales since then. Exxon, Libby-Owens-Ford, Olin Brass, G.M., several copper and aluminum suppliers, and other *Fortune* 500 companies all entered the industry in one way or another.

"But this was also an industry that small firms like SES could enter. The basic technology has been known for many years, so there are no significant patent barriers. Most components are in ample supply. Small-scale assembly is feasible with semiskilled labor. With a few hundred thousand dollars you could launch a local business. Estimates vary, but I think that by the early 1980s over three hundred companies were selling solar water heater equipment to contractors, to each other, and even to consumers.

"Several things have led to a shakeout. First, the oil shortage turned into a temporary oversupply, so fewer consumers currently fear big increases in their fuel bills. Second, high interest rates and an economic recession have put the building industry into a tailspin. Third, the resulting volume of solar system sales simply cannot support all the people who entered during the boom; some of them are falling by the wayside. My guess is that half the competitors have either withdrawn to other activities or failed, and another fifty will leave before the upturn. With total industry sales of, say, $100 million, there must still be a lot of mom-and-pop outfits in business."

P. Flannigan is more specific. "Many of the small firms that moved into this industry, and several of the big ones too, just don't understand marketing a product like solar water heaters. It's an unfamiliar product to most consumers, and an installation costs them between $3,000 and $4,500. So the consumer has to be educated before being sold. Most of our competitors don't know how to get that job done.

"That selling job is not easy. The margin in solar systems will not support direct selling by a manufacturer. The value of the fuel saved puts a ceiling on the price that can be charged. So you have to use plumbing or air-conditioning contractors who are already established in their locality. The real task is helping and inducing at least the more vigorous of these characters to sell solar systems. Remember, installation contributes at least 35 percent to the final cost. Maybe it is lucky for us that few of our competitors are ready to undertake that essential teaching task."

Ted Nielsen says, "The structure of our industry is changing. The local fly-by-night operators are folding up or looking for greener pastures. Fortunately, it is almost as easy to get out of this industry as it was to enter; there are no big factories with fixed overhead that must keep producing nor are there unfunded employee retirement claims that block liquidation. No one really knows how many have left, but I feel sure that four or five of the leading producers of total systems increased their combined share of the market from, say, 15 percent three years ago to 25 percent now. SES intends to be part of this elite group that builds market share while the going is tough.

"Concentration is taking place upstream also. Olin Brass, formerly a big manufacturer of absorber plates, has withdrawn. Libby-Owens-Ford dropped out even earlier. Exxon sold the Daystar company to American Solar King for much, much less than its total investment. And so it goes. Big-name companies remain active, but there are fewer of them. The industry seems to be moving toward a four-tier structure: (1) manufacturers of parts—controls, glass covers, absorber plates, and the like. Mostly, the parts we buy are off-the-shelf items also used for other appliances. Except for a few specialty items, these components are a small part of a large and diverse line of the manufacturer—for example, glass covers. (2) Producers of solar heating systems—we specify and assemble the parts and turn them into the things which make up a heating system. (3) Distributors—the regional marketing organizations that do all the things necessary to move the products from producers to the thousands of contractors who make installations in homes. A distributor provides regional warehousing of a variety of solar collector panels, stone-lined water heater tanks, valves, controllers, and other components that a home air-conditioning or plumbing supply house would not stock. (4) Contractors (dealers)—they sell a specific installed system to home owners and do the installation work. Of course, the separation between these four is fuzzy. For instance, absorber plate manufacturers such as Daystar also assemble completed solar panels. SES is both a distributor and a producer of solar heating systems. Some distributors also install systems. Nevertheless, the four-tier structure is now clearer than it was."

SES Strategy

The present SES strategy is summarized in an internal memorandum:

"A. We believe that in the foreseeable future that effective distribution will be the most sensitive step in the solar water-heating industry. Therefore, we will seek a strong position as a distributor as well as a producer of solar systems.

"B. Our strength as a distributor will be built upon the following:

1. Unusually complete written instructions for the proper installation of a solar system. The aim is to make it easy for a contractor to bid on and complete each job. Field engineers (salespersons) will be available to interpret the instructions for unusual jobs.
2. Prompt delivery to a contractor of any and all items involved in the installation of an SES systems.
3. Brochures for home owners and other selling aids which a contractor can use in reaching their customers.
4. Guidance on how home owners and contractors can arrange local financing. However, SES itself will not make such loans or endorse notes.
5. Modest quantity discounts and advertising tie-ins to encourage active contractors to push solar systems.

"C. We will expand our own distribution one region at a time. A strong base in large-volume regions is more important than wide coverage.

"D. SES R & D activities will be confined to designing systems which use available parts. This assumes that any major advances in absorber plates or other parts will be made available to SES because of our strong distribution in major markets."

Consistent with this strategy, SES does its own distribution in the southwest from its headquarters and plant in Houston. Also, it distributes to California, Arizona, and Nevada from a regional warehouse and office located in San Bernardino, California. The next target area is the southeast, where a regional office and warehouse are planned for Atlanta, Georgia. The son-in-law of an independent distributor in Florida has agreed to become the SES regional manager, but it will be at least six months before the Florida business is liquidated and he will be able to move to Atlanta. He is also having marital problems.

SES has an independent distributor in Albany, New York and one in Urbana, Illinois—each of which handles several other product lines. Sales in both regions are quite low. But, a New England sales representative who has made an outstanding record in commercial air-conditioning has told Ted Nielsen that she was looking for a position where she could exercise more initiative and would be glad to tackle solar systems. So, sales in these regions might improve.

Financing Company Growth

I. R. Resnik believes that SES has a good, long-run relationship with a venture capital firm named Vencap. At present, Vencap owns 45 percent of SES's common stock and officers of SES own the rest. Also, Vencap has loaned SES $800,000, which is covered by 8 percent subordinated notes and an option for Vencap to double its stock ownership at $4.00 per share.

"As SES expands its own distribution," says Resnik, "it will have to hold more inventory in the branch warehouses and probably more accounts receivable. We will certainly need another $200,000 in addition to retained earnings.

"Vencap will probably lend us the money *provided* we keep the risk to a minimum. Their representative on our board of directors is already bearing down on 'controls.' When we adopted our present strategy we heard a short sermon that I believe is the tip-off. It went something like this: 'Vencap is prepared to play a waiting game. I like your plan because it puts you in a position to market a breakthrough product, such as an inexpensive absorber plate, or to expand quickly if energy costs skyrocket. The critical part is to control your exposure until such favorable events occur. You have my blessing provided you come back to the board with a method for controlling the execution of the strategy.'"

Existing Controls

"SES has the usual annual budget, " continued Resnik, "but it is so strongly affected by sales volume, and sales depend so much on external factors that we can't influence, little real control results.

"There are two areas I watch closely. Most important is the size of the inventory. I watch that every week. If we don't ship, I make sure that we don't buy or make up panels. It's as simple as that. Accounts receivable, the second area, can't be turned off so easily but I do keep an eye on slow payments and jump in quickly. Sometimes there is a good reason for being slow, but our customers know that our bills must be paid.

"Another place where control is tight is quality of output in the plant. The specs are clear and Florio makes sure that the supervisors check these regularly. As a result, the workers have good quality habits.

"Our friend from Vencap, however, has something else in mind. He wants assurance that our product line is right, that our marketing effort is on target, and that we aren't caught short by unpleasant external events—the collapse of the 40 percent government subsidy, for instance. We won't get any more capital from Vencap until we install controls over things like that."

TABLE 1.
Solar Engineering Supply Condensed Balance Sheet
(in 1,000's)

Cash	$ 186	Accounts Payable	$ 434
Accounts Receivable	928	Notes Payable	630
Inventories	768	Accrued Items	207
Total	1,882	Total	1,271
Fixed Assets, net	821	Subordinated Notes	800
		Equity*	632
Total Assets	$2,703	Total Liabilities and Equity	$2.703

*Two hundred thousand shares of common stock outstanding.

Question

What controls should SES adopt to ensure that the execution of its strategy stays on track—as requested by the board member from Vencap?

MANAGEMENT OF CONVAIR[1]

The Corporation

By 1960 General Dynamics had become one of the great corporations of the country. Its sales were around two billion dollars and it produced, profitably, some of the most complex equipment known to man. Its major operating divisions were:

- Astronautic (Atlas Missiles)
- Electric Boat (submarines)

---

[1]For a fuller discussion of this period in General Dynamics history, see "How a Great Corporation Got Out of Control," by Richard Austin Smith in *Fortune,* January and February, 1962. The present case is composed of excerpts from these two articles. Reprinted by special permission; © 1962, by Time, Inc. All rights reserved.

- Forth Worth (B58 bombers)
- General Atomic (nuclear development)
- Liquid Carbonic (liquified gas)
- Electrodynamics (electric motors)
- Pomona (electronics plus Terrier missiles)
- Stromberg-Carlson (telephones, electronics)
- General Aircraft (leases or sells planes traded-in for jets)
- Canadair (aircraft)
- Convair

This case, reported in the January and February 1962 issues of *Fortune*, focuses on one product of one division, but the issues raised are basic to the entire scope of General Dynamics and to many other companies. The division—Convair—was by far the largest component brought into General Dynamics (in 1954); and the product—the 880 and 990 passenger jets—rolled up the largest loss ever achieved by a nongovernment enterprise on a single venture, around $425 million.

General Dynamics was founded by John Jay Hopkins. Under his inspiration net earnings, $600,000 on sales of $31 million in 1947, rose to $56 million on sales of $1.7 billion in 1957, the year of Hopkins' death. Hopkins was a man of great energy who kept posted on each division of this expanding empire largely by direct and unannounced visits. In 1953 he did bring in Frank Pace as executive vice-president "to have someone in the office to answer the phone" and especially to maintain Washington's confidence in the company. Pace had served as Director of the Budget, and during the Korean crisis as Secretary of the Army.

Aside from golf, the law, and the high order of intelligence, Pace and Hopkins were complete opposites: Pace temperate in all things, oratorical, deliberate, anxious to be liked, a product of the federal staff system, prone to rely on his second-in-command in the making of decisions; Hopkins volatile, creative, earthy, intuitive, ingrown, willing to listen but unwilling to share the making of decisions with anybody, a loner more likely to give the world the back of his hand than to extend the palm of it. In 1957 cancer caught up with Hopkins. His hand-picked board of directors decided (over Hopkins' strong objections) that Pace should be president. Hopkins died three days later.

Pace described the task of managing the enterprise he inherited in these terms: "When you have a company, employing 106,000 people, made up of eleven different divisons, each a corporation really in its own right, most of which were separate enterprises before they joined the organization, and headed by men who were presidents of corporations, with their own separate legal staffs, financial staffs, etc., all of these highly competent men—the only way to succeed is to operate on a decentralized basis. Our total central office in New York City was something like 200 people, including stenographers. This group can only lay out broad policy. Your capacity to know specifically what is happening in each division just cannot exist. If you did try to know everything that was happening and controlled your men that tightly, they would leave or would lose the initiative that made them effective."

Convair's Move into Commercial Jets

The Convair division was headed up in 1955 by General Joseph T. McNarney with John V. Naish as executive vice-president. Tough-minded Joe McNarney, ex-chief of U.S. forces in Europe, had always been pretty much of a law unto himself, while Jack Naish wore his fifteen years' experience in the airframe industry like Killarney green on St. Patrick's Day. The divison had already pulled off a successful commercial-transport program; the propeller-driven 240's, 340's, and 440's were world-famous. But what prompted Convair to consider making the formidable move into jet transports was a suggestion by Howard Hughes.

Hughes wanted jets for TWA; but before Hughes and Convair could agree on a design, Boeing and Douglas came out with long-range jet transports (the 707 and the DC-8) which scooped the market. Still determined to get into jets, Convair turned to the medium-range market. For this plan, Hughes proposed to buy 30 planes. After considerable engineering work, the executive committee of General Dynamics' board, headed by Hopkins, unanimously approved McNarney's program based on the assumption it would make money after 68 planes were sold, that potential sales of 257 aircraft could be realized, and that the maximum possible loss was only $30 million to $50 million.

By this time three airlines—TWA, Delta, and KLM—had already taken options to buy the 880. Now the committee instructed Convair to go ahead and get letters of intent from them within the next fortnight. The committee laid down only three conditions in authorizing the program: first, that GE guarantee the 880's engine; second, that the ability of the airlines to pay for the jets be investigated by an *ad hoc* committee of Pace, Naish, and Financial Vice-President Lambert Gross; third, that management was not to go ahead without orders in hand for 60% of the estimated 68-plane breakeven point.

The last provision proved to be quite flexible. The breakeven point on the 880 had been understated: after closer figuring, Convair raised it to 74 planes in May, up 6 planes in two months. When KLM did not pick up its option, the executive committee indulgently dropped its 60% condition, allowing Convair to go ahead with only 50% of the breakeven point assured. The new figure was made to fit the fact that by now Convair had only 40 firm orders (10 from Delta and 30 from Hughes).

A Doubting Thomas

Both Convair assistant division manager, Allen Morgan, and B. F. Coggan, the division manager, had informed management back in 1956, at the time 30 planes were sold to Howard Hughes, that the 880 was underpriced. Their conclusions were ignored then because of the difficulty of substantiating their cost estimates at so early a date. But now a year had elapsed, the 880's design was frozen, and components had been ordered preparatory to starting up the production line. So the cost of the aircraft could be figured with precision; it was an amalgam of money that *had* been spent on research and development and money that *would* be spent on materials, fabrication, and assembly. Usually about 70% of the material costs of an aircraft is represented by items bought from outside suppliers—the engines, pods, stabilizers, ailerons, rudders, landing gear, autopilots, instruments, and so on—with only 30% of the total material costs being allocated to the airframe manufacturer himself. The 880 ratios followed this general pattern. But when an engineer in Convair's purchasing division began totaling up the various subcontracted components, he came to a startling conclusion: outlays for the vendor-supplied components of each 880 totaled more than the plane was being sold for (average price: $4,250,000). He took his figures up the line, pointing out that when research and development costs of the aircraft (they totaled some $75 million) were added in, along with the 25 to 30% of the material costs allocated to Convair itself, nothing could be expected of the 880 program but steadily mounting losses. He recommended that Convair abandon the whole venture, even though the loss, according to his estimates, would be about $50 million.

Whether the engineer's recommendation and his supporting data ever reached New York headquarters is something of a mystery. In any event, when the engineer persisted in his analysis, Convair decided he was a crank and fired him—he was reinstated two years later after time had confirmed the accuracy of his judgments.

Target No. 1: United Air Lines

The sales problems that confronted Convair in 1957, however, were something that couldn't be sloughed off with the firing of a critic. At the start of the 880 program in March, 1956, the potential market had been estimated at 257 planes. By June of that year Convair had raised the figure to 342, but in September it was down to 150 after an on-the-spot appraisal had let the air out of the sales estimates for European airlines. These gyrations gave substance to an industry rumor that the division undertook a thoroughgoing market analysis only *after* commitment to the 880 program, but at least one point was clear about the "final" forecast of 150. The bulk of that number, as General Joseph McNarney, Convair's president, said at the time, had to be sold before July 1, 1957, or the 880's production line could not be economically maintained. The trouble was that an understanding with Howard Hughes had kept Convair from selling the 880 to anybody but TWA and Delta for a whole year. This had already caused the loss of customers who preferred a 707 or DC-8 in the hand to an 880 twelve months down the road. So in the spring of 1957, when Convair was at last free of the commitment, it had still sold no more than the forty 880's (to TWA and Delta) that started off the program. The success of that program, with only a few months to go before McNarney's July 1 deadline, now hinged on selling the remaining airlines, American and United.

Convair's first target was United, which it had listed as a prospect for 30 aircraft. For a time things seemed to be going Convair's way in its pursuit of this critical $120-million sale. Boeing, Douglas, and Convair were all in competition for the United contract, but Convair had the edge with its 880, for it was then the only true medium-to-long-range jet aircraft being offered. All Boeing could offer was essentially the long-range 707, too big and, for its seating capacity, 50,000 pounds too heavy to suit United. The size could be reduced, of course, and some of the weight chopped out, but not 50,000 pounds unless Pratt & Whitney could substantially lighten the engines, the JT3C-6's used on the 707 aircraft. With Pratt & Whitney unwilling to make this effort, United's board decided in favor of the 880 on September 27, 1957, subject to a final going-over by United's engineers.

Soon thereafter, United's President William Patterson called General Dynamics' Executive Vice-President Earl Johnson, whom Pace had put in overall charge of the jet program, out of a board meeting to tell him Convair was "in." But perhaps the most consequential call was one Pratt & Whitney's Chairman H. Mansfield "Jack" Horner then made on Patterson himself. Spurred on by Boeing, Horner had been galvanized into action, and now he wanted to know whether something couldn't be done about getting Boeing back in the competition, if Pratt & Whitney could come up with a lighter engine. Patterson referred him to United's engineers, who made very encouraging noises. They themselves had been pushing for Pratt & Whitney for just that. Both Boeing and Pratt & Whitney then went into a crash program, the former to scale down the 707.

Within a few weeks Boeing had come up with a new medium-range aircraft—the 720—45,000 pounds lighter than the 707. United then invited Boeing and Convair to cut their prices and both did, though Convair refused to cut below what Pace recently described as the "bare minimum." In November, United's chief engineer John Herlihy compared Convair's 880 and Boeing's 720 and then strongly recommended the latter. His reasoning: the commercial performance of the GE engine was an unknown quantity, while "we had the Pratt & Whitney engines in our other jets and wanted to regularize our engines if we could"; moreover, the narrower fuselage of the Convair 880 permitted only five-abreast seating, a shortcoming United had vigorously protested back in 1956 when Convair had first solicited its opinion of the 880 design; the Boeing 720, on the other hand, was wide enough for six-abreast seating, a difference of as many as 25 passengers at full load in the tourist section of a combination first-class ourist airliner. This meant, in Herlihy's view, that the 720 with its lower operating costs per passenger-mile was a better buy than the 880 with a $200,000 cheaper price tag. On November 28, 1957, United's board approved the purchase of 11 Boeing 720's with options for 18 more.

"Merely a Modification"

The loss of United meant a sharp reduction on the market potential of the 880, dropping it from 110 to 80 planes. Worse than this, Convair had a powerful new competitor in what had been its private preserve, the medium-range field. That competitor was now going to make it tough for Convair to sign up American Airlines just at the time when Convair expected to sell the airline 30 planes, nearly half of the 880's dwindling market potential. Discussions with American had been going on for some months, though pressure had naturally increased after United chose the Boeing 720 in November. But in January, 1958, American notified Johnson, who was in overall charge of the negotiations, that it too was going to pass up the 880 for twenty-five 720's.

In February, however, Convair was able to reopen discussions with American on the basis of a revolutionary new engine General Electric had just developed. Called a turbo fan-jet, it required 10 to 15% less fuel than a conventional jet to do the same job (under flight conditions) and provided 40% more power on take-off. The aircraft that Convair intended to use with these new engines, later designated the 990, was billed as "merely a modification" of the 880. It was a modification to end all modifications. The 990 had a bigger wing area than the 880 and a fuselage 10 1/2 feet longer; weighed over 50,000 pounds more; required an enlarged empennage, a beefed-up landing gear, greater fuel capacity, and stronger structural members; and was supposed to go 20 mph faster.

Many of these changes were imposed by American's hard-bargaining C. R. Smith, whose talent for getting what he wanted out of an airframe manufacturer was already visible in the DC-7. But Smith hadn't stopped with just designing the 990; he designed the contract too, using all the leverage Convair's plight afforded him. In it he demanded that Convair guarantee a low noise level for the plane, finance the 990's inventory of spare parts until American actually used them, and accept, for American's $25-million down payment, twenty-five DC-7's that had been in service on American's routes. The DC-7 was then widely regarded as an uneconomical airplane, 12% less efficient to operate that the DC-6, and, as Convair discovered, it could not be sold for even $500,000 in the open market. When General Dynamics reluctantly accepted this down payment, worth only half its face value, American signed up for twenty-five 990's with an option for twenty-five more.

"We Had to Go Ahead"

Looking back, director Alvord recently commented on the whole affair. "Earl Johnson brought back a contract written to American specifications with an American delivery date, but the plane was not even on paper. It was designed by American and sold to them at a fixed price. There was not even any competitive pricing." What is more, Alvord says, "the 990 was signed, sealed, and delivered without board approval. It was just a *fait accompli*. An announcement was made to the board that there would be a slight modification of the 880." Pace himself believed at the time that the 990 was only a slight modification. He now says, "If we had known at the outset that major changes would be needed, deeper consideration would have been given it."

The decision to go ahead on the 990 was an important turning point in the fortunes of Convair and of General Dynamics itself. The reasoning behind it has been stated by Pace: "When the Boeing 720 took away our sale to United, we found ourselves in competition with a plane just as good as ours. This is just what we wanted to avoid. The 880 seemed doomed. We had to go ahead with the 990 or get out of the jet business. American had not bought any medium-range jets . . . When the fan engine was developed, they told us, 'We will buy your plane if you produce a plane like the 990.' It was absolutely vital for us to follow American's wishes. We had to have another major transcontinental carrier. I thought I was taking less of a gamble than I did entering the 880 program."

But what this amounted to was that General Dynamics had now committed itself to a double-or-nothing policy, gambling that the success of the 990 (beginning with the American sale) would make up for the failures of the 880. The nature of this gamble is worth specifying, in view of the fiasco that eventuated:

The plane had been sold at a price of approximately $4,700,000. Yet nobody knew how much it would cost because its costs were figured on those of the 880, which were still on the rise and unpredictable.

The number of planes Convair must sell to put its jet-transport program in the black had gone up sharply. The breakeven point on the 880 had been 68 planes at the start (March, 1956), a figure that by 1958 should have seemed impossible of fulfillment. Nothing but dribs and drabs of sales to lesser airlines could be expected of the 880, for the "majors" (TWA, United, and American) had already been sold or refused to buy. Convair's commitment to the 990, which had a breakeven point of its own meant the division must sell 200 of the 880's and 990's to keep out of the red.

The success of the 990 depended largely on its being the sole plane on the market with a fan-jet engine. When it built the plane around the GE engine, Convair was confident that Pratt & Whitney would not make a fan jet. Barred from making a *rear* fan jet—GE's licensing agreement prevented this—Pratt & Whitney simply built a *front* fan engine. Boeing used this for the 720B, which took away a good deal of the 990's potential market.

The 990 was built without a prototype, or advanced model. General Dynamics had "lucked out," to use President Earl Johnson's phrase, on the 880 without testing a prototype. So now the company was again going to gamble that it could take a plane directly from the drawing board into production without any major hitches. Said Rhoades MacBride, by way of fuller explanation: "Our time for debugging the 990 was severely compressed because we wanted to take advantage of being first with the fan-jet engine. If we had built a prototype and flown it, we would have minimized our advantage in having the fan engine before Pratt & Whitney had it. We realized that if everything went right, we would be way ahead. If the 990 didn't fly as stated, we would be in terrific trouble."

"Our Basic Mistake"

Yet if ever a plane needed a prototype and plenty of time for testing, it was the 990. As Earl Johnson himself conceded recently: "Our basic mistake in judgment was that we did not produce a prototype to fly to virtual perfection. From a management standpoint we should have said, 'If you haven't the time to build a prototype, then you shouldn't get into the program.'" The 990 was an extremely fast aircraft, with short-field characteristics and a brand-new engine. The decision to go it without a prototype meant that Convair had committed itself to attaining the very high speed demanded by C. R. Smith—635 mph—the first crack out of the box. As it turned out, a lag of only six minutes in the 990's flying time on a transcontinental run of 2,500 miles was to result in C. R. Smith's canceling his contract because American wouldn't be able to bill the 990 as the "fastest airliner in the world."

"The Furnace Treatment"

Just before Convair undertook the 990 program, General McNarney retired and the division got a new president, hard-driving John Naish. Naish's succession clearly indicated that Convair was still an empire within General Dynamics' empire and would likely remain so. Pace had wanted the Convair job for Earl Johnson, the old Army buddy he'd made his No. 2 man. McNarney wanted Naish; McNarney got Naish. And the new Convair chief soon made plain his confidence he could handle anything that came along—if left strictly alone. As he said at the time: "The company has a great many people who like to solve their own problems. It believes in the furnace treatment—you throw people in the fire and you can separate the good metal from the dross very quickly."

Naish had already got a taste of the furnace treatment at Convair, for troubles were piling up on all sides. Total orders for the 990 were only 32, while those for the 880 were still stuck at 44. Overhead on the jet venture had risen as production of the Convair-made F-106 dwindled and the Atlas program, which also shared the San Diego facilities, had had to be moved to another plant on orders from the Pentagon. But these were just first-degree burns in comparison to the furnace treatment Convair's new head was about the get from Howard Hughes over the 880.

Hughes's vagaries had already caused Convair plenty of lost sales and missed opportunities. When the 880 got to the production stage, the Hughes group—TWA engineers and executives—had quietly set up shop in an abandoned lumberyard near Convair's San Diego headquarters and for a time Hughes caused more mystification than trouble. As 1959 wore on, however, it became increasingly difficult to get Hughes to commit himself on the final configuration (styling and arrangements) of his 880's and making it certain that overtime would have to be used to meet the tightly scheduled delivery dates of the 990's—they'd been promised to American for the spring of 1961—if their dates could be met at all. As a matter of fact, in September (1959) Sales Vice-President Zevely was already notifying the airlines that the 990 would be late.

Convair let more precious months slip by trying to humor Hughes before it came to a shattering conclusion: all his stalling on the final configuration of his 880's had its roots in the fact that he hadn't the money to pay for them on delivery.

Convair chose to pull his 880's off the line and put them out on the field. What made this decision so fantastic was that 13 of the planes were in different stages of completion. Now the economics of an aircraft production line are geared to "a learning curve," which simply means that labor costs go down as each production-line worker becomes familiar with his particular phase of putting the plane together. On the first 880 the learning curve was at its peak with labor costs of roughly $500,000, on the fortieth or fiftieth plane labor costs were designed to drop below $200,000. Thus removing Hughes' thirteen 880's from the line in *different stages* of completion meant that the learning curve for them would have to be begun again at the top—to the cost of Convair, not of Hughes.

"It's Not a Baby Any More"

This disastrous decision was made by Jack Naish, with an OK from Frank Pace and Earl Johnson. But even then New York was far from on top of the situation. Pace maintains that he never knew the 880 was in serious trouble until after the Hughes decision: "We knew we had problems, but there were no major difficulties as far as we knew. The information that came to us fiscally, in a routine fashion, through Naish and substantiated by Naish, would not have led us to believe the extent of the losses that were occurring." Earl Johnson is not even sure just when he himself became alarmed over the jet program. "It's difficult to answer that. It's like living with a child—when do you notice it's not a baby any more?"

The sad truth was simply that General Dynamics was still being run as a holding company with no real control from the top. Its headquarters staff had been kept at 200, and this, in Pace's view, "automatically recognizes that it is impossible to police the operation of the divisions." But even if there had been a will, the means of policing seem slender indeed. Pace had established no reporting system that could tell him quickly when a division was in trouble; the key figures were buried in pages of divisional operating statements. General Dynamics' Financial Vice-President Richard Knight is still overhauling the system of auditing the divisional books so as to prevent any doctoring of the figures to make a divisional president look good. In short, millions of dollars of publicly owned money could be on its way down the drain at Convair before New York was aware of it.

In a letter of May 10, 1960, addressed to General Dynamics' stockholders, Pace reported jet-transport charges of $91 million (as of March 31, 1960) but added "[We] have every reason to believe [the program] will be one of our most successful ventures." By mid-August, however, Pace's springtime optimism began to show the signs of an early frost. It will be remembered that from the very beginning the 880 had been grossly underpriced in relation to its material costs; now Convair had virtually given up trying to keep those heavy costs within the budgeted amounts. For almost a year San Diego had been abuzz with rumor that losses on the 880, "the sweet bird of our economy" as local citizens called the 880, might reach $150 million. Some 880 components had overrun their original estimates by as much as 300%.

Four months later (January, 1961) Hughes got his financing and Convair was confronted with the problem of completing his aircraft. And some problem it was. Since no two planes were in exactly the same stage of completion, they couldn't be put back on the production line. They had to be hand-finished on the field, at costs many times those prevailing on the line. Moreover, engineering changes had to be made—some Convair's and some Hughes'.

A $40-Million Discovery

By February of 1961, General Dynamics was beginning to reap the economic consequences of the disastrous Hughes decision. New York "discovered" that Convair had not only failed to write off all jet losses the previous September but had incurred additional ones. These, amounting to $40 million, spelled the end for Jack Naish and for August Esenwein, the executive vice-president Pace had put under Naish to try and control costs. "I felt," said Pace recently, "that if I couldn't get more accurate judgments from Naish than I had gotten, he ought to go." Then he added, "Whether these problems were passed on and not properly interpreted by Esenwien and Naish, I can't tell. There are conflicting points of view now that we go back into the problem. But we in New York didn't know the magnitude of the problem."

Regardless of whether New York knew then or not, the whole business community was shortly to learn how profound was Convair's trouble. The risky decision to build the 990 without a prototype began to bear some even more expensive fruit. Seventeen of American's twenty-five 990's had to be delivered during 1961, the first one in March. A flight test of this particular airplane in late January, 1961, four months later than the date scheduled in a previous announcement of Pace's, disclosed wing flutter and other problems that required rebuilding the landing flaps, the leading edge of the wings, and the outboard pylons. These were not too difficult to correct from an engineering point of view, but as General Dynamics' vice-president sadly remarked, "If you get into production with a plane whose design has to be changed, the magnitude of the troubles you then encounter becomes exponential." Moreover, these corrections now had to be made on overtime because of the tight delivery schedule to American. Ultimately this was to burden General Dynamics with an additional $116-million jet write-off.

The burning question, of course, is why New York *didn't* know the magnitude of the problem. Naish maintains he leaned over backward, because of his initial opposition to the jet program, to clear important decisions with either Johnson or Pace. Last fall a member of General Dynamics' executive committee, still puzzling over why New York had been so much in the dark for so long, pressed Pace on the point. He wanted to know why, even if Naish's information had been suspect, Convair's controller hadn't told Pace of the losses, or why he hadn't learned of them from MacBride, whom Pace had sent out early in 1961 to investigate, or from Earl Johnson, whom Pace had given overall responsibility for the jet program and sent to Convair in late 1958 and early 1959 when the division was plainly in trouble. Pace, at a loss to explain, wondered whether he ought to resign. No, said the director, and Pace needn't make any apologies. After all, he wasn't trained as a businessman. He (the director) made no apologies for not being able to walk into an operating room and perform like a surgeon. So Pace shouldn't feel badly about not being trained as a businessman.

The Wages of Sin

Unhappliy for General Dynamics, the departures of Naish and Esenwein did little to lighten the corporation's load of trouble. Nor was Rhoades MacBride, General Dymanics' No. 3 man whom Pace put in as acting president of Convair, able to bring the division under control (after ten months he too was to be washed out of office). There had simply been too many sins of commission and omission to be cured by chopping off heads in San Diego.

General Dynamics ran into trouble with American over the 990. The gamble, mentioned earlier, that Convair's engineers could guess the jet power needed to meet the speed and fuel requirements in the American contract, had failed. In addition, the 990 was already six months late, so in September, 1961, Smith canceled his order. Now the General Dynamics board was confronted by two choices, both bleak. It could turn back the uneconomical DC-7's Smith had induced them to accept in lieu of a $25-million down payment, then with the $25-million cash reimbursement as a cushion, cut the price of the 990 and try to sell it to other carriers; or it could try to get a new contract from Smith. A few audacious directors, including Crown, were for trying choice No. 1, but the opinion of the majority, as epitomized by one memeber of the board was: "Now let's not get C. R. mad. Earl Johnson knows him. Let's go and appeal to him."

The upshot was that Pace, Johnson, and Henry Crown [director] paid a call on Smith. There Colonel Crown related a little story about his having let a construction company off the hook even though, legally, he had had every right to hold them to a disasterous contract. Smith made no comment but when Pace and Johnson pursued the same thought he finally said: "I understand your problem, but I have stockholders. You told me, Earl, that the plane would go a certain speed." A new contract was signed with American and it was a tough one. The airline cut its order from 25 to 15 planes, with an option to take 5 more if Convair could get the speed up to 621 mph. Upwards of $300,000 was knocked off the price of each aircraft. With wind-tunnel tests completed, chances are now good that Convair will be able to meet the 621-mph specification.

But even as this article goes to press in mid-January, the end of General Dynamics' jet travail is not in sight. Howard Hughes has just canceled his order for thirteen 990's, an order that, surprisingly enough, Convair had accepted during the period when Hughes couldn't even pay for his 880's. SAS and Swiss Air have cut their original order from nine 990's to seven. Moreover, the market is just about saturated insofar as additional jet sales are concerned, even for a fine plane like the 880. As for the 990, it too has missed its market. To date only sixty-six 880's and twenty-three 990's have been sold, which puts Convair well behind Boeing's 720 sales in the medium-range market. Small wonder that when somebody suggests selling off Convair, a General Dynamics vice-president ruefully remarks: "Would $5 be too much?"

"This Has Hurt Us in Washington"

The failure of General Dynamics' management has had some serious collateral effects. As a member of the executive committee remarked: "The public has lost confidence in us. This has hurt us in Washington. We have to inject people of stature into the management." The company recently lost out on two of the three big defense contracts (the $400-million Apollo space-craft contract went to North American, Boeing got the $300-million Saturn S-1 booster system). Its executive committee has also failed to find a new chief executive officer, "a man forty years old with one hundred years of experience" as John McCone remarked in turning down the job, and this has further delayed General Dynamics' much-needed reorganization.

Though the great losses are now a matter of history, the subject of what went wrong with the company will no doubt be discussed for as long as there is a General Dynamics. "It's a grave question in my mind," said one of the company's senior vice-presidents, "as to whether General Dynamics had the right to risk this kind of money belonging to the stockholders for the potential profit you could get out of it. All management has to take a certain risk for big gains. But I don't think it's right to risk so much for so small a gain."

There are, however, larger questions of management's responsibility for the well-being of the corporation. That responsibility, in the jet age, is to keep management techniques developing at the same pace as the technologies they must control.

Question

What should Frank Pace have done to get better control at General Dynamics?

Part 6

CONCLUSION- ACHIEVING BALANCE

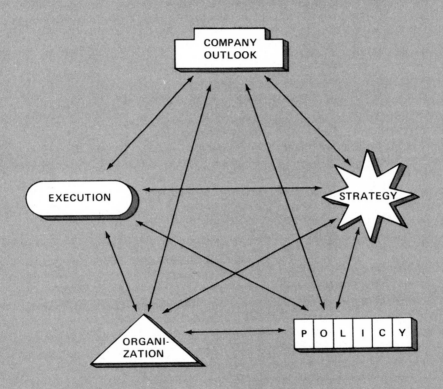

23 MANAGING MULTINATIONAL ENTERPRISES

The Total Task of Managing

To think sharply about a complex subject like managing, we usually divide the subject into parts for separate analysis. Thus, in this book we have shifted our focus successively from selecting strategy to defining policy, on to designing organization, and finally to guiding execution. This separate treatment helps in analysis, but also detracts from sensing the interconnection and the complexity of the total task of managing. Central managers necessarily give much attention to achieving a balance of the various actions they sponsor. They must build their company into an integrated whole.

In concluding, then, we want to put the parts back together again. We will do this in two ways—first, by reviewing the overall task of managing a multinational company and second, by discussing the integrating role of central managers.

The Attraction of Multinational Operations

"Go abroad, young man!" is the modern paraphrase of Horace Greeley's guide to opportunity. Companies, too, seek growth possibilities in foreign markets.

For years most U.S. firms were preoccupied with the vast free-trade area within American boundaries. In terms of time and communication, Los Angeles was then much further from Chicago than Paris or Tokyo is today. But, as national markets became more competitive, exports took on added attractions. Also, oil, copper, steel, and other industries needed large supplies of raw materials from abroad. Those pressures led to substantial exports and imports.

Then as foreign markets grew and nationalistic controls hampered trade, business moved to the next and current phase of fully integrated operations—both manufacturing and selling—in offshore locations. For example, over one-third of both sales and net income of Ford, IBM, Colgate-Palmolive, National Cash Register, H. J. Heinz, and Pfizer are generated outside the United States. Many other firms are also multinational in scope.

Such integrated operations abroad are growing rapidly, both for U.S. firms and for firms based in other countries. They create worldwide competition, with resources and expertise seeking opportunities in a highly adaptable fashion not confined to a country of origin. Most multinational companies start from a well-established domestic operation but seek to optimize both the source and the allocation of resources on a worldwide basis. They pose new challenges to our ability to manage.

This chapter deals with the *management* of companies that conduct manufacturing, selling, and related activities in several different countries. We will focus here on the issues that are particularly significant to multinational enterprises. Effective management of local operating units is assumed. This emphasis on "parent" operations serves two purposes: (1) it highlights the distinctive features of multinational companies, and (2) it illustrates the application of the basic analytical framework of the entire book to a different business.

STRATEGY OF MULTINATIONAL FIRMS

Multinational operation requires careful inclusion of the international nature of the business in the overall strategy. Important issues in formulating multinational strategy are the differential advantage to be obtained, the selection of countries with the greatest long-run growth potential, the balancing of risks, and the timing of expansion.

Differential Advantage Sought

A firm embarking on a multinational course needs synergistic advantage to offset the inherent costs of operating in more than one culture. Many of the policy, organization, and control decisions that a firm adopts tie back to the fundamental question of "why we think we can do it better" than a local national company.

Important among possible rationales for operating abroad are the following:

1. *Technical expertise*—manufacturing companies may go abroad to make use of the research and engineering already done for domestic operations. Clearly, one of the advantages Caterpillar Tractor has in its worldwide operations is its *engineering design* of heavy earth-moving equipment. *Processing expertise* is more likely a distinctive advantage for chemical and engineering companies. In some instances, as in pharmaceuticals, either the products or the processes are protected by worldwide patents, although even here the progressive updating of technology may be fully as important as the legal protection.

2. *Access to markets*—a worldwide company itself may provide an attractive market. Thus, "Nestlé uses so much chocolate in its numerous plants that it can provide an assured market for a large supply of raw material—cocoa beans." Or the company may have a widespread marketing organization and be able to dispose of much larger quantities than could any company in the country of origin; for example, Dole has a great advantage in disposing of Philippine pine-

apple. Perhaps a company has greater access to markets simply because of its superior marketing—a significant factor in Sears' success in Latin America.

3. *Capital*—especially in developing countries, the capital resources of a multinational company contribute to its relative strength. The ability to make large investments (coupled with technical expertise) has aided companies making everything from fertilizer to flashlights in India.

4. *Managerial skill*—hard to determine and often overrated, the managerial skills provided by a multinational company often provide it with a distinctive advantage. Philips' Gloeilampenfabrieken, the giant Netherlands electronics manufacturer, obviously owes part of its success to managerial ability; and the fifty-seven varieties of H. J. Heinz are world-famous for a similar reason. The French writer, Servan-Schreiber, picks managerial ability as the basis for *the American challenge* to the entire European business community. Currently, business analysts are wondering whether Japanese management style will produce unusual results in foreign settings.

If a company bases its international strategy on one or a combination of the factors just discussed, it must be sure that it does in fact have an advantage that is both relevant and continuing. For example, mass marketing techniques that are geared to suburban shopping centers can cause disaster in foreign countries. Production processes based on high labor cost are not necessarily optimum in countries with a large labor supply. Some of the "know-how" advantages are fleeting; local competitors will catch up. So, if in a long-run strategy rests upon a technological superiority, the multinational company must be reasonably confident that it can maintain its lead.

Defense rather than offense is sometimes the prime mover in multinational strategy. For years, a company making, say, radios or sewing machines may have exported to a South American or an African country. Then, local production or low-cost Japanese competition makes serious inroads. In this new environment, the company may have to choose between either establishing its own foreign plant or giving up a large segment of the market. But even if the strategy is initiated for defensive reasons, the company should have a clear advantage by which it hopes to keep a distinctive niche in each of the countries in which it operates.

Countries Attractive for Growth

Building a strong subsidiary in a country often takes years, and to obtain a significant industry position after other companies are entrenched is costly. Consequently, the multinational company needs some strategy to identify the kinds of countries that offer the greatest long-run potential. One metal container company, for instance, is setting up plants in developing countries—even though it may merely make bottle caps initially—in order to be established when the countries' real growth occurs. Other firms operate only where the per capita purchasing power is high. Less attractive countries may be identified by strategy as well. One rubber company, for instance, will have nothing to do with countries affiliated with the Soviet bloc.

A useful approach to identifying countries attractive for growth is careful appraisal of the following factors:

1. Estimate the potential demand for the major services the company expects to provide. This will be tied to industrial and economic development, living conditions, natural resources, population, education, comsumption attitudes, and other social and economic influences.
2. Assess the importance in each country of the distinctive strengths of the company. These strengths will include the differential advantages the company hopes to exploit. Also, weigh the strengths of prospective competitors and the likely responses of other key actors.
3. Predict the general environment and its associated risk. Important factors to consider in this connection are prospects for:

   - controls on foreign exchange
   - inflation
   - import and export restrictions
   - legislation against foreigners
   - expropriation and nationalization
   - onerous taxation
   - political upheaval
   - war
   - deterioration of financial, utility, and other services.

Analysis of this sort led a leading manufacturer of control equipment to concentrate its expansion in Western Europe, with secondary attention to Japan. All other parts of the world are served by exports from the United States or Europe. On the other hand, a large pharmaceutical manufacturer anticipates increasing pressure to manufacture at least the leading drugs locally. Consequently, it is setting up a large number of small local plants where much of the final fabrication and packaging is done. The company hopes that this localized activity will give it an edge in the importation of new and complex drugs (which carry wide gross profit margins) from the home country.

Building a Balanced Portfolio

A multinational firm must watch its risk and cash flow balance, as explained in Chapter 14. Some European companies,for example, are entering the U.S. market as a hedge against communist takeover of their government. At the same time, U.S. pharmaceutical firms are expanding in Europe partly because of the threats of even more U.S. government regulation of medical affairs. Large Japanese firms, which must import most of their raw materials, are clearly seeking several different sources as a protection against political disruption in any supplying country.

Similarly, the demands on scarce resources require an overall balance. A well-known advertising agency, for instance, announced that it was entering the international arena but soon ran out of experienced executives to send abroad. Consequently, it is confining its growth to northern Europe and Brazil. Capital also is a frequent constraint. Even large companies may be unable to finance vigorous growth in several countries simultaneously. Commitments already started in Australia may prevent a strong push into Japan. So the growth strategy must be kept in balance.

Timing of Expansion

Proper timing is also critical. Five years often elapse between a decision to manufacture in a given country and the efficient operation of a new plant. Acquiring government permits and building sites, engineering design, building construction, importing specialized equipment, hiring and training workers, establishing dependable sources of materials, overcoming start-up difficulties and shaping a viable social structure all take time. For this reason, many U.S. companies entered the European Common Market early, before trade barriers had been significantly reduced. Not all of these plants proved to be wise investments, but some companies built a strong position because they were ready to produce quality goods when the market opened up.

Multinational service organizations face a similar question of when to enter additional countries. Thus, for years all but two U.S. banks relied on "correspondents" for most of their foreign activities. Then, the growth of the Eurodollar market precipitated a great scramble for offices at least in London. In this instance, as with advertising agencies, multinational service organizations have delayed expansion until worldwide marketing and manufacturing organizations were well established. Industrial engineering and public accounting firms, on the other hand, have built strong positions by being the vanguard of economic development.

Political instability strongly affects timing strategy. Indonesia presents a classic problem of when multinational companies should enter a strife-torn area. Rich in human and natural resources, yet needing outside capital and expertise, Indonesia attracts investments of oil and other multinational companies. Nevertheless, serious losses have been incurred by companies that have entered the area under political regimes that were later overthrown. Comparable political difficulties have arisen in Central Africa. Here, companies anxious to get a foothold in the large potential market have often discovered that their early association with one political regime becomes a handicap at a later time.

In summary, recurring issues in multinational strategy include what services to perform, in which countries, with what balance, and at what time. Specific situations pose an array of additional angles, but these four issues give a sense of central management's strategy problems.

USE OF POLICY

The use of policy as a management tool is even more significant in multinational firms than in Stage III multidivision firms that operate within a single

country. In both types of enterprise, the operating divisions have their own policies. However, the multinational enterprise must distinguish clearly between
those facets of its activities in which it seeks synergistic benefits—and hence
needs centralized policy and coordination—and those activities that should not
be governed by central policy. Selectivity is crucial. Possible issues on which
multinational guidance may be warranted are illustrated below.

Standardization of Products

The degree to which products will be the same in various countries calls for
policy guidance. The most widely known product throughout the world is
Coca-Cola. The Coca-Cola Company has a strict policy that its product is to be
uniform, a standard that is difficult to achieve, since bottling is done by numerous independent local distributors in many countries. Product consistency and a
worldwide reputation take priority over local tastes. In contrast, Unilever permits its operating companies to adapt its soap and food products to the particular tastes and needs of the countries in which they are operating. This flexibility
permits local units to stress, say, margarine versus cooking oils in accordance
with national dietary habits.

Equipment manufacturers find standardization among countries difficult to
achieve. A U.S. food machinery manufacturer, for example, had to change all
dimensions from English to metric measurement; to simplify shop operations, it
also had to modify the specifications slightly. Electric motors, switches compressors, and even bolts that were purchased had to be adjusted to what was locally
available. Users of the machines wanted to be able to obtain repair parts quickly
and they preferred designs with which local workers were familiar. Consequently, the policy of this company is to have separate specifications for Europe
and for South America. IBM takes an opposite tack. The parts for its machines
are the same throughout the world. Such a policy is feasible because IBM has
long stressed providing its own service to customers, which includes assuming
the burden of maintaining an inventory of repair parts.

The choice of a product standardization policy, then, is influenced by company size and its volume of sales in each country, the importance of adapting to
local needs, and especially the strategy the company has chosen to make its services distinctive.

Regional Specialization of Production

A multinational company may concentrate production of each of its products in a plant and then trade among plants. Theoretically, this permits sale of a
full line in Country A, one product being made locally and the rest imported.
The same situation prevails in Countries X, Y, and Z. The advantage, of course,
is lower cost arising from making a large quantity of a single product in each

plant instead of a variety of products only in the volume needed in the local market. In practice, the trades do not balance neatly, but the central concept of regional specialization can be utilized. The major U.S. and Japanese automobile companies, for example, are shifting toward worldwide sourcing of motors; all of a particular type of motor will be made in Mexico or Brazil for shipment to local assembly plants in many different countries.

If the parts going into products are standardized, then regional specialization of parts manufacture is possible. IBM in Europe has made considerable progress in this direction.

Unfortunately, a regional specialization policy is difficult to apply. It relies on inexpensive and uninterrupted movement of goods across international boundaries; it assumes that product standardization and economies of scale are substantial; and it appplies only when the production capabilities of the various countries are compatible. Note also that a high degree of central coordination is required.

Transfer Prices

The prices at which raw materials, parts, or finished goods are transferred from one division of a company to another is always a troublesome problem. Transfers across national boundaries create additional difficulties. For instance, a high transfer price increases the profits earned in the exporting country and decreases the profits of the importer; this affects who pays more income taxes and which local managements "look good." The transfer price may also influence the choice of long-term investment, selling prices, and local allocation of effort among products. Consequently, a multinational company must have some policy regarding the value attached to goods (and services) moving from one operating unit to another.

Mobile Oil Corporation, for instance, ships crude oil from the Middle East to a refinery in the Netherlands and then ships the refined product from the Netherlands to Sweden for sale to consumers. The managers of Mobil's affiliates in each of the three countries and the respective national governments all naturally feel that their share of the final sales income should be higher. Where the profit shows up is not a matter of indifference to them.

Virtually all companies transfer at "market price" if such a figure exists for the product at the time and the place transfer occurs. Beyond that, policies differ sharply. Some firms use a negotiated price, a figure that presumably approximates what a competitive price would be. Others use direct cost plus a markup percentage set up by headquarters. A few use total budgeted cost, including a "fair" return on local investment. In some circumstances, the starting point is a budgeted selling price from which distribution and processing costs are deducted to arrive at the value of the product received.

A guide for multinational managers among this array of possible policies, we suggest, is to focus on the incentive effect of transfer prices. Put the variability—the residual profits—in those units that have the greatest maneuverability to make or lose money. For divisions performing a standard function (for example, pipelines in an integrated petroleum operation), set transfer prices to cover full costs and depend on budgetary control rather than "profit margins" for incentives.

Proportion of Local Ownership

All multinational companies are holding companies. They are parent companies only, investing in local concerns that are organized in conformity with the requirements of the particular country in which they operate. A major policy question in this regard is what share, if any, of each operating company should be owned by local citizens. Billions of dollars of present and potential foreign investment are affected by this issue.

Referring to our discussion of partially owned subsidiaries in Chapter 15, the parent company gains many advantages from 100 percent ownership—flexibility in assigning functions, freedom in setting transfer prices, avoidance of arguments about fairness to minority interests, simpler decision-making, and, by no means least, carrying the full risk and receiving all the net profits.

Full ownership, of course, means higher investment. The chief drawback of 100 percent ownership is the loss of potential incentive—stock ownership by local employees—but even this can be largely overcome by bonus plans and stock options in the parent company.

Multinational companies face an added dimension. *National pride* and *national economic independence* enter, often with heavy emotional and political overtones. The idea that a foreigner controls even a tiny part of the national gross product or the national employment can rally popular opposition. And if (1) a natural resource is involved and (2) a major sector of the economy is affected—as is true of copper in Chile and Zambia and oil in Libya—then governments can rise and fall on the ownership issue.

The alternative ownership arrangements are numerous. Simple variations start from full ownership by the parent, move to a minority local interest (the typical request of Brazilians, who want an opportunity to share in the profits of local companies), and extend to 51 percent (controlling) local interest. Moreover, different kinds of shares with various voting rights can be introduced, and options or contracts to gain control at a later date can be added. The ownership right, itself a social device, can be circumscribed by contracts with individuals or governments.

In communist countries, where private ownership of stock does not exist, long-term management contracts coupled with royalty or bonus payments sometimes take the place of ownership as we in the West know it.

From this array of possibilities, most multinational enterprises adopt a policy that gives them a consistent stand on this troublesome issue. Firms like IBM wish to use regional specialization and have a special reason for insisting on the flexibility that comes with 100 percent ownership. Also in this case rapid technological development makes avoidance of bickering over who deserves credit more significant.

In contrast, when the multinational company provides only technical expertise and the local firm carries complete responsibility for organizing production and marketing, a local ownership interest is fair and it generates incentive for local initiative that is essential for succcess. Who should eventually control the local operation depends on who will make the major *continuing* contribution—a matter hard to measure but at least it shifts the discussion from power to a constructive issue.

Exploitation of natural resources generates the most emotion. Here, rising nationalism makes 100 percent foreign-owned companies political untenable. An increasingly popular arrangement is to grant the multinational company control during the first twenty years or until it has recovered its investment plus, say, 20 percent profit per annum—and then to transfer majority ownership to local (perhaps governmental) interests.

These examples clearly indicate a close interdependence between a firm's strategy regarding products and countries and its policy on the sharing of ownership with local interests.

Optimizing Exchange Risks

Multinational firms inevitably face foreign exchange problems. Most transactions of each operating company will be in its local currency; but when goods are exported or imported and when dividends from local operations are returned to the parent company, the local money must be converted into foreign currency. Rates of exchange—the value of one currency in terms of another—do change, especially when a local inflation is creating balance-of-payments difficulties.

A common policy followed by smaller firms is to *ignore* exchange fluctuations. Under this approach, each local company seeks to maximize its profit, and transfers to the parent are made when surplus funds are available. It is hoped that exchange rates will be favorable, or at least average out over a period of time. The rationale for ignoring exchange fluctuations is that the firm will be more successful by concentrating on the business it knows than by dabbling where it is not expert.

An alternative and more sophisticated policy is to *minimize exposure.* This can be done is several ways: (1) Borrow locally to finance local operations so that repayments never get involved in foreign exchange. The catch, of course, is that only part of the total needs of the local unit can be borrowed, and interest rates may be quite high. (2) Rent buildings and other assets, thereby reducing local investment. Again, availability and cost limit the extent to which this can be done. (3) Hedge in forward exchange markets by "selling" a foreign currency to offset fixed obligations in that currency. For this, as for other methods, there is an expense involved in avoiding the risk.

In fact, firms often adopt a policy of *minimizing interest costs*, even though doing so may add to foreign exchange risks. Money is borrowed where the interest is low and is tranferred via foreign exchange to countries with high interest rates. When exchange controls hamper such direct movements, the same result can be achieved by either delaying or prepaying a settlement for goods that the multinational firm ships from one country to another. Since high interest rates frequently signal inflation and foreign exchange difficulties, such transfer of funds can increase exchange risks.

A still more daring policy is to deliberately *seek profits* from changes in exchange rates. Rarely will a multinational concern simply speculate in foreign exchange quite unrelated to its other business. However, it may feel that its intimate knowledge of some countries provides such a good basis for predicting rate changes that it is justified in shifting its holdings of these currencies in anticipation of future changes.[1]

The five policy issues discussed—standardization of products, regional specialization of production, transfer pricing, proportion of local ownership, and optimizing exchange risks—by no means exhaust the policy problems facing multinational enterprises. They do demonstrate that the concept of policy formulation can be helpful in dealing with the more unusual aspects of multinational operations as well as with the more common problems facing national companies that we examined in Chapters 6 to 13.

ORGANIZING MULTINATIONAL OPERATIONS

Geographic dispersion of the multinational enterprise intensifies most of the organization problems faced by domestic firms. The variety of languages, laws, loyalties, and customs require more adaptation and complicate integrated action. Basically, the problems are the same; the difference is one of degree.

Worldwide Departmentation

A multinational firm is a Stage III company (as defined in Chapter 17). The primary emphasis, of course, is on geographical divisions rather than product divisions. Normally, all activities in each country are placed under a single executive. Distance, national differences, and especially local political considerations

---

[1] Attempting to profit from changes in foreign exchange rates is similar to trying to outguess inflationary price changes. For policy restraints on such risk-taking, see pages 275–278.

accentuate the need for a coordinated, consistent posture in each country. But the stress on national divisions leave unsettled how these units tie into the over-all organization.

In many industries where production plants are small, both marketing and at least the final stages of production can be performed economically within each country. So here, the *regional* type of structure remains dominant and the national units report to an overall regional or world office.

For companies dealing with a single line of products that require large-scale operations, such as steel or copper, a basically *functional* structure works well. Each national unit is predominantly either marketing or production, so it can be assigned to an appropriate worldwide functional department.

Recently, worldwide *product* divisions reporting directly to the president of the parent corporation have become more common. This arrangement reflects increasing international competition focused on standardized product lines. Success depends on prompt adjustment to changes in supply or demand anywhere in the world. Improved communication and air travel now permit this sort of coordination.

As in domestic corporations, the choice of a regional, functional, or product structure should reflect the strategic emphasis the firm has selected. In multinational corporations, however, the ever-present need for coordination within each country often leads to mixed or matrix arrangements.

National or Regional Decentralization

Most multinational organizations are highly decentralized in some respects and centralized in others. Activities tied to consumers or operating employees—selling, granting credit, pricing, delivery, customer service, bookkeeping, warehousing, and the like—should be adapted to local conditions, and wide discretion in such matters should be exercised by managers of national units.

The benefits of synergy, on the other hand, usually come with centralized direction. For example, process and product knowledge, worldwide reputation for quality, and regional specialization of production can be fully utilized when they are centrally designed and controlled. Multinational firms whose strategies stress such concepts are committed to centralization on at least these key strategic weapons. Even a commitment to capitalize on managerial expertise implies that the techniques of planning, organizing, leading, and controlling will be stipulated by central headquarters.

The organizational task, then, is to sort out the kinds of decisions that need to be centralized from those that can be made more expeditiously in local units. And, having defined the dimensions of freedom at various levels, our multinational manager must make sure that the structure is understood by all executives—a substantial endeavor because of the diversity of backgrounds and expectations of the people involved.

Providing Expert Services Where Needed

A perpetual problem faced by multinational management is how to obtain full advantage of the expertise that exists within the company. How can the know-how of executives in the domestic operating divisions and the wisdom of central staff be incorporated into decisions in operating companies dispersed throughout the world?

The difficulty arises from several causes. The experts are busy with their primary assignments, and they give low priority to a request for advice from Calcutta or Copenhagen. Even when they do spare time for foreign matters, they have difficulty in communicating. Language, background, and unfamiliarity with local conditions make it hard for them to perceive the local situation and give advice that is realistic. Moreover, the local executives often lack sufficient training to sift and adapt the ideas they receive.

The most common device for overcoming this barrier is a *liaison staff* whose primary role is as communicator of pertinent questions to the experts and translator of answers to operating personnel. Such a staff might be attached to the chief executive of international operations or to regional managers. Unfortunately, experience with a staff of this sort is not always favorable. Both G.E. and Ford have created a large international staff, disbanded it, and recreated it. As with all staff, there is danger that persons far removed from the scene of action will become more bureaucratic than helpful.

An alternative is to try *lowering the communications barrier* itself. This may be done by increasing opportunities for travel, personal contact, and observation. Managers of domestic divisions may be given indirect or even direct "responsibility" for foreign activities similar to their domestic ones. Full-time task teams may be formed to study major problems. Cooperation may be explicitly added to performance appraisal factors. These and other devices are intended to create a "We're all in the same family" feeling.

Few multinational companies are happy with the spotty success they have achieved in getting good advice focused on local problems. Opportunities for improvement are rife in this facet of organization.

Coordination Between Countries

Shipping products from one country to another requires careful coordination. Multinational oil companies, for example, ship crude oil from half a dozen sources to several different refineries, which in turn ship finished products to a score of consuming nations. Or a company constructing a flour mill in South Africa imports specialized equipment that must fit the building erected on the spot. In each instance, activities in several countries must be closely synchronized.

This coordination task is complicated by its international dimensions. Usually a special organization unit is created to assure that misunderstandings are held to a minimum and that each country acts in a way that minimizes cost and optimizes income for the company. Oil companies often create a supply and distribution department devoted solely to this task. In other industries, a special scheduling unit is located at each plant, but it has international status. The manager of one such unit observes: "The mechanics are easy once you understand the needs and cost factors of each location; I spend most of my time being an international diplomat."

Again we see—as with departmentation, decentralization, and specialized services—that multinational coordination has its particular difficulties and intensities, but it is basically the same kind of phenomenon faced by managers of domestic firms.

KEY PERSONNEL

Operating units in each country will have their own personnel policy suited to local needs. To realize the potential benefits of their multinational affiliation, however, key technical and executive personnel must somehow acquire the best knowledge and skills available in the total system. Capturing this benefit is crucial to a successful multinational enterprise.

Use of Nationals as Executives

IBM follows a practice of filling all executive positions in the hundred countries in which it operates with local citizens. Two ends are served by this local use of nationals (that is, citizens of the country in which they work). Executives in each country know intimately the language and customs of their market and their workers. Moreover, nationalistic demands to give jobs to local citizens rather than foreigners are fully met.

But IBM is an exception. Virtually all companies agree that *most* local executives should be nationals, for the reasons stated. Complete adherence, however, restricts promotion opportunities. Under the IBM system, the best person available *in the total company* cannot be shifted into a vacancy unless that person happens to be a national of the country in which the vacancy occurs.

An alternative is to give nationals preference, but when foreigners are clearly better qualified, to place them in the positions. Still another variation used by one large oil company that wishes to "internationalize" its general managers is a clearly stated policy that no nationals will be appointed general managers in any country until they (1) serve a tour of duty in a foreign country and (2) agree to accept a transfer at a later date out of their native land. Because this guide is consistently followed, executives seek foreign assignments since they know this is the path of advancement, and local employees resist fewer general managers who are foreigners because they are not regarded as obstacles to advancement of local people.

A final alternative we should mention is maximum use of nationals *except* in the top *financial* position; the presumption is that a non-national in this job will be freer of local loyalties and more objective in appraising operating results.

Developing Multinational Managers

If nationals are to fill most, if not all, of the key positions in each country, the need for executive training is obvious. In the newer countries, especially, competent and dependable executives are very scarce. And, a core of senior executives qualified to move from one country to another, or to top staff jobs, needs even broader training.

The special requirements for a multinational executive include: (1) language; (2) sensitivity and adaptability to differences in culture, especially with respect to communication and motivation; (3) background in international trade and finance and in the economic problems of the country where assigned; (4) grasp of company procedures, technology, and successful practices; and (5) unusual degree of patience and tact combined with perseverance.

The first three of these special qualifications can be developed off-the-job; the company can assist by making time available and paying expenses of outside courses. Knowledge about the company is normally acquired on-the-job in a series of assignments including working in company headquarters and in key departments. Tact and perseverance, insofar as they can be consciously developed, call for personal counseling. And so a whole array of executive development techniques should be carefully combined to foster the growth of multinational executives.

Compensation of Executives in Foreign Assignments

Both the need to supplement local executive talent and the process of executive development call for assigning people outside their home country. Such working abroad complicates pay rates in two ways.

(1) Salary scales differ from country to country. For instance, using the official exchange rate, U.S. pay is about double the British pay for a similar job. So, should a Yankee working in England be paid by U.S. or British standards? And what of a Britisher in the United States? Of course, living costs, taxes, government benefits, social requirements, and the like do differ substantially, but few executives agree on the extent to which such factors offset the differences in cash salary.

(2) People living abroad want some things that they enjoyed at home but that may be costly in a foreign country. Brazilians in the United States find that domestic servants must be paid what they consider executive salaries, whereas North Americans in Brazil find that frozen vegetables are exorbitant. Few execu-

tives—and their spouses—are adaptable enough to quickly give up all of the particular living comforts they are accustomed to.

One large multinational firm meets these pay pressures as follows: (1) Executives' base salaries and their retirement accumulations are tied to what the job they hold would pay in their home country. The assumption is that the executives relate their salaries to standards in their native land and they plan to retire there. (2) In addition, they receive allowances for moving, extra living and housing cost, children's education, biennial trips home, and—if the location is unpleasant—"hardship."

This arrangement provides a consistent and "fair" pay in terms of a person's home base. However, two individuals from different countries might receive quite different total compensation for the same job, and this can become a source of irritation. (Americans' base salaries may be paid partly in local currency and partly in dollars in the U.S., so that their local scale of living will not conspicuously differ from that of their peers.) Also, if allowances are too liberal, the executives have trouble readjusting when they return home and receive only their base pay.

Whatever the particular system of allowances, clearly an executive away from home is a high-priced person. As international assignments become recognized as valuable steps on the way to the top, instead of an inconvenient way to save a few dollars, perhaps the premium paid to our mobile executives can be reduced.

CONTROLLING MULTINATIONAL ACTIVITIES

Distance and diversity of operating conditions also create problems of control within a multinational enterprise. The three dimensions of these control problems, discussed below, illustrate the special burden a multinational firm undertakes in addition to the normal control tasks in each of the operating units.

Understanding the Concept of Constructive Control

For cultural reasons, the control process is poorly understood in many countries. Often the significance of completing work on time and of maintaining quality is not accepted. Local life proceeds more casually; so when western control standards are imposed, the action appears to local workers as unwarranted and capricious.

Similarly, accounting records in many countries are scanty, inaccurate, and often manipulated to reduce taxes. Naturally, managers do not look to such records as aids to prompt coordination of activities.

In some cultures, business relationships are closely entwined with personal friendship, kinship, reciprocal favors, and *simpatico* feelings. In such situations objective appraisal and tough corrective action are too irritating to be tolerated.

A first step, then, for a multinational manager in securing control is to win acceptance of the concept. Executives in operating units must understand that survival in world business requires realistic objectives, performance standards based on these objectives, regular measurement of performance, prompt feedback of control data to people who can undertake corrective action, overall evaluation, updating of targets, and correlation of incentives with results. Without acceptance of this process, the best-designed control systems will achieve only moderate effects.

Operating Controls that Encourage Optimum Performance

Every multinational firm must have dependable, understandable accounting reports from each country. Due to local variations in bookkeeping practice, the establishment of a worldwide accounting system is no small task. But once in place, it does permit the introduction of annual and five-year budgets, measurement of growth in sales and profits, and other usual financial control devices.

Essential as such financial controls are, reliance on financial reports alone is especially dangerous in a multinational business. The opportunities and the difficulties in each country make necessary more complete and sensitive yardsticks. In addition to financial reports, criteria such as market share, government relations, quality maintenance, customer service, cultivation of new customers, physical productivity, employee training and turnover, plant maintenance, innovation and modernization, protection of assets from inflation, cooperation with other units of the company are all control measures that the multinational headquarters should watch in each country.

Frequent evaluation is inappropriate. A thorough semiannual review plus prompt evaluation of major changes or deviations from plans serve most multinational companies better than monthly reporting, which is likely to become routine.

Periodic Product Stream Evaluation

The controls just described help keep each operating unit "on course," but they do not check the continuing desirability of the course itself. This broader evaluation is difficult because most multinational firms sell the same product in different countries, ship materials or parts from one country to another, and in other ways seek synergistic benefits from joint activities. Separate controls in each country do not tell whether the desired overall benefits are being obtained.

Consequently, special studies that consolidate the incomes, costs, and investment from all countries dealing with a *product line* are needed. Since several lines are typically handled, at least when all countries are considered, a lot of unscrambling of assets and joint costs may be necessary. So the analysis becomes involved, too involved for routine periodic reports. Fortunately, a special appraisal, say every two years, is adequate because changes in product line or production strategy can only be made in relatively long time cycles.

With an analysis of how product lines are measuring up to original plans, a reappraisal also of markets, competition, technology, and other external factors is in order. This may lead to significant shifts in company strategy. And so we find ourselves completing the full management cycle of strategy, implementing plans, execution, and control—which provides the basis for a revised strategy and a new cycle.

SUMMARY

Managers in multinational companies face a variety of issues arising from the international climate of the total operation. Balancing these issues calls for unusual skill. While company *strategy* seeks to extend strengths in one country to many other markets, it requires judicious selection of countries where these strengths will be most beneficial. Additionally, it lays out the timing of international expansion.

Among the *policy* issues created by worldwide operations are the extent to which products will be adapted to local needs, regionalization of production, allocation of profits to different countries via transfer prices, participation in ownership of operating units by local nationals, and speculating on or avoiding foreign exchange risks.

Organization has to be adjusted to the strategy and geographical dispersion. To capture full synergistic benefits of technological expertise, uniform quality, or reorganization of production, decision-making must be centralized—whereas national differences may require that decisions related to people be decentralized. Special provision for communicating and coordinating is necessary to assure that the multinational advantages are attained.

Staffing with local nationals is desirable, but this creates a need for multinational training of executives. To provide such training, and in the senior levels to utilize exceptional talent, people must move across national boundaries. Whenever this is done, a prickly problem of salary and cost-of-living adjustments arise.

A multinational scope of operation increases both the need for and the difficulty of *control*. The underlying concept of constructive control has to be developed, realiable measures of tangible and intangible results must be created, and provision must be made for assessing integrated results as well as performance in each country.

Overshadowing these distinctive aspects of multinational management is the demonstration that the broard framework we have used throughout this book to analyze the central management tasks of national companies provides an equally effective means for thinking through the overall management framework of the most complex business enterprise yet conceived.

QUESTIONS FOR CLASS DISCUSSION

1. A leading U.S. office equipment company is considering a joint venture in the People's Republic of China. Copying machines, including a new fiber optics model, would be the only product line at present. The Chinese are primarily interested in reproducing technical drawings, statistical tables, and the like, rather than many copies of ordinary text. The U.S. company would provide product specifications, production expertise, and assistance in adapting product designs to Chinese needs. The U.S. contribution of capital would be in the form of production equipment. All output would be sold in China. Because China has about one-fourth of the world population, the potential market is large. However, other local firms will also be making copiers there, at least two with technical assistance from Japan. The projected financial return is satisfactory but not exciting, so the appeal for the U.S. company is "a foot in the door." Do you recommend that the U.S. company go ahead with the project?

2. Most multinational enterprises deal with products or raw materials. Recently multinational advertising agencies have had a spurt of growth. (a) Recognizing that advertising must be run in local media, use the local language, and appeal to local viewpoints, what differential advantage does a multinational advertising agency realize? (b) What kinds of policies, organization, and control will a multinational advertising agency need to provide the differential advantage you identified in your answer to (a)?

3. Fieldcrest Mills, Inc., is among the better known American manufacturers of towels, blankets, sheets, and related products. Fieldcrest does excellent styling and merchandising, but the domestic market is both mature and competitive. For growth, Fieldcrest is turning to Europe. A joint venture, with a completely new $50 million towel mill, has recently been organized in Ireland; ownership is 50 percent Fieldcrest, 25 percent Bank of Ireland, and 25 percent P. J. Carroll & Company—a diversified Irish corporation. The hope for low production costs rests on modern equipment, relatively low labor rates in Ireland, and especially on Carroll Company's approach to the restless labor relations in the country. (Recently, a labor strike closed all Irish banks for nine months.) Don Carroll, board chair, states, "As a principle, we would like to see all our activities constantly raising the amount of value added, constantly increasing the real income of employees through higher productivity. . . .Our view is the *greater disclosure of information to employees* as a basis for better understanding of the subtleties of the business and of the performance which is sought from them. . .will lead to better achievement by all. . .we can build an intrinsically healthier, sounder climate and achieve a more efficient performance. . . ." Fieldcrest's distinctive input will be the application of its styling and merchandising skills to the selling of the new mill's output throughout the European Common Market. What are the main risks for this new venture? What should Fieldcrest do to maximize its chances of success?

4. Multinational operations are faced with an additional array of uncertainties such as tariff charges, fluctuating foreign exchange rates and controls, different tax regulations, political upheavals, wars, varying growth rates, and additional sources of competition. Does the existence of these uncertainties mean that long-range programming (see Chapter 20) should not be attempted by multinational companies? If you do recommend use of long-range programming, explain how you would deal with these uncertainties.

5. British banks, and to a lesser extent German and Japanese banks, are making large investments in U.S. banks—sometimes owning control. This is disturbing to some U.S. citizens. (a) Is there any more reason for us to object to foreign ownership of some of our banks than for foreign countries to object to U.S. investors (typically U.S. banks) owning control of banks in their countries? (b) Should we establish a requirement that 51 percent voting stock in each U.S. bank remain in the hands of U.S. citizens? (c) Should we establish a requirement that, say, 75 percent of the officers be U.S. citizens? (d) Would your answers to the preceding questions be the same for hotels instead of banks?

6. How do the portfolio issues faced by a diversified U.S. corporation (see Chapter 14) differ from those of a multinational corporation?

7. One of the complications of multinational operations is the difference among countries in norms of ethical behavior and social responsibility. Both the formal standards (often expressed in law) and the strictness of their observance vary. (For example, wide differences exist with respect to bribery, tax evasion, treatment of workers, and agreements with competitors.) If you were working abroad for an England-based multinational company, which set of standards would you follow? What is the potential business impact of your ethical decisions?

8. Dow Chemical Co.'s senior executive in the Far East had misgivings when he was shown "the marketing organization in Korea. It was run by a retired, two-star general and everyone was sitting around reading newspapers." The executive from Dow had come to look at his company's $145 million investment in a chlorine plant (100 percent owned by Dow) and a vinyl chloride plant (50 percent owned by Dow and 50 percent by a Korean company). Neither plant has costs low enough to compete worldwide, but both were expected to do well in the booming Korean economy and to be protected by the government from any competition. But demand did not increase as had been expected and world prices for both chemicals dropped substantially. Then the Korean partners in the joint venture began to push for a rewriting of the contract so that the vinyl chloride plant would not have to purchase exclusively from the chlorine plant. Dow pushed for closer ties between the two units. It talked to the government about a merger of both companies. Nothing came of these talks. Both plants began to lose money. Dow filed lawsuits and began to try for a "de facto merger" by consolidating offices. The Koreans filed lawsuits in rebuttal. The Korean directors boycotted board meetings, so that no business could be conducted for a lack of a quorum. Although losses began to narrow as the economy picked up, the Korean executives who were retired generals had no interest in the merger. Dow

threatened to withdraw, but still invested another $30 million in working capital and plant modifications. When Dow's senior Far East executive attempted to talk with government officials, it turned out that the two key ministers had no interest in the situation. The Korean partners then offered Dow Chemical $60 million for the latter's total investment in the chemical operations. Should Dow accept to get out of "an aching process of continual arguments with a partner which brought no experience, clout, technology, or money to the joint venture"? (a) What risks has Dow run? How has it tried to minimize these? (b) What might Dow have done to avoid such unfortunate results? (c) Should Dow sell out for the $60 million offered?

9. An executive who had recently transferred from headquarters in Nashville, Tennessee, to a branch office on Sancerre, France, soon learned of the difficulties of working abroad. The unions were tough to deal with, it was impossible for her spouse to find work, they had to buy all new appliances, it was difficult to communicate with non–English-speaking plumbers. (The firm made plumbing equipment.) And there was *the problem*—the wine and cheese problem. A friendly tractor-company executive whose only exposure to wine in the States was mixing Cold Duck with beer at Illinois versus Iowa football games showed her his solution—a wine cellar which contained the famous white wine made from the Sauvignon Blanc grape (the smoky, almost flinty stuff—much like the best of Pouilly-Fume) and which allowed a comparison of the bolder bouquet of the latest Cote du Rhone pressing with the more complete, but less cheeky approach of a Haut-Medoc. And in Sancerre, the center of French goat's-milk cheese, the problem was to choose either *frais* or *demi-sec* and, further, to know when to order a young Pont L'Eveque or how to pick the right Port Salut or Camembert. *The problem* went beyond choice and comparison. It involved accounting for lunch, also dinner, dessert, and cheese. Did the expense-account scanners in Nashville know how important the correct selection was? If one didn't do it, one did not fit in and was thought of as coming from the sticks or, worse, the States—which sold no seats, nor pipe nipples, nor flushers in France. As an international manager, how should Mme. Dickson deal with this consuming problem?

10. One of several consulting firms engaged in forecasting political risks in various countries advised a commercial bank in the U.S. that the overall chance of political turmoil in Argentina was 42 percent during the succeeding eighteen months but that the bank, in loaning money to Argentinian companies, ran a significantly lower risk than did an industrial company which planned to open a manufacturing subsidiary in Argentina. The bank should be concerned with repudiation of its loan, but an industrial company faced "a slew of constraints." (a) Explain why making a bank loan would be safer than setting up a new subsidiary. What constraints might the manufacturing firm be facing? (b) What controls (see Chapter 22) might the bank install in an attempt to safeguard its funds? The industrial company? (c) Should U.S.-based firms stay out of countries with high political risks—Iran, Lebanon, Libya, Zambia, China, and Argentina, for example?

CASE 23
Maintaining Finland's Position in Metals

Finland's leading metal company, Outokumpu Oy (called OKO in this case), must decide how it wishes to position itself in the world metal industries during the 1980s. OKO has been an acknowledged leader in mining and refining technology but currently faces severe financial constraints.

Home Base

Finland is perhaps most widely known for its courageous fight for survival during World War II and for its ability through the diplomacy of neutrality to maintain independence ever since. Located on the Baltic Sea, with Russia on its eastern border and Norway and Sweden on its north and west, Finland serves as a buffer between the East and the West.

Geographically, Finland is larger than Great Britain or West Germany. But with a population under 5 million, it qualifies as one of the smaller of the small nations. Although about a third of Finland's length lies above the Arctic Circle, the Gulf Stream and air currents keep it warmer than other countries at the same latitude. Its major ports are open for shipping year-round.

For several decades now, manufacturing has displaced the traditional forestry and agriculture as the leading contributor to the total economy and to employment. Incidentally, Finland's per capita GNP is higher than Japan's and Great Britain's. Companies such as OKO have played a significant role in this development.

As with many small companies, imports and exports are especially important to Finland—close to one-quarter of GNP. Raw materials are the chief imports and manufactured goods the major exports. Although the Soviet Union is the single leading country in Finland's foreign trade (20 percent of the total), at least two-thirds of exports and imports are with Western nations.

By U.S. standards, Finland has a lot of government planning and government ownership. However, compared to its immediate neighbors, it places heavy reliance on private ownership and initiative. All the leading companies are expected to be economically viable and to earn a reasonable return on invested capital.

Synergistic Diversification

For the first thirty years of its existence, OKO was just a copper company, mining a relatively small deposit at Outokumpu. Since then three interrelated developments have drastically changed the scope of the company.

1. OKO has greatly expanded the numbers of different metals it mines and refines. In addition to copper, its major products are zinc, nickel, cobalt, and pyrite concentrates. Other metals are often associated in ore bearing these major ones, with the result that OKO also produces some chrome, lead, gold, silver, cadmium, and talc. Whenever a metal ore is found in commercial quantities in Finland, OKO will mine it. Moreover, having mined this ore, OKO proceeds to refine it into base metals—with only minor exceptions.

2. For several metals, OKO has integrated forward, adding still more value to the original resource. For instance, copper is converted into tubing, bars, sheets, wire, and other forms. Much of the company's chrome now goes into its stainless steel.

3. Compared with the major ore deposits of the world, Finland's deposits are neither very large nor very rich (a high percentage of metal). Consequently, throughout its history OKO has had to give much attention to productivity. In both mining (mostly underground) and refining, the most efficient and up-to-date technology is used. Since World War II, OKO has done pioneering R & D in metal refining. So successful has this effort been that OKO is able to license some of its processes and may be hired to consult refining plants in other countries. More than anything else, OKO's "flash smelting" process has made the company world-famous. Over half the world's new copper smelters are licensees of OKO. In addition, an X-ray analyzer of ore slurry is a key element in automated concentrators, and is even more widely used than flash smelting. OKO's "tramp iron detector," initially designed for use on crushers, has been converted into a security device against airport hijacking.

Note that all three of these developments—different metals, forward integration, and advanced technology—have been synergistic, and they have enabled OKO to sell most of its products abroad in the face of world competition. In fact, 78 percent of OKO sales are exports.

Recession: Impact on Financing

The diversification program just outlined enabled OKO to expand substantially in the 1960s and 1970s. In the past decade both sales and assets have grown more than fourfold. Much of this increase reflects inflation, but overall tonnage and employment did rise. The company is now divided into four operating divisions, and the relative importance of each is indicated in Table 1.

Unfortunately, profits have been much lower than the estimated net income that was used to justify the investment in new facilities. For example, the most recent major expansion into stainless steel is a technological success, but selling prices have dropped and this new plant is barely breaking even. During the last few years economic activity in Europe has been especially slow, and selling

TABLE 1.
OKO's OPERATING DIVISIONS AND MANAGEMENT

Division	Sales (million marks)*	Exports	Number of Employees	Management Comment on Profitability
Mining & Metallurgy	615	85%	5,060	Except for cobalt (prices and profits up dramatically because of turmoil in Zaire), the profitability remains unsatisfactory due to low prices of metals.
Copper & Copper Alloy	476	59%	1,838	Increased productivity has improved profitability, but a satisfactory level has not yet been reached.
Stainless Steel	429	75%	1,141	Profitability remains unsatisfactory due to low price level and continuing startup expenses.
Technical Export	307	97%	417	Profitability remains favorable. However, this year was unusually high due to large deliveries of smelter equipment to Soviet Union and the Republic of Korea. Preceding year sales were 175 million marks.
Central Management & "other"	8	94%	669	Includes R & D, which costs 3.2 percent of sales—primarily for exploration and metallurgical research.
Total	1,835	78%	9,125	

*For quick conversion, assume 4 Finnish marks equal 1 U.S. dollar.

prices for most metals and metal products have not kept pace with rising wage and interest rates. See Tables 2 and 3 for the most recent financial statements.

TABLE 2.
OKO INCOME STATEMENT
(in million Finnish marks)[*]

Gross Sales		1,835
Adjustments		79
Net Sales		1,756
Expenses:		
Materials and supplies	625	
Employee expense	523	
Other expenses	321	1,469
Operating margin		287
Deductions:		
Depreciation	156	
Other income & expense (net)	2	
Interest	101	
Foreign exchange losses	17	
Direct taxes	3	279
Net Earnings for the Year		8

TABLE 3.
OKO BALANCE SHEET
(in million Finnish marks)[*]

Assets		Liabilities & Equity		
Cash	52	Current Liabilities		831
Receivables	533	Long-term debt:		
Inventories	396	Bank loans	634	
Current assets	981	Loans from pension funds	111	
		Bonds	343	
		Other long-term debt	231	1,219
Fixed Assets	1,271			
Other assets	178	Reserves		111
		Stockholders' equity:		
		Share capital	283	
		Reserves	77	
		Retained earnings	9	369
	2,430			2,430

[*]For quick conversion, assume 4 Finnish marks equal 1 U.S. dollar.

OKO went heavily into debt to finance its diversification. Now that profits have not risen as expected, this debt is a serious burden. In fact, depreciation and depletion charge is less than necessary to replace capital so the situation is even more strained than the income statement shows. (Depreciation based on replacement values would have been 220 million marks, instead of the 156 marks used for the income statement.)

Because if this financial squeeze, the present central management has switched to a conservative investment policy during the last three years. In the OKO annual report, management says frankly, "In order to improve the financing situation, major expansion programmes will have to be shelved for the time being." Investments have been made (175 million marks last year) only to complete expansions already started and even more to improve productivity. Perhaps a clearer indication of the policy reversal is the drop in employment from a peak of over 10,000 to 9,100—a very significant action in a country where increased employment is a major social objective.

Present Options

No one is fully satisfied with OKO's present operations. In physical terms the volume is static, profits are very small, employment is down. So, central management must weigh alternative approaches to the future. The following threefold grouping suggests several possibilities. The various thrusts can, of course, be resorted into other combinations.

1. Continue the Present Strategy. This includes (a) focusing investments and R & D on improved productivity, (b) seeking to reduce the debt burden and improve the debt-equity ratio, (c) continuing to export products and services to the best markets currently available, and (d) deferring other expansion until metal prices and economic conditions improve and risk is reduced.

2. Stress Growth from Finland's Resources. OKO's growth through diversification was based on this approach. It involves (a) finding and mining Finland's mineral resources, (b) refining these ores into base metals by using advanced, sophisticated technology, (c) integrating forward into metal fabrication in selected areas to increase the value added, and (d) exporting products and services to the best markets available.

The copper ore deposits now being mined will be exhausted in about ten years, so intensive exploration will be necessary to maintain local supplies. For years local farmers and explorers have been encouraged to bring in rock samples.

The creativity of Finnish miners and engineers in taking full advantage of valuable resources has already been described. Note that under this strategy OKO's "domain" is defined by Finland's resources, not by potential world markets. Likewise, the outstanding technology has been developed primarily to improve local productivity; its salability abroad is a fortunate by-product.

3. Expand Abroad. This strategy would include (a) opening sales branches (in places such as Brazil, western U.S., South Africa, Korea) to promote the sale of technology, (b) developing more systematically the marketing of OKO's fabricated products—perhaps through the same sales branches, (c) contracting for long-run supplies of ore or ore-concentrates that can be refined in OKO's plants, and (d) looking for joint ventures with local foreign companies which can use OKO's expertise and/or products.

In exporting technologies, OKO can simply grant licenses, as it has done for its flash smelting process. Or it can *design* an entire plant. Or it can make much of the equipment in its own shops and sell that perhaps as parts of a total plant. Of course, OKO's future ability to sell technology in any of these stages depends on its continuing development of advanced techniques suitable to conditions in the users' country.

Central management has to recognize several influences bearing on its choice of strategic thrusts. For instance, because of the country's history and strict neutrality posture, Finland is wary of becoming very dependent on materials from a single nation. Finland is so small that it does not have much power in the international arena, and it does not want to be in a position where it can be pushed around.

OKO has long been sensitive to the needs of its employees. It stresses safety and has a liberal pension plan. On several occasions it has built up inventory rather than have a layoff. In exchange, there have been relatively few work stoppages.

In such a small country the supply of engineers is naturally limited, and the number of those who speak English or other world languages is even smaller. (Finnish, like Hungarian, has Mongolian antecedents rather than Greek or Latin, and it is hard to learn. The second language in Finland is Swedish.) So there are personnel constraints, as well as financial ones, on the number of different thrusts OKO can undertake.

Relationships between OKO and the Finnish government are close. In fact, in connection with the financing of various expansion projects, different ministries have bought stock, with the result that the government now has voting control. However, government officials rely heavily on the technical judgment of company management. Thus, at present the government is going along with the conservative strategy even though it would like to see an expansion of jobs and exports. On the other hand, if company management presents a new proposal which it believes is economically viable, the government would probably make additional capital contributions.

Question

Outline the future strategy that you recommend OKO pursue, and justify your position.

24 INTEGRATING ROLE OF CENTRAL MANAGERS

Each of the many managerial issues and tasks discussed in the preceding chapters deserves thoughtful attention. Sooner or later a central manager is likely to face all of them. Their full significance, however, lies in their contribution to a basic approach to managing a total enterprise. Each topic has been included because it fits into a framework for thinking about the challenge of overall, integrated management.

The following brief conclusion reemphasizes the central themes we have been unfolding. Individual chapters necessarily focus on separate facets. And there is always danger that we become so absorbed with these particular parts that the broader structure becomes blurred. To counteract this danger, we stress again the structure of the book as a whole. The selection of subjects and their sequence are significant; they present a mental framework—a way of thinking about a very complex phenomenon.

Three related themes deserve emphasis:

1. A way of moving from broad social-technological-political-economic developments to company programs tuned to these developments.
2. The design of balanced, integrated company programs in which (a) the several parts each contribute to a consistent central mission, and (b) the magnitude and timing of effort is realistically related to company size and resources.
3. Recognition that such programs have long-run viability only when they include a practical reconciliation of diverse social pressures; and that, in fact, managers have a critical and unique role in devising bases for continuing cooperation that give realistic implementation to social reforms.

FRAMEWORK FOR STRATEGY AND PROGRAM FORMULATION

The managers of an enterprise are bombarded with data—from the daily press, television, customers, vendors, trade periodicals, government publications, their own people, their own observations, and many other sources. Some device is needed to screen out what is relevant to the enterprise, and these bits of information then have to be related to practical action. Moreover, managers of going concerns are confronted with a host of "what do we do here" questions. And all these "inputs" appear in raw, unlabeled form. Clearly, a way of thinking is needed to bring some kind of order into the situation.

A framework for dealing with companywide problems has been presented in this book. It comes from a "general survey outline" used by a successful management consultant in several hundred companies, and it has also proved to be quite helpful to operating executives. Basically the framework identifies issues, puts them into logical arrangement so that the normal interactions can be readily seen, and provides a flow of thought leading from external opportunities to concrete company actions. Although the framework is easier to describe as a sequence of steps, in practice we grasp ideas and information as they appear and use the framework more as a sorting and organizing device. Then when opportunities are spotted, the framework guides us to additional angles that should be investigated.

Select Company Strategy

The guiding thrust of all central management action is the company strategy. Strategy defines the mission. It provides the justification for the company's existence as an independent social unit. And being the top statement of purpose, it is the end result in terms of which many other subgoals and activities are weighed.

Viewed another way, strategy identifies the key bases for company survival. It should specify (a) the domain; that is, the product arket niches the company seeks to serve, (b) the differential advantages that the company will use to establish an attractive position in this domain, (c) the major thrusts that should be started soon, and (d) the target results to be used in measuring accomplishments. No one of these elements alone is an adequate statement of strategy; each provides a necessary dimension to a meaningful, operational company objective.

To formulate strategy, we urged in Part 1 a three-pronged analysis. First, relevant factors in the whole dynamic environment can be brought into focus by concentrating on the outlook for the industry or industries in which the company functions. Careful review of the demand, supply, and competitive forces will yield a forecast of volume and profitability and will identify crucial factors for success in that industry. Second, an evaluation of the strengths and weaknesses of the specific company will indicate its ability relative to competitors to take advantage of opportunities uncovered during the industry analysis. Third, the likely response of key actors to company moves is predicted. Then in light of industry prospects, company strengths, and key actor analysis, central management selects propitious market and/or supply niches as its field for social contribution.

Formulating strategy calls for keen judgment in selecting key factors that warrant emphasis. The strength of strategy does not depend on an elaborate program. Instead its essence lies in singling out from numerous influences a few critical determinants. Companies will differ in the particular way each seeks distinctiveness. But unless a central management finds (and keeps up-to-date) some unique and attractive combination of the four dimensions listed above, its company will be unable to attract an inflow of resources essential for continued existence.

Diversified corporations control several business-units, *each* of which should establish its own strategy along the lines just summarized. These "companies" are the centers of action; most strategy is formed at their level. However, the parent company should have a strategy covering the portfolio of businesses it wishes to hold and the special inputs it will provide to give these business-units a differential advantage.

Use Policy to Elaborate Strategy

While strategy is selective in its points of emphasis, policy provides more complete coverage. Through policy we assure that "all the bases are covered." There will be policy guiding relations of the firm with all its main resource groups.

A policy is a standing guide for making decisions on a given subject. Each time a question arises regarding, say, price increases to match inflation or increased employment of blacks, we turn to policy for the established answer. Policy provides consistency of action and greatly simplifies the process of management. By establishing policy in all major functions of a company, we can create reinforcing effort throughout the enterprise.

Policy offers an important means for correlating many facets of a business with strategy. The work of each division and department can be reviewed for its compatibility with a new strategy, and policy can be adjusted wherever opportunity is found for strong supporting action.

The array of policy issues that we examined in Part 2 is listed in Figure 24-1. These issues are likely to be affected by a change in strategy. So a good way to begin this reconciliation of strategy and policy is to check each of these issues. Not every one of the topics listed will be significant for a specific company, and others may need to be added to deal with unusual resource groups; but the topics do identify issues encountered by many, many enterprises—profit and nonprofit alike.

Such a policy review for consistency with strategy elaborates the strategy. Occasionally this spelling out of strategy implications will raise problems sufficiently serious to require a readjustment in the strategy itself. More often, it flags the need for updating a traditional pattern of behavior in one or more departments.

Build a Supporting Organization

Strategy and policy must have an organization to carry them out. Both historically and conceptually, organization is a vehicle to execute strategy. So

FIGURE 24-1.

USE OF POLICY REVIEW TO INTEGRATE
COMPANY STRATEGY WITH OPERATIONS

Consider impact of strategy on policy for:

MARKETING:

    Product line and customer
    Pricing
    Marketing mix

HUMAN RESOURCES:

    Selection and training
    Compensation and benefits
    Industrial relations

CREATING GOODS AND SERVICES:

    Procurement
    Production
    Research and development

FINANCIAL RESOURCES:

    Sources of capital
    Allocation of capital

essential is the organization, in fact, that a weak or unsuited structure can nullify the best of plans.

To assure a good linkage between strategy and structure, we propose in Part 4 that the operating activities implied by a strategy and its associated policy be laid out first, and then that an organization be designed which suits these activities. The conclusions of such an exercise must be tempered, however, by the size of company and the available personnel. Size forces us to consider typical stages in corporate growth, and key personnel is a moderating influence on the variety of auxiliary services fitted onto the underlying operating units.

Organization design directly affects the prestige, power, influence, and compensation of key individuals. It has a great impact on their motivation. So part of the skill in effective organization design is to arrange managerial and other positions so that these motivators encourage people to work for success of the strategy—and not for some divergent or bureaucratic ends.

Guide the Execution

In one sense, selecting strategy, formulating policy, and designing organization are all preparatory. The action we can observe objectively is the actual activity of shaping and exchanging products, services, and diverse satisfactions. It is the execution of plans that really counts.

Central managers devote a significant portion of their energies to execution of plans—and first-line supervisors an even higher percentage. As outlined in Part 5, execution includes programming the action, providing leadership and motivation, and controlling allocations and results. It is the "make happen" phase of managing.

Two aspects of a central manager's role in execution call for continuing self-discipline. (1) Since central managers personally can be active in only a small part of total transactions, they influence execution largely by setting patterns for others to follow. Through their own behavior they create a leadership tone and they foster control practices, checking only occasionally to see that regular use is made of these control devices. In resolving specific problems central managers are as much concerned with precedent for the future as with the case at hand. Central managers guide execution primarily by helping to shape the customs and the values followed within their company and in its relations with resource groups.

(2) The external calls on a central manager's time may be heavy. Sometimes the manager can't escape seeing an important customer, arbitrating a personnel dispute, appearing before a Congressional committee, meeting with a Consumers' Protective Committee, negotiating a new stock issue, and a host of other worthy activities. The danger is that in responding to so many external requests for time the mission—the strategy—of the enterprise gets shunted aside. One of the main virtues of specific programs and well-designed controls is to keep primary attention focused on primary tasks to be accomplished each day. This means, of course, that we must see that the programs and the controls are regularly adjusted to match any changes in strategy.

Now, with this framework of strategy formulation, policy elaboration, organization, and execution—and the components of each—clearly in mind, we can deal with the disorderly bombardment of data and problems noted at the beginning of this section. The numerous inputs can be quickly placed into a meaningful, operational way of thinking about a complex endeavor. The framework becomes a powerful tool for keeping perspective and making use of the wealth of information and ideas available to us.

NEED FOR INTEGRATED TREATMENT

Reconcile Diverse Changes

The strategy→policy→organization→execution framework has an appealing, logical flow. Unfortunately, management problems cannot always be treated in this convenient sequence. The managers of any dynamic enterprise always face a cluttered, mixed-up situation.

In a normal company several forces contribute to this jumble. (1) Pressure for change may originate anywhere—not just with an opportunity for improved strategy. Perhaps the Urban Redevelopment Corporation offers us a downtown plant, or a salesperson has a great idea for advertising, or a control has failed to signal a shortage, or the government is challenging our fair employment practice, or we have an unexpected opportunity to hire an outstanding scientist. Such events may call for action anywhere in the total system.

(2) Diverse changes occur at the same time. With separate departments responding to their sector of the environment and pushing for their respective goals, one may be courting a foreign distributor while another is offering to increase local employment while a third is seeking a government subsidy.

(3) Moreover, a mixture if old and new often confounds the situation. This year's seniors must be taught while we are also designing new programs for entering freshmen or a new breed of systems analysts is working side by side with our traditional cost accountants.

This sort of bubbling, moving activity is fine *provided* changes in one place do not detract from efforts in another. Obviously, changes that reinforce each other, and thus yield synergistic benefits, are desired. Central management and other coordinating mechanisms have a never-ending task of reconciling the many changes that occur daily in a healthy organization.

One of the major contributions of a well-articulated strategy—with its supporting policy, organization, and programs—is to serve as the *basis for such reconciliation*. The diversity of the changes makes a central, preeminent rationale especially valuable. Proposed changes can be evaluated in terms of their contribution to the major mission. The very complexity of activities calls for such a synthesizing standard for coping with our environment.

Watch Magnitude and Timing of Changes

In the short run, company resources are always limited. A progressive management sensing new opportunities must be careful not to strain these capacity limits.

Accounting reports and financial budgets typically provide a mechanism for living within the firm's financial ability. More difficult to measure and to predict is the capacity of personnel to handle external pressures and opportunities. Meeting a deadline on new pollution controls, launching a new product-line, and developing a matrix organization all at the same time may be so confusing that important actions are missed. A thinly staffed division may be able to keep a mature operation running as usual but lack the capacity to switch production to foreign sources.

A related issue is the timing of changes. Clearly an effort to increase the employment of blacks will not mix well with an economy drive and consequent reduction of total personnel. A laboratory already running at capacity and considering a move is not ready for a new government contract.

The changes proposed in all these examples might be highly desirable when considered alone. But when they are combined with other changes, the total burden creates an overload. Here, again, the need for an integrated treatment is clear.

Central managers of business firms face pesky, ambiguous, intractable pressures involving a variety of values not immediately reflected on company balance sheets. Great skill is needed to respond to the topsy-turvy world in ways that reinforce each other and that are within the capacities of the enterprise.

UNIQUE SOCIAL ROLE

A third dimension of the work of central managers, in addition to focusing on the strategy→policy→organization→execution approach and keeping the company moving in an integrated fashion, is contributing to social development. They do this—not as an extra duty on the side—but as an integral part of directing company responses to its changing environment.

In the process of finding workable bases for getting necessary resources, central managers make a unique and valuable contribution to social problems. They help shape many reform proposals and provide practical tests of their feasibility. Of course, many reforms do not directly affect business operations—court reform, integrated education, and urban government are examples. In such areas, executives may be concerned citizens, but their positions in a corporation neither qualify them nor obligate them to be leaders. However, where a reform directly influences the conditions on which business is transacted—as in employment conditions, quality guarantees, and environmental protection—central managers and other executives make three kinds of contributions.

1. Managers Help Create the Conditions on which Cooperative Endeavors Take Place. Each strategy conceives of a joint undertaking involving services, jobs, markets, taxes, and so on. Each policy relating a company to its environment sets conditions on which exchanges will or will not be made. Each program lays out times and quantities when specific flows will occur. These interactions between a company and various interest groups are not incidental or charitable matters. They are necessary to performing a mission and to survival.[1]

As we have indicated repeatedly, managers want a continuing flow of resource inputs and continuing outlets for services and satisfactions that the company generates. Consequently, they give close attention to maintaining markets, building reputations, assuring supply, obtaining permissions, and the like. This kind of concerned behavior lies at the very heart of successful business operations.

Now, if any interest group wants to alter the conditions on which transactions occur—either to satisfy its own aspirations or under outside pressure—

---

[1] For expansion of this point see the discussion of the "resource converter" models on pages 2-7.

thoughtful managers try to devise a way the new conditions can be met without jeopardizing the cooperative venture they direct. All sorts of adjustments in conditions of work, material utilized, information provided to investors, side effects on ecology, and the like are hammered out in the frequent negotiations that take place between providers of resources and a company. Necessity forces some of the adjustments, while others are invented to attract better resources. Whatever the motivation, clearly the managers benefit from helping to create workable reforms.

Safety, shorter hours, paid vacations, company pensions, and air-conditioned offices illustrate improvements in working conditions many firms instituted to attract and retain workers. Product quality, often including guarantees, has long been a means of wooing customers. Stable earnings attract investors. These and many other business practices add to "the quality of life." Managers do not provide these conditions as a generous, emotional gesture. Rather, they try to put together a package of satisfactions that will assure a continuing flow of resources.

The tough, practical question is how much of what satisfaction it is possible for a business to offer. Managers are actual participants, along with the beneficiaries of a proposed added satisfaction, in creating specific answers to that question.

2. Managers Serve as Mediators for Competing Reforms. Worthy reforms often compete with each other. Consider the proposed goals for an electric power company as an example. Clean air, cool water, dependable and cheap electricity, low requirements for foreign exchange, beautiful countrysides, conservation of natural resources—are all commendable social objectives. But if we give unbridled priority to any one, several of the others will suffer. New technology may help, and power company managers have an obligation (and strong incentive, as noted above) to find improved ways to satisfy several of the listed objectives at once. Nevertheless, we know that a balance has to be struck in the degree to which the competing pressures will be met.

Central managers unavoidably serve as mediators in this balancing process. The firm as a resource converter—the power company in the preceding example—is the place where the competing pressures collide. For instance, environmentalists don't negotiate directly with consumers who are insisting on power for their refrigerators. Instead, each group puts pressure on the power company to serve its parochial desires. Managers of the power company would like to keep everybody satisfied, but they are caught in a squeeze. Consequently, the managers try to negotiate an agreement with each group that will satisfy some of the desires but not be so burdensome that the company cannot also make peace with other pressure groups.[2]

---

[2] In this example, several different quasi-judicial but nonetheless competing government agencies also get into the act. However, the main burden of initiating proposals for resolving the competing pressures rests with managers of the power company.

When managers make proposals to a resource supplier and when they reject other requests, they are acting in effect as mediators.[3] They are exploring how far to go along with the desires of each competing group. This is a hard and unpopular assignment. But managers should accept the role because (1) they know best what impact concessions in one direction will have on the ability of their company to satisfy other pressures, and (2) they have a strong incentive to arrive at a workable understanding (their company may shut down if agreement cannot be reached).

3. Managers Can Serve as Advisors on National Priorities and Institutional Changes.

Thus far we have pictured the manager as one who adjusts to new goals—not a person who sets goals. We believe this emphasis is correct, but we do not intend to rule out a manager's participation in the debate that typically surrounds the establishment of a new social standard. Today setting new standards usually centers on some kind of legislation.

Federal and state governments are playing an increasing role in social change. They make laws that press the laggards into line—on minimum wages, food quality, plant safety, and the like. They also initiate reform in such areas as equal employment, air and water pollution, social security, and financial underwriting. And in spending almost 40 percent of our gross national product, they support many causes.

In the arena where priorities get hammered out, business executives have a difficult and often conflicting role. As private citizens they are indeed entitled to voice their preferences on the directions national effort should take. And if their companies participate in filling a need, they are inclined to be more knowledgeable on that subject than the average citizen. A farmer, to pick another advocate, can speak from experience on the desirability of farm subsidies. However, the beneficiary such as a farmer can scarcely be expected to be impartial. So we rely on the legislative process to set priorities, and we look to interest groups for expert testimony and advocacy of their cause. The ethical problems involve the manner and the openness of pleading one's special interest.

A typical issue is society's decision as to the kind of environment it wants, with full recognition of the sacrifices necessary to achieve that end. Are consumers willing to pay more for poorer vegetables in a move to eliminate use of DDT? Should cities be built up rather than out so as to preserve the rural landscape? Do we want airports close to cities for the convenience of passengers or located far away to cut down the noise for city dwellers? Resolution of such issues cannot, and should not, be made by business executives alone. They can provide expert testimony about feasibility and costs, but if they have something to gain from the decision, they should appear as admittedly biased advocates.

---

[3] This proposing and rejecting may take place in a formal bargaining process if the interest group is represented by an official body. Or, it may consist of testing the attractiveness of a "package of satisfaction" among customers, suppliers, or workers responding individually.

Other interested parties should also be heard. And the social value decisions should be thrashed out in some legislative forum.

We believe that business executives should actively participate in setting social values, even though this joining in the debate makes them a target for those who disagree with the guides which emerge. The social forum needs the inputs which only business managers can provide; and managers are entitled to advocate a course convenient to them just as other interested parties should advocate their preferences.[4] But it is a mistake to think that the primary social responsibility of business is this sharing in the formulation of values—important though that may be.

The first responsibility of business is the generation of goods and services in harmony with the goals of society. When national priorities change, the business system must make a myriad of adjustments in the flow of goods and services. When growth and social attitudes bring particular aspects of our environment to a critical point, business must help find revised methods of producing the services people want while keeping the environment healthy. As the economy becomes more affluent and people's personal desires shift, business must devise ways of providing more opportunities to achieve self-expression, security, and other aspirations. This kind of constructive adaptation is a cardinal task of central management.

From a pragmatic view, managers play a major role in social change. They are not preachers but doers—as noted in the preceding paragraph. And this is a task they are uniquely well qualified to perform.

Permeating all three of the themes we have been summarizing—strategy→execution, integration, social change—is a strong emphasis on adjusting and adapting to future needs and opportunities. This emphasis makes managing a creative, rewarding endeavor.

---

[4] The concept of participating, but not dominating, in the establishment of social goals is vital. Much past criticism of business arose from unilateral, short-run decisions by business firms that were insensitive to the ramifications of their actions.

Part 7

COMPREHENSIVE CASES

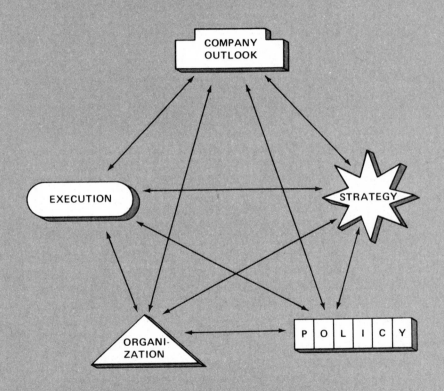

Comprehensive Case 1

FOURWINDS MARINA

Jack Keltner had just completed his first day as general manager of the Fourwinds Marina. It was mid-August and though the Marina slip rentals ran until October 30, business took a dramatic downturn after Labor Day. It would be unwise to change any of the current operations in the next three weeks, but he would have to move swiftly to implement some of the changes he had been considering—both short-range and long-range plans were sorely needed if the Marina was to survive.

The day before, Jack had been called in by Sandy Taggart, president of the Taggart Corporation, owner of the Fourwinds Marina and the Inn of the Fourwinds. Leon McLaughlin had just submitted his resignation as general manager of the Marina. McLaughlin and Taggart had disagreed on some compensation McLaughlin felt was due him. Part of the disagreement concerned McLaughlin's wife, who had been hired to work in the parts department but had spent little time there due to an illness.

McLaughlin had been the fifth manager in the five years that the Marina had been in operation. He had had fifteen years of marine experience before he was hired to manage the Marina. His experience, however, consisted of selling and servicing boats and motors in Evansville, Indiana, not in managing marinas. He took pride in running a "tight ship" and felt that the marina had an excellent chance in turning around after some hard times. It was fairly easy to keep the Marina staffed because the resort atmosphere was so attractive, and his goal was to have the majority of his staff on a full-time basis year round. Even though the Marina is closed from November until April there is a considerable amount of repair work needed on boats during those months. McLaughlin was told when hired that he had a blank check to get the Marina shaped up. This open policy, however, was later rescinded. He and his wife have a mobile home near the Marina, but maintain a permanent residence in Evansville. For the most part he puts in six full days a week, but has an aversion to working on Sunday. McLaughlin was an effective organizer, but was weak in the area of employee and customer relations.

Keltner had no experience in marina management either, but he was considered a hard worker willing to take on tremendous challenges. He joined the Taggart Corporation after four years as a CPA for Ernst and Ernst, an accounting firm. Functioning as controller of the corporation, he found that there was a tremendous volume of work demanded, necessitating late hours at the office and a briefcase full of work to take home with him most evenings. At this point,

Keltner lived in a small community near the Marina, but still had to commute frequently to the home office of the Taggart Corporation in Indianapolis, a ninety-minute drive from Lake Monroe. He had indicated that he hoped to move the offices to Lake Monroe, site of the Marina and Inn as soon as possible. Handling the accounting for the Marina, the Inn, and other Taggart Corporation interests could be done effectively at the Marina; the Inn and the Marina comprise 90 percent of the corporation.

Much of the explanation for the heavy workload lay in the fact that there had been virtually no accounting system when he first joined Taggart. He had first set up six profit centers for the Marina and was now generating monthly accounting reports.

The other principal investors involved in the Taggart Corporation besides Sandy (A. L. Taggart III) are William Brennan, president of one of the state's largest commercial and industrial real estate firms, and Richard DeMars, president of Guepel-DeMars, Inc., the firm that designed both the Marina and the Inn.

Sandy Taggart is a well-known Indianapolis businessman who is Chairman of the Board of Colonial Baking Company, one of the larger bakeries serving the Indianapolis metropolitan area and surrounding counties. He did his undergraduate work at Princeton and completed Harvard's A.M.P. program eight years ago. He is an easygoing man and appears not to let problems upset him easily. He maintains his office at the Taggart Corporation in Indianapolis, but tries to get to the Marina at least once every week. He kept in daily contact with Leon McLaughlin and continues to do the same with Keltner. He enjoys being a part of the daily decision-making and problem-solving that goes on at the Marina and feels that he needs to be aware of all decisions due to its weak financial position. Taggart feels current problems stem from a lack of knowledge of the marina business and lack of experienced general managers when they began operation five years ago. He also admits that their lack of expertise in maintaining accurate cost data and in controlling their costs hurt, but he feels Keltner has already gone a long way in correcting this problem.

Keltner has been intimately involved in the operation and feels that at a minimum the following changes should be made over the next 12-month period.

1. Add eighty slips on E, F, and G docks and put in underwater supports on these docks to deter breakage from storms. Cost, $370,000–410,000. Annual profits if all slips are rented—$110,000.
2. Add a second person to assist the present secretary-receptionist-bookkeeper. This will actually be a savings if the Indianapolis office is closed. Savings—$450/month.
3. Reorganize the parts department and install a new inventory system. Cost—$4,500. Savings—$3,700–4,500/year.
4. Keep the boat and motor inventory low. Boat inventory as of mid-August is approximately $190,000. It has been over $450,000.
5. Reduce the work force through attrition if a vacated job can be assumed by someone remaining on the staff.

6. Use E, F, and G docks for winter storage with an improved and more extensive bubbling system. Profits to be generated are difficult to estimate.
7. Light and heat the storage building so repair work can be done at night and in the winter. Cost—$18,000, which he estimates probably would be paid for from the profits in two winters.

Each of these changes would add to the effectiveness and profitability of the Marina operation and that was his prime concern. The operation of the Inn was under the control of another general manager and operated as a separate corporate entity.

As he reviewed the structure, background, and development of the Inn and the Marina he realized the extent of the problems that faced him in his new role of general manager and, at the same time, controller of the Taggart Corporation. Managing the Marina was a full-time seven-day-a-week job, particularly during the season. The questions uppermost in his mind were: (1) what would be the full plan he would present to Taggart for the effective, efficient, and profitable operation of the Marina? and (2) how would it be funded? The financial statements presented a fairly glum picture, but he had the available backup data to analyze for income per square foot on most of the operations and payroll data, for example, as well as the knowledge he had gleaned working with the past general managers and observing the operation of the Marina.

BACKGROUND DATA ON FOURWINDS MARINA

The Setting

The Fourwinds Marina and the Inn of the Fourwinds are located on Lake Monroe, a manmade reservoir over ten thousand acres in size nestled in the hills of southern Indiana. Both facilities are owned and operated by the Taggart Corporation, but are operated as totally distinct and separate facilities. They cooperate in promoting business for each other.

The Inn occupies some 71,000 square feet on thirty acres of land. It is designed to blend into the beautifully wooded landscape and is constructed of rustic and natural building materials. It is designed to appeal to a broad segment of the population with rooms priced from $33–$52 for a double room. The Inn is composed of 150 sleeping rooms—singles, doubles, and suites—and has meeting rooms to appeal to the convention and sales meeting clientele. The largest meeting room will seat 300 for dining and 350 for conferences. Recreation facilities include an indoor-outdoor swimming pool, tennis courts, sauna, whirlpool bath, a recreation room with pool tables and other games. Additional facilities include two dining rooms and a cocktail lounge. The Inn is open year round with heavy seasonal business in the summer months.

It is the first lodge to be built on state property by private funds. By virtue of the size of its food service facilities (in excess of $200,000 per annum) it qualifies under Indiana State Law for a license to serve alcoholic beverages on Sunday.

A brief description of the Pointe is also in order, as its development promises a substantial boost to the Marina's business. Located three miles from the Marina, the Pointe consists of 384 acres on the lake. It is a luxury condominium development, designed to meet the housing needs of primary and secondary home buyers. Currently seventy units are under construction. Twenty of these have been sold and down payments have been received on eighty more. These condominiums range from $35,000 to $140,000, with an average of $90,000. Approval has been secured for the construction of 1,900 living units over a seven-year period. The development has completed an eighteen-hole golf course. Swimming pools and tennis courts are now under construction. The Pointe is a multimillion dollar development by Indun Realty, Inc., Lake Monroe Corporation, and Reywood, Inc. Indun Realty is a wholly owned subsidiary of Indiana National Corp., parent firm of Indiana National Bank, the state's largest fiduciary institution.

The Fourwinds Marina occupies four acres of land and is one of the most extensive and complete marinas of its type in the United States. It is composed of the boat docks, a sales room for boats and marine equipment, an indoor boat storage facility, and a marine repair shop.

There are seven docks projecting out from a main connecting dock that runs parallel to the shore line. The seven parallel docks extend out from 330 to 600 feet into the lake, each at a right angle to the connecting dock. The center dock houses a large building containing a grocery store, snack bar, and restrooms and a section of docks used as mooring for rental boats.

At the end of the dock is an office for boat rental, five gasoline pumps, and pumping facilities for removing waste from houseboats and larger cruisers.

The three docks to the right of the center dock (facing the lake) are docks A, B, and C, which are designed for mooring smaller boats—runabouts, fishing boats, etc. A bait shop is on A dock. A, B, and C slips are not always fully rented. The three docks to the left are the prime slips (E, F, and G)—designed for berthing houseboats, large cruisers, etc.* There are a total of 460 rentable slips priced from $310–$1,155 for uncovered slips and $450–$1,690 for covered slips per season (April 1–October 30). Seventy-five percent of all the slips are under roof and are in the more desirable location, hence they are rented first. Electric service is provided to all slips, and the slips on E and F docks have water and trash removal provided at no extra cost. To the left of the prime slips are 162 buoys, renting for $225 per season. This rental includes shuttleboat service to and from the moored craft. Buoys are not considered to be a very profitable segment. The buoys require constant attention because they shift and break loose occasionally. Time is required to retrieve boats that break loose at night and during storms.

---

*E, F, and G are the most profitable slips and are fully rented. There is a waiting list to get into these slips.

Lake Monroe, the largest lake in Indiana, is a 10,700-acre reservoir developed by the U.S. Army Corps of Engineers in conjunction with and under the jurisdiction of the Indiana Department of Natural Resources. With the surrounding public lands (accounting for some 80 percent of the 150-mile shoreline) the total acreage is 26,000. It is a multipurpose project designed to provide flood control, recreation, water supply and flow-augmentation benefits to the people of Indiana.

The reservoir is located about nine miles, or a fifteen-minute drive, southwest of Bloomington, home of Indiana University, and a ninety-minute drive from Indianapolis. The Indianapolis metropolitan area has a population of over one million with some 5.25 billion dollars to spend annually. It is considered a desirable site for future expansion by many of the nation's top industrial leaders, as reported in a recent *Fortune* magazine survey. The city is the crossroads of the national interstate highway system with more interstate highways converging there than in any other section of the United States. Its airport can accommodate any of the jet aircraft currently in operation, and is served by most of the major airlines. The per capita effective buying income is $6,396, as contrasted with $5,668 for the U.S. as a whole, with almost half of the households falling in the annual income bracket of $15,000 and above. While approximately 75 percent of the customers of the Marina for boat dockage, etc. come from the Indianapolis area, it is estimated that there is a total potential audience of some 3.6 million inhabitants within a 100-mile radius of Bloomington.

The thirty-four acres of land on which the Fourwinds complex is located are leased to the corporation by the state of Indiana. The Indiana Department of Natural Resources distributed a prospectus seeking bids on a motel and marina on the selected site. Of the eight to ten bids submitted, only one other bidder qualified. The proposal submitted by the Taggart Corporation was accepted primarily because of the economic strength of the individuals who composed the group as well as the actual content of the bid.

The prospectus specified a minimum rental for the land of $15,000. Taggart Corporation offered in their bid a guarantee of $3,000 against the first $150,000 in marina sales and income and 4 percent of all income over that amount. For the Inn, they guaranteed $12,000 against the first $600,000 of income plus 4 percent of all room sales and 2 percent of all food and beverage sales over that amount.

An initial lease of thirty-seven years was granted to Taggart with two options of thirty years each. At the termination of the contract, all physical property reverts to the state of Indiana and personal property to Taggart. The entire dock structure is floating and is considered under the personal property category.

Prior to tendering a bid, the corporation visited similar facilities at Lake of the Ozarks, Lake Hamilton in Hot Springs, and the Kentucky Lakes operations. They received a considerable amount of information from the Kentucky Lakes managaement.

Sources of Income

Note: The Indiana Department of Natural Resources exercises total control over the rates that can be charged on slip rental as well as room rates at the Inn.

Slip Rental. Reservations for slips must be made by November 15 of each year or the slip is subject to sale on a first-come basis. Ordinarily all slips are rented for the year. Rental period runs from April 1 to October 30. Rental varies from $300 to $1,690 depending on the size of the slip and whether or not it is covered.

Buoy Rental. One hundred and sixty-two buoys are rented for the same April 1– October 30 season at a rate of $225. Shuttleboat service for transporting owners to and from their craft moored at the buoy area is available twenty-four hours a day. It is not a scheduled service, but operates as the demand occurs, requiring the use of a runabout and driver. The charge for the service is included in the buoy rental fee for the season. As long as the buoy field exists the shuttle service must operate on a twenty-four-hour basis in season.

Boat Storage—Winter. It is more expensive to remove a boat from the water than to leave it moored at the dock all winter. The prime rate for storage is based on the charge for the storage in the covered area of the main inside storage building. This area is not heated or lighted so repair work cannot be done in this building. An investment of about $18,000 would afford lighting and spot heating to overcome this drawback. When boats are stored they are not queued according to those needing repair and those not needing service. As a result, time is lost in rearranging boats to get to those on which work must be performed. The storage facility is not utilized in the summer months. The addition of lights in the facility would allow display of used boats for sale; these are currently stored out of doors. Rates for storage charges are:

- 100 percent base rate—inside storage
- 70 percent of base rate—bubbled area of docks covered
- 60 percent of base rate—bubbled area of docks open
- 50 percent of base rate—open storage areas out of water

Storage rate is computed by the size of the boat. A six-foot wide boat has a rate of $11. This is multiplied by the boat length to determine the total rate. So a twenty-foot long boat six feet wide would cost $220. Last winter the storage facility was filled. One hundred boats were stored with the average size somewhat larger than our 11 x 20 example. This rate does not include charges for removing the boat (approximately $110) from the water and moving it to either inside or outside storage areas. In the past there has been vandalism on the boats stored in the more remote areas of the uncovered, out of water storage. The Marina is not reponsible for loss, theft, or damage.

Boat and Motor Rental. Available equipment is up to date and well maintained and consists of:

- 15 houseboats—rental Monday to Friday, $450; Friday to Monday, $450
- 10 pontoon boats—hourly rental $30 for 3 hours; $50 for 6 hours
- 6 runabouts for skiing—$25–30 per hour
- 12 fishing boats—$18 for 6 hours; $28 for 12 hours

Maximum hourly rental is 13 hours per day during the week and 15 hours per day on Saturday and Sunday. (The rental rate does not include gasoline.)

It is not uncommon to have all fifteen houseboats out all week long during the height of the season (from Memorial Day weekend to Labor Day weekend). Pontoons are about 50 percent rented during the week. Utilization of runabouts is 50 percent while fishing boat usage is approximately 40 percent. The woman who operates the boat and motor rental for the Marina has a one-third interest in all of the boat rental equipment. The Marina holds the balance. Funds for the purchase of equipment were contributed on the same one-third to two-thirds ratio. Net profits after payment of expenses, maintenance, depreciation, and so on are split between the two owners according to the same ratio. The area utilized by the rental area could be converted to slips in the $750 range as a possible alternative use for the dock space. Rental income after expenses, but before interest and depreciation, was slightly less than $30,000 last season.

Small Boat Repair Shop. A small boat repair shop is located between C and D docks. It is well equipped with mechanical equipment and a small hoist for removing small boats from the water for repair at the docks. This facility is currently standing idle; one qualified mechanic could operate it.

Grocery Store. The grocery store is subleased and is operated effectively. Prices are those expected at a small grocery catering to a predominately tourist clientele. Income on the leased operation is approximately $750 per month.

Snack Bar. The snack bar is operated by the Inn of the Fourwinds and returns a 5 percent commission to the Marina on food sales. Currently it is felt that the manager of the snack bar is not doing a reliable job in operating the unit. The snack bar is sometimes closed for no apparent reason. Food offered for sale includes hot sandwiches, pizza, snack food, soft drinks, milk, and coffee. Prices are high and general quality is rated as good.

Gasoline Sales. Five pumps are located around the perimeter of the end of the center dock. They are manned thirteen hours per day, from seven A.M. to eight P.M., seven days a week. The pumps for the removal of waste from the houseboats and other large craft are located in this area. It takes an average of five minutes to pump out waste and there is no charge. These gasoline pumps are the only ones available on the lake, permitting access from the water to the pump.

Boat and Boat Accessory Sales Room. A glass-enclosed show room occupying approximately 1,500 square feet of floor space is located at the main entrance to the Marina property. Products from the major boatlines Trojan Yacht,

Kingscraft, Burnscraft, Harris Flote Bote, and Signa, as well as Evinrude motors are offered for sale. In addition, quality lines of marine accessories are available. The sales room building also houses the executive offices of the Marina and the repair and maintenance shops. Attached to the building is the indoor storage area for winter housing of a limited number of boats. Last year total boat sales were approximately $1,456,572. The boat inventory has been reduced from last year's $450,000—some lines have been removed while stocks of others that offered higher profit on sales have been increased.

Fourwinds Marina is the only operation in the state that stocks the very large boats. It is also the only facility in Indiana with large slips to accomodate these boats. With E, F, and G filled and a waiting list to get in, selling the larger, more profitable boats has become nearly impossible.

Marina Docking Area Facts

Dock Construction. The entire section is of modular floating construction. Built of smaller sections that can be bolted together, the construction is of steel frameworks with poured concrete surfaces for walking upon and styrofoam panels in the side for buoyancy. In the event of damage to a section, a side can be replaced easily, eliminating the need to repair the entire segment of dock. Electrical conduits and water pipes are inside the actual dock units. The major damage to the styrofoam dock segments comes from ducks chewing out pieces of the foam to make nests and from gasoline spillage that "eats" the styrofoam. An antigas coating is available. Damage from boats to the dock is minimal. Still, the docks require constant attention. A maze of cables underneath the sections must be kept at the proper tension or the dock will buckle and break up. Three people are involved in dock maintenance. If properly maintained the docks will have twenty to thirty more years of use. Original cost of the entire dock and buoy system was $1,476,398.

Winter Storage. Winter storage can be a problem at a marina located in an area where a freeze-over of the water occurs. It is better for a boat to remain in the water; water affords better and more even support to the hull. By leaving the boat in the water the boat cannot be damaged by the hoists used to lift boats and move them to dry storage. Because these factors are not common knowledge to the boat owner an educational program is required.

A rule of the marina prohibits any employee from driving any of the customer's boats. So, the marina needn't maintain a duplicate set of keys for each boat nor provide insurance to cover its employees. This means, however, that all boats must be towed, with the possibility the boats may be damaged during the towing.

Bubbling Process. To protect boats left in the water during the winter season, Fourwinds Marina has installed a bubbling system. Simple in concept, the system consists of hoses that are weighted and dropped to the bottom of the lake around the individual docks and along the perimeter line surrounding the entire dock area. Fractional horsepower motors operate compressors that pump air into the submerged hoses. The air escaping through tiny holes in the hose forces warmer water at the bottom of the lake up to the top, preventing freezing of the surface or melting ice that might have frozen before the compressors were started. The lines inside the dock areas protect the boats from being damaged by ice formations while the perimeter line prevents major damage to the entire dock area from a pressure ridge that might build up and be jammed against the dock and boats in high winds.

Questions

1. Do you foresee any social, technological, economic, or political *changes* in Fourwinds Marina's environment that are likely to have a major impact on its future success?
2. What do you predict will happen to Fourwinds Marina if it continues with the strategy and policy pursued during McLaughlin's tenure as general manager? (How sick is the patient?)
3. List the five or six most important "key actors" in this situation from Keltner's point of view. For *each* person on your list make a key actor analysis, as we proposed in Chapter 4, using information in the case and reasonable stated assumptions. (For this question, consider an institution such as a bank or a state department to be a "person.")
4. There are many changes which Keltner might make in the operation of Fourwinds Marina. Which of these changes might make a major impact on the future of the marina? Illustrate changes that may be desirable but are unlikely to have a major impact.
5. Within the framework established by your answers to the preceding four questions, what business-unit strategy do you think Keltner should propose to Taggart?
6. Assuming that Taggart approves the strategy you recommend in answering question 5, lay out a program for Keltner to follow during the next year. To the extent that time and available data permit, use the "basic steps in programming" listed in Chapter 20 to prepare this program.
7. Make a three-year financial projection (condensed profit/loss statements and condensed balance sheets) for Fourwinds Marina reflecting your answers to questions 1 through 6, and your proposals for financing the enterprise during this period.
8. On the basis of the limited information that you have on the history of Fourwinds Marina, what are the primary reasons for its unprofitable record to date? What might have been done to avoid the present financial plight?
9. Is it socially desirable to keep Fourwinds Marina in operation?

TABLE 1.
FOURWINDS MARINA
PROFIT/LOSS STATEMENT

Projected Operating Results
for Present Fiscal Year

Revenue:	Sale of new boats	$1,161,528	
	Sale of used boats	269,468	
	Sale of rental boats	25,576	
	Total sales		$1,456,572
Other income:			
	Service and repair	193,031	
	Gasoline and oil	121,994	
	Ship store	136,821	
	Slip rental	262,212	
	Winter storage	48,266	
	Boat rental	149,843	
	Other income		912,167
	Total income		$2,368,739
Expenses:	Fixed Costs		
	Cost of boats	$1,197,184	
	Cost of repair equip.	85,047	
	Ship store costs	96,607	
	Cost of gasoline	77,823	
	Boat rental costs	13,426	
	Total fixed costs		$1,470,087
Operating Expenses:			
	Wages and salaries	$342,231	
	Taxes	35,587	
	Building rent	87,174	
	Equipment rent	13,463	
	Utilities	28,074	
	Insurance	37,500	
	Interest on loans	313,965	
	Advertising	45,225	
	Legal expense	29,175	
	Bad debt expense	13,097	
	Miscellaneous	59,991	
	Total operating expenses		$1,005,482
	Total costs		2,475,569
	Operating loss		106,830
	Depreciation		183,510
	Total loss[*]		290,340

[*]This represents the total operating loss of the Fourwinds Marina in the present fiscal year. Fourwinds sold a subsidiary in the previous year (Boat sales firm in Indianapolis) on which it wrote off a loss of $413,370.

TABLE 2.
FOURWINDS MARINA
BALANCE SHEET

Projected for End of Present Year

Assets			Liabilities	
Current Assets:			**Current Liabilities:**	
Cash	47,787		Accounts payable	131,149
Accounts receivable	101,949		Intercompany payables	700,637
New boats	298,544		Accrued salary expense	13,358
Used boats	91,120		Accrued interest expense	30,574
Parts	79,943		Accrued tax expense	65,579
Ship store	4,111		Accrued lease expense	54,285
Gas/oil	3,939		Prepaid dock rental	267,699
			Boat deposits	6,432
Total Current Assets	631,393		Current bank notes	266,400
			Mortgage (current)	1,474,350
			Note payable to floor plan	338,325
Fixed Assets		Less Depr.	Note on rental houseboats	107,437
Buoys & Docks	1,476,398	473,175	Notes to stockholders	772,725
Permanent bldgs.	302,962	26,823	Dealer reserve liability	20,888
Office furniture	4,890	1,056	Total current liabilities	$4,252,838
Houseboats	208,703	23,447		
Work boats	61,207	1,980		
Equipment	108,630	58,113		
	$2,162,790	$594,594		
			Long term on houseboats	176,512
Net Fixed Assets	$1,568,196			
Other Assets			Common stock–1,500	
Prepaid Expense	4,410		shares at par value $1/share	1,500
Deferred Interest Exp.	37,981			
	$42,391		Retained earnings deficit	(1,485,157)
			Loss during current year*	(703,713)
Total assets	$2,241,980		Total liabilities	$2,241,980

*Loss during year ending March 31 is composed of an operating loss of $106,830 plus depreciation of $183,510, and a write-off loss of a sold subsidiary of $413,370.

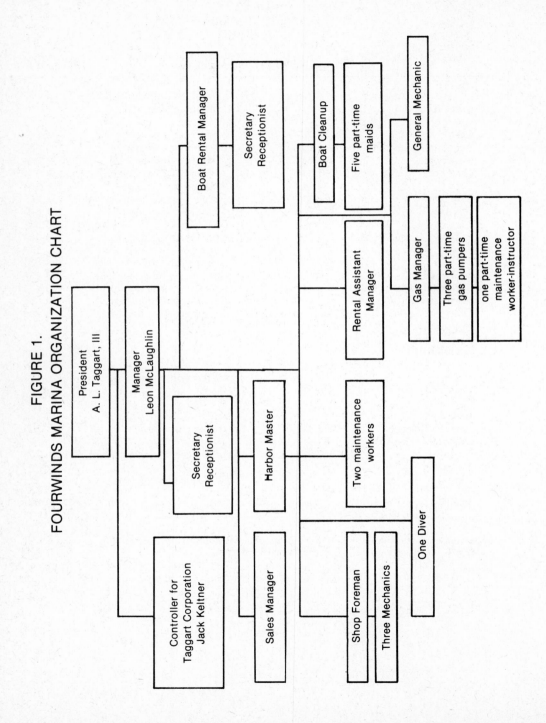

FIGURE 1.
FOURWINDS MARINA ORGANIZATION CHART

President
A. L. Taggart, III

Manager
Leon McLaughlin

Controller for
Taggart Corporation
Jack Keltner

Secretary
Receptionist

Boat Rental Manager

Secretary
Receptionist

Boat Cleanup

Five part-time
maids

General Mechanic

Rental Assistant
Manager

Gas Manager

Three part-time
gas pumpers

one part-time
maintenance
worker-instructor

Sales Manager

Harbor Master

Two maintenance
workers

Shop Foreman

Three Mechanics

One Diver

Comprehensive Case 2

CROSBY HOME SECURITY COMPANY*

"October 27th

"Ms. Jane Crosby
619 West 68th Street
New York, NY 10021

"Dear Jane:
"I am sorry to have to trouble you with a serious matter only two weeks after your father's unfortunate death, but my discoveries about the condition of his estate, in my capacity as executor, make it imperative that you be fully informed at once so that you can determine what course of action you may want to follow.

"As your father's personal lawyer for more than twenty years, I thought I was reasonably familiar with his financial and related matters. (You are probably aware that William Foster of Lincoln and Foster has long handled all legal matters for Crosby Home Security Company.) As executor of your father's estate, however, I have discovered that my knowledge was both incomplete and erroneous. I thought his estate would contain substantial funds and investments outside the business where, as you know, he owned 100 percent of the common (voting) stock. I was wrong. It is now clear that in the last several years he committed substantially all his personal wealth to Crosby Home Security Company in the form of loans subordinated to other company liabilities and also in supplemental equity investment. The unpleasant fact is that there is very little of value presently in your father's estate other than the company, life insurance payable to your mother, and the family home which is, fortunately, unencumbered by mortgage.

"What the estate tax problems may turn out to be in these circumstances is still to be determined and I won't trouble you with these matters now. I will simply say that establishing the estate tax valuation of a privately owned going business is a complex matter and depends on judgments, often controversial, about future earnings and net worth position. I will take up this whole subject with you on another occasion.

---

*We are indebted to Professor Melvin Anshen of the Graduate School of Business, Columbia University, for this case.

"This brings me to the heart of the situation. While your mother's financial security is protected by the life insurance, your grandmother and the three other members of your family who share in the ownership of CHSC's preferred (non-voting) stock are all dependent on the dividends that have been regularly paid on that stock since the company was incorporated in 1958. During the last four years, however, the business has been at best minimally profitable. Nevertheless, your father caused the company (through the board, which he controlled since the other directors were all company employees) to continue to pay the $4-per-share dividend on the preferred stock even when the dividend was not covered by earnings. One more year of this practice will put the business in an untenable working capital position. Further, I understand that minimum working capital stipulations governing outstanding bank loans would prohibit paying the preferred dividend unless working capital is strengthened. From now on, it seems clear, any dividends paid will have to be earned.

"You, as your father's only child, have inherited all the common stock. That stock will pay dividends, indeed will have any significant value, only if the company returns to the kind of prosperity it enjoyed prior to the time several years ago when your father's failing health made it difficult for him to give the close attention to daily management matters that used to be his dominant interest.

"The way the business has drifted during the years of his partial absence and what I have discovered in examining its financial statements and talking to its senior managers in recent weeks have persuaded me that there is no one presently employed by the company who is competent to take effective charge of its operation. The company is being run right now by a top management committee, but everyone, including the committee members, recognizes that this is at best a temporary device. Figure 1 shows the CHSC organization chart.

"I think there are three options for you to consider. One is to sell the business for whatever price it may bring in its present condition. The second is to recruit an experienced and competent manager from outside. The third is for you to come home and run the company yourself.

"I don't know what your attitude may be toward the idea of coming back to the town where you grew up and taking on the burden of running the family business. But I want to put the thought to you that your M.B.A. education and your management consulting experience in the past two years have gone a long way toward equipping you to handle this responsibility effectively, if you should choose this option. The only further persuasion I can put before you is that the net position of the company has been so reduced that a forced sale is not likely to yield any significant sum for the holders of the preferred and nothing at all for you as the owner of all the common shares. I doubt that a competent outsider could be recruited to manage the company unless you are prepared to sell such a person a substantial proportion of your common stock at an extraordinarily low price, thereby creating an attractive capital gain opportunity.

"Only the third option—coming home to manage the business yourself—

offers the possibility of assuring adequate continued income for your grandmother and other family holders of the preferred, as well as dividends and capital gain for yourself. It would also be, I know from my conversations with your father in recent years, the fulfillment of his hope that you would eventually return to succeed him as owner and manager of the business. Of course, he never anticipated the mortal heart attack that might require making this transition so soon and with the business in as bad shape as it seems to be.

"Let me know what you think and how I can help.

"Affectionately,

/s/Lucas Elder"

Jane Crosby

Jane Crosby received this letter two weeks ago as she was ending her second year of employment in the New York office of the management consulting firm of Hadley, Ford, and George, where she has just been promoted to the rank of senior associate. She is twenty-eight years old. She graduated from the Columbia Business School two years ago. Earlier, she earned an A.B. with a major in economics from Smith and then worked for two years as an economic analyst in a large New York City bank. She left the bank to get an M.B.A. because she thought she was blocked in a deadend staff position. Her post-Columbia management consulting experience has been interesting, varied, and financially rewarding. Promotion to the rank of senior associate puts her only one step away from a junior partnership in the firm, a level she hopes to reach in another three years. She has enjoyed her job and her life as a single woman in New York with a good salary, an attractive career line opening ahead, and a sense of independence with no family responsibilities.

Her father's heart attack and death occurred suddenly, although for several years he had been debilitated by a series of ailments which, in combination, had depressed his energy level and made it necessary for him to curtail substantially the time he devoted to the management of the business. Particularly since graduating from college, Jane enjoyed an unusually close relationship with her father. It was with his counsel and active encouragement that she left the bank to enter the Columbia Business School. She knew that he hoped the time would come when she would join him in running CHSC and ultimately take over full responsibility for managing the business. She had maintained a neutral position toward such a commitment, however, not being clear in her own mind whether she would ever want to leave New York City for Belleville, the Pittsburgh suburb where she grew up and where the family business is located.

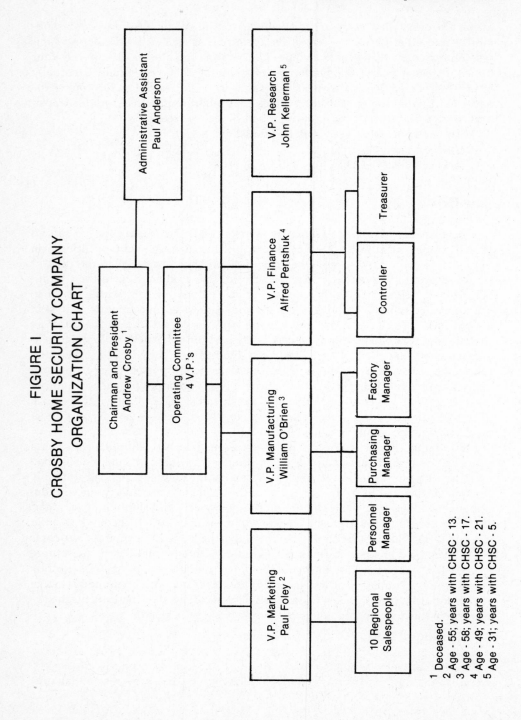

FIGURE I
CROSBY HOME SECURITY COMPANY
ORGANIZATION CHART

Chairman and President
Andrew Crosby [1]

Administrative Assistant
Paul Anderson

Operating Committee
4 V.P.'s

V.P. Marketing
Paul Foley [2]

V.P. Manufacturing
William O'Brien [3]

V.P. Finance
Alfred Pertshuk [4]

V.P. Research
John Kellerman [5]

10 Regional
Salespeople

Personnel
Manager

Purchasing
Manager

Factory
Manager

Controller

Treasurer

[1] Deceased.
[2] Age - 55; years with CHSC - 13.
[3] Age - 58; years with CHSC - 17.
[4] Age - 49; years with CHSC - 21.
[5] Age - 31; years with CHSC - 5.

As a result of her father's inclination not to press her for a decision, her own preference to postpone a decision she felt unprepared to make with confidence, and the family expectation that he would recover from his minor ailments, his fatal heart attack left Jane with no more than a surface acquaintance with the condition of the business. Lucas Elder's description of the situation he found in CHSC and in her father's estate was a quite disturbing revelation. With no clear sense of what should or could be done, she requested and was granted a two-month leave of absence from Hadley, Ford, and George and returned to Belleville to make her own evaluation of the condition and propects of the business in which she now owns all the common stock and wields sole control.

History of Crosby Home Security Company

Andrew Crosby founded Crosby Home Security Company in 1958 to manufacture and market a residential burglar alarm device which he had developed and patented. After graduating as an electrical engineer from the then Carnegie Institute of Technology in 1952, he was employed in engineering assignments by Westinghouse. His interest in developing a simple, easily-installed, and effective residential burglar alarm was stimulated when his parent's home was entered and valuables taken one night while his father and mother were asleep. Working on his own time he contrived such a device. When his employer expressed no interest in the system, he secured his own patent. Failing to persuade two electrical product companies to do anything with the product, he determined to launch his own company. He committed $100,000 inherited from his father and additional funds he borrowed from relatives, rented a factory building in his home town of Belleville, twenty miles from Pittsburgh, and opened for business as the Crosby Home Security Company.

The company prospered from the start. Andrew Crosby's design allowed simple self-installation by any home owner. "Electric Watchdog," as he called the device, was a battery-operated alarm signal consisting of a series of small remote sensors that could be readily attached to individual windows and doors and, after being switched on when a family retired at night, would ring a loud bell when an intruder raised a sensored window or opened a sensored door. The product could be purchased with any desired number of sensors and attached lengths of wire.

CHSC marketed the buglar alarm at a suggested retail price of $99.95 (including a standard kit of six sensors, wiring, battery, and alarm) through manufacturers' agents in regional markets who in turn sold to electrical and hardware retailers. "Electric Watchdog" was promoted in small-space advertisements in national home care and news magazines, in selected metropolitan newspapers, and in spot commercials on major city FM radio stations.

Sales and profits grew rapidly. In the late 1960s, the company developed and introduced under the trademark "Fire Alert" its patented residential fire alarm device activated by chemical smoke sensors located in individual rooms and hall areas. Designed—like "Electric Watchdog"—for self-installation by home owners, the product was distributed through the same channels. "Fire Alert" sales also grew rapidly.

During the next six years, sales of the two alarm systems almost doubled, reaching $22.1 million four years ago. Competition increased sharply in this period, however, and CHCS was compelled to spend more heavily for advertising and also reduce prices in order to hold its market position. As a result, earnings have been declining sharply.

Four years ago, the company added a third product to its home security line: an ultrasonic burglar alarm system that emits inaudible sound beams that, when interrrupted by an intruder, trigger an alarm. The system, trademarked "Silent Sentinel," was offered through the same distribution channels at a suggested retail price of $195.00. Sales of this product have been growing, at least partially, at the expense of "Electric Watchdog" sales. Competition developed even more rapidly than for earlier products, reflecting heightened public interest in home security products and entry into the market of several additional firms.

The dropoff in earnings during recent years, and the deterioration in financial position, are clearly shown in Tables 1 and 2. The performance of the three product categories is given in Table 3. Only in the past ten months has the decline been checked, as is indicated in Table 4. The company's top-level organization at the time of Mr. Crosby's death is shown in Figure 1.

The Home Security Market

The total home security market, including all types of intrusion and fire alarm devices, is estimated by trade sources to be in excess of $300 million annually at retail prices. This includes about $90 million in intrusion alarm systems, about $150 million in smoke alarm systems, and the balance in protective and alert devices for individual windows and doors. The market is believed to be growing at an annual rate of 20 percent. (These estimates do not include the market for comparable but more extensive and complex protective and alert systems for commercial and industrial applications.) At least a dozen companies, some national and others regional in scope, actively compete in the residential burglary and fire security market, in addition to a large number of local electric supply and repair retailers and individual "moonlighting" electricians who install "homemade," "amateur" alarm devices of their own fabrication.

A complex electronic security system requiring professional installation in a large suburban home can cost $3,000 or more. Simpler devices, many designed for self-installation, are available at prices ranging down to $100. Among the more elaborate systems offered by the three largest companies in the home security field (ADT, Honeywell, and Westinghouse) are combinations of perimeter devices (doors and windows) and indoor area motion "traps" (photoelectric beams, ultrasonic beams, and pressure mats under floor coverings). Critical concerns with complex systems are skilled professional installation and competent, prompt service. Critical concerns with simpler systems and unit devices are failure to perform as advertised and errors in self-installation by home owners.

Perimeter systems as first introduced required running wires from sensors equipped with magnetic switches, mounted on each protected door and window, to a central alarm unit. Charges for professional installation, including concealing wires for esthetic appearance, often exceed the cost of the system.

To eliminate the time or expense of extending wires through a residence, new wireless systems have been developed. In these systems each sensor or magnetic switch contains a battery-powered transmitter about the size of a pack of cigarettes. The transmitter sends a wireless signal to a central alarm unit. Installation by a home owner involves no more than attaching sensors to windows and doors and plugging the central alarm unit into the household electrical system. More sophisticated door sensors provide a time-delay setting which permits the home owner to enter and deactivate the system before the alarm sounds.

Although many protection systems are installed by professionals, a wide range of do-it-yourself kits are also available. There are many options for windows, doors, parked cars, and even personal transmitters. In addition to activating a horn or bell, devices which phone the police station are increasingly common. Smoke detectors, especially, have risen in popularity.

Evaluations of Position and Prospects for CHSC

During the first few days after she returned to Belleville, Jane Crosby reviewed CHSC's position and prospects with John Cunningham, senior vice-president of the company's principal commercial bank and the source of its short-term borrowing; William Foster, legal counsel for the business for many years; the four vice-presidents who constituted her father's top management team; and Paul Anderson, a young business school graduate, who had served as her father's assistant for the past year. With the exception of Anderson and John Kellerman, the head of research, these men had known Jane Crosby for many years and tended to treat her in a paternal style. In condensed form, here is what they told her.

John Cunningham. "This was a growing, prosperous business until your father's health began to fail a few years ago and he had to cut back sharply on the time he devoted to it. Until then, he was totally involved in every aspect of managing CHSC, and I mean *literally every aspect.* He was a good manager, so things ran well. Unfortunately, one result of his total involvement was that the other senior managers did what he told them to do. They never had to make decisions on their own. When he became a part-time manager and they *had* to make decisions, it turned out they weren't very good at it. So costs got out of hand, profits dropped, and the company became a less effective competitor at the very time the market was becoming more competitive.

"Trouble started growing about four years ago, but the last two years were absolute disasters. I kept hoping and expecting that your father's health would improve. I think you should know that it was only for that reason that I permitted the bank to extend the credit that appears on its balance sheet. The bank is in a secure position because the loans are well covered by pledged receivables and fixed assets. But it is our present intent to curtail and not to increase the commitment of credit. Further, we are not willing to countenance further payment of the preferred dividend until the total bank loan is reduced below $2 million. Even with the bank's financial support in a time of weak management, the company could not have survived without your father's investment of his own funds. And you must be aware that his loans have no specific security. That's a lot of money at high risk.

"I had a tough talk with your father at the end of last year, when the company recorded a devastating loss of $1.25 million. I made it crystal clear that costs *must* be brought into line. And he talked just as tough with his vice-presidents. And they *have* improved matters—to the extent that for the first ten months of this year they have accomplished about a break-even performance. That's not sensational, of course. But it looks pretty good compared to the previous year when they lost over a million dollars. (See Table 4.) It suggests that really capable management could restore the company to what it was when your father was in full charge.

"But now the problem is: Who is going to provide that kind of leadership? I tell you flatly that it won't and can't come from the present management group. They are good and faithful servants. They will follow a strong leader who knows what to do and how to do it. But when I've said that, I've said all the good I can say about them. I don't know, of course, how they view themselves or what political ambitions and jealousies may exist for individuals within the group.

"I understand that Lucas Elder has talked to you about *your* coming back here to run the business. Now, Jane, I've known you since you were a young girl and I guess that my long friendship with your father entitles me to a little of the prerogative of a quasi-uncle. I know it was your father's hope that you would come into the business with him and eventually inherit and run it. But, speaking strictly as a quasi-uncle, let me warn you that breaking in with your father in learning how to manage a prosperous, growing company and starting without him to restore a very sick company to a healthy state are entirely different things. I have no reason to doubt your ability—I am familar with your education and your consulting experience—but I wonder if you are ready for a challenge as big and complex and tough as this one. I really think you should consider selling the business. I don't know what you could get for it. But, on your instructions, I would be glad to explore the possibilities. Whatever you decide to do, I hope you will talk to me again before you take any action."

In reply to Jane Crosby's question about the company's competitive positions, the banker said, "I don't have an opinion worth respecting about that. I just don't know. I am certainly aware, as you must be, that the whole country is more conscious about and sensitive to security matters than it used to be. I've seen reports that sales of residential alarm and safety products and systems are on an uptrend. And I know that there are a number of companies including some big ones, actively competing for the business. But whether your company has a leading or a following position, whether its products are superior or inferior, whether their distribution is well planned and aggressively executed—I don't really know much about these matters. You ought to find out, of course. What I do know is that sales are flat, costs are high, capitalization is thin, borrowings are excessive, and profits are nonexistent. Since none of these adverse conditions existed only a few years ago when your father was the full-time CEO, I suspect that weak management explains much of the unsatisfactory situation. But I don't know for sure."

William Foster. "I'm afraid I have to tell you that you have inherited a very messy situation. It has been a sad experience for me to watch affairs deteriorate these last few years while your father was unable to give his full attention to the business. When his health began to fail, I was not optimistic about his recovering to the extent that he could resume active, full-time management of the company. This was not an easy subject to discuss with him, however, since he always insisted that his disability was temporary. I suggested more than once that he consider selling the business. That was when it was still profitable, although at a reduced rate compared to its earlier performance. But he brushed me off. Just wouldn't hear of it. He still looked forward to the time when you would join him in the business and he wanted to keep it going for you. He was also concerned about maintaining dividends on the preferred stock, on which family members for whom he felt a deep responsibility depended. That was why he pumped his own money into the business. I advised against that, but he insisted on doing it. He was a man who took such a responsibility very seriously. I wish now I had taken a much stronger stand.

"You will want to talk with the senior managers. It may be helpful for me to make some comments about them, based on my observation of their operation of the business during recent years when your father was on the scene only half-time or even quarter-time. The first point to be absolutely clear about is that these are totally loyal people. Paul Foley, Bill O'Brien, and Al Pertshuk have worked for your father for many years. They admired him and worked hard under his direction. He liked and trusted them. I suspect he never noticed that they were not the most aggressive and imaginative managers in the world because he was really running the whole show himself, developing the products, supervising their manufacture, planning the marketing, making all the financial decisions. He was a first-class manager himself, with one blind spot—he was a one-man gang. I talked with him about this once, a couple of years before his first illness, and tried to encourage him to delegate responsibility, both to develop these associates and to find out by testing them just how capable they really were. But it just wasn't his style. He agreed with me on the desirability of doing it, but he never let go of the reins. Until he had to. And then it was too late.

"What I've observed is that each of these three gentlemen is a pretty good first mate; not one of them has the qualities of a good captain. It took great pressure from the bank to force them into cost-cutting this year. How much fat they had allowed to collect in the business is indicated by the million-dollar difference in the first ten months now as against the same period last year. And I'd bet they still haven't come near to getting rid of all the fat there.

"Paul Foley is your typical good-fellow sales manager. He's a pal with the sales staff, plays golf and drinks with the customers. He's worried about the failure of sales to grow when the total home security industry has been expanding at a fast clip. You should ask him about the reasons for this situation, but you shouldn't get your hopes up about hearing an analytical, documented answer.

"Bill O'Brien started as a kind of factory foreman and then rose as the business grew. He's always out in the plant in his shirtsleeves; knows all the workers by their first names and their wives' and husbands' and kids' names, too; can fix any machine that breaks down. And then I have to ask myself, 'But he is a vice-president of manufacturing?' Bear in mind that I'm a lawyer, not an M.B.A. But I do legal work for several other companies and I have occasion to meet and talk with their managers. I have the notion that a vice-president of manufacturing needs a detailed understanding of costs and cost systems, inventory control standards and systems, policies and practices in procurement and personnel administration. Well, Bill O'Brien gets a little shaky in those areas. On the other hand, let something go wrong on the production line and Bill will work nights and holidays to get it fixed—and *he* will fix it. There are a lot of production managers who can't do that, and some who wouldn't even if they could.

"Al Pertshuk—well. Al goes back about tenty years in the business, to a time when all your father needed to back him up in handling money was a bookkeeper. I didn't know Al then; I hadn't begun to do the legal work for the business. But I'd bet he was a perfect bookkeeper. Never made a posting error, never missed a trail balance, never was caught short in an audit. But it was your father who handled financial matters with John Cunningham at the bank, not Al Pertshuk. I don't know that Al couldn't do it. He was never given the chance to try. But he makes the wheels go round in the office every day, sees that the records are kept, kept right, kept on time. He runs the budget and gets out the management reports when they're due, and I've never heard anyone complain about an error in them. That's a record he's likely to maintain until the day he retires.

"Then there's John Kellerman who has the title of vice-president of research. He's relatively new. Your father was the whole research department for many years, solely responsible for product development. Five years ago, when his health began to crumble, he hired John out of an assistant professorship in electrical engineering at Carnegie-Mellon and last year gave him the vice-presidential title. I assess John as a pretty good product tester and evaluator, but surely not an inventor and maybe not even a good product developer. Now that may be doing him a great injustice. But I do know the record since John has been here and what I have said is a fair reflection of the record. He's a nice young man, comes to work early, stays late, keeps a clean desk top. He really doesn't carry much weight in the business—not yet, at any rate. With his title, he's a member of the operating committee. But from what the other committee members tell me, he doesn't contribute much, just sits there and agrees with what is said.

"And there is also Paul Anderson. Your father hired Paul a couple of years ago out of Carnegie's Graduate School of Industrial Administration, to be a kind of administrative assistant to the president. He's an undergraduate electrical engineer with a master's degree in management and he's bright and well educated and probably twice as smart as anyone in the company—and he sticks his nose into everything that's going on and asks questions and gets people upset and mad as hell.

"On balance, I'm sure Anderson's an asset in the business, but he is pretty hard to live with. I've seen Bill O'Brien get so furious with him that he wanted to hang one right on the button of his jaw. But Paul was right about the matter they were arguing about, and eventually got Bill to calm down and admit he was right. I think your father hoped to break Paul in gradually and train and develop him over a stretch of years into a kind of executive vice-president. And now Paul is out there at loose ends with your father gone. He's administrative assistant to a nonexistent president. The vice-presidents don't know how to use him. He doesn't know how to use himself. Unless he is brought into some kind of organization structure soon, my guess is that he'll quit. And that might turn out to be a real loss to the business.

"Where does this all leave you? Well, I don't have a clear view of what you might want to do. You haven't asked me for my advice, but here it is anyhow. I think you should recruit a competent president from outside the company. To interest the right kind of person you'd have to make a stock deal—sell him or her some of the stock at a *very* attractive price, so that *if* the company gets back on the rails—healthy, growing, profitable—he or she could make a big fat capital gain by collaborating with you in selling the company when it's attractive enough to fetch a good price as a going concern. The ideal candidate would be an experienced and competent executive out of some Pittsburgh-area company, say about in the mid-fifties, who knows he or she isn't going to get the top job in the present company and wants a chance to build an estate before retirement. Allow five years or so to rebuild Crosby Home Security Company, and then put it up for sale. You'd probably have to sell the candidate half the stock you inherited—let's say 49 percent maximum so that you could be chair of the board and keep control. But it would be worth it, *if* you found the right manager, *if* the recovery were accomplished. Those are big ifs, but what's the alternative?"

Paul Foley. "Why have sales been flat for four years? Worse than flat? In the first place, total sales of the home security industry have been growing by at least 20 percent annually, so that our market share has been shrinking. And in the second place, we've been raising prices to cover rising costs. So level dollar sales have meant fewer unit sales. One other point should be made right at the start: We have one growth product, 'Silent Sentinel'; the two others have been stagnant at best and are really on the way down. What's the problem? That's a good question.

"I think it's a combination of things. First, while it's true enough that the total market has been growing, so has the competition. At least seven companies have moved into this business in a substantial way in the last five years—three of them are a lot larger than CHSC. I'm not even counting the fly-by-nights, the little electrical shops that are designing and installing their own security systems in their local neighborhoods. Each of these units is a peanut in size, but they add up to a substantial chunk of the total market. What I'm saying is that if you could see the operating figures of all the competitors, you'd discover that many of them are in the same box we're in, taking a smaller share of a growing market and not getting rich from the experience.

"OK, that's number one. Number two: We've got a couple of aging products. Not senile, not even obsolete—although getting into that condition. But aging, getting along in years; like me, I suppose. The good one is 'Silent Sentinel,' of course, but it can't carry the whole business and besides, we haven't got the production costs right on that one yet. So product-wise, we're not a strong competitor and we don't have an exciting story to tell to either the trade or the consumer.

"Three: A weak marketing system. I don't know how familiar you are with how we sell, but here's the picture. We distribute through manufacturers' agents, fourteen of them across the country, each with an exclusive franchise to handle our line in that region. We pay them a 5 percent commission on their sales. Each agent sells to between ten and twenty hardware and electrical supply wholesalers. The wholesaler's margin, or at least what we suggest, is about 10 percent of the selling price to the retailer. Wholesale distributors sell mostly to retail hardware and electrical supply stores. Our suggested price to consumers would give retailers a margin of about 40 percent on their selling price. What this adds up to is that our products are available to consumers in about seven thousand retail outlets across the country—theoretically available, that is: *if* every wholesale distributor of every one of our maufacturers' agents carried our line and *if* the wholesaler sold it to every one of the retail accounts. But they don't, of course. We don't have a precise sighting on our current retail dealer representation, but I'd guess it's in the neighborhood of three thousand stores, coast-to-coast.

"Now you can probably begin to see the dimensions of our problem. If you accept the trade estimate that retail sales of home security products amount to, say, $400 million and also accept my estimate that the retail value of our line is about double our factory sales dollars, say $45 million, then right now we have a market share in the range of 11 to 15 percent. Not too bad, you might think.

Except that five years ago, with the same dollar sales, we had better than a 15 percent share of a smaller total market.

"You have to recognize also that we don't represent important sales volume to anybody along our distribution channels. Divide $45 million in sales among three thousand retailers and you can calculate that our average dealer sells maybe $15,000 worth of CHSC products annually. Not enough to get the dealers interested in promoting them. They carry them, but they don't push them. All the push has to come from our own promotion to consumers—plus the override we get from the promotion of the big boys with the fancy security systems that need professional installation. By override I mean that their advertising gets a lot of people excited about burglary and fire protection, and then some of those potential customers have the shock of discovering how much those fancy systems cost—as much as $3,000 or more for a full-sized suburban home—and they go shopping for something cheaper. Some of those shoppers read our ads about self-installation and look for a store that carries our line. And we get some business on the bounce that way.

"Our special market niche is that we still have competitive products in the do-it-yourself segment of the total market. However, serious competition is now appearing in that segment from established companies. In addition, there are the electrician-moonlighters who rig up and install their own systems. Most of these amateur systems are no good. Either they're supersensitive and go off when the family dog takes a stroll through the house at night, or they're undersensitive and respond only to a three-alarm fire or an earthquake; they just give the whole industry a bad name. So conceptually we're not in a bad position—as of right now.

"But we're not going anywhere except backwards. We need improved products to give us news to excite the consumer market and our wholesale and retail outlets. We need to get our manufacturing costs down so we can make a decent profit, so that we can increase our advertising to consumers and the trade and strengthen our sales promotion effort through the trade, so that we can build sales and become more important to our distributors and dealers and get them more interested in displaying and talking about and pushing our line. And if we can do all this we will have a nice, healthy, growing, profitable business—the kind we had when your father was running this company. We're part of a growth industry. We still have a significant position in the industry. There's no reason we can't restore this company.

"It will take money, that's for sure. Where will it come from? Well, look at the recent record. When it became clear at the end of last year that we had to cut costs—just *had* to, to survive—we did it. We sold about a million dollars more product this year, with just about the same cost of goods sold dollars as last year. How? By laying it on the line to our factory workers and getting productivity up. That put a million dollars more on the gross profit line. Then we cut back our advertising budget by a hundred thousand, from $600,000 to $500,000—and that really hurt because, as I've explained to you, we get very little push through our distribution system. We have to *pull* our products through it by advertising and sales promotion to consumers and the trade. And we let two production engineers go. And that will hurt, too, because we need product development. But it was fish-or-cut-bait time for the whole organization, and we did these tough things.

"Can we cut more? This is where the arguments begin. I think we could get another half-million out of manufacturing costs at our present volume, but try and sell that to Bill O'Brien. We've never had a union in our plant, and he says we're begging for one, and then goodbye productivity. Or so he says. *His* idea is to take it out of selling and advertising. Well, we have ten salespeople. They don't deal with our manufacturers' agents. That's *my* job and I spend most of my time at it, all across the country. I've got to keep those agents feeling warm and friendly toward us, because every one of them handles other products, non-competitive with ours but many with bigger sales volumes that generate more commissions.

"Our salespeople work with wholesalers and retailers. They encourage wholesalers to pay attention to our line and push for more retail distribution. They do missionary work with retailers, try to get new outlets for our line, try to get displays in stores. The orders they take are funneled right back through our wholesalers. You can figure about $50,000 to $60,000 per salesperson in salary, commissions, and travel expenses. Any cut there would hurt sales. As for advertising, we ought to be sending more, not less.

"Al Pertshuk will tell you we could cut receivables by a million dollars and inventory by another million. Well, maybe we could get a little money out of inventory, but if we bear down on collections we'll lose sales. You've got to stretch payment periods and accept slow pay, too, to keep business these days. It's a shame to have to operate this way, but it's a fact of life. Al sits in his office and says it's easy to tighten collections. He doesn't know what conditions are like in the field. You've got to spend money out there to make money. We simply must be competitive, including payment terms. That's the way it is."

William O'Brien. "The basic problem is that we let ourselves get very sloppy when your father wasn't around to watch the nickles and dimes. We did things the easy way. We oiled every squeaking wheel with money. And all this slack caught up with us. Now I've taken the slack out of manufacturing. Look at the operating statement this year for proof. A million dollars more output with no increase in cost of goods sold, and this was in a time of rising material costs, too. But every loose screw has been tightened as far as it will go. The next contribution *has* to come from marketing. We simply don't need all those salespeople—not with our distribution system through agents and wholesalers. We could save a half-million dollars right there in selling expense. And some more in advertising. And we could tighten up on collecting receivables and cut down on our finished goods inventory. I bet we could take at least half a million dollars out of each of those areas. Then we could pay down the bank loans and get some breathing room.

"But we need new products, too. In the old days your father was the source of new product ideas and product improvements. I hate to say this, but I don't think John Kellerman can do the job. He's competent enough to work on the engineering side of existing products, but he's not an inventor. I think he should be replaced, even if we have to spend more money to get the right person for the job.

"Paul and Al will argue that we can cut costs even more out in the plant. It would be very dangerous to try to do this. This is union country here in the Pittsburgh area. We've operated all these years without a union because everybody out there in the plant liked your father and trusted him. I've tried to keep it that way, and so far I've succeeded. But we're at the outer limits of tolerance right now. We've put in production incentives. We've gotten rid of some lazy people who wouldn't go along. Pushing any harder would be asking for trouble. What we *could* do, if we had the money to invest, is put in some labor-saving equipment, automate some assembly processes. But even this would have to be done very slowly and carefully, with the displacement falling to people ready to retire. Otherwise, nothing but headaches all around."

Alfred Pertshuk. "We've made a million dollar improvement this year. With strong leadership, we could cut another million dollars. There's still fat in this organization. Look at receivables. Current dollar sales are about the same as they were four years ago, but we've got $800,000 more in receivables. You can't tell me that's necessary. Sure it's hard to go out there and press for prompt payment of bills. But our creditors beat on us and the only way we've been able to finance those receivables is to become slow-pay ourselves. I take the pressure on that. And don't think it doesn't hurt us on the prices our suppliers charge us. There are no bargains available to us anymore. Our suppliers pack that extended credit right into their prices to us.

"Look at inventories. Again, with our sales level, we've got almost half a million dollars more in inventory. It's not necessary. But when I point this out to Paul, he fights me. We sit around and discuss the situation in operating committe meetings, but we can't get agreement. The bank presses me to do something, but I don't have the authority to make it happen. We need a strong leader here, a real boss who can make a decision and stick to it."

John Kellerman. "The weakness in this business is in sales. We've got good products, competitive products. We've got a unique market position with our self-installation feature. But our products are priced too low and are sold ineffectually through that agent-wholesaler system. What we ought to do is to get rid of the agents, increase our salesforce, sell directly to wholesalers, and get our prices up to cover the added costs and make a profit. All Paul does is feed baloney to those agents, wine and dine them, play golf with them. Our own salesforce calling directly on wholesalers could do this job right and that's what we need.

"As for R & D, the problem we have really can be traced back to the time when your father was active in the business full-time. He developed our products all the way from original concept through engineering into production. He was totally responsible for our present three major products: 'Electric Watchdog,' 'Fire Alert,'' and 'Silent Sentinel.'

"He brought me into the organization five years ago to take over the responsibility from him. But before his persistent illness he resisted letting go of what interested him so deeply, and after his illness all the pressure on me as head of R & D was focused on two things. One was in making minor improvements in existing products to make them more competitive in ease of installation and in sensitivity of response to any type of security invasion stimulus. The other was to redesign existing products to make them easier and cheaper to manufacture.

"As a result, the R & D function has been largely staffed with people whose competence is in engineering development, not in product innovation. Now I hope you don't misunderstand me. We have—I guess a more accurate statement would be I have—two new product concepts on the drawing board which could obsolete everything now in the self-installation section of the home security alarm business, both competitors' products and our own. They involve the incorporation of microchips in alarm, signaling, and control systems.

"But we don't have the talent in our research staff to carry this concept through design, testing, and application. I need to add people. Instead, under pressure from the bank to cut costs, this year I took over $50,000 out of our budget. It's now at a quarter-million dollar annual level. It should be double that. With the right talent and a major focus on new products we would be in a position to revolutionize the business. And mark my words, someone in this industry will take this step. It had better be CHSC. I'd hate to be a follower when some other company takes the lead."

Paul Anderson. "Look, Miss Crosby, I'm quitting this job so I've got nothing to protect. I'll tell you exactly what the situation is here. There's no competent management. These people around here can't handle responsibility and don't want it. It's obvious to me that this company is loaded with unnecessary costs. But top management did nothing about the situation until the bank stepped in and told them what had to be done. So they made a first pass at the excess and knocked off a million dollars. There's at least another million that needs to go, but they won't make the effort.

"I'll tell you what you ought to do. You ought to fire your vice-presidents— all four of them. They were errand boys for your father, that's all. Then either hire some tougher people, if you're going to take charge here yourself, or hire a president who would do the recruiting. It's worth doing, too. Because under all this flab and stagnation and nonprofit operation, there's a good business in a growth industry. If I had some money I'd offer to buy it from you myself, that's how much I think of its possibilities.

"This business needs to be taken to pieces and redesigned from the ground up. We need a first-class talent in charge of R & D who can upgrade our line and introduce new products. Then we can really distinguish CHSC products from the crap that's peddled by moonlighting electricians. We could get a premium price for our products and still be far below the systems that are sold by companies like ADT, Honeywell, and Westinghouse.

"We ought to scrap our cumbersome, ineffective distribution system through agents and wholesale distributors. They're nothing by a bunch of order-takers. Year after year we keep trying to increae the number of retail dealers who carry our line. What for? Most of them sell only a few thousand dollars worth a year. We don't mean enough to them to get the attention and promotion we need. We ought to shrink the number of dealers. Pick out just the biggest and best in each territory, give them exclusive franchises, and then require them to promote and display. We ought to contract with them for cooperative advertising, say on a fifty-fifty basis, dollar for dollar. We should use our own salesforce to sell direct to the largest dealers. We should shrink our wholesale business the same way, pick out the best in each territory, and give them exclusive rights to sell to selected dealers other than the ones we sell to directly.

"And we ought to spend more on advertising, use spot television more in major markets. Our products lend themselves to a powerful visual selling message. We ought to engage a first-class advertising agency to dramatize that message.

"Where would all the money come from? Some of it would come from the commissions we've been paying those agents who don't really work to earn them. Some of it could come out of excessive receivables and inventories. Al Pertshuk is no powerhouse of a financial manager, but he's dead right about the money tied up in those areas that just isn't working for us. His trouble is that he has no clout. He calls attention to these problems, but he lacks the force to get results. And beyond the improvement in productivity this year, under great pressure from the bank, we could get at least another half-million in factory payroll economies. Bill O'Brien is afraid of unionization. Well, we ought to have the guts to accept the risk. If we end up getting organized, so be it. That wouldn't be the end of the world. It just looks that way to O'Brien because he's never had to run a union plant. Other people do it and prosper. We could, too, if we had to.

"Maybe this all sounds pretty brash to you. But I'm certain it could be done. Hell, I could do it myself, if you were willing to take the chance of putting me in charge. But I couldn't do it, nobody could do it, with those old-timers in charge of production and marketing and finance. All they know how to do is what they did in the old days. Anything new frightens them."

TABLE 1.
CROSBY HOME SECURITY COMPANY
ANNUAL OPERATING STATEMENTS ($000)

	Last Year	2 Years Ago	3 Years Ago	4 Years Ago	5 Years Ago	6 Years Ago	7 Years Ago	8 Years Ago	9 Years Ago	10 Years Ago
Net Sales	$22,385	$24,103	$25,888	$22,100	$19,487	$17,208	$17,655	$15,396	$14,217	$11,449
Cost of good sold	20,236	21,428	22,031	19,072	16,408	14,099	14,142	12,055	10,862	8,884
Gross profit	2,149	2,675	3,857	3,028	3,079	3,109	3,513	3,341	3,355	2,565
Selling, adm. and gen. exp.	3,089	3,254	3,236	2,497	2,533	2,185	2,313	1,909	1,663	1,362
Research and engineering	313	289	233	199	195	189	194	185	185	149
Pre-tax income	(1,253)	(868)	388	332	351	735	1,006	1,247	1,507	1,054
Income tax	–	–	155	133	136	224	406	570	682	527
Net earnings	(1,253)	(868)	233	199	215	511	600	677	825	527
(Percentages)										
Net sales	100.0	100.0	100.0	100.0	100.0	100.0	100.0	100.0	100.0	100.0
Cost of good sold	90.4	88.9	85.1	86.3	84.2	82.8	80.1	78.3	76.4	77.6
Gross profit	9.6	11.1	14.9	13.7	15.8	17.2	19.9	21.7	23.6	22.4
Selling, adm. and gen. exp.	13.8	13.5	12.5	11.3	13.0	12.7	13.1	12.4	11.7	11.9
Research and engineering	1.4	1.2	0.9	0.9	1.0	1.1	1.1	1.2	1.3	1.3
Pre-tax income	(5.6)	(3.6)	1.5	1.5	1.8	3.4	5.7	8.1	10.6	9.2
Income tax	–	–	0.6	0.6	0.7	1.3	2.3	3.7	4.8	4.6
Net earnings	(5.6)	(3.6)	0.9	0.9	1.1	2.1	3.4	4.4	5.8	4.6
Preferred dividends	$200	$200	$200	$200	$200	$200	$200	$200	$200	$200
Common Dividends	–	–	25	25	50	125	125	150	150	100

TABLE 2.
CROSBY HOME SECURITY COMPANY
END-OF-YEAR BALANCE SHEETS ($000)

	Last Year	2 Years Ago	3 Years Ago	4 Years Ago	5 Years Ago
Assets					
Current Assets					
Cash	$ 125	$ 186	$ 277	$ 362	$ 315
Accounts receivable (net)	3,127	2,943	2,736	2,326	2,165
Inventories (lower of cost or market)	3,976	3,830	3,895	3,577	3,128
Total current assets	7,228	6,959	6,908	6,265	5,608
Fixed assets					
Land (cost)	75	75	75	75	75
Plant and equipment (net)	1,285	1,360	1,515	1,427	1,655
Total fixed assets	1,360	1,435	1,590	1,502	1,730
Total assets	8,588	8,394	8,498	7,767	7,338
Liabilities and Net Worth					
Current liabilities					
Loans payable	2,600*	2,030*	1,597*	1,367*	1,123*
Accounts payable	2,815	2,270	1,814	1,582	1,451
Accrued payroll	188	176	162	140	128
Other accrued expenses	133	113	97	85	64
Accrued taxes			155	133	136
Total current liabilities	5,736	4,589	3,825	3,307	2,902
Notes payable-Andrew Crosby	1,000	500	300	100	50
Preferred stock (50,000 $1 par value shares, $4 annual dividend)	50	50	50	50	50
Common stock ($1 par value)	10	10	10	5	5
Retained earnings	1,792	3,245	4,313	4,305	4,331
Total liabilities and net worth	8,588	8,394	8,498	7,767	7,338

*Bank loans secured by accounts receivable and land, plant and equipment.

TABLE 3.
CROSBY HOME SECURITY COMPANY
OPERATING STATEMENTS BY PRODUCT CATEGORY ($000)

	Last Year			2 Years Ago			3 Years Ago		
	Electric Watchdog	Fire Alert	Silent Sentinel	Electric Watchdog	Fire Alert	Silent Sentinel	Electric Watchdog	Fire Alert	Silent Sentinel
Net sales	$ 9,562	$ 9,668	$ 3,155	$11,390	$10,936	$1,777	$12,822	$12,220	$ 846
Cost of goods sold*	8,128	9,205	2,903	9,795	9,624	2,009	10,770	10,331	930
Gross profit	1,434	463	252	1,595	1,312	(232)	2,052	1,889	(84)
Selling, adm. and gen. exp.*	1,879	648	562	2,010	750	494	2,075	861	300
Research and engineering†	25	56	110	20	34	125	—	—	88
Pre-tax income	(470)	(241)	(420)	(435)	528	(851)	(23)	1,028	(472)

*Both direct and indirect costs allocated by estimate.
†Additional research and engineering costs charged to new products still in development: Last year—
$122; 2 years ago—$110; 3 years ago—$145.

TABLE 4.
CROSBY HOME SECURITY COMPANY
OPERATING STATEMENT—TEN MONTHS ENDING OCTOBER 31ST ($000)

	This Year	Last Year
Net sales	$20,566	$19,587
Costs of goods sold	17,687	17,707
Gross Profit	2,879	1,880
Selling, adm. and gen. exp.	2,589	2,703
Research and engineering	225	274
Pre-tax income	65	(1,097)

Comprehensive Case 3

CROWN CORK—THE TOUGH MAVERICK (R)

For a quarter of a century, from the mid-1950s to 1980, Crown Cork & Seal Company, Inc., increased its sales and its earnings every year without interruption. In fact, during most of this period the earnings each three months exceeded those of the corresponding period a year earlier. The company moved from the verge of bankruptcy to sales of $1.5 billion.

This record is remarkable because (1) the company is substantially smaller than its leading competitors; (2) it operates in the very competitive, mature container industry, in which profit margins are narrow and precarious; and (3) the packaging revolution and technological changes have led to frequent shifts between metal, glass, paper, and plastic containers. By pursuing a strategy of not following the leaders, Crown Cork has found a way of obtaining the widest profit margin in its industry.

Uninterrupted growth cannot go on forever. Fierce competition and especially devaluations in Third World countries finally slowed Crown Cork. In 1981 and 1982 both sales and earnings have turned down.

Two questions naturally arise: What accounts for Crown Cork's success in a basically hostile environment? And, are the strategy and policies that worked so well in the past good for the future?

STRATEGY LEADING TO SUCCESS

Survival in a mature field such as the "tin can" business is never easy; growth and profitability are even more elusive. Four basic guidelines account for much, though not all, of Crown Cork's impressive showings.

1. Concentration vs. Diversification

The two leading producers of metal containers have actively diversified. Both American Can Company and the Continental Group (formerly Continental Can Company) expanded into a wide variety of packaging materials with an aim of being able to provide a customer with most, if not all, of its packaging requirements. Both companies have substantial research operations studying new forms of flexible materials, plastic containers, and printing and finishing techniques. The "business we are in" has expanded from traditional cans to active participation in the packaging revolution.

Moreover, Continental's interest in paper has led to major vertical integration back into forest industries. American Can has diversified into chemicals and an array of consumer products such as paper towels and tissues, paper cups, dress patterns, and food service products used in fast-food chains and elsewhere. Both companies are earning a higher rate of return from these "outside" activities than from their packaging business (including cans). Even National Can Corporation, a firm close to Crown Cork in size, moved into glass and plastic containers and has experimented with diversification outside of the packaging field.

In contrast, Crown Cork has stuck closely to its traditional lines of business. In fact, it has narrowed its focus to predominant emphasis on one part of the metal can industry—cans for "hard-to-hold products." These are notably aerosols, beer, and carbonated beverages, all of which must be held under pressure. This means that with minor exceptions, Crown Cork has no interest in packer cans for fruits and vegetables, cans for oil, and many other types of containers. (See Table 1.)

TABLE 1.
U.S. CONTAINER AND PACKAGING INDUSTRY

		Shipment Value in billions of dollars 1982
Paper and Paperboard		24.8
Corrugated & Solid Fiber Boxes	10.9	
Folding Paperboard Boxes	3.6	
Bags	3.0	
Sanitary Food Containers	5.3	
Fiber Cans, Tubes, Containers	1.5	
Set-up Paperboard Boxes	0.5	
Glass Containers		5.3
Metal Cans, Barrels, and Drums		10.7
Plastic Packaging		9.2
Flexible Packages	4.4	
Packaging and Shipping	4.8	
Total		50.0

Crown Cork's concentration on hard-to-hold products started at its founding in 1891. A shop foreman invented what we know as a soda bottlecap—a flanged disk of tin-plate with a cork insert to make a tight seal. To the present day, the company has been a leader in what is now called the "closures" segment of the packaging industry. Many competitors have entered the field, and twist-top, tear-tops, and an ingenious variety of plastic lids vie for consumer preference. But in this niche (50 billion closures per year) Crown Cork has remained an innovator and a low-cost producer.

A related facet of the business is the manufacture of filling machinery for use in customers' plants. In this highly automated operation, the containers and closures must be precisely integrated with the process of filling and sealing. And Crown Cork is a leading manufacturer of high-speed equipment used for this purpose. The volume of machinery sales and profits are cyclical, ranging from 6 to 12 percent of the total; but filling equipment helps keep the company abreast of the shifting needs of customers.

Nevertheless, in recent years metal cans have been the major product, as the estimates in Table 2 show. That is the area which accounts for most of Crown Cork's growth, and it is the area where present company management has chosen to bet its future.

TABLE 2.
CROWN CORK: ESTIMATED SOURCES OF SALES AND OPERATING PROFIT

	Total Company	Sales U.S.	International	Operating Profit Total Company
Cans	68%	90%	34%	60%
Closures	27	6	60	27
Machinery	5	4	6	13
	100%	100%	100%	100%

The product line strategy of Crown Cork is clear. It has elected to be a specialist rather than to diversify. In its particular niche, which has been the core of its business throughout its history, it seeks to outsmart its larger competitors by being expert and low cost. It meets threats from other types of containers by fighting them, not joining them. Fortunately for Crown Cork, the segment of its concentration has been growing, although uncertainties continue to appear—as we will discuss later.

2. Selective Service

A second facet of Crown Cork's strategy relates to the importance of containers to its customers. For all beer and soft-drink producers, the container costs more than its contents. Next to payroll, containers are their biggest expense item. Moreover, the appearance of the container plays a significant role in selling, especially in the supermarkets. Of course, reliable quality is vital for repeat sales, and this quality must be maintained on filling machines running at speeds of up to 1,200 cans per minute. Because of their bulk, inventories of empty cans are typically kept low; this means that reliability of delivery is crucial to keeping a plant in operation—thousands of cans week after week.

Crown Cork seeks to be an attractive supplier by responding promptly and personally to these customer needs. John Connelly, chair of the board, takes calls from any customer and follows up immediately. Other executives as well as salespeople do likewise, speeding a large portion of their time traveling to customer plants whenever problems arise. Since there is little difference in physical quality of cans from major producers, and pricing is so competitve there is virtually no margin for "deals," this personalized top-brass service becomes more important. Crown Cork tries to build its plant capacity somewhat ahead of customers' requirements so that it has capacity available to meet customers' peak requirements.

Soon after the two-piece aluminum can won customer acceptance, Crown Cork pioneered in the development of a two-piece steel can. This type of can is "drawn and ironed" so that the entire can except for the top is a single piece of metal. It is lightweight, economical because of the reduction in material required, and has no side seams or bottom joints that some health researchers think might contribute to lead poisoning. Crown Cork promoted and assisted in the development of production technology; and it invested millions of dollars between 1971 and 1977 in twenty-seven new production lines to serve its customers.

Limits on service do exist, however. As already noted, Crown Cork does not offer a "full-line" of cans, let alone other packaging materials. The presumption is that the products Crown Cork does offer are so important to customers they will seek out separate suppliers for these items alone. At first, the new two-piece can was offered only in steel and not in aluminum even though many large customers buy both. Reynolds and Kaiser aluminum companies produce large quantities of two-piece aluminum cans (they originated the product), and Crown Cork preferred not to be in a position where its metal suppliers could squeeze fabricating margins while making a profit in the base metal. Only in the last few years (when aluminum became plentiful) has Crown Cork offered both types of cans.

Moreover, Crown Cork has been unwilling to build a can manufacturing facility at a cusotmers' plant. The issue here is defense against the "self-manufacturer." Large customers especially in the beer industry may decide that they can make their own cans more cheaply than they can buy them. In fact, self-manufacture in relation to total cans produced increased from 19 percent in 1972 to 33 percent in 1981. The trend is serious because every can made by a user is one less sale for independent can producers. A compromise arrangement adopted by Crown Cork's competitors is to build a plant at the site of customer production and share with the customer the resulting savings from high-capacity utilization and transportation expense. Crown Cork has rejected such arrangements, which may involve an investment of $20,000,000, because it doesn't want to be dependent on a single customer for the efficient operation of a plant.

Crown Cork cherishes flexibility. It will go to great lengths to help customers by adjusting its schedules to meet their needs. But it is leery of being boxed in. It is selective about the areas where it participates and wants to play from relative strength.

3. No-Frills Expenses

Crown Cork has a simple approach to low-cost production; it spends money only to the extent that it has to. When John Connelly became president of the ailing firm twenty-seven years ago, he cut the payroll 24 percent, and the company has run on lean expense ratios ever since. Spartan offices, few secretaries, direct personal communication are symptomatic. The executive organization is simple, and senior executives spend much of their time in the plant or with customers. Staff units are small and close to the action they serve; the number of salespeople in a territory is trimmed to the number of active accounts.

Crown's approach to research and development is typical. Most of the attention of the small R & D staf is devoted to customers' problems—how to pack a new lacquer in an aerosol container, for example. In many packaging areas, the company prefers to be a quick follower rather than a pioneer. It has no think-tank in sylvan surroundings. Moreover, when confronted with the two-piece aluminum can competition, Crown Cork called on U.S. Steel (not its own personnel) to develop a sheet steel that could be processed in a similar fashion. Since the steel industry was threatened with losing much of its attractive tinplate business, it did most of the development work.

In its closures and machinery lines, Crown Cork operates at the forefront of technology. But development work is done within those divisions and is charged to their operating expenses. They are not expected to make big leaps into new fields.

A person working for Crown Cork has to like the work—because the hours will probably be long—and has to do it well. Saturday morning staff meetings are normal. The rewards are good for those who fit into this kind of regime; those who don't fit don't stay around.

Data on orders, prices, outputs, costs, and the like are known promptly, and problems are confronted on a factual and objective basis. The deadly parallel is often used in comparing plant performances. *Both* production and sales people are "responsible for profits" and both are expected to initiate corrective action when profits earned by a plant fall below target.

The net effect of this no-frills approach to expenses is a drop in selling and administrative expenses from 6.3 to 3.3 percent as indicated in Table 3. Crown Cork's more diversified competitors have comparable ratios ranging from 4.5 to over 10 percent. Although part of this drop reflects a change in product mix toward cans for large customers, the ratio is strikingly low. In one area, however, there is no holding back; the equipment in company plants is both modern and fast.

TABLE 3.
SELECTED CROWN CORK OPERATING STATEMENTS

	1982		1977		1972		1967	
	millions	%	millions	%	millions	%	millions	%
Net Sales	$ 1352	100.0	1049	100.0	489	100.0	301	100.0
Cost of Goods Sold	1215	89.8	906	86.4	407	83.2	242	80.3
Selling & Administrative Expense	44	3.3	35	3.3	21	4.3	19	6.3
Operating Profit before Interest & Income Tax	$ 93	6.9	$ 108	10.3	$ 61	12.5	$ 40	13.3

4. Foreign Spinoffs

A fourth pillar in Crown Cork's strategy is early entry into foreign markets. Cans and closures cannot be exported economically. Instead, Crown Cork has provided machinery (including rebuilt U.S. equipment) and production expertise to locally organized firms. Many of these companies are in developing countries, where the demand is primarily in bottlecaps.* Crown Cork had established these companies long before its U.S. competitors considered such locations worthy of attention.

These foreign subsidiaries are managed by local citizens in a highly decentralized manner. Having created a technological beachhead, each outpost must run its own show. There is no international vice-president at headquarters (which is consistent with the low-overhead philosophy mentioned above); the presidents of the Canadian and the European group do serve on the Crown Cork board of directors. And to a large extent, each foreign unit generates its own capital. In terms of people, markets, and capital, each becomes part of the local scene—even more than the local Coca-Cola bottler. It is, of course, on the spot if and when a local demand for cans develops. There is little attempt or need for multinational coordination.

With a relatively small amount of U.S. management attention, the foreign operations have grown over the years along with the total company. Income from foreign sales has ranged between 27 and 48 percent of the total over the last decade, and assets abroad account for almost half of the total. The trends are shown in Tables 4 and 5.

---

*Crown Cork has subsidiaries in the following countries: Canada, Mexico, Puerto Rico, West Indies, Argentina, Brazil, Chile, Colombia, Costa Rica, Ecuador, Peru, Venezuela; Austria, Belgium, France, Italy, Holland, Germany, Ireland, Portugal, Spain, Great Britain; Ethiopia, Kenya, Nigeria, Zimbabwe, Zaire, Morocco, Zambia; Indonesia, Malaysia, Thailand, Singapore, etc.

TABLE 4.
CROWN CORK & SEAL COMPANY, INC., OPERATING DATA
(in millions of dollars, except where otherwise indicated)

	1982	1981	1980	1978	1976	1974	1972
Net Sales	1352	1374	1460	1260	910	766	489
Cost of Goods Sold	1215	1208	1271	1095	784	655	407
Selling & Administrative Expenses	44	45	45	39	32	29	21
Interest Expense	9	12	15	11	4	7	4
Tax on Income	38	43	55	51	44	33	25
Net Income (excluding minority interests)	45	65	73	64	46	40	31
Shares of Common Stock (average in millions)	14	15	15	15	16	18	20
Earnings per share (dollars)	3.15	4.45	4.98	4.13	2.84	2.20	1.58
Net Income from Foreign Subsidiaries	12	29	35	22	15	15	13
Net Income from U.S. Operations	33	36	38	42	31	25	18
Number of employees (000's)	13	14	15	17	16	16	14
Plant & Equipment Expenditures	50	64	50	103	22	53	28
Ratio Net Income/Total Assets (percent)							
Foreign Subsidiaries	3.0	6.8	8.3	6.7	5.4	6.2	7.3
U.S. Operations	7.5	7.9	8.3	10.0	11.2	8.4	8.1
Common Stock Price (dollars/share)							
High	32	37	31-3/8	35-3/4	22-1/8	23	27-1/2
Low	22-3/4	25	22-7/8	22-1/8	16-7/8	13-5/8	18-1/2

TABLE 5.
CROWN CORK & SEAL COMPANY, INC.
COMPARATIVE BALANCE SHEET
(in millions of dollars)[a]

	1982	1981	1980	1978	1976	1974	1972
Total Company - Consolidated							
Current Assets	457	491	496	394	281	286	175
Plant & Equipment (net)	358	368	355	333	249	242	211
Investment & Goodwill	25	24	22	18	17	14	14
Total Assets	841	883	873	744	547	542	400
Current Liabilities	192	233	264	257	158	209	105
Deferred Income Tax	58	56	52	45	39	29	26
Long Term Debt	24	20	10	14	26	34	31
Minority Equity in Subsidiaries	7	7	8	8	7	9	8
Common Stock	70	73	63	76	78	86	97
Retained Earnings	490[b]	494[b]	466	345	238	176	133
Total Liabilities & Equity	841	883	873	744	547	542	400
Foreign Subsidiaries							
Current assets	253	300	297	221	170	156	82
Plant & Equipment (net)	147	127	118	104	99	89	96
Total Assets	400	427	415	326	269	245	178
Current Liabilities	104	131	133	96	77	87	37
Deferred Income Tax	8	9	11	11	10	7	6
Long Term Debt	9	0	0	2	1	7	9
Minority Equity in Subsidiaries	7	7	8	8	7	9	8
Retained Earnings (CC&S share)	225	222	193	159	132	91	69
Other CC&S Equity	47	58	70	49	42	44	49
Total Liabilities & Equity	400	427	415	326	269	245	178
United States Operations[c]							
Current Assets	204	191	199	173	111	130	94
Plant & Equipment (net)	211	241	237	228	150	153	115
Investments & Goodwill	25	24	22	18	17	14	14
Total Assets	441	456	458	418	278	297	223

TABLE 5. (Contd)

	1982	1981	1980	1978	1976	1974	1972
	United States Operations[c]						
Current Liabilities	88	102	131	161	81	120	68
Deferred Income Tax	50	47	41	34	30	22	20
Long Term Debt	15	20	10	12	25	27	22
Retained earnings	265[b]	272[b]	273	187	106	85	64
Other Equity	23	15	3	25	35	43	49
Total Liabilities & Equity	441	456	458	418	278	297	223

[a] Columns may not add exactly, due to rounding.
[b] Net after deduction for foreign currency translation of $74 million in 1982 and $35 million in 1981.
[c] Assets and liabilities assigned to U.S. operations are total company figures minus foreign subsidiaries.

COMPARISON WITH OTHER CAN COMPANIES

The results of Crown Cork's strategy look good when compared with its major competitors in the can industry. See Table 6 for growth and profit rates.

American Can diversified into other forms of packaging and also into a variety of consumer items such as paper cups, dress patterns, paper towels and tissues, and so on. At least half its present sales volume comes from these new lines which started from acquisitions rather than internal growth. Nevertheless, American Can's combined growth rate is lower than Crown Cork's, and its profit rate over the last few years has averaged about half that of Crown Cork.

Continental diversified even more than American Can. Even the name was changed from Continental Can to Continental Group. Less than half its revenue now comes from cans. The forest products division is a billion dollar per year enterprise. Unrelated lines include insurance and energy, each with a volume well over half a billion dollars per year. Up to four years ago, even with such acquisitions, Continental's growth rates in sales and profits were far behind Crown Cork's growth rates. During the last few years, however, Continental's nonpackaging activities have shown relative strength. At last, Continental's conglomerate efforts are beginning to pay off. Within the packaging industry (including operations in glass, paper, and plastics) however, Continental's broad base has not thrived as well as Crown Cork's specialized thrust.

National Can has zigged and zagged. Close to Crown Cork in size ten years ago, National Can diversified aggressively into glass and plastic containers and into a variety of food products. Not all these ventures were successful, and recently National Can management has returned to a focus on its "core business." In fact, National Can is now aggressively pushing containers for beer and soft-drinks—Crown Cork's favored domain. The net effect is that National Can has built volume; in 1982 it had sales of $1.5 billion compared with Crown

TABLE 6.
CROWN CORK & SEAL COMPANY, INC.
COMPARISON OF COMPANY SALES AND INCOME—1967–1981

Sales Index 1967 = 100

	Year	American Can	Continental	Crown Cork	National Can
	1981	318	372	456	698
	1980	316	366	485	709
	1978	262	282	418	442
	1976	207	247	302	417
	1974	190	221	254	323
	1972	132	157	162	216
		—	—	—	—
	1967	100	100	100	100
Base in $1,000,000	1967	1522	1393	301	220

Net Income Index 1967 = 100

		American Can	Continental	Crown Cork	National Can
	1981	101	336	344	311
	1980	113	288	389	692
	1978	158	161	341	262
	1976	133	151	245	260
	1974	131	142	211	253
	1972	73	103	166	177
		—	—	—	—
	1967	100	100	100	100
Base in $1,000,000	1967	76	78	19	8

Net Income as % of Sales

		American Can	Continental	Crown Cork	National Can
	1981	1.6	4.7	4.7	1.6
	1980	1.8	4.4	5.0	3.5
	1978	3.0	3.2	5.1	2.1
	1976	3.0	3.4	5.1	2.3
	1974	3.5	3.6	5.2	2.8
	1972	2.7	3.7	6.4	3.0
		—	—	—	—
	1967	5.0	5.6	6.3	3.6

Source: Standard & Poor's Industry Study.

Cork's $1.35 billion. Its profits are less impressive—$34 million compared with Crown Cork's $45 million.

These comparisons indicate that (1) during the 1960s and 1970s Crown Cork strategy enabled it to grow faster and maintain higher profit margins than its major competitors, but (2) in the early 1980s the relative advantage appears to be narrowing.

"THE PAUSE THAT REFRESHES?"

A close look at Crown Cork's present plight is critical. Are the difficulties that surfaced in 1982 temporary, or do they signal the need for a change in strategy?

In his annual letter to stockholders, Crown Cork's chairman says, in part: "We sold, produced and delivered more cans, crowns, machinery and other products than during any previous year in our history yet the dollar sales are down. . .

"In the United States economic conditions plus the effect of our industry's excess capacity has created bitter competition which has reduced our prices.

"Overseas every company has performed well. . .but when the results are restated in United States dollars profits sometimes are converted into losses. We have absolutely no control over the world's currency fluctuations."

These two forces, bitter competition and adverse currency fluctuations, are the primary villains—at least on the surface.

Increased competition is caused by several factors. (1) Crown Cork's growth and relative profitability has attracted additional capacity to serve the beer and soft drink markets. All three competitors are moving in; American Can, Continental, and National Can has each installed new, efficient two-piece can manufacturing machinery to serve this market.

(2) The rapid rise in popularity of two-piece aluminum cans has forced all competitors to replace old can-manufacturing equipment. Delay is no longer a realistic alternative. And when building new plants, each competitor is overly optimistic about the share of the market it will obtain.

(3) Meanwhile, self-manufacture of cans by large brewers is expanding. Between 1978 and 1981 self-manufacture of cans grew from 30 to 33 percent of total can shipments. This actually reduced the number of cans sold by independent producers from 63 billion to 60 billion. And most of this contraction occurred in the markets served by Crown Cork.

(4) Crown Cork's move to establish a differential advantage by making steel rather than aluminum cans has not been effective. As we will see, the cost of aluminum relative to steel has declined, instead of increasing as expected. The result is that Crown Cork does not have a differentiated product.

In effect then, Crown Cork now finds itself in a commodity-like market within the United States. Excess capacity of expensive, modern equipment in the plants of financially strong competitors leads to the "bitter competition" noted by Connelly.

Even more devastating to Crown Cork's 1982 profits have been sharp fluctuations in foreign currency values. In Crown Cork's strategy, international operations are expected to complement U.S. operations and to benefit from U.S. expertise. And within the various foreign subsidiaries this scheme is working reasonably well. Trouble occurs, however, in the consolidation of these foreign results back into U.S. dollars.

The magnitude of the profit write-downs due to currency adjustments is shown in Table 7 (income and losses stated in millions).

TABLE 7.

	1982	1981	1980
Foreign operations			
Reported net income	$ 12	$ 29	$ 35
Devaluation losses	30	11	3
Net before devaluation losses	$ 42	$ 40	$ 38
Return on foreign assets before devaluation losses	10.5%	9.4%	9.2%
Consolidated results			
Reported net income	$ 45	$ 65	$ 73
Devaluation losses	30	11	3
Net before devaluation losses	$ 75	$ 76	$ 76
Earnings per share before devaluation losses	$ 5.28	$ 5.22	$ 5.17

Almost all of these losses reflect a drop in the value of local currencies relative to the U.S. dollar in the hyperinflation countries of Argentina, Brazil, Costa Rica, and beginning in 1982, Mexico. The increase in 1982 over 1981 is due exclusively to Mexico.

So, foreign operations have indeed buttressed Crown Cork's position, but at the same time they have adjusted this narrow-margin business to severe risk.

FUTURE PROSPECTS

The wisdom of continuing any strategy depends in large measure upon the likely future circumstances in which it will apply. For Crown Cork, the outlook for pressure-resistant cans is crucial.

Crown Cork has been in the midst of a packaging revolution. Many products formerly sold in bulk are now further processed (trimmed, frozen, polished, precooked, glued, precut, and the like), placed in convenient-to-use containers, and labeled with enticing instructions. Usually such products are swathed in clear plastic and cradled in an attractive paper box. The change includes products ranging from soap to piston rings to pocket calculators. Nevertheless, Crown Cork persists in making cans and closures.

Moreover, in its own domain the can has been and continues to be threatened by substitutes. Environmentalists would like to legislate it out of existence. So Crown Cork's future is far from assured.

Growth of Underlying Demand

The U.S. consumption of both beer and soft drinks has been growing, as we see in Table 8.

TABLE 8.

Per-capita Consumption Per Year		
Year	Beer	Soft Drinks
1967	16.8 gallons	23.6 gallons
1972	19.5 "	30.3 "
1977	22.6 "	35.9 "
1981	24.6 "	39.5 "

If leisure lifestyles continue, and disposable income rises, the consumption of beer is expected to increase about 2 to 3 percent a year. So this outlook is favorable but not dramatic.

Soft drinks have recently replaced coffee as the leading national drink. The growth rate may be dampened as the proportion of teenagers in the population drops, but no one can be sure of what the present young guzzlers will prefer ten years hence. Currently, the sponsors of leading brands have launched the "Great Cola War of the 80s" which is expected to affect relative market position much more than total demand. Most forecasts project an annual increase in the total demand of about 3.5 percent.

Aerosol cans, Crown Cork's third market segment (about 15 percent of its total), experienced rapid growth from their introduction in the 50s to 1974. Then demand took a sharp dip, partly because aerosol packaging is relatively expensive and partly in response to a threatened ban for ecological reasons on the use of fluorocarbons as a propellant. Although demand has picked up again, substantial further growth is unlikely unless the ecological issues are resolved favorably.

Overall, for beer, soft drinks, and aerosol products, the U.S. growth-rate is estimated at about 3 percent per annum, barring shifts due to new ecological legislation. It is a mature market.

Battle of Materials

Not long ago every individual-size container for beer or soda was a glass bottle, and the bottle was returned to be refilled many times. There was no alternative. Then the metal can entered the picture. It saved the mess and labor of returning empty bottles, was lighter to handle, packed more closely, and didn't chip or shatter. The can companies and steel companies had to undertake a major educational campaign to persuade the consumer that a can did not affect the flavor of the product, but finally the tradition of the glass bottle was broken.

This switch to nonreturnable cans involved billions of containers and millions of dollars, as the data already presented indicate. But about the time it seemed likely that the soda bottle would follow the milk bottle into oblivion, the glass industry created the lighter-weight, cheaper, nonreturnable glass bottle. With a competitive product and a potential market many times the size of that of the old returnable bottle, the fight was on. Broadly speaking, the glass industry has been able to retain about one-fourth of the beer container business (with 96 percent nonreturnable bottles). In the soft drink field, the division between glass and cans is about the same.

Acutally, glass bottles are cheaper than cans. However, they weigh more, take more space, are slower to fill, and break occasionally. For the bottler, the difference in total cost is so narrow it usually will use the container which consumers like and that fits best into its market program. Four years ago Owens-Illinois introduced a plastic-shielded glass bottle. The shield helps to keep beverages cooler longer than a metal can does, and the bottle can be resealed. This improved package has been a major factor in checking the decline of glass containers.

A second continuing conflict is between steel and aluminum. When cans invaded the beverage field they were the traditional three-piece steel cans (a few conical tops never won an enduring position). Then around 1960, Reynolds and Kaiser aluminum companies moved in with their two-piece aluminum can. This can—now manufactured by all major can companies—has made rapid progress.

At first aluminum cans were more expensive than steel cans. And when Crown Cork and U.S. Steel succeeded in using steel for a two-piece can there was a good chance that aluminum would be priced out of the market. This did not occur because (1) the base price of aluminum fell, instead of rising as expected, thus narrowing the spread in raw material costs; and (2) many aluminum cans are recycled. Aluminum can makers have established about 6,000 recycling centers in the U.S. which handle a billion pounds of scrap aluminum annually. By 1981 half of the aluminum cans produced were made from recycled material. The net result of these two forces has been a 40 percent reduction in the price of aluminum cans during the last five years.

Aluminum makes a somewhat better-looking can than steel and it is lighter in weight. Its exceptional ductility simplifies the drawing and ironing process for production of two-piece cans.[2]

For all these reasons, in 1982, aluminum accounted for 95 percent of all beer cans, 75 percent of all soft drink cans, and 55 percent of total cans produced. Unless the world price of base aluminum increases sharply, steel has lost the beverage can market.

Currently, both American Can and Reynolds Aluminum are trying to find ways to use aluminum for food cans. (The absence of internal pressure leads to frequent denting of a thin-walled food can.) And, Continental is working on an "aluminum bottle" with a resealable cap—to compete with Owens-Illinois' "Plastic Shield" bottle.

One other storm-cloud on the materials horizon is the prospect for plastic bottles. Compared with glass, plastic bottles are lightweight, durable, almost unbreakable, and they can be formed into special shapes that have distinctive merchandising advantages.

In fact, Du Pont's PET (polyethylene tirepthalate) bottle has virtually taken over the large-size (2-liter) soft drink market. Experiments are underway to design a satisfactory single-service (8-ounce) PET bottle. However, the smaller size has a short shelf life and may affect the taste of the contents. (The difference in performance between the large and small sizes is primarily a function of the ratio of contents and surface exposure.) If these difficulties can be overcome, plastic will be a sharp competitor of regular-size glass bottles and probably would take some business from cans.

Several major firms are committing large research efforts on plastic bottles for this sixty billion unit beer and soft drink market. In addition to the Du Pont and Monsanto efforts, Dow Chemical is working with Owens-Illinois and Anchor Hocking has teamed with Coca-Cola on a plastic-coated glass bottle (returnable) that has a low breakage rate and is lightweight. Mitsubishi Chemical already has a bottle of the latter type. Imperial Chemical of England is also active.

Strength of Contestants

The way these future competitive forces will develop is strongly affected by the power and concerns of the major contestants—or actors. We have already noted that Crown Cork's U.S. competitors in steel can production—American Can, Continental, and National Can—are larger and more diversified. This is a capital-intensive industry. The number of direct competitors is small because large investments are required and profit margins unattractive.

---

[2]Crown Cork's machinery for making two-piece steel cans is easily converted to aluminum. Conversion of machinery designed for aluminum to steel would be much more difficult.

Moreover, the metal can industry has had chronic over-capacity. New capacity installed by self-manufacturers plus new capacity of aluminum can producers left excess machinery for the traditional three-piece steel can. During the early 70s American Can and Continental each dismantled old plants to reduce this depressing overhang. Now the rapid expansion of two-piece steel can lines creates unused three-piece facilities again. This is a tough climate for firms with limited capital.

Actually the competitors are more numerous. Two large aluminum companies, Reynolds and Kaiser, have obtained significant positions in the beer and soft drink markets. Four of the five leading brewers have large can plants, as do several food companies. And companies making glass bottles, such as Corning and Owens-Illinois, aggressively compete for the same end use. These are all powerful, sharp contestants.

Customers include large and relatively small firms. Bottlers of beer tend to be large and the industry is becoming more concentrated. In soft drinks the prevailing pattern of local franchises makes the number of customers much larger than might be inferred from brand concentration; the five largest firms get over 75 percent of the business, but they have several hundred distributors who actually purchase containers. Producers of aerosol products may be even smaller because they use aerosol cans for quite special markets. Nevertheless, containers represent a major expense for all these customers, and the buyers usually are very sophisticated in their purchasing.

Material suppliers are another set of actors. Materials account for roughly two-thirds of the cost of a can, so the dollar volume of materials consumed is very large. The big steel firms as well as the aluminum companies are vitally interested in this market. And as noted in the preceding section, at least five of the powerful chemical concerns are vying for advantage in a growing plastic bottle market.

By most standards Crown Cork is itself a large company. But compared with many of the firms whose actions impinge on its destiny, it is "just one of the boys."

In foreign countries the competitive picture varies widely. Because the market for cans and bottles is inherently local, each country has its own characteristics. Developing countries with low consumption in each locality, low purchasing power, and low labor costs typically use returnable bottles; this creates a demand for closures. In Europe the consumption of beverages is growing and there is a shift toward disposable containers; nevertheless, the size of individual purchasers of cans and closures is much smaller there than in the United States. Because of this diversity, a strategy for profitable growth varies from country to country.

Superimposed on this cast of actors are government regulatory agencies. The ones whose actions will have profound effect on the container industry deal with environmental issues.

686 PART 7 Comprehensive Cases

Environmental Protection

Containers for beer and soft drinks represent well over half of durable highway litter. The chief remedy proposed is a mandatory deposit to be repaid when the can or bottle is returned to the retailer.

Effective July 1983, New York became the ninth state to enact such regulations. Earlier action had been taken by Maine, Vermont, Massachusetts, Connecticut, Delaware, Michigan, Iowa, and Oregon. The New York law calls for a $.05 deposit on beer and soft drink containers, a $.01 retailer handling fee, and bans on detachable pull-tabs and plastic loops on six packs.

Experience in Oregon and Vermont, which have had such laws longest, indicates that (1) litter is substantially reduced, (2) total sales decline slightly, (3) consumers and especially retailers find the system something of a nuisance, and (4) prices have risen a bit to cover the additional cost of handling returned bottles. The impact on the type of container used is less clear. Originally it was assumed that the beverage industry would return to refillable glass bottles—virtually eliminating the use of cans. To some extent this happens. However, the recycling of aluminum cans is simpler for both consumers and retailers. The expectation now is that cans will win out, with single-use glass bottles the chief loser.

Opposition to these so-called "bottle bills" is also strong. Shortly after New York passed its mandatory deposit law, the voters in four other states (California, Colorado, Arizona, and Washington) defeated referendums calling for such legislation. Environmentalists are confronted by labor unions which might lose jobs and manufacturers which might lose sales. Emotions run high, lobbying pressures are intense. Probably the final outcome will be determined by the way politically active consumers balance a somewhat cleaner environment against the nuisance of returning cans and bottles.

CROWN CORK'S DISTINCTIVE RESOURCES

The future for Crown Cork is filled with uncertainties, as the preceding discussion indicates. The consumer industries it serves are basically mature, and a whole series of questions must be answered about the kind of containers which will carry products to those consumers. Moreover, the actions of powerful companies and political groups will profoundly affect Crown Cork; the extent and manner of Crown Cork's attempt to influence these actors will have to be decided.

As a further basis for assessing Crown Cork's future strategy, we should review several of its distinctive strengths.

1. Crown Cork is in a strong cash position. Its long-term debt is a mere 5 percent of equity, leaving large unused borrowing capacity. For the past three years, its net income plus depreciation has averaged $100 million per year.

Moreover, the company has a clear policy of paying no dividends to stockholders. So the cash flow is available for management's use.

The no-dividend (on common stock) policy—which runs back for more than two decades—is interesting, because in several years more cash was generated than was needed in the business. Instead of paying dividends, management elected to buy back common stock. The repurchase price has been around book value per share. From 1972 to 1982 the number of shares outstanding was reduced by 30 percent. Of course, this reduction has an effect on earnings per share; if the money used to buy back stock had instead been paid out as dividends, the earnings per share in 1982 would have been only $2.25 compared with the actual of $3.15.

2. The strong cash position has permitted the company to invest heavily in new equipment. During the past five years $323 million went into capital outlays. As a result, Crown Cork's plants are at least as efficient as those of its competitors, and it probably has in place more two-piece steel can capacity than all the rest of the industry combined.

3. The company's expense ratios are low and it has a tradition of lean operation. At the same time there is a tremendous morale built up around John Connelly, for many years president and now chair. Connelly is a Vince Lombardi-type of leader—demanding of himself and of others, generous to subordinates in need, inspiring subordinates through recognized success. Now 76, he continues to be the architect of company strategy.

4. The machinery division of the company, in addition to being profitable, provides valuable insight into customer problems. When it sells and services high-speed filling equipment, it must keep tabs on where expansion is planned and what competitors are offering. This helps Crown Cork keep on its toes.

5. The foreign subsidiaries provide Crown Cork with a widespread base for using its technological expertise. To date, the benefits have been predominantly on the sale of closures. However, if and when foreign subsidiaries can market, say, two-piece cans, Crown Cork will already be an established local vendor.

TABLE 9.
U.S. VERSUS FOREIGN OPERATIONS
(in millions)

	U.S.	Europe	All Other	Total
Sales to customers	781	304	273	1.352
Operating profit	59	19	38	115
Assets (excluding cash, etc.)	429	170	211	840
Capital expenditures	14	10	26	50
Depreciation expense	26	6	8	40

Comprehensive Case 4

ALLYN INSURANCE AND REAL ESTATE, INC.

Henry "Hank" Allyn III thought again about the assignment given him by his father and decided that he had to come to some conclusion about either selling the family firm to Coldwell, Banker & Co. (the nationwide real estate subsidiary of Sears, Roebuck & Co.) or, as a second option, to accelerate his company's growth by acquiring a local insurance agency that was up for sale. *Of course,* Hank thought, *I could reject both ideas and try to persuade my father and the other directors that we should go on as we have in the past and grow by depending upon our own resources.*

ALLYN'S PRESENT BUSINESS

Allyn Insurance and Real Estate is the oldest and largest firm of its kind in Williamston, a Southeastern city with a metropolitan area population of some 700,000. The company conducts a real estate brokerage service and also is an independent insurance agency.

As a *real estate broker*, the firm helps both commercial and residential clients with the sale or purchase of buildings and land. For a client, Allyn Real Estate can appraise a property, advise the owner as to a suitable selling or buying price, list and promote the property, show it, and assist with insurance and mortgages. The firm also manages properties. It advises as to rents; sees to repairs, and to the collection and disbursement and expenses; and maintains expense, revenue, and tax records. In addition, the company invests in real estate on its own account, aids companies with relocation of their personnel when large plants or offices are moved, and sells time-sharing investments in resort properties.

As an *insurance agent*, the company sells several types of insurance: property and casualty insurance, life insurance on or to the officers of companies, and workman's compensation and group medical insurance—to local manufacturing companies, hospitals, automobile agencies, newspaper and magazine publishers, and printers. Its sales agents call on clients and, based on these contracts, the firm processes applications, decides the risk associated with various clients, and then places the insurance with appropriate carriers (not all insurance companies accept high-risk customers). It also processes claims, often appraises claims for accidents, advises clients on risk-management (should the client be self-insured? should it install sprinklers? should it prohibit smoking in certain areas? should it change exits?), and generally assists clients who are in distress.

Allyn Insurance and Real Estate represents about thirty different insurance companies and so can provide a wide selection of policies and a wide range of service to its customers.

Allyn Insurance and Real Estate has operated in Williamston for over eighty years. Its most substantial growth has occurred in the last forty years under the direction and control of Hank Allyn's grandfather, who specialized in the insurance arm of the firm, and then Hank's father, who grew up in and managed the real estate part of the company. Hank himself has worked for the past four years in the commercial insurance activities of the company but has been taken off his regular duties to investigate the merger offer from Coldwell, Banker, and the possibility of acquiring the Koch Insurance Agency.

Financial results for the company are shown in Tables 1, 2, and 3. These reveal the current financial situation of the company, its capital structure, the various sources of funds, the returns on investment and on sales, growth of the firm, and trends in major expense categories. Hank's father is particularly proud of the changed percentage of sales and income attributable to the real estate division and of the growth in net worth.

The region in which Allyn Insurance and Real Estate provides its services is one of the ten most rapidly growing areas in the United States. Population growth has averaged 3.6 percent per year for the past twenty years and is widely predicted by knowledgeable forecasters, including the U.S. Bureau of the Census, to continue this rate of growth for twenty more years. Total commercial, tourist, government, and industrial activity is growing even more rapidly than is the population—about 6.2 percent per year in real dollars (adjusted for inflation). Property and income tax rates are low in comparison to the average of the fifty states. Thus there is an unusually favorable economic and tax climate. This has not gone unnoticed by competitors of Allyn Insurance and Real Estate, nor by the users of its services.

Favorable prospects for the region and for service firms should be interpreted in light of major changes that are occurring in the real estate business and the insurance industry. The provision and sale of insurance is undergoing major disruptions in established patterns. These changes are, at the moment, mainly in the planning and pilot-plant stages. But there is little doubt that the efforts will increase and that, within a decade, product and service offerings of financial, insurance, and financial-service firms will be greatly changed and that new forms of competition will appear. For instance, major nationwide banks are selling insurance—both commercially and on the retail level. Merrill Lynch, Sears, Roebuck & Co., and Shearson-American Express combine stockbrokerage, insurance sales, real estate services, credit cards, personal financial advice, and certain banking services in one organization. Traveler's Insurance offers a complete financial planning package to and through the independent insurance agencies which have been its traditional sales arm.

According to analysts quoted in *The Wall Street Journal*, Merrill Lynch and Coldwell, Banker, as well as Marsh and McLennan and Fred S. James Company

TABLE 1.
PROFIT AND LOSS STATEMENTS
(in thousands; percentages are approximate)

Year	Present (6 mos.)	%	Last Year	%	Preceding Year	%	Five Years Previous	%
Revenue								
Real Estate	$4,400	70	$ 7,260	66	$5,640	63	$4,000	54
Property Management	315	5	440	4	360	4	300	4
Insurance	1,560	25	3,300	30	3,000	33	3,100	42
Total	$6,275	100	$11,000	100	$9,000	100	$7,400	100
Expenses								
Commissions	$2,878	46	$4,340	39	$3,240	36	$2,300	31
Personnel Salaries	1,320	21	2,600	23	2,300	25	1,990	27
Other Personnel Exp.*	376	6	700	7	530	6	440	6
Occupancy								
Rent	313	5	650	6	600	7	600	8
Other†	125	2	230	2	160	2	140	2
Selling								
Advertising	310	5	700	6	600	7	384	5
Other‡	110	2	200	2	160	2	130	2
Telephone Svce.	100	2	190	2	180	2	140	2
Administrative								
Interest Exp.	150	2	250	2	230	3	210	3
Postage	60		130	1	100		60	
Office Supplies	60		150	1	110		70	
Other**	48		100	1	70		50	
Total	$5,850	93	$10,250	93	$8,300	92	$6,514	88
Operating Income	425	7	750	7	700	8	886	12
Profit Sharing Fund	65	1	200	2	160	2	220	3
Net Income before Income Tax	$360	6	$550	5	$540	6	$666	9

* Payroll taxes and insurance.
† Taxes, insurance, depreciation and leasehold amortization.
‡ Listing expense, entertainment, bad debts, travel.
** Contributions, dues, training, education, professional services.

(the real estate subsidiary of Trans-America Corporation), are acquiring local real estate companies across the country. They are setting up national real estate systems that will use the powerful marketing tool of national TV advertising and an array of new financial products to help sell homes. These companies predict that small, unaffiliated "mom and pop" real estate companies will be close to extinct within twenty years.

Market shares in *real estate* sales and brokering in the Williamston area are indicated in Table 4.

TABLE 2.
INCOME STATEMENT—INSURANCE DIVISION
(in thousands; percentages are approximate)

Year	Present (6 mos.)	%	Last Year	%	Preceding Year	%	Five Years Previous	%
Revenue								
Insurance								
Commissions*	$1,342	86	$2,805	85	$2,760	92	$3,007	97
Life Insurance								
Commissions†	156	10	364	8	180	6	—	0
Other Income	62	4	231	7	60	2	93	3
Total	$1,560	100	$3,300	100	$3,000	100	$3,100	100
Expenses								
Commissions Paid	172	11	297	9	275	9	155	5
Personnel Salaries	950	61	1,980	60	1,750	59	1,550	50
Other Personnel Exp.	110	7	220	7	220	7	160	5
Occupancy								
Rent	125	8	270	8	270	9	220	7
Other	47	3	95	3	90	3	40	1
Selling								
Advertising	16	1	33	1	45	1	60	2
Other	95	6	190	6	180	6	105	3
Telephone Svce.	60	3	180	5	90	3	90	3
Administrative								
Interest Exp.	45	3	60	2	55	2	50	2
Postage	25	2	65	2	65	2	55	2
Office Supplies	10		30	1	25	1	30	1
Other	5		30	1	25	1	25	1
Total	$1,660	106	$3,460	105	$3,090	103	$2,540	82
Operating Income	(100)	(67)	(160)	(5)	(90)	(3)	560	18
Profit Sharing Fund		0		0		0	126	4
Net Income before Income Tax	$(100)	(6)	$(160)	$(90)		(3)	$434	14

*Property and Casualty, Group Medical, Workman's Compensation.
†One agent sold only life insurance; she earned only a commission—which amounted to 50 percent of the company's revenue. Other agents were guaranteed a base salary and fringe benefits plus a commission—if earned above the draw.

THE COLDWELL, BANKER & CO. OFFER

Coldwell, Banker, a national real estate chain recently acquired by Sears, Roebuck & Co., proposes to increase its efforts in the Williamston region by purchasing all the stock of Allyn Insurance and Real Estate. Coldwell, Banker

TABLE 3.
BALANCE SHEET
(in thousands)

Assets	Current	Five Years Previous
Current Assets		
Cash	$ 700	$ 720
Accounts Receivable	2,900	1,900
Notes Receivable*	1,100	600
Prepaid Expenses	380	280
Total	$ 5,080	$ 3,500
Investments		
Realty Joint Ventures	995	600
Limited Partnerships	60	80
Total	$ 1,055	$ 680
Fixed Assets (net of depreciation)		
Land	$ 800	$ 800
Buildings	560	660
Furniture & Fixtures†	2,200	1,400
Leasehold Improvements	950	690
Total	$ 4,510	$ 3,550
Other		
Advances to Officers	$ 150	$ 100
Cash Value of Life Insurance	160	90
Total	$ 310	$ 190
Total Assets	$10,955	$ 7,920

Liabilities & Net Worth	Current	Five Years Previous
Current Liabilities		
Escrow and Customer Accounts	$ 590	$ 330
Accounts Payable	1,760	980
Notes Payable	620	370
Current Portion, Long-Term Debt	530	290
Accrued Liabilities (Due within One Year)		
Payroll Taxes and Insurance	700	440
Bonuses	90	40
Deferred Commissions Payable	920	360
Other	70	90
Total Current Liabilities	$ 5,280	$ 2,900
Long-Term Notes Payable	$ 825	$ 850
Equipment Purchase Agreements	225	150
Real Estate Mortgages	775	1,170
Total Liabilities	$ 7,105	$ 5,070
Stockholder's Equity		
Preferred Stock‡	$ 120	$ 120
Common Stock	240	240
Retained Earnings	3,490	2,490
Total Equity	$ 3,850	$ 2,850
Total Liabilities & Net Worth	$10,955	$ 7,920

*90 days or more past due.

†Includes a collection of paintings and sculptures—recently appraised at $2.5 million. Purchased over the years by Mrs. Allyn and her mother-in-law at a cost of less than half of the appraised value.

‡Noncumulative, preferred as to distribution of assets.

TABLE 4.

	% Market Share (present)	% Market Share Gain or Loss over the last 5 years
Allyn Insurance and Real Estate	14	+6
Small, Smart and Associates[*]	13	+5
Real Estate Executives[*]	9	+1
Century 21[†]	8	−2
Red Carpet[†]	5	−8
Merrill Lynch[†]	3	0
Chase and Company[*]	2	+1
Aquilano Associates[*]	2	+1
Others (about 75)	44	−4

[*]Local and regional companies—privately owned.
[†]National firms.

currently has one branch in Williamston which does a fair commercial business, but little in residential real estate. It proposes to utilize three of the present ten branch offices of Allyn Insurance and Real Estate, combine three others into one, and move four branch offices into Sears stores in two of the newer regional shopping centers in the area. In doing this, it will increase the number of agents in each branch from about twenty-five to a minimum of fifty and will also introduce its own cost-control, sales, and management systems.

Since Allyn's real estate division has grown by using a strategy of selling only higher-priced properties to upper and upper-middle class residential clients and to older and well-established local and regional companies, the purchase by Coldwell, Banker and the relocation of two Sears stores will bring about a change in domain. The change will also affect the present branch managers who are widely believed in local and real estate circles to be one of the two major strengths of Allyn Insurance and Real Estate. The second strength to be considered is extensive participation in community cultural and charitable affairs by Henry Allyn, Jr.—Hank's father—and by several of the branch managers.

Branch managers' activities include selecting, training, encouraging, and supervising the sales agents in the various branches. The managers do not list or sell property. They help their agents do so through their attention and encouragement.

Hanks' cousin and sister—who are agents in the commercial real estate section—can remain with Coldwell, Banker in its separate commercial group, which is one of the strongest commercial real estate coalitions in the country. Both have told Hank that they would not be displeased with the merger and that their 20 percent share of the Allyn stock would be voted in favor of the merger. Hank's aunt, however, is strongly opposed to the merger. She inherited 15 percent of the shares. Although not active in the company's operations, she is an active board member and the proprietress of the best-known and highest-priced ladies' specialty retail shop in the city.

Another 10 percent of the stock in the company is owned by two vice-presidents in the insurance division. They acquired it through an incentive plan which had been set up by Hank's grandfather and then discontinued. Henry Allyn, Jr., owns 55 percent of the shares. If the Coldwell offer is accepted, Henry Allyn, Jr., Henry Allyn III, and the two vice-presidents would have to agree not to engage in real estate or insurance activities in the Williamston area for five years.

The Coldwell, Banker plan is to discontinue the insurance division of Allyn Insurance and Real Estate and absorb its work and personnel into Sears' Allstate Insurance Company. Hank has not talked with the two vice-presidents about this plan, but he assumes that they are opposed to the merger.

Coldwell, Banker proposes to pay, in cash, $10,500,000 for the stock of Allyn Insurance and Real Estate. This is a high price-earnings multiple above that common in other service industries, but in line with multiples paid for real estate firms that have been acquired recently.

Coldwell, Banker justifies this price by considering entry to the Williamston market. Of course, individuals can become local real estate agents with very little capital investment. The real barriers are the time needed for an individual sales agent to build his or her own clientele and position—about three years—and for a company to develop a preferred position in the community through the community efforts of its chief executives. Work for charitable organizations, nonprofit service organizations, local public authorities, and recreational groups is necessary. It generally takes at least five years for this kind of activity to result in a well-established, recognized position so that referrals to the brokerage firm will be made by bankers, lawyers, accountants, town fathers, business leaders. Acquiring a going concern allows a company to leap these barriers.

BUYING THE KOCH INSURANCE AGENCY

The results of the insurance arm of AIRE have not been favorable for several years (see Table 2). This unhappy situation is generally explained by Robert Eggert, head of the insurance division, his predecessor, and other insurance agents of the company to be the consequence of a policy change on the part of the large insurance carriers, such as Traveler's, the Hartford Group, and Aetna Life & Casualty.

"Four years ago our percentage of the insurance premiums paid by Williamston Country Club amounted to $19,000. For the same amount of work on our part to process claims, analyze risks, recommend carriers, and place the insurance we will receive about $14,300 this year," said Mr. Eggert. "The insurance companies have cut the premiums they charge by this much, which reduces our commissions from them. They are accepting considerable losses to keep the cash from the premiums flowing in. A recent report in *Best's Review* shows that expenses for companies which underwrite property and casualty insurance are now 115 percent of the revenue they get for providing this kind of insurance. What has happened is that the firms are making so much money from their investments that they are willing to sell insurance at a loss to bring the money in. And, of course, our expenses have risen—not fallen.

"The way to overcome this is to double the size of our insurance operation and to cut the number of carriers we deal with from thirty to five so that we will have more clout with the insurance company and can get a performance bonus for the premiums we bring in. I expect that gross revenues for the insurance division would soon be three times what they are now if we go ahead with this acquisition."

Henry Allyn, Jr., says, "I not only need more clout with the insurance companies—which we will get if we double our business—but a manager who can make the division efficient. Ed Koch runs his agency with half the number of employees that we have."

As a way of expanding the total insurance sold and simultaneously obtaining the services of Mr. Koch to manage the combined operations, Henry Allyn, Jr., has discussed with Mr. Koch the purchase of the Koch Agency.

The Koch Agency generally sells the same types of insurance policies as Allyn Insurance to a similar clientele. Mr. Koch proposes to move all the insurance work into a building which he owns. Headquarters of the Allyn activities will remain where they are (about two miles away). The space made available at headquarters will be used to expand the real estate division, to add a mortgage investment operations, and to increase the size of the executives' offices.

Mr. Koch has supplied a minimum amount of information about the financial situation of his company (see Table 5). He wants to be bought out for cash at a price which is a multiple of 1.75 times the prior year's revenues.[1] Henry Allyn, Jr., and Mr. Koch have had extensive discussions and negotiations. The 1.75 times multiple seems to be his minimum price. "We've talked enough," he says. "I'll settle for 50 percent in cash and 50 percent of the stock in a new insurance company which we can set up as a joint venture."

JOINT VENTURE WITH KOCH INSURANCE

Henry Allyn, Jr., says, "If we move at all, a joint venture is the only practical way to proceed with Koch. Koch might sell for 1.75 times this year's revenues of, say, $1,700,000. But that comes to $3 million which neither the Allyn family nor company has now. Besides, the main asset we need is Koch himself as the manager.

"I have sounded out Coldwell, Banker on our keeping the insurance part of Allyn Insurance and Real Estate, which is not what they are after. They will let

---

[1]Two large, publicly-owned, insurance brokerage firms bought smaller local firms at prior year's revenue multiples of 1.23 and 1.76 times respectively earlier in the year.

TABLE 5.
REVENUES AND PROFITS, KOCH INSURANCE AGENCY

	Gross Revenue	Pre-Tax Profit
Current Year (6 mos.)	$ 864,000	$ 32,000
Last Year (12 mos.)	2,004,000	69,000
Preceding Year	2,120,000	85,000
Preceding Year	1,800,000	108,000

Current Assets/Current Liabilities = 1.34/1
Pre-tax Profit/Net Worth = 16%
Total Debt/Net Worth = 1/1
Current Assets/Total Assets = 67%

(The information in this table was supplied by a well-known, regional accounting firm which rendered its opinion with no reservations.)

TABLE 6.
MEDIAN RATIOS—SERVICE INDUSTRIES[*]

Ratio	Insurance Agents & Brokers	Real Estate Agents & Brokers
Current	1.0	1.1
Quick	1.0	0.7
Sales/Receivables	2.3	12.5
Total Debt/Net Worth	5.4	2.3
Percent of Profit before Taxes/Net Worth	14.8%	11.1%
Percent of Profit before Taxes/Total Assets	2.9%	2.6%
Sales/Total Assets	0.9	0.9
Current Assets/Total Assets	72%	43.8%

[*]Source: Robert Morris Associates statements.

us keep—actually spin off—all insurance operations with related assets and liabilities for the net book value of the assets involved. Roughly such a spin-off would involve, in thousands:

Current Assets	$1,500	Current Liabilities	$1,300
Fixed Assets	800	Amount deducted from payment to Allyn stockholders	1,000
	$2,300		$2,300

"Those assets and liabilities are what we would put into the joint venture, along with our total insurance organization and customer relations. And all of us would be free to stay in the insurance business. Koch would put in his company, which we estimate looked something like this at the end of last year, also in thousands:

Current fixed assets	$578	Current liabilities	$431
Fixed assets	284	Net worth	431
	$862		$862

"The combined revenues of the two organizations last year were $3,300,000 plus $2,044,000, or $5,304,000. If Koch can help the combined operations earn 3.7 percent in profit before tax, which is the rate he is earning this year, the new venture would make almost $200,000. Any improvements in margins or volume would add to that.

"The real crunch, of course, is that Koch sees his contribution to the joint venture as only 50 percent of his selling price. The other 50 percent, about $1,500,000, would have to come out of the cash we would receive from Coldwell, Banker. Even for pro football players, that's a hefty bonus for signing a contract."

Hank Allyn had a final word with his younger brother, James, who said, "We would be better off to shrink the insurance business to two specialties. Life insurance still pays—although not as well as it should. My specialty of selling insurance and writing performance bonds for the construction industry is also profitable. It will bring in about $250,000 in revenues this year. All the expenses— including my salary, direct costs, and a heavy chunk of general overhead—won't amount to more than $225,000 for the year. Skilled clerks or underwriters are in heavy demand in this area. The sales agents we let go could take some clients with them, so they wouldn't be badly off. Of course, grandfather would turn over in his grave if this happened; insurance certainly built this business for the family. Maybe the companies will come to their senses and try to make a profit from writing policies.

"Should we trade the family name for money?"

Comprehensive Case 5

REED SHOE COMPANY[1]

Reed Shoe Company was organized nine years ago to produce and market specially-designed and recreational footwear. From first-year sales of $150,000 and a net loss of $55,000, the company progressed to third-year sales of $750,000 and its first profit—$25,000. The growth continued, and two years ago the company was able to enlarge its equity capital base by selling 100,000 shares of common stock with a net realization to the company of $3.75 per share. Sales topped $5,000,000 last year with post-tax profit of $245,000. Its founder and president, Tom Reed, believes the company has now reached a critical point in its development. He is convinced that he has to make fundamental decisions which will determine the character of the business for at least the next decade.

LEARNING THE SHOE BUSINESS

Tom Reed joined his family's business, Yankee Shoe Company, immediately after graduating from Dartmouth's Tuck School of Business with a major in marketing. The company was then directed by Tom's father and uncle, Franklin and Nathan Reed, who were the third generation of owner-managers of a New England shoe manufacturing business. Throughout its history, Yankee Shoe Company had concentrated on a conservatively-styled line of men's shoes that featured comfort and durability. In the years following World War II, when the men's shoe industry began to give greater emphasis to style, Tom's father and uncle refused to follow the trend. In their view, styling introduced a risk that they wished to avoid. They were confident that there would always be an assured, if limited, market for "sensible" shoes that were comfortable when new, that were designed and built for long life, and that could be resoled and reheeled repeatedly without losing their shape. The result of the undeviating application of this policy was a steady volume of sales year after year with equally steady profits. The company's shareowners, all family members more interested in assured dividends than in growth, were satisfied with this performance.

A year after Tom entered the family business his father died, leaving the direction of the company wholly in the hands of his uncle. Tom spent that year

---

[1] This case was written by Professor Melvin Anshen, Graduate School of Business, Columbia University.

and the next at the head office in Boston, "learning the business" by sitting in on management meetings, participating in the budget process, analyzing production costs, accompanying salespeople calling on the independent retail shoe stores which carried the Yankee line, and talking with the purchasing agent and the factory manager about their responsibilities and problems. He then became a salesperson, first in the Midwest and later in Southern and mid-Atlantic territories. After five years in the field, he was promoted to the position vacated by the retiring sales manager, with responsibility for supervising the company's twelve sales representatives, and he began to participate in the general management of the company under his uncle's leadership.

In this role, Tom became increasingly frustrated by Yankee Shoe's commitment to conservatively-styled "comfort" shoes. While he agreed with the judgment that there would always be a profitable market for such shoes, he saw little opportunity for significant growth in sales and profits. He expected style to have growing importance in buying decisions for men's shoes in the years ahead, parallel to the rising interest in style in all men's apparel. He also saw a trend toward special-purpose shoes, constructed and styled for specific uses. One area especially drew his attention: the mounting consumer interest in a variety of athletic and recreational activities in which the old-fashioned, all-purpose "sneaker" was beginning to be displaced by shoes uniquely designed for specific uses: in basketball, tennis, sailing, and in the newly-popular activity of jogging. He believed that this whole area held possibilities for rapid growth, with interesting opportunities for those companies that moved in early and established strong brand "images."

Drawing on his experience as a college athlete (varsity basketball and tennis at Dartmouth) and in the shoe business, and working with a friend who was a chemical engineer, Tom developed and patented a process for forming a "sandwich" of honeycomb sponge rubber bonded between flexible, fibrous "breathing" plastic sheets, which would serve as an unusually resilient, supportive, light, and comfortable innersole for athletic footwear. The material has a unique capacity for retaining its shape when subjected to sudden shocks and repetitive twisting stresses and strains. Tom had a few dozen pairs of canvas-top shoes made up with this innersole material for trial by tennis and squash players of his acquaintance. Their favorable appraisals led him to conclude that indeed he had developed a distinctive material for sports and recreational shoes, at least equal to and probably superior to anything then on the market. He visualized its application to a variety of specialized shoes which, with colorful external styling to accord with the trend in sports and recreational clothing, would meet excellent consumer acceptance.

Tom's discussion of this potential development with his uncle met a stubborn refusal even to consider enlarging the scope of the business. His uncle argued that much of the apparent market was likely to be a "fad" of temporary duration. Further, athletic and recreational footwear used different materials and manufacturing techniques than the company's traditional line and would require substantial investment in new equipment, as well as new manufacturing skills. Also, these types of shoes were usually sold in sporting goods stores, rather than in shoe stores, and therefore would require additional sales representatives and advertising support. "Why take such a risk?" his uncle asked. "We've got a nice, steady, assured business with an established and respected name. Why move into an area that we know nothing about, that isn't even likely to be an enduring market?" Tom's talks with his uncle became increasingly acrimonious, and it became clear to Tom that their basic attitudes were so antagonistic that he would be better off and happier outside the business.

LAUNCHING THE NEW COMPANY

After eleven years with the family firm, Tom decided to resign and organize his own company to manufacture athletic and recreational shoes for men and boys. He negotiated an amicable agreement with his uncle to purchase the Yankee stock he had inherited from his father for $200,000, a sum that he judged sufficient to launch his new business and see it through what he anticipated would be its difficult early period. He decided to focus first on a line of tennis shoes, and then expand to other sports and recreational categories.

Tom employed a part-time styling consultant whose shoe-design studio served several large shoe companies. To minimize his initial investment in fixed assets, he contracted with a small plastics company to produce his bonded rubber-plastic sandwich material. This he shipped to a leading New England manufacturer of a diversified line of athletic shoes with idle factory capacity; the manufacturer contracted to produce the Reed line of tennis shoes with a minimum-quantity guaranteed output.

Tom's next step was to persuade one of the Yankee sales representatives to join him in his venture, taking compensation partly in a modest salary and partly in stock in the new company. He budgeted $40,000 for an advertising campaign, using the services of a Boston advertising agency to prepare small space ads that were placed in the Eastern editions of several sports and tennis magazines and in regional magazines along the Atlantic seaboard from Boston to Florida. The advertisements featured the unique design characteristics and distinctive styling of Reed "Air-Tread" tennis shoes.

A headquarters office was opened in Boston where Tom installed as office manager, bookkeeper, secretary, and general factorum, his cousin, Phyllis Reed, who had just graduated from Wellesley and was looking for a job in a small business where, as she said, she "could get involved in everything." With all these arrangements in place, Tom and his one sales representative, Joe Ferguson, went "on the road" to sell Reed tennis shoes to specialty tennis shops and general sports equipment retailers in the New England, mid-Atlantic, and Southern territories.

"The results in the first few months," Tom Reed later reported to a friend, "were better than my worst fears and worse than my best hopes. We had a great product, but nobody knew it. We gave retailers an opportunity to take an attractive 50 percent markup on retail (100 percent on their cost), selling them styles for nets after cash discount of $9.00, $12.00, and $15.00, with suggested retail prices of $17.95, $23.95, and $29.95. We were telling our story to amateur tennis players by advertising in magazines with good coverage of the amateur tennis market. But there were lots of tennis shoes already in those stores, many with well-known brand names that retailers and tennis nuts were familiar with. You had to believe in the comfort and playability of our shoe to buy it, and you had to wear it to believe in it. It was a tough sell. But Joe and I found a few stores willing to place initial orders with a return guarantee for unsold stock, and we slowly began to get favorable word-of-mouth support. Sales really started to move in the second year. It was a good thing I had that $200,000 nest egg, however, and no money tied up in plant and equipment, because it was a traumatic time financially, with more dollars going out than coming in.

Midway through the second year, when rising sales encouraged confidence that the business was moving ahead, Tom negotiated his first bank loan, purchased a small vacant shoe factory in Haverhill, Massachusetts, leased machinery, employed a crew of experienced workers and a plant supervisor, and became a full-fledged manufacturer of tennis shoes. "It was a high-risk throw of the dice," he later said, "but I felt I had to take the chance. I was getting murdered on that contract manufacturing deal. There was no leverage on volume, no way to make a profit out of growth. I just had to sink money in a fixed asset base.

"We didn't try to produce our own sandwich innersole material—that didn't happen until the following year when we could make another fixed investment—but we did start to build our own shoes. We still lost money, but we pushed sales up to half a million dollars and I thought I could begin to see that famous light at the end of the tunnel.

"I was working myself silly, of course, I was still on the road selling, along with Joe Ferguson and another salesperson I had hired. But I was also back at the factory, working with my plant supervisor to organize the machinery and the workflow, and in the office teaching Phyllis how to be a bookkeeper—something she didn't learn at Wellesley, but she's a quick learner—and then teaching her how to be at least a rudimentary treasurer and controller and credit manager and office manager, too. I was also purchasing agent for materials and parts, not to mention personnel manager and advertising manager. I guess I didn't see much of my wife and kids through that year and a half. And I worried a lot about the whole structure collapsing on my head. There were times in there when I thought I was somehow working an eight-day week in seven days."

In the third year, Reed Shoe Company sales pushed above $750,000 and the firm earned its first profit. A development of even greater importance for the business was the growing popularity of jogging, a recreational and health activity that expanded explosively two years later. Tom Reed discovered jogging as a health-enhancing activity for himself at this time. He also discovered that his patented innersole could be incorporated in a running shoe as advantageously as in a tennis shoe. So the "Air-Tread" jogging shoe was introduced as the company's first significant line extension. By last year, when sales topped $5,000,000, 80 percent of the sales were generated by the jogging line, the balance coming from tennis shoes. The growth of the jogging line is shown in Table 1.

TABLE 1.
UNIT SALES OF REED "AIR TREAD" TENNIS AND JOGGING SHOES
(thousands of pairs)

	Total	Tennis	Jogging
5 years ago	104	83	21
4 " "	190	114	76
3 " "	235	94	141
2 " "	308	93	215
Last Year	345	69	276

THE JOGGING SHOE INDUSTRY

Precise data on the jogging population and on its purchase of shoes and clothing are not available. Trade papers frequently estimate that from 20 to 25 million Americans are regular joggers (double the number of two years ago). Annual purchases of special jogging shoes and clothing are believed to aggregate almost $500 million. In a market dominated in earlier years by such foreign brands as Adidas and Puma from Germany and Tiger from Japan, U.S. brands such as Nike, Brooks, New Balance, Etonic, and Reed are now active competitors. Nike claims first place with 33 percent of the total jogging shoe market against second-place (formerly the leader) Adidas with about 20 percent. In addition to the 25 million joggers, industry analysts believe that another 7 to 10 million Americans find jogging shoes so comfortable, and possibly so colorful as well, that they wear them regularly as general-purpose shoes. Although some analysts feel that the figures cited above are as much as 25 percent high, the market is clearly substantial.

The design and construction of jogging shoes has become a technology of considerable complexity. Competing brands each claim to offer unique advantages derived from such features as aerated, cantilevered, and wedge soles; laced and solid bodies; straight and flared heels; and special arch support structures. The styles of jogging shoes receive as much attention as their construction, with brilliant tones, decorative stripes and swirls, and other colorful trimmings.

Specialty retailers concentrating on running shoes and associated clothing and gear are expanding rapidly, often by the franchise route. One such organization, Athletic Attic, Inc., based in Jacksonville, Florida, claims to have 140 outlets, with new franchised units opening at the rate of one per week. Special-focus magazines (*Runner's World, The Runner,* and *Running Times*) provide editorial content of interest to all classes of runners from neighborhood joggers to long-distance racers, including evaluations of footwear and other items, articles on health and medical topics, and related subjects. These publications carry advertising for shoes, clothing, chronographs, and many other items for male and female runners of all ages, all levels of skill and commitment, and all running environments—urban, suburban, open country, on- and off-track.

Retail distribution channels for jogging shoes and clothing are not clearly defined, nor is there any agreement among trade sources about the relative volume of merchandise moving through different categories of stores. In addition to outlets specializing in jogging shoes (a growing number of which are adding clothing for joggers), special-line retailers (identified previously as "tennis shops") and general sporting goods stores promote jogging shoes and equipment. Traditional shoe stores feature jogging shoes. Department stores display jogging shoes in their shoe departments and jogging clothing in other departments (often identified as "recreation" or "leisure" departments), as do such chain organizations as Sears, Montgomery Ward, and J.C. Penney. In all these diverse outlets, jogging shoes are available at prices ranging from about $15 at the low end to as high as $50, and clothing is offered in a comparable range. Retail markups range from 40 to 50 percent of selling prices, but are often reduced to 25 to 30 percent for special promotions.

Some industry analysts are skeptical about the likelihood of maintaining the recent growth rate in the jogging market. They are optimistic, however, about two other possibilities. One is the application of special construction features, and special styling also, to shoes for other sport and recreational uses. This spring, for example, shoe trade sources report that the exploding popularity of soccer is opening a large new market opportunity. They estimate that as many as four million adults, youths, and children are playing soccer.

Some athletic shoe manufacturers anticipate that the market potential in soccer shoes, assuming continued growth at the existing rate, would compare favorably with that in running shoes. To support their growth forecasts, they cite additional television coverage of soccer games, and the recent growth of youth and adult amateur soccer leagues at a 20 percent annual rate. They also call attention to the attraction of soccer as a high school competitive sport in a period of severe budgetary constraint for school athletic programs. A high school can field an entire soccer squad for little more than the price of a ball, compared with the $300 required to outfit one football player.

The leading company in the soccer area is Adidas. Its print advertising features well-known professional players. It also has secured the endorsement of NASL for three models of soccer shoes. Eltra Corp.'s Converse division, long established in the athletic shoe business with particular emphasis on basketball shoes, has extended its line to football, baseball, running, and soccer shoes. Its advertising manager defines its primary soccer target as the youth market, players "who, for the most part, have not made a commitment to one particular brand." It uses endorsements (secured in return for payments from Converse for every pair of Converse soccer shoes purchased) from the United States Soccer Federation and the American Youth Soccer Organization, with a combined membership of 800,000 in over 100 member soccer leagues.

Two companies whose growth is closely tied to jogging (New Balance Athletic Shoes and BRS Inc. with its Nike line) are believed by trade sources to be planning expansion into soccer shoes. (Nike jogging sales are reported to have grown from $25 million to $150 million in the past five years while its product line expanded from 10 to 72 models.) Brooks Mfg. Co. is reported to be ready to commit $50,000 for print advertising for soccer shoes in the mid-Atlantic and Northeast markets.

The second broad area for growth is the invasion of the stardard shoe market by high-style special-construction shoes which consumers find more comfortable and attractive than slip-on leather "loafers" for all-day wear. "Your basic man's shoe," says one enthusiast, "really hasn't changed for a couple of hundred years, beyond substituting machine for hand production. We have the makings of a footwear revolution in what first appeared to be strictly an engineered shoe for runners. We can put comfort and style together as they have never been joined and we can do it at a price that will permit middle-income people to own half-a-dozen pairs of shoes where they used to think two pairs, one black and one brown, were all they needed."

REED SHOE COMPANY ORGANIZATION

In carrying out his responsibilities as president of Reed Shoe, Tom Reed relies on the advice of three friends he persuaded to join his board of directors when the company added to its equity capital by the sale of 100,000 shares of common stock. Clement Fairweather is a senior vice-president of the bank that loans money to help finance the company's current operations. John Beggs is chairman and chief executive officer of a diversified manufacturing company. Hale Allyn has taken early retirement for health reasons from a management consulting firm and occcupies himself on a part-time basis by serving as an outside director of several small companies.

"These are wise and experienced men," Tom comments. "They have a knowledge about business operations that adds a valuable dimension to my own abilities. Further, the fact that they are not involved in the pressure cooker of the company's daily operations, as I am, gives them a different sighting on the company's situation and prospects than mine. Our board meets quarterly, usually for half a day. In addition, I talk to them individually between meetings, whenever something comes up on which I'd like to check my ideas with an independent point of view. They're personal friends of mine, but they tell me frankly what they think and don't pull their punches when they believe I'm about to make a mistake or haven't evaluated all aspects of a situation.

"Of course, they serve another purpose, too. Their presence on the board impresses some of the stockholders, gives them a little more confidence that we know what we're doing. Don't get me wrong. I'm still the largest stockholder and the ultimate boss of the whole operation. But I can't conceive the circumstance in which I would make an important decision without asking their counsel."

The fifth member of the board is Joe Ferguson. "Joe's a director because he was in on this adventure from the start," Tom said. "But his experience is narrow, wholly in sales, and he doesn't contribute much to board discussions."

The formal organization structure of Reed Shoe Company below the board of directors is shown in Figure 1. In reality, Tom Reed notes that additional boxes with his name in them should be added above the positions of sales, production, and finance managers because he actively directs each of these functions. "That is one of the problems that makes this a critical point in the development of the business. Up to now I have spent a lot of time with each of these managers and am involved in all significant decisions in each of these areas. While the thought may cross your mind that I am reluctant to delegate responsibility to the three individuals concerned, the truth of the matter is that they are relatively inexperienced in handling the responsibilities attached to their jobs.

"Joe Ferguson is 38 and up to last year when I designated him as sales manager he had spent fifteen years as a shoe salesperson, including his time with Yankee Shoe before he came in with me at the start of Reed Shoe. He's a good sales representative and is totally committed to the company. But he knows little about being a sales manager, especially in such areas as recruiting, training, supervising, and compensating salespeople. If you appraise him against the broader responsibilities of a marketing manager, you have to conclude that he is lacking in experience in all aspects of profit management, including budgeting and pricing. Moreover, if we move into some of the new kinds of merchandise and retail stores I am considering, he starts as a novice.

"Sam Adams is 45. His education did not go beyond high school. He got a job at Yankee as an apprentice shoemaker and worked up to be a supervisor. He's a good supervisor. But if you put his ability and experience up against a competent production manager, about the best you can say is that he has native intelligence and a desire to learn. He doesn't know much about cost analysis or budgeting. He has no experience in union negotiations. And his knowledge of machine technology is self-taught, derived wholly from working with shoe machinery.

"As for Phyllis—well, she's just a great person, probably far superior to me in general intelligence. But she majored in French at college and never laid eyes on an accounting record or a balance sheet until she came to work here. Everything she knows about finance and control she learned from me and from a couple of night-school courses in accounting she has taken at our local community

FIGURE 1

REED SHOE COMPANY
Organization Chart

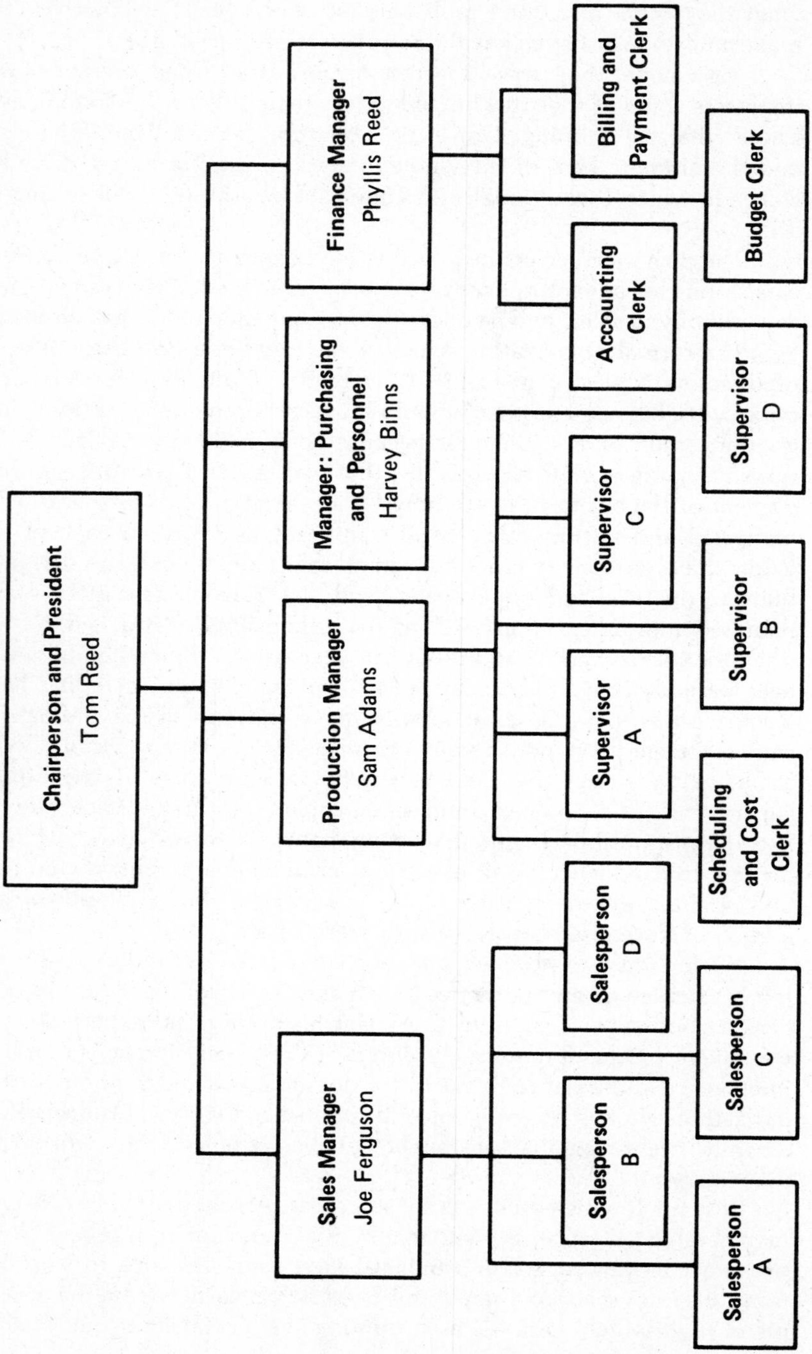

college. She's so smart and learns so fast that I'm confident that in, say, five years she could be a competent treasurer and controller for a business of the size Reed Shoe might be at that time. But she can't do that job right now without my leaning over her shoulder and answering her questions. She can't deal with our banker. She just lacks credibility with him. He likes her all right, but he doesn't have confidence in her as a corporate treasurer.

"Up to now, the business has simply been too small to carry the salaries of fully qualified managers in these three important functions. I've had no choice; in all but routine daily activities it has been necessary for me to function as chief cook and bottle-washer. We are now at a stage in our growth where this situation can't continue. I'm doing too much. I don't have enough time to be an adequate chief executive officer. I don't have time to plan for the future of the business. But that future is right on our doorstep and either I am going to make the critical decisions or circumstances are going to make them for me, possibly in ways that may not be advantageous for the business.

"I'm going to have to recruit fully-qualified, experienced managers for the three functions and superimpose them above Joe Ferguson, Sam Adams, and Phyllis Reed. If the business continues to grow, as I am confident it will, it can carry the burden of the salaries required to attract people of the quality I want. But there is always the risk of making mistakes in hiring. On top of that, it's not going to be a popular move with Joe, Sam, and Phyllis. They think they are doing okay. I doubt that they realize how much of their responsibilities I have shouldered. And I want to keep them as seconds-in-command who may ultimately replace the outsiders I bring into the firm. I'm not confident I know how to explain and justify this move to them in a way they will accept. It's a very delicate matter."

FUTURE POSSIBILITIES

Tom Reed sees the prospects of Reed Shoe in the following terms. "Here we are at $5 million in sales. That's a long way from where we started. But, in the other direction, it's a long way in the running-shoe business from Nike, Adidas, and Puma, and even some of the smaller companies that are considerably larger than we are. We've begun to get distribution through a fair number of retail outlets, both general sporting goods stores and specialty running shoe retailers. We've got a great product. On its merits, it's at least equal to the best on the market. We're beginning to get consumer recognition in the markets where we have distribution. But so far those markets are limited to the Eastern Seaboard. So where do we go from here?

"One possibility is to reach out for national distribution, either in one big move or region by region. If the latter, then I suppose our next move should be into the Midwest. But even regional expansion would require a major investment in manufacturing capacity—an investment, I judge, of at least a million dollars. We obviously don't have that kind of money. We'd have to go into debt financing; possibly we could sell some more stock, although I know investors are not exactly waiting around to buy the stock of a small operation like ours in an industry like this. Furthermore, the immediate effect of such a move on profits is likely to be negative. Unit production costs rise in the first phase of expansion, though later we should realize substantial economies of scale. Sales and advertising expense would go up, too. An interruption of the growth of bottom-line earnings would surely make some of our stockholders nervous. I guess it would make me nervous, too.

"When you start to think in these terms, you have to evaluate prospects for the industry. It's been through three years of absolutely phenomenal growth. But there are those who say that practically all the potential joggers in the American population are already out there jogging and the number of new recruits for this truly splendid activity will be limited to what is provided by population growth.

"Of course, there are also those who say that jogging will turn out to be a fad—like bowling—and will tilt down hereafter, maybe falling to half its present volume, possibly even further. If that should happen, it's going to be a real jungle of a business because the big established firms are not going to give up volume without one hell of a fight. I guess it's practically inevitable that that fight would focus on prices and margins, and that would be tough for a business of our size because we don't realize the kind of economies of scale that the big operators enjoy. I figure that for shoes of comparable quality and style, our unit production costs are at least 10 percent higher than the big firms' costs. If it didn't totally knock us out of the ring, it could at least make us into a not-for-profit business. And that's not the kind of business I want to run. I like profits.

"But there are other possibilities all around. For example, there are a growing number of people buying jogging shoes who never do any jogging. They simply like their comfort and their style. I know men, and some women too, who wear them just about every day strictly because they are light, easy on the feet, and they look great. There's a big potential market that has sort of created itself. Nobody's advertised running shoes for everyday wear. But we could do that. If we got serious about it, it would certainly mean we would have to try for distribution through regular shoe stores. It would be a tricky promotional job—telling a persuasive story about general use of what most people think of as a special-use type of shoe. And we couldn't expect to keep this market for ourselves. It's open to every other company in the business. It's open to the regular shoe companies, too—companies that have never made a running shoe.

"Then there are other sports and recreational markets. We started out with tennis shoes, picked up running shoes, and now most of our customers are joggers. We could make a bigger effort in the tennis market. It's still growing. We've never tried basketball shoes. All of a sudden soccer is booming. We could design, produce, and market a line of shoes for some or all of these markets. All it takes is guts, enthusiasm, and, of course, money. Lots of money—exactly how much would depend on whether we try to exploit these possibilities one at a time or all at once.

"I've got some bigger ideas then these. As you have probably observed, joggers like to wear special clothing, especially clothing carrying the same brand name as the shoes they prefer. There is no market-attitude reason why a line of specially-designed clothing under the Reed name would not be received favorably by people who wear or know about Reed running shoes. Whether we could offer some unique or distinctive features, comparable to our patented 'Air-Tread' innersole and other shoe construction components, is speculative. But we could certainly style our jogging clothing with the best of the competition. Again, as with expansion in our shoe business, this would mean additional investment in production facilities—and we should certainly bear in mind that we come to the clothing business with no experience in manufacturing technology. Of course, we could also contract out our clothing production, retaining responsibility for its styling (for which we would have to employ a specialist) and its promotion and marketing. That would be simpler and within our reach.

"There's at least one other possiblity that is worth examining. That is not to do any of these things. Maybe I should have said there are two possibilities, because there are two quite different ways of not doing any of these things. The first way is to abandon all these ambitious notions of continued growth and settle for being the kind of modest-sized business we are right now. Be a small specialty shoe company; don't look for major growth. In fact, be a Yankee Shoe Company in the tennis and jogging shoe business. You could make a nice living out of it and you could really relax and enjoy life. I could turn over full responsibility to Joe and Sam and Phyllis in their areas. They could handle, or learn to handle, without much help from me, what they are now doing in the business of our present size. And I could free up my time for my family and take up golf seriously.

"The business would probably be profitable enough to let me take winter vacations in the Caribbean and all that. My wife would surely vote for this strategy. But I doubt that it would keep me satisfied very long. After all, I got out of Yankee Shoe because it was exactly that kind of comapny. If I'd stayed there I would have taken over from my uncle in a few more years and lived exactly that kind of life. But I find the idea of a vigorous, growing company stimulating and satisfying. I resist the notion of stagnation.

"The other possibility is to sell out and look around for something else to start. My banker has steered a couple of prospective buyers my way. I could sell this business and let someone else struggle with the problems of growth. And I could put the money into another business that would give me the kind of challenge I seem to respond to. How much could I sell for? Well, take a look at our recent performance and our balance sheet and make your own judgment. (See Tables 2 and 3.) I think my board would go along with just about any reasonable purchase proposal. Speaking of my board, it might be interesting for you to talk to my three outside directors and get their perspective on these matters."

TABLE 2.
REED SHOE COMPANY
END-OF-YEAR BALANCE SHEETS
($000)

Assets	Last year	2 years ago	3 years ago	4 years ago	5 years ago
Current Assets:					
Cash	$ 38	$ 31	$ 48	$ 27	$ 22
Accounts receivable—less reserve	452	382	327	125	53
Inventories—lower of cost or market	1,137	924	672	335	204
Prepayments	58	52	45	22	15
Total current assets	1,685	1,389	1,092	509	294
Fixed assets at cost:					
Building—pledged under mortgage	480	365	290	290	260
Machinery and equipment	230	205	158	112	58
Other	53	38	22	15	12
	763	608	470	417	330
Less accumulated depreciation	176	129	98	58	26
Total fixed assets	587	479	372	359	304
Total Assets	2,272	1,868	1,464	868	598

Liabilities and Equity

	Last year	2 years ago	3 years ago	4 years ago	5 years ago
Current Liabilities:					
Notes payable	$ 325	$ 210	$ 150	$115	$ 50
Current installment of long-term debt	40	30	13	13	13
Accounts payable	276	217	147	107	40
Accrued expenses	323	256	168	114	55
Income taxes payable	155	127	78	45	24
Total current liabilities	1,119	840	556	394	182
Long-term debt:					
Mortgage on building	230	200	149	162	175
Less current installment	40	30	13	13	13
Total long-term debt	190	170	136	149	162
Stockholders' equity:					
Common stock—par value $1	300	300	300	200	200
Paid-in capital	275	275	275		
Retained earnings	388	283	197	125	54
Total stockholders' equity	963	858	772	325	254
Total Liabilities and Stockholders' Equity	2,272	1,868	1,464	868	598

BOARD MEMBERS' VIEWS

Banker Fairweather had the following things to say about Tom Reed and Reed Shoe Company: "If you want to understand Tom Reed you have to grasp some

TABLE 3
REED SHOE COMPANY OPERATING STATEMENTS
($000)

	Last year	2 years ago	3 years ago	4 years ago	5 years ago
Net sales	$5,185	$4,310	$3,057	$2,298	$1,150
Cost of goods sold	3,630	3,090	2,232	1,632	828
Gross profit	1,555	1,220	825	666	322
Expenses	1,043	828	546	528	248
Selling, administrative and general	931	738	469	463	207
Other	112	90	77	65	41
Income before income taxes	512	392	279	138	74
Federal and state income taxes	267	201	137	67	31
Net income	245	191	142	71	43
Dividends	140	105	70		
Transferred to retained earnings	105	86	72	71	43

fundamental things in his makeup. First, he has a good inventory of the kinds of personal resources that are absolutely essential for developing a business from scratch. He's ambitious for success, he has a lot of energy and drive, and he likes to get personally involved in every nook and cranny of operations. And he's capable, by which I mean that he understands what makes a business go, he sees the relationships between income and outgo, and he can motivate people. They like to work for him.

"He's always thinking bigger than where he is at any moment. When this business was barely launched he was thinking of hitting the $5 million sales mark. Now that he's accomplished that goal he's thinking about tripling it. And if he got to that target he'd be busy setting up a still bigger objective. That's a good thing in a manager. It can also be a bad thing, particularly if the problems generated by size and rapid growth begin to strain the management resources of the individual and his organization. And that's exactly where this business is right now.

"As to opportunities for the company, I think it is beginning to attain a size where further success will begin to take a little skin off some of the competition in the running shoe industry. There are some big animals in that industry. And they are not going to like Reed Shoe's taking business away from them, especially if the total market for the industry levels off or even shrinks, as I think there is a good chance of its doing. I'm not saying I think jogging is a fad that will disappear. But I believe there's a fair likelihood that it isn't going to grow much more and that it may well shrink. How far? Who knows? Even the cessation of growth will make the competition a lot stiffer than it has been so far. Shrinkage would really put pressure on the firms in the industry.

"But putting a brake on Tom's enthusiasm isn't easy. Our bank isn't eager about financing that kind of high-risk growth. I doubt that any other sensible banker would be. I've told Tom this, but I'm not sure he hears me because he doesn't want to hear me. I'm getting into a potentially awkward position. As a banker, I don't want to see a good customer like Reed Shoe overextend itself in a chancy market situation. As a director, with responsibility to non-manager stockholders, I'm disposed to urge caution. But as a friend of Tom Reed, I hate to see his ambition and desire constrained, and he probably would not accept such counsel. I can visualize his inviting me off the board if push comes to shove, and it's not clear what my proper course of action would be in such a situation."

John Beggs has a different view of the company's situation and prospects: "If there is one thing I've learned in my thirty years in business, it's to give encouragement to a capable manager who believes enthusiastically in his own ideas. You mustn't let a conservative banker throw cold water on his plans for growth, for invading new markets, for expanding and diversifying into new product areas. I've had to put up with a certain amount of that kind of restraint in my own operation and I can remember a couple of really glittering opportunities that got away from me as a result. I'd hate to see that happen to Tom. He's a real entrepreneur and he needs to be encouraged, not held back.

"Is the kind of growth he visualizes in the ways he plans to get it possible? Is it feasible? I think a qualified yes is not an unreasonable answer to both questions. The qualification is only partly a reflection of market uncertainties. There always are market uncertainties. The larger consideration in my judgment is Tom's ability to delegate responsibility. He probably talked to you—as he talked to us in board meetings—about bringing in experienced, qualified senior managers. There's no doubt in my mind that he needs such staff reinforcement. But there *is* a doubt about his ability to delegate to them, while retaining control.

"This is where a lot of successful small business people fail. I'm very sensitive to this problem because I faced it myself. Whether Tom can change his style is problematical. But he surely has a chance. I've been talking to him about it. I think he understands what's involved. And I'm in favor of supporting him if he wants to push ahead."

Hale Allyn's comments were in the following vein: "A common mistake I find among managers—especially among managers of small businesses like Reed Shoe—is to overestimate their competitive resource strengths and underestimate their resource weaknesses. They fall in love with their own products, especially if they invented them. And they're inclined to plan for the future on the assumption that they will make this or that advantageous innovation while competitors will keep on doing just what they have been doing. The result of this kind of thinking is always an attractive projection of successful growth. They don't recognize how critical their implicit assumption may be. And when competitors also innovate, the results turn out to be less cheerful than the anticipation.

"I think Tom is inclined to make both of these mistakes. The Reed running shoe is a very good product. But is it superior to its larger competitors—in the minds of consumers out there in the marketplace? I really doubt that it is. Does the company have the marketing muscle to fight for a growing share of consumer purchases? I doubt it. Are its production costs in line with competitors' costs? Its material costs? Its marketing costs? Here I have no doubt at all— they're not. At Reed's present and even near-future scale of operations they can't be.

"If you accept these judgments, then what explains the company's growth from ground zero to where it is now? Well, the whole market has been exploding in recent years. If you could place a product of even fair quality in a fair number of retail outlets in this kind of expanding market environment your sales would be bound to grow. But if the market stops growing, that situation will change. And that's where a 'me-too' product backed by a company that is relatively weak in promotional and distribution resources and operates at a substantial cost disadvantage starts to suffer. Is this what lies ahead for Reed Shoe? There's a real chance that it is.

"What about building growth on identifying and exploiting new markets, along the lines of Tom's ideas for other specialty-shoe applications, and also invading the market for standard shoes with a more comfortable and stylish substitute? They're interesting ideas all right and there may well be real market opportunities there. But what does Reed Shoe bring to the competitive battle that is superior to the resources the big companies in the running shoe business can commit? They probably see the same opportunities. And they start with existing resource advantages. They've got more money. They've got stronger brand recognition among consumers. They've got more extensive and more intensive retail distribution. They've got management depth. Tom's ideas may well be sound ones. But it's at least speculative whether he has or can acquire the resources to capitalize on them.

"Speaking as an outside director, before I'd be inclined to support Tom's ideas for continued rapid growth in the ways he sees that growth evolving, I'd like to get him to sit down and lay out a real thorough plan—a professional approach, rather than a dream made up of equal parts of hope, inspiration, and courage. I'd like to see a specific, bullet-biting analysis of comparative resource strengths and weaknesses. He could do this with the help of his board. The strategy should be detailed on paper. He should make an action program and a financial projection, too (how much money would be required when, and where it will come from in relation to internal cash flow and external supplements). This is a great way to separate dream from harsh reality.

"Tom has the ability to do this kind of planning. Does he have the discipline? He never has stood still long enough to start doing it. He ought to take the risk of delegating responsibility to his present management group to run the existing business 'as is' for at least a few months—they surely won't destroy it; it has good momentum—and focus close to 100 percent of his attention on some hard, realistic, detailed thinking about the future, with a view to developing just the kind of plan I've been describing. Put it on paper, not just words but numbers, too. Then he should review it with the board, after we've had a chance to study it. From that would come a plan we could have confidence in.

"Will he be willing to do this? Look, I've been his friend for a long time, and I honestly don't know. What I do know is that if he doesn't do it, I am one director who is not going to support him, and if this means resigning from his board, I'll resign. In the circumstances, it would be an act of pure friendship to do just that, but of course he might not see it that way."

Comprehensive Case 6

AMAX ALUMINUM COMPANY[1]

AMAX, Inc., faces a major question of what to do with its wholly-owned subsidiary, Amax Aluminum Company. The subsidiary has a voracious appetite for capital investment, but its earnings to date have been unimpressive. World developments in the aluminum industry cloud the future.

AMAX EXPANSION STRATEGY

AMAX deals with minerals and energy resources. At the time of this case, the end of 1973, it has $1.7 billion in assets and will report record sales of over $1.3 billion. The aluminum subsidiary accounts for 16 percent and 28 percent of these impressive sales.

Because Amax Aluminum competes for capital and attention with other subsidiaries of AMAX, a brief sketch of AMAX total operations is called for. The scope of the nonaluminum operations and the major expansions are summarized below.

AMAX has always dealt with several different metals since it was formed by the 1957 merger of the American Metals Company, Ltd., and the Climax Molybdenum Company. American Metals was a miner, processor, and trader of nonferrous metals and minerals, including copper, lead, zinc, precious metals, and potash. The company also held major investments in two large African copper mining concerns, but did not manage these concerns directly. A subsidiary owned and operated the largest secondary copper smelting facility in the United States.

In terms of sales, the Climax Molybdenum Company was barely a tenth the size of the American Metals Company, Ltd. at the time of the merger, but Climax's earnings were almost 90 percent those of the American Metals Company. The source of Climax's earnings was the huge Climax, Colorado molybdenum mine, which in 1957 supplied almost half of the non-Communist world demand for molybdenum. Molybdenum is a vital ingredient for many types of high-strength hard steel alloys.

Following the merger AMAX diversified even more. In 1963, AMAX gained

---

[1]This case is based primarily on two much longer cases, AMAX-MITSUI (A) and (B), prepared by Edward M. Graham and Yoshihiro Tsurumi (ICCH Numbers 9-375-350 and 9-375-388). It is positioned in late 1973.

claim to a major deposit of high-grade ore at Mt. Newman in Western Australia. By 1956, it was determined that at least one billion tons of ore was recoverable from the Mt. Newman location. In 1967, final agreements were made for a consortium of American, Australian, British, and Japanese companies to create a joint venture to exploit Mt. Newman. AMAX would hold 25 percent equity paticipation in the venture. One of AMAX's partners in the consortium included, Mitsuitoh Pty., a joint venture of two Japanese trading companies, Mitsui and C. Itoh. Mitsuitoh held 10 percent of the project. This was the first time in history that Japanese interests participated in a major Australian minerals venture.

In 1969, AMAX acquired the Ayrshire Colleries Corporation, an independent coal-producing company in the United States. The acquisition of Ayrshire, accomplished by exchange of AMAX preferred stock for Ayrshire common, gave AMAX control over large reserves of coal located largely in the Midwest and in Wyoming and the Rocky Mountain area.

In 1973, by exchange of AMAX preferred stock for the acquired companies' common stock, AMAX acquired the Banner Mining Company and the affiliated Tintic Standard Mining Company. These companies owned a large copper ore deposit in Arizona. The ore body was leased by the Anaconda Company, which operated a large copper mine to exploit the body. AMAX for years had sought to engage in copper mining in the United States. At the time of the acquisition of Banner and Tintic, AMAX formed a partnership with Anaconda, to be named the Anamax Company, to expand the mine.

An AMAX executive who played a major role in the expansion and diversification of AMAX's activities was Ian MacGregor. Following the 1957 merger, Mr. MacGregor was made vice-president in charge of new business development and in this role he led AMAX's efforts to establish itself in the aluminum industry. Later, as chief executive officer, he played a key role in the formation of the Mt. Newman consortium and oversaw the acquisitions of the Ayrshire, Banner, Tintic Standard companies. A native of Scotland, Mr. MacGregor's first job was in British Aluminum's management training program. His early experience with the British Aluminum industry was to be very valuable to Mr. MacGregor in his career with AMAX.

Most of these developments involved joint ventures. Often the economical size of operation was so large that no one company wanted to invest the necessary capital in a single venture. In other siutations, a partner was needed to assure markets or managerial skill. In the natural resource area, such coalitions are common.

ENTRY INTO ALUMINUM INDUSTRY

During the first years of its existence, AMAX was able to generate earnings faster than it could reinvest them. In 1960, for example, earnings after tax were

$41 million, while dividends and capital expenditures less depreciation were $24 million.

In order to utilize its growing liquid assets, AMAX management asked Mr. MacGregor in 1960 to investigate new businesses that the company might enter. The objective was to find businesses which would provide the company with greater long-term growth potential than existing investment opportunities, but which were congruent with the company's expertise in minerals and metallurgy.

Analysis by Mr. MacGregor and his associates indicated (1) that the long-run growth potential of the aluminum industry was greater and the prospective return on investment higher than those of other major metals and minerals based industries. Moreover, economic studies showed (2) that the existing integrated aluminum companies in North America were more highly leveraged than were most other American manufacturing companies, and the possibility existed that these aluminum firms would experience difficulty in financing the expansion of capacity required to serve a growing demand for aluminum products. Thus, MacGregor believed that new entry could occur in the aluminum industry without disrupting the stability of the industry.

Entry into the industry did pose some problems, however:

1. "Upstream" aluminum companies (bauxite mining, alumina production, and primary aluminum reduction), which were generally more profitable than "downstream" operations, were highly capital intensive and the minimum scale for economic operations was very large.[2]
2. Entry at the level of bauxite mining or alumina production appeared virtually impossible. The known reserves of bauxite in the early 1960s were almost entirely controlled by the established integrated companies—ALCOA (U.S.), ALCAN (Canada), Reynolds (U.S.), Pechiney (France), Kaiser (U.S.), and Alusuisse (Swiss)—and these companies were not eager to share their bauxite operations with a major new entrant.
3. Entry at the level of primary reduction was only slightly less problematic. Over 85 percent of primary reduction capacity in North America was controlled by ALCOA, ALCAN, Reynolds, and Kaiser. There was no free market for alumina, and hence the alumina for a primary reduction mill would have to be purchased from the integrated producers. Because a primary aluminum reduction facility must be operated continuously, even a brief interruption in the supply of alumina could result in severe adverse effects on the economics of operating the facility.
4. The aluminum industry had historically been subject to cycles of undercapacity and overcapacity. Were AMAX to construct and operate integrated "upstream" facilities but fail to establish a secure market for its output of ingot, during a period of overcapacity AMAX might have to "dump" its ingot at distress prices.

---

[2]The main stages in aluminum production are: (1) Mining of bauxite (aluminum ore), (2) concentrating and transforming the bauxite into alumina, (3) "primary reduction" of alumina into ingots of 99.5 percent pure aluminum, (4) conversion of ingots into foil, wire, sheet, bars, and other extrusions. Scrap aluminum is refined by "secondary reduction," and then moves into stage (4).

A tentative conclusion of MacGregor was that if AMAX were to enter the aluminum business, its first thrust should be into "downstream" operations via acquisitions of existing businesses. "Downstream" the industry was less concentrated and less capital intensive than "upstream" but also less profitable. However, once a "downstream" market share had been firmly established, the company could integrate "upstream."

An opportunity to enter the aluminum industry via "downstream" acquisition came in 1962, when the U.S. Department of Justice blocked the proposed acquisition of the Kawneer Company by Kaiser Aluminum and Chemical Company and the proposed acquisition of the Apex Smelting Company by ALCAN. Kawneer was one of the nation's leading fabricators of architectural aluminum products supplied to the commercial construction industry. Apex was a leading secondary smelter of aluminum whose main business was to produce aluminum alloys from processed scrap.

AMAX was able to reach an agreement with the owners of Apex and Kawneer to merge their companies into AMAX. These companies not only provided an initial entry for AMAX into the aluminum business, but also provided AMAX with technical personnel experienced in aluminum operations.

Further "downstream" expansion took place the following year when AMAX acquired the Hunter Engineering Co. Hunter was a major producer of aluminum siding for the mobile home industry and of other mill products.

Having secured a "downstream" base in the aluminum industry, Mr. MacGregor began to consider thrusts toward "upstream" integration. Of paramount importance was to secure a supply of alumina.

The first effort failed. A consortium led by Kaiser Aluminum was being formed in 1963 to exploit the underdeveloped Gladstone bauxite deposits in Queensland, Australia, but MacGregor was initially unable to convince the partners in the consortium to allow AMAX to join.

A second chance to gain access to the Gladstone alumina arose when Mr. MacGregor learned that Howmet Corporation was considering building a primary reduction plant in the state of Washington. Howmet, a recent U.S. acquisition of Pechiney of France, wished to integrate backward for the same reasons as AMAX. But Howmet's needs could not keep a primary reduction plant of economical size busy. So Howmet and AMAX joined in a 50-50 venture—the construction of a 228,000-ton plant which cost over $150 million. The special appeal here was that Pechiney, Howmet's parent, was a member of the Gladstone consortium and could provide the new venture with Gladstone alumina!

Acutally, ALCOA of Australia found that it had excess capacity on its western Australia alumina plant, and it was glad to sign a long-term contract with AMAX to supply alumina to the new plant.

So by 1965 AMAX was, indeed, an integrated producer of aluminum. But it was buying rather than producing its own alumina. At that time all its aluminum operations were consolidated in a single company, Amax Aluminum Company. This new company has continued to expand its sheet, extrusion, and other "downstream" capacity. The growth of Amax Aluminum Company and its current financial position is shown in Tables 1 and 2. In just eleven years Amax has moved from zero to a significant position in the industry.

TABLE 1.
AMAX ALUMINUM COMPANY INCOME STATEMENTS, 1969–1973
($ millions)

	1969	1970	1971	1972	1973
Sales	280	277	287	311	373
Costs & operating expenses	217	219	232	249	296
Selling & general expenses	25	27	28	30	31
Depreciation & amortization	9	10	11	11	11
Taxes, other than income taxes	4	4	5	5	5
Earnings from operations	25	17	11	16	30
Other expense & income, net	2	2	1	1	2
Income taxes	12	7	4	6	12
Net earnings	11	8	6	9	16

TABLE 2.
AMAX ALUMINUM COMPANY BALANCE SHEET, Dec. 31, 1973
($ million)

Assets		Liabilities & Equity	
Cash & equivalent	2.7	Current liabilities	48.8
Accounts receivable, net	71.5	Long-term obligations due to AMAX, Inc.	20.0
Inventories	59.2		
Other current assets	.31		
Total current assets	136.5	Total liabilities & equity	68.8
Investments in 50% owned companies, at equity	9.9	Shareholders equity	200.6
Plant & equipment, net	119.4		
Other assets	3.6		
Total assets	269.4	Total liabilities & equity	269.4

Two additional bold moves by Amax Aluminum are still pending. One is the mining of bauxite and production of alumina in a newly discovered site at Kimberley, Western Australia. This is planned as a huge operation costing around $750 million, with an annual output of alumina large enough to equal the entire demand of Japan in 1975. But Amax Aluminum has not yet been able to muster the consortium large enough to support the venture, partly because of an excess capacity situation in the aluminum industry in the early 1970s. (The list price of primary aluminum actually declined from $.27 per pound in 1967 to $.25 in 1972.)

The second plan involves a 50-50 joint venture with the Mitsui Company, Ltd., of Japan, for the construction of a primary aluminum reduction facility in Northwestern Orgeon. This plant would have an annual capacity of 187,000 tons, and cost at least $250 million. A contract for power from the Bonneville Power Administration has been signed and construction was about to start when a dispute with the State government of Oregon over environmental aspects arose. Late in 1973, it was unclear if and when this project would move ahead.

AMAX PORTFOLIO PROBLEM

In the autumn of 1973, Mr. MacGregor reluctantly told Mr. Robert Marcus, executive vice-president of Amax Aluminum, that the board of directors of the parent company, AMAX, Inc., probably would not provide funds for the continuing growth of the aluminum subsidiary. Both Mr. Marcus and Mr. MacGregor, now head of AMAX, Inc., had worked strenuously to build the aluminum company to its present position.

The change in heart arises from two considerations—(1) the portfolio squeeze which AMAX, Inc., faces, and (2) new doubts about the outlook for the aluminum industry.

From 1967 on, substantial capital commitments were required by AMAX in its operations outside the aluminum subsidiary. The Mt. Newman iron ore mine began operations in 1967, and over the four years 1967–1971 required well over $100 million from AMAX, 25 percent owner of the mine. By 1971 the mine had become the largest single supplier of iron ore to Japan.

In 1967 the Urad Mine, an old molybdenum mine located about thirty miles north of Climax, Colorado, was reopened, requiring $25 million in capital investment over the years 1967–1971. In the longer term, AMAX was developing a third Colorado molybdenum mine to exploit reserves discovered in 1965. This mine, Henderson Mine, when it comes onstream in the mid to late 1970s, will rival the Climax mine in yearly output. It will require capital expenditures of upwards of $400 million over a five to eight year period beginning in about 1971. Also, "downstream" molybdenum processing facilities are in need of modernization and expansion. Through the 1970s the expansion and modernization of molybdenum operations are expected to cost AMAX at least $500 million.

Additional capital is needed to expand coal production. By 1972, AMAX had become the fifth largest producer of coal in the United States. In 1973, shipments began from the new Belle Ayr South mine in Wyoming and the new Ayrshire and Wabash mines in Indiana. By the end of 1973, over $65 million had been spent on coal mine expansion and development of new mines, and through the remainder of the 1970s over $200 million more is due to be spent.

AMAX expects to incur other capital costs through the 1970s. Purchase and rehabilitation of a zinc plant in Illinois is budgeted at $26 million. Entry into the nickel business has long been sought by AMAX, and acquisition and rehabilitation of a nickel refinery in Louisiana is budgeted at $53 million.

The effect of so much expansion of activities has resulted in capital expenditures tripling between 1967 and 1973, as shown in Table 3. As is indicated, total yearly capital expenditures exceeded net cash flow after dividends during these years, requiring AMAX to raise outside capital. The resulting capital structure is shown in Table 4. Stockholders equity is now less than half of total assets. Long-term obligations are about 75 percent of equity, which is high for a mining company.

TABLE 3.
CAPITAL DEFICITS OF AMAX, 1967–1973
($ millions)

	1967	1968	1969	1970	1971	1972	1973
Internal sources of capital:							
Earnings after taxes	57	69	82	73	55	66	105
Depreciation & amortization	57	25	27	37	39	42	48
Total	78	94	109	110	94	108	153
Uses of capital:							
Dividends paid	30	30	32	36	36	37	45
Increases in working capital	22	2	-6	26	83	41	-12
Capital expenditures & acquisitions	86	103	147	189	142	157	265
Total	138	135	173	251	261	235	298
Deficits of internal sources	−60	−41	−64	−141	−167	−127	−145

AMAX's board of directors now feel that the investment opportunities open to the corporation outstrip its ability to raise capital. So, recently the board has been putting pressure on Mr. MacGregor (now CEO) to limit future expenditures only to those areas which have the highest potential return on investment.

The success of the various sectors of AMAX's portfolio is indicated in Table 5. From 1969 through 1973, most sectors have grown faster than aluminum in sales volume, and all have outstripped it in profitability related to sales. Even in 1973, a good year for most businesses after price controls were removed, Amax Aluminum earned only 8 percent on stockholders equity (see Tables 1 and 2).

Clearly, a picture of unusually favorable prospects for aluminum will be necessary if Amax Aluminum is to take priority for capital over other sectors of AMAX's portfolio.

TABLE 4.
AMAX, INC., BALANCE SHEET DEC. 31, 1973
($ millions)

Assets		Liabilities & Equity	
Cash equivalent	288	Current liabilities	257
Accounts Receivable, net	193	Long-term debt	441
Inventories	178	Reserves & other long-term liabilities	174
Other current assets	13		
Total current assets	672	Total liabilities	872
Plant & equipment, net	890	Stock & paid in capital	289
Other long-term assets	150	Retained earnings	551
Total assets	1,712	Total liabilities & equity	1,712

TABLE 5.
AMAX SALES AND EARNINGS BY PRODUCT LINE

	1969	1970	1971	1972	1973
Sales (in $ millions)					
Molybdenum & Specialty Metals	155	145	108	114	179
Copper, Lead, Zinc	275	294	215	270	571
Fuels	19	98	96	119	134
Iron Ore	8	25	39	45	60
Chemicals	21	23	27	20	22
Aluminum	280	277	287	311	373
Total Company	758	862	772	879	1,339
Ratio of Earnings from Operations to Sales*					
Molybdenum & Specialty Metals	35%	36%	26%	25%	26%
Copper, Lead, Zinc	6	6	4	8	13
Fuels	5	10	14	16	13
Iron Ore	50	52	59	56	63
Chemicals	-5	17	15	25	27
Aluminum	9	6	4	5	8
Total company	12%	13%	11%	13%	16%

*Earnings from Operations are before income tax, exploration expense, and unallocated corporate expense. Exploration and corporate expenses are about 5 percent of sales.

OUTLOOK FOR ALUMINUM INDUSTRY

The basic aluminum industry has experienced significant growth during the post-World War II period, as is reflected in Table 6. Worldwide expansion has been even more impressive than in the United States.

TABLE 6.
TRENDS IN U.S. BASIC ALUMINUM INDUSTRY
1950–1973
(thousands of tons, except price)

	Primary Production	Recovery from Scrap	Metal Imports	Metal Exports	Price Primary Ingots
1950	719	228	177	11	$.16.6 per pound
1955	1,566	334	178	21	.21.9 '' ''
1960	2,015	407	153	37	.26.0 '' ''
1965	2,755	769	527	65	.24.5 '' ''
1970	3,976	940	350	79	.28.7 '' ''
1973	4,530	1,060	508	230	.25.3 '' ''

Demand for aluminum in the United States is closely tied to general business conditions. As Table 7 indicates, growth in demand depends on growth in construction, automobile production, use of two-piece aluminum cans, extension of electric power lines, and a wide variety of other uses.

Because of very high fixed costs required for the production of aluminum, and the need for continuous production once a reduction plant is in operation, manufacturers press hard to sell their full capacity. Thus, even a small excess capacity above demand tends to drive down selling prices. Contrarily, when demand exceeds capacity, prices tend to move up substantially.

The demand and supply balance is a worldwide issue. While normally local demand is met by local production (at least in the industrialized countries), aluminum will be shipped from country to country when large price differentials develop. The countries which participate in this game are shown in Table 8.

TABLE 7.
U.S. ALUMINUM SHIPMENTS TO MAJOR MARKETS,
1973

	% share of total tons
Building-Construction	25
Transportation	20
Consumer durables	8
Electrical	13
Machinery & equipment	7
Containers & packaging	14
Miscellaneous	6
Total domestic	93
Exports, metal & products	7
Total shipments	100

TABLE 8.
WORLD PRODUCTION OF PRIMARY ALUMINUM BY COUNTRIES–1973*
(1,000 metric tons)

U.S.	5,077
Japan	1,574
U.S.S.R.	1,480
West Germany	856
U.K.	487
France	450
Other European countries	849
Canada	332

*Figures in the table are not exactly comparable with those in Table 6 and 10, due to differences in definitions, metric versus short tons, etc. However, comparisons *within* each table are reliable for our purposes.

Reliable information on effective capacity for primary aluminum production is hard to obtain, especially from countries such as U.S.S.R. One estimate of current world capacity is 12.6 million tons per annum. However, we do know that even companies such as ALCOA rarely run at capacity except for brief periods; in 1973, ALCOA ran at 94 percent both in the U.S. and worldwide. Informed estimates are that, if past consumption trends continue, there will be a worldwide shortage of capacity by 1978. Within the United States, consumption may outrun capacity even earlier unless new capacity is constructed. A few proposed new plants have been announced, the largest being the projected Amax Aluminum-Mitsui plant in Oregon; but all of these are subject to environmental clearances, availability of power as anticipated, and so on.

The costs of purchased inputs are rising. Between 1970 and 1973, for example, in the U.S. aluminum industry, salaries and wages have risen 36 percent, purchased materials 8 percent, and energy 24 percent. Government controls on selling prices created a cost-price squeeze in early 1973, and only larger volume enabled companies to improve their overall results for the year. However, with the removal of controls, prices had jumped 25 percent by December, and further substantial increases are expected.

The aluminum industry is concentrated but nonetheless highly competitive. The major companies in primary production in North American are listed in Table 9. Although the Amax Aluminum venture is number five on the list, the volume is far behind the leaders. ALCOA, the U.S. leader, earned only 4 to 5 percent on invested capital during 1969–1974. (The "experience curve" did not work out here because Amax Aluminum with only a small fraction of ALCOA's experience has done somewhat better.)

Outside the United States, the largest aluminum producer is clearly Pechiney of France. Its total revenues for all kinds of products in 1973 will be close to $3 billion. Pechiney along with the companies listed in Table 9 account for about 60 percent of world capacity for primary aluminum. Companies fully as large as Amax Aluminum are operating in Japan, Switzerland, Belgium, Norway, and West Germany. All such companies face the same economic pressure to operate as near capacity as possible.

TABLE 9.
PRIMARY PRODUCTION OF MAJOR NORTH AMERICIAN ALUMINUM
COMPANIES,
1973
(in thousands of tons)

ALCAN (Canadian)	1676
ALCOA (U.S.)	1652
Reynolds	1084
Kaiser	847
Intalco*	228
Anaconda	218

*Owned 50-50 by Amax Aluminum and Howmet.

AMAX ALTERNATIVES

AMAX has several alternatives in the action it may take with regard to Amax Aluminum and still live within its general objective of making no further investment in aluminum activities.

1. *Maintain the status quo.* This would involve reinvesting depreciation so as to maintain equipment, but any new ventures would have to call for very small amounts of capital. Basically Amax Aluminum would simply wait for improvements in industry conditions, realizing that some loss in market position would probably occur as more aggressive competitors made new thrusts.

2. *Set up Amax Aluminum as a quasi-independent company.* The aim here would be to decentralize financing as well as operating management. Amax Aluminum would be free to go directly to the capital markets for such long-term loans or other advantages as it could justify. Probably, to make this arrangement viable, the current debt Amax Aluminum now owes its parent, AMAX, would be converted into equity. This would give Amax Aluminum much more flexibility in rearranging its capital structure. Amax Aluminum would "paddle its own canoe." This might increase the risk for the common stockholder (AMAX), but presumably would also increase the potential long-run value of the stock.

3. *Sell the entire company.* This would not only stop a capital drain but actually increase the funds AMAX has available to invest in other sectors of its portfolio. The question here is who might buy Amax Aluminum and why? The company has over a quarter of a billion dollars in assets. Few potential buyers have the cash of this amount to invest in a single aluminum enterprise. Large

U.S. aluminum companies (and probably Pechiney) would be prevented from buying a competitor because of antitrust laws. The big mining concerns have attractive alternatives just AMAX does. Amax Aluminum's earnings record is scarcely one that will excite the very large institutional investors. So finding an eager buyer will not be easy.

4. *Look for a partner, or partners, with lots of capital.* Investors and owners of mineral deposits often follow this approach. The new investors provide the capital necessary to make the moves which will bring the venture to economic fruition. Of course, with the addition of each new partner the original owner's share of the total pie goes down. If Amax Aluminum is to continue the kind of aggressive course which has built it present position, sources of large amounts of capital must be found.

Other alternatives, or some combination of the above types, must be explored. The evaluation of each will be strongly influenced, of course, by the specific "deal" that can be negotiated. Also, an assessment of the future prospects for aluminum, and AMAX's continuing interest—if any—in Amax Aluminum must be weighed.

POSSIBLE DEAL WITH MITSUI

One evening recently in a Manhattan restaurant, Mr. MacGregor and Mr. Marcus (executive vice-president of Amax Aluminum) were talking about the future of Amax Aluminum, a subject they had discussed many times before. Marcus had been reviewing the reasons why he continued to be optimistic about long-run propects, and then the conversation turned to possible buyers of the company.

"I have considered approaching Pechiney," commented MacGregor. "The problem is, I am not sure that they would be able to buy in cash. We would want cash—we need it—and they are not extremely liquid."

"Maybe a Japanese firm would be willing to buy us," ventured Marcus.

"Why would one want to?" asked MacGregor.

"Well, when I was over there talking to Mitsui about the Oregon plant, I had the distinct feeling that they badly wanted sources of aluminum outside of Japan," said Marcus.

Out of that exchange has come a decision to carefully consider Mitsui as a potential buyer. With so much at stake, a "key-actor" analysis is obviously called for.

Mitsui Company, Ltd., is one of the ten largest general trading firms in Japan. Each of these firms deals in a broad array of goods and services; a popular (and correct) Japanese saying is, "General trading companies handle everything from peanuts to guided missles." While there are some 5,000 trading firms in Japan, the ten largest do 80 percent of the trading volume. Their combined annual turnover corresponds to 30 percent of the Japanese Gross National Product.

Within Japan, a general trading company traditionally (1) markets the output of its manufacturing company clients, (2) procures raw materials for its clients, (3) helps finance inventories and accounts receivable. The company may also transport, warehouse, insure, and provide other services to manufacturing clients and to distributors. Internationally, the general trading companies are the main marketing organizations for worldwide exports, and the main procurement agencies for imports—here again with a full array of services to facilitate international movement of goods. In addition, they use their very extensive telecommunication systems to make all sorts of commodity trades which have no connection with the Japanese economy. Incidentally, the competition between the general trading companies themselves is very keen.

The dominant position of the general trading companies, however, is eroding. As manufacturing firms have become larger and financially stronger, they are taking over more of their own procurement and marketing. Especially the firms selling products which require technical services to consumers, such as color TV sets and automobiles, obtain better results by closer relationships with users. The general trading companies are so diversified that they lack the specialized knowledge and interest that is desirable for complex products.

The general trading companies, such as Mitsui, have tried to counteract this lessening of interest in their traditional role by taking on manufacturing activities themselves. Being well aware of growth in demand for new materials and products, and where shortages are likely to arise, the trading companies have stepped in to fill the gaps. In the international arena, much of the attention has been in mining and oil because Japan is notably lacking in natural mineral resources.

Production of primary aluminum has had rapid growth in Japan, expanding more than threefold in the last eight years, as shown in Table 10. Mitsubishi, the largest general trading company, entered the field in 1963 and within ten years has expanded to become third in the industry. Mitsui, its rival, did not enter until 1968 and still occupies a minor position. The current capacity of the five primary producers is given in Table 11.

TABLE 10.
PRIMARY ALUMINUM PRODUCTION IN JAPAN
(thousands of tons)

1966	373	1970	930
1967	517	1971	983
1968	611	1972	1,221
1969	819	1973	1,355

Even with the past expansion in capacity, the Japanese aluminum industry has been plagued with a chronic shortage of ingots during 1973. There are at least 300 firms engaged in fabricating aluminum, and the scramble for domestic

TABLE 11.
CAPACITY OF JAPANESE PRIMARY ALUMINUM PRODUCERS, 1973
(tons per annum)

Nippon Light Metals*	380,000
Sumitomo Chemicals	377,000
Mitsubishi Chemicals	217,000
Showa Denko	261,000
Mitsui Aluminum	83,000
Total primary capacity in Japan	1,372,000

*Nippon Light Metals is 50 percent owned by ALCAN of Canada, and through this connection has access to ALCAN's bauxite. All the other companies must negotiate long-term contracts for bauxite or alumina from foreign suppliers. There is no domestic bauxite, and no general trading company or producer has its own captive source of bauxite or alumina anywhere in the world.

or imported ingots has been wild. Against such a background, Mr. Marcus hopes Mitsui will show an interest in Amax Aluminum.

There are no announced plans for expanding primary aluminum capacity within Japan, in spite of the supply and demand situation just cited. Probably a major restraint is air pollution. As Japan has industrialized and greatly increased the number of automobiles on the road, pollution has become serious. With its large population, new industrial sites are scarce. And unless a nonpolluting source of electricity can be developed, government officials are unlikely to approve major additions to present reduction plants.

The Japanese government, largely through the powerful Ministry of International Trade and Industry (MITI), will have to endorse plans of any Japanese company to invest in the aluminum industry at home or abroad. MITI seeks an orderly development of the entire economy. In this connection, it would like to reduce dependence on foreign producers for basic raw materials.

The government is under several other pressures which have a bearing on what Mitsui will be permitted to do. Japan has been exporting more than it imports, leading to very large accumulations of foreign exchange. To correct this trade imbalance, other national governments are putting pressure on Japan to relax obstacles to imports and to invest abroad with much less eagerness. The Japanese government naturally is concerned about the impact of any such moves on domestic employment, especially since *lifetime* employment is a pillar in Japanese personnel practices.

A foreign investment of the size necessary to buy Amax Aluminum, or even half of it, will certainly require MITI's O.K. A variety of large commitments for foreign raw materials have been made, but through 1973 no investment even approaching the potential Amax Aluminum magnitude has been made for the processing of materials outside of Japan. If consummated, the transaction would represent the largest direct investment in the United States by a Japanese corporation in history.

So, the proposal Mr. Marcus is trying to develop would have to clear at least three hurdles. (1) The investment must be endorsed by MITI, in terms of Japan's national interests. (2) Mitsui must consider the investment an attractive business proposition, consistent with its general objectives. (3) AMAX must consider the price it receives more attractive than holding or disposing of the assets in some other way.

"Remember," Mr. MacGregor said to Mr. Marcus, "you will have to convince Mitsui that the company is more attractive to them than it is to us. And, they have an even wider range of portfolio alternatives than we do. From our angle, shares of stock in aluminum companies are now selling at about book value. Our ROI is better than most, so I think we should get a premium over book value."

APPENDIX A

History of Mitsui

The house of Mitsui is one of Japan's oldest business firms, marking its humble beginnings in 1616. At that time, the Mitsui family belonged to the samurai class of warrior noblemen, with the head of the family holding the title of Lord of Echigo, in Japan's feudalistic system. A long period of warring had just recently come to an end, causing Mitsui Sokubei Takatoshi, the latest heir to the Mitsui peerage, to reflect deeply upon the future of the Japanese society. He reasoned that if a long period of peace were to be forthcoming, the foundations of the samurai class, which were based on war, would be undermined significantly. He decided, therefore, that the future of his family lay not in the nobility but in what he saw as the next emerging elite, the merchant class.

Not long after the Meiji Restoration (which is what the defeat of the shogunate and the 1868 reinstallation of the emperor is called), Japan was fully involved in its own industrial revolution. For its base primarily as a financial institution, Mitsui added various manufacturing firms, creating a group of companies which were centered around the bank. As the output from these manufacturing firms continued to grow, the importance of the trading function of the group increased accordingly. Mitsui Bussan Kaisha Ltd., which was formed in 1878 as the trading arm, was charged with the responsibility of obtaining for Mitsui's firm, and other manufacturing firms, the necessary goods for production, and then marketing those goods both domestically and internationally. These products included mostly textiles and machinery. The Mitsui Group was granted large coal interests by the Meiji regime. This placed the Mitsui Bussan in the center of both domestic and international trading activities in the metal and chemical areas.

To facilitate scouting out and taking advantage of business opportunities around the world, Mitsui Bussan built a strong information system on an international level, an information network that is still a major factor in Mitsui's success today. In the aftermath of the Russo-Japanese War, 1904–05, Mitsui Bussan expanded into a number of investments in the "Yen Bloc," which incuded Japan, Manchuria, Korea, and later much of the rest of the Chinese Mainland. With the predominant position in the Yen Bloc, and with a strong foothold in the rest of the world, the firm was by far the largest general trading firm in Japan, conducting, in 1932, 13 percent of Japan's total foreign trade, and more than 50 percent of Japanese transactions of some commodities, such as coal and machinery. The House of Mitsui had business connections with literally hundreds of firms in Japan. The core group, controlled by a holding company, Mitsui Honsha, was composed of "ten 'first line' subsidiaries, thirteen 'second line' subsidiaries, as well as more than eighty listed sub-subsidiaries, in 1942. In addition, there were whole sub-empires including textile, cement, paper, automotive, and electrical interests] in which Mitsui had substantial interests but wished to keep separate from the Honsha structure."[3]

The Japanese defeat in World War II
changed the shape of the House of Mitsui dramatically, as it did for all the "zaibatsu" (the fully integrated mammoth industrial concerns). Citing excessive monopolism as the largest problem of Japanese society, the Supreme Commander for Allied Forces in the Pacific (SCAP), General Douglas MacArthur, ordered in 1946 the holding companies of the zaibatsu to dismantle operations, and limited the size and scope of the subsidiaries.

The Reemergence of General Trading Firms after World War II[4]

The fact that the large general trading companies had acquired such an expertise in international trade was a major factor in their resurgence after the war. International trade after the war evolved in several steps. From 1945 to 1947, the Allied General Headquarters (GHQ) handled the imports and exports for defeated Japan. The GHQ imported products and channelled them to the International Trade Agency of the Japanese government, which in turn rationed them to the various companies. In order to obtain imported products for the purpose of resale in Japan, the trading firms that were allowed to operate competed fiercely to handle products outside of their traditional lines of business. At this point, the only skill needed by the trading firm was the ability to file and process the proper procurement and sales forms with the Government.

As a result of this move toward taking on products outside the traditional scope of given trading firms, some firms established different departments for

---

[3]John G. Roberts, *Mitsui: Three Centuries of Japanese Business* (New York: Weatherhill, 1973), p. 354.

[4]Based on accounts contained in Yoshi Tsurumi, *The Japanese Are Coming: A Multinational Interaction of Firms & Politics* (Cambridge, Massachusetts: Ballinger Publishing Co., 1976).

the handling of different products, in anticipation of the re-establishment of private trading. Private trading, it was hoped, would include not only imports, but exports of machinery and chemical products as war reparation payments to Japan's Asian neighbors.

In 1948, a relaxation of the restrictions against private international trading came about, but because of the severe dollar shortage in Japan, the importers in Japan were forced to conclude many barter deals. In exchange for crude sugar, products such as ammonium sulphate fertilizer, iron slabs, and whale oil were exported. Accordingly, in order to survive, the trading firms had to develop both the internal communications network and the outside contracts to offer barter deals more quickly than their competitors. This pressure also caused many of the fragmented, single-line trading companies to merge.

The next step in the evolutionary process which saw the full re-emergence of the general trading firm was the establishment of the "Linking Trade" policy by the Japanese government. In order to encourage trading firms to export manufactured goods vital to Japan's development, the government, in 1953, began to link these exports to import licenses of the lucrative consumer and luxury-type goods. Such things as whiskey importation were linked to a firm's achieving its export quota of chemical and heavy manufacturers. This policy, which lasted into the late '50s, caused an even greater diversification of product line for the trading firms, and because quotas of goods were involved, inevitably led to a stronger concentration among trading companies.

The Linking Trade policy was not singularly responsible for this concentration, however. A series of severe "downs" in the business cycle in Japan forced many of the more poorly capitalized trading firms into bankruptcy. The need to find capital with which trading firms could expand into different product lines, often through merger with smaller companies, also caused considerable concentration. Mitsui Bank, along with the banks of the other former *zaibatsu* groups, helped their respective trading companies over the financial crunch. That crunch was indeed formidable, in that the average gross margin during this period was 2 to 3 percent, while selling and administrative expenses of trader's firms amounted to around 1.3 percent of gross sales. Average collection days of receivables were around 110 days. Even a slight downturn in the economy and the performance of a trading company's customers could cause bankruptcy.

Mitsui's own resurrection occurred within this context. After the war, the many trading departments of Mitsui Bussan were split apart and the managers of the individual departments started their own single line trading firms. Because the GHQ prohibited the use of the old *zaibatsu* names, there was no official "Mitsui Bussan" immediately after the war. As the business environment changed, and multiline businesses became necessary, the former Mitsui departments merged into five large groups, headed by a Mitsui manager. Contacts were kept close between the former members of the group. It was in 1958 that Mitsui & Co. (Mitsui Bussan Kaisha) was formally re-established.

Present Activities of Mitsui

Fortune's lists of the largest industrial corporations and largest banks outside the United States give an indication of the present activities and size of Mitsui interests.

Mitsui & Co.	Sales	Net Income	Employees
Mitsui Mining & Smelting[1]	$ 868 million	$ 11 million	12,721
Mitsui Petrochemicals	526 million	(15 million)	4,804
Mitsui Engineering & Shipbuilding	1.01 billion	40 million	16,319
Mitsui Toatsu Chemicals	939 million	1 million	9,511
Mitsui Mining[2]	734 million	2 million	1,680

[1]Nonferrous metal refining.
[2]Coal mining.

Mitsui Bank is ranked 18th among the largest banks outside the United States with assets of $27 billion, loans of $14 billion, net income of $46 million, and stockholder's equity of $586 million.

Comprehensive Case 7

SCI-TECH ASSOCIATES[1]

When Jane Sherrill left the office of president Carl Thompson of Cyril Electronics, Inc., last March, she knew that she had just been handed the greatest opportunity of her life. What she didn't know was whether it would be an opportunity for a major advance in her career or an opportunity to fall on her face.

The opportunity just handed Sherrill was the presidency of Sci-Tech Associates, a small electronic components company located in El Monte, California. Cyril had recently acquired Sci-Tech from its three owner-managers in an exchange-of-stock transaction. "We bought this company," Thompson told her, "for two reasons. Number one, they supply us with two components that are critically important to our business—patented items not available from other suppliers—and they have repeatedly fouled up delivery schedules. Also, their quality control has been erratic. We need what they make, but we can't tolerate their shipping failures and their slipshod production and inspection standards. And neither can their other customers for the same components. Number two, we think they have outstanding scientific and engineering capabilities but weak management. We think we can turn the business around and make a fine return on our investment. At the same time, we can solve the problems they've been creating for us. Your assignment is to do both of these jobs."

JANE SHERRILL

Sherrill is a confident, tough manager. She had, in effect, run away from a very conservative home to attend a large university—working and borrowing to pay expenses. This experience removed any trace of the "dependent female" syndrome. She decided that she could get ahead fastest by obtaining a master's degree from Columbia University's business school, with a major in marketing. Finding an attractive job, however, proved to be more difficult than she expected. Due to an economic slowdown the year she graduated, job offers were scarce; also she sensed that being a female with only campus work experience did not impress recruiters with the drive that she felt.

[1]This case is based on two longer cases on Sci-Tech Associates written by Professor Melvin Anshen, Graduate School of Business, Columbia University.

The one company that showed a strong and persistent interest in her was Cyril Electronics. Surprised, because she had understood that this Fort Custer, Michigan, company insisted on an undergraduate engineering degree together with an M.B.A., Sherrill suspected that Cyril was out to hire at least one woman. A company visit revealed that the company had no women as managers nor as engineers. Nevertheless, the recruiters stressed their need for marketing expertise, so—with some apprehension—she moved into the engineer's world.

In fact, Sherrill has been placed in challenging and varied jobs. A first assignment as a market analyst used her specialized knowledge and also gave her an opportunity to bone up—nights and weekends—on an essential technical background in electronics. Being project manager of a new computer facility and doing M.B.A. recruiting added variety. These she followed with product management and later she became marketing manager for the Specialty Products division. By age 32, when she got the Sci-Tech assignment, she had an impressive record of successes. When asked by her friends about how marriage might fit into her life plan, she had a standard response: "I haven't missed it so far. As the politicians like to say, I'm keeping my options open."

Underneath Sherrill's assured exterior manner were two gnawing uncertainties about her own abilities for the new job. (1) She had never been a general manager and was unsure how she would act as a young boss—very young in the eyes of many of her older subordinates. (2) She had never prepared and staked her reputation on a written strategic plan. Suddenly the distinction between a staff report and a manager's report which she had to execute loomed large. How to prepare the report, how to win support of her colleagues for it, how to sell it to top management became very real questions. The following account of the *processes* that Sherrill used to meet these two challenges reveals some success, some luck, and some fumbling which showed her inexperience.

SCI-TECH ASSOCIATES

Sci-Tech Associates was organized nine years ago by three electronics engineer-scientists, two of whom were employed in middle-level staff positions in large West Coast electronics companies while the third was an associate professor in a leading California engineering school. Bernard Ash and Mark Feldstein had been classmates at California Institute of Technology, and they remained in close social contact during the next fifteen years while they rose to department-head level in their respective organizations. Conrad Woodworth had known Ash and Feldstein slightly while he was a teaching assistant at Caltech, working toward a doctorate. After joining the faculty of another California engineering school, he did consulting with the company for which Ash worked. Through this relationship he renewed his acquaintance with Ash and Feldstein, an acquaintance that developed into close friendship.

The three men often talked about cutting loose from their jobs and starting their own electronics businesses. Ash and Feldtein were increasingly frustrated by the rigidities of the formal organization structure and the procedures of their companies. Woodworth's restlessness was fueled by his mounting disinterest in teaching and his hostility to the pressure to build a publication record as a requirement for a tenured appointment. Beyond this, all three men wanted a stock-ownership position that would give them the chance to realize substantial capital gains.

Finally the three decided to launch their personal moonshot. They formed Sci-Tech Associates, Inc., with a capitalization of $700,000. Stock ownership was split evenly three ways. Ash and Feldstein each supplied $350,000, part from their own savings, part borrowed on personal notes from members of their families. Woodworth's contribution was his assignment to the company of three patents he held on electronic devices. Bernard Ash was designated president of the new firm, Mark Feldstein treasurer, and Conrad Woodworth director of research. In practice, they agreed to operate as equal partners, with all decisions made cooperatively.

The partners decided to try producing and marketing Woodworth's devices themselves. They leased a small plant in El Monte, purchased the necessary equipment, hired a small workforce, produced sample units, and went out to solicit orders from California electronics companies.

They sold a few small orders for the devices and then a larger volume of repeat orders. The flow of incoming orders was erratic, however, and after six months they concluded that the business could not be profitable without a steady volume of bread-and-butter work as a basic revenue source while the market for the patented products was developing and while Woodworth was working on two other promising components. Subcontracting work for the electronic firms they were already contacting was the quickest source of such stabilizing income. It involves competitive bidding and thin margins, but it does pay for the overhead. Ever since this first grasp for stability, Sci-Tech has done subcontracting in addition to making its patented components.

Sci-Tech produces a variety of electronic components: hypersensitive unitary and interlocked-series switches, high-speed electronic-impulse transmitters, and elements for incorporation in sophisticated microvoltage regulating and measuring systems. About half of its sales have been generated by these patented products. Last year Sci-Tech sold such products to seven companies. The single largest customer, accounting for slightly more than $1 million in sales, was Cyril Electronics, which used Sci-Tech's hypersensitive switches in several of its advanced process-control systems. Among the other customers for Sci-Tech's proprietary products were Ampex, Intel, National Semiconductor, and Texas Instruments.

Customers for Sci-Tech's proprietary products, with the exception of Cyril, did not maintain a stable relationship with Sci-Tech or purchase in large quantities. They appeared to follow the strategy of using Sci-Tech as a high-technology resource for certain unique components incorporated in the early marketing stage of their own advanced products. Then, for products that developed high-volume sales, they shifted to inhouse manufacture of comparable components.

The reasons for this erratic use of Sci-Tech products, according to Ash and Feldstein, were varied. They included high cost for large volume orders, unreliable quality, difficulties of coordinating deliveries with customer's production schedules. As already noted, Cyril Electronics also was unhappy with these matters, but Cyril preferred not to get involved with inhouse design and production—at least prior to the Sci-Tech acquisition.

The subcontracting part of Sci-Tech's business generated a growing volume of sales from a diversified and constantly shifting group of customers, one of which ordinarily accounted for more than 20 percent of the total of this type of Sci-Tech's business.

The partnership mode of top management has continued at Sci-Tech. All three men—Ash, Feldstein, and Woodworth—discuss all major decisions. In daily operations, Woodworth clearly runs the research effort, whereas Ash and Feldstein often overlap. Generally, Ash spends more time on production and Feldstein on marketing and finance, although both respond to any pressing problem. The employment of a production manager—Ivar Sunderberg—facilitates this top management flexibility.

Sci-Tech's growth has been steady but not as fast as hoped, and its ability to earn a profit has been even more disappointing to the partners. The operating results for the past five years, shown in Table 1, are far below what the partners envisaged when the company was formed, and their working relationships have begun to erode as a consequence.

The original plan was to build a record of profitable growth and then "go public," including some of their own shares together with new stock in the public offering. The mediocre profit performance prevented this step and by the time of the acquisition the partners had become increasingly pessimistic about future prospects. Woodworth was critical of both the marketing effort for the proprietary devices he developed and the quality of factory supervision over their production. Ash and Feldstein complained that Woodworth appeared to be more interested in the scientific novelty of his developments than in their potential for volume marketing. Ash and Feldstein were also beginning to bicker about their overlapping responsibilities for production, marketing, and finance. All three were disappointed by the continuing dependence of the business for a substantial share of its gross revenue on low-margin subcontracting activities which developed no proprietary security.

Cyril Electronic's proposal to acquire Sci-Tech Associates therefore occurred at a time when the mutual disaffection of the three owners was threatening to become a serious destabilizing factor in the business. The terms of the offer were, in the circumstances, attractive. Cyril proposed to (1) exchange its listed stock at market value (trading at eleven times per-share earnings) for Sci-Tech stock valued at net worth per share, (2) give the three owners five-year

TABLE 1.
SCI-TECH ASSOCIATES: OPERATING STATEMENTS
(in thousands)

	Last Year	2 Years Ago	3 Years Ago	4 Years Ago	5 Years Ago
Net Sales:					
Proprietary Products	$ 4,917	$3,543	$2,580	$1,760	$1,308
Subcontracts	5,208	4,145	3,467	3,125	2,555
Total Sales	10,125	7,687	6,047	4,885	3,863
Cost of Goods Sold	8,782	6,667	5,184	4,287	~~3,863~~ 3257
Operating Profit	1,343	1,020	863	598	586
R & D Expense	600	450	450	300	300
Selling & Administrative Expense	626	402	323	260	192
Net Income before Tax	117	168	90	38	9444
Income Tax	52	72	32	15	36
Net Profit	$ 65	$ 96	$ 58	$ 23	$ 58

SCI-TECH ASSOCIATES: BALANCE SHEET
END OF LAST YEAR (in thousands)

Cash	$ 63	Loans Payable	$ 238
Accounts Receivable	1,515	Current Installment of Long-	
Inventories	925	Term Debt	57
		Accounts Payable	1,056
		Accrued Items	729
Total Current Assets	2,503	Total Current Liabilities	2,080
Property & Equipment		Long-Term	720
(net of depreciation)	1,226	Stockholders'Equity:	
		Common Stock	700
		Retained Earnings	229
		Net Worth	929
Total Assets	$3,729	Total Liabilities & Net Worth	$3,729

employment contracts, continuing their existing salaries and fringe benefits, (3) give them a potential for bonuses based on sales and profit increases during the employment contract period, and (4) install a new president to provide highly qualified top management direction. The three partners would have the titles of senior vice-presidents in the Cyril subsidiary. The proposal was accepted and became effective in March of this year.

Management in Transition

Understandably, the executives of Sci-Tech were uneasy about what their new president, named by Cyril Electronics, might do. That she was more than ten years younger than they, a nonengineer, and a woman added more uncertainty. When, after a week of getting acquainted with people and facts, Sherrill indicated that there would be no immediate rocking of the boat, tension turned to relief—even enthusiasm.

Sherrill quickly decided that a tightening up of present activities would be a necessary base for any future strategy. Consequently, she set specific targets for the rest of the year—including a 50 percent reduction in late deliveries, a 75 percent reduction in quality failures and re-work requirements, a $300,000 reduction in costs, and a pre-tax income target of 4.1 percent of sales (compared to 1.2 percent the preceding year).

In keeping with past practice, the three partners began discussing the reasonableness of these targets. Sherrill cut them off, saying: "Look, we all know that the recent performance of this business has been no better than mediocre. It certainly hasn't achieved the goals you had in mind when you started the business. You have an opportunity now, with Cyril's backing, to achieve these goals. If this business realizes its full potential, your employment contracts will give you extraordinary bonuses during the next five years. As far as I am concerned, my neck is on the block. I've started to build a good career in Cyril and I don't intend to spoil it by failing in this assignment. All of us therefore have a powerful motivation to succeed. But we must recognize that Sci-Tech is no longer a game or an ego trip, if it ever was. You believe, and Cyril believes, that there are valuable resources in this business. So let's quit horsing around and get to work."

In addition to the specific targets for the year, Sherrill asked for written suggestions for the longer term strategy of Sci-Tech. Parts of the immediate program were assigned to each of the senior vice-presidents, while Sherrill undertook primary responsibility for drawing up a strategic plan to be submitted to the president of Cyril in December. A weekly management meeting was set up to share information on progress and problems, but she made it clear that each person was expected to proceed vigorously with his and her assignment.

The Senior Vice-Presidents

This "immediate program" gave Sherrill further opportunities to talk with and observe her three associates. She had already received a preliminary evaluation of each of them from John Leonard, the Cyril vice-president who negotiated the acquisition. The following are highlights from the information that Sherrill picked up during her first few weeks at Sci-Tech.

Conrad Woodworth. "He is close to the model of a pure scientist," Leonard had said, "except that he has this itch for big money. When his interest is hot, he may work straight through the night. He's independent, likely to resent direction, firmly committed to the notion that a better mousetrap will find its own market."

In Sci-Tech's laboratory, when Sherrill first met the research staff—which included four Ph.D.'s and six holders of master's degrees—Woodworth was particularly enthused about one device undergoing tests. "This little gizmo can revolutionize high-speed transmission of electronic impulses. It could transform the future of this company." Responding to Sherrill's question about when the device would be ready for demonstration to potential customers, Woodworth explained, "There are a couple of problems we haven't quite solved. But I'm sure we will—maybe next Monday, maybe six months from now." And as to problems that might arise in quantity production, "I haven't any idea. That's Bernie Ash's job. And Bernie hasn't seen this yet. If I show him something new he wants to jump right into the factory before we've eliminated all the bugs. We've had trouble like that before. So we've learned to keep our mouths shut about something new until we know it's ready to fly. Until then, my policy is to keep it top secret. Sometimes I wish I could erect a Chinese Wall around this lab."

In response to Sherril's further probing, Woodworth continued, "This business is off on a wrong track. We should never have gotten mixed up with that subcontracting crap. It uses our resources at their lowest level of skill and their lowest market value. In my opinion, we ought to throw the whole subcontracting nonsense out the window and concentrate our attention on building our own business."

Bernard Ash. Of the three senior vice-presidents, Ash showed the best grasp of what has to happen in production to make the business go. But he is not really intrigued with a smoothly-running shop. Instead, he—and Feldstein too—likes to work with engineers in customer companies to discover how Sci-Tech components can radically improve the performance of customer products.

Nevertheless, it was Ash who first provided Sherrill with a thorough look at Sci-Tech's production facilities. With production manager, Sunderberg, they toured the air-conditioned, immaculate, quiet shop. About forty workers were either monitoring automated machines or operating delicate controls on other precise equipment. Another forty workers, dressed like nurses in white smocks and caps and latex gloves, were occupied with miniaturized assembly operations observed through microscopes.

Sunderberg explained that the entire factory force was paid on a straight salary basis and rather proudly noted that management-employee relations were such that three efforts to unionize the group in recent years had been unsuccessful. The plant worked a single shift, with occasional overtime. Quality control was incorporated within production operations, with employees spot-checking their own work. Because of the irregular receipt of orders, the same group of employees worked on both proprietary products and subcontract job-orders. "We could expand output 50 percent on the site. Doubling output would require moving to a new location."

In response to Sherrill's question about cost control, Ash showed her worksheets that he and Sunderberg kept on each order. "These figures are our personal estimates of what it actually cost to get each order produced. Some run smoothly, others cause headaches, overtime, and therefore expense. Of course, with a single shop producing different kinds of products, the allocation of overhead is a judgmental matter. But we do need total cost figures, especially to help us prepare bids on subcontracts.[2]

On another issue Ash explained, "Our organization is more informal than what you probably have at Cyril. Connie Woodworth runs the lab because that's where we need him and that's where he wants to be. As far as Mark Feldstein and I go, things are all mixed up. I spend quite a bit of time on sales and Mark occasionally dips into production. He is technically treasurer, but in reality we both work on that job. It has worked so far, but maybe you'll want to make some rearrangements."

Mark Feldstein. Feldstein gave the impression of being tougher and more abrasive than his former partners—ready to shoot from the hip. His aggressiveness probably provided the push that the trio needed to launch Sci-Tech. John Leonard suspects that "he starts a lot of things going and then gets interested in something else, leaving a lot of debris behind him. But he has real talent if you can keep him focused."

"Our marketing setup is simple," Feldstein explained. "Bernie Ash and I get the orders for the proprietary products; the salespeople bring in the subcontracts. Of course, in a small organization like ours it's not quite that clean. Bernie or I are always in on the subcontracts, at least in the bidding, and the salespeople help maintain contacts with proprietary customers—our midwest rep, for example, keeps in close touch with Cyril Electronics. He damn well better, now that they own us.

"At the top level we are a mess. The three of us had the cockeyed idea that we would run this business as equal partners. It hasn't worked. It never does. We spend hours trying to reach agreements. That means the third person often yields when he is still convinced he is right, or the decision is put off which may be worse. I've told this to Bernie and Connie repeatedly, but they like things as they are."

---

[2]The cumulative totals on these job cost sheets indicated that subcontract job-orders accounted for the following percentages of Sci-Tech's overall results: net sales, 51.4 percent; cost of goods sold, 61 percent; direct labor costs, 53.8 percent; material costs, 52.7 percent; production overhead costs, 63.4 percent. The operating loss on subcontracts last year was estimated at 2.8 percent of subcontract sales; the operating profit on proprietary products was estimated at 30.3 percent of proprietary sales.

Responding to Sherrill's questions about budgets, Feldstein said, "We've prepared quarterly profit and loss budgets for years. Our banker likes them. But frankly they don't mean much. You've probably noticed that the actual figures jump around a lot. That's because of the irregular way orders come in and shipments are made. It's the orders that really count, not the budgets, so we don't pay much attention to them. By holding our inventories low we've kept Sci-Tech solvent, although I must admit our customers would be happier if we carried large stocks which they could order at the drop of a hat whenever they shuffle their own schedules around. I don't think budgets are the way to solve that problem."

Short-Run Response

The response to Sherrill's "immediate program" was good. It focused effort on a series of soft spots in Sci-Tech's operations that everyone agreed should be improved. Equally important, morale picked up for several reasons. The normal early anxiety about what the new owner would do was relieved; nobody was fired and no quick-fix remedies were imposed. Rather, Sherrill was a friendly person (to people throughout the organization, not just her immediate associates), open to suggestions, and she asked probing questions that needed to be asked. At the same time, she accepted the role of final arbiter; in spite of her inexperience, a feeling of unified direction was injected.

People at the top level knew that several long-run issues remained open. But there was agreement on immediate needs, and working hard on them absorbed energy that could easily have turned into grousing. There was little time for idle hands to find mischief. And, Sherrill saw decreasing evidence of irritation among the former partners.

Operating results also improved. By the end of October, Sherrill was able to prepare an estimated operating statement for the year which showed that tightening up was, indeed, paying off. (See Table 2.) There had been a few cutbacks, but primarily the organization handled a larger volume of business without a proportional increase in expenses. Also significant was an improvement in customer service. Most delivery commitments to customers, and notably to Cyril, were being met on time. The rate of quality defects had dropped dramatically. So the financial gain had not come from a sacrifice in these intangible items.

Sherrill was now confident that the first-year hurdle under the new ownership would be cleared with flying colors. Yet she was aware that the current energy level would be difficult to sustain. The "new boss" stimulation would wear off, and she had not yet been forced to make an unpopular decision. Even more worrisome were the long-run prospects for the company with its obvious management weaknesses and its dual-line operation.

TABLE 2.
SCI-TECH ASSOCIATES: OPERATING STATEMENTS
ACTUAL LAST YEAR—ESTIMATED THIS YEAR*
(in thousands)

	Last Year	Estimated This Year
Net Sales		
Proprietary Products	$ 4,917	$ 6,300
Subcontracts	5,208	6,100
Total Sales	10,125	12,400
Cost of Goods Sold	8,782	10,600
Operating Profit	1,343	1,800
R & D Expense	600	700
Selling & Administrative Expense	626	700
Net Income before Tax	117	400
Income Tax	52	200
Net Profit	$ 65	$ 200

*Based on 10-month actual.

The Longer View

Most of Sherrill's time during her first six months at Sci-Tech was devoted to preparing the long-range strategy which Cyril's president wanted by the end of the year.

The written suggestions from the senior vice-presidents provided little help. They repeated personal preferences which Sherrill already knew and made "straight-line" projections with scant attention to threats, risks, and resource requirements. On her own part, Sherrill studied the company outlook in depth. She visited managers and engineers in both customer and noncustomer organizations, talked with editors of trade magazines, and spend several days with Cyril's headquarters research staff. From these and other sources she explored trends in the industry, evolving technology, economics of make-or-buy decisions, and life cycles of proprietary products in electronics.

Within Sci-Tech she observed the scheduling and purchasing process, followed an incoming order through its entire progression, talked with employees about their work on subcontracts, and accompanied salespeople on customer and cold canvass calls. Also she talked with Sci-Tech's banker about risks and trends in the electronics industry and why some companies succeed where others fail.

Another essential input to this study was an assessment of the long-run contributions that her three senior associates might make to Sci-Tech. Sherrill concluded that Woodworth was an extraordinarily talented scientist whose personal contributions were essential to the continuing development of the proprietary business. However, his insensitivity to market needs and production problems, as well as disinterest in research administration, disqualified Woodworth as head of R & D. A much better arrangement would be to name a new R & D director with Woodworth as chief scientist.

Feldstein, she concluded, was an able technical sales representative, and an acceptable but not outstanding marketing manager. But he possessed neither the training nor objectivity of a good finance and control executive; and if Feldstein objected to turning over these functions to a more qualified person, Sherrill was willing to risk losing him. Ash, with proper direction, could serve well as production vice-president, but Sherrill doubted his ability to handle either procurement or personnel in a rapidly growing business. Here, too, another vice-president probably would be needed.

Fortunately, long-run financing was available from Cyril Electronics *if* a plan could be prepared that offered potential returns commensurate with its risks.

Strategic Options

From this analysis and numerous "what-if" notes to capture her own thoughts, Sherrill concluded that Sci-Tech faces two basic options. One is to continue the existing dual commitment to proprietary components and to subcontracting. This is a relatively safe, slow growth course. Because of the narrow profits on subcontracting, the returns are likely to be modest. Looking five years down the road, Sherrill projected doubling the sales volume under this strategy, with pre-tax income in the range of 5-7 percent of sales (compared with 3.2 percent estimated for this year).

The second option is to stop taking subcontracting orders and concentrate the full capabilities of Sci-Tech on the design, production, and sale of proprietary components. While cutbacks in factory employment would be faced next year, a vigorous building of added strength in R & D, procurement, personnel, finance and control would be launched. With this focused strength, and the new products Woodworth was conjuring up in his laboratory, Sherrill projected a trebling of profits in three years and trebling that figure again in the succeeding three years. This is a more risky operation than the first, with a much higher growth and profit potential.

An unknown was the inclination of Cyril Electronics executives to take risks on Sci-Tech's development. President Thompson said that he wanted *both* an assured source of critical components for Cyril's other divisions *and* a rich return on the initial investment. But a tradeoff between the two objectives was not stated. Sherrill believed that she could get no clear answer on this issue until Thompson and his colleagues face spelled-out alternatives. "They don't know the answer," Sherrill quipped, "until I pose the question." Consequently, Sherrill planned to lay out both options in her forthcoming report.

Sherrill prepared a draft of her report, her first strategic plan, which she planned to send to Thompson early in December. It had to be weighed in terms of psychological impact and tactical considerations, as well as rational arguments. Before making final revisions in the document, Sherrill wanted to test the reception and obtain the advice of her senior vice-presidents. The principal elements in the draft are outlined in the following excerpts and paraphrases.

I. Strategic Choices

A. The development of Sci-Tech can be charted along either of two strategic courses: (1) continue the existing dual commitment to proprietary products and subcontracting; (2) discontinue subcontracting (complete jobs presently under contract but accept no new orders) and concentrate all resources on proprietary products.

B. The first option is a low-risk strategy. It will provide satisfactory continuing fulfillment of one of Cyril's two objectives in acquiring Sci-Tech: assured supply of Sci-Tech's components, on time and meeting quality specifications. It has a high probability of earning moderate sustained profits and a moderate sustained rate of return on Cyril's investment. At this level, it will not achieve Cyril's second acquisition objective: a high rate of return on its investment in Sci-Tech. This option will require a small additional investment by Cyril three years hence (about $1 million) to assist in financing the projected steady, slow growth in sales through the next five years, but will be substantially self-financing. It will retain Sci-Tech's present senior managers and management structure, both of which are adequate to meet the administrative needs associated with this option.

C. The second option is a high-potential but high-risk strategy. It opens the way to a rapid development of the business, with a good possibility for up to tenfold growth in sales and a corresponding increase in profits in the next five to seven years and a high return on Cyril's initial and subsequent investment. This option will certainly involve substantial losses of sales and income in at least the first two years following its adoption. It will require large supplemental investments by Cyril because it cannot come close to being self-financing. It will also require recruiting several new senior-level executives and might result in the resignation of one or two of the three founders of Sci-Tech.

D. There is no acceptable "middle" strategy that would preserve the low-risk feature of the first option while also developing the full potential of the second option. Successful implementation of the second option will require undivided concentration of Sci-Tech's present resources—and additional financing and organizational resources—all targeted on satisfying the demands created by the option.

II. Recommendation

I recommend corporate approval of the second option: rapid phasing out of all subcontracting; prompt recruiting—from Cyril if possible, from outside if necessary—of the required new top-executive resources; a corporate commitment to meet the indicated long-term financial needs for a high-growth business; and accepting operating losses for two years of the magnitude described below.

III. The Dual Strategy: Subcontracting Plus Proprietary Products

A. While cost allocations between subcontracting and proprietary work have been unreliable, it is reasonably clear that subcontracting was never better than a breakeven operation until this year. More important, the subcontracting business is so intensely competitive, Sci-Tech's profit-to-sales ratio on subcontracts can never be much higher than the present level. This competitive environment will not change in the foreseeable future.

B. Subcontracting uses Sci-Tech's skills at both managerial and worker levels. The same skills applied to the division's proprietary products would yield high-profit returns.

C. The presence of subcontracts in the factory workflow inevitably lowers workers' and supervisors' concern for high quality in proprietary work. The same people handle both types of assignments. It is not feasible to segregate either the two types of work or the personnel who do the work.

D. There is, of course, a positive rationale for retaining subcontracting. It absorbs overhead costs. It provides greater continuity of employment for factory personnel. It contributes to stability of annual revenues. These considerations tend to offset the risks associated with proprietary products in the volatile electronics field.

E. On balance, continuation of the dual strategy is a relatively low-risk option. Its real cost is the extent to which it will stunt the growth and profit potential of the business, which can be attained only through a total commitment of all resources on exploiting the division's present and future proprietary products.

IV. The Proprietary Concentration Strategy

A. Sci-Tech's uniquely valuable resource is its ability to invent, develop, manufacture, and market certain state-of-the-art proprietary electronic components; hypersensitive switching devices, high-speed electron-impulse transmitters, and microvoltage measurement and control elements. The central core of this resource is the inventive and developmental genius of Conrad Woodworth. His talent is irreplaceable. Of supporting, but less valuable and clearly replaceable, usefulness are the talents of Bernard Ash and Mark Feldstein. Sci-Tech's present proprietary products represent only a first step in the potential development and exploitation of the organization's capabilities.

B. The market for Sci-Tech's proprietaries includes major segments of the electronics and computer industries, with additional potential in other end-product industries in which very high-speed electronic devices will be used. These are all high-growth markets. Equally important, they are all markets in which component performance characteristics and quality are more important than price. Profit margins of component producers who stay at the leading edge of rapidly advancing technology are extraordinarily wide once high-volume semi-automated manufacture has been established.

C. Given Sci-Tech's capability and the size and growth rate of these markets, why has Sci-Tech's development to date been so slow and its profitability so low? Several factors combine to explain this mediocre performance:

1. The diversion of top management time and energy to subcontracting, as noted above.
2. The inability of Conrad Woodworth to recruit and direct a first-quality research group and his reluctance to accept market-oriented guidance in focusing the R & D strategy. He is close to the classic case of the solo genius who is most effective when allowed to work alone.
3. The lack of first-rate managerial skills. Bernard Ash is, or with proper leadership could be, an effective manager of production. He is an amateur, to the point of being naive, in personnel administration. Mark Feldstein is, or with proper leadership could be, an effective marketing manager. He is an amateur in the finance and control area. Ash may be willing to acknowledge his limitations. Feldstein probably is not.

D. An organization plan which would overcome the managerial weaknesses and give Sci-Tech the managerial strengths it needs to take full advantage of its potential is shown in Figure 1. The success of the proprietary strategy depends on Sci-Tech's ability to maintain a strong position at the leading edge of evolving technology in the component area. This leadership, in turn, depends on the introduction of competent senior management in R & D, finance and control, and personnel administration. It further depends on the willingness of Cyril corporate to accept at least two years of operating losses while Sci-Tech backs itself out of subcontracting and strengthens its base for exploitation of its proprietaries, and also to make substantial further investments in senior management and in manufacturing facilities. Finally, it depends on Sci-Tech's ability to absorb the shock of the breakup of the three-man founding group.

E. The projection of proprietary sales under the proprietary-only strategy (see Table 3) rests on the following assumptions:

1. Sci-Tech's presently-marketed components, in existing and improved technological modes, will not be made obsolete in the next several years by new developments or lose sales because of customer's decisions to self-manufacture comparable devices. Recent discussions with customer engineering managers and other knowledgeable electronic industry sources indicate low probability of technological obsolescence for two years, with rising uncertainty thereafter. Self-manufacture is becoming less of a threat as Sci-Tech improves its quality and delivery performance.
2. The projected sales increase for proprietaries to $13 million in two years and $22 million in three years assumes completion of development and entry into production of Woodworth's multiphase triode coupling. The potential market for this revolutionary device is estimated to be as large as $100 million annually, based on discussions with customer engineers and other electronic industry sources, if it performs as anticipated and if it is susceptible to semi-automated production. I believe both of these requirements will be met within the next twelve months. If this belief is realized, the sales projection is minimal.
3. Cyril must be prepared to finance rapid growth. Under the projection in Table 3, $1 million to $1,500,000 will be needed next year to supplement mortgage financing of a new plant and office building and to cover anticipated operating losses. Equity capital to keep Sci-Tech in a position to obtain short-term bank loans at favorable rates will also be needed—probably $500,000 two years hence and perhaps $1 million the year after.

FIGURE 1.

SCI-TECH ASSOCIATES:

PROPOSED ORGANIZATION FOR PROPRIETARY STRATEGY

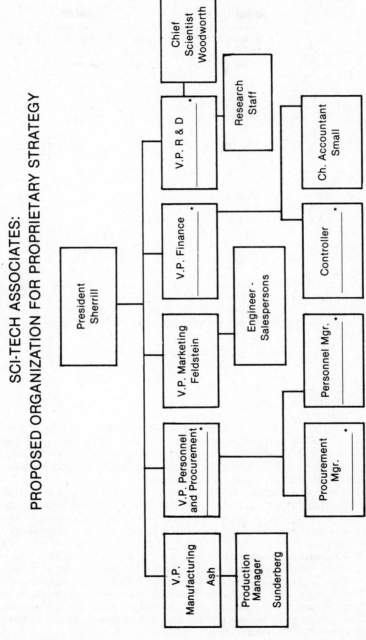

*To be recruited from outside Sci-Tech, possibly from Cyril.

TABLE 3.
SCI-TECH ASSOCIATES: ALTERNATIVE BUDGETS FOR NEXT THREE YEARS
(in thousands)

Net Sales:	Assuming Continuance of Existing Dual-Line Strategy			Assuming Focus on Proprietary Products[*]		
	Next Year	2nd Year	3rd Year	Next Year	2nd Year	3rd Year
Proprietary Products	$ 7,500	$ 9,000	$10,500	$ 9,700	$13,000	$22,000
Subcontracts	7,500	9,000	11,000	2,600	—	—
Total Sales	15,000	18,000	21,500	12,300	13,000	22,000
Cost of Goods Sold	12,400	15,000	18,000	11,300	11,400	16,000
Operating Profit	2,600	3,000	3,500	1,000	1,600	6,000
R & D Expense	800	900	1,100	1,300	1,800	2,500
Selling & Administrative Expense	800	1,000	1,200	900	1,200	1,400
Net Income before Tax	1,000	1,100	1,200	(1,200)	(1,400)	2,100
Income Tax	460	510	550	—	—	100
Net Profit	$ 540	$ 590	$ 650	$(1,200)	$(1,400)	$ 2,000

[*]Completing presently booked subcontracts and seeking no new subcontract jobs.

V. Summary

A. Sci-Tech has been its own worst enemy in serving its most attractive market—the users of its proprietary products. However, correction of delivery and quality shortfalls—already well underway—coupled with prompt refinements of its existing products should enable the company to build and retain a much higher proportion of this attractive business.

B. The potential new market for the kind of state-of-the-art components Sci-Tech already has in its laboratory is both large and profitable. Commiting balanced resources—undiluted by low-margin subcontracting—to this attractive growth market can convert Sci-Tech into a significant generator of profits for Cyril Electronics.

C. The fundamental consideration in choosing a strategy for Sci-Tech is Cyril Electronics' objective in owning Sci-Tech. The dual strategy at best would assure Cyril of a reliable source for certain critical components used in other divisions, with only a moderate long-term return on its investment. The proprietary strategy, if successful, would represent a bold thrust into a new technological area yielding high growth and high long-term return on the original and supplemental investments.

Advice of the Vice-Presidents

Sherrill asked her three senior associates to meet with her at Sci-Tech's empty office on Saturday following Thanksgiving Day. She devoted the first hour to reviewing orally the content of her draft report, stressing the rationale behind it and showing the financial estimates and proposed organization. She omitted her assessment of the three vice-presidents. Instead, she made the case for bringing in new senior management in terms of utilizing the special capabilities of each of the three men in their most advantageous contribution to the long-run success of the business.

"What I intend to do," she concluded, "unless you see strong reasons to the contrary, is to lay both strategic options before Carl Thompson, and recommend that he adopt the second one. If we focus all our efforts on proprietary products, I believe Sci-Tech can become a $60 million business in five or six years, with a 20 percent pretax income. If we stick with our present strategy, I think we are unlikely to see sales of more than $25 million, with a pretax profit-to-sales rate around 8 percent. O.K., what do *you* think?"

While what she heard in response didn't surprise her much, neither did it give her much comfort. Mark Feldstein spoke first.

"I think you have described two basic ideas—one of them good and the other lousy," he said. "The good idea is to get rid of subcontracting and concentrate on our own products. When we started, we were too small to do that; we had no margin of safety, no reasonably secure income base. But we're not in that vulnerable position now, expecially with Cyril standing behind us. So I think it's the right way to go and I don't think the risks are all that great either.

"But your bad idea is—and I'm not going to pull my punches on this, Jane— that you are proposing to take the management of the business away from the three of us. I don't give a damn about all your smarmy talk about using our talents where they'll help the business most. What you are proposing to do is obvious: demote Connie out of running R & D, demote me out of running finance, and demote Bernie by taking procurement and personnel away from him. Put it all together and what your plan amounts to is a scheme to take the management of the business away from the three of us. That is exactly what I feared would happen when we sold Sci-Tech to Cyril. But I didn't think it would happen this fast. You've been around here eight months and you're ready to get blood on your knife. I don't really blame you personally for this. You were sent here by Thompson to do this job exactly this way—and you're doing it per orders from headquarters."

Sherrill said quietly, "I wasn't sent here by Carl Thompson to do anything but help to make this business a success, Mark. And I think the four of us, working together, have made an excellent beginning this year. What I'm trying to do now is take a longer look forward and decide how to make a small success into a big success."

"Fair enough," he replied. "Then let's take your specializing strategy as it stands and the four of us continue to manage it. I think we've shown we can do it. But let me make one thing crystal clear. If you make this recommendation to Thompson to bring in new top management, I'm not going to stay around to see if he approves it. You can count me out right from the moment you make such a proposal."

Without arguing the point with him, Sherrill said to Ash, "Bernie, what do you think?"

"The first thing I think," said Ash, "is we shouldn't get so excited until we've got something that's worth being excited about. Calm down, Mark. If Jane really has a good idea for the business, it would be stupid for us to try to kill it on the grounds of loss of personal power, status, and similar nonsense. If this business grows the way she thinks it might and if it makes the kind of money she has projected—well, we've got employment contracts that will put a good share of those profits into our personal bank accounts. Speaking for myself at least, it wouldn't bother me a bit not to be involved in managing personnel and procurement if I was also getting rich.

"But will we get rich? As I see it, the choice Jane has laid on the table is between continuing to run a business we understand and launching ourselves into a total commitment to an extremely risky venture. The first option may not be very exciting, but the business is growing, it's starting to return to a respectable profit. And it will make more. The second option strikes me as a trip to Las Vegas—we might hit the jackpot, but we could lose our corporate shirt. I don't want to lose my share of that shirt.

"Isn't there a third option, Jane? Why can't we keep and even expand our subcontracting business and at the same time try to build a proprietary business that grows even faster than the subcontracting line? Then, if we hit a dry period in the lab, which can always happen, we would still have a reasonably secure foundation in subcontracting and our established proprietaries. Maybe we won't get as rich as we might if your second option works perfectly. But maybe also we don't get as poor as we might if it fails."

"Before I try to answer," Sherrill said, "I'd like to hear what Connie thinks."

"That's easy," he replied. "I think it's a great idea, and I think we should do it. Subcontracting isn't what we got in business to do. I'd welcome getting rid of my whole administrative job and being free to put all my attention on research. As for you, Mark, I should think you would be glad to concentrate on either finance or marketing. You can't really give both jobs the attention they'll require in a rapidly growing business. If you prefer finance to marketing, I'm sure Jane would see no difficulty in revising her proposal by putting you in the v.p.-finance position and recruiting a new marketing manager."

Without indicating her own reactions to their comments, Sherrill pushed the three to assess her proprietary strategy in greater depth, with particular emphasis on what successful execution of the strategy would require in each of the functional areas for which they were responsible. The ensuing discussion identified no substantial problems that she had not herself explored in her own analysis. At the end of the afternoon she said, "Let's call it a day. This has been very valuable to me. I want to think over what you said and I'll let you know what I decide to do."

Early in the following week each of the men came to her office for a followup conference.

Mark Feldstein told her, "When I said I would quit rather than give up the finance and control function, I meant it. I endorse without qualification the proprietary strategy. Equally without qualification, I am opposed to bringing in a top management team. I'd be willing to reconsider my decision if you are willing to accept Connie's suggestion that I keep the top job in finance and control and let an outsider take over the marketing job. Otherwise, it's the end of the road as far as I am concerned."

"Mark, I don't think that would be advisable," she replied. "This is a high-risk strategy, as you recognized. I think we can lower the risk if we apply our best resources where they can make the greatest contribution. In my judgment, you can be most valuable to this business as head of marketing. If you view this as a demotion you are totally misreading the situation. It is simply a specialization of talents to handle all of the complex needs of the business with maximum effectiveness. If you can't see it that way, I'm sorry. I don't want to lose you, but it is your decision. Think it over for a while. After all, Carl Thompson might throw the whole proposal in the wastebasket."

"Jane, I don't think you understand the full implications of what I'm telling you," he said. "When I say I'll quit if you propose your scheme, I don't mean I'll simply walk out and leave behind everything I've helped to build here. I'll take a piece of this business with me, a substantial piece, at least one and a half million dollars of annual sales, to put a figure on it. That represents our present business with two good customers for our own products. In one of those companies my brother-in-law is director of purchasing. In the other, a college classmate is chief of production engineering. I developed the business with these customers, and you better believe it goes out the door with me. I'm sorry to be this rough on you, but you're acting pretty rough with us."

"Thank you for telling me, Mark," she said. "You've given me something to think about."

Connie Woodworth said, "The more I think about what you outlined, the more I like it. I especially like the idea of being relieved of responsibility for managing the research group. As chief scientist, without the administrative burden, I'll be doing exactly what I always wanted to do."

"Suppose we lose Mark," Sherrill said, "would that upset you? I'm not prepared to give him the finance and control position, as you suggested. I just don't think it's the best way to use his abilities for the business."

"Well, I really threw out the possibility to calm him down," he said. "I understand your point of view. If he goes, he goes."

"Suppose he goes and takes a million dollars or more of business with him?"

"Did he threaten to do that?"

"Let's not view it as a threat, but as a possibility."

"Well, I don't think it's likely to happen. We've got unique products—superior to any alternatives. He can't take that business elsewhere. It doesn't make sense to me."

"So you're prepared to accept that risk?"

"Absolutely."

Bernie Ash said, "I'm still very bothered by your either-or approach. I don't see the need to lock ourselves into this absolute choice. I don't understand why we can't set a middle course, with greater emphasis on our own products but still retain some subcontracting as a backstop. It's probably the conservative in me."

"What bothers me about what you term a 'middle course,'" said Sherrill, "is that it really isn't a middle course. It's just continuing to do what we have been doing, dividing our attention, our resources, and our management time and energy between a slow-growth, low-profit subcontracting business and what could be a high-growth, high-profit proprietary business. The record of this company demonstrates that the combination just doesn't fly very well. We've improved our performance in the last six months, but we're close to exhausting the important possibilities for improvement."

"Well, maybe so. But what I see as a middle course is a deliberate tilt toward the proprietary side of the business, without letting go of subcontracting completely."

"How strongly do you feel about this?"

"I'm very concerned. But you're the boss and I'll go along with any decision you make."

"Are you bothered about what Mark said?"

"Yes, I am. A little. Maybe more than a little. But I can live with it. I want to do what's best for the business, not what's best for any one of us, especially if what's really involved is status. I don't give a damn for status. I wish Mark didn't either, but I guess he does."

"Suppose he quits and takes a million dollars or more of the business with him?"

"I don't believe he would do that. I've known Mark Feldstein a long time. He talks tougher than he acts."

"Suppose this time he really acted?"

Ash took a deep breath. "We can live with it."

APPENDIX A

Cyril Electronics, Inc.

Cyril Electronics, Inc., is a multinational manufacturer of a broad line of electronic and related products, including data communications equipment, telephonic equipment, integrated circuits, and computer peripheral products. International business last year accounted for about 25 percent of sales and 30 percent of pre-tax profits. Key operating and financial data for the last five years appear below:

	5 Years Ago	4 Years Ago	3 Years Ago	2 Years Ago	Last Year
Sales ($ million)	872	958	1,098	1,349	1,621
Operating Margin/Sales	16.5%	13.2%	17.8%	18.4%	18.9%
Net Profit Margin/Sales	6.0%	3.9%	7.1%	7.6%	7.8%
% Earned/Total Capital	11.2%	6.8%	12.5%	13.1%	14.6%
% Earned/Net Worth	12.8%	7.3%	13.7%	14.8%	16.3%

Comprehensive Case 8

STONE RIDGE BANK

Like most other U.S. banks, Stone Ridge Bank is facing one of its most crucial decisions in its long history. Instead of continued expansion, aiding, and consequently benefiting from, the economic growth of its region, Stone Ridge must sharpen its focus if it is to survive. The board of directors has asked Spencer Smythe, Jr.—an investor and part-time consultant—to help it decide how to respond to an offer to buy the branch network of Stone Ridge Bank. The following pages summarize the information that Mr. Smythe has gathered.

THE STONE RIDGE BANK

For many years Stone Ridge has been one of the two leading commercial banks in the region—its history can be traced back to 1856. The stockholders and directors include members of the leading families in the area. Conservative management helped Stone Ridge survive the bank crisis of the 1930s, and astute officers achieved an attractive earnings record, especially during the 1960s and 1970s.

The bank performs all the usual commercial banking activities. (1) For its corporate customers engaged in commerce and industry, Stone Ridge accepts demand and time deposits, makes loans with various kinds of security and conditions, does lease financing, provides automated payroll services, buys and sells foreign exchange, does cash management and funds transfer functions, advises on short-term investment of excess cash, and the like. Many of these functions are also performed for local government units and other institutions. (2) For individual consumers, Stone Ridge provides checking accounts and various kinds of savings accounts, makes installment loans and real estate loans, offers travelers checks, safe deposit boxes, credit cards, and similar services.

Located over a thousand miles from the major financial centers of the U.S., Stone Ridge has long served as an intermediary between Wall Street and the little fellow in the hinterland. It shares a strong regional pride, and regards its New York and West Coast bank correspondents as convenient sources of help for regional development. In fact, especially since World War II, the region has had a significant influx of industry, and Stone Ridge has been an active participant in this development. Stone Ridge, with less emphasis on consumer and agricultural banking, has benefited more than competing banks from this industrial growth.

Affiliated with the bank is the Stone Ridge Trust Company (both are owned by a holding company). The Trust Company oversees the estates of many prominent local citizens and is the epitome of conservative respectability. Stone Ridge Bank operates under a state charter and is a member of the Federal Deposit Insurance Corporation.

Stone Ridge Bank's earnings statement for last year and the year-end balance sheet are shown in Table 1. With $2.2 billion in assets and about 2,000 employees, Stone Ridge is a big frog in a middle-sized puddle; it is proud and conservative.

TABLE 1.
STONE RIDGE BANK CONDENSED INCOME STATEMENT
(in millions)

Operating Revenues:	
Interest and fees on loans	$171
Interest and dividends on securities	29
Other	42
Total operating revenues	242
Expenses:	
Salaries and other personnel expenses	34
Interest on deposits	110
Other interest expense	42
All other expenses	36
Total operating expenses	222
Income tax	3
Total expenses and tax	225
Net income from operations	$ 17

Condensed Balance Sheet, at Year End (in millions)

Assets		Liabilities and Equity	
Cash and due from banks	$391	Deposits:	
Federal government securities	121	Demand	$618
State and local obligations	125	Savings and other time	936
Federal funds sold	310	Federal funds purchased	406
Mortgages and loans	1,123	Other borrowed funds	51
Direct lease financing	92	Other liabilities & accruals	64
Land, buildings and equipment	39	Total liabilities	$2,075
		Common Stock	38
		Retained earnings	88
		Total equity	126
Total assets	$2,201	Total liabilities & equity	$2,201

A NEW BALLGAME

In a few short years the setting in which Stone Ridge Bank succeeded so well has changed drastically. The old order passeth—for banking everywhere.

Disrupting Forces

New technology has altered bank services and internal operations. Computerized bookkeeping has lowered operating costs significantly when large volumes are processed; this changes optimum bank size. Electronic-communication links across the nation make feasible centralized credit files, plastic credit cards, automated transfers of funds, and new forms of cash management. Automatic teller machines lower deposit and withdrawal costs and, more important, make cash available twenty-four hours a day in many locations. A further possibility is the use of interactive TV for home banking. Such changes as these are modifying the role of branch offices of banks and are moving us toward a checkless society. And with satellite communication, some of the techniques can be applied nationwide and even worldwide.

Deregulation has dramatically changed who competes with whom. For example, savings banks now are permitted to engage in activities previously confined to commercial banks; they can offer checking accounts and make commercial loans. The commercial banks are now permitted, through affiliates or other ties, to offer securities brokerage services, real estate brokerage services, life insurance and casualty insurance, and so on. In turn, the brokerage houses such as Merrill Lynch and the insurance companies such as Prudential are invading commercial banking turf. The provide personal checking accounts, auto loans, credit cards, and an array of related services.

In addition, deregulation has extended the geographical reach of commercial banks. For years, each bank was restricted to a single state, and often by local legislation to a single county or city. These barriers are breaking down. Bank holding companies are buying up banks in several states. Big New York and California commercial banks are buying chains of out-of-state savings banks with the clear intention of converting these into branches of a nationwide system. Already the big banks have regional offices which ferret out industrial and commercial loan opportunities—as do the large life insurance companies. With competing brokerage firms and insurance firms well established on a national basis, and deregulation in vogue, most people in the financial industry believe that nationwide banks will soon be here.

The combination of *deregulation plus new technology* is especially disruptive to traditional banking. New, cheap communications, for instance, make the management and control of far-flung branch offices much easier. Similarly, tying automated teller machines located thousands of miles apart into centralized accounts for individual customers is now possible; your friendly banker may even follow you abroad.

Double digit *inflation* forced interest rates up (so that lenders could recover at least as much purchasing power when the loan was paid off as they gave up when the loan was made). This pressure, plus deregulation and an associated change in Federal Reserve policy, led to a crumbling of traditional interest rate ceilings.

The resulting wide *interest rate fluctuations* have led to massive flows of capital in and out of banks—notably the savings banks. Also, banks and other institutions with fixed interest assets but varying interest costs often have gyrating profit or loss. Both these forces affect a bank's capacity to make loans. In addition, high interest rates have attracted nonbank lenders into the arena; General Electric Company, for instance, has billions of dollars for leasing and business loans of many kinds. The high and fluctuating interest rates likewise make corporate treasurers more vigorous in watching their bank balances, government security investments, and financing fees. The days of large inactive balances kept with the banks are gone.

Changing Competition

The inflexibility of the former regulated banking system, mixed with a good measure of conservative inertia, opened the way for more venturesome invaders. "Financial services" became a fashionable target for strategic planners in nonbank companies.

American Express Company, a well-known example, expanded its international travelers check and booking agency business into credit cards and insurance, and it has acquired small commercial banks and is poised to enter nationwide banking when legislation permits. Merrill Lynch converted its stockbrokerage business into an array of financial services including investment banking, insurance, and the equivalent of a checking account. Prudential Insurance Company acquired a brokerage firm, and now Prudential Bache claims to give individuals "complete financial service." Sears, Roebuck & Company, with its millions of credit card holders and long experience in automobile insurance, acquired a major stockbrokerage firm and a nationwide real estate company; it clearly seeks to use its reputation for reliability to move into a wide range of consumer financial services. As noted above, G.E. has moved into industrial loans and leasing.

These examples indicate that much of the competition which banks will face in the future will come from nonbank companies.

Within the banking industry itself, many consolidations are taking place. To gain lending power and to obtain economies in operations, formerly independent local banks are merging into statewide chains. And to operate in several states, bank holding companies are acquiring commercial (or savings) banks in other states. These mergers do require approval of federal regulating boards, but in the current deregulation climate restraints are being relaxed.

The merger movement is going so fast that some analysts are predicting that before long U.S. banking will be dominated by only a few very large and powerful megabanks. Commercial banking in England and Canada has such a structure. Such a development would run counter to a well-established tradition in the United States. In 1837, President Andrew Jackson abolished the second Bank of the United States in a Populist move against the money centers of the northeast coast. This feeling was strong well before our antitrust doctrines and legislation was formulated. A deep-seated fear of the size and the concentration of power in only a few sources of funds has fostered the thousands of independent banks we now have.

The current mood, however, is that (1) electronic communication and processing have made large-scale financial organizations so efficient that concentration is irresistible, and (2) aggressive competition among a few giants will force modernization of services, a search for available markets, and narrow profit margins. Indeed, the argument runs, the mobility of both borrower and lender now greatly increases competition compared with the horse-and-buggy days when one or two local banks enjoyed a local monopoly.

Much of the current merging of banks and other financial institutions is an effort to be positioned, defensively or offensively, to survive in the new realignment. The specific form of future competition is uncertain. So there is a lot of jockeying and getting ready to jump. The number of banking and non-banking organizations laying plans to seize a big piece of the pie is so great that severe competition with a future shakeout is inevitable.

Plight of Regional Banks

Regional banks such as Stone Ridge Bank must decide where and how they wish to fit into the future banking structure. Among the broad options each bank has are these four:

1. *Expect to become a part of a megabank organization.* With this aim, the regional bank should develop assets that will be attractive to merger partners—such as a large customer based in a growing area, or unusual skills or preferred locations. Since the bank will become only a part of a larger organization, overall balance is not so important as outstanding strength in one or more activities that will be vital in the new setup.

2. *Become an aggressor.* Typically this involves identifying a niche—for instance, a particular service like credit data (see Case 22) or a special industry—and then seeking to become the dominant supplier in that niche. Probably some acquisitions will be necessary and in the process the bank shifts its identity from a region to a more specialized domain.

3. *Defend a special piece of turf.* Here the assumption is that in some activities regional firms can be more effective than national (or local) organizations. So, the regional bank develops topflight capability in those activities and tries to erect some entry barriers to forestall incoming competition.

4. *Build a cooperative processing organization.* To offset the economies large banks enjoy, several local and regional banks can form a central processing company to do computer work, purchasing, and the like for the entire group. Such associations already exist in several parts of the country. By becoming a part of one or more coalitions, the independent units counter the power of large competitors.

Each of these options involves uncertainties. The environment may not change as predicted; the bank may not build the strengths it wants; the timing may be wrong. Perhaps more than one option could be pursued at the same time. And, of course, the bank could assume that the wave of national centralization will pass and that the wise strategy is to hold tight until legislation and loyalties again favor regional banking.

DECLARATION OF INDEPENDENCE

When considering its strategic options, Stone Ridge Bank made an early decision to maintain its independence. The chair of the board of directors (a former president) explains: "We enjoy a unique position in our region. We are the oldest bank, the strongest financially, number two in assets, number one in earnings. We have always been active in regional development. Our people come from the region and know its history and traditions. We are proud of the region and our share in its growth.

"Because of this strong position, our board decided when all this merging started that we would follow an independent course. We don't need a lot of help from big organizations. Of course, we work through our correspondent banks to provide top service to our customers, but we don't need them to tell us what to do. So we have discouraged the feelers about merger and other forms of affiliation. At the same time, we don't assume that we can tell other established banks like ourselves how to run their businesses. That means we are not out on the prowl looking for a bank which we might take over.

"There is also the matter of integrity. Stone Ridge is more than a fairweather friend. The east coast capitalists are eager to support a venture where the economy is strong, but then disappear whenever they estimate that they can earn a quarter of a percent more someplace else. Their commitment to the region is not genuine and continuing. Local people have learned that they can't trust outsiders in the sense that outsiders do not provide dependable help. In comparison, Stone Ridge is committed. We've been here over a century and we intend to be here for the next hundred years."

Other directors share the chair's feeling that Stone Ridge Bank can serve its region best by maintaining its independence. That view, however, leaves open the question of how much Stone Ridge should adjust to current changes in banking technology and competition.

Financial Counselor Concept

Mr. Bruce Wallender, president and CEO of Stone Ridge Bank for the past year, wrote a memorandum outlining the "financial counselor concept" when he was still senior vice-president in charge of loans. This plan deals directly with the issue of the bank's distinctive service in the face of increasing competition. The following is a digest of the points Mr. Wallender made at that time.

A. In the industrial and commercial area, Stone Ridge should concentrate on the "middle market"—that is, companies with sales of $5 million to $100 million. The advantages of this concentration are:

1. Typically these companies cannot afford to employ specialists in the various branches of finance. Consequently they need the kind of technical advice and assistance which we can provide. In contrast, the large *Fortune* 1000 firms have inhouse specialists who deal directly with money center organizations.
2. A significant number of companies of this size have headquarters in, or close to, our region. Many already do business with us.
3. Several big New York and California banks are already trying to make loans and provide special services to this "middle market"—operating through small regional offices. However, the personnel turnover in such offices is high and they have difficulty developing the personal relationships which we enjoy.

B. We should seek to provide these customers with a full range of banking services—including short- and long-term loans, lease financing, collection services, short-term investments, cash management, direct payroll transfers, letters of credit, and foreign exchange. The advantages of providing a variety of services are:

1. Fees for services can be an even greater source of bank income than net interest on loans—especially because outside competitors, noted in A3 above, use low rates as a primary wedge in securing business.
2. By providing good services at competitive prices we will forestall nonbank competitors from getting a "foot in the door" of our legitimate customers.

C. We should go even further and become "financial counselors" to this set of customers. Financial counseling includes:

1. Studying the total financial needs of each company, and advising its officers on such matters as capital structure, risk protection, ways to finance expansion, options in restructuring the sources of capital, credit management, cash management, financial controls, and the like.
2. Interpreting and explaining the significance to the company of new legislation and regulations in the financial field and summarizing national and international forecasts of economic conditions.
3. When a company can benefit from a financial service that Stone Ridge does not itself provide (e.g., public sale of securities, foreign banking connection, Eurodollar loans), using our contacts to obtain that service for the company.

Mr. Wallender summarized: The advantages of financial counseling are in providing our customers with a service they will have difficulty obtaining elsewhere and creating an entry barrier for our get-rich-quick competitors.

This financial counseling concept was presented to the board and warmly endorsed. Perhaps even more significant was the selection of Mr. Wallender as the new president of the bank. In making this choice, the board in effect adopted the strategy which Mr. Wallender advocated. Loan officers of the bank have been redesignated "Financial Counselors" but no other explicit moves have been made in this direction.

Pressure on Retail Business

Since taking over the top spot at Stone Ridge Bank, Mr. Wallender has faced a more pressing issue of what to do about the dwindling profit on the bank's retail business (transactions with individual consumers and small businesses). The vice-president in charge of Stone Ridge's sixty branches explains: "First we were hit with unprecedented interest costs. Balances in checking accounts, a good source of funds, have been shifted to NOW accounts on which we pay high interest, and depositors will shift on to money market accounts when those rates are even higher. With the deregulation of interest rates on savings accounts, the cost of these funds is creeping up, too. So the days are gone when the retail part of the bank generates low-cost funds which the industrial loan officers can lend often at a percent or two above the prime rate.

"It is true that we now collect some fees for small balances, checks, and the like. But the catch is that our operating expenses are rising faster than the fee income. Personnel costs and rental expenses at each branch are going up and up, and competition is forcing us to keep open longer hours. We have automated some, but it will take several years to recover the installation costs.

"I have finally come to the conclusion that the only way we can keep our expenses even close to those of the banks with many branches all over the state is to join—or perhaps create—a coop servicing company. If all of us who want to stay independent can pool our overhead, we could lower processing costs considerably. Stone Ridge could be a leader among a group of other financially strong local banks in such a venture. By picking our associates carefully we could avoid any appearance of weakness.

"The installment loan business has so many competitors that the margins have gone out of that, too. Again expense reduction is essential. Thank God for Visa. Local people like to have a card with the Stone Ridge name on it, and we make some money on their slow pay balances.

"Our leading competitor has bought up small banks or opened new branches all over the state. That puts it ahead of Stone Ridge in deposits. It has enough volume to help on overhead expenses. It is anybody's guess, however, just how it'll make out in the long run. A coop service organization would help us meet that competition, and at the same time we could maintain our independence."

Opportunity to Exit

What to do with the retail end of the bank has suddenly become a pressing question. Stone Ridge has received an informal offer to buy all its branches and the business connected with them. The offer comes from First National Bank, which is strong in the opposite end of the state. First National has recently acquired several savings banks and wishes to build a network of branches that will blanket the entire state. Acquisition of Stone Ridge branches would be a major step in this plan; they would give First National real strength in an area where it now is unrepresented, and the association with Stone Ridge's image would lend prestige to the entire expansion program. The combined network would make First National the main rival of the state's largest bank in retail banking.

Although the specific details have not been examined, the basic proposal is clear. Stone Ridge would sell its retail banking business to First National for $40 million net gain. More specifically, First National would take over all the *deposit liabilities* at the branches—that is, the checking and savings accounts of individual depositors. It would also *buy* the equipment, buildings, and other physical assets of the branches, the automobile and other installment loans arranged at the branches, the home mortgages that were arranged at the branches, and in general other banking services provided by the branches to individuals. The *net* difference between (1) the liabilities that First National assumes, and (2) the book value of the assets transferred, plus the purchase price of $40 million, would be settled in cash.

Furthermore, the proposal provides that all Stone Ridge personnel engaged in retail banking would be transferred (with the pension reserves) to First National. Stone Ridge would agree not to solicit retail banking business during the next five years, and its name would be removed from the branches. First National would not solicit during the next five years industrial or commercial deposit accounts in the territories presently served by Stone Ridge branches.

A few qualifications and exceptions have been noted. Business and industrial customers now served through Stone Ridge branches would be given the option of banking with the main office of Stone Ridge, and officers of such customers could transfer their personal accounts to the main office if they so wished.

Mr. Wallender says, "The immediate effect of such a transaction would be a $40 million (less tax) increase in our equity. Also we would have the income earned on that sum to add to our operating profit. Last year we earned only $1 million on our retail operations, so you might say that we aren't sacrificing a lot.

"However, the proposal would have a more profound impact on Stone

Ridge than would show up in the financial statements of the first year. We must think about the long-run prospects for our piece of the retail banking business. That industry is mature, highly competitive, with narrowing profit margins. According to Professor K. R. Harrigan, we have three options: (1) Become a large volume, low-cost operator—and hold on through the period when weaker competitors drop out. (2) Find a protected niche that we can dominate. (3) Sell out quickly while someone else is still interested in such assets as we possess.[1] Stone Ridge is not big enough to try the first option on a national basis, and we have not discovered a protected niche. That leaves only the third option—sell soon.

"The trouble with that reasoning is the impact of selling on the rest of the bank. We are talking about giving up over one-third of our deposits—shrinking the bank personnel and physical presence in the region even more. A contraction of that size *could* have a devastating effect on our remaining personnel and on our public image. Some people would view us as losers.

"There is a personal angle, too. I hate to go down in history as the president of Stone Ridge who started to retreat almost as soon as he got into office—in fact, gave up a very large part of the business that others before me worked so hard to create. Statues are not built for people who draw back so that they lose less money than they otherwise might."

The chair of the board is also concerned. He says, "Cutting the size of the bank is a serious matter. You lose your status as a leader. Stone Ridge has helped to set a progressive business climate for the region. We've preached confidence, hard work, venturesomeness, and growth; in our own actions, we followed what we preached. Now, if we give up on retail banking, throw in the towel for the most conspicuous part of our business, what sort of respect will our opinions deserve and get?

"It is true that combining operations with another bank within the state is not like selling out to a large national organization of some sort. Our branches would continue to be staffed by local people serving local needs. In this respect, it is just that Stone Ridge's role would be smaller. If at some future time, First National gets swallowed up by an east coast megabank the onus will not be on us. But we would escape criticism because we no longer would be considered important."

A shareholder's opinion is expressed by the president of Stone Ridge Trust Company: he is personally trustee of several estates owning large blocks of the holding company stock and is a respected director of the bank. "First National's proposal gives Stone Ridge Bank an opportunity to concentrate on what it can do best. The 'financial counselor' concept fits the primary strength of the bank and also reinforces the Trust Company. That will build Stone Ridge in circles which really count.

---

[1]*Strategies for Declining Businesses.* Lexington, MA: D.C. Heath & Company, 1980

"I realize that selling the branches to First National would make us smaller and less prominent. However, the sale would remove us from an area which is likely to become a dogfight, and the purchase price—although too small—would be a cushion to earnings that the bank will need to retool and redirect its resources on the industrial and commercial markets. I don't see another attractive bidder on the horizon, and we should not pass up this chance."

Tooling Up for Financial Counseling

Mr. Charles Farnum was promoted to take Mr. Wallender's position when Mr. Wallender became president of the bank. Mr. Farnum, a long-service employee of Stone Ridge, is enthusiastic about the financial counseling concept and has prepared a private list of steps to carry it out.

1. Appoint a New York representative of Stone Ridge Bank, probably an economist who would keep the bank informed on the latest economic and financial forecasts, and would inform the bank of any new kinds of services being offered by large banks or nonbank companies that will compete with Stone Ridge financial counseling.
2. Employ and train future counselors, preferably M.B.A.'s with good connections in the region. Include present loan officers in training to ensure breadth of service.
3. Consider appointment of lawyer or tax specialist as inhouse expert to advise counselors.
4. When ready, launch P.R. campaign, focused on the business community, about Stone Ridge service.
5. Have systematic and comprehensive plan for market development. Target all potential accounts and assign to specific counselors. Develop form for systematic records and annual review of status of each existing and potential account.
6. Develop method of income and cost analysis for each account.

Mr. Farnum explains that this program is still in the planning stage. Mr. Wallender has indicated that he wants to be sure that he understands the total bank and is recognized as a total bank person before he pushes his own pet project. Also, because of the squeeze in interest rates, Mr. Wallender has urged all officers to keep expenses in line with income, and several of the above steps will involve additional expense.

A note just received by Mr. Smythe from Mr. Wallender says: "Am concerned about a leak or rumor of the First National offer. This would create problems with both customers and employees. So would like to have your recommendation as soon as possible."

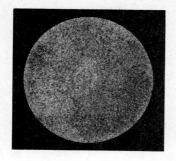

SELECTED
BIBLIOGRAPHY

CHAPTER 1: Social Responsibility and Central Management

Anshen, M. *Corporate Strategies for Social Performance.* New York: Macmillan Publishing Co., 1980.

Carroll, A. B. and F. Hoy. "Integrating Corporate Social Policy into Strategic Management." *Journal of Business Strategy* (Winter, 1984).

Drucker, P. F. "The New Meaning of Corporate Social Responsibility." *California Management Review* (Winter, 1984).

Mintzberg, H. "The Case for Corporate Social Responsibility." *Journal of Business Strategy* (Fall, 1983).

CHAPTER 2: Forecasting Attractiveness of an Industry

Armstrong, J. S. *Long-Range Forecasting: From Crystal Ball to Computer.* New York: John Wiley & Sons, 1978.

Makridakis, S. and S. Wheelwright (eds.). *The Handbook of Forecasting.* New York: Wiley Interscience, 1982.

Porter, M. E. *Competitive Strategy: Techniques for Analyzing Industries and Competitors.* New York: The Free Press, 1980, Chapters 1, 7–13.

Utterback, J. M. and E. H. Burack. "Identification of Technological Threats and Opportunities by Firms," *Technological Forecasting and Social Change* 8, 7–21, 1975.

CHAPTER 3: Assessing A Company's Competitive Strengths

Bylinsky, G. "The Game Has Changed in Big Computers." *Fortune* (January 25, 1982).

Harrigan, K. R. "Barriers to Entry and Competitive Strategies." *Strategic Management Journal* (October, 1981).

Porter, M. E. *Competitive Strategy: Techniques for Analyzing Industries and Competitors.* New York: The Free Press, 1980, Chapter 3.

Steiner, G. A. *Strategic Planning.* New York: The Free Press, 1979, Chapters 8 and 9.

CHAPTER 4: Predicting Responses of Key Actors

Allison, G. T. *Essence of Decision: Explaining the Cuban Missile Crisis*. Boston: Little, Brown, 1971.

MacMillan, I. C. *Strategy Formulation: Political Concepts*. St. Paul: West Publishing Company, 1978.

Mazzolini, R. *Government Controlled Enterprises: International Strategy and Policy Decisions*. New York: John Wiley & Sons, 1979, Chapter 8.

Porter, M. E. *Competitive Strategy: Techniques for Analyzing Industries and Competitors*. New York: The Free Press, 1980, Chapters 4–6.

CHAPTER 5: Selecting Business - Unit Strategy

Hofer, C. W. and D. Schendel. *Strategy Formulation: Analytical Concepts*. St. Paul: West Publishing Company, 1978, Chapters 3 and 5.

MacMillan, I. C. "Seizing Competitive Initiative." *Journal of Business Strategy* (Spring, 1982).

Quinn, J. B. *Strategies for Change: Logical Incrementalism*. Homewood, IL: Richard D. Irwin, 1980.

Rothschild, W. E. *Strategic Alternatives: Selection, Development and Implementation*. New York: AMACOM, 1979.

South, S. E. "Competitive Advantage: The Cornerstone of Strategic Thinking." *Journal of Business Strategy* (Spring, 1981).

CHAPTER 6: Marketing Policy — Product Line and Customers

Day, G. S. "Strategic Market Analysis and Definition: An Integrated Approach." *Strategic Management Journal* (July, 1981).

Garda, R. A. "Strategic Segmentation: How to Carve Niches for Growth in Industrial Markets." *Management Review* (August, 1981).

Heany, D. F. "Degrees of Product Innovation." *Journal of Business Strategy* (Spring, 1983).

Jain, S. C. *Marketing Planning and Strategy*. Cincinnati: South-Western Publishing Co., 1981.

CHAPTER 7: Marketing Mix Policy

Abell, D. F. and J. S. Hammond. *Strategic Marketing Planning: Analytical Approaches*. Englewood Cliffs: Prentice-Hall, Inc., 1979.

Kotler, P. *Marketing Management: Analysis, Planning, and Control*, 5th ed. Englewood Cliffs: Prentice-Hall, Inc., 1984, Chapters 15–22.

Luck, D. J. and O. C. Farrell. *Marketing Strategy and Plans*. Englewood Cliffs: Prentice-Hall, Inc., 1979, Chapters 7–10.

CHAPTER 8: Research and Development Policy

Collier, D. "Linking R & D and Strategic Planning." *Journal of Business Strategy* (Fall, 1981).

Galbraith, J. R. and R. K. Kazanjian. "Developing Technologies: R & D Strategies of Office Product Firms." *Columbia Journal of World Business* (Spring, 1983).

Ruggles, R. L. "How to Integrate R & D and Corporate Goals." *Management Review* (September, 1982).

Tushman, M. L. and W. L. Moore (eds.) *Readings in the Management of Innovation.* Boston: Pitman Publishing, Inc., 1982.

CHAPTER 9: Production Policy

Jelinek, M. and J. D. Golhar. "The Interface Between Strategy and Manufacturing Technology." *Columbia Journal of World Business* (Spring, 1983).

McMillan, C. J. "Production Planning in Japan." *Journal of General Management* (Summer, 1983).

Skinner, W. *Manufacturing in the Corporate Strategy.* New York: John Wiley & Sons, 1978.

Strobaugh, R. and P. Telesio. "Match Manufacturing Policies and Product Strategy." *Harvard Business Review* (March, 1983).

CHAPTER 10: Procurement Policy

Corey, E. R. *Procurement Management.* Boston: CBI Publishing Company, 1978, Chapters 1–4.

Harrigan, K. R. *Strategies for Vertical Integration.* Lexington: D. C. Heath and Company, 1983.

Moore, F. G. and T. E. Hendrick. *Production/Operations Management*, 8th ed. Homewood, IL: Richard D. Irwin, 1980, Chapters 17–20.

Schonberger, R. J. "Transfer of Japanese Manufacturing Management Approaches to U.S. Industry." *Academy of Management Review* (July, 1982).

CHAPTER 11: Human Resources Policy

Devanna, M. A., *et al. Human Resource Management: Issues for the 1980's.* New York: Center for Career Research and Human Resource Management, Columbia University, 1982.

Foulkes, F. K. *Personnel Policies in Large Non-Union Companies.* Englewood Cliffs: Prentice-Hall, Inc., 1980.

Pigors, P. and C. A. Myers. *Personnel Administration: A Point of View and a Method*, 9th ed. New York: McGraw-Hill Book Co., 1981.

Strauss, G. and L. R. Sayles. *Personnel: The Human Problems of Management*, 4th ed. Englewood Cliffs: Prentice-Hall, Inc., 1980.

Sweet, J. "How Manpower Development Can Support Your Strategic Plan." *Journal of Business Strategy* (Summer, 1981).

CHAPTER 12: Financial Policy — Allocating Capital

Gale, B. T. and B. Branch. "Cash Flow Analysis: More Important Than Ever." *Harvard Business Review* (July, 1981).

Helfert, E. A. *Techniques of Financial Analysis*, 5th ed. Homewood, IL: Richard D. Irwin, 1982, Chapter 4.

Schoeffler, S. "Capital-Intensive Technology vs. ROI: A Strategic Assessment." *Management Review* (September, 1978).

Seed, A. H. "New Approaches to Asset Management." *Journal of Business Strategy* (Winter, 1983).

Van Horne, J. C. *Financial Management and Policy*, 6th ed. Englewood Cliffs: Prentice-Hall, Inc., 1983, Chapters 5–12.

CHAPTER 13: Financial Policy — Sources of Capital

Fruhan, W. E. *Financial Strategy: Studies in the Creation, Transfer, and Destruction of Shareholder Value*. Homewood, IL: Richard D. Irwin, 1979.

Helfert, E. A. *Techniques of Financial Analysis*, 5th ed. Homewood, IL: Richard D. Irwin, 1979.

Piper, T. R. and W. A. Weinhold. "How Much Debt Is Right for Your Company?" *Harvard Business Review* (July, 1982).

Van Horne, J. C. *Financial Management Policy*, 6th ed. Englewood Cliffs: Prentice-Hall, Inc., 1983, Chapters 17–23.

CHAPTER 14: Portfolio Strategy

Dionne, J. L. "Corporate Strategy." *Journal of Business Strategy* (Summer, 1983).

Harrigan, K. R. *Strategies for Declining Businesses*. Lexington, MA: D. C. Heath and Company, 1980.

Heany, D. F. and G. Weiss. "Integrating Strategies for Clusters of Businesses." *Journal of Business Strategy* (Summer, 1983).

Hofer, C. W. and D. Schendel. *Strategy Formulation: Analytical Concepts*. St. Paul: West Publishing Company, 1978, Chapters 4 and 7.

Rumelt, R. P. "Diversification Strategy and Profitability." *Strategic Management Journal* (October, 1982).

CHAPTER 15: Corporate Input Strategy

Dundas, K. M. and P. R. Richardson. "Implementing the Unrelated Product Strategy." *Strategic Management Journal* (October, 1982).

Hamermesh, R. G. *Making Strategy Work*. New York: John Wiley & Sons, 1984.

Nees, D. "Increase Your Divestment Effectiveness." *Strategic Management Journal* (April, 1981).

Normann, R. *Management for Growth*. New York: John Wiley & Sons, 1977.

Pitts, R. A. "Strategies and Structures for Diversification." *Academy of Management Journal* (June, 1977).

CHAPTER 16: Mergers and Acquisitions

Bradley, J. W. and D. H. Corn. *Acquisition and Corporate Development*. Lexington, MA: D. C. Heath and Company, 1981.

Ebeling, H. W. and T. L. Doorley. "A Strategic Approach to Acquisitions." *Journal of Business Strategy* (Winter, 1983.)

Salter, M. A. and W. W. Weinhold. *Diversification Through Acquisition*. New York: The Free Press, 1979.

Song, J. H. "Diversifying Acquisitions and Financial Relationships: Testing 1974–1976 Behaviour." *Strategic Management Journal* (April, 1983).

Steiner, P. O. *Mergers: Motives, Effects, Policies*. Ann Arbor: University of Michigan Press, 1975.

CHAPTER 17: Matching Organization and Strategy

Chandler, A. D. *Strategy and Structure: Chapters in the History of the American Industrial Enterprise*. Cambridge: M.I.T. Press, 1962.

Davis, S. M. and P. R. Lawrence. *Matrix*. Reading, MA: Addison-Wesley, 1977.

Horovitz, J. H. and R. A. Thietart. "Strategy, Management Design and Firm Performance." *Strategic Management Journal* (January, 1982).

Yavitz, B. and W. H. Newman. *Strategy in Action*. New York: The Free Press, 1982, Chapters 9 and 11.

CHAPTER 18: Governing the Enterprise

Andrews, K. R. "From the Boardroom." *Harvard Business Review* (November 1980, May 1981, November 1982).

Boulton, W. R. "Effective Board Development: Five Areas for Concern." *Journal of Business Strategy* (Spring, 1983).

Mueller, R. K. *New Directions for Directors: Behind the By Laws*. Lexington, MA: D. C. Heath and Company, 1978.
Vance, S. C. *Corporate Governance*. New York: McGraw-Hill Book Co., 1983.

CHAPTER 19: Executive Personnel

Brady, G. F., R. M. Fulmer and D. L. Melnich. "Planning Executive Succession: The Effect of Recruitment Source and Organizational Problems on Anticipated Tenure." *Strategic Management Journal* (July, 1982).
Leontiades, M. "Choosing the Right Manager to Fit the Strategy." *Journal of Business Strategy* (Fall, 1982).
Rappaport, A. "How to Design Value-Contributing Executive Incentives." *Journal of Business Strategy* (Fall, 1983).
Schein, E. H. *Career Dynamics: Matching Individual and Organization Needs*, Part 3. Reading, MA: Addison-Wesley, 1978.
Yavitz, B. and W. H. Newman. *Strategy in Action*. New York: The Free Press, 1982, Chapter 10.

CHAPTER 20: Short-Range and Long-Range Programming

Lorange, P. *Corporate Planning: An Executive Viewpoint*. Englewood Cliffs: Prentice-Hall, Inc., 1980.
O'Connor, R. *Planning Under Uncertainty: Multiple Scenarios and Contingency Planning*. New York: The Conference Board, 1978.
Steiner, G. A. *Strategic Planning*. New York: The Free Press, 1979, Chapters 12–14.
Stonich, P. J. "How to Use Strategic Funds Programming." *Journal of Business Strategy* (Fall, 1980).
Yavitz, B. and W. H. Newman. *Strategy in Action*. New York: The Free Press, 1982, Chapter 7.

CHAPTER 21: Activating

Adizes, I. *How to Solve the Mismanagement Crisis*. Homewood, IL: Richard D. Irwin, 1979.
Kanter, R. M. *The Change Masters*. New York: Simon & Schuster, 1983, Chapter 8.
Tichy, N. M. *Managing Strategic Change, Technical, Political and Cultural Dynamics*. New York: John Wiley & Sons, 1983, Chapters 7–10.
Yavitz, B. and W. H. Newman. *Strategy in Action*. New York: The Free Press, 1982, Chapter 8.

CHAPTER 22: Controlling Operations

Horowitz, J. H. "Strategic Control: A New Task for Top Management." *Long Range Planning* (June, 1979).

Hurst, E. G. "Controlling Strategic Plans." In P. Lorange, *Implementation of Strategic Planning*. Englewood Cliffs: Prentice-Hall, Inc., 1982.

Jelinek, M., J. A. Litterer and R. E. Miles (eds.). *Organization by Design: Theory and Practice*. Plano, TX: Business Publications, Inc., 1981, Section 7.

Newman, W. H. *Constructive Control: Design and Use of Control Systems*. Englewood Cliffs: Prentice-Hall, Inc., 1975.

Yavitz, B. and W. H. Newman. *Strategy in Action*. New York: The Free Press, 1982, Chapter 12.

CHAPTER 23: Managing Multinational Enterprises

Channon, D. F. and R. M. Jalland. *Multinational Strategic Planning*. New York: Macmillan Company, 1978.

Fayerweather, J. "Four Winning Strategies for the International Corporation." *Journal of Business Strategy* (Fall, 1981).

Gladwin, T. N. and I. Walter. "How Multinationals Can Manage Social and Political Forces." *Journal of Business Strategy* (Summer, 1980).

Hamel, G. and C. K. Prahalad. "Managing Strategic Responsibility in the MNC." *Strategic Management Journal* (October, 1983).

Robock, S. H., K. Simmons and J. Zwick. *International Business and Multinational Enterprise*, 3rd ed. Homewood, IL: Richard D. Irwin, 1977, Part 5.

CHAPTER 24: Integrating Role of Central Managers

Gluck, F., S. Kaufman and A. S. Walleck. "The Four Phases of Strategic Management." *Journal of Business Strategy* (Winter, 1982).

Pascale, R. T. and A. G. Athos. *The Art of Japanese Management: Applications for American Executives*. New York: Simon & Schuster, 1981.

Waterman, R. H. "The Seven Elements of Strategic Fit." *Journal of Business Strategy* (Winter, 1982).

Yavitz, B. and W. H. Newman. *Strategy in Action*. New York: The Free Press, 1982, Chapters 13 and 14.

INDEX